MW01027523

Coming Out, Moving Forward

COMING OUT, MOVING FORWARD

Wisconsin's Recent Gay History

R. RICHARD WAGNER

WISCONSIN HISTORICAL SOCIETY PRESS

Published by the Wisconsin Historical Society Press
Publishers since 1855

The Wisconsin Historical Society helps people connect to the past by collecting, preserving, and sharing stories. Founded in 1846, the Society is one of the nation's finest historical institutions. *Join the Wisconsin Historical Society:* wisconsinhistory.org/membership

Photographs identified with WHi or WHS are from the Society's collections; address requests to reproduce these photos to the Visual Materials Archivist at the Wisconsin Historical Society, 816 State Street, Madison, WI 53706.

Front cover images, clockwise from left to right: David Clarenbach, Dick Wagner, Henry Lufler Jr., Tim Carpenter, Tammy Baldwin, and Kathleen Nichols, from the author's collection; Lou Sullivan, Lou Sullivan Papers (#1991-07), Courtesy of Gay, Lesbian, Bisexual, Transgender Historical Society; participants in Milwaukee's Wisconsin AIDS Walk, Archives Department, University of Wisconsin–Milwaukee Libraries; participants in the 1973 International Women's Day March, Judy Greenspan Papers, Acc. No. 2015/383, University of Wisconsin–Madison Archives

Printed in Canada

Cover designed by Percolator Graphic Design
Typesetting by Wendy Holdman Design

24 23 22 21 20   1 2 3 4 5

Library of Congress Cataloging-in-Publication Data

Names: Wagner, R. Richard (Sociologist), author.
Title: Coming out, moving forward : Wisconsin's recent gay history / R. Richard Wagner.
Description: Madison : Wisconsin Historical Society Press, 2020. | Includes bibliographical references and index. | Summary: "Coming Out, Moving Forward, the second volume in R. Richard Wagner's groundbreaking work on gay history in Wisconsin, outlines the challenges that LGBT Wisconsinites faced in their efforts to right past oppressions and secure equality in the post-Stonewall period between 1969 and 2000"—Provided by publisher.
Identifiers: LCCN 2019049807 (print) | LCCN 2019049808 (ebook) | ISBN 9780870209277 (hardcover) | ISBN 9780870209284 (ebook)
Subjects: LCSH: Gays—Wisconsin—History.
Classification: LCC HQ76.3.U58 W335 2020 (print) | LCC HQ76.3.U58 (ebook) | DDC 306.76/609775–dc23
LC record available at https://lccn.loc.gov/2019049807
LC ebook record available at https://lccn.loc.gov/2019049808

♾ The paper used in this publication meets the minimum requirements of the American National Standard for Information Sciences—Permanence of Paper for Printed Library Materials, ANSI Z39.48-1992.

For Hank, Will, Paula, and Mark

This 1989 cover of *In Step* magazine from Milwaukee highlights the twentieth anniversary of Stonewall as an enduring marker. *IN STEP*, JUNE 8–21, 1989

Publication of this book was made possible
in part through generous gifts from:

Mr. Charles Bauer and Mr. Charles Beckwith
David Bedri and Jon Sorenson
Sue Riseling and Joanne Berg
Paula Bonner and Ann Schaffer
Frances Breit and Julie A'cci
Gary Brown and Paul Hayes
Barbara Constans and Deb Rohde
Paul Gibler and Thomas DeChant
Bob Dowd and Marge Schmidt
Julie Eckenwalder and Constance Anderson
William and Lynne Eich
Renee Herber and Tamara Packard
Joanne Holland and Margie Rosenberg
Kim Karcher
Scott and Mary Kolar
Donald Lamb
Phil Levy
Hank Lufler and Mike Gerdes
Katharine Lyall
Scott and Megin McDonell
Eileen Mershart and Sarah Hole
Mike and Sally Miley
Anne Monks
Richard Petran
Purple Moon Foundation, Inc. – Dale Leibowitz
Timothy Radelet
Mary Lou Roberts
Susan Schaffer and Joan Hinckley
Robert Stipicevich and Scott Short
Mary Strickland and Marie Barroquillo
Howard Sweet
Mike Verveer
William Wartmann
Mark Webster and Ryan Brown
Susan Zaeske
Jaime Zimmerman

Contents

FOREWORD

TAMMY BALDWIN

US SENATE, 2012–PRESENT

I first met Dick Wagner in 1984, after returning to my hometown of Madison, Wisconsin, following my graduation from college. Eager to become involved in the local political scene and searching for mentors, I had been cold calling local officials in my new neighborhood and seeking opportunities to work on campaigns and learn the ropes. I was invited to a gathering of local progressive elected officials, labor union leaders, and civil rights and environmental activists to strategize about candidate recruitment for city council and school board seats to be contested in the spring 1985 elections. We met on the second floor of a popular local establishment, Mother's Pub, which had long been a gathering spot for local progressives. I observed how much respect Dick had earned from his fellow progressive leaders. Following a discussion about the issues the group hoped to advance, we broke into small groups. Dick Wagner and Kathleen Nichols, both out LGBT members of the Dane County Board of Supervisors, led a discussion on opportunities to advance policies, initiatives, and ordinances to counter discrimination against our community. I nervously approached their working group, having come out in college about a year earlier. That day, Dick became my role model and mentor, and a lifelong friendship ensued.

Dick Wagner, who obtained his doctorate in history from UW–Madison, was then working in state government and serving as an elected supervisor for his near east side Madison district on the Dane County Board. I took delight when he shared stories of his graduate training. In that pre-Internet era, the research for his dissertation on prostitution permitted, in fact necessitated, that Dick work in the library stacks near books on non-normative sexual behavior and orientation, which, at the time, usually presented the subject of homosexuality as a disorder. No doubt, this experience played a pivotal role in Dick's search for an alternative narrative more reflective of his own experience. At social gatherings in the 1980s and 1990s, usually hosted at his historic Madison home, Dick would share tidbits from his extensive collection of news clippings, correspondence, and other archival materials depicting gay life and culture in Madison and the surrounding region. He knew he had a book waiting to be written of heretofore untold stories. Little did he know then that it would require two volumes.

Of my own coming out story, I wrote the following for a speech delivered at a Madison Gay Pride Rally in 1989:

> During the year after I came out, I grabbed anything I could find to read which gave what I was going through some social and historical context. I needed to ground myself, to discover I was not alone. And I was amazed and so proud of what I learned when I read. The dignity and courage of people in our movement. And I was so angry that no one had ever let me know about these things before. No one in my educational background told me about Stonewall, when years ago, gays in New York City united to resist nightly acts of police oppression and that this event signaled the beginning of the contemporary gay liberation movement. And no one told me about Elaine Noble, the first openly lesbian member of a state assembly, or of Harvey Milk who became the first openly gay person elected to the San Francisco Board of Supervisors and was later assassinated. No, the Stonewall rioters, Elaine Noble, and Harvey Milk were people who I found out about from other Gay and Lesbian people who took the time to make films, write books, and tell others about our history.
>
> We can celebrate the fact that we have begun to reconstruct our history and to document our contributions to this world. And we can be proud that we had Stonewall, Elaine Noble, Harvey Milk and the countless others who've broken ground in other areas, and that we can still cherish their words and their work.
>
> Yet the challenge to us is implicit. We must continue to learn about our history, our many and vital contributions to our own freedom and the freedom of others. And we must continue to share that history, to speak out about it, to make our nation's and our world's history whole (and truthful) by including our part in shaping it.

This two-volume work reflects a lifetime of meticulous research and a sensitivity to reading between the lines in public sources. Dick Wagner makes our state's history more complete by including our part in shaping it. He also presents the opportunity for young people growing up all over Wisconsin and the Midwest in this century to know that they are not alone and that they stand on the shoulders of people who came before them and paved the way for the progress we have made in recent years.

Washington, DC, 2019

FOREWORD

STEVE GUNDERSON
US HOUSE OF REPRESENTATIVES, 1980–1996

Wisconsin's commitment to national leadership goes back to 1851 when the state adopted as its motto one simple word: "Forward." Despite bumps in political, economic, and social history, the state's citizens have sustained their commitment to progress. I remember years ago when a seasoned Wisconsin politician told me, "You can call them Democrats or Republicans. But if you draw a line from La Crosse to Green Bay, the people north of that line have always been progressives." Add Madison and Milwaukee to the mix and you have a state committed to national leadership in many issues—including human rights.

Wisconsin's values include a deep commitment to integrity. And as a state created through the settlement of people from many different nations, we came to know and celebrate diversity—and the value of every individual—long before our own time.

As a youngster growing up in Wisconsin, I was taught by my family, my schools, the 4-H, and even our faith that everyone was different and everyone was good. One of the real gifts of growing up in rural farm country is that there were just no options for discrimination. Everyone was needed and everyone needed to do their part.

When I first entered politics in 1974, I described myself as a "Lincoln Republican." Lincoln's historical commitment to individual freedom, equal opportunity, and a limited government created my political values. As a young man seeking to understand and accept my sexuality, I was challenged to reconcile my faith and my politics. In doing so, I realized that both compelled me to stand up for the rights and the value of every person created by God. And it was the Wisconsin value of integrity that told me to be myself in an open and honest way.

One thing about us Wisconsin folks: we tend to "live and let live." We just don't talk about things like sexual orientation. But that changed during the AIDS epidemic. Some of my best friends—some of the finest people I will ever know—lost their lives to AIDS. That was bad enough. Learning that certain churches would not hold their funerals became for me a clarion call to public action. And so, in my own way and in my own timing, I became a national voice on something other than education and dairy policy. In my own way, I carried forward Lincoln's commitments to equality and opportunity for all.

Looking back on my political history, I was in Congress just long enough to participate in the debate over the Defense of Marriage Act. My political instincts pushed me to find compromise and common ground. When my proposals to find ways to provide the same legal protections to same-sex couples without the use of the word *marriage* were rejected by my party's leadership, I realized this was a political fight rather than a serious attempt at public policy. And so I became the only Republican in that Congress to oppose the legislation. The words most people remember from my speech on the floor of the Congress are, "I stand here today with respect and with love for each of you as fellow members of the human race. All I ask in return is that you don't intentionally make me any less worthy than you."

History teaches us. We learn from our mistakes, and we learn from our good and visionary deeds. We learn those values which endure over time to define us—as a people, a state, and even a nation. The book you are about to read records and shares an important chapter in our state's history. Like me, you will learn that progress is not swift. Progress happens only when a set of common values provide the foundation for courageous people to move forward in ways that make our world a better place for those who follow.

The Wisconsin motto guides us forward. Our history confirms that Republicans and Democrats have combined to make this state what it is today: a leader in many areas, including equal opportunity and protection for every one of our citizens.

Arlington, Virginia, 2019

Coming Out, Moving Forward

INTRODUCTION

I n *We've Been Here All Along: Wisconsin's Early Gay History*, I outlined the repressive nature of Wisconsin's laws and societal attitudes regarding homosexuality in the pre-Stonewall period. Nevertheless, some small number of gays, lesbians, and other gender nonconforming individuals found ways to emancipate themselves from these strictures during this era. They developed and presented their identities and built social networks to support one another. With incredible conviction, they faced the headwinds of dissent and persisted toward the goal of equality.

In *Coming Out, Moving Forward: Wisconsin's Recent Gay History*, I explore how the state's LGBT community overturned a century and a half of oppressive legislation and capitalized on Wisconsin's distinctive politics to position the state in a singular place in American gay history. In 1982, Wisconsin became the first state to enact a gay rights law, and to date it has been the only state to elect three out members of Congress: Steve Gunderson, Tammy Baldwin, and Mark Pocan. In addition to these political achievements, and often supporting and interacting with them, Wisconsin made intellectual and social developments that tell the story of lesbian, gay, bisexual, and transgender life in the state. Understanding the agency of the actors responsible for these advancements is crucial to understanding Wisconsin's gay history. This volume covers the decades of the 1970s, 1980s, and 1990s, and some threads are followed into the twenty-first century to demonstrate the aftermath of certain key events. While this is not a comparative study, I have included references to works in the broad field of LGBT scholarship to provide a context for the developments I discuss. Though national events certainly did influence the state, many Wisconsin LGBT activists appear to have been primarily driven by their own circumstances in creating and seizing opportunities for advancement.

Most history assumes we are not sexual beings. Gay history, on the contrary, insists on integrating sex into history. Thus, I do not skirt material about sexual activity, since it is central to the history of sexual identity. This content is not presented erotically, though at times it may be playfully

1

addressed. Another component in the history of sexual minorities is the social structures that facilitate sexual life. While this is not my main focus, it would be a truncated history if I failed to demonstrate how gay social life occurred and how it was constructed—both from within, by members of the community, and from without, by those who sought to shape it and understand it (and, all too often, negate it).

As I stated in the first volume, I wish that this work could encompass all Wisconsin gay history. As a gay man, I feel most comfortable and competent in dealing with issues of male homosexuality, yet I have tried to be inclusive of lesbian, bisexual, and transgender voices where the record exists. I am sure a feminist perspective would reveal many other nuances, as would more stories from bisexual, transgender, and other gender nonconforming individuals, all of whom are underrepresented here. Because I cannot claim to speak for anyone whose subject position and life experience is different from my own, I try to tell stories using individuals' own words, relying (as always) on primary sources including interviews and first-person accounts. There is always more work to be done, and I hope scholars will continue to bring these missing voices and histories to the surface.

Prior to the twenty-first century, the LGBT community was known variously as the gay community or the gay and lesbian community. At times I use the term *gay* to be inclusive of non-normative individuals without regard to gender. The significant inclusion of bisexuals and transgender individuals occurred only in the last decade of the twentieth century. Thus, I have chosen to use the acronym LGBT to refer to the community described in this book, and I have avoided the more contemporary addition of letters such as Q, I, and A in the acronym. After Stonewall, many gay men and lesbians worked together in the liberation struggles.

The story of Wisconsin's recent gay history centers on a series of brave individuals who, with very meager resources, achieved remarkable progress in the realm of gay rights. They did this by actively and openly interacting with major institutions and changing the stories about gay life in the state. Similar developments occurred in a handful of other states, but the story of the upper Midwest, and particularly Wisconsin, needs to be understood and added to the more well-known histories of the coasts. Since LGBT voices have been so marginalized in our history—both in Wisconsin

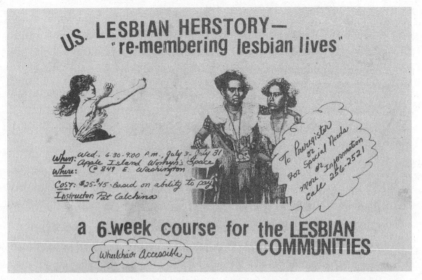

This six-week course on lesbian "herstory" conducted by Pat Calchina at Apple Island Womyn's Space in Madison was an example of community-based historians ending the erasure of LGBT lives from history. Louis Stimac offered a similar course on gay history in Milwaukee. ARCHIVES DEPARTMENT, UNIVERSITY OF WISCONSIN–MILWAUKEE LIBRARIES

and in the nation—I have tried to bring them to the fore so readers can appreciate the personal significance of their lives and struggles. While I was not able to include as many stories as I'd like, I have incorporated many pioneer voices and names. It is my sincere hope that other historians will take on the research and writing of more of this history. As poet William Butler Yeats wrote in his momentous poem "Easter 1916" about the Irish rebellion of that year, it is now "our part to murmur name upon name."

1

STONEWALL STIRS THE STATE

We were going to be a new kind of homosexual, not buying any of the old sick stuff. . . . We were making history, we were supposed to be making history.

—RON McCREA, EARLY WISCONSIN
GAY ACTIVIST, ORAL HISTORY[1]

Gay people, particularly the younger ones, were no longer begging for gradual change. They were demanding change right now and were prepared to fight for it.

—ELDON MURRAY, "GAY LIBERATION:
FIVE YEARS AFTER STONEWALL," 1974[2]

The June 1969 action at the Stonewall Bar in New York City, where gays "rioted" in response to a licensing raid by police, became a signal to homosexuals all across the country that a new activist response to legal and social oppression was possible. Individuals in some areas saw the signal and responded; others did not. Wisconsinites, from a state deep in the heartland but with a progressive tradition, received the signal and immediately took up the challenge.

The Stonewall riots have assumed a mythic place in gay history and are surrounded by other myths. One bit of lore is that Judy Garland's funeral contributed to the riots. Indeed, Garland was an icon for older, likely closeted homosexuals of the time who hoped they could be magically transported over the rainbow to someplace better. But David Carter, in his admirable *Stonewall: The Riots That Sparked the Gay Revolution*, has shown

4

that Garland's death did not influence the actions of those who fought back against the police on those New York nights.[3]

Wisconsin's gay activists of the 1970s frequently used Stonewall as a marker in their memories of the battle for rights. In 1974, Eldon Murray, a key figure in Milwaukee's gay community, wrote a long article in *GPU* (Gay People's Union) *News*, "Gay Liberation: Five Years after Stonewall." Among other resonating memories, he recalled a leaflet circulating in Greenwich Village in mid-July after the riots that stated, "Do you think homosexuals are revolting? You bet your sweet ass we are." Murray retrospectively understood that older gay groups such as the Mattachine Society were too conservative in their attempts to garner attention or inspire action in the 1970s. He wrote, "Perhaps without fully understanding it, the old homophile movement had laid the groundwork and raised consciousness of the gay community to the point where a liberated outlook was possible." In a *GPU News* editorial of October 1971, Murray noted that these earlier organizing efforts relied "primarily on fellowship and education to achieve the aims and goals of our minority." Other social activist movements of the 1950s and 1960s, such as those for black civil rights, the peace movement, and the hippie explosion, had paved the way for a new activist gay liberation effort. As Murray saw it, "Gay people, particularly the younger ones, were no longer begging for gradual change. They were demanding change right now and were prepared to fight for it."[4]

About the aftermath of the riot Murray wrote, "Only a few persons realized that a momentous change had taken place." Mainstream media in Wisconsin did not devote much reporting to the New York bar raid and subsequent developments. To read about the Stonewall riots, I can remember going to Snappy's Place, an old-time newsstand shop on King Street in Madison, and buying the *Village Voice*, which covered that summer's events, many of which happened in and around Greenwich Village. Jeremy, an early writer on gay liberation in

The sense of Stonewall as an uprising shows in this button featuring two clenched fists, a symbol used by leftists and minority groups throughout the twentieth century. WHS MUSEUM 1984.242.59

Wisconsin who, like many gay early activists of the period, did not list his last name, also wrote about having to use the *Village Voice* as a source. Don Schwamb, who has chronicled Milwaukee's gay history and was active in gay rights in the 1970s, recalls, "The Stonewall events of 1969 allowed more homosexuals to come out of the shadows and demand to be seen as people with rights just like other 'minorities.'"[5]

Murray recollected that during the summer after Stonewall, "several small meetings were held in Milwaukee as an attempt to start a local gay organization." Nothing came together quickly, but by fall 1969, several Milwaukee gay writers were contributing to *Kaleidoscope*, the local underground paper, which put out a gay supplement that winter. Gay news items came primarily from the national Liberation News Service. A more formal organizational effort in Milwaukee would not occur until spring 1970.[6]

In Madison, news of Stonewall also galvanized people. Mike Lutz remembered the activist groups and, specifically, the Dow Chemical riots on the Madison campus in the late 1960s. As one of eight persons who attended the first gay organizing meeting in Madison on November 5, 1969, Lutz recalled, "Then Stonewall happened, and everything changed that June." Chuck Bauer, one part of the Madison power couple of gay entrepreneurs known as the Chucks (along with his partner, Chuck Beckwith), recalled, "Stonewall [was] a big deal," because homosexuality had been "unspeakable" when he was growing up. Bauer said attending the post-Stonewall meeting in Madison was "how I came out, scared to death to walk through the door."[7]

Stonewall truly resonated with Wisconsin's early activists. This was shown during the First National March on Washington for Lesbian and Gay Rights in October 1979, ten years after Stonewall. Both the Milwaukee and Madison gay communities organized buses to take participants to the nation's capital. The Milwaukee committee for the march reached out to feminists in a flyer with a banner that read, "SISTERS—we need you," and below that, "Yes! We have marched for the ERA with our straight sisters. Isn't it time that we demonstrated for our long overdue lesbian and gay rights? As lesbian mothers in this country, we do not even have the right to raise a family—our children can and are daily stolen from us by the courts." The Madison committee, cochaired by prominent lesbian activist Kathleen Nichols, created a flyer that read, "After a decade of incredible growth in local and regional activity, joining forces is necessary for movement expansion." It was time, the committee argued, "to demonstrate the size and determination of our movement." Madison Mayor Joel Skornicka endorsed the march for protection of "civil rights," urging "all Madison residents to support the March in whatever way they can." Madison's WORT radio broadcast parts of the speeches live, and Madison's "Glad to Be Gay" cable TV program showed taped highlights. A story in the December issue of *Gay Madison* reported that over sixty Madisonians had attended the march.[8]

On Stonewall's twentieth anniversary in 1989, the event was still producing echoes around the state. In July, the lesbian publication *Leaping La Crosse News* proudly featured a story titled "Lesbian Started Stonewall Riots." Based on reporting in *Lesbian Connection* magazine, it drew on a Human Rights Campaign Fund letter that featured the lesbian who refused to be put into a police patrol car on the night of the riot, one of the first acts of resistance. The incident, though reported in the *Village Voice* of July 3, 1969, had been largely ignored.[9]

For the twenty-fifth anniversary of Stonewall, Milwaukee's gay magazine *In Step* carried stories of Wisconsin residents who went to the New York celebrations. Julie Marie Totsch drove from Racine with lesbian bumper stickers on her truck. She reported, "Amazingly the bar that started it all was difficult to find." Tom Salzsieder, active in gay sports in Milwaukee, went to the companion event, Gay Games. He recalled that a release of thousands of yellow balloons for AIDS victims "was a really touching moment." Stonewall marked a sense of beginning for gay liberation and became a touchstone for Wisconsinites as they saw a new road—and a new struggle—open before them. A new age was beginning.[10]

GAY ACTIVISM IN MADISON

The Madison meeting that Chuck Bauer described as his door to gay activism took place in the fall of 1969. The meeting was held at St. Francis House, the campus Episcopal center, which had a long-standing association with the Madison gay community. A gay social circle, consisting mainly of graduate students, had formed in the 1950s and 1960s around an early pastor at St. Francis House who provided hospitality to many gay men and supported gay efforts during the 1970s. Later in the decade, the

Madison Gay Center moved into low-rent space in the Episcopal center's basement, and St. Francis House advanced a two-thousand-dollar loan to help establish its early operations, which included counseling and referrals to gay-friendly professional services. In 1977, Reverend William Landram, the pastor of St. Francis, returned from the Integrity Convention in San Francisco, a national gathering of Episcopalians on gay rights, and suggested that Madison's religious gays, including Catholics, Episcopalians, Lutherans, and Presbyterians, should form an organization and meet at St. Francis House. From this idea sprang Madison's ecumenical Integrity/Dignity group, whose religious ministry continues to this day.[11]

Another gay organizing meeting in late 1969 led to the formation of the Madison Alliance for Homosexual Equality (MAHE—pronounced "may," or alternatively, "may he," as in "may he come out"). The group's first meeting was attended by people from both the campus and the town, but they were exclusively gay men. "It was an exciting time," attendee Jess Anderson later recalled. "As individuals our best answer to all political challenges is to come out, to be known as widely as possible as the people we actually are." A 1970 statement from MAHE printed in the Wisconsin underground paper *Kaleidoscope* affirmed, "There is a fresh new breeze of moral change bringing with it a new life style, new ideas about sex, . . . and most important to us, a new homosexuality."[12]

In spring 1970, the group discussed whether it would be politically or socially focused but soon took up community action. Members set up a card table at the University of Wisconsin (UW) Union to distribute coming out pamphlets. When someone lodged a complaint that the group was "distributing pornography," campus police seized the materials and threw the table aside. Ultimately, the Wisconsin Student Association came to the group's rescue, explaining that MAHE was a legitimate campus organization with a right to distribute literature.[13]

MAHE adopted a goals statement in 1969: "We are an organization dedicated to the creation of a society characterized by responsible sexual freedom. . . . We believe the public should be educated as to the true nature of homosexuality, and that this education will benefit people of all sexual orientations. . . . We do not seek tolerance; we demand human dignity and respect." To achieve these goals, MAHE sought the active participation of Madison's homosexual community. The group shared information about

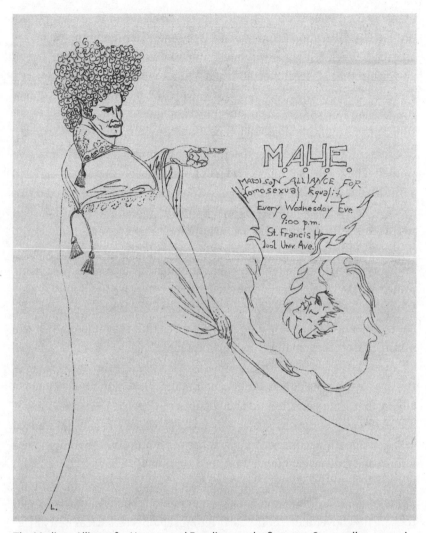

The Madison Alliance for Homosexual Equality was the first post-Stonewall gay organization in Wisconsin, formed in the fall of 1969. The countercultural sensibilities of the group can be seen in the long hair depicted in this image. WHI IMAGE ID 59037

homosexuality by speaking to students in gay-friendly classes, promoting gay-friendly social gatherings, and providing mutual support groups. It also created a dormitory counseling program aimed at students "who would otherwise receive no help for fear of exposing themselves to repression and harassment."[14]

The Gay Sisters group of Madison was also founded at St. Francis House in spring 1971. The group's separatist focus was clear from the outset: "The present Gay Liberation Front [a spin-off of MAHE] is predominantly male, and the women felt the need for a group of their own to work with the gay group that is already established." In a 1972 article, "Memoirs of a Tired Lesbian," author Judy Greenspan recalled that forty men and just two women were present at the first gay meeting she attended in March 1971. "Men are slow in recognizing the lesbian presence," said Greenspan. She therefore held a meeting specifically for lesbians, which drew twelve women. The resulting group, Gay Sisters, was also occasionally referred to as the Madison Lesbians or the Sisters of Safo [sic]. The group shared office space with the Gay Center on North Hamilton Street, and it held dances twice a month and provided workshops. In presenting their speakers' bureau to potential venues, the members stated, "The analysis of homosexuality should not be left solely in the hands of medical and academic professionals." Gay Sisters advertised using posters with the slogan "Gay Women Love Is Just a Kiss Away." It also wrote a statement denouncing "homosexism"—a term it did not define but that may have meant the sexism of homosexual men toward women.[15]

In 1972, Greenspan wrote, "Lesbianism is a greater threat to the reactionary institutions of this society than male homosexuality." Acknowledging that same-sex attraction had historically been considered a type of social deviance, she asserted that lesbianism had been virtually ignored for sexist reasons. She commented, "It is the most humiliating thing to be a lesbian and not have your very existence seriously believed." Greenspan also took feminism to task: "When lesbians finally surfaced in women's liberation, our coming out created a tremendous shockwave that is still rocking the movement." Some early feminist pioneers, such as Betty Friedan, did not want to be visibly welcoming to lesbians, fearing that to do so would taint feminism. Greenspan noted some Madison lesbians would participate only in feminist Women's Center events, and others would join in lesbian-only events.[16]

In 1970, MAHE picketed the Eastwood (now the Barrymore) Theater's showing of *The Boys in the Band*, a movie based on Mart Crowley's play of the same name. Many early gay activists criticized the movie because of its unfavorable portrayal of homosexuals as heavy-drinking, self-loathing stereotypes. One Madisonian remembered being appalled by this line from

Some lesbians in Madison, correctly perceiving that men dominated the early gay organizations, broke away to form Gay Sisters. The party advertised on this 1971 poster shows their efforts to create social as well as political spaces for lesbians. WHI IMAGE ID 59053

the movie: "You show me a happy homosexual and I'll show you a gay corpse." MAHE crafted a statement that argued, "The overall effect is to regard Crowley's characters as neurotic and pathetic individuals who elicit an audience's sympathy and pity rather than its empathy and understanding." During the group's leafleting, some members recalled, "High school boys were cruising up and down the streets in their cars hollering 'faggot.'" Yet, many would look back on these picketing tactics, borrowed from other activist movements, as a great early accomplishment.[17]

In 1973, the Madison Theater Guild put on a production of *The Boys in*

This lineup of Gay Sisters members in 1971 includes Sara Hummel (far left), Judy Greenspan (third from left), and Kathryn Burzinski (fourth from left). UNIVERSITY OF WISCONSIN–MADISON ARCHIVES IMAGE 2019S02026

Early Madison feminist organizers, left to right: Sandy Torkildson, Judy Greenspan, and Karla Dobinski. UNIVERSITY OF WISCONSIN–MADISON ARCHIVES IMAGE 2019S02027

the Band, and MAHE members picketed once again. Though the Gay Liberation Front was invited to hold a panel after the play, they rejected the offer because "the play as it stood was too destructive for them to associate themselves with it in any way." In a gay community newspaper profile that same year, early gay activist Ron McCrea contended that local gay social life was freest "at home parties—and few of them in Madison resemble the morose birthday wake which is the setting for 'Boys in the Band.'" In contrast to this free atmosphere, he explained that "for the majority of time, gay people cope with moving in a society which they feel is prepared to fear, despise, ridicule, or pity their lives but not to understand them."[18]

Later, activists in the capital city would repeat this pattern to decry other negative depictions of homosexuals. In January 1980, gay Madisonians picketed the movie *Cruising*, which included stereotypical portrayals of gay men. Two months later, the low-budget movie *Windows* came to Madison, featuring a psychotic lesbian portrayed as a murderer; she even killed a friend's cat and stowed it in the fridge. The local gay press claimed it represented "a clear and present danger in Madison" by contributing to bigotry and crimes against homosexuals. Lesbians and gays sought a boycott of the movie and picketed two theaters where it appeared. As Nichols reported in *Gay Madison*, some protesters "decided passive picketing was not enough and decided to sit in." Police arrested seven protesters one night at a local theater and another twenty on a different night at East Towne Mall. Nichols and another early activist, Barb Constans, were among those arrested, and Karla Dobinski of the Wilson Street Law Office and other progressive lawyers volunteered to do their legal work. The charges against the twenty were dismissed, and most of the seven paid small fines or accepted community service as a punishment. One picketer performed his forty hours of community service by volunteering at the ALL-GAYS Crisis Line, a phone counseling service for gays.[19]

In what was likely the first gay pride–related celebration in Wisconsin, MAHE Day was held on the first weekend of May 1970. Described as a group coming out, the event was held to break down stereotypes and develop new and positive images of gays. Borrowing techniques from the civil rights and antiwar teach-ins, gay activists offered workshops on the Madison campus, where, as Dale Hillerman, future leader of the Gay Center, wrote, "gay activists felt most at ease." While many of the early members of MAHE came from the world of campus activism, Hillerman explained, "from the beginning the gay movement contained a much larger range of political ideas and life styles than those provided by movement people, for many gays who did not consider themselves activists in the traditional sense became involved." At MAHE Day, talk sessions and panels discussed gay lifestyles and institutions. Presenters included MAHE members, a sociologist, and a member of the campus ministry.[20]

Those in the early iteration of MAHE wanting more political focus reorganized as the Madison Gay Liberation Front (GLF). They called for a national convention to be held on Thanksgiving in 1971, described as "the most crucial event in the Madison movement." Several hundred men and

St. Francis House, the UW–Madison campus Episcopal Center, was an early locus and supporter of gay organizing. The message of love on this poster emphasized that the movement was about more than sex. WHI IMAGE ID 59049

GAY LIBERATION LOVES YOU VERY MUCH.

EVERY WEDNESDAY AT 8:00
ST. FRANCIS HOUSE
1001 UNIV. AVE.

women attended with folks coming from Boston, New York, Austin, and Seattle, among other cities, facilitating early national cross-fertilization for Wisconsin's nascent movement. A workshop on sex was the most heavily attended. As Hillerman wrote, it "directly focused on sexual practices" as many people felt uptight about male-male touching and affection and feared the consequences of erotic homosexual involvement. Workshop participants asked questions about whether one had to identify as a homosexual to engage in same-sex activities.[21]

Another important workshop, though it drew only a few attendees, focused on gay community centers and how to define them. Dale Hillerman, director of the Gay Center in the early 1970s, saw communication, support, and inclusion as key elements for successful community centers. He believed "our greatest insecurities and dependencies arise when we have isolated ourselves from other people, when we fear interacting with others." According to Hillerman, "The conference opened many students to the possibilities of gay caucuses for law, medical, [and] social work students." Early activist Gridley Hall, for example, would later help to organize the gay law school students at UW–Madison. MAHE member Jess Anderson praised the conference's overall "positive results."[22]

In the early 1970s, the GLF established a gay center in Madison. In its first years, the Gay Center was used primarily by those in their twenties and thirties, which was also the age range of the staff members. In November 1972, for example, the center had five hundred calls and five hundred people walk in to use its resources. During this time, at the suggestion of the Madison Student Co-op, the GLF and its counseling center moved into 10 Langdon Street, a former sorority house, with a number of other groups such as the People's Office, which offered copy services for countercultural groups, and a women's writing collective. The hectic atmosphere was less than ideal for counseling sessions, and when the lease expired, another site had to be found. For the six months from July to December 1972, the center was located on North Hamilton Street, and a social membership including dances was used to raise money. Finally, the Gay Center was established in an office on the second floor of 550 State Street, and by July 1973, the space was serving a thousand people a month, with over half the contacts identifying as gay. While the GLF had maintained close ties to the campus, according to Hillerman, "only twenty-seven percent of

In the early 1970s, Gridley Hall was one of the Madison activists pushing for an amendment to the city's equal opportunities ordinance including language on sexual orientation. FROM THE AUTHOR'S COLLECTION

our contacts came from people who identified themselves as part of the
university community."[23]

The counseling staff was integral to the Gay Center's success, as staff
members were able to explain the clinic to curious parties and respond to
many people's fear of exposure. As Hillerman wrote, counseling staff also
held "workshops for medical students, family practice residents, nursing
students, and the staffs of mental institutions." Many of the counselors
gained skills through a series of sessions with a community counseling
group called Noah's Ark. The Gay Center also greatly benefited from
working with a group of psychiatric residents and social workers, many
of whom were involved in the campus psychiatric services. Several graduate students from the school of social work did field placements at the
Gay Center, and the university therapists' experiences at the Gay Center
added to their professional development in understanding gay issues. In
1973, the university's Psychiatric Institute published the first issue of the
journal *Forum* with symposium on homosexuality as its theme. Dr. Leigh
Roberts, chair of the Department of Psychiatry, posed the question "Homosexuality: Variance or Deviance?" Both Hillerman and Greenspan had
pro-gay contributions included.[24]

Creating gay social spaces outside of the bars, like this advertised picnic, was an important undertaking of early gay organizations like the Gay Center in Madison.
WHI IMAGE ID 59231

The center attempted to address many needs in the community, such as group counseling for married men and support for parents and families of gays. Gay health issues, particularly venereal disease (VD), were recognized as a concern. While general information sessions had been held several times a year in the early 1970s, they had a limited effect. One of the graduate students organized a VD screening clinic with cooperation from city and state health officials and members of the Madison medical profession. The clinic opened at the end of August 1973, providing many benefits to the community, such as educating gays about venereal diseases, determining the community's health needs, and providing experience on responsiveness to the medical professionals involved. The center also referred people to the Blue Bus Clinic, which would continue the work once the center ended its program.[25]

The Gay Center also served the needs of lesbians. The Gay Sisters group would use the space for coffeehouses, dances, and concerts, and the Lesbian Switchboard provided information and referrals. In the mid-1970s, these separate programs merged and the organization became the Madison Gay and Lesbian Center. It continues today as OutReach, cementing the legacy of MAHE, the GLF, and the Gay Sisters.[26]

GAY ORGANIZING IN MILWAUKEE

By spring 1970, Milwaukee was ready for its first formal gay organization. Posters were placed in bars and advertisements in *Kaleidoscope*. An initial meeting at UW–Milwaukee saw a turnout of between eighty and one hundred people and resulted in the selection of a steering committee "for the purpose of securing [gay and lesbian] rights thru positive courses of action." An early committee on legal counseling was also formed "to assist gays who are hassled by the police."[27]

Some radical members who later formed the GLF in Milwaukee initially joined in campus protests, including a strike against the Cambodia bombing and the 1971 Labor Day Peace Parade. Such actions led some members to question tactics; most of the leftists at the early meetings formed an amorphous group to support various protests, while other activists felt the need for structure and focus. One group that formed out of the early meetings was a UW–Milwaukee student group called the Gay Liberation Organization, which quickly evolved into the Gay People's Union (GPU). The GPU was most often described as the largest and most active of Milwaukee's gay groups. Some women in the group left and formed the Radical Lesbians.[28]

Several years later, *Bugle American* ran a profile of Milwaukee's gay community that described three other groups of gay activists: an informal New Gay Underground comprising mostly leftists who joined in protests, the Radical Queens, and the Homosexual Freedom League. In addition to these groups, several gays from Milwaukee attended the 1970 Black Panther Party's Revolutionary People's Constitutional Convention in Philadelphia. Upon their return, when their report was not welcomed at a Revolutionary People's gathering in Milwaukee, they proclaimed, "No revolution without us." Another group of gay artists called themselves

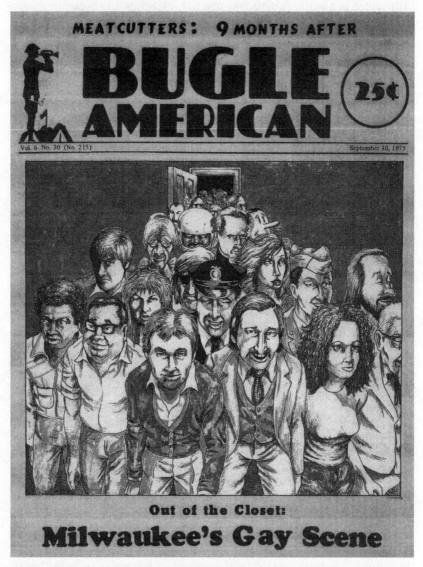

The cover illustration of the 1975 *Bugle American* special issue depicted a diversity of Milwaukee's gay community. *BUGLE AMERICAN*, SEPTEMBER 10, 1975

Le Petit Bon-Bons and argued in their "anti-manifesto" that "gay people have a responsibility to sabotage seriousness." A final group mentioned in the press was the PTA, "a secret social club of middle-aged male homosexuals." Though not officially confirmed, some members suggested that perhaps the acronym stood for Poor Tired Aunties.[29]

A viewpoint articulated by the *Bugle American* in 1975 stated, "Because Milwaukee is a conservative community, marches and picketing were never deemed effective." This characterization might seem strange for a city that had a Socialist mayor as recently as 1960. However, by the mid-1970s, longtime Democratic mayor Henry Maier and longtime police chief Harold Breier had created a climate of civic repression in Milwaukee, in part due to black activism over open housing. But the city's gay community did not always act conservatively. A 1970 UW–Milwaukee production of *The Boys in the Band* was subject to a follow-on gay satire produced by Milwaukee's GLF, though few in the audience stayed through the performance. One reviewer wrote, "By attempting to show gays as victims of straight oppression, GLF was betraying everything that *The Boys in the Band* had carefully reinforced in the straights' minds."[30]

In 1980, the Milwaukee Coalition to Oppose Violence Against Lesbians and Gay Men picketed the films *Cruising* and *Windows*. The leaflet to picket *Cruising* at the Downer Theatre complained that it "plays on all the old stereotypes about us." Gay men crossing the line to see the movie disappointed picketers, who were mostly women. The picket of *Windows* took place at the Esquire Theatre on Wisconsin Avenue and drew a group of one hundred protestors. Nevertheless, the cautious views of Milwaukee's early gay community would set it on a different path than Madison's more politically active gay community.[31]

MILWAUKEE'S GAY PEOPLE'S UNION

In Milwaukee during the 1970s, gays undertook a broad and vigorous program for community education and media outreach. Activist speakers were sent by the GPU as far as Beloit College and Carroll College in Waukesha. An invitation for a radio show led the GPU to sponsor what was believed to be the first regularly scheduled, scripted gay radio program in the nation, *Gay Perspective*. The show aired on WZMF from February to

July 1971 and then for another year on WUWM. In October 1971, the GPU launched *GPU News*, a monthly magazine that would be published for the rest of the decade. In 1972, the group also worked with the *Milwaukee Journal* to mitigate the unwanted exposure of gays in the press. Early in the year, several gay people committed suicide after their arrests for homosexual activity were reported in the paper. Alyn Hess, an early Milwaukee activist, claimed that the publication of a name "was tantamount to killing the person." Hess noted, "We confronted [the *Journal*] and asked them if they had to print every misdemeanor if it caused suicide. They have never published the like since."[32]

Five individuals were listed on the initial board of directors when the GPU's articles of incorporation were filed, a courageous and difficult decision given that state laws still criminalized sexual perversion. They were Gerald Earl Meyers, Michael Mitchell, Eldon Murray, Louis Stimac, and Donna Utke. According to a retrospective on the group from 1975, the "GPU barely got off the ground. When it incorporated, members could hardly find any lawyers who would not charge them double the usual fee for incorporation." Four banks turned the group down as it attempted to open an account. When it filed with the IRS seeking tax-exempt status, the group was rejected multiple times. At the time, there was only one gay tax-exempt group in the country, the Gay Community Services Center of Los Angeles. The LA group had to accept an IRS proviso that it would "not advocate homosexuality as a sexual orientation or lifestyle, and that none of your programs will ever be so conducted as to encourage or facilitate homosexual practices to a consequential degree." Hess, GPU president in the early 1970s, felt "this attitude on the part of the IRS indicates that [the GPU] has been denied its application solely because it's gay."[33]

A beloved figure in Milwaukee's gay community, Hess was active in the GPU and participated in many other gay rights efforts in the 1970s and 1980s. In a 1980 letter criticizing a national TV special on gay power, he wrote, "We want the right to live openly and proudly with members of our own sex and to express our affection publicly as all other people can. We want protection from discrimination by those intolerant bigots who wish we did not exist." Hess was also credited with bringing about the Milwaukee Gay Rights Ordinance in 1980. After his death from AIDS on March 31, 1989, Hess's home was donated to the Milwaukee AIDS Project at his

Eldon Murray (left) and Alyn Hess (right) were two of the pioneer leaders of Milwaukee's gay community. ARCHIVES DEPARTMENT, UNIVERSITY OF WISCONSIN–MILWAUKEE LIBRARIES

request. His obituary in the statewide gay and lesbian newspaper *The Wisconsin Light* ran with the headline "The Legacy of Alyn Hess Will Be with Us Forever" and noted his "refusing to apologize for his Gayness, holding his head up high and showing us the true meaning of dignity." Both the mayor and county executive of Milwaukee issued laudatory statements on his passing, and the successor to former police chief Harold Breier attended the funeral at All Saints' Episcopal Cathedral.[34]

In April 1972, during Hess's tenure as president, the GPU hosted delegates to the Midwest Homophile Conference in Milwaukee. The Midwest was one of three national homophile regions, along with the East and West. Four years earlier, the North American Conference of Homophile Organizations had met in Chicago with twenty-six groups represented. As the Milwaukee underground press reported, a "Homosexual Bill of Rights" had been adopted at the 1968 conference. More than one hundred delegates attended the 1972 Midwest conference, including the Cleveland Gay Alliance, Chicago GAA (Gay Activists Alliance), Kent State (Ohio) Gay Liberation, Minneapolis Gay House, Notre Dame Gay Alliance, Columbus (Ohio) GAA, Michigan State, and the University of Illinois Champaign–Urbana. The *Milwaukee Journal* captured the spirit of the event when it

"you are a child of the universe
no less than the trees and the stars
you have a right to be here ..."

mid-west
homophile
convention

milwaukee, wis.   april 8·9,'72
G.P.U. P.O. BOX 90530 milwaukee, wis. 53202

Milwaukee showcased its early liberation efforts by hosting the 1972 Midwest Homophile Convention. ARCHIVES DEPARTMENT, UNIVERSITY OF WISCONSIN–MILWAUKEE LIBRARIES

began its coverage stating, "Two national homosexual leaders said here Saturday that homosexuals must take the offensive against discrimination, saying that passive acceptance of society's attitudes was no longer acceptable."[35]

Sessions were held on Saturday at the Sheraton Schroeder Hotel and on Sunday at the UW–Milwaukee Student Union. Speakers for the Saturday noon banquet lunch were Barbara Gittings, editor of the national lesbian publication *The Ladder*, and Frank Kameny, an astronomer who had been fired from the federal government during the lavender scare and the president of the Washington, DC, Mattachine Society. Gittings told delegates that "the gay liberation movement was good for the straights as well as the gay community. It brings all of us, especially the straight society, to a reconsideration of love as a primary value—love, not marriage." A Saturday evening cocktail party was held at the gay bar Your Place on First Street, and on Sunday a Farewell Event took place at the Stud Bar on Fifth and Michigan featuring 25-cent beer.[36]

A session titled "Working with the Religious Community" would have a significant impact on gay activism efforts in Wisconsin. The Chicago delegates pointed out that the repeal of Illinois's sodomy laws, the first such repeal in the nation, "had been supported by Chicago-area churches."

This early 1970s ad for Your Place highlights an early claim by one of Milwaukee's longest running gay bars. ARCHIVES DEPARTMENT, UNIVERSITY OF WISCONSIN–MILWAUKEE LIBRARIES

Big enough to 'party-party,' but small enough to do your own thing.

YOUR PLACE

813 South 1st Street, Milwaukee

The Notre Dame Gay Alliance had published a letter written by a local priest defending homosexuals in their campus newspaper, the *Observer*. The GPU reported that a local minister had helped them establish contact with the *Milwaukee Journal*. The engagement and leveraging of religious support beginning in the early years of the 1970s would be very important in passing groundbreaking legislation in the 1980s, from consenting adults laws to state gay rights to hate crimes inclusive of sexual orientation. The support of clergy and local religious institutions was a significant element in this effort.[37]

In its 1974 annual report, the GPU cited work with the Milwaukee Council on Religion and the Homosexual and the Salvatorian Justice and Peace Commission Task Force on Gay Ministry. In early 1973, the Salvatorian group, based in Milwaukee, accepted a commission from the Catholic National Federations of Priests Councils to develop "guidelines and models" for ministry to gays. Later, the national group passed two resolutions calling for an end to civil laws criminalizing actions between consenting adults and opposing the use of homosexuality as the basis of discrimination in the areas of "employment, governmental service, housing, and child rearing involving natural or adoptive parents."[38]

On February 9, 1974, the GPU sponsored Masqueraid, a Mardi Gras ball at the Bradley Pavilion's Performing Arts Center. It was important for gays in Wisconsin and elsewhere to show same-sex couples dancing as a public display of how out they could be. The *Milwaukee Journal* reported one attendee saying, "It shows that gay people are together enough and have enough solidarity to come out in the open like this." There was a special award for most lavish costume, and people were certainly decked out that night, as I myself observed when attending a different event at the Performing Arts Center. The *Journal* reporter wrote, "Many of the guests were attired in costumes that would have done justice to any Cecil B. DeMille epic." The ball would lose $750, but the energy and public presence were thought to be well worth it.[39]

On October 11, 1974, the GPU opened a new center for venereal disease control. The *Milwaukee Journal* noted it was part of "an effort to stem a growing incidence of syphilis in the Milwaukee area, primarily among homosexuals." Three funding sources supported the effort: the GPU, the City of Milwaukee Health Department, and the Gerald Meyers Foundation.

The clinic was at the Farwell Center at 1568 North Farwell Avenue, the locus for many GPU organizing activities, and eventually evolved into the Brady East STD Clinic, known as BESTD. The center was open from 10:00 p.m. to 1:00 a.m., with those hours chosen according to Hess, then GPU head, "because that is when many of the city's homosexuals frequent the gay bars and are more available for tests."[40]

PROFILING MILWAUKEE'S GAY COMMUNITY: THE *MILWAUKEE JOURNAL*

Two remarkable journalistic efforts give important glimpses into early Milwaukee gay life. The first occurred at the end of February and the beginning of March 1972 when the *Milwaukee Journal* ran six days of articles in a series titled "The Gay Revolution." Since this metropolitan paper had the state's largest circulation with both city and state editions, its influence was far-reaching. The series was spearheaded by Neil Rosenberg, a twenty-seven-year-old staff reporter, and its articles, which ran on the front page of the city/state news section, were accompanied by a *Journal* artist's sketches. The apprehension many interview subjects felt about being out was reflected in a caution to readers: "Unless otherwise noted the names of persons identified as homosexuals are fictitious." Supposedly, the follow-up letters to the editor were 85 percent favorable to the series. One letter writer identified as H. C. K. of Milwaukee responded, "Of all the minority groups, the gay community has been the least understood. The information given in your articles has given me a positive attitude towards the gay people." Another writer tagged as M. C., a self-identified homosexual, wrote, "Perhaps in the near future, as a result of more series like yours, homosexuals will be able to come out." A third writer, E. O., thought the series was "enlightening and overdue."[41]

The *Journal* series was ahead of the times in including a major part of one article on transsexuals, in which Rosenberg reported that the "first sex reassignment in Wisconsin was performed last Sept. 28 in Lutheran Hospital." The patient, a male transitioning to female, "had to go through exhaustive counseling before the decision was made." Though the article brought this group to light, it ran with the negative headline, "Sex Identity Ills Cause Problems." That the story included both transsexuals and transvestites reflected the societal tendency to conflate them, despite the categorical difference between those concerned about gender identity and those who favor clothing of the other sex. Regarding transvestites, the series reported on a visiting county judge from Hudson, Wisconsin, who dismissed a Milwaukee case against a twenty-one-year-old who was arrested for wearing women's clothing. The man appeared for his trial wearing a pink blouse, magenta skirt, black hose, rouge, lipstick, and a wig tied in pigtails. The judge ruled that the man's behavior was private conduct guaranteed by the Constitution, writing, "I don't see how we can legislate what a person is to wear." But elsewhere in Milwaukee, Judge Christ Seraphim stated, "I feel that any man who dresses like a woman tends to cause a breach of the peace even if he is just walking down the street." Transvestites continued to be arrested in Milwaukee during this period.[42]

One of the most poignant comments was expressed by a Milwaukeean named Roger, who was one of five homosexuals of the so-called "closet minority" profiled by Rosenberg in the first article of the series: "I would love to be a 24-hour human being. I would like to be able to be true to myself every minute of the day, every day of the week, not to have to be someone at work, and then someone else after work." Roger had researched literature on homosexuals, but he said, "The books were horrible. All they talked about was the way rats acted in cages. What good did that do me?" Roger attended GPU meetings and went to gay bars three or four times a week. He was still searching for a sense of completeness. "I want to be part of the whole world," he wrote. "I see too many gays who hide in the homosexual world." Another interviewee, a twenty-six-year-old college graduate named Mike who was active in the GPU, said, "I feel they [heterosexuals] are sick, and I am healthy." Two years later, the *Journal* and other state papers would report on the American Psychiatric Association's decision to stop classifying homosexuality as a mental disease.[43]

Another article in the series focused on Milwaukee law enforcement agencies as predators and oppressors. Dominic Frinzi, one of two attorneys identified who represented homosexuals, complained, "Police in Milwaukee used to lie naked in hotel rooms with the door open to entrap homosexuals." He noted most arrested were charged with lewd and lascivious behavior but pled down to disorderly conduct, a misdemeanor. James

Shellow, another attorney who had handled hundreds of cases involving homosexuals, called the Milwaukee vice squad cops "constructive victims" because their conduct patrolling homosexual hangouts precipitated contact with the law. Captain John Davis, head of the vice squad, saw homosexuals as both criminals and sickos; he said, "By enforcing such laws we bring [homosexual behavior] to the attention of the courts, which have the prerogative of seeking psychiatric help or aid for the individual." Most cases ended up in the courtroom of Judge Seraphim, who "often ridiculed and taunted" the accused. In response to the article, the judge later said, "I don't necessarily approve of their act—I may even deplore them—but far be it from me to start a war on homosexuals."[44]

While harassment by police and others was ongoing, some gays fought back, as one of the men profiled in the first article in the series attested: "Last summer, according to homosexuals here, several gangs of youths began a series of attacks on homosexuals in Juneau Park, a longtime meeting place. The attacks became so frequent and devastating that a group of homosexuals formed a vigilante committee to patrol the park. They eventually tracked down one of the gangs and in the ensuing fight, a gang member was pitched through a plate glass door of the Knickerbocker Hotel." The piece concluded, "The attacks on homosexuals soon tapered off."[45]

A final article in the series was headed "Churches Easing Stand on Gays." Reverend Wilbur C. Cain of the Ebenezer Lutheran Church on South Thirty-Fifth Street was featured and described as "one of the prime movers behind the formation" of the Council on Religion and the Homosexual, a group that sought to involve understanding clergy with the gay community. The great need for this work was shown in a four-year-old document circulated by the Wisconsin Conference of the United Church of Christ to three hundred pastors. It regarded homosexuality as "an arrested form of development and as such is a pathetic, second rate substitute for normal masculinity." While encouraging fairness and understanding, the statement continued, "It does not deserve encouragement, glamorization or rationalization." If God is still speaking, as today this denomination's welcoming stance toward gays indicates, apparently he had not yet said enough by this time.[46]

The article also highlighted two churches serving the gay community. One was the St. Nicolas Orthodox Church, a campus mission near

Marquette, and the other was the Milwaukee Metropolitan Community Church, whose pastor said, "We consider the homosexual a child of God." However, the article pointed out that the two churches were "mostly ignored by the homosexual community," perhaps not surprising in a city dominated by Lutherans and Catholics.[47]

Despite many drawbacks in the series, such as dealing in stereotypes and conflating transsexuals and transvestites, it firmly established that there was a gay community in Milwaukee, with multiple institutions and organizations. It engaged in actual research on the gay community, permitted gays to speak in their own words, and showed them as organized and organizing. The series also proved that major institutional actors in the larger community, such as the *Milwaukee Journal*, parts of the clergy, and some major trial lawyers, were beginning to interact with the city's gay community in ways that would not have been expected in pre-Stonewall times.

PROFILING MILWAUKEE'S GAY COMMUNITY: THE *BUGLE AMERICAN*

Three years later, in September 1975, the *Bugle American*, an alternative weekly, published a special issue called "Out of the Closet: Milwaukee's Gay Scene," filling sixteen pages with related articles. Several were written by Dave Pettinari as his professional project for a master's degree at Marquette University. The series also included a couple of gay national wire features from Liberation News Service, a leftist alternative to the Associated Press. The *Bugle American* had, in 1974, started to run occasional columns from the GPU called *Gay Perspective*. There was no disclaimer about fictitious names, though often only first names were used. With the intention of reaching the "non-gay community" of Milwaukee, this special issue noted that while "sheer visibility after centuries of oppression has finally taken some of the fear out of being gay . . . gays are still very much oppressed educationally, psychologically, physically, socially and politically."[48]

One of the articles in the special issue bore the headline, "Banishing the Gay Stereotype." However, the articles sometimes seemed to reinforce the stereotype, for instance with sidebars on homosexual biker/leather clubs. A part of one story featured attorneys who defended those arrested for "tea

Banishing the Gay Stereotype

by Dave Pettinari

A person can be a homosexual and not be gay. The difference is the degree to which one's thinking is liberated. Some integrate their sexuality with other aspects of their lives. That is, they give up repressing their sexuality and come out into the open.

Others lead double lives and pretend to be heterosexual. The secret lifers are the men and women who wear wedding rings and laugh at queer jokes. Men feign drooling when the boss shows them a stag movie at the office party. They can never bring their lovers to a company picnic or, if young, to a prom at school.

It is difficult to go to work or school for eight hours a day and repress part of a personality. It is hard for a closet gay to come home to watch on TV the heterosexual commercials which say nothing else is valid.

Dennis was studying to be a Catholic priest. He was thrown out of the seminary when he took a liking to one of the head administrators. One of the other priests, who was the man's lover, found out. He got Dennis dismissed.

Dennis said probably 40% of the men in this seminary were secret lifers. "You eat together, socialize together and have a common goal. Of course there will be sexual contacts among the members." He is not sorry about leaving: "They hypocritically told us 'Be your sick, perverted self, but hide it, hide it, hide it!' " He no longer feels comfortable hiding it, and is not ashamed to discuss it.

Dennis is often invited to parties. His hosts assume he will bring a girl. If he brings John, his lover, they are often not invited again. The assumptions that people act on bother him: "Everybody assumes that everybody else is heterosexual. But one out of ten men you meet on the street is not."

Gary, a gay businessman, is not pleased that society determines a role for a person before he has a chance to make a determination for himself. "When you realize you are homosexual, you have to throw away much of what you learned as a child. Gay men are brought up to direct themselves toward having a family. Gay women are brought up to plan for their children. When you conclude that many of society's designs are not valid ... you have questioned them and found them wanting, it becomes relatively easy to question other values in society. It becomes necessary to set up your own code of what is right and wrong."

In his own case, Gary said, his clients who know his sexual preference are not bothered. "People don't give a damn if you fuck ducks, as long as you make money for them," he said.

It is impossible to draw a personality profile of a gay person. However, some are gay-happy, some gay-sad. The gay-happy are well-adjusted, sensitive people who feel comfortable with their sexual and human identities. The gay-sad have not yet overcome an oppressed state of mind. One who is in constant fear of being found out will undergo psychological trauma leading to neuroses.

Nothing is more likely to make a person sick than to be constantly told he is sick. Until recently, psychiatry has treated gays as despicable deviants, even though in 1936, Sigmund Freud wrote: "Although homosexuality is assuredly no advantage, it is nothing to be ashamed of; no vice, no degradation, it cannot be classified as an illness." The American Psychiatric Association recently dropped homosexuality from its list of mental aberrations.

Gary, the gay businessman, feels that most gays are more mentally stable than non-gays: "There is a life crisis that occurs when a person realizes he is gay, parentheses, different. Society tells him he is a criminal because he has natural feelings. Society tells him he is sick ... he is coming along when he finally admits, 'This is where I am. I am attracted to people of the same gender. I accept myself for what I am.' "

Transvestitism has often been erroneously restricted to gay people. "A gay female is supposed to be a butch and the gay men are supposed to dress in women's clothing," Gary said.

"This does happen in the gay community, But statistically, it can be shown that there are more heterosexual men into wearing women's clothing." The statistics say one in five transvestites are gay people.

A distinct culture has arisen which is the gay community's way of making their sexuality visible so they can find one another. They also flaunt it for the straights. If it can be seen, it can become an issue and be talked about.

Those who feel the need to broadcast their sexual lifestyle

The Lavender Lady at Brady Street's Gay Kissing Booth
Photo by Dennis Darmek

This article from the *Bugle American* features a photo of the Milwaukee Gay People's Union's "Kissing Booth," with men happily providing services for the bargain price of 25 cents at the Brady Street Festival. *BUGLE AMERICAN*, SEPTEMBER 10, 1975

room" sex—encounters that occurred in public lavatories—and proceeded to list popular Milwaukee "tea rooms." Another article titled "Gay Health Spas" noted that such establishments had orgy rooms with wall-to-wall mattresses. A story called "The Bar Scene" included the observation that "though gay bars are located in tacky neighborhoods, the interiors are absolutely beautiful." A sign reading "One at a time" outside a gay bar's men's room required an explanation for the reader: "The sign is a source of some confusion for straights participating in the fashionable practice of gay bar-hopping. The sign is a dig at Milwaukee's Police Department's Vice Squad, or as some call it, 'The PROD Squad,' Pervert and Restroom Observation Detail." In another example of articles delving into stereotypes, one included comments from John, a gay Marquette student: "Gay men affect limp-wristed silly savages to the amusement of their fellow gays." But for him such gestures had a use. "If the sauna at Marquette is a little crowded, you just do a little camp and they [the homophobes] clear out."[49]

Several interview subjects also spoke about the intersections between religion and homosexuality. Dennis, a Milwaukeean and former Catholic seminarian who had taken a male lover, made clear that the Catholic university was not the only place harboring gays in the church. He guessed 40 percent of the seminary students were homosexual, saying, "They [the administration] hypocritically told us, 'Be your sick, perverted self, but hide it, hide it, hide, it!'" Another article focused on a "gay mass" held at the UW–Milwaukee Newman Center. The service was begun by a local chapter of Dignity in March 1975. Dennis commented, "If supposed Christian people at the liturgy in non-gay churches knew I was gay, I would be rejected." A man referred to as Father Mike said the mass but would permit only his first name to be used in the article because, he said, "If you print my last name my parishioners will have me removed. I feel sorry that their concept of Christianity and acceptance of individuals is so narrow."[50]

The article "GPU: 5 Years of Teaching" featured the Gay Kissing Booth set up at the Brady Street Festival, an eastside hippie countercultural festival where, as the paper stated, "the curious meets the outlandish." Alyn Hess explained, "The kissing booth was there to point out that gay people can kiss in public," and he was delighted that Waukesha barbershops were still talking about it. Joseph Schuman, one of the staffers of the kissing booth, wrote a letter to the *Milwaukee Sentinel* about the coverage, proclaiming that the joyous affirmative message behind the booth was, "Destroy your fear: Kiss a queer."[51] Throughout the *Bugle American*'s coverage, there was a preference for portrayal of a movement rather than a community. The underground press was credited with the first positive presentation of gay life in Milwaukee, and one reader was quoted as saying, "It is helpful to learn gay history."[52]

Sizing Up the Coverage

The *Milwaukee Journal* and the *Bugle American* presented their gay information quite differently. The *Journal* sought to inform its presumably
mostly straight readership about the new phenomenon of an active gay
community in the state's largest city. It had ready access to elected officials
and was able to provide experts on opposing sides of issues such as illness
and religion. In contrast, the *Bugle American* presented Milwaukee's gay
scene as part of a broader liberation effort and often referred to it as part of
a "revolution." In taking this social revolutionary view, the *Bugle American*
delved much more into the sex lives of gay Milwaukeeans than did the *Milwaukee Journal*. In some ways, the *Bugle American*'s series was more one-
sided in its coverage; for example, only sympathetic religious voices were
cited, while the voices of law enforcement officials were mainly negative.
Despite these differences, both papers presented homosexuals as a new minority that could be talked about in similar contexts as other minorities.[53]

Both series give us an intriguing look at some numbers. Using data
from Alfred Kinsey's 1948 report, *Sexual Behavior in the Human Male*,
the *Milwaukee Journal* estimated that out of a population of 1.4 million in
metropolitan Milwaukee, "40,000 to 100,000 persons are homosexuals."
This estimate was much higher than that of Dr. E. R. Krumbiegel, the
city's health commissioner, whom the *Journal* cited as guessing "there are
about 5,000 homosexuals in Milwaukee." The paper concluded, "Whatever
the exact number, it is clear there is a sizable number of homosexuals in
the Milwaukee area." The *Bugle American* wrote, "Milwaukee, although
a crushingly conservative community, is on the verge of at least tacit ac-
knowledgement of its estimated 25,000 gay citizens." Whatever the actual
number, Milwaukee in the early 1970s was certainly home to a larger gay
population than the number the Milwaukee Crime Prevention Commission had estimated in the 1940s—several hundred people.[54]

Of the potentially tens of thousands of homosexuals living in Milwaukee in the mid-1970s, however, only the slightest fraction were involved
in gay causes, communities, or movements. In 1974, the GPU's annual report listed 140 members, up 50 percent since the previous year. Yet, other
organizations had smaller numbers. Only twenty-five or thirty people attended gay mass at the Newman Center, between fifteen and thirty people

belonged to the Metropolitan Community Church, and just ten gay folks belonged to St. Nicolas Orthodox. Biker clubs, an alternative to the bars, were likewise small. One strictly gay club had twenty-six members, but only half of the members owned bikes. Frokers club had ten full members and two pledges. Vipers had six local members and a dozen associate members from outstate. The Argonauts were seven men, but none owned cycles at that time.[55]

At this time, the most popular gay institutions in Milwaukee were those that opened the avenues to gay sex. The city's gay bars were described as "booming" and were often standing room only. The other large institutions were the city's three gay health spas, otherwise known as "the baths." As the *Journal* reported, "One club claims 1500 members; another 1000 patrons; the third a mere 700." Gay Milwaukeeans attended these social venues in numbers that far exceeded those in any political groups.[56]

METROPOLITAN CITIES AND BEYOND

While exhibiting some differences, the early gay community efforts in Milwaukee and Madison displayed some similarities. Most of the actors in these early gay movements were young, twenty-something, and male. In both cities, more leftist members split off from the initial gay groups and tried to form broad fronts with other liberation movements. But as a *GPU News* editorial noted, some leftist groups did not welcome homosexuals. The enduring groups from the early days in Wisconsin were those that focused exclusively on "homosexual welfare and equal rights."[57]

Both cities' early organizing efforts set up speakers' bureaus or committees to publicize homosexuality. According to the 1974 GPU annual report, speakers associated with the group had addressed twelve hundred persons that year. Call lines for information and referrals were set up in both cities. Both communities also established publications primarily aimed at their own members—*GPU News* in Milwaukee and *Gay Renaissance* in Madison—though members found them difficult to maintain. The publications provided content similar to that established in the 1950s by *ONE: The Homosexual Magazine*, published in San Francisco for a national audience. The communities in Madison and Milwaukee also set up gay libraries as resources for homosexual information, perhaps as a response to the reluctance of public libraries to display gay material on open shelves, or perhaps because gays were reluctant to use such resources when they were available. As a personal example, when I was a graduate student in Madison in the 1960s doing research on progressives who tried to reform prostitution, I had a legitimate reason for being in the social deviance section of the stacks of Memorial Library. Of course, I could sidle over and read the materials on homosexuality, but I never thought of checking them out. Similarly, one gay man in Appleton in the latter part of the 1970s admitted he stole homosexual material from the library rather than checking it out.[58]

In the early 1970s, Wisconsin was quickly linked into the national circuit of traveling gay speakers, and these visits often heartened early Wisconsin activists. Many national speakers came to the Midwest to hit Chicago and Minneapolis, and Wisconsin made a logical in-between stop, not because of its cornfields or dairy barns but because Wisconsin's gay activists were eager to hear their messages and gay or gay-friendly audiences would show up to attend their speeches.

Some appearances were simply fortuitous. In March 1974, Morris Kight, director of the Los Angeles Gay Community Service Center, came to Milwaukee on business to help one of his program directors and, while in town, made an appearance at a regular GPU meeting and attended a reception where he spoke about the twenty-seven programs hosted by the center in California. Other appearances were planned as part of celebratory or political events. For Milwaukee's Gay Pride Week in 1973, the GPU booked a presentation by Del Martin, cofounder of Daughters of Bilitis and coauthor of *Lesbian/Woman*. Jack Baker, former student body president at the University of Minnesota, spoke to a crowd of five hundred in Oshkosh during 1973 as part of his campaign "to promote the same-sex marriage issue."[59]

Many speakers came to Wisconsin as part of academic lectures or conferences. In early April 1974, Dr. Frank Kameny from the Washington, DC, Mattachine Society spoke in both Milwaukee and Appleton. He also lectured at the UW–Madison Law School one afternoon and gave a public address in the Memorial Union that evening. Dr. Bruce Voeller, early director of the National Gay Task Force, spent three days in Wisconsin in June 1976, speaking in both Madison and Milwaukee. Voeller and lesbian author Ginny Vida gave keynote addresses to the Symposium on Gays and the Law at UW–Madison sponsored by the Madison Committee for Gay Rights, with fifty people in attendance from around the state. The event was funded by the Gay Law Students and the campus student government. The report on the conference noted the possibility of gay groups forming in La Crosse and Beloit. Voeller's later successor at the National Gay Task Force, Steve Endean, would speak in Wisconsin in 1980.[60]

Elaine Noble of Massachusetts, the nation's first out state legislator, spoke in Madison in 1977 at the Eighth National Conference on Women and the Law. In 1979, Alan Bell, a researcher at the Indiana Institute for Sex Research founded by Alfred Kinsey, spoke at UW–Milwaukee on a visit sponsored by the UW–Milwaukee Gay Students Association, the Campus United Ministries, and the Counseling Center of Milwaukee. He had co-authored a recently published study called *Homosexualities* with Martin Weinberg. Bell contrasted his Milwaukee experience with a recent trip to the University of Nebraska where a court injunction was sought to prevent him from speaking.[61]

Outside the two metropolitan cities of Madison and Milwaukee, the Fox River Valley area appears to have had one of the most active gay communities in the 1970s. As noted previously, Kameny visited Appleton to address the Fox Valley Gay Alliance (FVGA) in April 1974. The Alliance was formed in December 1972; by 1977, the Lawrence University Committee for Gay Awareness appears to have replaced the earlier Alliance. In November of that year, the committee sponsored a weekend series of programs and workshops. In her keynote address, Miriam Ben-Shalom, president of Milwaukee's GPU, urged the crowd of about a hundred to continue the struggle for "the right to our dignity as human beings."[62]

In 1973, the *Fond du Lac Reporter* published a two-part series on the Fox River Valley's gay scene. Both the article's author and the gay interviewees remained anonymous. The FVGA founder, "Simon," who appeared to be the main source of information in the series, had moved to the valley a year prior after being involved with Milwaukee's gay community. Simon described the FVGA as composed primarily of members under thirty from Fond du Lac, Oshkosh, and Appleton. He emphasized that they were not a militant group. While no true gay bars existed in the valley at this time, one Appleton bar did host a "gay night" once a week. (In 1981, the gay bar 1101 West would open in Appleton and become an anchor for the valley's gay community.) "Gays are definitely a minority," the *Reporter* journalist wrote in 1973, "but not like minorities as most people tend to identify them. They have no visible differences from the typical person." In a somewhat concessional view, Simon remarked, "The key to successful gay living is simply to accept the fact that it is a heterosexual society." Later in the same year, Brian Salchert of Fond du Lac wrote a letter to the editor of the *Fond du Lac Reporter* seeking to educate people about homosexuality. Salchert wrote, "Hiding ourselves from ourselves does no one any good, I know. . . . Neither ignoring nor ignorance cures."[63]

In the mid- to late 1970s, the FVGA worked with area libraries to make publicly available "a more expanded and contemporary selection of materials related to the gay theme." The Appleton Public Library agreed to carry *GPU News* among its periodicals, and its library director also agreed to purchase more materials "reflecting an honest view of the subjects concerning homosexuality and the gay life-style." Still, an anonymous "Letter from Fox River Valley" sent to *GPU News* in November 1979 read, "You will have to prove to me that these Wisconsin cities [Oshkosh, Appleton, and Green Bay] are not inhospitable, intolerant, and outright hostile to gay and bisexual persons. . . . The occasional (perhaps even frequent) anti-gay and Gestapo-like police tactics simply add to the arrogance and bigotry which is already here."[64]

Merle Miller visited Whitewater, Wisconsin, to speak in 1973. While primarily there to discuss his biography of Harry Truman, Miller agreed to speak informally in the afternoon at the religious center about his 1971 book *On Being Different: What It Means to Be a Homosexual*. The book had been published as a long-form essay called "What It Means to Be a Homosexual" in the *New York Times Magazine* on January 17, 1971. In Wisconsin, the *Milwaukee Journal* had picked up the multipage piece, running it on February 21, 1971, in its Insight section. Whitewater was the same place where, the previous year, a dozen "gay students had met for about four sessions or so—and then had faded away." The *GPU News* report on Miller's Whitewater presentation stated, "There seems to be no gay presence at this school of 8,500." No posters had advertised the talk because, as the campus ministry facilitator said, when they put some up for the earlier meetings, "people simply tore them down as fast as they were put up."[65]

GPU News may have been harsh in its judgment about the gay presence on Whitewater's campus. Just a year earlier, in 1972, the student paper ran a story called "'Gay' G.I. 'Undesirables,'" a review of a play called *The Undesirables* written and produced by Richard Mence, a Whitewater student. The play's theme revolved around a court martial trial about which the reviewer in the student paper wrote, "The accused is a homosexual which is considered prejudicial to order and discipline." The staff writer thought the play was well written: "The dialogue was especially good— using language native to the gay community and that which is at home in a military installation." In the play, the accused is raped by a drunken comrade who refers to him as "Aunt Alice." The reviewer found the scene "somewhat shocking but not sickening." One hopes the shocking part was the rape, not the same-sex activity. Overall, the reviewer presented the discharge and treatment of gay military persons as "an undesirable but realistic problem."[66]

During the 1970s, a GPU organized at UW–Stevens Point. By July 1980, the group was established enough to host a statewide gay networking conference to improve communication among groups around the state. The impetus for the conference was a May 1980 Midwest Conference of the Lesbian and Gay Communications Network. The Stevens Point GPU sponsored an opening night dance and a closing picnic with a pig roast. This led to the birth of the Wisconsin Lesbian and Gay Network (WLGN), which held an annual conference in Stevens Point for several years. The conference was attended mainly by outstate contacts, though a few Milwaukee and Madison members were present.[67]

The annual event brought national speakers to Stevens Point, including Madison's Karla Dobinski, at that time a board member of the National Gay Task Force, as the main speaker in 1981. In 1982, with the conference theme Flaunting Our Virtue, Leonard Matlovich, who had been discharged by the US Air Force for homosexuality, spoke, as did Madison activist Judy Greenspan. In 1983, speaking on the theme We Shall Go Forth, featured presenters were Barbara Grier, a pioneer of lesbian publishing, and Ann Bannon, a lesbian author. The 1984 conference, with the theme A Vision of Boundless Means, featured Tom Chorlton, director of the National Association of Gay and Lesbian Democratic Clubs, and Denise Matyka, director of the Wisconsin Women's Network. Matyka had attended UW–Stevens Point and knew WLGN was "really a lifeline" in Stevens Point.[68]

The Stevens Point community also sponsored an annual Lesbian/ Gay Awareness Week. During the month of March 1984, a gay awareness banner flew across Main Street. Music and lectures were the highlights of what Stevens Point GPU advisor Ernest Clay called a "very successful week." Then a backlash set in. A Lutheran minister took out an ad in the local paper denouncing the homosexual lifestyle as "grotesque" and saying that gays did not "know when to shut up." The police chief, Joseph Flandre, piled on. He condemned "the homosexuals in this community openly flaunting a sign across Main Street advertising this illicit conduct that all true Christians oppose." The chief may not have realized that Wisconsin's consenting adults law had passed in 1983 decriminalizing homosexual acts. In contrast, Stevens Point's mayor Michael Haberman met with gay activists and agreed to promote police sensitivity training and the appointment of gay men and lesbians to local government bodies.[69]

Sandra Lipke was a driving force in the Stevens Point gay community. A native of Racine attending UW–Stevens Point and studying political science, Lipke came out while a student and was active in the community in the late 1970s and early 1980s. A cofounder of WLGN in 1980, she was an advocate for gay communities in the nonmetropolitan areas of the state. She believed the typical "Madison response" of organizing a march on public streets did not occur throughout most of Wisconsin because most areas did not have a critical mass of out lesbians and gays. Lipke believed that fear and isolation were strong deterrents for potential gay activists in rural areas. "If you're living somewhere and 30 miles away is the Posse Comitatus," she said, referring to a patriot militia active in parts of central Wisconsin, "you are not about to go out and educate your local sheriff." In addition to the Posse, Lipke also knew of a "local vigilante group" operating in central Wisconsin. Still, she believed, "we can be successful in taking those risks. They have to be educated risks, though."[70]

Lipke's hope was that WLGN could connect the most isolated gay Wisconsinites. Another WLGN spokesperson, Kay Sprinstroh, echoed her concern: "Once again many of the members of our minority are getting the message that coming out is an invitation to violence." A case in point was not too far off in Sparta. A reputed, though dubious, rumor that gays were planning to hold a candlelight vigil and march in the town provoked an egg- and firecracker-throwing crowd of two hundred in February 1984. A local resident, photographed with egg in hand, was reported as saying, "I'll tell you what, no one around here likes queers." Lipke would later become one of several activists from Stevens Point involved in the early organizational efforts to create an Eleanor Roosevelt Political Action Committee for lesbians and gays in Wisconsin. By the end of the 1980s, WLGN was no longer active, and gay Wisconsinites were calling for a new statewide group.[71]

UW–Platteville also saw gay organizing efforts in the late 1970s. Initially called the Gays and Lesbians of Platteville (GLOP), the group changed its name to the Gay and Lesbian Alliance (GALA). The founder, Mark Prestegard, had been attacked after leaving a bar in Madison and said he "didn't know where to turn after returning to school." It made sense to start a support group on the campus of five thousand in a town of ten thousand. When the group sought recognition as a campus organization, it was met with some resistance from faculty members as well as from a local pastor, but a tie vote that would have denied recognition was changed at the last minute. The Platteville group created a speakers' bureau from its ranks to present to classes on campus, and group outings were made to Dubuque, the closest city with a gay bar. Coming out in 1979, then-student Callen Harty joined the group and "quickly became one of its most active members, going into classrooms to talk openly and honestly about my sexuality, my struggles with accepting myself, my hopes for finding love in a world where not everyone finds it." In one instance, when a professor used the term *faggot* in class, Harty objected and got an apology. As a known out person on campus, he remembered people throwing beer bottles at him for just walking down the street.[72]

Not all speakers' bureau efforts were successful. In Kenosha in 1972, some GPU speakers at UW–Parkside drew only three people. A reporter for the campus paper came to the event imagining that campus biases against gay people would increase after the talk. He wrote, "I couldn't have imagined that a person who was Gay should have the rights I have and be allowed to express himself in the manner he desired." However, by the end of his article, the reporter had changed his mind, writing, "People need awakening in order to help change old values and attitudes. . . . I sincerely hope at some time you can talk to a person without looking at their sexual beliefs in determining if they are a good person or not."[73]

As the GPU morphed into more of a community institution during the 1970s, activities on the UW–Milwaukee campus continued both in the campus press and with a new Gay Students Association. In November 1971, the *UWM Post* ran a profile titled "Student Describes Life of Homosexual." After debunking stereotypes, the gay man being interviewed said, "I wasn't necessarily looking for sexual pleasure with men because I was gay; I was looking for love and affection only male companionship could give me." The campus publication *crossroads* ran a four-part profile series called "Being Gay: One Experience" in the spring term of 1974. "Mike," twenty-five, described as a recent UWM graduate, had come out to a number of friends during his days on campus. "I want to tell people I'm gay," he said, "because I want people to know that I am real, that I am deep, and with respect to all of these things, I am also gay." He did go to gay bars but was not willing to walk down Wisconsin Avenue carrying signs. "No gay can escape being hassled," he reported. "Almost all of the arrests are brought about by police entrapment." In one response to the series, a letter writer said that being gay is "just like being a woman or a black or a third world worker, revolutionary in the most radical sense. Understood fully, it is a rejection of the entire white-penis-power structure. . . . In the truest sense of the word, homosexuals are an abused minority."[74]

The following year, in fall 1974, a furor erupted over an antigay column in *crossroads*. Peter Ehrmann, a self-described member of "the gentry," felt straights were "entitled to fidget when the fetishists insist on advertising themselves in a loud and obscene manner and even worse when they demand their quirks be accepted as a normal, standard procedure. . . . Specifically I have in mind the so-called 'Gay Liberation' associations, which have been making whoopee on the socio-political fronts." Particularly offensive to him were gay rallies, dances, and media events. He argued that minority groups should "exercise discretion."[75]

The campus Gay Students Association, Alyn Hess on behalf of the GPU, and Louis Stimac, one of the GPU's founders, all responded with letters. Regarding Ehrmann's contention that tax money supported student dances held on campus, Hess gave a strong riposte, pointing out that gays paid taxes to "a government that tells us we are criminal, denies our rights to do in private what we like, and puts us in jails." The student group argued that gays organized to present the validity of their sexuality against the oppression of the straight world. Claiming they would not be patronized, they warned Ehrmann, "Be prepared to feel very uncomfortable, our closets have no more doors."[76]

The first four issues of *Gay Comix* were published by Denis Kitchen in Princeton, Wisconsin, reflecting the strength of the state's underground press. Since sexual presentations were banned from traditional comic shops, the magazine was marketed at head shops around the country. *GAY COMIX* NO. 1, 1980

Perhaps the most unusual outstate spot of gay creativity was the Krupp Comix Works at No. 2 Swamp Road in Princeton, Wisconsin. The workshop was the creation of Denis Kitchen, native of Racine, who founded the *Bugle American*, Milwaukee's underground newspaper, in 1970. Kitchen, a cartoonist and publisher, wanted to diversify the cartoon world. The Comics Magazine Association of America had formed the Comics Code Authority in 1954 during the McCarthy period to self-police the industry, and the authority strictly forbade the depiction of sex perversion in comics. Newsstands and drugstores would not sell comic books without the Code's seal of approval. By 1973, Kitchen had relocated to an old barn in Princeton and begun creating underground comics without Code seals that were sold primarily in head shops. In 1980, he produced a thirty-two-page underground publication called *Gay Comix*, which featured sexually explicit depictions of gay sex. Priced at $1.50, the publication proclaimed "Adults Only" on the cover. Kitchen recruited gay cartoonist Howard Cruse as the comic's editor. Cruse, who also contributed cartoons to the early issues, would go on to become one of the most well-known freelance gay cartoonists in the country. The Kitchen Sink Press published four issues of *Gay Comix* in Wisconsin before the publication moved out of the state. While Milwaukee and Madison established gay liberation structures that would have continuity, many manifestations of visible gay activity could be found outside these metropolitan areas.[77]

Milwaukee Council on Religion and the Homosexual

As shown in the newspaper series discussed above, Milwaukee had a depth and breadth of gay activity. In February 1972, Reverend Wilbur C. Cain initiated the Milwaukee Council on Religion and the Homosexual (CRH). The model for such a council had been created in San Francisco in 1964 when progressive clergy had engaged with homophile activists. Cain shared materials from the San Francisco model with Milwaukeeans. Among the six individuals invited to the first gathering were Eldon Murray and Donna Utke, both of whom were among the original organizers of the GPU. According to founding documents, the purpose of the council was "to foster and promote a continuing dialogue between the religious community and homosexuals." Cain became chairman and Utke was recording secretary.

They decided to grow the group through personal contacts rather than using more widespread publicity efforts.[78]

Cain may have felt the need for company in the fight for recognition of better treatment of homosexuals. On February 28, 1972, he was among the few speakers at a meeting of the Assembly Judiciary Committee on Assemblyman Lloyd Barbee's bill liberalizing state sex laws. The bill had been introduced in the previous three sessions and was having its first hearing. Barbee began by stating, "The state has no business dealing with a person's sexual practices in or out of the bedroom or in or out of the park." Cain was featured the next day in both Milwaukee daily papers. He was quoted as saying, "The present statutes do not allow adequate personal dignity nor protect human worth in those individuals which choose to live a different style." Other speakers at the hearing were Eldon Murray of *GPU News*, Michael Mitchell of the GPU, and Professor William Gorham Rice from UW–Madison speaking for the Wisconsin Civil Liberties Union. Despite its historic import, the hearing was not a major event: only four of the eleven committee members showed up and no opponents spoke. No vote was taken.[79]

Many CRH meetings were held at the Church for All People in Milwaukee, but some took place at Cain's summer retreat in Dousman or his house on South Thirty-Fifth Street in Milwaukee. Meetings were never large, with an average of eight to fourteen people in attendance. As meeting notes show, an ongoing topic was how the church could minister to homosexuals, especially to "religiously inclined gays" and to "so-called respectable gays." Another question was whether congregations could accept such ministry. Various studies were discussed including George Weinberg's *Society and the Healthy Homosexual* and Wainwright Churchill's *Homosexual Behavior Among Males*. In 1973, the CRH prepared an informational bulletin and members advertised themselves as willing to accept speaking engagements for church groups. That year, the committee also had a presence at the Brady Street Festival. As part of the weekend's events, the council held a service at the Church of All People at Twenty-First and Highland.[80]

Cain believed the church should defend those who experienced discrimination and be the instrument for "the consecration of diverse gifts." At the same time as he helped found the CRH, Cain distributed a document that stated, "The Church has within its embrace sinners of every sort. Not one has achieved instantaneous sanctification. . . . Thus it would not seem right in my sight that arrogance more than compassion, demand the impossible of the invert before he come into the grace, or remain under, the grace of God." In the early 1970s, Cain also attended classes at Concordia Seminary in St. Louis, which hosted homosexual speakers from the local Mandrake Society. As an advocate for gay acceptance within his denomination, Cain published a letter in *Advance*, a national bulletin of the Missouri Synod, to inform readers about Milwaukee's CRH.[81]

Cain formalized his thinking in "The Church as Advocate for the Gay": "The problem of the homosexual wanting to be gay and also God's is not a simplistic categorization of 'sin and grace' or 'Law and Gospel.'" He drew on the experience of Christian professionals who had found that using the "confess and be cured" tactic seldom worked. The church should not ask for "the negation of one's self." In a section of his document titled "God's Grace for the Gay," Cain argued, "Jesus was much more compassionate than he was judgmental." He cautioned people against taking the cultural context and translation of certain biblical verses too literally. For Cain, repealing the laws criminalizing homosexuality would be a pastoral call to stand for justice against those who were the targets of discrimination.[82]

Cain's paper included footnotes with positions from two of the major Lutheran denominations: the American Lutheran Church and the Lutheran Church in America. While maintaining that homosexuality was contrary to God's will, these denominations refrained from condemning the homosexual person. Cain was following the work of the Association of Lutheran Physicians, Attorneys and Clergymen (ALPAC) in the Missouri Synod, which was developing statements on homosexuality to be used by pastors. In fact, *Badger Lutheran*, the paper of the Greater Milwaukee Federation of Lutheran Churches–Missouri Synod, had reported in 1972 on the work of ALPAC, mentioning one pastor (possibly Cain) who was in favor of homosexuals receiving medical help rather than five-year prison sentences as under Wisconsin state law. Cain hoped ALPAC would conduct a more in-depth study that could involve the gay community, but he was disappointed. On July 10, 1973, both of Milwaukee's daily papers ran headlines announcing that the Missouri Synod condemned homosexuality. Reverend Karl A. Barth, president of the South Wisconsin District, had led the committee proposing the language of condemnation.[83]

Cain left Milwaukee for further seminary study in the fall of 1973, and Reverend Charles Schinlaub, a Methodist minister, assumed the CRH chairperson's duties. Among the meeting minutes taken in 1974, the committee observed that there were four ministers in Milwaukee who would perform gay marriage ceremonies. In June 1974 at the annual conference of the United Methodist Church in Wisconsin, where the CRH staffed a booth, CRH member Steve Webster of Madison spoke on the need for a homosexual ministry. In June 1974, the *Milwaukee Journal* ran a feature on the CRH, and Schinlaub noted, "The group is just about at the point of collapsing most of the time." Salvatorian Brother Grant-Michael Fitzgerald, who was active in promoting churches' acceptance of gays, viewed the CRH as only "a Kaffee Klatsch type thing." By the fall of that year, the CRH disbanded due to a lack of support. However, by 1976, Schinlaub was able to report that the CRH's efforts during the 1974 Wisconsin Methodist Conference had paid off when the conference supported "decriminalizing private noncommercial sexual acts between consenting adults."[84]

A New Wave of Activism Hits Wisconsin

When a national wave of gay activism formed after Stonewall, Wisconsin's gay community was ready to join the movement. While the "new kind of homosexual" in the state belonged to a younger generation, gays and lesbians were able to build on the networks established by earlier activists. For example, MAHE formed at St. Francis House, which had previously been the site of an earlier gay social network. Homosexuals in Milwaukee placed posters in gay bars to recruit attendees for their organizing meetings. They also advertised in Milwaukee's underground newspapers such as *Kaleidoscope* that had shown interest in gay news in the pre-Stonewall period.[85]

Importantly, Wisconsin's new gay activists were not afraid to assert their rights. From MAHE's early picketing of *The Boys in the Band* to the GPU's speakers' bureau that sent gay presenters as far as Beloit, a new public discourse about homosexuals was evident in the state in the early 1970s. Many national gay and lesbian speakers visited cities such as Appleton, Stevens Point, Platteville, and Whitewater, showing that the discourse occurring in Wisconsin both attracted national attention and generally provided a welcoming climate. Perhaps the great UW tradition of sifting and winnowing ideas, which withstood Chappleism's attacks in the 1930s and McCarthy's witch hunts in the 1950s, shaped the welcoming climate on campus. As in many states, Wisconsin's urban centers had the most resources and provided much of the movement's energy. But gay communities from all corners of the state responded to Stonewall.

This post-Stonewall activism was just the beginning. As the gay community continued to grow in size and strength, homosexuals would find multiple ways to amplify their voices. And as the community defined objectives and developed strategies to achieve them, the state's political establishment would continue to shape its response.

2

A State Debate on Homosexuality

*In Wisconsin homosexuality is not a crime. Nor are certain
homosexual acts.*
> —David Adamany, Amicus brief for Paul Safransky
> before the Wisconsin Supreme Court, August 1973[1]

*Lesbianism is a greater threat to the reactionary institutions of this
society than male homosexuality.*
> —Judy Greenspan, *Memoirs of a Tired Lesbian*, 1972[2]

One of the most important post-Stonewall public dialogues about
LGBT persons in the state began in 1972 when Paul Safransky, an
out gay man, was dismissed from his job at Southern Colony, the state's
residential institution for the mentally impaired in Racine County, where
he worked in the residential cottages for older boys. His case became an example of Wisconsin's gay community standing up for itself and marshaling
its resources, few as they were, to engage in a significant debate about the
status of gay people in the state. The dialogue over this incident involved
high-level civil service bureaucrats, the Wisconsin Civil Liberties Union
(WCLU; part of the ACLU), the State Personnel Board, a Dane County
Circuit Court judge, the Wisconsin attorney general, and the Wisconsin
Supreme Court. *GPU News*, the state's gay newspaper, would describe the
case in March 1973 as "the first challenge in the history of Wisconsin to the
state's right to fire a person because of homosexuality." And because *GPU
News* was distributed nationally, the case received some national attention

47

and was picked up by *The Advocate*, a national gay publication. However, the intricacy of the legal details and rulings defied coverage in many press accounts and even in later scholarly references.[3]

Before getting into the specifics of the Safransky legal case, I believe it's important to explore what the testimony reveals about those charged with running this particular institution, their treatment of patients, and their attitudes toward homosexuality. John Garstecki, the superintendent of Southern Colony at the time, had a very negative opinion of homosexuals. Under cross-examination by a member of the State Personnel Board, Garstecki stated, "I would have terminated any avowed homosexual [employee] solely on the basis that he admitted he was a homosexual." In a slightly more broad-minded statement, he said, "I do not object to homosexuality any more than I object to other forms of lifestyle that are not in the mainstream of society." Yet he thought having homosexual staff impugned "the integrity, mission and responsibility" of the institution. In his testimony, Garstecki admitted, "In 22 years I have had to make decisions involving 6 to 8 incidents involving homosexuality involving employees. All resigned and did not require dismissal." However, his statement clearly implies that dismissal would have been his choice if those employees had refused to resign.[4]

Staff who worked alongside Safransky in the treatment area for teenage boys consistently remarked in their testimony that same-sex sexual activity took place among the residents of the institution. Richard Testard, an aide, observed that one seventeen- or eighteen-year-old boy "had been caught in the act several times and had been reprimanded." Like others called to testify to the State Personnel Board, which reviewed Safransky's firing, Testard was not specific in his description of such acts. Patricia Dolan, a registered nurse at Southern Colony, commented, "You will find youngsters who get involved in homosexual activities in any institution." Carol Feist, a supervising nurse, stated, "I knew there were some homosexual acts at the institution." Even Safransky admitted to having found young men engaged in homosexual acts at the Colony. He claimed to have "found five boys in my unit engaged in homosexual acts," two of whom were reported as being involved in a second incident. Even Superintendent Garstecki admitted, "I am aware that some residents engage in homosexual activity."[5]

Gender norms were also rigidly enforced at the institution, to the detriment of any transgender or gender nonconforming youths. Employee Shirley Lamborn testified that one boy "did have some feminine actions and did like to wear female clothing. He had been found to have worn women's clothing before." She also mentioned another boy who liked to "dress up in female clothes" and said, "I have heard that male residents try to put on female clothing."[6]

Staff members admitted to responding with different levels of discipline when confronted with these cases. The aide Testard stated that the official discipline was "restriction to the unit for a period of time and loss of token points." But he also added, "The nurses and Dr. Fredrickson [a staff doctor] told me to ignore a child's question as to why he shouldn't engage in homosexual acts because attempted guidance would give the child reinforcement for continued behavior." Safransky said, "I stopped them and sent them to their rooms, talked to each one separately, fined them and reported to my supervisor." Lamborn told the State Personnel Board, "If a male attempts to dress up with balloons or Dixie cups to imitate a woman we are trained to resolve the situation. We remove the items quietly. Female attire is removed from male units immediately."[7]

Garstecki refused to accept behaviors that deviated from the supposed traditional norms. He discussed homosexuality with Dr. Rusch and Dr. Ganzer, the assistant director and the director of mental hygiene, respectively. "Both of these doctors who are psychiatrists," Garstecki said, "state homosexual activity is not to be encouraged but should be discouraged by staff effort." In outlining his policy as it pertained to patients, he explained, "When a resident is determined [to be gay] by psychiatric examination and medical information, I seek their transfer to Central State Hospital at Waupun. We have sent a number of homosexuals there." As Garstecki explained, "If 20 percent to 30 percent of the residents were homosexuals, I would recommend their transfer to Central State at Waupun." Thus, both gay employees and patients were eliminated from the institution under Garstecki's administrative practice and policies.[8]

Safransky would challenge this homophobic regime and become the eye of the storm around which this early post-Stonewall Wisconsin debate on LGBT rights centered. He was not the stereotype of a gay man lurking in the shadows but a new kind of out gay activist. He was in his mid-twenties at the time of his dismissal from Southern Colony in June

1972. After graduation from high school, he had attended Union Grove Teachers College for two years and then taught for another two years in Kenosha. He claimed to have been gay since he was fourteen in the early 1960s. In his testimony, he disclosed that he was a member of Milwaukee's Gay People's Union. In fact, two years after the trial, in 1974, he would be elected to the GPU's board. Safransky described it as "an organization professing the freedom of homosexual activity."[9]

Safransky's decision to appeal his firing and eventually bring his case to the public eye was costly. An editorial in the November/December 1973 issue of *GPU News* described the personal cost for standing up to the anti-gay attitudes of Southern Colony, stating, "A great amount of courage and self-sacrifice went into his decision." He was out of work for over a year, though he filled out seventy-five job applications, because employers were reticent to hire him after finding out about his job discrimination case. The editorial continued, "Paul Safransky is fighting this battle not only for himself but for every other gay person employed in the public sector." On October 31, 1974, after Safransky had exhausted his appeals with the state, the *Milwaukee Journal* reported, "In what is believed to be a precedent, a Milwaukee man is challenging the state's right to fire an employee because he is a homosexual."[10]

As an out gay man, Safransky felt he should not have to hide his life, and he claimed, according to the testimony, "that he was entitled to his own life style." Even though some of Safransky's coworkers said they were "disturbed" by his orientation and that it made them "very uneasy," Safransky did not back down. "It bothered me that other staff members discussed their private heterosexual family lives," he stated, "but I listened and did not tell them to stop." Safransky was determined not to accept a double standard based on sexual orientation.[11]

FIRED FOR A GAY LIFESTYLE

Nevertheless, Safransky's out lifestyle offended his coworkers, who reported him to their supervisors for discussing his private life. Eventually, these reports reached the ears of Superintendent Garstecki, who ordered an investigation. Safransky's supervisor, Patricia Dolan, a registered nurse, held a supervisor–employee conference on June 28, 1972, in which she recalled that Safransky "felt entitled to his lifestyle just as others are entitled to their lifestyle." She filed a report. On the next day, a disciplinary conference was held by the personnel officer, Mark Hoover, which was attended by the union representative, the acting director of care and treatment, and Dolan. Safransky first heard about the conference when he came to work that day. Hoover offered Safransky a chance to resign, but he refused. This response did not fit into the pattern of resignations that had been established at the institution when these circumstances arose, but many gay men, particularly gay activists, were refusing to bow to such pressure since Stonewall.[12]

On July 18, Garstecki fired Safransky. Garstecki's letter stated the reason for the dismissal was

> due to problems associated with your homosexual life style. . . .
> Specifically, you admitted at a disciplinary hearing conducted on
> June 29, 1972, that you were an avowed homosexual. This confirma-
> tion of your life style has caused a substantial concern in that you
> have openly discussed your activities with co-workers and in the
> presence of residents.

The letter gave Safransky ten days to appeal the action to the State Personnel Board.[13]

Safransky not only refused to resign but also refused to accept his dismissal. He appealed to the State Personnel Board and secured help from the WCLU. Todd J. Mitchell, a young Milwaukee-area attorney who volunteered with the Wisconsin ACLU, would argue his case. The hearing was held October 27, 1972, with Safransky and Mitchell present in addition to Safransky's coworkers and the superintendent with his state attorney.[14]

In their State Personnel Board testimony, the witnesses, coworkers, and supervisors who provided testimony during the hearing stated that Safransky never made any sexual advances or overtures directed at co-workers or residents. From their comments, it was also clear that he never discussed his or others' sexual activities but simply talked about gay life. This, it turned out, was at the core of their complaint. Coworkers conveyed how uncomfortable they were made by hearing about Safransky's gay life-style. They also expressed concern about the impressionable residents of

Southern Colony, who might be misled by hearing or seeing aspects of this gay lifestyle. Some indicated that Safransky was an unpaid go-go dancer at a gay bar. Upon an objection to questions relative to his off-duty life, the prosecuting attorney's questioning was restricted; however, none of the testimony about Safransky's off-duty activities was stricken from the record. The only member of the board who appeared to be seeking fairness in the trial was new appointee Percy Julian, a black Madison attorney who had been appointed by Governor Patrick Lucey and taken office in January 1971. Julian, however, would later recuse himself from voting on the case, as he himself was active with the WCLU.[15]

The state's summation of its case by attorney Robert Kletzien, representing Garstecki and Secretary Wilbur Schmidt of the State Department of Health and Social Services, presented a view that was a little less harsh than Garstecki's: "Mr. Safransky, of course, has admitted that he is a homosexual. It has been shown that he has discussed his homosexual lifestyle with other employees. Perhaps that factor in and of itself does not justify a discharge." But he went on to state that the main factor in the firing was that Safransky "does not in the opinion of our staff present the proper adult image in accordance with appropriate standards of society today." The state's case for dismissal of the appeal basically rested on the presumed bigotry of straight society.[16]

"I think the testimony indicates that the discharge was discriminatory," Attorney Mitchell contended in his summary. "There was no proof that Paul's conduct in any way related to his homosexuality adversely affected any of the residents. . . . We feel that Paul has a right to discuss his private homosexual lifestyle, his activities, just as much as any heterosexual person." In a powerful closing statement, Mitchell argued,

> Although a homosexual may be unpopular, it's just not possible and consistent with our basic American principles to make any right or benefit or privilege or employment contingent upon a person's popularity or unpopularity in the case of a homosexual. I think Paul and any other homosexuals are entitled to the same benefits under law, that same protection that the constitution guarantees and the same right of due process for fair employment.[17]

On February 2, 1973, the State Personnel Board, by a 3 to 0 vote, issued
its ruling in favor of Garstecki and upheld Safransky's firing, with Charles
Beecher of Janesville, William Ahrens of Muskego, and John Sharpe of
Kenosha voting. Most disturbing among their findings, and something
that would become a key point in future legal contention, was the statement "that homosexual activity is contrary to the generally recognized and
accepted standards of morality." That a state body would feel compelled
to create a Wisconsin state moral standard from a single case reflects an
assumption that such views would go unchallenged. This was an under-
estimation of the state's newly emboldened gay community.[18]

David Adamany Brings Gay Reinforcements to the Circuit Court

One member of the state's new gay community was the attorney David
Adamany, who entered the case at this stage to submit an amicus or
"friend of the court" brief for the appeal from the State Personnel Board.
A University of Wisconsin professor of constitutional law, Adamany was
a Lebanese-American native of Green Bay with an undergraduate degree
and law degree from Harvard University. He also held a PhD in political
science from UW–Madison. In 1973, Adamany was in his late thirties and,
while perhaps not formally out, was known in Madison's gay circles. The
Capital Times and GPU News both reported that Adamany's brief was filed
on behalf of the Gay Liberation Front (GLF), though the court documents
simply list him as the friend of the court without any organizational at-
tribution. The GLF did help raise money in the city's gay bars; GPU News
reported that funds "to cover the court fees and other expenses of this brief
were donated by the Student Bar Association of the UW–Madison Law
School and members of the Madison gay community." Adamany would
also work with ACLU lawyer Todd Mitchell to prepare briefs for the appeal
to the Wisconsin Supreme Court.[19]

Many years later, after his service in Wisconsin, Adamany would continue a distinguished academic career in law and go on to be the first out
campus president of Wayne State University in Detroit and then of Temple
University in Philadelphia. In 1998, when Adamany received a UW–Madison

UW–Madison political science professor David Adamany argued the first gay rights case before the Wisconsin Supreme Court. In the process, he came out to his political patron Governor Patrick Lucey, who appointed him secretary of the Wisconsin Department of Revenue. UNIVERSITY OF WISCONSIN–MADISON ARCHIVES IMAGE 2019S09705

Badger Pride Distinguished Alumni Award, he would recall a man who had been a student in the 1970s approaching him in a West Hollywood restaurant to thank him for discussing cases on gay rights in his constitutional law course. Adamany reflected, "The incident brought home to me how the smallest things we do may have the profoundest effects on people."[20]

Under Wisconsin law, appeals from the State Personnel Board were directed to the Circuit Court in Dane County. The *Capital Times* noted that Safransky's case was "the first litigation in Wisconsin raising the question of a homosexual's right to hold public employment." Judge William L. Jackman held a hearing on May 17 and issued his decision on May 29. In his brief decision, Jackman found creditable evidence for the first eight of the board's findings and went into more detail discussing the ninth, "that homosexual activity is contrary to generally recognized and accepted standards of morality." Judge Jackman noted, "Morality refers to the principles of right and wrong conduct. While homosexual activity is probably not rare, it is not conduct that is generally accepted as normal among the great majority of persons. . . . It may be a manifestation of mental illness or disturbance of varying degree."[21]

The judge did concede a little ground for gay rights, though not full rights. He stated that "the plaintiff asserts a constitutional right to be a homosexual and we have no quarrel with his right, so long as he confines his talk and activity to other than working hours and with some semblance of privacy." Thus, Jackman rejected Garstecki's view that gay persons had no rights but thought it best if these rights could be exercised in a closet. Jackman dismissed the appeal by Safransky and affirmed all of the State Personnel Board's findings. Essentially, the judge joined the Southern Colony staff, Superintendent Garstecki, Secretary Schmidt, and the State Personnel Board in basing employment for gay individuals on popular attitudes about their lifestyles. In 1973, Wisconsin had no appeals courts, so the next step for the case was the state supreme court.[22]

AN EARLY ALLY LEAVES THE FIELD

While the case was going to appeal to the Wisconsin Supreme Court, the gay community was thrown a curve ball by an ally. In October 1972, Ed McManus, executive director of the WCLU, had said of the Safransky case, "We are ready to go all the way on this." However, in an article by Eldon Murray, the *GPU News* of November/December 1973 reported, "In an incredible about-face, Wisconsin Civil Liberties Union Foundation has voted to drop its funding of the Paul Safransky employment discrimination case now before the Supreme Court." At what was described as "a stormy board meeting" on October 13, 1973, Murray reminded the WCLU Foundation of its prior commitment to go all the way. Murray accused the Foundation of "shabby and despicable treatment" of Safransky. He charged, "You have let down Mr. Safransky, your own attorney who has worked long and hard on this case, and the entire gay community."[23]

The WCLU action was poorly timed. Murray's article reported that "a hastily put together committee of five WCLU attorncys met over a luncheon and voted to drop the funding for the case." Neither the client nor the GPU was notified of the meeting; the WCLU informed them of the decision three days before the deadline for filing intentions of appeal, which required a $250 fee. Safransky and friends of the GPU frantically raised the filing fee. An additional estimated $750 would be required to print the briefs; in fact, the bill came to $1,000. The total cost of the appeal, outside

WCLU LETS DOWN GAYS

In an incredible about face, Wisconsin Civil Liberties Union Foundation has voted to drop its funding of the Paul R. Safransky employment discrimination case now before the Wisconsin Supreme Court.

At a stormy board meeting on October 13, Eldon E. Murray, member of the board of directors of Gay People's Union, reminded the Foundation directors of their original commitment to "go all the way on this." He accused the Foundation of "shabby and despicable treatment" and said, "In spite of your action here today, this case is already going forward and we (Gay People's Union) will raise the necessary funds even if we have to collect money in the gay bars in tin cans."

After stressing the importance of the case to every employed gay person, he said, "You have let down Mr. Safransky, your own attorney who has worked long and hard on this case, and the entire gay community."

One board member responded with an apology, saying, "We evidently made a financial commitment to you that we simply cannot carry out. We still believe in the merits of the case."

In July of 1972, Paul R. Safransky, a homosexual, was fired from his job as houseparent (CONTINUED ON PAGE 5)

The Wisconsin Civil Liberties Union supported the 1972 gay employment discrimination case in its early stages, but later backed out due to financial constraints and perhaps other considerations, leaving the gay community to carry the burden. GPU NEWS, NOVEMBER/DECEMBER 1973

of attorney fees, was estimated at $2,000, a staggering sum at the time. The GPU set up a defense fund to raise the money.[24]

Murray noted, "One board member responded with an apology saying, 'We evidently made a financial commitment to you that we simply cannot carry out. We still believe in the merits of the case.'" However, not everyone at the WCLU may have believed so strongly in the case. *GPU News* argued that the WCLU discussion showed that "no board member had read any of the briefs or testimony in the case although all testimony had been available to them over a year." While the WCLU discussed the case with attorney Todd Mitchell, it did not permit either Safransky or Murray (who had gotten wind of the meeting and joined it in haste) to speak or make their case. Eventually, the two stalked out of the meeting saying, "Go to hell."[25]

The *GPU News* story written by Murray reported that the GPU had given the WCLU one hundred dollars to help with expenses and had paid half of the printing bill for the briefs. Murray vowed the GPU would go forward with its support of the case and "raise the necessary funds even

Gay People's Union
presents in cooperation with
The River Queen
402 N. Water St.

LIBERATED TOGETHER
all Girl Band

Saturday, Dec. 8 at 10 P.M.
You get a free drink for $1. donation
Proceeds for Safransky Defense Fund

The hat was passed in gay bars in Milwaukee and Madison to raise money for the defense in the case of Paul Safransky, who was fired in 1972 for being openly gay at Southern Colony, the state institution in Racine County at Union Grove. ARCHIVES DEPARTMENT, UNIVERSITY OF WISCONSIN–MILWAUKEE LIBRARIES

if we have to collect money in the gay bars in tin cans." *GPU News* was happy to report that some subscribers had sent donations to ensure that "all workers are protected from persecution."[26]

In the same issue, an editorial lamented the fact that the WCLU "deserted" Mr. Safransky and the gay community, while also admitting the

WCLU Foundation's concern was about the money, "which in all fairness they do not have." "We do have allies in this case," the editorial stated. "We must here give credit and praise to attorneys Todd Mitchell and David Adamany who have agreed to waive their attorney fees in this case. They believe so strongly in the merits of the case that they are willing to make such a donation."[27]

Some thought the WCLU wanted out before the case was appealed to the supreme court because it had concerns about legal strategy. It could be argued that a gay man who wore facial powder and mascara was perhaps not the most sympathetic client to advance equal rights. The fact that a county's circuit court had upheld the blatantly discriminatory findings of the State Personnel Board was bad enough, but if the state supreme court upheld the same findings, Wisconsin's employers would be legally allowed to discriminate against gay people.[28]

An Appeal for Equal Rights

Between the circuit court decision on May 29, 1973, and the filing of the supreme court appeal on June 15, Governor Lucey asked David Adamany, one of his longtime trusted advisors, to become secretary of the Department of Revenue. Adamany felt the need to come out to the governor as a gay man before accepting the appointment, as he intended to continue with the Safransky case. He did not wish to give the governor any surprises, and as a cabinet member in the executive branch, he would have to obtain permission from the court to participate in a case in which the state was a party. Lucey had no problem with Adamany continuing the case.[29]

Before the supreme court, Adamany and Mitchell framed the case for Safransky by claiming that his dismissal was based solely on his status as a homosexual. Their argument in the appellant's brief stated, "In no case has the Wisconsin Supreme Court held that mere status as a homosexual is sufficient to constitute just cause." The brief presented the court with constitutional issues specific to the Fourteenth, Ninth, and First Amendments, as well as the status of the national debate raging about homosexuality. While other documents, like Garstecki's letter, had referred to Safransky as a "confirmed homosexual" or "avowed homosexual," both considered negative language, this brief specifically used the term "self-avowed homosexual" to refer to Safransky, demonstrating his gay pride. This language demonstrated that being out was a form of self-liberation and personal agency—a clear distinction from the way homosexuals had been presented as criminals or sickos at trials in the past. The brief claimed:

> The sphere of constitutionally protected interests includes the right
> to hold specific employment . . . [and to] deny these rights to a person
> because of his race, religion, sexual preference, or beliefs, no matter
> how unorthodox or repulsive to the majority of citizens, or because
> of any other reason having no direct relationship to his job perfor-
> mance, is to deprive that person of life, liberty or property without
> due process of law.[30]

In support of this argument, the brief cited a 1969 California case and a 1971 District of Columbia case, among others. In these two cases of admitted sexual activity, the first involving a man who had sex with men and the other a woman who belonged to a swingers club and had sexual relations with male members, courts ruled that the government needed to show a clear effect on job performance. Additionally, the brief mentioned a recent May 1973 Maryland case in which the decision argued, "The time has now come for private, consenting adult homosexuality to enter the sphere of constitutionally protected interests. Intolerance of the unconventional halts the growth of liberty."[31]

Since the record from the earlier trial had included Safransky's off-duty associations with other gay men, his lawyers argued that his constitutionally guaranteed rights of freedom of association were violated. The brief also argued that his ability to talk about his lifestyle should have been protected under free speech rights under the First Amendment. Regarding the controversial ninth finding ("that homosexual activity is contrary to generally recognized and accepted standards of morality"), the brief maintained that the "State Personnel Board has no judicially cognizable expertise" in so finding and that the "record is devoid of evidence about what are 'generally recognized and accepted standards of morality.'" Even if the State Personnel Board had the expertise to arrive at such a finding, it would have needed an evidentiary hearing and record to have the finding judicially supported.[32]

Here the brief made its major argument: "The question of 'generally recognized and accepted standards of morality' is a controversial question of fact in today's fast changing society." The attorneys supported this argument with an overwhelming evidence of "indicators of greater acceptance or tolerance of homosexuality and homosexual activity in our society." Rather than starting with academic experts, they began by listing examples from the media, citing prime time television episodes from shows such as *Marcus Welby, M.D.*, *The Bold Ones*, and *60 Minutes*. The movie *Sunday Bloody Sunday* was also listed. The brief concluded that the "open portrayal of homosexuality is a clear indication that the public's standards at least condone and encompass open discussion of homosexuality." Next, to show the changing standards in the media, the brief cited Ann Landers, who had commented on homosexuality in her national advice column, which appeared regularly in the *Wisconsin State Journal*. Also cited was the free circulation of gay magazines and newspapers, specifically mentioning those circulated by Milwaukee's GPU.[33]

Finally, the brief addressed public policy changes in attitudes toward private sexual acts: "Law may be a measure of society's standards. Eight states have eliminated from their statutes former proscriptions which applied to sodomous and sexual acts." The brief cited two gubernatorial commissions appointed by Governor Lucey, which "within the year urged repeal of prohibition against private sexual conduct by heterosexuals or homosexuals." Perhaps the justices were surprised by one precise legal argument made in the brief:

In Wisconsin homosexuality is not a crime. Nor are certain homosexual acts, such as mutual masturbation of adults in private. Members of the same sex may kiss privately without running afoul of our law. They may live together without legal sanction. . . . Only anal and oral intercourse are proscribed and these are banned for heterosexuals as well as homosexuals.[34]

Finally, the brief cited academic evidence to counter Judge Jackman's foray into homosexuality as mental illness. The brief claimed that modern psychiatry had moved beyond such views, which had been based primarily on "pre-1957 studies conducted among psychiatric patients, prisoners, and others institutionalized for non-conforming behavior. The pre-1957 studies are now in disrepute precisely because of the bias of the sample of persons studied." Once the brief had been submitted on behalf of Safransky to the supreme court, it was the state's turn to respond.[35]

THE WISCONSIN ATTORNEY GENERAL VILIFIES HOMOSEXUALS

The brief on behalf of Attorney General Robert Warren claimed Safransky was not dismissed solely on his status as a homosexual, maintaining that Safransky's discussion of his orientation and acts such as wearing feminine makeup in the workplace had created problems in his working relationships and his duties as a "houseparent."[36]

The attorney general's brief did support the argument that "homosexuality is outside the generally accepted standards of morality," stating, "Homosexuality is abnormal." While it grudgingly admitted that "there is a conflict of opinion among psychologists, psychiatrists and social workers as to whether homosexuality is an illness," the brief maintained that "they are in agreement that the homosexual needs treatment for his deviant behavior and that homosexuality is not regarded as socially or morally acceptable by the majority of Americans." The brief also claimed, "The general population has a well-known disgust for homosexuals and refers to them as queer or strange." Thus, in this view, constitutional rights should be trumped by majority disapproval.[37]

Perhaps the most despicable and unfounded argument in the attorney general's brief was: "Many homosexuals are child molesters and also prey on mentally retarded persons and non-consenting adults." The state cited a 1969 medical dictionary that described homosexuality as a "sexual perversion," though the word *perversion* had been deleted in the 1972 edition. The brief stated:

> Historically, homosexual activity has been one of subtle persuasion [or] entrapment and in many cases the innocent victim has been a minor or mentally retarded individual. . . . History confirms that homosexuals . . . do possess an aggressive desire for sexual gratification and seek children, young adults, adults who are indisposed by

intoxication or who are in dire need for funds, and persons who do not have full mental faculties.

One slight concession was made with the admission that "not all homosexuals are pedophiles." However, the attorney general painted a thoroughly negative depiction of both homosexuals and homosexual activity.[38]

Passages from the Bible as well as writings by St. Thomas Aquinas, John Calvin, and contemporary doctors of theology were cited in the state's brief. Regarding Finding 9, the brief argued, "An administrative tribunal can take notice of matters of common knowledge and of commonly accepted scientific facts." Finally, a judge was quoted from his decision in a 1969 case: "Any schoolboy knows that a homosexual act is immoral, indecent, lewd, and obscene. Adult persons are even more conscious that this is true." Thus, the attorney general relied on a variety of tired traditional judgments against gay people. Now, the decision was up to the Wisconsin Supreme Court.[39]

THE SUPREMES SPEAK: A SPLIT DECISION

The brief on behalf of Paul Safransky concluded with two requests: that the circuit court order affirming the findings be reversed and that the order of administrative dismissal from employment be set aside and Safransky be reinstated. *GPU News* stated the importance of the case in its November/December 1973 editorial: "Every gay person who is employed in the public sector must live with the constant threat of dismissal for no other reason than sexual preference. Many private employers also feel that if the state can discriminate in this matter, they are free to do the same."[40]

The Wisconsin Supreme Court decision, delivered on March 5, 1974, was a partial victory for gay rights advocates but not for Safransky. On several main issues the court, in the opinion written by Justice Leo B. Hanley, ducked, saying these were not matters to be decided in this instance. The court reasoned that "the question of whether an individual may be terminated for his homosexual status is not an issue and need not be determined." Additionally, the decision read, "This court need not herein determine whether mere association with other homosexuals during off duty hours is constitutionally guaranteed."[41]

Regarding the controversial Finding 9 on the immorality of homosexuality, the court's opinion correctly observed, as argued by the appellants,

> No evidence was submitted as to this finding. Therefore, the finding
> is not supported by evidence. . . . We are satisfied that there is credible
> evidence to support all the findings of the Board with the exception of
> the finding as to the accepted standards of morality. As to the Board's
> finding that homosexuality is contrary to the accepted standards of
> morality, we hold that whether homosexuality is immoral or not is
> irrelevant to the determination of the case.

Thus, the justices threw out the attorney general's appeal to the Bible and
the theologians. In addition, the supreme court showed little sympathy
for Superintendent Garstecki's blanket presumptions about prohibiting
homosexuals' employment. The court reasoned there had to be a clear
connection between job duties and performance and that mere status as a
member of a group was not sufficient to justify dismissal.[42]

Unfortunately, the supreme court accepted the state's contention that
the job of a houseparent required "the projection of the orthodoxy of male
heterosexuality." The court felt that "an individual fulfilling the position
of houseparent cannot discuss homosexuality in the presence of his wards
without at least communicating an idea of tacit approval of such action."
While Adamany was glad the court tempered the lower court's legal findings, the decision, disappointingly, favored keeping LGBT persons in the
closet and ignoring out gay activism.[43]

THE GAY COMMUNITY'S REACTION

In response to the court's decision, activist Louis Stimac penned a letter to
"my Gay Brothers and Sisters," urging them to come to GPU to share their
indignation. In his view, "The Wisconsin State Supreme Court declared
we had the right to starve to death. . . . The men sitting in their long black
dresses felt [Safransky] did not portray the proper male image. Robes? You
say. To paraphrase gay Gertrude Stein, 'a dress is a dress is a dress.' . . . I
wouldn't let them judge a tiddly wink championship."[44]

GPU News carried a story on the decision written by Sheila (Lou)

Supreme Court Upholds Gay Firing

by Sheila Sullivan and Alyn Hes

On March 5th the Wisconsin Supreme Court handed down its unanimous decision in the Paul R. Safransky versus the State Personnel Board case. They upheld the judgement of W. J. Jackman, Circuit Judge for Dane County, that the State Department of Health and Social Services had found substantial evidence to warrant Safransky's discharge.

The court did not support the Board's finding "that homosexual activity is contrary to the generally recognized and accepted standards of morality." Thus the case was supposedly decided on factors other than morality. However, in this article we will attempt to show how standards of heterosexuals normalcy have crept into the case.

The court's contempt for the appellant, Paul, was shown in the fact that neither he nor his attorneys were notified of the decision prior to its release to the press. Thus, Paul heard of his defeat from friends who had heard the news on the radio. Mr. Todd Mitchell, Paul's attorney, had to call the court to find out about the decision after being notified by GPU that the news was being broadcast.

In the decision, written by Justice Leo B. Hanley, it was stated that one of the duties of Paul as houseparent was "to direct the patients to a proper understanding of human sexuality." "Such an understanding," the decision reads, "required the projection of the **orthodoxy of male heterosexuality**. Consistent with the projection of normalcy of **heterosexuality by the houseparent** was the requirement that he project the unorthodoxy of male homosexuality to the patients under his care." (emphasis by GPU).

Responding to Paul's claim that his dismissal for his self-avowal of homosexuality and discussions of his gay lifestyle was a denial of his First Amendment right of free speech, the court ruled that "an individual's First Amendment rights are necessarily limited by the manner and place of their exercise."

The decision cited the findings in the Acanfora case where a known homosexual teacher, transferred from a classroom teaching position to a non-teaching position because of his unrestrained off-duty advocacy of his homosexual way of life, which read:

"The instruction of children carries with it special responsibilities, whether a teacher be heterosexual or homosexual. The conduct of private life necessarily reflects on the life in public. There exists then not only a right of privacy, so strongly urged by the plaintiff, but also a duty of privacy. It is conceded that it would be improper for any teacher to discuss his sex life in the school environment. . . ."

Acanfora case fails to understand that a heterosexual teacher who mentions either "husband" or "wife" is discussing sex life implicitly. The mention of a teacher's child, of love, of marriage, all constitute a discussion of sex life. However, Paul's discussion of clothing, wigs, plucking hair and "dancing and different things," have been interpreted to mean sex life. Are we going insane or are they?

The Acanfora case was cited again in the ruling.

"As a result of the distinguishing obligations which a person assumes upon signing a contract to teach children, the standard must shift to accord with the goals of the educational process. The question becomes whether the speech is likely to incite or produce imminent effects deleterious to the educational process. Such speech is not within the bounds of the 'protectable' and the Board of Education is not precluded from taking reasonable action with respect to it."

When the mixed Supreme Court verdict in the Paul Safransky case was announced, the pair of Milwaukee activists Sullivan and Hess urged further efforts in the *GPU News*. GPU NEWS, APRIL 1974

Sullivan and Alyn Hess attempting "to show how standards of heterosexual normalcy have crept into the case." "Paul's discussion of clothing, wigs, plucking hair, and 'dancing and different things,' have been interpreted to mean sex life," they wrote. "Are we going insane or are they?"[45]

While the supreme court justices thought they had kept their decision narrowly focused, gay activists realized a larger conversation was required. Early activists understood that this case about employment discrimination at a Wisconsin institution raised broad societal questions. Sullivan and

Hess wrote, "What is left out of the case is the fact that there are all of our future gay brothers and sisters trapped into a heterosexual brainwashing educational system without any open gays or drag queens to let them know that there exists a great variety in adult sexuality." Fueled by this anger, members of the GPU attended a Milwaukee School Board hearing in May 1974, faulting the school system's report on sexism "for not including homosexuality in its studies of discrimination in the schools" and charging that "present curriculum places homosexuality in the category of being abnormal." Though discrimination was still a present threat, these actions, and the public nature of the Safransky trial, showed that the public sphere was finally opening up to such discussion and debate.[46]

KEEPING THE EARLY DEBATE GOING

Other parts of the gay community were also finding ways to bring the fight to the larger community. The staff of Madison's Gay Center used their vigorous speakers program to gain access to courses on the UW–Madison campus, especially in sociology, social work, and human sexuality. They spoke to students about their "own experiences, as intelligent people not showing pathology," in an attempt to "crack their image of what gay people were supposed to be all about." An article in the *Capital Times* in early 1973 claimed that over a period of several months, speakers from the Gay Center had appeared on sixteen panels before more than one thousand people.[47]

In 1972, a teacher and students at Madison East High School invited the Madison GLF to a workshop on sexual identity/orientation during the school's intersession. Among other speakers, they invited Judy Greenspan, who was then a twenty-year-old out lesbian, feminist, and UW–Madison student. The principal stopped the plans cold and brought the issue to the council of high school principals, claiming a need for a policy on homosexual speakers. The policy they landed on was a total ban; it was approved by the elected school board at a hearing on June 7, 1972.[48]

To challenge the ban, Greenspan ran for the school board in the spring election of 1973. "I will run on a platform advocating the right of gay people to both speak and exist openly without harassment in the public schools," she said. "To deny gay people the right to represent themselves by speaking in the schools is to deny students the right to hear about homosexuality

In 1973, Judy Greenspan ran for the Madison School Board as an out lesbian on a gay rights plank among other issues. She is believed to be the first out lesbian in the nation to run for elected office. WHI IMAGE ID 59050

Judy GREENSPAN

for SCHOOL BOARD

* PASSAGE OF THE HIGH SCHOOLS BILL OF RIGHTS

* AN END TO DISCRIMINATORY PRACTICES AGAINST WOMEN

* SUPPORT OF THE RIGHT OF GAY PEOPLE TO EXIST OPENLY AND SPEAK IN HIGH SCHOOLS

Authorized and Paid for By FRIENDS of JUDY GREENSPAN – Martha Pietzik, treasurer

from the real experts, the gay people themselves." According to the *Capital Times*, she noted the irony that "as a lesbian she is not permitted to enter public schools without the principal's permission, but as a candidate she has already been invited to speak at Memorial High." Greenspan also advocated for the rights of teachers and students to be openly gay without fearing suspension or the loss of their jobs. She promised to "exact an apology from the Board for the abuses heaped on both the GLF and the high school students." In the February 1973 issue of *Whole Woman*, an early Madison feminist paper, she wrote, "Running openly as a lesbian and a feminist is going to be a hard job. I hope my sisters will actively participate in the campaign."[49]

As part of her campaign, Greenspan also urged "counseling on birth control and abortion, and self-defense classes for high school women." She proclaimed, "My campaign has broadened to include women's rights, equal representation and education for residents of the inner city . . . and advocacy for the High School Bill of Rights." Although the *Daily Cardinal* (UW–Madison) endorsed her in the race, she barely lost in the March 6 primary and her showing in the nine isthmus wards was strong. Greenspan brought a lesbian perspective to the sphere of public debate, stepping out into the spotlight during the same period as the Safransky case.[50]

STATE DEBATE OFF TO A ROARING START

When community funds were needed to support Paul Safransky's appeal to the Wisconsin Supreme Court, the social organizations that had developed in and around gay bars came to the rescue—and these institutions had existed in the community since the 1950s and 1960s. When David Adamany came out to Governor Lucey, it was not the first time Lucey had dealt with the issue of homosexuality. In 1966, the Wisconsin Young Dems had given him a taste of how the new issue was trending among the younger members of his party.

Some of Wisconsin's early gay activists excelled at managing the state's public discourse. Safransky asserted a claim for equal employment rights and was willing to seek the proper appeals of his firing. Adamany showed courage in filing the amicus brief at the circuit court and in coming out to Governor Lucey before the supreme court took up the matter. Adamany also masterfully framed the appellant's brief, allowing the court to set aside the insidious finding that homosexual status alone could be used to deny public employment. Many people, then and now, have focused only on Safransky's loss of his job as an outcome of the trial, but this view ignores how the larger debate framed issues about homosexuality in general, not just about one individual. It is well worth noting that the Wisconsin judges in 1972 showed a reluctance to accept that homosexual status alone could disqualify a man from his job.

The state's political establishment did not quite know how to handle this new wave of activism. John Garstecki at Southern Colony continued to dismiss gay employees. Madison's high school principals decided to ban gay speakers, though UW–Madison and other college campuses welcomed them. Greenspan emerged as a local lesbian voice in Madison's school board race.

Yet change was slow to come. The state's attorney general still quoted the Bible to support negative attitudes against gays. And several judges, such as Jackman and Hanley, simply made decisions that ducked the issue. Judges were now a bit more circumspect in their comments, but still fairly hostile in their decisions. At the circuit level Judge Jackman wanted homosexuals to stay in their private closets rather than be public about their identities. Wisconsin Supreme Court Justice Hanley ducked the question of homosexual immorality in upholding the firing of a gay man for not presenting the right male image. Meanwhile, in the state assembly in 1971, Representative Barbee had introduced sex reform legislation that would specifically include male homosexuals and their employment rights. And in 1977, just before he left to become ambassador to Mexico, Governor Lucey would denounce singer and antigay activist Anita Bryant's attacks on gays.[51]

The state debate sparked by the Safransky matter ignited Wisconsin gay activists even further in the endeavor to remedy their legal status as criminals and outcasts who could be denied the rights of citizens.

3

FORGING A GAY AGENDA

*Basically when stripped of emotionally charged sexual overtones, the
homosexual question is a matter of civil rights. A group who differs
from the majority only in sexual preference should not be oppressed.*
                                                —MILWAUKEE JOURNAL, 1977[1]

*This Foundation shall defend the civil rights of homosexual men and
women, and shall pursue the legal integration of homosexuals into
society enjoying the full rights and privileges of all other members of
this society without restriction due to sexual and/or affectional preference. It shall foster pride in the lesbian and gay community, and shall
seek to educate both that community and the society in which it exists
about the nature and needs of homosexuals.*
                                                —ORGANIZING STATEMENT OF
                                        MADISON COMMUNITY UNITED, 1978[2]

F ollowing Stonewall, gays and lesbians in Wisconsin—like those across
the nation—were trying to work toward the goal of liberation from
both an oppressive past and a bleak present. Several decades later, conservatives, including US Supreme Court Justice Antonin Scalia in *Lawrence v.
Texas*, would write about "the so-called homosexual agenda" or "the gay
agenda" in pejorative terms as something that threatened the sanctity of
the family. (This conservative characterization has been pimped by claiming the *truly* gay agenda was making everyone's wardrobe and décor simply
fabulous!) Yet the historical process of agenda-setting in the nation and in

Wisconsin during the 1970s and 1980s was not clear-cut, despite national gay leaders speaking in Wisconsin in the early 1970s.[3]

Wisconsin gay men and lesbians knew that their sex lives should not be criminalized and thus believed an agenda should include the repeal of criminal statutes. Only a few states had accomplished this prior to Stonewall, usually through the general penal law reform recommended by the American Bar Association. Wisconsin had not repealed its criminal statutes because it had reformed its own penal laws before the American Bar Association's reform model drew attention to victimless crimes, including those that violated morality laws where there was consent between the individuals involved. Most Wisconsin gay men and lesbians had experienced discrimination and felt they should not be victims of prejudice. Existing state and federal nondiscrimination laws gave them a model. Many persons in same-sex relationships felt their status should be recognized. In addition, many early activists wanted to affirm gay identity and shine a light on the gay community's gifts to American culture and to spread this word into the educational system. How these desires translated into specific strategies and actions would vary across the nation. Wisconsin's own unique history would inform how its gay community built a political agenda in the state.

THE *MILWAUKEE JOURNAL* BECOMES AN ALLY

The *Milwaukee Journal*, which had been virulently homophobic in the 1950s, came out for gay rights in 1977, though admittedly with a great deal of caution. In a July 8, 1977, editorial titled "Liberty and Homosexuality," the paper voiced support for nondiscrimination in employment, housing, and public accommodations on the basis of sexual preference. The work of the Milwaukee Gay People's Union (GPU) in media education, especially in building contacts with the *Journal*, appeared to be paying off.[4]

The paper's use of the term *preference* over the more contemporary term *orientation* reflects the evolving views of the day on whether homosexuality was a choice or a natural-born trait. Because of the "lack of academic information" on the subject, the paper felt "the homosexual personality has yet to be adequately studied." It did note that the American Psychiatric Association had removed homosexuality from its list of

Liberty and Homosexuality

Should homosexuals be given legal protection against discrimination? The question is explosive. Most people easily affirm that every person should have the right to be different. But many who advocate safeguards against discrimination by sex, race or religion find that deeply felt emotions and esthetic repugnance impede tolerance for homosexuals.

Some worries about homosexuality are legitimate. Most people, after all, are not gay. The majority has a strong interest in promoting heterosexuality, the cornerstone of family life and a necessary practice for the human species to continue. With justification, for example, most parents do not want their children exposed to teachers proselytizing a gay lifestyle or flaunting homosexuality with dress. And all people want to be protected from sexual molestation — whatever the sexual preference of the predator.

These valid concerns should be addressed by specific regulations: in the first instance, classroom guidelines preventing teachers — homosexual or otherwise — from peddling personal sexual values; in the second, criminal laws against sexual assault.

But how about homosexual teachers who simply stick to their teaching assignments? Should parents shield students from meeting homosexuals in the classroom out of fear that somehow children will model themselves on the teachers and become homosexual?

That fear seems irrational — although separating irrational fears from legitimate concerns can be difficult. It is complicated by lack of scientific information. The homosexual personality has yet to be studied adequately. Psychiatrists differ on the roots of sexual preference — on when it is established and whether it can be changed. Several years ago, the American Psychiatric Association removed homosex-uality from its list of disorders. That was a humane attempt to ease the stigma that brings great pain to homosexuals. But psychiatrists remain divided on whether homosexuality is an illness or simply a variant of sexual behavior.

Nonetheless, some common fears about homosexuals are clearly irrational. There is, for example, no evidence that gay people are guilty of sexual assault more often than straight people. And research has not shown that homosexuality is "catching," in the sense that firmly grounded heterosexuals can be seduced into permanently embracing the gay life. Likewise, there is no evidence that children taught by homosexuals become homosexual.

Basically, when stripped of emotionally charged sexual overtones, the homosexuality question is a matter of civil rights. A group of people who differ from the majority only in sexual preference should not be oppressed. To begin with, there should be fuller protection of privacy through repeal of outdated laws regulating sexual acts between consenting adults in private (a step that would benefit heterosexuals as well as homosexuals). At the same time, homosexuality should not be ground for discrimination in housing, public accommodations and jobs. For example, they should — with prudent regulation — be allowed to teach.

That is a long way from saying that society should condone or approve homosexuality. But it is affirmation of the right of homosexuals — like all other people — to be different. Except in circumstances where there is evidence of a clear threat to society, a homosexual's rights should be fully protected. This is essential not only to safeguard a minority but also to maintain the integrity of a nation that prizes liberty and justice.

The *Milwaukee Journal* published a separate state edition that circulated in most counties around Wisconsin. Its endorsement of homosexual rights in 1977 marked a major step forward in the state debate. MILWAUKEE JOURNAL, JULY 8, 1977

disorders, but the paper believed it could be either "an illness or simply a variant sexual behavior."[5]

The editorial also expressed concern over how to separate irrational fears from legitimate concerns about homosexuality. One concern, which was described as "valid," was that the "majority has a strong interest in promoting heterosexuality, the cornerstone of family life and a necessary practice for the human species to continue." The editorial continued, "Most parents do not want their children exposed to teachers proselytizing a gay lifestyle or promoting homosexuality with dress." This view echoed the line laid down by the Wisconsin Supreme Court in the Paul Safransky case. "But how about homosexual teachers who simply stick to their teaching assignments?," the paper continued. "Should parents shield students from meeting homosexuals in the classroom out of fear that somehow children will model themselves on the teachers and become homosexual?" No, the *Journal* responded; that was an "irrational fear." "Basically," the editorial stated, "when stripped of emotionally charged sexual overtones, the homosexuality question is a matter of civil rights. A group who differ from the majority only in sexual preference should not be oppressed."[6]

Lest its readers think the paper had gone too far, the editorial pointed out that nondiscrimination legislation was "a long way from saying that society should condone or approve homosexuality." However, it concluded with a balanced statement: "Except in circumstances where there is evidence of a clear threat to society, a homosexual's rights should be fully protected. This is essential not only to safeguard a minority but also to maintain the integrity of a nation that prizes liberty and justice."[7]

THE MADISON GAY RIGHTS ORDINANCE

While state nondiscrimination legislation seemed a distant dream even with the *Milwaukee Journal*'s nascent support, Wisconsin's gay activists did not put all their eggs in one governmental basket, especially in the capital city. In Madison, new efforts began on November 8, 1973, at the meeting of the Madison Equal Opportunities Commission (EOC). As the meeting began, Chairperson Ann Nelson introduced a group of six gay advocates—Karla Dobinski, Rob Anderson, Steve Klapisch, Sara Hummel, David Bryant, and spokesperson Ron Albers—who wanted to add several protected classes to the existing equal opportunities ordinance. According to the National Gay Task Force, only three cities in the United States had adopted nondiscrimination ordinances based on sexual orientation by the end of 1973. Madison would become one of the first dozen cities in the nation to do so.[8]

Madison's original EOC ordinance had been adopted in 1963 with then Mayor Henry Reynolds breaking an 11 to 11 tie in the Madison City Council by voting in favor of the ordinance. By the early 1970s, when the commission had grown to include fifteen members, *sex* and *class* were added to the original categories of *race, creed,* and *national origin.* Now, in 1973, these six gay activists were proposing that the protected categories expand even further.[9]

The advocates were associated with a variety of Madison's early activist organizations, including the Gay Liberation Front, the Gay Law Students, and the Lesbian Law Students. Since the reform movements of these days were often linked to one another, the advocates also had associational ties to a progressive labor group in the Memorial Union Labor Organization as well as ties to women's groups, including the National Organization for Women, the Rape Crisis Center, Whole Woman, the Woman's Action Movement, and the Women's Law Students, and other progressive groups such as the Tenants Union, the Wisconsin Student Association, and the National Lawyers Guild.[10]

Although he was not present for the meeting, Ricardo Gonzalez, an LGBT community member, was an active member of the EOC. Gonzalez, a Cuban immigrant, worked for Green Giant in Ripon and had run unsuccessfully in 1972 as a Democrat for the state assembly. After a friend introduced him to gay circles in Madison, including the Jenifer Street group, a network of supportive gay men active in the 1950s and early 1960s, he moved to Madison and became a state affirmative action officer. In 1974, he would open a gay dance bar called the Cardinal Bar on the east side of Madison's isthmus in what had been an old railroad hotel bar.[11]

At the meeting on November 8, 1973, the six gay advocates requested that the categories *sexual preference*, *economic status*, *marital status*, and *educational association* be added to the EOC ordinance. The EOC minutes did not record any specific listed cities, but other places having already adopted nondiscrimination ordinances were Seattle, Washington, and East Lansing, Michigan. As Albers noted, early ordinances might use *sexual preference* or *sexual orientation* for the protected class. One commission member asked Albers if he knew of any cases of discrimination concerning sexual preference presented to the EOC that had been turned down. Albers said he knew of no such instances, but he was aware of cases in which discrimination existed with regard to sexual preference.[12]

Since the current ordinance prohibited discrimination on the basis of class, the committee discussed the possibility that any of the groups seeking protection by enumeration might be interpreted as being covered simply by their definition as a protected class.[13] Precedent had been set for this in slightly earlier EOC discussions about long hair. Similar discussions had taken place almost a century earlier as well. When the English aesthetic movement was popular in the late nineteenth century, the long hair of Oscar Wilde was one of his physical attributes most often satirized. The Wisconsin press had even noted that, once convicted, Wilde's famous long locks were shorn. In Madison in the 1960s, when student antiwar activist Paul Soglin was arrested, his long hair was also shorn while in jail. Since flowing locks on males had become associated with both activism and the counterculture in those days, the EOC had grappled with the question of whether long-haired males constituted a protected class under the existing antidiscrimination ordinance. Clearly the Madison commission was struggling with what and how *class* could and should be interpreted. The commission began the drafting process for possible ordinance changes, eventually adding the category *physical appearance* to cover the question of hair length, along with other physical attributes.[14]

On February 14, 1974, Albers appeared before the commission again, this time representing the Gay Liberation Coalition, along with Bob Honig, Karla Dobinski, Sylvia Forney, Terri Schmidt, Rick Davis, Bob Dishmond, John Lindert, Steven Webster, and Jeffery Blum. Working with the commission on the ordinance was Henry Gempler, who as assistant city attorney helped draft changes and may have researched the legal precedent in other states to determine how these changes might be possible under Wisconsin statutes. Albers pointed out that *sexual orientation* was the standard term used in other municipal ordinances, and it was again noted that the several municipal ordinances that included the term did not have the general class provision that Madison already had.[15]

In the winter of 1973–1974, at this same period, I was running in a special election for a seat on the Madison City Council. Though I was not yet formally "out" in the press, other gay Madisonians helped me in my campaign. In my campaign literature, I took a clear stand on the two main issues of our gay agenda. I would "seek to abolish laws which regulate victimless crimes and control private morality," and I stood against "discrimination based on status, race, sex or sexual preference." Following Judy Greenspan's race, my campaign was among the earliest in Wisconsin to use material pushing the gay agenda. My opponent, who won the close election, also supported nondiscrimination measures, though she did not feature them in her literature.[16]

Dick Wagner, shown here going door-to-door, ran for the Madison City Council on a gay
rights plank in 1974. FROM THE AUTHOR'S COLLECTION

By its November 14, 1974, meeting, the EOC was considering a draft
ordinance that included the term *sexual orientation*, which would be defined as including "homosexuality, heterosexuality, and bisexuality by
preference or practice." Alder Michael Shivers moved to add "transsexual
and transvestite" to the definition, and the commission passed the motion. By meeting's end, the commission recommended that the proposed
changes proceed through the mainline political process of consideration
for adoption by the city council.[17]

At the next EOC meeting on December 12, James Yeadon, co-president
of the Gay Law Students Association, presented "a letter and statement
requesting that transsexualism and transvestism be removed from the
definition of 'Sexual Orientation.'" The motion to delete by Alder Michael
Christopher passed. The minutes report an assertion that "transsexualism
would be protected under 'sex' and transvestism would be protected under
'physical appearance.'" Many years later, Yeadon told me those involved
thought including transsexual in the definition of sexual orientation
would complicate passage of the proposed addition.[18]

As mayor, Paul Soglin was willing to lead the City of Madison in progressive innovation, but he also was a thoughtful political practitioner. One conversation between Soglin and Reverend James C. Wright before the ordinance changes were introduced played a key role in advancing the proposal. Wright, in addition to his position as director of the EOC, was an associate minister at Mt. Zion Baptist Church, one of the city's most prominent African American congregations. Wright was a civil rights pioneer and had worked during the 1960s to create Madison's original Equal Opportunities Ordinance. His support for adding *sexual orientation* to the ordinance served to counter the argument that expanding protections to gays would somehow dilute protections for those already covered, such as African Americans. As a minister, his support also made a statement that some churches were opposed to discrimination against gays.[19]

Surprisingly, there was no public debate about these additions to the ordinance. The EOC revisions were adopted at the Madison City Council meeting of March 11, 1975, with no dissenting votes. Mayor Soglin noted

Reverend James Wright was director of the Madison Equal Opportunities Commission and a pastor at Mt. Zion Baptist Church. His early support for the Madison gay rights ordinance was crucial to its passage. WHI IMAGE ID 67947

During his first term as Madison's radical new mayor, Paul Soglin was a key supporter of the city adopting a gay rights ordinance in early 1975. PHOTO BY EDWIN STEIN, *WISCONSIN STATE JOURNAL*

there was little opposition because of the good work done by the EOC. Madison thus joined the first dozen communities in the nation banning discrimination toward gays. Perhaps even more remarkable, the newspapers of the following day did not even note the changes. The Madison GLF had achieved a major accomplishment, but the change to its equal opportunities ordinance did not mean that Madison was suddenly a sexually tolerant community.[20]

At about the same time that the EOC's nondiscrimination additions were enjoying broad support, the city was engaged in a furious debate about sexual acts between consenting adults. Ministers and other opponents of massage parlors, which had become highly visible in the community, launched a crusade against them as blatant examples of sex for sale and immorality. By a petition drive, they presented the Madison City Council with a choice to adopt an ordinance regulating massage parlors or to put such an ordinance to a referendum. Soglin believed this was a maneuver to bring out voters who would vote against his reelection at the spring general election.[21]

On January 28, 1975, the city council decided to adopt the ordinance rather than hold a referendum. In response, the opponents of sexual regulation presented their own petition for a charter ordinance that would prohibit the city council from regulating private acts by consenting adults. The city council held a special meeting on February 17 to weigh the options. In the end, the council decided to put two referendums to the voters in April. One measure would ask if citizens wanted to repeal the newly adopted ordinance regulating massage parlors, and the other would ask if they wanted to prohibit the Madison City Council from regulating the sexual conduct of consenting adults.[22]

In the April election, Soglin, a strong supporter of adding sexual orientation to the city's nondiscrimination ordinance, was reelected with 61 percent of the vote. The results of the referendums did not follow suit; the massage parlor referendum was passed with 59 percent in favor of regulation, but support for allowing consenting adults to be free of legislation regarding their sexual conduct garnered only 47 percent. The election results showed that even in Madison, majority support for sexual privacy rights and the repeal of penalties for victimless crimes had not been fully achieved; no one knew what challenges might still arise.[23]

MADISON COMMUNITY UNITED

The year 1978 marked a turning point for Madison's gay community. During the decade following Stonewall, various gay political organizations came and went. Two institutions emerged as the most enduring: the Gay Center and the Gay Law Students Association, the latter associated with UW–Madison's law school. Both proved remarkably steady and are still in existence today. In 1978, they were joined by Madison Community United, which lasted for twenty years until merging with the (by that time renamed) Gay and Lesbian Center to become today's OutReach.

The United was created in response to an Anita Bryant–inspired attack on Madison's early gay rights ordinance. In 1977, Bryant led the attack against a Dade County, Florida, ordinance on nondiscrimination on the basis of sexual orientation by demanding a popular vote on the issue. This prompted other antigay reformers to demand referendums on such ordinances in other cities, and a number were repealed in this manner. Madison's gay rights activists were concerned because of the successful 1975 referendum on regulating massage parlors.

Even so, Madison was prepared to join the fight against Bryant even before local threats appeared, and the Anti–Anita Bryant Bash was held on May 1, 1977. The rally was endorsed by the Wisconsin Student Association, the American Workers Party, Young Socialists Alliance, the Committee Against Racism, the Center for Conflict Resolution, the Green Lantern Eating Co-op, and numerous downtown elected officials. Alder Yeadon helped bring six hundred people to the Great Hall in the Memorial Union. Among the speakers were Representative David Clarenbach, Mayor Soglin, and Yeadon himself. During the Dade County fight, Soglin had sent a supportive letter to the Dade County Commission, which passed the ordinance, citing Madison's positive experience. He wrote, "Protecting the basic rights of Madison's minorities, including gay people, has been beneficial to all residents of this city."[24]

In December 1977, the Madison underground newspaper *Take Over* reported on the efforts of a local pastor to repeal the city's nondiscrimination sanction. In the mainstream press, Pastor Wayne Dillabaugh of Northport Baptist Church announced a campaign to revoke the ordinance, which he claimed to be an example of "permissive immorality." The min-

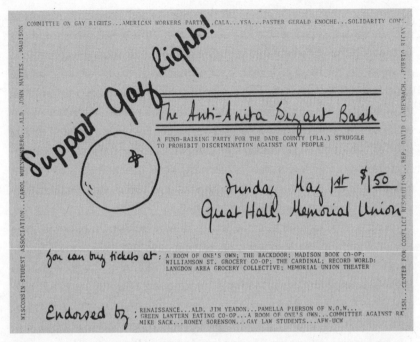

When the equal rights ordinance of Dade County, Florida, was under attack by Anita Bryant in the late 1970s, the Madison community organized to send funds to help save the nondiscrimination measure. WHI IMAGE ID 121045

ister also vowed to focus his attacks on homosexuals in politics. The *Milwaukee Journal* suggested that his threatened crusade "could produce an ugly McCarthy-like atmosphere." Dillabaugh asked Dane County Sheriff William Ferris for a weapons permit and to be made a special deputy; he claimed that he'd been harassed after he was charged by the district attorney with abusing a five-year-old child by administering severe corporal punishment. Ferris refused, explaining, "We have no people deputized who are not law enforcement people." The sheriff might have been particularly concerned by this request because some gay rights supporters claimed that Dillabaugh had called for the execution of homosexuals.[25]

Dillabaugh was joined in attacking the ordinance by Pastor Richard Pritchard, who wanted to repeal the ordinance protections on employment in "certain sensitive vocations, such as teaching, school administration and religious organizations." One locus of their efforts was the Dane County Association of Evangelicals; the group started a petition to permit discrimination, stating, "We oppose the acceptance or promotion of homosexuality as a sexual alternative" and "homosexuality should not be promoted as an acceptable life-style in the public school system." The evangelicals compared acceptance of homosexuality to acceptance of the American Nazi Party. They also sought to carve out an exception from the ordinance for public service organizations, presumably government employment and utilities. A total of seventeen names were listed on the petition, but it had only eleven signatures. These small numbers may reflect the relatively low numbers of evangelicals in Madison, a town that was dominated by Lutherans, Episcopalians, Presbyterians, Unitarian Universalists, Congregationalists, and Catholics.[26]

With a local mimic of Anita Bryant in Madison's own backyard, the city's nondiscrimination policy protecting gays and lesbians was under direct threat. Among the organizers of the United in 1978 were Kathleen Nichols, coordinator of the Madison Committee for Gay Rights; EOC Commissioner Gridley Hall; Ricardo Gonzalez, owner of the Cardinal bar; and Barbara Lightner, who would later become staff coordinator for the United. The first meeting, just like the earlier Madison Alliance for Homosexual Equality, took place at St. Francis House, this time with 240 attending. An early draft of the bylaws described the organization's general principles:

> This Foundation shall defend the civil rights of homosexual men and women, and shall pursue the legal integration of homosexuals into society enjoying the full rights and privileges of all other members of this society without restriction due to sexual and/or affectional preference. It shall foster pride in the lesbian and gay community, and shall seek to educate both that community and the society in which it exists about the nature and needs of homosexuals.

The group's dedication to gender parity was shown in the establishment of executive co-secretaries (later changed to co-conveners), one man and one woman. The United also created a religious committee and reached out to churches and synagogues through training sessions. Henry Dudek, a founder of Madison's Integrity/Dignity chapter (a gay ecumenical group that included Episcopalians, Catholics, Lutherans, and Methodists) gave a talk at this first meeting called "Addressing Religious Issues." In a comment to the press, Dillabaugh asserted, "I think they [members of Madison's gay community] are running scared. I think they ought to—because this community is sick and tired of their liberal politics and their sexual perversion."[27]

, That May, Ginny Vida, the media director for the National Gay Task Force, was in Madison speaking at Gay Awareness Week. To encourage the Madison community in the fight, she said Bryant and her ilk had "catapulted gay rights into the fore." She continued, "Now is the ideal opportunity to generate talk about the gay movement and send the stereotypes down the tube. We have to confront these fears head-on." Following Vida, mayoral aide James Rowen described Dillabaugh's antigay campaign as "a serious threat to some of the most basic traditions in Madison; the kind of traditions that make Madison, I think, a unique, very tolerant community." Rowen added that Dillabaugh's threat to "name names of homosexuals" was "reminiscent of the era of Sen. Joseph McCarthy." Reverend Thomas Woodward of St. Francis Church indicated that a "broad-based group of the city's religious, service and community organizations is being assembled to safeguard the ordinance." On May 10, the United launched a petition drive "showing community support for civil rights, particularly those of gay men and lesbians."[28]

Along with the drive for signatures, the United created rousing songs and chants for the street marches and rallies that were part of the campaign. One undated chant sheet aimed at a leader of the Moral Majority included the lines:

One, two, three, four,
Jerry Falwell's out the door!
Five, six, seven, eight,
We're United—gay and straight.

Another song, to be sung to the tune of the "Battle Hymn of the Republic" and aimed at local antigay clergyman Richard Pritchard, went:

We've seen this preacher clearly and he will not do us in,
We've got the men and women and together we will win;
The closets will not hold us, we're too strong to be locked in,
Seven days a week.

A favorite song performed at Madison's gay and lesbian rallies during this period was the Holly Near song with the lyrics,

> We are a gentle, angry people,
> and we are singing, singing for our lives.[29]

Dillabaugh, whom some called "our local Anita," hoped to spark the repeal effort with a three-day God and Decency Rally at his church in July 1982. The highlight was to be a born-again Christian jumping from a plane into the north-side church's backyard as part of a "Skydiving for Christ" show. Two prominent fundamentalist preachers, one a Baptist who had led a similar repeal effort in St. Paul, were to speak. The event was not a success; the preachers drew only eighty to a hundred attendees while a concurrent gay rights rally at Brittingham Park drew six hundred. Other local preachers did not join in the weekend's events. When Dillabaugh folded his tent and left town in 1983, much of his repeal effort fizzled.[30]

Rodney Scheel, pictured here with a bullhorn, brought the "party hardy" bar crowd to the political cause of defending Madison's nondiscrimination ordinance at the MAGIC (Madison Area Gay Interim Committee) Picnic. *ROD'S NEWSLETTER, 1989*

The Brittingham Park event was organized by the Madison Area Gay Interim Committee (MAGIC) as a picnic and spearheaded by popular gay bar owner Rodney Scheel. Scheel had been holding similar social events for his bar patrons since the Back Door Picnic of 1973. For the Brittingham Park event, Scheel persuaded social venues Lysistrata, Going My Way, the Pirate Ship, the Back Door, and the Cardinal to join as MAGIC sponsors. He knew how to design fun, attractive events, and he was credited with bringing the party-hardy boys, who frequented gay bars, into the effort to save the ordinance by framing the event as a large community rally. MAGIC picnics continued to be held for many years after 1978, though with a less political focus, and included events such as a water-balloon toss and high-heel drag races. Brooks Egerton, editor of *Gay Madison*, observed that these gay pride events were "where we celebrated our differences from mainstream America—the differences in values, roles, [and] histories that make us lesbian/gay and proud."[31]

Among the speakers at the 1978 picnic were Clarenbach, Yeadon, and Wright, director of the Madison Equal Opportunities Commission. In his stirring remarks, Wright said,

> This is a day for concern . . . and not a day for despair. And although there is afoot a diabolical movement to systematically destroy the rights so gained in this community, . . . with the cooperative effort we will be able to not only come through this particular battle victorious, but we will come through with a greater solidarity and a greater purpose than ever before to champion the civil and human rights. . . . We know what happened in Dade County, in Wichita, in St. Paul, in Eugene, Oregon, and we are not going to let that happen here in Madison.[32]

The success of repeal efforts in several other state capitals was not lost on Madison's gay rights advocates. The Madison EOC, in early 1979, issued a twenty-two-page report on the evangelicals' petition full of legal citations and noted the repeal efforts in Florida and Minnesota. The report noted that job performance, not status, was the basis for the Wisconsin Supreme Court ruling in the Safransky case. This information validated David Adamany's conviction that the State Personnel Board's ruling against Safransky, which was based solely on his status as a homosexual and not

the magic picnic

A CELEBRATION OF THE LESBIAN AND GAY COMMUNITY

JULY 14, 1979 • NOON — 7:00 P.M.
BRITTINGHAM PARK, MADISON, WIS.

FOOD • DRINK • DANCING • GAMES • FUN

DONATION $5 FOR FOOD AND DRINK
CHILDREN UNDER 12 W/ADULT $1
SPONSORED BY MADISON'S LESBIAN AND GAY COMMUNITY

For many years, the MAGIC picnic was held in Madison's Brittingham Park, conveniently located near the Washington Hotel with its LGBT watering holes and the Boys on the Bay "gayborhood" on Lake Monona Bay. WHI IMAGE ID 59228

The MAGIC picnic, which started as celebratory event for gay and lesbian bar patrons, grew to become a large community event featuring a water balloon toss and a high-heel drag race. Here Rodney Scheel (center with bullhorn) helps to coordinate events at the 1984 picnic. FROM THE AUTHOR'S COLLECTION

on his performance, needed to be contested. Since the 1975 passage of the sexual orientation provision in Madison's nondiscrimination ordinance, the report noted, seven complaints had been filed on that basis, with two settled, two withdrawn, two dismissed, and one pending.[33]

The issue finally was put to rest when the EOC recommended that Madison not change its nondiscrimination ordinance to exempt teachers or others from the sexual orientation classification, urging the city to "take no action which would in any way reduce the rights of homosexuals to be free from employment discrimination." The city council accepted the EOC's report in January 1979. Reverend Wright and Mayor Soglin had worked closely with liberal clergy members and the United strategists to lobby the council for a positive result. The United would proclaim, "Madison was the first of the targeted cities to stop repeal."[34]

As the threat to repeal the ordinance receded, the United decided to continue as a functioning organization; its members were "unwilling to dissolve just because a crisis was over." A cross-section of both lesbian and gay folks and political establishment leaders continued to serve on the board. Soglin and Clarenbach served, as did Woodward and Reverend Vernon Forsberg. The group's headquarters was located at the YMCA on North Brooks Street, just behind St. Francis House.[35]

Starting in 1980, the United's coordinator was Barbara Lightner, who had returned to Madison in 1978 from San Francisco where she no doubt was abreast of that community's efforts. After many weeks and months fighting Dillabaugh, Lightner worked to broaden the gay community's reach and was appointed to the police department's Committee on Community–Police Relations. In her role as United coordinator, she served as an advocate for gays and lesbians, filing complaints with the EOC. Later, as part of the Wisconsin Privacy Coalition, she lobbied the legislature on behalf of the gay agenda and trained others in how to lobby. In 1982, however, the United's board requested her resignation based on "growing incompatibility with the changing goals of the organization." As United board member Duane Kolterman observed at the time, the organization had moved from being a "socially activist membership organization formed in time of crisis, to a stable and ongoing social services agency." The shift to social services meant the group would no longer be as political as it was at its founding, since funding was dependent upon public grants, which could be administered only to organizations with nonprofit (and thus, generally nonpolitical) status. Upon Lightner's departure, the board commended her for "her incomparable efforts . . . on behalf of the lesbian and gay community."[36]

Over the years, the United made a noticeable impact in Madison's gay and lesbian community. It established a nonalcoholic coffeehouse with movie screenings, a gay nurse's alliance, and the Alive 'N' Well Health Fest '80, which held workshops on lesbian and gay health. In 1982, the city granted the organization funding for a crisis hotline with the phone number ALL-GAYS, or 255-4297. The phone line provided referrals and peer counseling. The United also undertook the first police sensitivity training program in the state and pushed Madison's police and fire departments to hire gay men and lesbians. These people became some of the earliest uniformed out homosexuals in the state. Police Chief David Cooper and Fire Chief Ed Durkin were both receptive and supportive of these efforts.[37]

The United also developed a program to deal with attacks on gay men. A September 1981 article on gay assaults in the underground paper *Free for*

All quoted Lightner as saying, "If this gets any worse, we're going to have to call it a crisis." The article listed tales of discrimination and abuse, including one of a gay man who was called names and shoved by strangers on the streets and on a Madison bus. The article writer observed, "Gay men, the most frequent victims of gay-related assault . . . may feel ashamed at not having been able to defend themselves." According to records kept by the Dane County Committee on Sexual Assault, twenty-one cases of gay sexual assault were reported in 1980, and the first six months of 1981 already showed that another twenty-six had been reported. To effect change and provide support, the United produced a brochure on gay assault and harassment that helped victims find places to report incidents.[38]

For the 1979 mayoral election, as Soglin was ending his first stretch in city hall and did not plan to run for another term, the United's political action committee sponsored a mayoral forum—perhaps the first held by gays and lesbians in Madison. "Amazingly," read a report by the United, "all the candidates appeared, and we endorsed the best." The committee selected the more radical candidate, James Rowen, who campaigned in gay bars, but he lost the election in a close vote to the liberal Joel Skornicka.[39] In 1982, in another agenda-defining effort, the United became involved in the Dane County Board races. The organization developed an issues program that included the promotion of statewide gay rights and a consenting adults bill, opposition to the recently introduced federal Family Protection Act that would cut funding for entities promoting homosexuality (including local governments, such as Madison and Dane County, with nondiscrimination laws), creation of a training program for county personnel on lesbian and gay issues, establishment of special in-services on gay issues for sheriff's deputies, and the development of alcoholism treatment programs for the gay community. One of the United's chief goals was to ensure that supervisors who voted in 1980 to approve the county nondiscrimination law on sexual orientation did not lose elections over their vote. Almost all were reelected, and the number of out members on the county board rose from two to three.[40]

The United also pushed the city to lobby at the state level on behalf of the passage of the sexual privacy (consenting adults) bill and the nondiscrimination bill on the basis of sexual orientation. In the early years, the United platform covered two full pages, including a request for the city to seek qualified gay and lesbian candidates for employment, as well as steps to improve community–police relations and social services interactions. Recognizing that not all gay needs were politically oriented, the organization in 1981 helped conduct trainings for 250 health-care professionals and assisted in blood screenings held in various taverns and bookstores in the city. The prevalence in this period of adult bookstores as locations for promiscuous sex contrasted with Milwaukee's many baths and fit the Madison community's self-identification as the supposedly more bookish city, as it was sometimes called, tongue-in-cheek, the "Athens of the Midwest."[41]

In 1983, the United Political Action Committee (UPAC) was involved with a number of City of Madison races and held a fundraising brunch on Jenifer Street. From these and other efforts, donations were later made to support mayoral candidate Joseph Sensenbrenner and alder candidate Anne Monks, a lesbian. One alder was attacked for his support of the city council funding the United. While he lost, most alders supportive of gays won. In 1984, UPAC again geared up to work on elections. It sought to work with like-minded groups such as the Wisconsin Lesbian and Gay Network, the Wisconsin Democratic Party's Gay and Lesbian Caucus, and the Eleanor Roosevelt PAC. Linkages were also sought with the local Women's Political Caucus PAC, the Madison Democratic Socialist PAC, and the Community Fair Share PAC.[42]

From its beginning, the United tried to maintain what was termed "a perspective beyond lesbian and gay issues." The organization's slogan was "United we stand; divided, they pick us off—one by one." This was a reference to the Lutheran pastor Martin Niemöller's famous statement about the Nazis' attacks on a sequential list of targeted groups. Though not mentioned by Niemöller, the Nazis' list included homosexuals, in addition to socialists, trade unionists, and Jews. A piece of artwork used frequently in early United materials was an image of clasped hands set with a quote by James Baldwin, the black gay novelist, from a letter written to Angela Davis, the black radical leader and communist. Baldwin's powerful opening to his "Sister" was, "One might have hoped that by this hour, the very sight of chains on Black flesh, or the very sight of chains, would be so intolerable a sight for the American people, so unbearable a memory, that they would themselves spontaneously rise up and strike off the manacles." Echoing Niemöller's sentiments, Baldwin said of Davis,

You look exceedingly alone—as alone, say, as the Jewish housewife in
the boxcar headed for Dachau, or as any one of our ancestors, chained
together in the name of Jesus, headed for a Christian land. . . . If we
know, then we must fight for your life as though it were our own—
which it is—and render impassable with our bodies the corridor to
the gas chamber. For, if they take you in the morning, they will be
coming for us that night.

When the United sought to bring Audre Lorde, the black lesbian poet who
had been nominated for the National Book Award for Poetry in 1973, to
Madison, the organization reached out to the Madison Urban League and
the Afro-American Studies Department.[43]

Susan Green, the coordinator for the United in the mid-1980s, had
worked with the Gay Rights National Lobby serving as a Midwest field representative, volunteered with the Madison Institute for Social Legislation,
and coordinated alternative families and labor projects. Upon moving to
Madison with her partner, Kathy Patrick, who was active with Wisconsin
NOW, Green began revitalizing the United and undertook new projects
related to its social services focus. One was building a broad community
coalition when Big Brothers Big Sisters denied the application of Brooks
Egerton, a gay man, to be a big brother. Even though they had a waiting list
of three hundred kids due to a shortage of volunteers, the organization had
a policy that denied gay applicants: "Big Brothers/Sisters of Dane County
will not knowingly match homosexuals or bisexuals with Little Brothers
or Little Sisters." Through research, discussion, collaboration, and per-
suasion, Green led the Big Brothers Big Sisters organization to a policy
change in 1986 that permitted gay men and lesbians to be seen as suitable
"family" for underprivileged kids. She commented, "I am very pleased that
we were able to negotiate successfully so that the issue could be resolved
without further legal action." Green was also an early champion for the
rights of persons with HIV/AIDS. At the 1993 Queer of the Year Awards,
Green was praised for "her courage and passion for social justice." The
United would go on to expand its gay family work by building a support
network for gay parents.[44]

The early efforts of the United showed the success gay and lesbian organizing could achieve. They made Madison one of the first communities

in the nation to turn back an Anita Bryant–type attack on a local sexual orientation nondiscrimination ordinance. From there, the group defined a broad social agenda for the lesbian and gay community and proceeded to develop programs and resources to implement these goals.

MILWAUKEE FIGHTS GAY-TARGETED LAW ENFORCEMENT

For decades, institutions in Milwaukee that provided sexual opportunities for gay men had been the targets of ongoing harassment by law enforcement. *GPU News*, believing it was "open season on the gay community," prominently featured Milwaukee's gay health clubs and baths when they were raided multiple times starting in summer 1978. The city's vice squad conducted one raid in May 1978 with the assistance of thirty or forty uniformed officers. Of the sixty patrons at the Broadway Health Club, eighteen were arrested, mostly for sexual perversion (formerly the state sodomy statute). In the raid, doors were broken down and one attendant was beaten with flashlights. The assistant district attorneys tried to get the arrested individuals to plead guilty to lesser charges, but these still left them with criminal records.[45]

GPU News reported in its July 1978 issue that on June 7, four vice squad police officers interrupted and shut down an informal auction to benefit a legal defense fund for gays facing police harassment at a gay bar on the grounds that there was no licensed auctioneer present. Five patrons received summons, but eventually the charges were dropped. Two days after the auction raid, *GPU News* reported, thirty-two parking citations were issued to cars parked in the vicinity of the Inferno, a gay bar. In addition to publicizing this police harassment, Milwaukee's gay community fought back in other ways. Community leaders immediately contacted mainstream press representatives with pleas "to safeguard and advance the defense efforts of the individual persons victimized in the raid" by refraining from publicizing hearsay reports until actual charges had been made. In July 1978, two more gay health clubs were raided, resulting in eleven additional arrests. The police entered the clubs without warrants because they had undercover agents inside. Those arrested were charged with lewd and lascivious conduct, and most were placed on six months' probation.[46]

In order to fight back, the GPU established a legal defense fund with

Alyn Hess as its chairperson. It raised over seven thousand dollars from mid-1978 to early 1979. In February 1979, more raids occurred and six men were arrested, but the district attorney's office referred them to the city attorney's office for civil disorderly conduct charges. The assistant district attorney said there were usually half a dozen such arrests each week, made in restrooms, bookstores, parks, and other locations. In January 1980, *GPU News* quoted a source that claimed as many as fifteen arrests were made nightly at some adult bookstores. That month, another health club was raided. This time District Attorney E. Michael McCann announced that he intended to prosecute all future arrests for violating the state law on sexual perversion, a felony charge. Attorney James Wood of Milwaukee contended that "McCann's remarks constituted an open invitation for police to continue their systematic violation of civil liberties." That the district attorney was applying criminal charges to homosexuals, even though the sexual perversion statute with its prohibition on oral sex also applied to heterosexuals, was made apparent by McCann's comment: "I don't think there can be abnormal acts between married people." In July 1980, another health club was raided with the use of undercover vice squad cops. *GPU News* observed that this raid occurred on the eve of the Milwaukee City Council's meeting to consider a gay rights ordinance.[47]

A citizen's letter published in the January 7, 1982, issue of the gay paper *Our Horizons*, "Response to D. A. McCann," criticized the district attorney's attitudes. The anonymous missive accused McCann of being "sourly bigoted, and with horse-blinder prejudice." For the article writer, McCann's double standard was clear: "More than twelve percent of all married people, after eight years of marriage, will have indulged in perverted sex acts." The "blind irresponsibility" of the district attorney was also attacked: "Complaints by the gay victims of anti-gay harassment have been systematically disregarded by the District Attorney and his staff." Even as late as 1988, *The Wisconsin Light* ran an editorial titled "McCann Must Enforce Law Fairly, Evenly."[48]

In July 1978, Hess published a satirical piece, "Scenario for: 'The Great Bath Raid'" in *GPU News*. Hess made clear, "If anyone in the Police Department expected that this (or any other) raid will cause gays to crawl back into their respective holes, they are sorely mistaken—and twenty years too late." Hess believed the value of the raids was to remind gay people "once again of the dangers of a police force which is both secretive and irresponsible." He thought the Milwaukee police tactics "were not only outdated by any responsible standard of police routine, but they were also haphazard and sloppy."[49]

The GPU went further and in late 1979 established a hotline "for gays who are regularly arrested by undercover Milwaukee police on such charges as sexual perversion, lewd and lascivious behavior, disorderly conduct, loitering, prowling, etc." It also created a wallet-sized card with legal defense information. *GPU News* felt sure that there was "selective enforcement of these laws against the gay community." The paper called the vice squad "the clown brigade" and decried the entrapment of gays as squandering police resources when people were afraid to walk alone in their neighborhoods. Police harassment was a theme of the 1980 gay pride march in Milwaukee, in which 150 people walked from Juneau Park to MacArthur Square. Quoted in a *Milwaukee Journal* article, one gay man watching from the sidelines expressed the fears of many who were "too afraid" to join, asking, "Where are the 30,000 others?" The march and rally, sponsored by the GPU, featured lesbian activist Miriam Ben-Shalom, who used her speech to say, "We want the police off our backs."[50]

One target of the community's anger was Milwaukee Police Chief Harold Breier, whom *GPU News* referred to as serving a lifetime term "senility notwithstanding." The publication thought the chief and district attorney were engaged in a vain attempt against so-called threats to "public morality (whatever that is)," and it urged gays to join the Coalition to Oust Chief Breier. The coalition presented petitions with a combined thirty-six thousand signatures to the Milwaukee City Council. Breier struck back using a McCarthy-era attack, saying the coalition was spearheaded by the "'revolutionary Communist Party' consisting of homosexuals and the former head of Milwaukee's Black Panthers." For Breier, the members of the United Workers Organization, a community organization, were the Communists, and the members of the GPU were the homosexuals.[51]

The Women's Coalition also joined in the attack on Breier, perhaps because he had been slow to respond on the issue of rape. Women Against Rape (WAR) spotlighted the Milwaukee group's efforts. They were incensed that Breier had once said he "believed that many rapes reported to the police were not really rapes at all." Breier responded to the movement to oust him by saying, "I guarantee you these three groups won't force me to retire. They can take those petitions and stick them in their ear." Breier retired in 1984 after the state legislature statutorily curbed his powers in response to these complaints about his misuse of power. The new police chief opened a dialogue with the gay community, and the alliances forged in the fight against Breier would only help spur the movement.[52]

THE GAY SEXUAL REVOLUTION VS. THE GUARDIANS OF MORALITY

Before Stonewall, many Wisconsinites had been silent about homosexuality. According to a 1986 *Isthmus* article, young men had very few places where they could be supported, guided, and encouraged "to explore their own bodies, thoughts and desires." However, in the post-Stonewall era, Wisconsinites created spaces where sexuality could be explored within the gay community. Still, the boundaries of what that exploration might entail clashed with the state's former norms of morality and behavior.[53]

The Milwaukee police were not totally delusional in thinking they had more responsibility when it came to enforcing morality laws. As shown in the previous chapter, the number of fun-loving patrons at Milwaukee's baths and crowded bars far overwhelmed the number of members in the city's gay political organizations. As the number and visibility of Milwaukee's gay bars exploded in the 1970s and 1980s, that city became the center for baths in the state. Milwaukee and Madison bar owners also organized trips to gay bars in Chicago, such as Gold Coast, which was known for its hardcore leather scene.

An increase in gay sexual activity in Milwaukee was suggested by press reports on a surge of sexually transmitted diseases (STDs) among gay males in the pre-AIDS era. In 1974, the *Milwaukee Journal* noted "a growing incidence of syphilis in the Milwaukee area, primarily among homosexuals. . . . 65 since the beginning of the year . . . indicate[s] that the Milwaukee area [is] in the midst of an outbreak." At the time, about half of the patients with syphilis were suspected to be gay.[54]

The gay community responded to the prevalence of STDs by establishing health options for testing and treatment. The GPU venereal disease clinic opened in 1974 and remained functional for over forty years;

eventually it became permanently located on Brady Street and was known as the Brady East STD Clinic, or the BESTD Clinic. During its early years, it operated on an annual budget of ten thousand to fifteen thousand dollars and was staffed by volunteers, including Dr. Roger Gremminger, its medical director. Early board members included Mark Behar and Sue Deitz, and key players included volunteers Ross Walker and Erv Uecker. Gremminger recalled that, during the pre-AIDS days, he "worked diligently to control gonorrhea, syphilis, giardiasis, amebiasis, warts, and hepatitis B." In 1989, Gremminger donated the building on Brady Street to the nonprofit corporation, removing any concerns about future lease payments.[55]

Another event in 1974 sparked additional press revelations about the region's sexual activity: the suicide death of Robert Jones, age forty-eight, president of Waukesha Memorial Hospital. The press described Jones as a bachelor who took his life shortly after a party at his home. Jones graduated from UW–Madison in 1949, after which he earned a master's degree in hospital administration from Columbia University, and in 1958 the Waukesha Junior Chamber of Commerce had named him the Outstanding Young Man of the Year. After his suicide, the county coroner undertook an inquest to obtain sworn testimony and investigate the social implications of having three teenage bartenders for a party of thirty- to thirty-five-year-old bachelors. The coroner was looking into the corruption of juveniles and sexual perversion based on supposed statements Jones had made that he would kill himself if the youths did not spend the night at his home. In the press, the coroner referenced the party's possible similarity with a "homosexual torture and killing ring" in Texas. The district attorney and sheriff's department followed up with a secret John Doe probe, and five criminal complaints were issued on sixty-one counts of morals charges, including sexual perversion. The district attorney, after noting that Jones had been involved in the "contamination" of boys, expressed "concern that there had been no complaints by either the young people or their parents." Other offenses had allegedly occurred at a Boy Scout campout at Jones's country estate. Press accounts mentioned that multiple orgies had been uncovered in the investigation.[56]

In Madison, which did not have established bathhouses, erotic bookstores, sometimes referred to as "porn dens," were the most popular locations for sexual liaisons. The *Capital Times*, in a 1986 series on pornography in Madison, reported that booths in "video arcades are a source of casual, anonymous gay and straight sexual encounters." The paper called two well-known stores with basements and back rooms "the most convenient places to turn" for the libidinous. The stores were rumored to be owned by an Illinois porn distribution company. "The activities have taken place for years," the *Capital Times* reported, "far more blatantly in years past, with hardly any notice taken of them. . . . For $5 worth of tokens, [customers] can enter—singly, in pairs, sometimes in threesomes—a video booth where they can close a door, watch a sex film and have their pleasure at the same time."[57]

By 1986, when AIDS became an issue, the city health department was successful in getting cooperation from the stores for educational campaigns on safe sex and providing free condoms. The *Capital Times* reported, "The gay bars in Madison where sex once was freely and openly available now display signs warning of unsafe sex, urge the use of condoms and even show videos on AIDS dangers." These videos appeared on the same screens that showed triple X gay male sex videos. The same story reported that La Crosse health officials undertook similar sexual health education efforts for their adult bookstores.[58]

The *Capital Times* also reported on solicitation at the bookstores, reporting that "gay hustlers are a frequent presence in these stores, ready to enter a booth with anybody who can flash a $20 bill." The paper obtained the story from an ex-hustler who frequented these establishments, though the reporters declined to pay the $50 requested by the hustler, despite his insistence that "you get more when you pay for it." The twenty-six-year-old man, who used the pseudonym "Jason," admitted he started going to bookstores at age sixteen and was not much older when he began hustling "because I was broke." He observed, "Casual sex among strangers was much more open and commonplace in the bookstores 10 years ago." Jason said twenty dollars resulted in some fondling, and anything else was more like fifty to seventy dollars; on a good night, he claimed he could earn three hundred dollars.[59]

In January 1974, the *Milwaukee Star Times*, a black community paper, profiled an ex–male prostitute named Harry Davis who had abandoned "the homosexual lifestyle" after working the Milwaukee streets for several years. The headline was "'Gay Life' Was No Life at All." Various sources disagreed about how much male prostitution existed in Milwaukee at this time. That spring, the situation would heat up when District Attorney McCann decided to charge men who had several prostitution arrests. McCann claimed that Milwaukee "has a problem with males selling their services that has surfaced in the last five years." In response, County Judge Terence Evans dismissed charges of male prostitution that May, claiming state law did not provide for men to be prosecuted for that offense. Within two weeks of Judge Evans's ruling, Circuit Judge Christ Seraphim convicted a man for offering to perform an act of sexual perversion with a vice cop. Seraphim was quoted as saying, "I'm now also recognizing that we have male prostitution."[60]

It's possible the anti-prostitution effort led to less hustling, because a 1976 *Milwaukee Journal* story ran with the headline, "Gays Thrive Here, but Male Prostitution Scarcely Exists." The story claimed that law enforcement and gay community leaders both agreed male prostitution "is apparently close to nonexistent in Milwaukee. . . . The temperament of the city simply does not welcome and nurture prostitution for gays." Yet by 1981, the *Journal* suggested that the city's reputation had changed when it ran a story headlined "Big Increase Seen in Gay Prostitution." That February, Louis Stimac, director of the Gay Counseling Service, spoke at UW–Milwaukee and estimated that five or six hundred full-time or part-time gay prostitutes lived in Milwaukee. Stimac believed the city's transvestite prostitutes primarily had heterosexual customers.[61]

In 1989, the *Milwaukee Sentinel* published an article with the headline, "Male Prostitutes, Clients Frequent Third Ward Area." After describing the putative efforts of offering money for some action between a reporter and unwitting drivers, the writer noted, "This scenario is repeated regularly in the area, observers said. . . . Members of the Historic Third Ward Association Inc. fear unwarranted paranoia about homosexual prostitution could keep developers and potential residents from the area." Milwaukee police observed, "Homosexual prostitution is more prevalent in the Third Ward than other parts of the city, but on nowhere near the scale of female heterosexual prostitution citywide." At a subsequent meeting with the *Sentinel*'s editors, gay community members complained that the article was not balanced.[62]

The situation in Madison differed from that in Milwaukee. Madison's premiere gay entertainment venue was the Hotel Washington Complex, operated by Rodney Scheel, who, as a booklet celebrating the establishment's tenth anniversary proclaimed, was "committed to quality entertainment and leisure activity for Madison's Gay Community." Two of the hotel's four venues were gay-focused—the New Bar, the city's most popular dance bar, and Rod's, a basement bar that held leather/Levi–themed events. The hotel also contained Something Different, a store with "toys for boys and tools for men" and not a little artistic flair. Later, a patio bar was added to the complex, and in good weather it was used for the plentiful buffet supper of the weekly Sunday Beer Bust. Lewis Bosworth, who had suffered through the gay purges at UW–Madison in the 1950s, now served as editor of Rod's newsletter, which was sent to some twelve hundred devotees. Rod's was known for the underwear remnants decorating its basement ceiling pipes—the establishment's unspoken commando policy meant that some of those unfortunates caught wearing underwear in the bar would have the pair snipped off them at either side of the waist and added to the bar's involuntary underwear donations. Rod's tenth anniversary booklet noted, "Five years of underwear weighs 446.5 pounds." The undergarments were eventually removed from the pipes as they posed a potential fire hazard.[63]

In 1996, an accidental fire tore through the Hotel Washington Complex, ending the life of the gay mecca. Off-duty firefighter Ronnie Greer, who had a history of distributing antigay literature in Madison, said, "I'm not sorry about some of the businesses that are gone now." His remarks were denounced by Mayor Paul Soglin. A vigil of five hundred people gathered on the steps of the State Capitol to mourn the loss to the community. The many gay couples who had met at the hotel felt a strong personal loss. Steve Webster, a member of the Council on Religion and the Homosexual, and others organized an interfaith service of remembrance at the University United Methodist Church. Antigay picketers shouting "shame" greeted worshippers as they entered the church.[64]

In addition to bathhouses, gay bars, and erotic bookstores, personal ads in local newspapers also provided gay Wisconsinites with opportunities to make sexual contacts. In a 1986 issue of the Isthmus, for example, a self-proclaimed "GWM [Gay White Male], Good Looking, dark blond," advertised that he was seeking an "in shape straight acting-G/BiWM

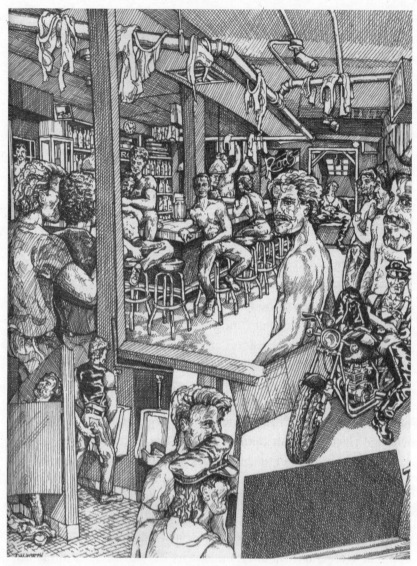

This cover illustration for the tenth anniversary issue of *Rod's* newsletter portrays the leather/Levi–themed bar's unofficial "no underwear" policy. Two snips, one down each side, could shed any bar-goer's offending garment, which was then hung from the overhead pipes. After several years, the fire department ordered the removal of the underwear as a fire hazard. *ROD'S* NEWSLETTER, 1989

[Gay/Bisexual White Male]." The seeker's interests included tennis, rac-
quetball, and movies. Later in Milwaukee, Alternative Connections Inc.
would use the tag line, "A Matching Service for Same-Sex Relationships
and Friendships."[65]

Not all profligate sex in this era took place in commercial locations.
One farm in a rural township in southern Wisconsin during the 1980s and
1990s was famous for its annual "Bivouac" parties where guests could stay
all night if they brought a tent, camper, or bedroll. The party was listed in
the *Isthmus* and *Gay Chicago*. Attendees were encouraged to "dance your
ass off" during this night of "Relationship Amnesty."[66]

CRUISING VENUES GET THE POLICE SPOTLIGHT

In the early 1990s, complaints surfaced that Madison's Olin-Turville Park,
a longtime cruising area for gay men just a mile from the State Capitol,
had become, as Sunny Schubert of the *Wisconsin State Journal* described
it, "an *au naturel* no-tell motel for gay men." Madison police sent officers
on horseback into the wooded park and ticketed illicit activity. The gay
community members using the park were thought to be "a minority who
thumb their noses at the concept of public decency." One gay man, in a
letter to the editor of the *State Journal*, asserted that closeted and married
homosexuals used the park because out gays could meet at bars and other
social outlets. The problem, as Schubert explained it in her piece, "becomes
particularly acute in the summertime." When police checked the license
plates in the park's parking lot, they discovered many cars from outside
the city, reputedly from as far away as ninety miles. A proposed Unlawful
Trespass into Parks ordinance, which would have permitted harassment of
gay men who cruised in parks, was rejected in 1996 by the city council. Gay
alder Mike Verveer led the fight against what he called "an unconstitutional
swipe at everyone's civil rights and liberties." As recently as 2009, police
were still dealing with these issues in the park, which the *State Journal* noted
had "been home to public sexual activity for nearly 20 years." The city's
Parks Department experimented with allowing dogs into the park for a
month in autumn 2009, something which was generally prohibited, but a
member of Bay Creek's neighborhood association said the increased foot
and paw traffic "seemed to have only a minor impact" on the cruising.[67]

B. B. Clarke Beach on Madison's near east side was known for after-gay-bar skinny-dipping parties in the 1970s. Later, lesbian activists claimed the space in the daylight for the shirt-free movement. FROM THE AUTHOR'S COLLECTION

Celebrating gay pride with a pink triangle banner on the house, young politician Mike Verveer (left) joins Dick Wagner in holding a colonial-era flag of resistance. FROM THE AUTHOR'S COLLECTION

Other cities in Wisconsin also saw burgeoning cruising and sex activities in parks in the years after Stonewall. My first volume on gay history in the state, *We've Been Here All Along: Wisconsin's Early Gay History*, recounted how arrests in Waukesha's Frame Park caused an uproar in the state's pre-Stonewall days. In 1986, another Milwaukee suburb confronted a similar problem as Underwood Parkway at Camp Wil-O-Way in Wauwatosa broke into the news. Wauwatosa Chief of Police Roy Wellnitz told statewide gay newspaper *OUT!* that gay activity in the area had "simply gotten out of hand." While admitting it was not "a choice assignment," he sent undercover operatives who arrested twenty-seven men between June and October. Wellnitz hoped the onset of winter would discourage further activity.[68]

In 1987, Wauwatosa police said they had "received scattered complaints about homosexual activity in the area [for years], but the activity increased and became more flagrant last summer." Some fifty men were arrested from 1987 to 1988, including a high school teacher, a suburban pastor, a director of patient services at a nursing home, a parochial school principal, and a school psychologist. They ranged in ages from twenty to fifty-nine, and most were residents of either Milwaukee or Waukesha Counties. Some lost their jobs. Most were cited for disorderly conduct and paid civil forfeitures. Undercover plainclothes officers were used to entice the men into chargeable actions. One man identified as "Richard," a computer operator, told the *Milwaukee Journal*, "I go to the parks once or twice a month on the average. It's a place to go and meet other gay people." However, he claimed he did not engage in sexual activities while in Underwood Park.[69]

In August 1986, Ralph Navarro of the gay Cream City Business Association told the press, "Our problem, from a civil liberties perspective, is enticement. In too many of these cases, the undercover officer involves himself in highly alluring activity." Navarro offered the theory that public places such as parks were used by "closet homosexuals" who might be afraid to visit gay bars. He said the association opposed casual sex in public places by both heterosexuals and homosexuals. "We in the gay community say: put uniformed police patrols in these places regularly," Navarro said, "and that will stop it." The proposed solution upheld the law and sought to end sexual activity in public without the entrapment of gay men.[70]

In 1994, the Madison police crackdown on Club 3054 became a cause célèbre. The bar's basement level was well known to be pretty wild, featuring "Underwear Night," wet jockstrap contests, and buttocks prints on the ceiling. Police had reported public oral and anal sexual acts occurring there as well. The owner, Cheri Becker, claimed she never encouraged, permitted, or condoned sex on or off her premises. She disagreed with some of the city's charges but accepted a sixty-day license suspension with the bar's doors shut and agreed to the permanent closing of its basement. The club did not last long after this. Newspaper accounts indicated that a concerned gay man complaining about "unprotected sex in the bar" might have sparked the matter. The city denied that their actions were discriminatory toward homosexuals and focused instead on public health. With growing awareness of AIDS and the fears that came with it, not many in the gay community objected to some restraint.[71]

While lesbian sexual activity attracted less notoriety than gay sex, there was one aspect of their liberation that did appear in the press—the shirt-free movement. In October 1976, the Madison alternative newspaper *Take Over* published an article about one incident: "The Lesbians played baseball at Olbrich Park, but when spectators went topless one of those little old puritans with spyglasses called the cops." The unfortunate officer who responded to the call had some notoriety for previously having shot a cow that had escaped from the Oscar Mayer slaughterhouse. The officer showed discretion and left when his presence caused even more of the group to strip. In 1991, *The Edge*, another Madison alternative paper, published an article titled "Shirt-Free Victory." Three women reporters wrote about the "Shirt-Free Revolution," which they saw as a struggle for social equality. For them, "the issue of who gets to decide where and when and how women's breasts can be seen" had begun "an important dialogue on how we view women's bodies." A number of Madison lesbians had pressed the issue, and in response, the city park superintendent, on advice from the city attorney, had agreed that public beach lifeguards would not cite women for not having their breasts covered. Lifeguards would call police only "for behaviors that create a disturbance, including men's harassment of women with or without shirts." The paper's published comments from eleven on-the-street interviews showed mixed reactions, even among females, to the shirt-free movement.[72]

Gay men and lesbians (and quite a few heterosexuals, too) embraced the sexual revolution that began in the 1960s. As they worked in the following decades to create new spaces where sexuality could be expressed, gays and lesbians too often faced outdated law enforcement strictures as they pushed the boundaries. Police and some district attorneys had long-established patterns of enforcing morality laws against gays. The community worked to build its own defenses, publicize harassment by agents of the law, and address outdated policies.

BISEXUALS SORT OF WELCOME

Though there is less in the historical record about bisexuals than about gay men or lesbians, Wisconsin's bisexual community did begin to organize in the early 1990s. Recent scholars such as Lisa M. Diamond, author of *Sexual Fluidity: Understanding Women's Love and Desire* (2009), and Ritch C. Savin-Williams, author of *Mostly Straight: Sexual Fluidity among Men* (2017), have brought more nuance to discussions about bisexuals. In a number of interviews, Diamond has suggested that the numbers of bisexually active individuals far exceeds those who are exclusively homosexually active. Savin-Williams urges society to embrace a greater range of sexual orientations than just lesbian, gay, and bisexual. Both of these views harken back to Alfred Kinsey's heterosexual–homosexual scale, which ranked sexual orientation on a scale of 0 to 6. A number of both gay and lesbian activists from the first decades of Wisconsin's liberation movement later demonstrated fluid bisexuality by entering into successful heterosexual marriages. Some indicated that they had never been "perfect sixes," or full homosexuals, on the Kinsey scale. One referred to himself as a gay activist because he thought his attraction to men needed defense, while his attraction to women did not require activism.[73]

In April 1991, the Madison-based *Feminist Voices* newspaper featured an article attributed to the Bisexual Women's Support Group. The organization was formed in the early 1990s so that bisexual women would have a safe place "where no one will point a finger and say, 'You—out of the pool.'" The group welcomed both students and non-students of all ages. Role models of prominent bisexuals such as actor Cary Grant, musician Leonard Bernstein, tennis star Billie Jean King, entrepreneur Malcom Forbes, and singer Joan Baez were discussed. The group made the claim that "bisexual women are seldom understood by either heterosexual or lesbian women and are often denied an existence by both." The author wrote: "Once in a gay bar someone came up and confronted me with, 'What are you?' I felt as if I wasn't welcome. I was an intruder who didn't belong." She felt the shock of being rejected "because of my lifestyle is more painful when it comes from someone in the women's community or the lesbian community. . . . It is hard to believe that I don't exist, and that the other bisexual women I know in Madison don't exist."[74]

The support group met weekly on a drop-in basis to counteract such bias and to build a community of shared experiences. They were supported by the Campus Women's Center. The woman who facilitated the group, going by the pseudonym "Melinda," told a reporter from the *Capital Times* in a series later in 1991 that the gay community sometimes characterized bisexuals as either kinky or trying to have the best of both worlds. Toni Phillips, who had moved to Madison from the Bay Area two years earlier, was quoted in the series as saying that Madison lagged behind San Francisco in providing support for bisexuals. He noted, "My sexuality is defined as bisexual, but culturally I'm gay." Another bisexual quoted in the series was William, a UW–Madison professor identified only by his first name, who had sexual relations with men during the time between his two marriages as a relief and a release from his first divorce. Some fourteen years later, he still found himself "much more comfortable around women and gay men than with 'so-called' straight men."[75]

Janet Hyde, professor of psychology and a vice chancellor at UW–Madison, was featured in the *Capital Times* series as the author of the 1979 textbook *Understanding Human Sexuality*. She also taught a human sexuality class on campus. Hyde wondered why so many people described themselves as being attracted to only one sex when she believed all humans start out being able to respond to males or females. She concluded, "The reason is that the social stigmas are so great against bisexuality and homosexuality, that most of us end up heterosexual."[76]

In the same series, Michael Dixon of the Ten Percent Society, UW–Madison's gay student organization, said the organization encouraged bisexuals to join, although he knew of no members who admitted to being one. Jane Vanderbosch, executive director of the United, argued for efforts to bridge the mistrust: "We cannot silence another community the way we've been silenced. I don't know how we're going to build this coalition, yet we're in the process of doing it." She perceptively saw that "the issue is seen in political terms, not in sexual ones."[77]

In November 1992 in Madison, the first issue of *Bi-Lines: A Newsletter for the Bisexual Community* was published by Bi?Shy?Why?, a loosely structured bisexual organization active since April of that year. The publication

Bi-Lines

A newsletter for the Bisexual Community published at Bi-Monthly intervals by **Bi? Shy? Why?** PO Box 321, Madison, WI 53701-0321

Welcome to the second edition of Bi-Lines, the newsletter from Bi?-Shy?Why? Bi-Lines is here to update you on news of our organization, to inform you of upcoming events, to get the word out about issues that concern bisexuals, and to be a forum for our creative expression. Bi?Shy?Why? is a group of bisexuals from the Madison area who meet regularly to discuss issues, network, share information, organize political actions, and socialize. We are a loosely structured group of friendly people who welcome anyone interested in bisexual, lesbian, or gay issues to drop in and join us. Come to our meetings on the first and third Monday of each month, from 7:00-9:00pm at our new location, the Lesbian, Gay, and Bisexual Campus Center, 336 W. Dayton. For updates or more information contact Bi? Shy?Why? at P.O. Box 321, Madison, WI 53701 or call 265-3344.

Bisexual Women's Support Group

A Bisexual Women's Support Group will be held at The United, 14 W. Mifflin St. on the 2nd and 4th Wednesdays of the month, on a drop-in basis. The first meeting was Wednesday, February 10, from 7:00-8:30pm. This group is for bisexual women to come together in a supportive environment to share experiences. Some of the goals of this group include:

•To provide an environment that allows us to simply be bisexual without the expectations of either lesbian or heterosexual communities.

•To provide a place to explore the meaning of a bisexual identity specifically as it relates to women.

•To provide a place that is non-judgmental about the diversity of bisexual women's coming out processes.

•To cultivate empowering and positive images of bisexual women.

•To provide networking information to those who wish to reach out to the larger bisexual community.

If you would like more information about this group, call Melinda at 231-2150 or the United at 255-8582.

It's Our Anniversary

Goofy is 50. Laugh-In is 25. And Bi?Shy?Why? is 1 year old! No fooling! We will celebrate our one year anniversary on April 1, 1993. To celebrate this event, our regular meeting on Monday, April 5 will be an anniversary party. We have all effected change during the past year in the Madison area and it is time to celebrate our success. Our organization has helped over 150 members find and help each other deal with bisexuality in our lives. Our outreach has placed spokespeople on several local boards, in classes, and workshops, and helped give a bisexual name, face, and voice to public education. We have influenced decision makers and our opinion is now sought by other local organizations. On April 5 let's get together to look back with pride on all that we have done in our first year and to renew our enthusiasm to move forward. Yippee! Hooray for us!

Bi?Shy?Why?, one of a few organized bisexual groups in the nation, was founded in Madison and published a newsletter titled *Bi-Lines*. BI-LINES, FEBRUARY/MARCH 1993 featured bisexuals telling parts of their own stories via nonfiction, fiction, and poetry. Money to start *Bi-Lines* came from a grant provided by the Ten Percent Society. A couple of years later, bisexuals were included when UW–Madison formed the Lesbian, Gay, and Bisexual Issues Committee in 1994. After its initial start, the group raised money by participating in the annual MAGIC picnic donating volunteer hours that earned them approximately 6 percent of the event's proceeds. Over its four-year history, more women than men appear as contributors in *Bi-Lines*. By 1993, the staff noted that their mailing list had "grown dramatically" and expressed the sentiment that "there is a growing bisexual community in Madison." The publication, which favored the more inclusive term *queer* in many of its usages, continued into 1996.[78]

Bi?Shy?Why? offered both women's and men's support groups as well as a combined group. During its first year, the organization claimed to have 150 members. *Bi-Lines* reported that Bi?Shy?Why? was among nine bisexual groups at the 1993 national march and that gay fathers in the group chanted, "We're here, we're queer, we're in the PTA." A Wisconsin chant was "M-I-L-K, Drinking milk will make you gay. Don't be cruel, don't be mean, we're just a bunch of dairy queens." Group members were featured on Madison's *Sunday Night Out* radio show, and a photo of members marching with their banner was published in *BiNet News*, the newsletter of the national bisexual group. Madison group members were also sometimes featured in the BiNet Midwest newsletter published out of Minneapolis.[79]

The group dealt with what it saw as biphobia from the gay and lesbian communities. For example, in a 1993 Lesbian Variety Show, an annual event showcasing lesbian music performers, some lesbians accused Bi?Shy?Why? of "invading lesbian space, stealing lesbian energy, and lessening lesbian personal safety." Trying to smooth things over, the Campus Women's Center sponsored a lunch dialogue for lesbians and bisexual women. In the November 1993 issue of *Bi-Lines*, Bi?Shy?Why? member David O'Donnell argued, "In a world where compulsory heterosexuality is violently enforced and biphobia among gays and lesbians is often strong, outing one's bisexuality can help move society from its limited 'straight or non-straight choice.'" A more positive view of the relationship between gay men, lesbians, and bisexuals was expressed by Scott M. in the

Members of the Madison bisexual group Bi?Shy?Why? pose with their banner. UNIVER-
SITY OF WISCONSIN–MADISON ARCHIVES, *DAILY CARDINAL* LGBTQ IMAGE COLLECTION, UAC68

February/March 1993 issue of *Bi-Lines*. After observing that his friends "equally cover the Kinsey scale," he noted, "It is only the gay and lesbian population who have taken bisexuals into their movement (sometimes willingly, sometimes with hesitation)." One sign of inclusion in Madison was the addition of two members of Bi?Shy?Why? to the United's board; one of the two, Greg Hines, eventually became president. Additionally, Frontiers, a local older gay men's group, several times invited Bi?Shy?Why? members to speak to their group.[80]

During the early 1990s, the Milwaukee bisexual group Bi Design met at the Counseling Center of Milwaukee and offered peer support groups. For several years, bisexuals participated in the speakers' series at the UW–Milwaukee Union sponsored by Milwaukee's GayLesbianBisexual group. Both Milwaukee's and Madison's bisexual groups marched in Milwaukee's Pridefest in 1995. Dennis Bunch, a Milwaukee man who described himself as "a Radical Leather-Faerie" with the fey name of "Queer Scout," published several letters in the BiNet Midwest newsletter, describing his work as encouraging gay groups to "be inclusive of [the] Bisexual and Transgendered person."[81]

The interactions between gays and lesbians and bisexuals in Wisconsin revealed plenty of tensions, but since heterosexuals were generally no more welcoming to bisexuals than they were to homosexuals, the limited organizational support and partial welcome for bisexuals came from the gay and lesbian community, which valued inclusion.

LOCAL ACTIONS SHAPE THE GAY AND LESBIAN AGENDA

Following Stonewall, Wisconsin's gay community had initially focused on starting pro-LGBT organizations, many of which were related to university campuses. Timidity often kept real or full names from being used. This rapidly changed in the late 1970s. Some of the state's opinion makers were also changing their tune, as shown in the *Milwaukee Journal* editorial of 1977 endorsing civil rights for gay people. Yet this change of opinion was more a recognition of homosexuals as a minority than an embrace of the gay community. With emerging conceptions of personal liberty and rights, some of the population felt the now-acknowledged minority should not suffer discrimination. Yet disapproval of gay people themselves and of their sexual lifestyles remained quite strong.

Nevertheless, Wisconsin's lesbians and gays and, as time progressed, its bisexuals and trans persons, did not wait for approval as they expanded and fought for their own sexual geography. This led to many clashes, especially as gay males in urban centers pushed the boundaries of acceptable behavior. Wisconsin gays were vocal against what they viewed as selective police enforcement in the Milwaukee bath raids, crackdowns in public parks and bars, and entrapment. In response to these and other acts of harassment, Milwaukee's GPU established a legal defense fund and helped oust the Milwaukee police chief. Gay leaders spoke out against entrapment, and the Milwaukee's district attorney's double standard was criticized. The gay community and its allies took steps to better organize and win local victories, and initial steps were taken for local political involvement in electoral races. These efforts would become building blocks in a statewide effort.

As the next chapter details, the gay community would also find a voice in politics, both from their ranks and from allies who would fight on the front lines as lawyers, councilpersons, and elected officials working to legislate for much-needed change as they began to build a statewide coalition.

4

FIGHTING FOR OUR RIGHTS

The government doesn't have the right to tell you who to go to bed with.
— Donna Burkett, who with her female partner applied for and was denied a marriage license in 1971 in Milwaukee[1]

In very few other cities besides Madison could a self-confessed homosexual like James Yeadon be considered anything but a protest candidate.
— *Badger Herald* (UW–Madison), February 14, 1977[2]

M any actors contributed to the implementation of a gay agenda in Wisconsin. The civil rights and women's rights movements provided examples for how a minority or identity group could organize and engage political power structures. Many of the state's early gay activists had previous involvement in the civil rights and antiwar movements, marching for open housing in Milwaukee or joining welfare rights demonstrators at the State Capitol. While a very few in the community sought to turn their backs on the world of politics and took an isolationist, communal tack, most would follow the model earlier established by the homophile movement of claiming equal rights as a minority community. Engaging in this fight with Wisconsin institutions required the gay community to change perceptions and forge strong political links.

BUILDING STATEWIDE POLITICAL LEVERAGE

Wisconsin's first statewide gay political effort took place in the fall 1976 elections, which included partisan races for US Congress and the state legislature. "Realizing the only way they are to achieve freedom through the legislative process is by seeing that candidates sympathetic to their cause are elected," *GPU News* observed, "gays have for the first time taken wide measures in the political arena." The effort was two-pronged. To begin, *GPU News* published interviews with candidates for legislative seats in three districts on the east and near north sides of Milwaukee where there was a recognized gay voter base. Since multiple candidates were running in these predominantly Democratic districts, the interviews were published in the September issue of *GPU News* before the primary vote on September 14. The results for the candidates who got through the primaries appeared in the October issue before the November elections.[3]

These interviews, published under the heading "Assembly Candidates Speak Out," were crucial in educating voters, particularly gay voters and gay-friendly voters, about their advocates. James Moody and Barbara Ulichny, two of the four candidates vying for the open seat in Milwaukee's Twenty-fifth District, were profiled. Moody had spent four years in the San Francisco Bay area while earning a PhD in economics at Berkeley and in 1968 had worked for presidential candidate Eugene McCarthy. Moody described himself as "staunchly liberal with respect to human rights, rights of expression and lifestyle" and felt state laws should change to "eliminate discrimination of any sort based on race, sex, or sexual preference." Passing consenting adults legislation was on his agenda, as was the issue of child custody and hospital visitation rights for gays. Ulichny, a local woman who graduated from Milwaukee Lutheran High School, was a state vice-chairperson for the Wisconsin Civil Liberties Union (WCLU) and highlighted the organization's fight against gay discrimination in housing and over child custody. She said, "I would be willing to co-sponsor consenting adult in private legislation as well as anti-discrimination legislation based on sexual orientation." Moody came in first in the election, with Ulichny a close second. He would go on to win a special election to the state senate the next year in 1977, and Ulichny would take over the assembly seat. Moody later continued on to Congress where he was a cosponsor of federal nondiscrimination legislation on the basis of sexual orientation.

Agenda setting in Wisconsin proved to have long legs, as politicians from Wisconsin took their gay-supportive positions to the national level.[4]

In Milwaukee's Eighteenth District, Lloyd Barbee chose not to run for reelection in 1976. Marcia Coggs, who had managed Barbee's previous election, ran instead. She was the widow of Reverend Isaac Coggs, who had served in the assembly before Barbee and had served on the Milwaukee County Board. Coggs had served on a state consumer advisory panel on insurance and brought that experience, as well as her experience as an African American, into her *GPU News* interview: "I was surprised at how often gays are discriminated against when obtaining life, health, and auto insurance. They pay much higher rates just because they are gay. . . . As a minority member I have lived with discrimination all my life and if elected will be happy to co-sponsor consenting adults in private laws and anti-discrimination laws based on sexual orientation." Coggs won the Democratic primary in the Eighteenth District, beating Robert Swan, who had run against Barbee in 1974 and had nastily attacked him for his support of gay rights. Coggs's victory, like Barbee's, indicated that many of Milwaukee's black voters did not object to African American candidates who supported gay rights.[5]

Only one of the five Democratic candidates running in Milwaukee's Twenty-sixth District conducted an interview with the *GPU News*. William Lemieux was a member of Holy Rosary parish and a parochial schoolteacher in the Archdiocese of Milwaukee. Like Moody, Lemieux had also worked for McCarthy in 1968. "On gay issues," *GPU News* reported, "he takes the same position as Eugene McCarthy who said, 'Who sleeps with whom is not the concern of the state nor is it my concern.'" Lemieux estimated that sexual discrimination against gays "would disenfranchise a conservative estimate of 3,000 persons in my district." He pledged, "I am not only willing to co-sponsor the consenting adult in private law and the anti-discrimination law based on sexual orientation, I am willing to work hard and long to assure passage of these laws." Lemieux ran a good race but lost to Steve Leopold, a liberal Democrat who would become a steadfast supporter of the gay community. Though no interview with Leopold was published (he presumably missed the opportunity), he was favorably noted by *GPU News* among the list of pro-gay candidates. In the next session, Leopold was a cosponsor of the consenting adults bill and its floor manager.[6]

Perhaps most remarkably in this election, the Milwaukee candidates who intended to appeal to gay voters had quickly learned the issues and understand how the gay community framed them. Almost all referred to "consenting adults in private" as the language for decriminalizing sodomy and other sex acts. Additionally, these candidates knew that vocalizing support for nondiscrimination legislation on the basis of sexual preference/orientation was the next most important goal. The variance in nondiscrimination language continued to show the evolving terminology between *preference* and *orientation*, both nationally and locally. The fact that these key items on the gay agenda in Wisconsin were commonly known both within and outside the gay community demonstrated good political progress.[7]

In October 1976, the GPU sent a statewide survey on gay issues to nearly 250 state legislative candidates. Of those, 210 chose not to respond. The survey made clear that a lack of response would be considered a negative response. Though only 8 percent of candidates responded, this was about twenty more candidates than had previously made comments about gay issues on the record. Most were from the urban areas of Milwaukee and Dane County, and some were from the state's smaller cities. Two candidates responded to say they would oppose the measures on the GPU's list.[8]

The 1976 survey issues were as follows:

1. Repealing the sex laws against consenting adults in private

2. Nondiscrimination on the basis of sexual preference in employment, housing, public accommodations, public service, and credit

3. Views on child custody, adoption, visitation, and foster parenthood as they affected gays

4. Concerns that state-regulated enterprises not be permitted to discriminate

Candidates who answered three of the four agenda items favorably were put on the approved list. Though it may seem surprising today, the overall group of pro-gay agenda candidates comprised fifteen Republicans and ten Democrats.[9]

Certainly a number of the Republicans running in heavily Democratic districts, especially in Milwaukee, had to be considered long shots. In one state senate district, the Twentieth in Sheboygan, both opposing candidates in the general election responded to the GPU survey and obtained a favorable rating. While some respondents may have been just filling in the blanks on their returns, a number of Republicans were genuine supporters of the gay agenda. Among them was Lyman Anderson, incumbent from the town of Oregon in southwestern Dane County, who had a gay son. Anderson later lost the seat to then-Democrat Jonathan Barry, who would go on to be a supporter of gay rights even after he switched to the Republican party. Another Republican with a favorable rating in 1976 was Steve Gunderson from Osseo, near Eau Claire. He would go on to win a seat in Congress and, in the 1990s, become one of three out congresspersons from Wisconsin, winning reelection in 1994 as an out gay man.[10]

The results of the GPU survey were published in *GPU News* in the form of a list of twenty-five candidates favorable to the gay agenda who had survived the primaries. The magazine also urged homophile organizations to "follow up on candidates in their area." Its November issue noted that the GPU "also disseminated the results to the non-gay press with limited results." The magazine reported, "It has been an interesting political year for Wisconsin gays. For the first time politicians are turning to the homosexual community for help. In five districts they are seeking the homosexual vote discovering that we have an impact in the outcome in those districts." In December, reporting on the election results, *GPU News* wrote, "Wisconsin gays were generally pleased with the results of the election. Over half of the candidates on record in favor of gay rights were elected, and all of the candidates actively supported by gays won." The list of winners included fourteen assemblypersons and five state senators. It also contained names not mentioned in the first published group of survey results—more candidates from Milwaukee and Dane Counties, and Representative Richard Flintrop, a not-yet publicly out gay man from Oshkosh who may have been tardy in responding to the survey.[11]

The 1976 election provided the GPU with a dose of political reality. While some candidates were willing to address gay issues, what mattered was the number of legislators needed to pass controversial legislation on sexual matters. Following in the footsteps of Lloyd Barbee, Representatives Marcia Coggs and David Clarenbach introduced a comprehensive sex reform bill early in the session. Felicitously numbered Assembly

Bill (AB) 69, the bill included a full laundry list of measures including repealing criminal penalties for incest, allowing same-sex marriage, lifting restrictions on advertising for birth control, permitting first cousins to marry, repealing laws against prostitution, and repealing laws against consenting adult acts in private. At the time, the activist community was stepping away from a full legislative frontal attack that conjoined all sexual issues, and this was a "holy card" effort by Clarenbach and Coggs to simply put the issues into view rather than move them forward. Alyn Hess, president of GPU in 1976, was quoted as saying, "We have backed such legislation in the past, but we have come to realize that our efforts can best be spent on approaches that do not create an atmosphere of hysteria." Roger Durand, the head of the Wisconsin Alliance for Sexual Privacy, said he hoped the "bill would die quietly and quickly. . . . Regardless of the merits of such legislation, past history shows us bills that lump controversial matters together get nowhere." Indeed, the bill died after introduction. Durand was working on another bill, which would focus solely on consenting adults to be introduced on February 10, 1976, by Representatives Clarenbach and Flintrop.[12]

Over the years, gay political organizing in Wisconsin would result in the formation of many different groups that advanced the community's agenda. The United Political Action Committee (UPAC), formed in 1979, was for many years Madison's lesbian/gay PAC. In 1982, the Lambda Political Caucus formed in Milwaukee. By 1984, there was a lesbian and gay caucus in the state's Democratic Party. In December of that year, *OUT!* would publish an article arguing that "feminist [and] gay votes were felt" after the 1982 election. Several years later, Milwaukee's Lambda Rights Network formed in response to the election of Governor Tommy Thompson in 1987. The next decade would see the establishment of the Human Rights League PAC, Center Advocates, Action Wisconsin, Equality Wisconsin, and Fair Wisconsin.[13]

FROM CAMPAIGNS TO LEGISLATIVE PROGRESS

The political activity in the 1976 legislative races and revised tactics for focused rather than comprehensive sexual reform legislation resulted in some progress during the next legislative session. In February 1977, with the reintroduction of a consenting adults bill, *GPU News* announced that a new statewide lobbying effort had begun for decriminalizing gay sexual behavior: the Wisconsin Alliance for Sexual Privacy (WASP). The alliance formed as a statewide gay and lesbian lobbying group, motivated by the recommendation (reported a month earlier) from the Special Committee on Criminal Justice Standards and Goals of the Wisconsin Council on Criminal Justice that private sex acts be legalized. The recommended measure was adopted only after heated debate. Sister Dorothy Wood of Milwaukee commented, "I believe in morality, but I don't believe you can legislate it." Percy Julian, who had been on the State Personnel Board in 1972 during the Paul Safransky case, was now head of the special committee.[14]

On March 30, 1977, the UW–Madison student newspaper the *Daily Cardinal* reported on a hearing before the Assembly Judiciary Committee for the new AB 323, the bill for consenting adults legislation. The hearing opened with Clarenbach's challenging and provocative question: What statute have "most members of the legislature violated?" Cries of, "Speak for yourself, David!" greeted the query. Mark McNary of the UW–Madison Gay Law Students Association quickly followed with, "To the best of my knowledge, we're the only organized criminals in the law school." Unitarian Universalist minister Tony Larsen, who was active in the Racine-Kenosha WCLU, asserted there were differing church positions: "Some churches forbid oral sex or fornication or homosexuality. My church does not. The state should not act as the religious authority." Reverend Judith Michaels of UW–Milwaukee's Campus Ministry claimed that "telling people what they can do in the privacy of their own bedroom" was an immoral act. Out Madison Alder James Yeadon quipped, echoing former president Nixon, "I'm not a criminal, I'm not a crook." Attorney Karla Dobinski argued that even if not enforced, the sex statutes formed the basis for discrimination against gay people.[15]

On May 3, 1977, the Assembly Judiciary Committee voted for the first time in state history in favor of Sexual Privacy Bill AB 323 by an 8 to 5 vote. The favorable votes included three Democrats on the GPU winners list. The five negative votes comprised both Democrats and Republicans. The only Republican in favor was John Gower from Green Bay. Among the Republicans opposed was state assemblyman Tommy Thompson from Elroy.[16]

On May 5, the assembly voted in favor of the bill at a second reading by a vote of 54 to 44, and *GPU News* reported that "the gay community thought victory was at hand." However, passage still required a third reading and final vote in the house. At that session, opponents made charges that the bill would legalize prostitution. Amendments were offered, and the bill was tabled and finally referred back to the Assembly Judiciary Committee on May 11. A class of sixth graders in the public gallery stymied part of the debate over amendments as members were reluctant to discuss sex acts and related language in their presence. Meanwhile, a Racine radio host stirred up new debate. Supporters of the bill had cited many groups with positions supporting the decriminalizing of victimless crimes, including the American Psychiatric Association, the American Medical Association, and the National Council of Churches. With a lack of precision and overstatement, supporters had, however, claimed specific support for AB 323, which of course most of those national organizations had never heard of. The bill was shelved for the summer, and Speaker Edward Jackamonis undertook an investigation of the claims at his own request. A twenty-one-page report was prepared that showed the endorsements were "in principal" if not "specifically" related to the bill. Durand of WASP felt the report "cleared the air" on the issue. However, in part due to the delay, the bill did not pass in this legislative session.[17]

YEADON BUILDS A STRONG TRADITION FOR WISCONSIN

In fall 1976, District Eight, a student-dominated area that included Fraternity Row on Langdon Street, had a vacancy on the Madison City Council. For a midterm vacancy, the city council selected from those who applied. Out of fourteen applicant candidates, on October 12, after three hours of candidate presentations and eight ballots, the council selected Yeadon by a vote of 14 to 7. He was described in the *Renaissance* newsletter, published by the Madison Gay Center, as a gay activist since the founding of MAHE. Raised in Manitowoc, Yeadon would be claimed by the Parents and Friends of Lesbians and Gays of Manitowoc as their own, with roots at Lincoln High School. As a member of the UW–Madison Gay Law Students Association, he helped frame the revisions in the Madison Equal Opportunities Ordinance and appeared several times before the city's

Equal Opportunities Commission (EOC). He himself became a member of the EOC representing the gay community in 1975 after passage of the Madison nondiscrimination provisions. After his election, Yeadon felt his visibility meant he was "walking on a tightrope." Potential rivals were watching for any mistakes.[18]

Publicly, Yeadon tried to downplay his gay activism. Yeadon told the *Daily Cardinal*, "I'm a vegetarian and I'm gay, but they're not something I'm going to push on anyone else." Asked about the statement, Yeadon replied, "I meant that these are things I'm into but I'm not saying everybody should be into them. I'm willing to educate people on those issues, but I won't say that everybody has to be gay or a vegetarian." His other political work involved the struggles of the Memorial Union Labor Organization and the United Farm Workers. Yeadon would later recall he didn't have a gay agenda but "wanted to be honest with people about who I was." A few nicknamed him the "alderfaggot," and he kept a file of death threats. Yeadon maintained a law practice from his home at 123 West Gilman, which would later be the home of both Clarenbach, the advocate for a series of state pro-gay bills, and Earl Bricker, who helped organize the UPAC and later became an out Dane County board supervisor. The house was part of the Mansion Hill neighborhood in the Eighth District, which spawned a number of lesbian and gay officials. It no doubt deserves a pink landmarks plaque.[19]

In the city council elections in spring 1977, Yeadon ran for a full term. The *Renaissance* newsletter in the March issue ran a headline, "Yeadon Campaign Fag-Baited by *Badger Herald* Editors." The *Badger Herald* was then the conservative student newspaper. The February 14 issue ran an interview of Yeadon and his two rivals the day before the spring primary. *Renaissance* described the interview itself as "reasonable," but on the editorial page, Yeadon was attacked as one of the "political loonies" and "certifiable head cases." On the eve of the election, the paper blasted Mayor Paul Soglin as a "recycled radical" and "political transvestite." Then the editor noted, "However, Madison's political oddities are not confined to the mayoral race. . . . In very few other cities besides Madison could a self-confessed homosexual like James Yeadon be considered anything but a protest candidate." The paper charged that Yeadon "had cleverly waited to reveal his sexual perversities until after he was appointed by the Council."[20]

Madison Alderman Jim Yeadon, who had worked on the 1975 gay rights ordinance, was appointed to the city council in 1976 and elected in the spring of 1977, making him the fourth out gay elected official in the nation. UNIVERSITY OF WISCONSIN–MADISON ARCHIVES IMAGE S00928

The editorial provoked a letter of protest in the *Herald*, which was reprinted in *Renaissance*, expressing "dismay over the irresponsible treatment of all gay people and Alderperson Jim Yeadon." The writers challenged the *Herald*, "Yeadon has never hidden the fact that he is gay. In fact, he has always been quite open about it, and was an active member of the Gay Law Students while a student at the University." The letter was signed by Dennis Carlson and David Carter of the Madison Committee for Gay Rights; Eve Mokotoff and Mary Bethold of the Lesbian Switchboard; Mark McNary of the Gay Law Students Association; attorney Karla Dobinski; Reverend William Landram of St. Francis Episcopal Church; Eric Bingen, a Wisconsin Student Association (WSA) senator; Joel Federman, vice president of the WSA; and Kathy Anderson of the United Council of Student Governments. The list of signers showed the continuously changing names of gay organizations and leaders in town and the ongoing success of finding sympathetic allies.[21]

Of Yeadon's appointment by the council, the letter stated, "If the Common Council saw no reason to publicly question his sexual orientation, it is to their credit." The letter drew a subsequent response from the *Herald*'s chief editor Robert Ritholz, who said he did not see how those arguing for openness on sexual orientation could complain about "my mention of Yeadon's sexual proclivities." Unless Ritholz had special sources, it was unlikely he knew anything about Yeadon's particular sexual "proclivities" that should have been distinguished from his sexual orientation. The editor also contrasted Madison with other places: "For example, imagine a self-confessed homosexual running for alderman in a city like Chicago or Houston." The *Herald*'s use of "self-confessed" had echoes of sin being attached to gays. Of course, their crystal ball was clouded, for Houston would go on to elect a lesbian mayor in 2010 and Chicago in 2019.[22]

Before the letter was published, Dennis Carlson, one of the chief signers, spoke with Richard Voss, the editorial page editor of the *Herald*. As *Renaissance* reported, Voss stated that the paper "did not support equal rights for gay people." Further, "There are some of us on staff who feel that you people shouldn't be allowed to walk the streets. And there are those of us who certainly feel that you shouldn't be allowed to hold public office." Yet time and again Wisconsin voters, especially in Madison and Dane County, would show the *Herald*'s views were not shared widely.[23]

For *Renaissance*, "the best reply to the fag-baiting campaign against Jim Yeadon is to help him beat dormitory resident and frat man Robert Eskta April 5." According to *GPU News* in May 1977, Eskta "made Jim's homosexuality a campaign issue bringing it up again and again when meeting with 'Frat Houses.'" Yet as Yeadon observed, the district had a growing number of left-leaning housing co-ops as well as fraternities. Yeadon came in first in the February primary among four candidates. He won the general election in April by a good margin, beating Eskta by 1,555 to 1,090 votes.[24]

Yeadon continued his council work and traveled to Milwaukee to be a featured speaker at the GPU meeting of September 1977. The GPU was interested in the efforts to elect openly gay persons. In January, *GPU News* had featured out Massachusetts Representative Elaine Noble as Gay Person of the Year. In 1974, Noble became the first out lesbian in the nation elected to a state legislature. Among their presentation of her work was her belief, "We can never expect other liberal people to speak for us. It is our responsibility to speak for ourselves." The *GPU News* story said, "Her sensible feeling that gay people must themselves be responsible for promoting their own ameliorative legislation naturally leads to the necessary corollary that homosexuals organize themselves, back candidates, raise money, and seek to influence the process of power, in short to join the political system as to influence it." Noble visited Madison in March of that year to speak at the Eighth National Conference on Women and the Law, which featured a Lesbian Law Section.[25]

Yeadon did not seek reelection in 1979, citing the time demands of the alder job. He thought people had judged him on his performance. "It's a relaxed city here. People deal with me as though I'm just another alder-person. I've never emphasized being gay and neither has anyone else." Yet he remained a believer in having gay people elected to office, and "hope[d] another gay person [would] run for his seat." In fact, the Eighth District would see a whole procession of gays and lesbians serving on the city council and the county board, starting a tradition of out gay officials in the state's capital.[26]

DEFINING THE ISSUES: FAMILIES AND MARRIAGE

While the Wisconsin state legislative agenda had become highly focused on consenting adults and nondiscrimination legislation, the broader gay agenda addressed more issues. In October 1973, Jack Baker, a former University of Minnesota law student who had served two terms as student body president, spoke at UW–Oshkosh on behalf of same-sex marriage. He and his partner, Michael McConnell, had used a loophole in 1970 to obtain a marriage license from Blue Earth County, Minnesota. Baker believed that gay "stereotypes are so deeply embedded in society that in order to unembed them you have to just hammer away." The campus paper reporting on the event stated that Baker "wasn't quite the screaming queen" and the "audience reaction seemed to be one of polite distance. Their questions showed how little many knew about gay liberation and occasionally exhibited an overall nervousness." Later in the decade, there would be a Gay Students Association at UW–Oshkosh with regular meetings and counseling services. The *GPU News* story on Baker's Oshkosh speech had optimistically begun with the speaker's prediction, "Same-sex marriages will be legal in the United States within a decade."[27]

Several months earlier, the magazine had reviewed an article in the *Yale Law Review* that discussed the pros and cons of "The Legality of Homosexual Marriage." One theory advanced was that once the Equal Rights Amendment (ERA) had been ratified, a strict interpretation of the amendment language "could easily give homosexuals the right to marry persons of the same sex." As we now know, the ERA ratification failed.[28]

Wisconsin's actual experience had shown that several couples were impatient for the state to get around to marriage equality. In September 1971, Donna Burkett and Manonia Evans applied unsuccessfully to Milwaukee County Clerk Thomas Zablocki for a marriage license. Burkett, twenty-five at the time, had grown up on Milwaukee's North Side and viewed herself as a tomboy. After graduating North Division High School, she took some college and technical school classes and then joined the US Army. Posted in Alabama in the 1960s, she had to confront an openly segregated society. When she returned to Milwaukee, she became an activist, marching with Milwaukee's Father James Groppi for open housing in 1968 and attending GPU meetings. She worked in an auto factory for decades as she shunned employment where she might have had to wear a dress. Burkett met Evans at a gay bar on the north side. She would recall, "I did not believe the government had any business telling me who I could marry." The couple's quest was featured in the November 1971 *Jet* magazine published in Chicago.[29]

After being refused a license, Burkett and Evans applied to Federal court claiming that the denial of marital benefits, including inheritance rights and joint tax filings, did not afford them constitutional equal protection of the law. The complaint read, "The legal increments of marriage ought to be shared irrespective of generic differences, to wit: mutual fulfillment and happiness and the equal opportunity to share in the benefits of the law as those in heterosexual unions blessed by the civil marriage contract." Federal judge Myron Gordon dismissed the suit over technical legal issues. While the suit was pending, a public question-and-answer forum held in early December drew a crowd of one hundred persons, predominantly black, to UW–Milwaukee. When asked, the couple stated they would not be playing husband/wife roles. Their response to possibly raising adopted children to be gay was that any children they had "would be raised as people." Not deterred by the official turndown, they proceeded to wed on Christmas Day surrounded by 250 friends. The marriage was presided over by Father Joe Feldhausen in St. Nicolas Church according to the rite of the Holy Eastern Orthodox Catholic Church. Feldhausen, a Milwaukee native, had also marched with Father Groppi for civil rights.[30]

In 1973, *GPU News* reported another gay wedding had taken place at a private residence in Green Bay, officiated by Father Bob, a Roman Catholic priest whose full name was not given. The grooms, James Riske and Nick Gagalaino, wore matching gold shirts and white slacks, and each had a double rose corsage. In 1977, Garth Wangemann and Roy Badger formed a family after they met at UW–Milwaukee. The couple would wait thirty-seven years for their union to be recognized when they were among the plaintiffs in the successful Wisconsin same-sex marriage case in 2014. Badger noted, "After nearly four decades together, Garth and I had kind of lost hope we'd ever be able to get married—it always seemed like such a long shot."[31]

With the United now refocused as a social service agency, in the early 1980s, a group of activists formed the Madison Institute for Social Legislation (MISL), taking up the issue. For MISL, the unofficial status of underground marriages was insufficient. These activists wanted an official formal recognition of family status even if marriage equality was not yet a part of it. MISL was headquartered at the Wil-Mar Center on Jenifer Street, and among its activists were Barbara Lightner, Kate Nolan, and Jerri Linn Phillips, strong and determined women who had formed families. In a brochure, MISL answered the question, "Why does Madison need an Alternative Family Ordinance?" The group defined *family* as inclusive, stating, "Any family is composed of people who are committed to each other in terms of mutual support, caring and love. Alternative families need and deserve the same rights and benefits afforded to those families related by blood, marriage or adoption." In pursuing the goal of local legislation, MISL circulated a petition on the issue. In the tradition of seeking allies, the organization received a grant from the Wisconsin Community Fund for a project that sought to achieve alternative family benefits through labor contracts. One of its successes was to have the Madison Police Union seek recognition of nontraditional families through collective bargaining in 1987. The *Isthmus* nominated MISL in 1984 for an Americanism Award.[32]

The Madison EOC established an Alternative Family Rights Task Force in fall 1983. Three MISL members served on the Task Force: Kate Nolan, Duane Kloterman, and Joyce Wells. On September 20, 1984, more than

150 people turned out at a forum on the proposal for alternative families legislation. Kathy Christensen from the Labor Farm Party spoke about alternative family benefits such as bereavement leave that had been negotiated with Madison General Hospital as part of their labor contracts. Cheri Maples, a Madison police officer, testified that though family health insurance was available to her, she could not provide access to her partner or her partner's children. Though present at the birth of their son by her partner, she stated, "I have no legal rights in authorizing medical care for him. I have no legal rights in terms of access to health records, to school records." Earlier, the task force had heard testimony from Brooks Egerton about a hospitalized gay man who was not able to register his lover to direct his medical care, as he himself was medically unable. The parents moved the man to an out-of-state hospital against the recommendation of physicians.[33]

The forum was met with protests. Several self-proclaimed Christians spoke in opposition, citing biblical verses about Sodom and Gomorrah. They trotted out a familiar argument: "I will state again that I am against your movement because, if we have all such people that call themselves family, we wouldn't have many children. Would we? So let's not do away with the American family which has made America what it is or was." Another protester claimed, "They have AIDS, this disease, because of what they are doing." At the forum, 37 people spoke or registered in opposition, while another 126 spoke or registered in support.[34]

Likely on the minds of attendees was a situation that had arisen a few months prior. In 1984, lesbians Alix Olson and Martha Popp applied for and were denied a family membership with its special rates at the Madison YMCA. They were seeking access for themselves and their children. As the YMCA persisted in its denial, MISL helped the couple put together a news conference and made the matter public, starting a battle that lasted for several years. Their efforts were recognized by MISL with the Red Rose of Courage award. In 1985, MISL sponsored the First Annual Alternative Families Recognition Day Picnic.[35]

MISL also began efforts in the Madison Metropolitan School District to recognize alternative families. Within the school district, MISL had found that social workers ranked higher than teachers in sensitivity to alternative families. One concern they voiced was making libraries "a place where students could find materials responsive to the needs of alternative families." Another concern was the failure to get records to noncustodial, nonbiological parents in same-sex co-parent families. One parent noted, "My children's most basic reality is completely ignored by the society they live in—it is crazy making. Even if a teacher doesn't like the gay culture, she/he needs to attempt to validate a child's life experience." Working toward a better understanding of and rights for alternative families would be ongoing.[36]

The EOC Task Force completed its work in early 1985. It issued a "Statement of Desirability and Feasibility" for alternative families legislation, noting the "differential treatment that existed appears to be directed primarily towards 'several classes' of individuals against whom the present Madison Equal Opportunities Ordinance purports to prohibit discrimination." Among its findings were "psychological, social, and economic harm to persons grouped in alternative families." They recommended that the city register alternative families, in lieu of non-available marriage licenses, so the parents and children could be recognized by schools and other public institutions. The main areas where redress and rights should be extended included health care, memberships, co-parenting, housing, and personnel policies. The EOC report offered information on lesbian and gay families that became instrumental in moving the fight for family rights to drafting ordinances proposed to the Madison City Council.[37]

A GAY REPUBLICAN CHAMPION FOR ALTERNATIVE FAMILIES

The Madison City Council leader on the alternative families issue would be Jim McFarland, first elected to the council in November 1986 at a special city election. He resided with his then partner, Rick Villasenor, an anti-ROTC campus activist, and represented the same Langdon Street district earlier held by LGBT Alders Yeadon and Monks. McFarland, a Republican, identified himself as a "fiscal conservative" but stated that "on the social issues, I'm pretty liberal." He credited gay rights organizations for mobilizing on his behalf because of his alternative family proposals. He was praised in the press for coming out "as one of two openly gay Republican elected officials in the country" and for introducing Villasenor as his lover at public events and in the press.[38]

Jim McFarland, elected to Madison's city council in 1986, was the second out Republican in the nation to hold elected office. He was a champion for a local ordinance to
recognize alternative families with same-sex partners and to confer domestic partner
benefits. FROM THE AUTHOR'S COLLECTION

After his reelection in spring 1987, in July of that year McFarland circulated a draft alternative family ordinance to other alders and secured six
cosponsorships. McFarland cited the example of the City of Berkeley, California, which had adopted a similar ordinance. MISL was busy during the
rest of the year organizing support. In November, a report from the EOC
authored by McFarland named the YMCA membership issue as "just one
example of the problems current law creates for alternative families." It
also noted the EOC's finding that alternative families face discrimination
and a double standard. The report cited the case of Janice Czyson and Crystal Hyslop, in which Czyson's employer would not grant sick leave when
the couple's children were ill because she was not the biological parent.
The report concluded, "The EOC believes that it is time to recognize that
in reality there are many ways in which human families are formed."[39]

Opposition to changes came from the YMCA of metropolitan Madison
and from attorney and Alder Ron Trachtenberg, who wrote in a Greater
Madison Chamber of Commerce newsletter, "Since alternative families do
not have the social and legal obligations of traditional families, they are

not entitled to and should not receive traditional family subsidy status." Mayor Joseph Sensenbrenner, who had previously sought gay support and money, threw cold water on the ordinance in a 1988 New Year's Day news story in which he was quoted as saying, "I haven't seen any drafts I can support." Immediately, a number of gays and lesbians threw their support to former mayor Paul Soglin, who was contemplating a return to the mayor's office. Soglin would go on to win the spring 1989 mayoral election against Sensenbrenner.[40]

The matter was again taken up at the city council's meeting on August 2. A Madison police officer in support of the ordinance noted that 7 percent of the force was gay or lesbian, stating, "We are hired to do the business of protecting and serving this community, yet we are still treated as second-class citizens." In opposition, Madison citizen George Koski claimed the proposal "concocted a pseudo-matrimonial blue-light special." I was noted as a gay public official arguing that the community needed the ordinance to fight the homophobia represented by the "Die Fag" graffiti painted on the near east side. At the meeting, 217 citizens registered in favor, and 63 registered as opposed. The YMCA continued to oppose it.[41]

The next morning, the *Wisconsin State Journal* reported, "Council Goes Halfway on 'Kate & Allie' Law" with the adoption of two of the four alternative family provisions. The council voted 15 to 5 to open family zoning categories to households consisting of unmarried couples with their children and to extend sick and bereavement leave to city employees of a designated family partner member. With an 11 to 9 vote, the council rejected a provision on public accommodations discrimination that would have covered memberships for private organizations such as the YMCA. A provision for health care for city employees' domestic partners was also shot down, 12 to 8, over arguments about cost. By these measures, the city did establish official recognition of the existence of such new families. McFarland called it a mixed bag.[42]

Efforts would continue. The Village of Shorewood Hills to the west of Madison would put in a domestic partnership provision for its swimming pool in 1990. That same year, Mayor Soglin and Alder McFarland introduced a more comprehensive ordinance to adopt provisions on public accommodations and register all local Madison domestic partners. In

2008, Dane County would also adopt an alternative families registry. Part of this strategy was to show and document that there were indeed sizable numbers of lesbian and gay couples when state legislation was sought.[43]

DEFINING THE ISSUES: GAYS IN THE MILITARY

While perhaps not as high on the agenda as other issues, the existence of gays in the military was an issue in Wisconsin even in the 1970s, as shown by the case of Miriam Ben-Shalom. Born in Wisconsin and having converted to Judaism, she served in the Israeli army as the driver of an armored personnel carrier. Back in Wisconsin, she began her American military career in 1974 with the Eighty-fourth Training Division of the Army Reserves based in Milwaukee. She became one of the first two female drill sergeants in the division. Ben-Shalom was discharged in 1976 for being an admitted lesbian, and she sued for reinstatement.[44]

Ben-Shalom believed hers was "a civil rights case." She stated, "The army is taking away my right to work and forbidding me to live my lifestyle." Ben-Shalom credited Leonard Matlovich, who came out in a 1975 *Time* magazine story that profiled his own discharge from the Air Force and his fight for reinstatement, with encouraging her to come out. Unlike so many military personnel who had left quietly, she chose to fight. On the issue of serving in the military, Ben-Shalom felt the community met the idea "with such silence or hostility as to make your head spin." She attributed this to a hangover of the anti–Vietnam war sentiment, and felt she was "accorded second-class citizenship." In fact, she stated, "Gay and lesbian veterans are intelligent, sensitive people. Most are proud to be Americans, despite having had their futures marred because of dishonorable discharges." Ben-Shalom would serve the gay and lesbian community as president of GPU during the 1980s and as a frequent speaker for her cause.[45]

In May 1980, Judge Terence Evans of the US District Court for Eastern Wisconsin, a former Milwaukee County prosecutor and circuit judge who had been appointed by President Carter to the federal bench the year before, overturned her discharge and she became the first lesbian to win reinstatement. Judge Evans's ruling was based on the First, Fifth, and Ninth Amendments to the Constitution. In the decision, he wrote, "While the law remains unsettled as to whether private sexual conduct between consenting adults is protected by the right to privacy . . . the court believes that constitutional privacy principles clearly protect one's sexual preferences in and of themselves from government regulation." The judge was advancing the concept that one's sexual orientation was a matter that could not be legislated. He also wrote, "The Court is satisfied from the record that her sexual preferences had as much relevance to her military skills as did her gender or the color of her skin." This placed gays on the same plane as other classes claiming equality. Evans wrote, "For much of our history, the military's fear of racial tension kept black soldiers segregated from white."[46]

The judge further observed that upholding the dismissal would mean that "no soldier would dare be caught reading anything that might be construed as a homosexually oriented book or magazine. No soldier would want to be observed in the company of any person suspected of being a homosexual. Most importantly, no soldier would even want to make any statements that might be interpreted as supporting homosexuality." He ruled that such activities are protected by the First Amendment. Find-

Miriam Ben-Shalom was discharged from the military for being a lesbian and conducted a series of court fights for reinstatement. *DAILY CARDINAL*

ing the army process "offensive by this court," Judge Evans ordered Ben-Shalom's reinstatement, but the army refused to comply with the district court. Ben-Shalom did receive an award of $991 in lost back pay but failed to gain contempt damages. In 1987, the US Court of Appeals upheld the lower court's decision. In September 1988, Ben-Shalom successfully re-enlisted until another federal appeal court ruling in August 1989 threw her out once again. At this point, though she continued to fight, she had exhausted her legal options. Judge Evans's ruling in favor of gays in the military did not hurt him, as President Bill Clinton appointed him to a seat on the United States Court of Appeals for the Seventh Circuit, the court that had both upheld and overruled him.[47]

In 1993, newly elected Wisconsin state representative Tammy Baldwin generated a legislative round robin letter to the Wisconsin congressional delegation as the issue of gays in the military surfaced in the early days of the Clinton administration. The letter urged support for "efforts to end discrimination in the military service." Twenty-two state legislators, Democrats and Republicans, signed, including the assembly speaker and the senate president. Baldwin's press release noted the Wisconsin National Guard Adjutant General Jerald Slack commented that "as long as National Guard members perform their jobs and abide by the rules of conduct there should be no discrimination based on sexual orientation."[48]

A STRONG TRANS VOICE EMERGES FROM MILWAUKEE

Lou Sullivan was born Sheila Sullivan in Wauwatosa, Wisconsin, in 1951. During his youth, Sullivan dreamed of becoming a writer and from age thirteen kept a journal. Transgender historian Susan Stryker calls his journals "one of the most complete and compelling autobiographical accounts of a transsexual life ever recorded." Signing as Sheila Sullivan, he would write articles on transgender issues and theory that were published in Milwaukee's *GPU News* during the 1970s. Late in his life, he would publish *From Female to Male: The Life of Jack Bee Garland*, a biography of a turn-of-the-twentieth-century transsexual from California. Stryker observes that "Sullivan has been posthumously lionized by the transgender movement that took shape in the years since his untimely death at age 39—and rightly so." A modern dance by trans choreographer Sean Dorsey titled *Lou* was performed in 2009 to critical acclaim.[49]

Sullivan recalled that when he was fourteen, he dressed as a boy wandering the Milwaukee factory districts, something he thought he would not be able to do dressed as a girl. At sixteen or seventeen he walked down Wisconsin Avenue singing "We Shall Overcome" with a male friend. After high school he had a boyfriend, whom he noted presented as a homosexual and with whom he lived in a rented apartment on Brady Street, Milwaukee's nearest equivalent to San Francisco's Haight-Ashbury neighborhood. The prevailing assumption at the time was that a trans person, once transitioned, would be heterosexual. For Sullivan, "awakening came for me when a beautiful gay guy came up to me in the street in the fall of '71." Forthrightly, Sullivan wrote in *GPU News*, "I've always thought of myself as a male homosexual (try and figure that one out—I can't)."[50]

Sullivan's Milwaukee experiences nourished his burgeoning sense of social justice. In 1967, he joined Father Groppi's marches for a fair housing ordinance and participated in a Students for a Democratic Society (SDS) protest, though he noted that in conservative Milwaukee, while there was plenty of yelling, no one crossed against the red light. In fall 1969, Sullivan went to the antiwar march on Washington. The next May he was part of the sit-in at the UW–Milwaukee student union over the Kent State protests.[51]

In 1970, Sullivan became employed as a secretary at the UW–Milwaukee Department of Slavic Languages, where he dressed as a male. When the celebrity transsexual Christine Jorgenson spoke on campus in March 1973, he attended and found the lecture "pretty interesting." Perhaps moved by the lecture, in April 1973, Sullivan went to his first GPU meeting. Sullivan biographer Brice Smith notes, "GPU and Milwaukee's gay community offered Lou a safe space for sexual experimentation, provided him with an unparalleled sense of belonging and laid the foundation for his future FTM [female-to-male] activism." That fall Sullivan would be elected, uncontested, as GPU secretary. Through GPU, Lou would learn about community organizing and help the organization to become more inclusive for trans people.[52]

Sullivan, cross-dressed, also explored Milwaukee's gay world, going to bars such as the River Queen, the Factory, and the Wreck Room. He complained that when he met a man he was interested in, he had to find a bisexual or make a gay one "heterosexual." Stryker notes, "Sullivan deeply identified with the drag queens he met in the city's bars. He saw in them a reflection of his own situation as a masculine subject who presented a

Lou Sullivan was a transgender man who befriended Eldon Murray in Milwaukee's Gay People's Union and eventually became one of the foremost national advocates for trans persons. Here he is pictured in 1974 before attending the GPU's drag ball. LOU SULLI-VAN PAPERS (#1991-07), COURTESY OF GAY, LESBIAN, BISEXUAL, TRANSGENDER HIS-TORICAL SOCIETY

feminine image to the world." In Milwaukee, the drag queens and one lone preoperative male-to-female transsexual were all the trans community he found.[53]

After moving to San Francisco in 1975, Sullivan sought medical help to transition but was denied access to medical therapy and procedures because it was presumed all FTM would be heterosexual. Here Sullivan had to break ground to find help, and he was eventually successful. Sullivan wrote that "information for the female-to-male transsexual is practically non-existent."[54]

The historian Stryker notes that Sullivan used his community organizing skills, gained through his work with the GPU in Milwaukee, to become "the hub of the organized FTM community in the United States" in the 1980s. In *A History of Transsexuality in the United States*, trans historian Joanne Meyerowitz describes how Sullivan "found himself at the center of new FTM networks." Sullivan organized correspondence networks and get-togethers and edited an FTM newsletter. He is credited with laying the basis for the largest FTM organization in the United States, simply known as FTM. His work in bringing FTM trans people into the public view was successful in getting the medical profession to drop what it had seen as the "assumed contradiction between gender identity and sexual orientation." Perhaps his key contribution was insisting that utilizing personal agency against the medical establishment could result in progress.[55]

Sullivan would have one more fight to wage. In 1987, he was diagnosed with AIDS and had to wage a new battle to educate medical personnel on how transsexual AIDS patients should be supported. According to biographer Smith, he was the first FTM known to contract AIDS. His panel for the AIDS quilt, with the date of his death of March 2, 1991, would say, "One man who made a difference, you are missed—FTM." Several trans historians note that in his journal Sullivan wrote, "You told me I couldn't live as a gay man, but now I am going to die like one."[56]

FIGHTING RACISM AND HOMOPHOBIA

The establishment of Black and White Men Together (BWMT) Milwaukee on Sunday, November 24, 1980, showed how closely Wisconsin was tied into national gay trends. The Milwaukee group was founded just months after the first chapter of Black and White Men Together was formed in San Francisco. There were fifteen in attendance in Milwaukee, and three, including the host, who held the event in his home, were designated as founding coordinators. The organization would flourish in the 1980s with nearly one hundred members.[57]

As explained in an early newsletter, the group's purpose included offering "an opportunity for socializing between black and white gay men in an atmosphere which is conducive to forming friendships and which provides support for ongoing relationships." They viewed interracial gay couples as a minority within the minorities of race and sexual orientation. Their larger purpose was "to actively engage in the struggle for racial understanding in Milwaukee, the Milwaukee area, and the Nation, especially in the gay community." The sometime tag on the newsletter was "A Gay Multi-racial Organization for All People."[58]

The Milwaukee membership application reiterated the BWMT's aim "to confront the racism found at all levels of our society." Annual dues were ten dollars, and members had to be eighteen or older. The application included the statement, "It is my understanding that my membership is a matter of confidentiality." The early newsletters refer to members only by first name and last initial, though this practice was dropped after several years. Alyn Hess was a prominent member. The group met at the Holy Angel Fellowship Hall at Twelfth and Atkinson.[59]

Meetings were mainly social but included some more formal programs. Professor Louie Crew from UW–Stevens Point spoke at the first banquet in 1981, which he attended with his African American partner, Ernest Clay. Crew's address, "Love with Justice," cited Rosa Parks and Nat Turner as examples of committed social activists. Former state representative Barbee addressed the group in February 1985, and his remarks on the "tyranny of heterosexuality" were warmly reported in the newsletter. Later that same year, the group invited representatives of the Milwaukee Police Department to speak, noting this would not have been possible under the previous chief.[60]

The newsletter featured items that appealed across racial lines. When it reported in April 1984 that former vice president Walter Mondale was now supporting a federal nondiscrimination bill, it also mentioned that presidential candidate Jesse Jackson supported a similar measure. In fact, Jackson's support for the bill was why many gays in the multicultural political organization, the Rainbow Coalition, including myself, voted for him in the Wisconsin primary, helping him achieve a decent third place in a state whose African American population was only 4 percent. In reporting on a book about Martin Luther King Jr. and the March on Washington, the newsletter made sure to note that the contributions of black gay pioneer Bayard Rustin to the civil rights movement were included.[61]

One of the most poignant items in the 1984 newsletter was a two-part piece by a young black man titled "Mom, Dad: I'm Gay!" As a member, he was now at least eighteen but asserted he knew he was gay at age eleven during the mid-1970s, describing himself as a "classic sissy" who was always writing poetry. As a teen runaway, he saw a poster with services for gays at the Farwell Center in Milwaukee. When he visited, a manager at the center showed interest in him, calling him a "chocolate drop." Another black gay man alerted him to a gay youth group that met at UW–Milwaukee, and he became a regular. During his time with the group, he "learned that the other kids didn't turn me on as much as the MEN, the guys who were running the meetings." He was appreciative of the environment that BWMT Milwaukee created, commenting, "Only recently have I received any meaningful moral support."[62]

The Milwaukee chapter was also active in hosting other BWMT groups. In 1984, the Great Lakes Regional Network of BWMT celebrated the Milwaukee group's fourth anniversary. Irwin Rothenberg, guest speaker from the Memphis group, urged the audience of one hundred, "Black and white gays must work together in politics." He said his chapter had rap groups "exchanging real experiences" across racial lines. The regional gathering also included workshops, a business session, and singing. Hess had reworked a couple of songs. To the tune of "The Navy Hymn" ("Eternal Father, Strong to Save" by John Bacchus Dykes), he created the "Black and White Men Together Hymn" with these simple lyrics: "We are the men who integrate, Loving each other and feeling great!"[63]

In 1987, BWMT Milwaukee hosted the seventh annual convention of the national BWMT association. Members from thirty chapters around the nation convened in Milwaukee from June 28 to July 5, 1987, with the theme Celebrating Our Life, Liberty and Happiness. As most attendees were expected to fly in through Chicago, the event began with march-

Michael Lisowski (right), a leader in the Milwaukee chapter of Black and White Men Together, and Russell Webb (left) attended the 1985 Gay Pride Parade while in New York City for the BWMT national convention. In the background is gay elder Bayard Rustin, who helped organize the national march for civil rights at the Lincoln Memorial in 1963.
PHOTO BY D. A. LEONARD, SCAN COURTESY OF THE UNIVERSITY OF NORTH CAROLINA PRESS

ing as a delegation in the Chicago Gay Pride Parade. This parade always attracted good followings from both Milwaukee and Madison and was a prime reason Gay Pride was not always celebrated in late June in either city. Joseph Beam, who edited an anthology of twenty-nine black writers titled *In the Life*, provided the keynote. Other speakers included Ron McCrea and Earl Bricker, both veterans of Governor Anthony "Tony" Earl's administration, and David Fair, vice president of the National Union of Hospital and Health Care Employees. Michael Lisowski, a longtime Milwaukee gay activist, called the planned caucuses "the highlight of every convention." A press release for the convention stated that the event was organized "so that there will be places where inter-raciality is fostered and gayness is accepted."[64]

MILWAUKEE GAY RIGHTS ORDINANCE

Alyn Hess, prominent in Milwaukee's gay activist scene, expressed ambivalence about a gay rights law for Milwaukee. In a 1978 letter to Louis Stimac, an equally long-toiling activist, Hess declared that law reform "will have little effect on what people really do." He believed the effort was "just a show of strength of our movement." He compared "traditionally conservative" Milwaukee with Madison, which had passed its nondiscrimination ordinance a few years earlier. Madison, with a countercultural mayor and an openly gay man on the city council, was simply a different place. Was Milwaukee ready for change? "Not now," Hess concluded.[65]

Stimac, in his reply, showed no ambivalence about the benefits of a possible law and thought such efforts were attempts to protect certain classes and "a deterrent to those who would harm." He cited the incident where Hess himself was forced to move by his landlord because he was a homosexual. Stimac saw value in reaching out to "heterosexual politicians who arc leaders" because "they will often vote for homosexual rights." Yet he too agreed that 1978 was too soon for Milwaukee. He feared that if the political groundwork was not laid, "there is too much probability of [a measure being] reversed in a referendum." This was at the high point of the Anita Bryant repeals. In just a couple of years, however, things would appear much brighter.[66]

In 1980, clergy from several denominations asked the Judiciary and Legislative Committee of the Milwaukee City Council for changes to the city's civil rights law. The requested change would bar discrimination in city employment on the basis of sexual orientation. The moving force behind the request was the Committee for Fundamental Judeo-Christian Human Rights composed of representatives of mainline churches including the United Methodist, Presbyterian, American Lutheran, Episcopalian, United Church of Christ, and the Roman Catholic church. Leon R. Rouse coordinated the group, and Father Jack Murtagh of the Milwaukee Archdiocese; John Greg, clerk of the United Presbyterian Church; and Reverend Paul Fluke of Plymouth UCC appeared to make the group's case. Hess, speaking for the GPU, described incidents of discrimination in employment by the city: "Some employees live in fear of their superiors finding out they are gay."[67]

The chief focus of the draft ordinance was on the city itself as an employer and those businesses doing public works for the city under contract or as suppliers of goods and services. One alder suggested that housing discrimination be included as well. A Mr. Garnien of the city's Civil Service Commission argued that the city should wait until state and federal legislation had been passed. Several more hearings were planned. On June 20, Police Chief Harold Breier testified against the law, claiming his department would not hire gay men. When a minister testified that there were gay police officers in Milwaukee, Breier responded that he was "positive there were no homosexual members of the Milwaukee Police Department."[68]

In June, the Judiciary and Legislative Committee recommended the council take it to a vote. As the city was weighing the ordinance, tireless advocate Michael Lisowski published a letter in the *Milwaukee Journal*. He decried recent letters that implied gays were destructive of family life, informing readers of the gay logo that proclaimed, "We are family," and citing his own experience as a caretaker for his elderly grandfather during his final years, which was only possible because he was not married. With emotion, he implored, "Don't try to preach to me about or lecture me about decaying family standards."[69]

The council debated the bill for an hour on July 8 and was "frequently interrupted by shouts from more than 100 supporters and opponents in the gallery." In response to opponents quoting the Bible, supporter Alder Kevin O'Connor said he turned to the Bible to find love and quoted from the Gospel of John. Other strong supporters were Alders Marlene Johnson and Sandra Hoeh. One opponent, Alder Richard Spaulding, challenged the idea that it was possible to prohibit discrimination on the basis of sexual orientation yet also disapprove of homosexuality. The proponents' argument stressed the basis of personal privacy rather than sexual rights, a key factor in the Wisconsin discussion. Spaulding's remark, "If I say to a person, you can be a homosexual but don't practice it, I am a hypocrite," was greeted with "Amens" by fundamentalists in the galleries. Alder Wayne Frank opposed the measure over a concern for day care centers that receive city funding and might thereby be forced to hire homosexuals who could influence the young.[70]

The ordinance covered employment discrimination but did not cover housing or public accommodation, and it defined sexual orientation as "heterosexuality, homosexuality, bisexuality, a history of such preference or an identification with a preference." To mollify opponents and gain support, an amendment was added by a 9 to 7 vote that said, "Extension of these provisions does not in any way condone the practice of persons whose affectional or sexual preference is towards persons of the same gender." The measure was adopted 10 to 6 and signed by Mayor Henry Maier without public comment.[71]

After passage, Reverend Frazer Lawton of the Milwaukee Baptist Church took the lead on a petition seeking repeal, but it did not succeed. Following Milwaukee's action, the Common Council of the City of Waukesha voted to place the measure on file and take no action on a request to adopt a similar ordinance.[72]

DANE COUNTY, TOO

From the time the City of Madison adopted its nondiscrimination ordinance in 1975, there was the possibility that Dane County, which encompassed the city, might also pass one. Under Wisconsin law, cities that, like Madison, were corporate bodies had home rule and could ban discrimination in housing and employment within its boundaries in all instances. Counties, by contrast, were civil divisions bound by state statutes; they could, however, set their own employment policies. Expanding Madison's gay progressive politics to Dane County was part of a larger effort to expand the city's liberal influences to a larger political scope. Madison supervisors, though not all left-leaning, constituted half of the county board and provided a good base.

In late 1979, having served as president of the Marquette Neighborhood Association, I decided to run for an open county board seat. David Clarenbach, who had once been my roommate on Mansion Hill, helped gather signatures on my nomination papers, and in spring 1980, I began serving on the Dane County Board. A county nondiscrimination ordinance was high on my agenda. Some groundwork had been laid by the county board in the previous session to broaden the Affirmative Action Ordinance to become an Equal Employment Opportunity Ordinance. The old ordinance covered *race, religion, color, sex, handicap, age,* and *national origin.* The aim was to add *sexual preference, marital status,* and *physical appearance.* Supervisor Judith Blank had been working on drafts and served as chief sponsor, while supervisor Lynn Haanen and I assisted as floor managers. On August 21, 1980, the board was scheduled to take up the proposed ordinance change. Expecting religious concerns, I placed copies of Milwaukee Archbishop Rembert Weakland's column supportive of nondiscrimination that had appeared in the Milwaukee *Catholic Herald* on each supervisor's desk.[73]

Nine persons testified on the ordinance, mainly supporting the change. Among them were veteran gay activists Gridley Hall, Barbara Lightner, and Leigh Roberts. Also speaking in support was Dane County District Attorney James Doyle Jr. Letters in favor were read into the record by Chairman Rod Matthews from the Madison Federation of Labor (AFL-CIO), showing that allies, once again, were key to change. Thirty-three who registered in favor chose not to speak.[74]

Board conservatives sought to turn the measure aside by deleting all references to specific classes, arguing for a general statement that Dane County would not discriminate. This motion failed with 15 in favor and 21 against. A motion to indefinitely postpone the vote also lost, 4 to 32. Adoption of the nondiscrimination act passed by a vote of 28 to 8 of the forty-one-member board, with several members who would have voted in favor absent. Among the pro votes were several well-known local Republicans including Bea Kabler, Jeff Wiswell, and Lyman Anderson, the "grandfather" of the Dane Republican Party. At the end of the meeting, Judith Blank invited the board, which had a tradition of going for drinks at the end of the evening, to nearby gay bar Going My Way to celebrate.[75]

Success and Boldness

As the decades of the 1970s and 1980s progressed, a full-bodied political activism became evident both to the gay community itself and to the larger body politic. Gay and gay-friendly legislators and activists developed a state legislative agenda with optimistic yet realistic priorities. They communicated this agenda through party platforms, electoral surveys, the media, and planned testimony at governmental hearings. While the immediate concerns were the consenting adults bill and legislation on nondiscrimination based on sexual orientation, other agenda items included family recognition, military inclusion, and fighting racism.

The gay and lesbian communities' political skills were further honed in electing out gay candidates and passing nondiscrimination ordinances at different municipal levels. Part of this success came from reaching out to allies in progressive labor and in the mainline and Catholic religious community. Milwaukee and Madison, the state's primary urban centers, served as the power base. Racine, Oshkosh, Stevens Point, La Crosse, and Eau Claire also provided support. A considerable number of Wisconsin Republicans proved open to supporting gay rights.

Yet a careful reading shows that the support was based on the minority status of Wisconsin homosexuals and did not signal an embrace of the gay community itself. The majority, with its own conceptions of liberty and rights, felt the now-acknowledged minority should not suffer discrimination. Statements in *Milwaukee Journal* editorials, the language added to the Milwaukee nondiscrimination ordinance, the failure of the legislature to pass consenting adults legislation, and the *Badger Herald*'s fag-baiting showed that disapproval of homosexuals and their sexual lifestyles remained quite strong.

Wisconsin's newly recognized gay and lesbian minority showed it could mobilize using limited resources, find progressive allies, gain access to the halls of power, and effect change in public policies. While gay men had dominated some of the earliest community efforts, lesbians came into the fore of organizing efforts. Bisexuals and transgender and transsexual persons also began to find a voice, pointing to a future when their interests would join together.

5

LGBT Media Get the Word Out

Unfortunately little is known about Lesbians except that which society has told us, which we are finding out to be false.
—Barb C., "Between Closets," *Amazon* (Milwaukee), November 1972[1]

Gaining control of the media is essential for gaining control of our lives.
—Mark McNary, *Renaissance* (Madison), 1976[2]

I n 1977, the early gay liberation film *Word Is Out: Stories of Some of Our Lives* challenged the invisibility of homosexuals. The documentary featured the experiences of some twenty-six gay men and lesbians ranging in age from eighteen to seventy-seven. One of the filmmakers, Peter Adair, a gay man, wanted to challenge the stereotypes created by outsiders. "What a state of affairs," he recalled. "One's reference for 'What was Gay?' was a few nasty images, and if you were lucky, your immediate circle of queer friends." Among the filmmakers was Rob Epstein, who would go on to make many excellent movies on the gay community. *Word Is Out* had a limited theatrical distribution, but it did play at the old Majestic in Madison and was later broadcast on PBS. Moving from Oscar Wilde's 1890s "love that dare not speak its name" to breaking the verbal and sexual silence on gays was a major undertaking of the new liberation movement.[3]

The gay men and lesbians who were now coming out had a great task ahead of them: to construct a community. Scholars of the nation-state have shown that nations and communities are not a presumed reality to be taken for granted but are social constructs that are imagined and discovered by their own inhabitants. A key tool in forming community coherence is media, and from the nineteenth century into the twentieth, this largely meant the printing press. Rodger Streitmatter in *Unspeakable: The Rise of the Gay and Lesbian Press in America* examined the phenomenon of gay media and concluded, "Because we exist everywhere but each of us must consciously identify himself or herself as a gay person, newspapers and magazines are uniquely important in our social movement." Knowledge through words and stories would inform the imaginations of LGBT Wisconsinites as they furthered sexual identity and created community.[4]

The realization that everyone in the 1970s and the 1980s, gay or straight, was dealing with massive ignorance about alternative sexuality and gender identity created a major task for both the national and Wisconsin gay communities. In a prologue to the book companion to *Word Is Out*, film subject Adair's mother observed about her two homosexual children, "They discovered who they were and began to feel the enormous relief and strength of their self-recognition and honesty—and freedom." She observed that friends of the family would still not directly confront her children's orientation. "They can't seem to realize that my children's homosexuality is not just a statement of sexual preference," she said. "It is their identity."

Through a chronological survey of LGBT newletters, newspapers, magazines, and other media this chapter explores how Wisconsin gays, lesbians, and to some extent its bisexual and trans communities, attacked ignorance and created lasting community. This chapter explores how Wisconsin gays, lesbians, bisexuals, and transgender persons attacked ignorance about homosexuality through a chronological survey of LGBT newsletters, newspapers, and other media.[5]

PUBLISHING FOR AND BY THE LGBT COMMUNITY

LGBT journalists throughout state were at the forefront of communicating factual information about homosexuals, bisexuals, and trans persons. Their media efforts helped define the community. Editors of the many Wisconsin gay and lesbian publications had a great responsibility. Their selection of stories would describe gay lives not only to the LGBT community but also to potentially larger straight audiences. What they included would define the boundaries of who we were. Were leather bikers and drag queens included? What about bisexuals and transsexuals? Would the stories of both rural and urban persons be told?

Outside of specific organizations' newsletters designed for a limited internal audience, several types of gay publications in Wisconsin were in print. The first was a general newspaper or magazine format. These publications often included artwork, fiction, and poetry, with coverage aimed toward a broad gay community. Publications in this category included *GPU News, Renaissance, Gay Madison, OUR HORIZONS, OUT!*, and *The Wisconsin Light*. A model that editors could draw on, if they were aware of it, was San Francisco's *ONE* magazine, which had been the national homophile community's magazine in the 1950s and 1960s. Another was the alternative newspaper that sprang up, usually with a countercultural bias, during the late 1960s and early 1970s. For example, the *Red Star Express*, the paper of the Milwaukee Revolutionary Youth Movement, carried a story in the December 1970 special women's issue, "Say It Loud, Gay Is Proud." It is doubtful many gay persons were reading this publication.[6]

The second type was a more socially oriented publication, popularly called the bar rag, distributed in local bars. Some bar rags included news features. Most showed multiple photos of gay men enjoying themselves at the bars. Bar calendars of daily specials and comprehensive directories of bars were regular features. Some bars also had their own newsletters proclaiming, "Hot, Gay Action!" *Rod's* newsletter, associated with the Hotel Washington in Madison, was a popular monthly publication. *In Step* and *ESCAPE* were also among this type, though over time *In Step* expanded well beyond its origins. *Quest*, another publication focused on social life, sprang up in the Green Bay area in the 1990s. It was described by publisher Mark Mariucci as a gay shopper with bar gossip and free personals. It too would expand its coverage in the twenty-first century to include news and feature stories, especially after the demise of *In Step*.[7]

A third type of publication was a limited number of Wisconsin publications specifically focused on women, such as *Scarlet Letter, Amazon, Hag Rag*, and *Leaping La Crosse News*. Many of these arose out of women's collectives and relied on a dedicated volunteer staff, a model that proved difficult to sustain. Forays were also made into local cable shows and radio programs, though the records for many of the earliest of these have been lost as videotape and audio recordings were erased by reuse or lost due to a lack of archival interest.

The editors and collectives who published this rainbow of offerings were mostly volunteers. They knew they had to aim at a niche market, one that they were helping to create through the publication. At a time when most Wisconsin gay organizations had memberships in the hundreds or fewer, these media publications could reach a much larger audience. *OUT!*, one of the most vigorous, printed and distributed up to ten thousand copies per issue around the state in the mid-1980s. Clearly, gay media played a major role in shaping and defining gay community.

Where Wisconsin writer Ralph Warner in the 1920s and 1930s had to present his gay life through innuendo, those now writing in the 1970s and 1980s could and would be explicit. How they pushed boundaries would sometimes put them at odds with the mainstream media and other forces. This was just as much the work of gay liberation in Wisconsin as political organizing.

SCARLET LETTER, 1971–1972

A collective located at 10 Langdon Street, at the time the site of the Madison Gay Center, published this small, short-lived women's newsletter whose aim was to provide "an open forum for women of differing viewpoints to discuss ideas and problems." The collective in its first year joined the Madison Sustaining Fund, a community fundraising umbrella for alternative groups. The newsletter published some poetry, including some lesbian-themed items by collective member Suzanne (many writers in this and other publications used their first names only or a pseudonym).[8]

In the third issue, Judy Greenspan wrote an article titled "Come Out, Come Out, Wherever You Are." She recounts how it took her four years to be able to say, "I'm gay. I say that now without fear or hatred of myself and my own sexuality. I say it with joy and with a tremendous love for all my gay sisters." She recalled reading about gay liberation happening in

In 1971, lesbians in Madison published *Scarlet Letter*, claiming the Nathaniel Hawthorne title to show a shamelessness in being out about their sexuality.
WHI IMAGE ID 144445

SCARLET LETTER

MAY 1971 ~~~ 15¢ ~~~ VOL. 1, NO.1

New York. Greenspan described how the Madison Gay Sisters group was growing and that she now had the strength to walk down the street holding a woman's hand. She went to gay liberation meetings and spoke on gay liberation panels. In September 1971, she wrote, "Finally gay sisterhood is blooming all over this country. And our lives will never be the same."[9]

In the March/April 1972 issue, a unique feature stated that "the most exciting & creative interaction going on these days among women in Madison is on the walls of public toilets stalls." The bathroom described as the most prolific was in the University Y across from the Women's Center. One woman wrote, "I love this bathroom & all of you." Another women wrote, "Next step: Out of the (water) closets, into the streets." One simply added, "Come out sister." The dialogue continued with, "Lesbians are so far-out, fight on." Others included "Being gay is fun" and "Gay Sisterhood is Powerful, come out."[10] Though *Scarlet Letter*'s run was short, it captured a snapshot of the lesbian scene in Madison during the early years of gay liberation.

GPU NEWS: 1971–1981

In October 1971, the first issue of *GPU News* appeared in Milwaukee as a monthly magazine put out by the Publication Committee of the Gay People's Union. Previous to this, the GPU had distributed a mimeographed newsletter called *Take Heed*. In the first issue, the magazine vowed to "act as a news gathering service for the gay community" and monitor "homosexuality in the media." It urged readers and volunteers, "If you see or hear homosexuality discussed on television, radio, newspaper, or in a magazine, please note the source and call." While admitting all publications relied on advertising, the new magazine tried to indicate its serious, elevated tone with an advisory that it would "not accept ads which solicit. After all, G.P.U. is not a dating or mating service." In later years, personal ads would appear.[11]

In 1974, the magazine explained the magazine's new logo of entwined double lambda stick figures as relating both to classical Greek culture, a time when homosexual love was considered normal, and its use as a chemistry notation for "reacting substances . . . [which] symbolizes a change of state and release of energy." For their activist readers, the editors explained, "becoming liberated releases gay pride and gay power." The use of the two lambdas also suggested working and marching together. Its use as a sexual symbol was explored in a cartoon signed "by alyn," presumably Alyn Hess, in a subsequent issue. The cartoon showed one traditional lambda asking a contorted lambda, "What are you doing?" The response showed the contorted lambda practicing yoga by putting knees up to shoulders, "something useful." A frame showed the overlapping legs of the logo forming an *M* for Milwaukee.[12]

In June 1976, Liberation Publications of Milwaukee was formed as a legally separate entity from GPU and became the nonprofit owner of *GPU News*. With subscriptions at six dollars per year, *GPU News* grew in circulation and size up to forty-eight pages. In 1977 the publication claimed subscribers in every state and in Canada. They even exchanged subscriptions with the Japan Gay Center of Tokyo. Articles ranged from those on gay votes to the Mr. Club Baths Contest. Although most content reflected the gay male community, lesbians were not excluded. Social science articles included one headed, "Researchers Find Children of Lesbians No

Different." Arson directed at gay bars appeared along with news of the local venereal disease clinic expansion. The magazine closely followed political developments in Wisconsin and the nation. Though it provided national coverage and writing for a national audience, the magazine had a regular Milwaukee Update section.[13]

Some boundaries were pushed in August 1976 when the magazine carried Michael J. Mitchell's "Erotic S&M Among Gays." Mitchell, then living in Chicago, had worked on *GPU News* for two years and had served on GPU's board. He argued ritualistic pain had been around since ancient civilization. For him, consensual S&M in mutual fantasy "is universal in its scope and application as it knows no limitations except those imposed on it by the parties involved." Following the article was an editor's note: "It is not the object of this article to encourage the practices of S&M. Rather it is presented in the hope that a better understanding of the basic philosophy and rituals of S&M will lead to a greater sexual freedom for all persons."[14]

Editor Eldon Murray, one of the original founders of GPU, was the driving force behind the magazine. A stockbroker by profession, Murray felt he could be a contributor for gay Milwaukee because his clients did not care whether he was gay, just that he made money for their stock accounts. A native of Indiana born in 1930, he served in Korea and settled in Chicago after the war, later migrating to Milwaukee. In February 1971, he worked on a gay radio show, *Gay Perspective*, that ran for a few years in Milwaukee on WZMF. Later, Murray was active with Seniors in a Gay Environment in Milwaukee.[15]

Murray brought his views to the magazine's readers through editorials. In his first editorial, Murray wrote that in "the process of achieving freedom for the homosexual" the magazine would "carry forward the ideas of education and fellowship." Announcing in July 1976 that *GPU News* was being sent to selected Wisconsin libraries, he wrote that this was an "effort to reach the gay population of our home state. Equally important is that we reach and educate the non-gay public." Murray believed because of either benign neglect or outright censorship, "not one public library in the state of Wisconsin save the Milwaukee Public Library carries *GPU News* or any other gay periodical." In December 1976, the magazine announced that the Appleton Library upon request of the Fox Valley Gay Alliance had agreed

Producing *GPU News* from Milwaukee for a decade was a hands-on job for editor Eldon Murray (left) and his crew of other volunteers. ARCHIVES DEPARTMENT, UNIVERSITY OF WISCONSIN—MILWAUKEE LIBRARIES

to carry *GPU News*. In July 1980, Murray's editorial again reminded readers, "Communication is indeed the essence of liberation, and it requires a continuous flow of both information and commitment."[16]

During its sixth year, in October 1976, Murray observed that the gay community was in many ways not a community at all "but a multitude of rich and ever-varying subgroups, each with its own contributions to make to the growing concept of gay identity. It is growing in size as more and more closet doors swing open, and even the closets themselves have changed much in the past five years." For Murray, the term *gay* was not gendered and included gay men and lesbians. He much preferred it to the "clinical" word *homosexual*. In 1977, observing the progress that was already made, Murray warned, "Passive optimism may be today's great threat, for no one should think that the march of history is irreversible." He stated, "More are urgently needed to swell the ranks" of those fighting for gay liberation.[17]

After January 1981, *GPU News* ceased publication despite the formation of a Friends of *GPU News* to aid with financial contributions. A letter by Murray indicated the shuttering was due to a loss of volunteers. He noted that just a few years before, they had twenty-eight volunteers, but they were now down to seven with the recent resignation of a key staffer: "Several have moved from the area and many have left because they no longer have the free time to spare." He closed, "We can all be proud of the ten years in which we operated to provide gay people and their friends with a quality gay news/magazine. Yours in liberation."[18]

Lou Sullivan, a Trans Presence at *GPU News*

One of Murray's contributions to *GPU News* was to bring new voices to the fore, including female-to-male (FTM) trans writer Lou Sullivan, whose work as an early trans activist is profiled in chapter 4. Sullivan's early article, published in the August 1973 *GPU News* under his given name, Sheila Sullivan, was structured as a fictional exchange with a feminist friend, Dorothy. In what transgender historian Susan Stryker noted as "one of the first published engagements with the feminist critique of transgender identity," Sullivan argued to feminists: "You're trying to press straight standards on transvestites which just won't work." Several times in the article, Sullivan used the compound pronoun "he she," explaining that it was futile "to only dress up alone in a locked room, hoping no one will ever see, afraid to open your mouth in regard to any topic coming close to your secret." Yet there was a danger in coming out, especially for the FTM, who, as he commented, is "left wide open for rejection by family and friends, physical harm, denial of use of public and private facilities, easy prey." Compellingly, he wrote, "You ask him to come alive to the world so the world can kill him."[19]

　　Sullivan's next contribution to *GPU News* in February/March 1974 expanded on what he perceived as a feminist attack: "The presence, or even the thought of male transvestites, drag queens and female impersonators provokes angry protestations within the feminists and other liberation movements across the country." His argument, bolstered by current scholarship on gay and trans issues, was that feminists find "their little girl playing with a chemistry set much more acceptable than their son rocking his Tiny Tears to sleep."[20] Reflecting on the feminist argument that women are accorded lower status than men, Sullivan noted, "The transvestite has not been able to integrate his femininity into his self-image as a man and for good reason: in our society it is nearly impossible to possess feminine appearances and behaviorisms and yet retain a male standing." For this reason, a feminine man "immediately gives up the sacred status of being a man."[21]

Sullivan's final contribution to *GPU News* came in 1978 after he had relocated to San Francisco, a review of *Emergence: A Transsexual Autobiography*, a firsthand account of an FTM transsexual by Mario Martino. Sullivan wanted the book "to present a human being I could understand," but Martino, a former nun named Marie, presented his story more like

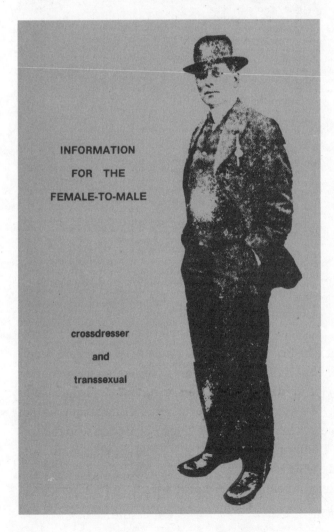

INFORMATION

FOR THE

FEMALE-TO-MALE

crossdresser

and

transsexual

In his book *Information for the Female-to-Male Crossdresser and Transsexual*, Lou Sullivan lent his pen to breaking the ignorance about female-to-male trans persons. ARCHIVES DEPARTMENT, UNIVERSITY OF WISCONSIN–MILWAUKEE LIBRARIES

In this copy of *Information for the Female-to-Male Crossdresser and Transsexual*, Lou Sullivan penned an inscription to Eldon Murray. Sullivan's mention of his "awful secret desire" demonstrates that internalization of transphobia could be as pervasive as internalized homophobia. ARCHIVES DEPARTMENT, UNIVERSITY OF WISCONSIN—MILWAUKEE LIBRARIES

ILLUSTRATIONS

January 1987
To my dearest friend Eldon Murray—
the first person to whom
I confided my "awful secret
desire" .... in 1973
Lou Sullivan

2nd Edition, 1985

by L. Sullivan
1827 Haight Street #164
San Francisco, California 94117

"an appointment schedule than the revealing diary it could have been." For Sullivan, the book's disappointment lay in the emphasis on Marie's sexual attraction for women rather than on Martino's body image. Sullivan commented, "We still need a transsexual story that will show us (not tell us about) a person in a state of male/female confusion who can sort out the problem." Sullivan's biography of Jack Garland, published in 1990, may have helped to fill that gap.[22]

Murray remained a mentor and friend to Sullivan after Sullivan moved to California, and he even sold Sullivan the typesetting machine he had used for *GPU News*. As chapter 4 details, Sullivan would go on to become a founding member of FTM networks on the West Coast, even editing an FTM newsletter. His early work on *GPU News* set him up for a successful career as a trans writer and highly visible early promoter of the FTM trans community.

AMAZON, 1972–1984

For over a decade, *Amazon* served the Milwaukee women's community as a feminist magazine with strong lesbian content. *Amazon* began in May 1972 as a newsletter by a UW–Milwaukee English professor and a student in Women's Studies with a mimeograph machine. A few years later, Professor Angela Peckenpaugh was at some pains to disprove the myth that *Amazon* started over a kitchen table, a proverbial woman's space. She insisted, instead, that it had begun in a professional context. Soon after its founding, a collective of students took over the magazine, and it found a home with the Milwaukee Women's Coalition located on Kenwood Boulevard. Like similar publications, it likely garnered funds through donations and relied on volunteers.[23]

As the collective explained in the April/May 1980 issue, "The Amazons were tribes of women who governed themselves. . . . So we call our paper *Amazon* as a tribute to these women and as a challenge to male society. We are claiming our history; we are claiming our culture." This editorial note put them squarely in the separatist camp. There was no mandate on style, but writers would frequently use variations such as *wimmin*, *womyn*, and *womon* to avoid including "men" and "man." In its first iteration, the magazine bore the tagline "A Feminist Journal" and concentrated on the Milwaukee women's community with some national articles. Starting with a few eastside and downtown distribution points, it gradually expanded to forty or so spots where it was available for free as well as by subscription.[24]

Amazon covered general women's topics such as the Equal Rights Amendment (ERA), menstruation, childbirth, rape, martial arts, sexism in education, abortion, keeping your own name, and sex education. The magazine became a member of the Feminist News Exchange, and almost every issue contained lesbian content. Much of it had to do with educating women, straight and lesbian, about the myths and facts of lesbianism. In the sixth issue, a section signed Barb C. was titled "Between Closets." She wrote, "Unfortunately little is known about Lesbians except that which society has told us, which we are finding out to be false." Barb C. noted that the struggle to rightly understand lesbianism might be difficult for any woman: "The *Amazon* will deal with gay issues not only to help our straight sisters but also [to help] other gay sisters who may be confused, misled and bothered by the myths and stereotypes that are still misrepresenting lesbians." One article from October 1973 tackled the issue "How to Identify a Real Lesbian," while another in the same issue covered lesbian mothers having children taken away. A prose poem in March 1973 by Karen, titled "SISTERS?," raised the matter of whether straight women would accept their lesbian sisters. "But will we fight their oppression? What do we do to change social attitudes and laws that discriminate?" The conclusion was, "We will lose our lesbian sisters for we keep expecting them to help us solve our problems but don't do a damn thing to help them solve theirs."[25]

Other features were on lesbian mothers, lesbian health issues, and, with an article titled "N.O.W. Embraces 'Dykes,'" the accepted terminology for lesbians. It also covered a lesbian writers conference, lesbian poets in Milwaukee, and reviews of lesbian books. Miriam Ben-Shalom's fight to remain in the military as an out lesbian was an ongoing topic of interest. One provocative article from March 1973 was titled "Random Thoughts of a Lesbian/Feminist Masturbator." Another, "DYKETACTICS!," introduced a local collective of lesbians "committed to actions which will raise public consciousness and electrify the imaginations of the gay and women's communities."[26]

Lesbians told poignant personal stories. One Green Bay woman, Kitty, talked of becoming so depressed after ending a painful relationship that she began abusing alcohol and valium. After getting sober, she came to Milwaukee, which she termed "Dykeland USA," and "met some wonderful Milwaukee womyn." Vicki wrote of noticing her attraction to women in the fifth grade. When she rejected her presumed path of marrying a nice Jewish boy, a would-be "Rock Hudsonberg," her mother's advice was, "I hope you're going with nice Jewish girls."[27]

Amazon also devoted space to the Wisconsin chapter of the National Lesbian Feminist Organization (NLFO). The national organization had been founded in March 1978 at a national meeting in Los Angeles. Fifteen women attended a follow-up meeting on July 23, 1978, at the offices of the Milwaukee Women's Coalition with only lesbian members having voting rights. This resulted in the constitution of a local chapter. On November 10–12, 1978, a state conference was held at UW–Milwaukee with "over 100 wimin attending." Wisconsin was the first state to hold a state convention of the NLFO. Colleen, reporting for *Amazon*, commented, "It was for me the most exciting, powerful, and productive celebration of sisterhood I have ever witnessed." She met "Wisconsin lesbian feminists from small towns" across the state. An important topic of the convention was lesbian co-parenting. To avoid "patriarchal decision-making," resolutions were passed using a discussion/consensus method that led to "an overall feeling of power and success."[28]

In the mid-1970s, the magazine included numerous features on Grapevine, described as a Lesbian-Feminist Action Core that formed in spring 1974 and lasted over sixteen years. Grapevine met at the Women's Coalition space and offered counseling for lesbians through the women's crisis line. The group held classes on the lesbian experience and maintained a bibliography of lesbian literature. It also sponsored dances on the first Saturday of the month and held yard parties to raise money. One Grapevine member, Barb, who served on a panel that discussed the stereotypes of lesbians as man-haters, noted in *Amazon*, "Man-hating doesn't come from Lesbians. In my life there are no men to hate. You can't hate someone you're not involved with." Issues addressed included whether lesbians should build a separate community or continue to work with their non-lesbian sisters.[29]

A major bulwark of the feminist community in Milwaukee was Sister-Moon Feminist Bookstore and Art Gallery, founded in 1976 by Karen Voltz, a member of Grapevine, with money from her divorce. *Amazon* encouraged readers to "matronize" their advertisers, such as SisterMoon. Books were shelved by theme and included feminist theory, herstory, parenting, lesbianism, and much more. *Amazon* cited SisterMoon as an important role model for women-owned and women-operated businesses. It was also important that the store was "blatantly alternative" with the word *feminist* boldly visible on its sign. When it closed in September 1983, SisterMoon was appropriately mourned with an *Amazon* cover. An expiring bookstore lease triggered the final decision, but burnout was the real reason behind the closure. As Voltz remarked, "I had worked hard and struggled for the movement but now there was nothing left of me to give." She moved 275 miles away to the Northwoods of Wisconsin seeking healing and taking with her memories of the "wonderful womanspace."[30]

Another lesbian-run feminist institution that gained special affection in the pages of *Amazon* was DOE Farm, or Daughters of the Earth Farm, located near Norwalk in the Driftless Area and owned by the Wisconsin Womyn's Land Cooperative. Its eighty acres, called "some of the prettiest land east of the Mississippi" by *Amazon*, were purchased in April 1977. To use the land, one had to be a member, initially at the annual cost of two dollars per one thousand dollars of gross income. Members worked to conserve the land and develop farming skills. As *Amazon* reported, DOE Farm was based on the belief that that "patriarchal culture is a death culture, unconsciously (or consciously) raping, polluting, and slowly killing the earth." Two hundred fifty members had joined by 1980. The fees they paid for camping and classes helped to pay the mortgage. Members raised goats for milk, grew vegetables, and built trails.[31]

As an all-womyn environment, DOE Farm promoted the rebuilding of feminist culture "with a minimum amount of contamination/interference from the straight patriarchal value system." As a rule, "there would be no intrusions by men, for none were welcome on the land." DOE Farm also provided a resource to isolated rural women where battered women shelters and lesbian centers were too far away to access. It was a space to recover from burnout and a place to heal. A July 1980 story featured one woman's experience. When she and friends awoke in their trailer to the sound of a hundred chickens, they laughed because they had chosen to park in the dark five feet from the henhouse. The friends enjoyed the communal fire ring and looked forward to the solar heated showers they were building.[32]

In 1978, *Amazon* brought a new topic to its pages. Transsexuality had been on the boundaries of the community but had never been addressed in its pages. On March 11 that year, the collective staged an open conversation on transsexuality and feminism, with the caveat that they realized "transsexuality is a polarizing issue in the women's community." The "rap" lasted four hours and was attended by fifty women and "guests"—a presumed reference to the five male-to-female transsexuals in attendance. The transsexuals shared their journeys, and the discussion was heated. One writer's perception was that "each of the five transsexuals who were there seemed to have accepted the societally defined expectations of male and female 'roles.'" These conceptions of *female* to the feminists of the collective seemed like "some mythical perception." One commented, "Just changing the body and sexual characteristics *reinforces* the rigid sex roles, it does nothing to change the structure of society."[33]

In general, the collective members did not support whatever gender or gender role people felt most comfortable in. One asserted, "We all have the right to question the feminist motives and values of transsexuals." The writer for *Amazon* deplored the infighting and "that we 'women-identified' women must resort to this old patriarchal tactic of oppression." Yet her conclusion, since in her understanding they came from totally different worlds, was, "As a lesbian/feminist, a totally woman identified woman, I will never accept a surgically transformed woman as my sister." Another saw it as just another ploy to destroy womynspace. Still, one had scrawled an inclusive message on the graffiti board: "All women are beautiful no matter how they got that way." In the end, the subject proved too divisive, and *Amazon*'s 1978 foray into the transsexual community was its last.[34]

While most of the male-focused bar magazines did not include women, and most women's magazines did not cover men, *Amazon* did raise an issue that was not infrequently expressed by lesbians. Gay men were thought to be isolated from society and less

The lesbian back-to-the-land movement occurred across the nation, and Wisconsin's experiment in a safe women's space, DOE Farm, operated by the Wisconsin Womyn's Land Cooperative, occurred near Norwalk. WHI IMAGE ID 144583

nurturing and supportive than lesbians, who found support among the feminist community. In praising the strength of women who provided one another support, *Amazon* expressed pity toward gay men. A 1975 article opined, "How wonderful this [feminism] is, [it] can further be realized by contrasting it with the situation of gay males. For them isolation from the rest of society is still almost exclusively the rule. There is no corresponding male support group for them—men [are] still being shackled with medieval ideas of what constitutes masculinity. Since lording it over a female is central to the male physique, male homosexuals are most obviously unmasculine."[35]

As with many ventures run by a collective and powered by volunteers, publication could be erratic. Issues were missed, and some were shorter than planned because contributors failed to meet deadlines. Readers were informed in November 1974, "We are at the ends of our ropes time-wise, energy-wise, and organization-wise." In October 1976, staff observed, "Spiritual and emotional support have sustained Amazons for four years, with numerous burnouts along the way." The staff felt it was important to establish a means for feminists' communities to support each other, "economically as well as spiritually."[36]

Over its twelve-year existence, the magazine went through three major periods. In its second period, beginning in October 1976, a new tag was adopted: "A Midwest Journal for Women." The staff's view was, "There is no other feminist publication in this part of the country that shares our goals." Attendance at the 1979 Women in Print Conference, held in Chicago, had fostered this view. They believed theirs was a "Midwestern voice." The editors hoped the magazine, now a bimonthly, would be able to pay contributors who would be able to hone this voice. Though *Amazon* strove to become recognized as a regional publication, it never truly achieved that goal. Some articles did cover regional stories, and a few regional contributors did appear, but the listed distribution points remained mainly in Milwaukee with a few around the state.[37]

JAMAKAYA: AN ENDURING VOICE IN LGBT JOURNALISM

During the winter of 1978–1979, *Amazon*'s collective system collapsed. and seven months went by without an issue. In July 1979, it relaunched with its third and final tagline, "Milwaukee's Feminist Press," and was staffed by two editors. Soon, Jamakaya (J. M. Dombeck), who had served as a counselor on the Women's Crisis Line and an office manager for the Milwaukee Women's Coalition, became the sole editor. One of her delights up to the end of the magazine's run was the SISTERNEWS feature of bits and blurbs from Milwaukee and elsewhere. Jamakaya believed the publication was "a vital communications tool and a vehicle for documenting our history: our social events, artistic achievements, political struggles and future ambitions." Noting only a limited number of consistent lesbian journalists in the state, she urged other women to write for LGBT community publications and "lighten our load, sisters." For her efforts at *Amazon*, she was given a Milwaukee Cream City Brick Pacesetter award. After Jamakaya left, the magazine appeared to be back to a floating collective for its publication. More items in later issues came from national sources; the poetry came from New York and other non-Wisconsin places. The last issue of *Amazon* was February/March 1984. In 1986, it would be reborn in a new iteration, the *Hag Rag*, which is profiled later in this chapter.[38]

Jamakaya would prove to be one of the enduring writers and historians of Wisconsin's LGBT community. Later she would muse about viewing "LGBT history from the trenches," recalling from her days as a "baby butch" that she had started out as a "'bad' lesbian feminist doing things that organizational leaders often disapproved." This included distributing copies of *Lesbian Nation* at a right-wing ladies' gathering against the ERA. Her master's thesis at UW–Milwaukee, "The Women's Coalition of Milwaukee, 1972–1987," received the Theodore Brown Award for Distinguished Graduate Research and Writing. As she wrote in *The Wisconsin Light*, "Until we take our own lives and contributions as feminists seriously . . . how can we expect to be taken seriously by others or by history itself?" In 1988, the National Gay and Lesbian Press Association gave her an award for covering current news for her *The Wisconsin Light*'s coverage of the Jeffrey Dahmer serial murder case. Her 1988 book *Like Our Sisters Before Us: Women of Wisconsin Labor* won an award from the International Labor Communications Association. Her tongue-in-cheek title for a possible memoir was "Rascals, Rogues, Vagabonds, and the Truly Pathological: Women I Have Loved." Jamakaya was still regularly contributing columns to various gay publications into the second decade of the twenty-first century.[39]

RENAISSANCE, 1976–1978

The *Renaissance* newsletter developed out of the Madison Gay Center, itself nominally rebranded as Renaissance in 1976, with a dedicated group of volunteers who constituted the Newsletter/Publications Committee. (The center would rebrand again when it became the Gay and Lesbian Center later in the decade.) *Renaissance* was preceded by *Free for All*, an alternative paper with occasional newsletter items that started in March 1973 and ceased publication in 1975. Appearing that month was an article, "The Right to Be Gay," that described the latest efforts of the Madison Gay Liberation Front. Calendar events informed the community of various happenings. The alternative paper's bounds included a piece called "Bisexual Chic." Another, titled "Gay Rap," described taking a straight friend to a gay bar to see the reality of gay life, which included straight men yelling "faggot" at bar patrons. The publication also reported on a UW Extension gay conference on the Invisible Minority, keynoted by Professor Dr. Leigh Roberts of UW–Madison's Department of Psychiatry. [40]

In the first year of the *Renaissance* newsletter, John Lindert was editor. Contributors included local journalists Ron McCrea and Jacob Stockinger. The works of Madison gay poets, including Credo Enriquez, Richard Herman, Lenny Tropp, and Steve Miller, appeared in its pages. The newsletter also sought more women's coverage in later years under the editorship of Lewis Bosworth. Arlys Bowler was appointed the Woman Editor, and her poems and those of other women appeared near the end of the newsletter's run. The newsletter paid $3.50 for published articles and poems but was free to readers. Its editorial philosophy was laid out in the February 1978 issue: "In a city with gay talent and vitality, like Madison, much can be shared with a community newsletter. We would like to present a format as diverse as the people who read it." [41]

Publication could be irregular. In June 1977, an editorial note after a hiatus of several months assured readers, "No, the Newsletter has not folded." A monetary contribution from the new gay bar Going My Way had helped. The November 1977 issue noted that *Renaissance* now accepted advertising. Among the ads, the Soap Opera, a State Street shop, promoted its "scentuous" bath toys and oils. Other ads came from gay bars and local bookstores. *Renaissance* often contained a counseling report from the Gay

Center and political news. One concern expressed by writer Mark McNary was that "news coverage of events important to gays has never been good." He closed his piece with the assertion, "Gaining control of the media is essential for gaining control of our lives."[42]

Two notable articles from this period were "The Dynamics of Drag" and "The Gay Poor: A Challenge for the Gay Liberation Movement." In another article, Lenny Tropp profiled two gay men, a couple who were developmentally disabled, noting, "Their tenderness transcends this confining stereotype." Jon Hall contributed a series on gay historiography. David Smith reviewed gay books and discussed library resources on gay material, including a small library of sixty books at the Gay Center. Smith complained of the difficulty of finding a gay book at the University Bookstore with the observation, "Let's face it, these people are afraid of homosexuals." A bit later, he would remedy the dearth of gay material by starting Four Star Fiction and Video. Gay venues and events were often promoted in the newsletter. In 1977, *Renaissance* boosted the Arena Repertory Theater, a new gay theater group, performing at Freedom House on Winnebago Street. It also promoted the Gay Arts Festival set for May Day in the Great Hall of Memorial Union.[43]

In January 1978, Chuck Rhodes, director of counseling at the Gay Center, wrote an opinion piece titled "Get Your Priorities Gay." He felt the most destructive oppression was from within. He touted the advice of a button he owned: "Nobody Can Make You Feel Inferior without Your Permission." Rhodes cited the 1975 Madison referendum on massage parlors as an example of how liberals cannot protect gays from harassment by the right. He urged readers to think about more than "having new cha-cha heels or a hot trick." Highlighting the accomplishments of the Gay Center, "one of the oldest gay service centers in existence in this country," he noted new programs, including a gay men's social group. His plea was for gay men "to take care of yourself and plot your own destiny."[44]

One way in which readers took care of themselves was to find community through the newsletter itself. A letter writer from Boyceville, Wisconsin, a village of less than a thousand in Dunn County, believed that "organizations like yours will help to break down the years of prejudice that we've all been living with for many years." Others felt more isolated. "The Other Side/'Beautiful Is Ugly'" told the story of a self-described

Sketch by Steve Applequist

Gay Arts Festival Set for May Day in Great Hall

The gay community is invited to contribute its talents to a Gay Arts Festival scheduled for Sunday, May 1, in the Great Hall of the Memorial Union.

The all-day festival will include dance presentations, poetry readings, musical performances, and theater. Gallery areas are also planned so that artists and craftspersons may exhibit their work. "Gay Arts" embraces all work by gay artists and performers--not necessarily on gay themes.

Several groups and persons have already committed themselves to participate. The Arena Theater will present portions of the play "Coming Out," including a Madison segment based on the "62 Purge" interview in the last Renaissance Newsletter.

Lesbian and regional participation is desired. Help of all kinds is invited for coordinating the various parts of the festival, including art, film, music, and photography committees.

The event is being sponsored by the Madison Committee for Gay Rights. To get in on the planning of the festival, call David Smith at 251-2937.

Help Keep the Gay Center Working for You—Send a Contribution Today!

Name_____

Address_____

City_____State_____Zip_____

_____ $10 and up
Individual membership

_____ $5 Basic membership
(Newsletter and postage only)

_____ $300 and up ($25 per month)
Benefactor membership

_____ $120 and up ($10 per month)
Sponsor membership

_____ $50 and up ($4 per month)
Sustaining membership

_____ $15 and up
Household membership

The Gay Arts Festival of 1977 harkened back to the first gay pride event in Madison on May Day in 1970 and foreshadowed many years of the Lesbian Variety Show to come.
WHI IMAGE ID 59163

handsome man who lamented, "Alas, I'm the bright yellow wrapper that catches people's eye." His complaint, which he felt was akin to the plight of airline stewardesses, was that "many people take it for granted that the only satisfaction 'heavenly numbers' want out of life is to be admired for their beauty and handled like a rubber blow-up fuck doll."[45]

The January 1978 issue of *Renaissance* was titled "LAST GASP?" The staff, while claiming the newsletter was exciting and important, worried that with at least four staff members leaving Madison, "the newsletter is in danger of dying, just when its potential for growth seems very great." Within a year it would be gone. This penultimate issue would also be the venue for the great "Disco Debate." McCrea, who deplored the disco scene as low on political consciousness, argued that many gays had sworn off the bars, but "[we] return because there are no safe or promising alternatives; because Madison, for all its tolerance, is not yet a gay city prepared to integrate gay people into mainstream social life." A bar scene that he thought reflected the hedonistic straight singles scene provoked his remark, "We call this liberation, but we've only learned to wear our oppression well."[46]

In his response, Tropp, a DJ at Going My Way and the Cardinal, thought the bars were where you rubbed shoulders with your peers. For Tropp,

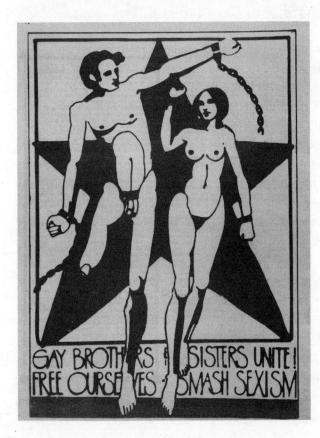

The presentation of nudity and the broken chains on the back cover of the 1978 *Renaissance* newsletter emphasized the theme of liberation in this early Madison gay and lesbian publication. WHI IMAGE ID 59237

claiming Dionysian antecedents, "Real Gay disco . . . is a wonder to be-
hold." For him, disco was "action, ceremony, living theatre . . . gesture,
prose in motion . . . dance/trance." Tropp admitted his comments applied
less to Madison where disco bars doubled as cruise bars, and he compared
McCrea to an old pining grandmother. In the last issue of *Renaissance* in
February 1978, McCrea responded, rejecting "emotional fascism" toward
anyone showing "evidence of gay dissatisfaction with the bar scene as our
major social outlet." McCrea reemphasized his point that gay energies
poured into disco were "not a substitute for a gay politics or a gay culture."[47]

Though it folded after only three years, the *Renaissance* newsletter
was an important communication tool for early gay activists in Madison.
Assuming a gay audience, it sought to raise both the cultural knowledge
and political consciousness of the community.

GAY ENDEAVOR, 1978, AND GAY MADISON, 1979–1982

The demise of *Renaissance* in February 1978 prompted efforts in Madison
to keep a gay/lesbian publication in print. Unfortunately, there was only
one issue (March) of *The Gay Endeavor: A Publication for Gay Women and
Gay Men*. The staff, described as a collective, included Lewis Bosworth,
who also edited *Rod's* newsletter, and activists Kathleen Nichols and Abbey
Hill. Its single issue covered news from Rhodes of the Madison Gay Center
on counselor training and support groups; the results of a questionnaire
on gay issues sent to political candidates from the Madison Committee
for Gay Rights; and the newly opened Lysistrata Restaurant, whose aim,
according to the founders, was to appeal to the "widest common denomi-
nator" of feminists. The editors were frank about the amount of effort it
took to put out a quality publication: "After this edition some members
of the original staff find it necessary to leave the collective for personal
reasons." The hope was that other members of the gay and lesbian community would "become involved as contributors and staff members," but
this was not to be.[48]

The demise of *Renaissance* and the failure of its short-lived successor created a vacuum in Madison's coverage of the gay community. For a
few years in the late 1970s, Madison Community United had published a
newsletter on regular 8 ½" x 11" paper. In 1979, it shifted to newsprint and

The Gay Endeavor

A PUBLICATION FOR GAY WOMEN AND GAY MEN • MID-MARCH 1978

.INTERVIEW:
  SOGLIN and NICHOLS
. a warning from Louisiana
. SAPPHO

Though it was published for just one issue, the *Gay Endeavor* of Madison was produced in an ambitious magazine format.
WHI IMAGE ID 59224

was renamed *Gay Madison*. With a staff of volunteers, its existence was tenuous. Issues were irregular despite the claim that it would be published either monthly or bimonthly. Its main revenue came from small ads sponsored by gay-owned and gay-friendly businesses. The October 1979 issue, its eighth, raised the question of whether this might be its last. Since the newspaper was "distributed to selective national publications, often providing their only source of gay news from Madison," the editors worried that exciting progress would go unreported. But the initial crisis was overcome, and *Gay Madison* continued until 1982.[49]

The writing in the early issues of *Gay Madison* was still generally of the newsletter variety, and its link to the United was stated in every issue. Sandra Finn-Curkeet served as the first editor. She was followed by Peter Klehm in 1981, and in 1982, Brooks Egerton joined as assistant editor and Lynda Wannamaker joined as a coordinating editor. Contributors included Klehm, Nichols, Caryl Bentley, Lance Green, Barbara Lightner, Jim Taylor,

GAY MADISON

Number 9   December 1979   Madison, Wisconsin

Madisonians in national march

By Duane Kolterman

On Sunday, October 14, about 100,000 people from all over the country marched on the nation's capital to demand lesbian and gay rights. The spirited crowd of lesbians and gay men, as well as some of our parents, children and friends, marched from the Mall, near the U.S. Capitol, past the White House, and to the Washington Monument. There, an exciting five-hour rally was held, featuring a wide spectrum of speakers and entertainers, and emceed by lesbian comic Robin Tyler.

Among the speakers were poets Audre Lorde and Allen Ginsberg, N.O.W. president Ellie Smeal and vice president Arlie Scott, San Francisco City Supervisor Harry Britt (appointed to take the place of Harvey Milk, who had worked hard to organize the March prior to his assassination), U.S. Representative Ted Weiss (D-NY), and a representative of Washington Mayor Marion Berry. Toward the end of the rally, the crowd was particularly inspired by the speeches of Kate Millett and Flo Kennedy. Music was provided by Meg Christian, Mary Watkins, Holly Near, Tom Robinson and others, and signing for the hearing-impaired was available throughout. The rally was broadcast live nationwide via Pacifica Radio/National Public Radio, and carried locally by WORT-FM.

Coming 10 years after gays took to the streets of New York in the Stonewall Rebellion, the National March for Lesbian and Gay Rights was not the largest gathering of lesbians and gay men in American history, but it was the most diverse. Never have the more than 20 million lesbian and gay Americans been so well represented—economically, socially, politically, ethnically, demographically and geographically. By bus, plane, train or car, people came to Washington from every state, and from

several foreign countries as well. Many Third World Lesbians and gays attended a five-day conference held in D.C., and their contingent led the march.

Banners, signs and chants ranged from the militant to the frivolous, and gay marching bands from Los Angeles and Houston accompanied the marchers. Over 60 Madisonians were in attendance, as well as many others from Milwaukee and elsewhere in Wisconsin. In addition, a camera crew videotaped the day's events for "Glad to Be Gay," Madison's gay TV program.

After the excitement which the march and rally generated in all of us, the woefully inadequate press coverage, both locally and nationally, was a tremendous disappointment. Even a tear-gas attack on the last of the marchers escaped the notice of journalists. The attention paid to the National March might be compared to that paid to the Pope, who frequently drew much smaller crowds, but was always front-page news.

An offhand remark by a Washington police officer appears to have been the source of attendance reports of 250,000 at the rally itself, while even National Park Service estimates of 25,000 were rejected by the Press Connection. Since then, the attendance estimates have stabilized at 25,500 to 150,000.

The National March on Washington for Lesbian and Gay Rights elicited no statement from President Carter, no action by Congress, and little nationwide awareness of the strength, demands or oppression of lesbians and gay men. Yet, the extensive local, regional and national organizing for the March is a big step toward our achievement of full freedom and dignity, and the thrill of participating in this unprecedented event will remain with us always.

Holly Near tells us: 'Take it with you . . .'

By Sarah Schuyler

It isn't art for art's sake. Not only do the little hairs rise up on the backs of our necks while we listen to Holly Near concert but what is most important is that we listen to the political lesson we learn there and silently promise ourselves that we will obey when Holly sings "Take it with you wherever you go." Holly repeatedly reminds us that the most important task for everyone is to organize, like Nicolia who "worked inside a factory," and stay with the fight.

"Everyone needs to do what they do best," she says. "Music is what we do best, and we're here to refuel you for your own work." This is exactly what Holly and her friends do, with a musical virtuosity and a

spiritual purity that made her November third concert in Madison probably the closest thing to a religious experience many of us who were there have had in a long time.

Holly Near, pianist-composer John Thomas, and American Sign Language interpreter Susan Freundlich came to Madison billed "On Tour for a Nuclear Free Future." We have Madison's own women's music production company, Fallen Woman, the Alternative Power Alliance, the Black Hills Alliance, and the University of Wisconsin Women's Studies department to thank for bringing her here.

The tour is raising money for antinuclear organizing and women's music production. An audience of two thousand men and women came to hear her at the UW Stock Pavilion.

"I was raised on a farm, Holly told us, "so I feel very much at home in the Stock Pavilion." Her political development began back on the farm when her mother ran as a Socialist candidate for mayor of their small town. As a woman, Holly has grown over the years by working for different political issues. The variety of songs she sang Nov. 3 illustrate her growth.

In the '60s she was an anti-war activist. "No More Genocide in My Name" is a good example of her work from this period. The theme of racial genocide tied in as well with the anti-nuclear cause, as she told about Native Americans hired to mine radioactive fuels and about the Vietnamese who have been relocated at the poisonous Love Canal.

When Holly came out as a lesbian ("Imagine My Surprise") she began an emphasis on the feminist and gay struggles. She gave women's concerts because she felt the need for women not to overlook the oppression of women in general and lesbians in particular. It's a point she became most controversial at that point because men felt "left out" or "discriminated against." The fact is that for feminists and lesbians to have the courage to struggle against discrimination, especially when there is so far to go, they find their most __ing support from one another. Holly is saying today is that realizing men and women, gay and straight are too vital for all of us not to __.

The Tour for a Nuclear __ different kind of stat__

CONTINUED __

This issue of *Gay Madison* reported on city residents who attended the first national march for gay rights in Washington, DC, on the tenth anniversary of Stonewall.
GAY MADISON NO. 9, DECEMBER 1979

Janice Czyson, Steve Starkey, Henry Dudek, Susan Christenson, Tom De-Chant, and Steve Deathrage.

The last issue of *Gay Madison* in September 1982 included a bold announcement: the editors were forming a new paper. The new publication, independent from the United, was to be called *OUT!*, and its intent was to rely on "subscriptions, advertisements and contributions for financial support." The publishing team was to be a collective "staffed primarily by the folks who have brought you *Gay Madison* for the last seven months." Of the separation, the editors stated their desire to "to assume full responsibility for controversies we, as journalists, easily and often encounter in our work." It noted, "One such controversy, of course, is the charge of discrimination, presently still in its filing stages, against Verona publisher Henry Schroeder. Schroeder refused to print *Gay Madison* on grounds of 'pornography and obscenity.'" The Cardinal Bar hosted a benefit for the new venture.[50]

In its final months, editors Klehm and Egerton had raised the journalistic quality of *Gay Madison* and reached for a more significant level of news. Prior to the 1982 Democratic gubernatorial primary, the paper ran features on candidates Anthony Earl and James Wood, both of whom had favorable positions on gay issues. The paper also started to publish poetry, some of which, while certainly not pornographic, was explicit about mentioning body parts. The move to separate from the United was parallel to gay activist Barbara Lightner's resignation from the United as the organization moved from a focus on social activism to the delivery of community social services.[51]

LEAPING LA CROSSE NEWS, 1978–2007

For more than twenty-five years, *Leaping La Crosse News* was published in western Wisconsin and served as the primary media for an active community of lesbians. Similar to Milwaukee's *Amazon*, it was fueled by individuals associated with the area's colleges. In 1978, a handful of women began holding monthly potlucks in the La Crosse area that quickly grew to attract up to thirty or forty women. Soon, the group began publishing a newsletter for the National Lesbian Feminist Organization, a chapter of which briefly existed in Wisconsin. It eventually branched out, publishing poetry and general information in addition to local lesbian events.[52]

The founding mother, listed in the first issue of November 1978, was Jill (the publication did not use last names during this period, but a later issue identifies her as Jill Davy). The publication included the schedule of the monthly potlucks and featured other social events, some of which were hosted by the Friends of Tattoo's, the women's bar, opened in 1980, where lesbians could dance. Among other early community programs in La Crosse, *Leaping La Crosse News* publicized a lesbian erotic poetry reading that drew fifty attendees. Also featured were music events in the area produced by Out and About Women. Mary O'Sullivan and a woman who went by the name Lois joined the publication efforts in 1981. O'Sullivan taught English and worked with reentry students, mostly women seeking to reenter the job market, at Western Wisconsin Technical Institute. Concerned that the women "were getting slotted into traditional female occupations with low pay," O'Sullivan found funding and became the first coordinator of the Women's Opportunity Center in 1978. O'Sullivan was also involved with the local NOW chapter, and she recalled that 90 percent of the women she networked with were "dikes." When O'Sullivan joined the publication in 1981, the name *Leaping La Crosse News* was established as a play on Meg Christian's song "Leaping Lesbians," which O'Sullivan introduced at dinner parties to test out whether other women guests might be lesbians, too. Another name associated with the newsletter's production, Joy Holthaus, is known because she became a public figure when Governor Earl appointed her to the Governor's Council on Lesbian and Gay Issues in the mid-1980s.[53]

After a couple of years, *Leaping La Crosse News* reached more than two hundred women. Annual subscriptions were first six dollars and then eight, and donations could be left with the bartenders at Tattoo's. Costs totaled about eighty dollars an issue, and the editors admitted, "The *LLN* is usually on the brink of bankruptcy." One benefit was "Italian Night at Tattino's," which promised food and dancing to good tunes. An auction in October 1989 raised $680, which exceeded the editors' wildest dreams.[54]

While primarily social, *Leaping La Crosse News* also carried some political news. Positioned on Wisconsin's border with Minnesota, it covered the Twin Cities but overwhelmingly focused on politics in Wisconsin as they affected the gay and lesbian community. One writer reporting on the 1987 National March on Washington noted, "It was fun to march with the Wisconsin group, as everyone seemed to notice the banners that said 'Wisconsin—the Gay Rights State,' and there was applause, smiles and gestures of support." The newsletter proudly covered the 1989 GALVAnize (Gay and Lesbian Visibility Alliance) March in Madison where all seven of Wisconsin's openly gay and lesbian elected officials were introduced, noting that this was the highest number of out elected officials in any area of the country.[55]

Shortly after the passage of the Wisconsin gay rights law in spring 1982, *Leaping La Crosse News* became invested in seeing the law fully implemented. In the October 1983 issue, it took the La Crosse Community Housing Resources Board to task for a brochure that failed to include lesbians and gays. The board's response that the brochure had mentioned sex and marital status (a provision adopted at the same time as sexual orientation) cut no ice with the publication. It responded, "Sorry CHRB, that doesn't do it."[56]

Though it closed its doors in 2007, *Leaping La Crosse News* had nurtured a separatist lesbian community that was self-assured but not particularly militant. Its portrayal of a smaller city's lesbian community was fun and fulsome.

OUT!: 1982–1987

OUT!, started by *Gay Madison* editors Peter Klehm and Brooks Egerton, published its first issue in November 1982. Klehm was listed as coordinating editor (and later publisher) and Egerton as associate editor (and later editor). The duo represented an independent, nonprofit collective of lesbians and gays in Madison. Klehm would depart in September 1984 after "two years of toil for the cause of lesbian/gay journalism."[57]

The paper sought to cover all of Wisconsin, and the first issue included a story on small-town gay life. The staff believed that "even in the national gay press you're not going to find a lot of stuff that's pertinent to a small town in Wisconsin." Egerton explained, "In Wisconsin, roots are taking hold in a rural gay presence that's very uncommon in this country." While the initial issue used the tagline "Madison's Lesbian/Gay Newspaper," the next issue expanded it to "Wisconsin's Lesbian/Gay Newspaper."[58]

The paper reached all corners of the state, with distribution points

Peter Klehm (left) and Brooks Egerton (right) transformed *Gay Madison* from an organization newsletter into *OUT!*, a statewide gay newspaper that was published monthly.
ISTHMUS, NOVEMBER 25, 1983, PHOTO BY GLENN TRUDEL

for free copies in Appleton, Beloit, Green Bay, Fond du Lac, Kenosha,
La Crosse, Oshkosh, Racine, Sheboygan, Stevens Point, Superior, Waukesha, Wausau, and multiple points in Madison and Milwaukee. It was also
available through subscription, and the staff pushed advocates across the
state to request public libraries to carry the paper in their periodicals section. When the librarian at Rice Lake rejected a subscription to the paper
as "too sensitive," she was overruled by the library board. With its fourth
issue, the paper published a comprehensive Lesbian/Gay Guide to Wisconsin with bars, baths, counseling and support groups, bookstores, health
services, friendly religious groups, sport groups, Alcoholics Anonymous
groups, gay chorales, campus groups, and political groups—an invaluable
statewide resource. Outside the larger cities, the most frequent guide entry
for a place was the gay bar.[59]

In its inaugural edition, the paper opened with the statement, "We
will continue to strive to present an equal balance of male and female
issues." Women were well-represented. Feminist activists Crystal Hyslop
and Carolyn Kennedy were part of the collective, and Kathleen Nichols

OUT!

OUT!, Inc.
P. O. Box 148
Madison, WI 53701

Wisconsin's
Madison's Lesbian/Gay Newspaper

Vol. 1, No. 3————January 1983———————(608) 251-0698, 256-8204————————*FREE—But Please Subscribe!*

The Lesbian Center:
Beyond Survival to a New Sense of Self

By Barbara Lightner

To speak of Madison's Lesbian Center is to speak of an organization which has experienced many changes and yet always maintained dedication, commitment, and perseverance. Recent years have seen a lull in activities, but the Center today is full of a renewed energy, a broadened commitment of life and an openness that has been difficult to sustain in the past.

The signs of the Center's new sense of itself are everywhere—in its highly successful pancake breakfasts, in its sponsorship of events with other lesbian and gay organizations, and in its plans for creating a calendar of social events in a city where there has been little opportunity for lesbians to be with lesbians just for the fun of it.

In a recent interview, Jeanne Fondrie and Leslie Wilmot of the Lesbian Center discussed some of the reasons for the Center's vitality. Of primary importance, Wilmot said, has been the current general climate of repression and the sense of solidarity it has created among lesbians in Madison.

That solidarity has been frustrated, however, by the closing of the feminist restaurants Lysistrata and the Main Course, the closing of the gay disco Going My Way, and the perceived lack of welcome accorded lesbians at the new gay bar, Sam's. By providing space both physical and mental, the Center has become a place where lesbians can come together in an expression of solidarity.

A new openness in policies and programs is another invigorating factor for the Center, Wilmot believes. In the past, the Lesbian Center had been plagued by an image of "patrolling the kingdom"—because of its emphasis on lesbian feminism, for example, and a policy requiring all events to be chemical-free.

Though women at the Center said their intention was not to patrol, but

The Lesbian Center: The Changer and the Changed

to provide alternatives not otherwise available in Madison, many lesbians felt that they were not welcome—a state of affairs that women now involved at the Center are determined to change.

According to Fondrie, the policy on sponsoring chem-free events is now of particular concern. This policy, perhaps more than any other, created a sense of alienation among lesbians. Center members once thought it important to provide an alternative to the bars—but few lesbians participated in organizing and attending these events. The closing of bars where women could come together in women's space adds to the need to re-evaluate, says Fondrie.

There is also a growing understanding, Wilmot believes, that the Center should not cater exclusively to feminist lesbians. She notes that lesbians have "separated ourselves, and there is a need to integrate again."

The group is also examining its relationship to other lesbian and gay or-

ganizations in Madison. Fondrie points out that in the past the work of lesbians at the Center went into keeping the Center alive. In this situation, there was little time for coalition work and, though there was some co-sponsorship of events, most of it was in name only.

Now, however, Fondrie and Wilmot believe that it will be possible to do some coalition work, although they note that the Center in no way intends to diminish its responsibility to provide "alternative, women-only space for any women who can appreciate being at a woman-only gathering." Work with other groups

will not be the central focus in the Center's new identity, however.

As proof of its pudding, the Center is conducting a survey to determine what it can best do to serve Madison's lesbian community. The survey has received wide distribution, being passed out at the November Holly Near concert in an attempt to reach lesbians beyond the Center's network. According to Wilmot, the survey will be used as a "place to start" in developing Center activities.

Organized through general monthly meetings, the Center presently has 10 to 12 core women, along with many others who participate from time to time. The structure is collective and open so that lesbians can participate according to their time and interest, in a way that discourages accumulation of power. Both Fondrie and Wilmot stress that all lesbians are welcome at the meetings.

Presently, the Center provides a Wednesday evening drop-in at its office in the Wilmar Community Center, 953 Jenifer Street. A pool tournament, a Valentine's Day dance, and a pancake breakfast are currently on the Center's calendar. Plans for a monthly coffeehouse are beginning to take shape, as are workshops which the survey indicates will be of interest to the lesbian community.

Becoming involved in the Lesbian Center, obtaining a copy of the survey questions, or asking for further information is only a phone call away. Interested lesbians may call 257-7378 or drop in Wednesday evenings from 6 to 9 p.m.

Barbara Lightner is a former community services director of the United and a sometime poet.

Lawyers, Guns and Money

By Duane Allen

Despite both a 1982 state law and a 1979 Faculty Senate resolution prohibiting discrimination on the basis of sexual orientation, the FBI and the U.S. military continue to recruit on the UW-Madison campus. Neither the FBI nor the military will hire open lesbians and gay men.

The UW's position on the use of University Placement Services by organizations which discriminate against gays and lesbians was set out by Chancellor Irving Shain in October. That position, in effect, says that the University will not enforce the non-discrimination law unless ordered by a court to do so.

Shain claims that state laws banning discrimination cannot be applied to federal agencies like the FBI. Attorney Mike Liethen of UW Legal Services says that Shain's "statement resolves the issue in the short run, but it hasn't been resolved in the long run."

But this "short run resolution" means that heterosexuals will continue to have more job opportunities than lesbians and gays—at least as far as some federal agencies are concerned. And this "short run" may turn out to be a long one. The University is moving slowly to constitute a committee to look further into this

matter, and there are questions about who is—and who is not—acceptable to serve on the committee.

One argument that the committee will have to consider is put forward by Mark Borns, Student Bar Association president. Borns says that it is true Wisconsin can't dictate to federal agencies. "However, can federal agencies use state property when they openly discriminate? When they do, it's certainly against the *policy* of the law, if not the letter. And it may turn out to be against the letter, too."

Hidden Agenda

The hidden agenda for the University in the controversy is federal money. Research grants and contracts come to the UW from the discriminating agencies. Shain's statement permitting the FBI and the military to continue recruiting was made five days after the Defense Department said it would issue no more contracts to universities which bar military recruiting.

Other universities which had non-discrimination policies have already begun to back down on the recruitment issue. Temple University recently reversed its non-discrimination position, and Columbia, Yale, Harvard and UCLA may be in the process of doing so.

The Gay Men's Chorale gave a rousing holiday performance at the University Bay Meetinghouse in December. See page 4

See page 4

would contribute articles. Sue Burke became an important contributor of Milwaukee stories. Cristina Montes de Oca served for a long period as the sales representative. In April 1983, staff member Molly Doane authored an editorial, "Power Together." She wrote, "Like it or not, we are considered one 'homosexual' community to the outside world, and sometimes must present a unified front of information in order to influence that world." Her belief was that "by combining resources, lesbians and gay men can better begin to forge the coalitions necessary to overcome homophobia."[60]

In November 1983, for its first anniversary, the paper published a spoof sheet titled "IN!" Articles purportedly covered topics such as "Breeders Support Group Forming," "Wisconsin Records Its First HETS Death," and a "Straight Revolt at Stone Hearth" (across the street from the gay bar The Back Door). In addition to the spoof, staff reported a successful effort of steadily improving journalism, serious newsgathering, and improved credibility. The paper reprised the "IN!" spoof for its April Fools issue in 1984 with the story "Heterosexual Awareness Week Promises Much."[61]

By the second issue, the press run for *OUT!* was five thousand per issue, and by the end of the first year, it was at ten thousand. Though the paper was free at various locations, a year's subscription could be had for ten dollars. At one point, five hundred people had subscribed. A complimentary letter on the first issue, playfully headed "Keep It Up," praised the poetry and photo spread. Small grants were received from the Wisconsin Community Fund, the Chicago Resource Center, and the Wisconsin Student Association at UW–Madison. An issue in 1984 cited costs of three thousand dollars an issue, which would translate to a yearly budget of around thirty-six thousand dollars. Ad revenue provided 80 percent of the paper's revenue. Madison's feminist bookstore A Room of One's Own contributed a regular review of recommended reading on lesbian and gay topics, and Jeff Kirsch and Jane Vanderbosch reviewed gay and lesbian books.[62]

In 1986, Milwaukeean Sue Burke became editor. She had started as a volunteer reporter covering Milwaukee. Burke also worked on the *Sherman Park News*, was an officer in the National Organization for Women, and later joined the Governor's Council on Lesbian and Gay Issues. Kirsch became the Madison editor under Burke, and during the last days of the paper, he was listed as sole editor. Tim Tillotson of the Blue Bus Clinic coordinated regular gay health columns, including early information on the developing AIDS crisis.

OUT! was one of the Wisconsin gay publications to cover transsexuals. In the fourth issue, editor Brooks Egerton authored a piece, "What Do Gays and Transsexuals Have in Common?" He argued that because some gays feel they have now achieved "normal" status, they want distance from those who are still viewed as outsiders. The issue arose around "Theresa," a trans woman who was denied public welfare funds for reassignment surgery. Egerton observed those who cited fiscal constraints against funding the surgery are the same ones who cite fiscal constraints to deny gays and lesbians domestic partner benefits. Egerton panned deprogramming as false for both gays and transsexuals and called for solidarity. He ended with, "I'd like to think that Theresa, too, will be believed someday when she says she's a woman."[63]

The same issue included a piece by "Dragonfly," titled "What Does a Sex-Change Operation Change?" Dragonfly was acknowledged as a member of a Madison circle of "dykes, fairies, and friends." He argued that oppressive gender roles and inhuman standards of gender did not serve society and that we should not blame the person seeking to change his or her gender identity. Instead, "Our blame should be aimed instead at the mindless system we've all been crushed into, in which our differences become threats and don't receive the affirmation they deserve." The issue continued its coverage of transsexual issues with a story on a transsexual prisoner at the state prison in Waupun.[64]

By the fifth issue, the paper faced a crisis because it had outstripped its fundraising capacities and could not print all the news it had gathered. Two staffers were working full time, and volunteers gave countless hours, but everyone feared burnout. Motivating the call for support was the belief that "here, in the only state in the nation with a gay rights law, we must sustain a newspaper. How else do we get information about the work of Wisconsin's many lesbian and gay service and political groups?" The editors thought the need was great because the mainstream media suffered from "myopia," with hardly any favorable coverage of gay news.[65]

At the beginning of *OUT!*'s fifth year, the paper admitted it had weathered several financial crises and had a high turnover rate, but it was still standing when many alternative publications had failed. A letter to readers stated, "If this situation continues, we may not be able to." While the paper was fiscally sound, the Madison-based journalists were dealing with exhaustion and fatigue. The paper had also assumed the onerous duty and was now publishing obituaries of AIDS victims. This was during a time when mainstream media obituaries were often silent about AIDS. In July 1987, the paper announced that "*OUT!* is once again at a critical point in its history." A renewed call for volunteers and financial aid tried to sound hopeful. But the paper folded shortly after with the August 1987 issue as its last. Kirsch would go on to become editor of *The Wisconsin Light*, which took up the mantle for *OUT!* later that year.[66]

OUR HORIZONS: 1981–1982

The publication *OUR HORIZONS* was printed in Milwaukee beginning in September 1981. Initially produced in magazine format, it later switched to a tabloid layout. Shalom Enterprises, a business that also provided secretarial services, published it with Ralph Navarro as editor and Kevin Conaty and Rick Urban as associate editors. In January 1982, the publishers of *OUR HORIZONS* recognized Jamakaya of *Amazon* for her help in getting their publication on the road. The magazine acknowledged "the negative manner in which gay men have [treated] and continue to treat most women. We recognize the chauvinistic nature of men and cringe in acknowledgment at the narrowmindedness of gay men." Despite this statement, the magazine's coverage did not extend to women, perhaps because it lasted less than two years.[67]

Navarro had studied for the Catholic priesthood but abandoned seminary when he came out. Navarro was active in the gay community since 1980, and his obituary notice in the *Milwaukee Journal* described him as "one of the undeniable leaders in the early stages of the local gay movement." He helped found the Cream City Business Association, a gay and lesbian business group, and the Milwaukee AIDS Project. In December 1981, Navarro reported on a speech he had given to the Cream City Business Association, "A Very Gay Vision." Navarro explained, "It must be recalled that there is a difference between being gay and being a homosexual." "Gay vision" was not a "fantasy of you as the center of attention

Ralph Navarro was an early Milwaukee activist with the Cream City Business Association who also published *OUR HORIZONS*, a short-lived gay magazine.
CREAM CITY SPECIAL EDITION, SEPTEMBER 1983

in a six-month orgy!" but had to do with "your level of consciousness" as a gay-identified person. He specifically charged gay men to challenge "macho orientation and acculturation." His vision for Milwaukee included gay businesses working together, significant money flowing to gay and lesbian charities, and people being supportive of one another.[68]

OUR HORIZONS covered a range of topics and issues. Michael Lisowski wrote on political topics, including an article detailing Congress bowing to the Moral Majority by overturning the District of Columbia's law decriminalizing gay sex. In 1991, he would run as an out gay man for the Milwaukee School Board. Roger Gremminger, a doctor at the the BESTD Clinic, had a regular column on gay medicine. In addition to talking about disease treatment, Gremminger reported on his work with the Gay Public Health Worker's Caucus. One session the caucus sponsored was "The Gay Patient—Straight Health Care." Too often, it was reported that straight health-care providers harassed gay patients. Gremminger was elated to report in 1981 that Stan Matek, an openly gay man, had become president of the American Public Health Association at the national conference to which he had been a delegate.[69]

The December 9, 1981, issue claimed that another gay paper, *ESCAPE*, had lifted items from *OUR HORIZONS*, including its rather complete directory of bars and community organizations. The same issue posed the question, Why were there two gay/lesbian publications for Milwaukee? It reported on a meeting of the two editors and that they concluded with the agreement that "there was a need and value for both." According to *OUR HORIZONS*, "The purpose of *ESCAPE* is to provide Milwaukee and Wisconsin with coverage of socially oriented events and to bolster the

focus on certain bars." *ESCAPE* editor Erin Criss believed "that the social life of gay people is very important and they look to learn as much
as they can about it." In contrast, Navarro wrote, "*OUR HORIZONS* . . .
exists to provide people with news and news features about life as it im-
pacts the total gay/lesbian community." The publication was associated
with the National Gay Press Association. This enabled the magazine to
publish updates on the efforts to stop the antigay Family Protection Act.
Navarro believed that "what is most important is the building and uniting
of the Gay and Lesbian communities of Milwaukee and Wisconsin." To
reach a statewide readership, he asserted, "We need good writers in all of
Wisconsin's major cities."[70]

The last issue, dated February 5, 1982, led with a notice, "Until Later,"
that claimed this would be a temporary suspension of the paper. The
editors observed that the newspaper had been blackballed by select gay
bars, and both the Milwaukee Journal Company and radio stations had
refused their advertising. In its defense, they stated that the paper had been
founded to fill a void, presumably since the demise of *GPU News*. They
felt its purpose had been "to provide a source of local and national news
so that the growing groups within this state would feel a keen relationship
to the national and international gay/lesbian communities." Included was
a note on the expected and real interaction of Wisconsin's gay community
with national ideas and trends. "With expanding positive role models,"
the editors wrote, "people might begin to feel ever more comfortable in
relating to each other both professionally and personally."[71]

One consolation on the exit was that Navarro reported that *ESCAPE*
had agreed to expand coverage of news features that could lead to a unity
of focus within the community in one publication. Taking a final bow,
Navarro pledged his continuing community-building efforts would be
focused on the Cream City Business Association and the newly formed
political action committee, the Lambda Political Caucus.[72]

ESCAPE: 1982–1983

ESCAPE, begun a few months after *OUR HORIZONS*, had a very different
purpose from that of its once rival. Essentially, it functioned as a "bar rag"
focused on Milwaukee, but it was actually published in Chicago by a gay

Escape

Volume 1, Number 8 — Thursday, January 13, 1983 — **WISCONSIN**

Volleyball league is forming in Milwaukee
Page 3

Milwaukee has first gay-lesbian film fest

By Albert Williams

Milwaukee's first gay and lesbian film festival will be held Thursday, Jan. 27, through Saturday, Jan. 29, on the University of Wisconsin-Milwaukee campus.

The event is sponsored by Lavender Commitment, an on-campus gay arts group. "Milwaukee didn't have a gay film festival," said Lavender Commitment's Carl Szatmary, so his group, which had presented occasional screenings, set out to stir up interest in a festival at one of the city's movie theaters. After meeting with no strong response, says Szatmary, "We decided to just do it ourselves"—rent the films, arrange for the location, and publicize the festival.

The offerings range from commercial features to short, independent, sometimes experimental work. Thursday's films are geared especially toward women, Friday's program should appeal equally to lesbians and gay men.

The main features Thursday and Friday may strike some as questionable choices—*The Killing of Sister George* (1969) and *The Boys in the Band* (1970). Both films have been attacked as perpetuating stereotypes of gays as unhappy, unstable, unfaithful and unliberated. Certainly, they reflect the preliberation plight of homosexual lives.

Sister George (Thursday), based on Frank Marcus' play, is the tragi-comic account of a British TV soap opera star whose character is "killed off" after her public (lesbian) behavior becomes intolerably outrageous—and after her female boss takes a shine to her lover. The movie version has been disavowed and condemned by playwright Marcus and his wife, Jackie—herself a lesbian activist and arts critic for *London Gay*

News—for sensationalizing the play, in particular with what they consider a gratuitous sex scene between Susannah York (as "Sister George's" girlfriend) and Coral Browne (as the employer). There is no sex scene involving "Sister George" herself because the actress refused to do one. That actress, Beryl Reid, is the main reason for seeing the film. Reid created the role on stage. It was her first dramatic role (she was known as a variety performer until then), and she was brilliant in the part: gutsy, hilarious, and overwhelmingly moving. *Sister George* was directed by Robert Aldrich, whose other films include *Whatever Happened to Baby Jane* and *The Dirty Dozen*.

Accompanying *Sister George* on Thursday's bill are: *Pictures for Barbara* (1980-81), by California filmmaker Barbara Hammer, a celebrant of independent feminist spirituality and strength in opposition to the violence of the outside world; Hammer's *Super Dyke*, *Farewell to Charms*, by Carla Pontiac (1980), which, says Pontiac, "questions the goals of love and romance as a woman's ultimate fulfillment and offers the possibility of a richer and more challenging lifestyle"; and *I'm Not One of Them*, by Jan Oxenburg, whose films, writes critic Michelle Citron in *Jump Cut*, explore lesbianism in a broadly political context, "having to do with ideological mechanisms of socialization, male-female gender differentiation, cultural notions of romantic love, and being an outsider."

The Boys in the Band (Friday), like *Sister George*, is based on a hit play. Set among the New York East Side gay crowd, Mart Crowley's comedy recounts the activities at a gay party into which walks a (questionably) heterosexual friend

of the host. Full of venom, self-pity, pot, booze, and movie trivia, the "boys" lacerate themselves and each other. If nothing else, *Boys in the Band* serves as a testament to how far we've come. Featuring the original New York cast (including Leonard Frey, Kenneth Nelson, Cliff German, Laurence Luckinbill, and Donald Coombs), it remains one of the finest pieces of ensemble acting in movies. Its director, William Friedkin, gained notoriety with a later gay-themed film, the brutal and exploitative *Cruising*; this film, however, showcases his main strength as a filmmaker—capturing the interaction between characters and their environment.

Also on Friday's program, a more recent and less unbalanced view of a gay male relationship: *We Were One Man*, French director Philippe Vallois' 1978 drama about a reclusive Frenchman who is brought out of his shell by his attraction to a wounded Nazi soldier during World War II. The film won the Silver Hugo at the 1980 Chicago International Film Festival, and also has been shown at the Cannes and Berlin festivals and the San Francisco and New York gay film festivals.

Foolish Things, by New Zealand's Peter Wells, will not be shown as previously announced.

Saturday's program is definitely a mixed bag. *Greetings from Washington, D.C.*, by Lucy Winer, is a buoyant documentary of the 1979 National March on Washington for Lesbian and Gay Rights, winning praise for its adroit handling of a volatile theme with sensitivity and uncompromising artfulness. And *Whatever Happened to Susan Jane?* (1982), by Marc Huestis, revels in the San Francisco drag-punk scene, contrasting its present-day "outsiders" to the characters in a '50s youth training film, *The Outsider*, which

film fest

The Boys In The Band

is intercut with Huestis' own footage.

All programs start at 7:30 p.m. at the University of Wisconsin-Milwaukee Student Union, 2200 E. Kenwood Blvd. Thursday's and Friday's screenings are in the union's Wisconsin Room, Saturday's in the Fireside Lounge. A suggested donation of $3 ($2 for students) is requested.

Illustration by Garth

Men from motorcycle and leather/Levi's clubs all over the upper Midwest will gather in Green Bay, Wis., for *Winterquest '83* Jan. 14-16. This is the 9th annual Winterquest, hosted by the Argonauts of Wisconsin L/L club. Joe Maffeo, in charge of registration for the affair, told *Escape* that registrations are coming in strong—local housing is full, and area motels are filling up. The new host is Friday Jan. 14, at the Body Shop bar in Green Bay, with a welcoming party and late registration. An anniversary party will be hosted by the Castaways M.C. of Milwaukee in the clubhouse. Saturday morning eye-openers will be hosted by the Minneapolis S/M club. After lunch, a program of games begins, including "Las Vegas style gambling," said Joe—where you can sell your clothes for gambling "money"—and a scavenger hunt. In the evening, the Body Shop will host cocktails, followed by a banquet. An after-hours party Saturday will be hosted by the 1301 bar of Appleton. Sunday morning eye-openers will be hosted by the Black Guard of Minneapolis. Along the way, noted Joe, there will be plenty of "extracurricular activities. It's sure to be an action-packed weekend—said Joe. "We just have fun." For more information, contact the Body Shop at (414) 435-5476.

Music Update
Kim Zweibohmer

Happy New Year and best wishes for a healthful, happy time in '83—dance music-wise!

One album that's a must for your collection is Sylvester's *All I Need* (Megatone). This finds him in his glory, with his most consistent, interesting album since the late '70s. There are fast songs—"Be With You," "Won't You Let Me Love You"—and slow funk like "All I Need" and the two real killers, "Don't Stop" and "Tell Me," which peak in glorious harmony. Of course, there is a rock cut, "Hard Up," which makes this album work so well. Hot!

Modern Romance's "The Best Years of Our Lives" (Atlantic 12-inch), not as effective as their last album, sounds like a pop single—much like ABC. It's mixed by Richie Rivera, who contributes a long, dark break-down passage and reverses the layout on the B side. Give it a listen.

Divine's "Shoot Your Shot" (O 12-inch) should please the cult that made "Native Love," a long-term sleeper hit; this has a much more energetic feel. Also, the flip, "Jungle Jezebel," is a rap that renews the meaning of "vicious."

And finally, a new "old" song gearing up for lots of club play is "The Beat Goes On," by Orbit (Atlantic/RFC). The old Sonny and Cher number gets a drastic update with synthesizers and vocals. Very clever and very rhythmic.

Top Fifteen

1. IT'S RAINING MEN	Weather Girls
2. NIPPLE TO THE BOTTLE	Grace Jones
3. THE LOOK OF LOVE (remix)	ABC
4. LIES	Thompson Twins
5. PLAYING FOR TIME	Madleen Kane
6. MIND WARP (all cuts)	Patrick Cowley
7. THRILLER (all cuts)	Michael Jackson
8. ALL I NEED (all cuts)	Sylvester
9. SHE HAS A WAY	Bobby "O"
10. I'M SO EXCITED	Pointer Sisters
11. THE HARD LOVER	Loverde
12. KEEP THE FIRE BURNING	Gwen McCrae
13. PASS THE DUTCHIE	Musical Youth
14. DO YOU REALLY WANT TO HURT ME?	Culture Club
15. MICKEY	Toni Basil

This issue of *ESCAPE*, published from Milwaukee but with Chicago ties, features the gay and lesbian film festival—one of the long-running gay cultural events of Beer City.
ESCAPE, JANUARY 13, 1983

publisher. Its early distribution consisted of an insert in *Gay Life*, also published in Chicago. In a letter to readers, the publisher noted, "The tie between Wisconsin and Illinois is a strong and beneficial one—socially, politically, and economically." The list of ties included Milwaukee contingents in Chicago's Gay and Lesbian Pride Parade, sports enthusiasts going to one another's events, and bar crawl parties. Wisconsin's leadership in the gay rights bill, in decriminalizing sodomy, and in promoting interaction between gay leaders and elected officials meant "more gay news—news that readers in and out of Wisconsin need to know."[73]

An important Milwaukee connection for *ESCAPE* was Ron Geiman, a sales associate, photographer, and writer. For some months, Geiman's Wisconsin column covered bar crawl updates and small pieces on gay news. Paul Cotton also wrote gay news stories for *ESCAPE* after the demise of *OUR HORIZONS*, traveling around the state to follow leads. Popular Milwaukee DJ Kim Zweibohmer covered music, and Tom Salzsieder, a founder of the gay Saturday Softball Beer League, covered gay sports, with many teams sponsored by local gay bars. An extensive daily calendar listed bar events. The paper also covered the Holiday Invitational Tournament bowling festival, with many teams also sponsored by the bars.[74]

More regular news coverage included a cover article on Milwaukee's first gay and lesbian film fest in January 1983 and a report by editor Erin Criss on bartending in the Douglas Dunes gay resort in Michigan. Though the newspaper ran only through 1983, it showed the strong desire to have gay publications circulate both news and socially focused items.[75]

IN STEP: 1984–2003

With the demise of *ESCAPE*, publisher Ron Geiman launched a new Milwaukee-based publication in February 1984 that shared some of the features of a bar rag but was much more substantial in the gay news it carried. Initially, Dave Iraci served as co-editor/publisher, but after a year, Geiman was left as both editor and publisher. His tenure would last until 1995. Both men were victims of AIDS. Iraci died at the age of thirty-three in 1990. Geiman would live many years HIV positive. Upon Geiman's passing in 2004, director of the Wisconsin AIDS Support Network Doug Nelson said, "He really captured the essence of the community and its growth."[76]

In Step's regular distribution was eight thousand copies, though the publication had a rocky start with a three-month hiatus in its first year. A survey in 1984 claimed readership was at thirty thousand with a large percentage of readers who did not identify as gay. Many of the same venues distributing *OUT!* also distributed *In Step*. The magazine came out bi-weekly on alternate Thursdays, presumably in time to make weekend plans based on the information it carried. Of its dual purpose as a news outlet, Geiman indicated that the "social/lifestyle magazine was not intended to compete with *OUT!*" in news.[77]

During its first year, the magazine was known as *WisconsIN Step*, a nod to its statewide reach. Later it would be known simply as *In Step*. The directory of gay bars and organizations included in each issue reflected establishments across the state, with a heavy emphasis on Milwaukee. The magazine accepted advertising, but the editor made clear that "the appearance by anyone or any advertiser in this magazine does not reflect one's own sexual orientation whatsoever." Additionally, the editor reserved "the right to refuse advertisements . . . considered to be exploitive of the gay and lesbian community." One example of this was clubs with discriminatory policies of hosting "gay nights" one or two evenings a week.[78]

Editor Tom Rezza, subsequently called "one of the premier Gay artists in Wisconsin," contributed "Gay Side" cartoons and many cover illustrations for this and other gay publications. Geiman's regular column, Steppin' Out, featured social news. The magazine sponsored bar crawls, and pictures of gay men and, occasionally, women appeared alongside the announcements. Writers who had contributed to previous gay publications also wrote for *In Step*: Kim Zweibohmer on music and Tom Salzsieder on Jock Shorts, a sports column. A fun feature was Graffiti, where short messages were printed for free. One such post read, "Madison: Yes, that was the other *In Step* editor eating a dog biscuit and licking boots. *One Who Knows*."[79]

Antler (Brad Burdick), a poet who had recently returned to Milwaukee from San Francisco, submitted poems for publication. One titled "Bringing Zeus to His Knees" described a bare-chested boy sun-basking at a disarmament rally. One of the best lines reflected in the title spoke of "the dazzling sight of naked boyhood armpits and chest and belly and face that would bring Zeus to his knees."[80]

WISCONSIN STEP

WIs

February 9-22, 1984
Volume 1, Issue 1

DEVOTED TO THE HEARTLAND'S GAYS & LESBIANS

— Our Premiere Issue —

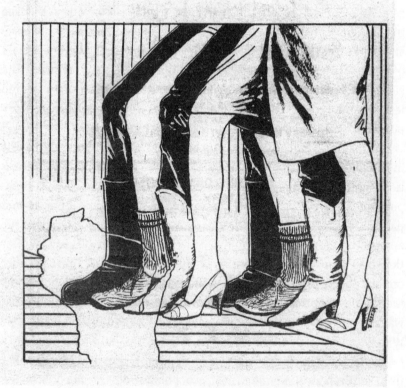

The premiere issue of *In Step* showed LGBT people marching "Forward" for rights. It echoes back to the *GPU News* logo of multiple lambdas marching together. *IN STEP*, FEBRUARY 9—22, 1984, COURTESY OF TOM REZZA

W. W. Wells III was a regular contributor. In 1989, under his Juicy Bits byline, he ran a spoof piece, "1069EZ Gay Income Tax Return." Among the choices of filing status was "presently single but filing jointly with the 5 boyfriends I had during the year." Among the imagined deductions were "a) flowers if purchased to cover-up indiscretion, b) gave lover my dessert, and c) was nice to his parents over Christmas (estimated deduction worth $213.40)." If you flirted with your lover's ex-boyfriend, you were to add thirty-five dollars to your taxes.[81]

In addition to covering gay news in Wisconsin, *In Step* weighed in on issues in its editorials. It supported a recommendation by the Governor's Council on Lesbian and Gay Issues to have Governor Tony Earl create a full-time gay liaison position. It deemed it newsworthy when Milwaukee's first "open window" gay bar opened in the M&M Club in 1984. In 1984, the magazine published "*In Step*'s Program for Our Concerns," penned by Geiman. Among the ten concerns listed were housing for low-income AIDS patients, the passage of the Equal Rights Amendment, and the pressing need for a national gay rights law. Also on the list was "an active, on-going building of an overall 'Network' between all the state's gay and lesbian groups." From the beginning, the magazine had strong AIDS coverage, with back-to-back articles in April and May 1984 titled "AIDS Find Reported" and "AIDS Is Here." It was not lost on the editors that the epidemic hit Wisconsin coincident with its publication.[82]

In 1984, Kathleen Nichols, who was cochair of the Governor's Council on Lesbian and Gay Issues, remarked that *In Step* was just a publication for "barflies," a comment that was refuted in the next issue of the magazine. While they admitted *In Step* was a "lifestyle, social, and entertainment oriented magazine," the editors maintained that *In Step* was an important facet of the well-rounded coverage of Wisconsin's gay and lesbian community. The editorial, titled "Barflies," stated bars and other social settings were the front line for gay interaction. Regarding boundaries, the editors stated, "We are not a sleazy publication—and for the record—we don't show genitals. Occasionally something 'borderline' may appear, but that is always weighed against the rest of what we publish." In later years, ads for gay phone-sex lines would appear.[83]

The editorial comment went on the offensive and noted, "Realistic assessment of the size of the 'activists/politically correct' gay and lesbian community are not very high. If members of all the state's gay and lesbian organizations were totaled up and all the duplicates (those belonging to more than one organization) were weeded out, the tally would bring embarrassing results." Miriam Ben-Shalom also joined the editors in critiquing the barfly comment as a faux pas by a political roué. Ben-Shalom claimed it would throw out of the movement the 95 percent who were not part of any organization and demanded Nichols's resignation from the Governor's Council on Lesbian and Gay Issues.[84]

The barfly identity question would be an ongoing issue in the magazine. In 1990, John Jahn would write in a letter that one should not assume that Milwaukeeans who do not crowd into the gay bars "somehow don't want to participate in the community." Jahn had marched with five thousand others in the city's gay pride parade but also agreed "there could have been more of us marching that day." His conclusion, implicitly critical of bar patrons, was that "there will always be those of us who may get the Gay Liberation message and choose to ignore it anyway." Geiman had strong ties with the party-hardy crowd through his stories on gay bar life around the state, but he was a serious and politically aware contributor to the creation of knowledge about Wisconsin gay life. When he became ill in 1995, the magazine transitioned to new owners and a different format, finally ceasing publication in 2003.[85]

HAG RAG, 1987–1993

Begun in 1987 in Milwaukee, *Hag Rag* bore the tagline "Wisconsin's Lesbian-Feminist Press." An early issue included a cover illustration with the caption, "CRONE: Great Hag of History, who has Dis-covered depths of Courage, Strength, and Wisdom in her Self." *Hag Rag* was a successor to *Amazon* and had some of the same staff. One of the new editors observed the previous publication had ended in burnout, with a loss of writers and a decrease of fervor for the cause: "Part of the old guard, the radical feminists who founded it, went off and did other things." *Hag Rag* sought to pick up the challenges of political education, feminist theory, and analysis of lesbian feminism to counter Reaganism and creeping conservatism. "We want to combat that slide back into the closet. We have to keep struggling,"

said another editor. The Crone's Nest collective that published it included .
Mary Frank, Betty Edwards, Doreen Riley, Justice Fire, and Lance.[86]

Issues were proudly "produced and controlled entirely by lesbians."
There was a sliding scale for subscriptions from six dollars to fifteen dollars annually for the bimonthly publication. It covered the National Conference of Witches and included a health column, At Your Cervix. *Hag
Rag* welcomed submissions dealing with "lesbophobia, separatism, class
and economics, feminist analysis, [and] the world wide lesbian conspiracy." Initially begun in Milwaukee, by the January 1988 issue and with the
move of one of the editors to Madison, the magazine "decided to expand
our format to include news and calendar coverage of the entire state. If
you know of individual wimmin or dyke organizations in other areas of
Wisconsin," it continued, "please let us know." It also called for articles
on "creating lesbian community" and "creating rituals for community
building." One question in this vein was, "Can Girl Scout ceremonies be
adapted to Dyke Scouts?"[87]

Mary Frank, a Milwaukee member of the collective, contributed "Myths
about Separatism" in which she claimed, "Separatism is the way we discern
and remove our Selves from the patterns of patriarchy." It was "a positive
choice to live free." For Frank, "What Separatists have in common is that we
want most of all to be with other Lesbians, and not with men." She believed
that "'out' Separatists are rare and ostracized by other Lesbians nearly as
often as we are harassed by men," and she "soon realized that Separatists are
the 'bad girls' of the Dyke community. . . . In Milwaukee," she continued, "I
can count the 'out Separatists' I know on two hands." Frank feared that "the
myths of Separatism permeate our lesbian community, acting as a cancer
to weaken and divide us from other women."[88]

The magazine also covered Madison's annual Lesbian Variety Show,
held for many years at the Barrymore Theater. Chris Buss had gotten the
idea after attending a lesbian festival in West Berlin provocatively named "I
Got This Way From Kissing Girls." The initial show in 1986 was held at the
senior center where five hundred people crowded into a room with a capacity for three hundred. After it shifted to the Barrymore, dyke artwork was
displayed in the theater lobby, and a group of women known as the Raging
Hormones took the stage partially nude, despite garnering criticism for
being politically incorrect. According to *Hag Rag*, they thought of it as

$1.50

VOLUME 3   NUMBER 3
NOVEMBER-DECEMBER 9988

HAG RAG

WISCONSIN'S LESBIAN-FEMINIST PRESS

New Rage Thinking

Fight Back!

"Dykes to Watch Out For" in This Issue

Hag Rag, an openly lesbian feminist magazine, replaced the earlier *Amazon* as a women's magazine from Milwaukee. Based on the cover art, Amazons were still a part of the collective imagination. *HAG RAG*, NOVEMBER/DECEMBER 1988

"mooning the patriarchy." A review of the 1987 show noted that twenty acts were squeezed into three and a half hours, featuring the musical duo of Lynette (known by her first name) and Jane Reynolds. Merle Graybill showed a documentary slide show on the work experience of black womyn with a score by Sweet Honey in the Rock. The next year, praise went to musicians the Hardly Sisters, Kelly White, and Mary Waitrovich. That year, people were turned away because the house was full. Several years later, Jamakaya would complain that the now five-hour show was overlong.[89]

The September/October 1988 issue of *Hag Rag* was heralded as the "Lesbian Sex Issue." Collective member Lance wrote "The Discussion of Sex in the Lesbian Press" based on a paper she had presented at the Society for the Scientific Study of Sex. She recalled her days at *Amazon*, which was "produced by some very hard-working lesbians who rarely felt comfortable identifying the paper as a lesbian newspaper, trying instead to appeal to 'all women.'" Given the editors' timidity, *Amazon* could "hardly be expected to address the topic of lesbian sex." She believed that "we NEED to talk about our sexuality, our sexual behaviors and practices." Topics on her list included orgasms, sex toys, the "G" spot, abuse, and power. Lance believed the lesbian press was the proper place to discuss sexuality despite what she termed ambivalence "to boldly go where no lesbians . . . have gone before." In the same issue, Sue Burke contributed a review article titled "*Lesbian Sex* and *Lesbian Passion*: Laugh a Little and Improve Your Sex Life." Her thesis in reviewing the two books was "Lesbians don't have enough sex, don't have enough variety in our sex, don't know how to talk about sex, don't know how to ask for sex." She noted that JoAnn Loulan, a psychotherapist and sex educator known as "the Dr. Ruth of dykedom," was coming to Milwaukee to present a comedy show, "What's So Funny about Lesbian Sex?"[90]

In the November/December 1988 issue, Mary Klobucar of Madison contributed an article on self-defense, "Frozen in Fear or Filled with Power?" For her, "Inside each of us is a wise and strong self who has the power and energy to protect and defend herself. Until violence against women and children stops, we each need to nurture this self." Klobucar was identified as "a second-generation Lesbian feminist" and director of the Chimera Self-Defense program at Madison's Rape Crisis Center.[91] The same issue included an article by Justin Fire and described the social scene during a summer evening at the Beer Garden, a popular lesbian bar in Milwaukee. The author went "to shoot the shit for a while, flirt, and catch up on everybody's news." The pleasantness of the evening was upset when a "bunch of puds" entered the dance floor. An asterisk explained that *puds* or *pudbusters* was a local terminology for "dickbrain," meaning the type of men who went to a lesbian bar to leer and be obnoxious. It was also explained that *jerk* was local terminology equivalent to "pee pee head" or "dickstick," derogative terms for obnoxious men. In this instance, after a lesbian and her friends pushed back, the bartender threw the men out. Whether this slang usage was used more broadly than in Wisconsin needs further research.[92] *Hag Rag*, which continued publication until 1993, marked a bold and memorable foray into some of the more provocative topics of feminist lesbianism.

AMONG FRIENDS: 1985–1989

Among Friends was the work of Jay Hatheway (formally listed in the masthead as Joseph G. Hatheway Jr.), at the time a graduate student and teaching assistant at UW–Madison. Its tagline ran, "Networks and Resources for Gays and Lesbian of Rural Wisconsin." Hatheway envisioned *Among Friends* as an organization, of which he was director, whose purpose was "to connect rural gays through a newsletter and help them form social networks to ease their loneliness—right in their own hometowns." The monthly publication, though initially offered at no cost, subsequently carried an annual cost of ten dollars, a fee that would vary over its life. The format shifted between a newsletter and a magazine format. It had articles of general interest, lists of support professionals willing to work with gays, calendars of events, and a personal contacts column.[93]

Hatheway grew up in Iran and Italy and served as a Green Beret until a court martial and a less than honorable discharge for homosexuality ended his military career. On living in Wisconsin, Hatheway remarked, "My attitude is essential, this is a state in which it's legal to be gay, so let's be gay. I've never lived in an environment where the law says you can be gay, so let's enjoy it." There was a little flurry when the state's tourism effort adopted the slogan "Wisconsin—You're Among Friends." Madison's

Among friends

October 1987

News Magazine
for Gays and Lesbians of the Upper Midwest

Inside:

Beginnings

George Segal's
"Gay Liberation"

Cleanliness is
next to . . .
Impossible!

Book Reviews

While the cities of Madison and Milwaukee had many gay media publications, *Among Friends* was aimed at a more isolated rural audience that needed both news and referrals to friendly service providers. *AMONG FRIENDS*, OCTOBER 1987

Capital Times ran a story headline, "Will New Tourism Slogan Make Us the 'Gay State'?" Hatheway planned to thank Governor Thompson for the publicity.[94]

Hatheway stated, *"Among Friends* is an attempt to reduce isolation. How do you meet other gays and lesbians if you live God-knows-where?" He believed that "loneliness makes people neurotic, it makes them do crazy things. Gays are not unstable. It's the kind of society we're socialized to." By its own description, subscribers tended to be older males who were socially isolated. In 1986, the mailing list approached twenty-five hundred, and the paper claimed contacts in 108 communities in Wisconsin.[95]

Beck Schwitz, identified as president of Baraboo Area Gays and Lesbians, wrote an article on "Small Town Advantages" in March 1986. The same issue included a list of towns that had informal support groups, including Ashland, Rhinelander, Ripon, Platteville, and Rice Lake. At that time, all these towns had colleges that may have helped the local atmosphere. An April 1988 issue profiled Ron Bodoh and his partner Larry Henke. Ron was well known for his uniquely carved quartz crystals that were sold by mail order. Larry was a jewelry designer. Together, they had restored an old school house in the rural town of Albion for their home business.[96]

In October 1987, the magazine acknowledged five months of silence since its previous issue. The situation was described as "touch-and-go." Hatheway noted with the demise of *OUT!*, his publication was now the only statewide gay and lesbian publication. The orientation would now be both rural and urban with the tagline, "News Magazine for Gays and Lesbians of the Upper Midwest." This was the case for the next brief period of several more issues before the publication closed its doors.[97]

THE WISCONSIN LIGHT: 1987–2000

For a decade and a half, *The Wisconsin Light* would be the mainstay newspaper for the LGBT community in Wisconsin. The first issue appeared November 20, 1987, with its masthead bearing the banner, "Give the People Light and They Will Find Their Own Way." Publisher Jerry Johnson and executive editor Terry Boughner were life partners who put their hearts, souls, and minds into the endeavor. The first issue displayed a triangular logo over the words "Serving America's Gay Rights State" and was dedicated "to the Lesbian/Gay community of all Wisconsin." "Wish us luck, Gay/Lesbian Wisconsin," Johnson and Boughner wrote, "in giving you a paper worthy of the Badger State." With these words was the clear assumption within Wisconsin that a state gay community existed and even thrived.[98]

Though *Among Friends* editor Jay Hatheway had claimed his paper would pick up the mantle for *OUT!*, the initial issue of *The Wisconsin Light* named itself as successor: "The Wisconsin Light Succeeds OUT!" Some continuity was maintained by asking *OUT!*'s last editor, Jeff Kirsch, to be the new paper's Madison editor. Marc Haupert, Bob Melig, Karen Colleran, Peter Johnson, and Ron Geiman were also credited with helping to launch the new paper. They pledged themselves to objective reporting and to seeking the talented writers they believed the "Wisconsin Gay/Lesbian community has available to it and in such abundance." The article on the launch promised, "In pursuit of excellence, LIGHT will determinedly seek to become a forum for ideas of the most diverse nature and of every kind."[99]

The Wisconsin Light's understanding of its role was explicitly described in its first editorial: "We, as other papers do, will be a voice of the Lesbian/Gay community to itself and to the world." This important work was designed "to let our community continue the ongoing process of creating its own definition of itself, thus removing that power from the words and hands of others." The paper saw its role as pivotal for the community "in its efforts to be informed and in its desire to define itself."[100]

The first issue included the story "Wisconsin Marches on Washington DC" by Bill Meunier, who would become an important gay political journalist in the state. The article reported on the Wisconsin contingent marching in the Second National March on Washington for Lesbian and Gay Rights, which took place on October 11,1987. As Meunier reported, Badger pride and identity was shown through the chant, "WIS-CON-SIN the Gay Rights State." He wrote, "Throughout the March route, many of the thousands lining the street joined in the chant as gays and lesbians from throughout America saluted our state and expressed their appreciation for the hope we have given them."[101]

The price for an annual subscription was fifteen dollars, and it came with a number of regular features. Four Star Fiction and Video in Madison, the Schwartz Bookshops in Milwaukee, and Webster's Books in

VOLUME ONE NO. 1 NOVEMBER 20, 1987   FREE

Give the People Light and they will find their own way.

The Wisconsin Light

MILWAUKEE HOSTS H.I.T.

Jeff Clark, Banquet Chair and member of the Board of the Holiday Invitational Tournament (HIT) talked enthusiastically with LIGHT about the up-coming bowling tournament.

"We are," he said, "the oldest Gay bowling tournament in the country. We call ourselves the Granddaddy of them all." Though other such tournaments are held across the country, "We started it all", he said.

That's quite an accomplishment and this will be the ninth such tournament for HIT. Clark said that some 50 teams, 250 bowlers, are expected in Milwaukee over the Thanksgiving weekend (November 25-29). They'll be coming to the Cream City from such places as New York City, Cincinnati, Dallas, the West Coast and points in between.

While the competition is intensely serious, there will be plenty of fun beginning with a Welcome Party on the 25th at Jo's Place bar. On Thursday, there'll be another welcome party at "Dance, Dance, Dance."

But the "big bash" will come Saturday night at the Crystal Ballroom of the Marc Plaza Hotel, which is serving as the host hotel for the tournament. This is the Awards Dinner and will begin with cocktails at 5:00 p.m., followed by dinner at 6:30 p.m., with the ceremony and entertainment at 8:00 p.m.

This year's entertainment will include HIT Company '87, a lip-synch group, the Cream City Chorus, and Mr. and Miss Gay Wisconsin, Scott and Miss M.

Awards will include trophies for first, second and third places, Doubles and Singles events, Team Events and All Events.

The winners will receive $1000.00 for first place, $500.00 for first place Doubles, $300.00 for first place Singles and $200.00 for first place in All Events. ▼

KASTENMEIER ADMITS ERROR IN VOTING

Washington, D.C.- Congressman Bob Kastenmeier (D-Madison) stated in a press release issued November 13, 1987 that he had erred in his vote approving the anti-Gay language of Senator Jesse Helms.

According to the statement issued by Kastenmeier, "When the House asked for a conference with the Senate on the Labor-HHS-Education appropriations bill, it agreed to a motion offered by Congressman Dannemeyer of California to instruct the House conferees to agree to language offered by Senator Helms and accepted by the Senate to prohibit the use of Federal funds appropriated to the Centers for Disease Control to provide information or prevention materials and activities that promote or encourage, directly or indirectly, homosexual sexual activities.

"As a member of the House, I have cast thousands of votes and I feel able to justify three votes. However, the sheer volume of votes and time constraints may cast doubt upon how wisely, how well thought out, each vote is made. In this instance, I, along with the rest of the Wisconsin delegation, voted for the motion to instruct the House conferees. I did so because of privacy concerns and I do not believe that the Federal government should promote any form of a life style.

"Since casting this vote on October 20, I have given this matter further thought. The homosexual community has been the subject of considerable discrimination and "gay bashing." It causes me concern that the Helms language will be viewed by the gay community and others as a further effort to discriminate against the homosexual community by preventing information from being distributed in the campaign to try to reduce the incidence of AIDS. Mention was made during the brief House debate on this vote that very graphic information is being distributed in New York in order to instruct people on how they could avoid getting AIDS. While some are offended by this information, it is arguably necessary in order to bring home the harsh facts of AIDS.

"Upon reflection, considering all, I do not feel that supporting the Dannemeyer motion can be justified. My vote, therefore, was the wrong one." ▼

KENNEDY NAMED TO HIGH COURT

WASHINGTON, D.C. (WBS) - Anthony Kennedy, judge of the 9th Circuit U.S Court of Appeals, was nominated by President Reagan on November 11, 1987 to the Supreme Court. He is Reagan's third nominee to fill the vacancy on the high court.

According to Legal Times reporters Aaron Freiwald and Terence Moran, Kennedy was on the verge of being nominated to the court on October 27 when he was passed over in favor of Douglas Ginsburg. The report states that Kennedy failed to get the nod when key conservative senators read Kennedy's opinion in a case upholding a Navy policy banning Gays. In the case, Beller v. Middendorf, Kennedy wrote that "the Navy's blanket rule requiring discharge of all who have engaged in homosexual conduct is perhaps broader than necessary to accomplish some of its goals ..."

"Upholding the challenged [Navy] regulations is constitutional," concluded Kennedy, writing for the three-judge panel, "is distinct from a statement that they are wise."

Continued on Page 15

SAL MINEO: SEE STORY ON PAGE 9

Madison may become the third city in the country to pass an alternative families ordinance, which would extend traditional family benefits to gay and lesbian couples, unmarried heterosexuals and people with disabilities and their attendants.

Chief sponsor of the bill, District 8 Alderman Jim McFarland, publicly announced that he is gay in a November 4 interview with The Capital Times. McFarland becomes the fourth openly elected official in Dane County to announce his or her homosexuality.

McFarland believes that the alternative family ordinance has a "good chance" of passing. It currently has six other sponsors besides McFarland and needs only five more votes to achieve a majority on the 22-member City Council.

A public hearing will be held on the issue on January 5, before the matter comes up for a council vote. In the case of a tie, Mayor Joseph Sensenbrenner would cast the deciding vote. So far, Sensenbrenner has not given his opinion on the proposed piece of legislation.

If the bill were to become law, alternative families would be able to rent housing in areas which have only single-family zoning, receive sick and bereavement leaves granted to traditional families, get health insurance coverage if one member is a city employee and obtain family memberships in public organizations.

Berkeley and West Hollywood, California are the only two cities in the country which have currently passed such legislation.

McFarland joins a group of approximately twenty public elected officials in the country who have openly declared their homosexuality and is one of only two Republicans in the group. Madison and Dane County currently have more openly gay/lesbian publicly elected officials than any other city or county in the country. The Dane County list also includes District 6 County Supervisor Dick Wagner, District 2 Supervisor Kathleen Nichols and District 8 Supervisor Tammy Baldwin.

McFarland is a senior at UW-Madison majoring in International Relations and hails from Wauwatosa. His lover, who accompanied him at a press conference the morning following the publication of the Capital Times interview, is Rick Vilasenor, also a UW-Madison, senior, who has been active in the Task Force for ROTC Reform and has been President of the Ten Percent Society, the UW-Madison lesbian/gay student organization. ▼

TESTING POSITIVE MAY BREAK UP A RELATIONSHIP

Researchers at the University of California in San Francisco reported in the October 9 issue of the Journal of the American Medical Association that Gay men in San Francisco who test positive for AIDS antibody were "more likely to have their primary relationship break up."

The research project, supported in part by the National Institute of Mental Health, studied 502 Gay and bisexual men in San Francisco between November 1984 and November 1986. By November 1986, 40.8 percent of the men had taken the antibody test and more than half of those tested positive. According to the researchers, "significantly higher rates" of unsafe sex were reported by this group -- and those who tested negative or who did not take the test -- in November 1984 before the antibody test was available.

"The results of this study indicate that antibody testing may have useful public health outcomes," said the researchers. However, noted the researchers, those who tested positive suffered "potentially adverse mental health" problems, including "significant increases in stress and depression."

—Lisa M. Keen ▼

The first issue of *The Wisconsin Light* featured the Holiday Invitational Tournament, or HIT, a bowling event hosted in Milwaukee. For the home city of Laverne and Shirley, a more appropriate gay event could hardly have been designed. *THE WISCONSIN LIGHT,* NOVEMBER 20, 1987

Milwaukee contributed to the paper's list of bestselling gay and lesbian books. Gremminger became a medical columnist. Jamakaya, the prolific lesbian writer, provided Sister News and Views and later her own byline column. Dr. Karen Lamb had a regular column, often focused on health and AIDS issues. By the 1990s, the paper carried the syndicated cartoon

Dykes to Watch Out For by nationally known writer Alison Bechdel. The *Light* carried much more advertising than previous gay media, which contributed to its stability. The publisher, Johnson, was also listed as handling advertising. The paper was successful in getting gay professionals who offered mainstream services to buy ads.[102]

Publishing the first issue was not without drama. Three days before press time, the printer backed out. Though the job had been approved by the shop manager, the owner discovered it was a "sinful" publication and refused to go ahead. Due to the short turnaround, there was no choice but to take the paper to Chicago. The second issue's editorial, "Bigotry Snaps Its Head," deplored the "snot-nosed bigotry" that led this and another printer to refuse their business. The editors noted the paper "is no one's idea of a porn mag, no 'hot' pictures, no stories of simmering sensuality." They concluded, "It is these people who are the true perverts, the seducers of the young. To combat this sickness must be our top priority."[103]

Yet financial realities could impinge on editorial preferences. In a May 13, 1988, piece from The Editor's Desk, Boughner explained some of the economics of the "free" paper. Each issue cost several thousand dollars to produce. To date, they had not broken even. The publisher and editor had sunk five thousand dollars of their own money into the project during the first six months. All labor was on a volunteer basis; the mainstay had to be advertising. Boughner made the difficult decision to print the phone-sex ads with the claim, "We don't accept all of them and work closely as may be with these advertisers to make the ads as tasteful as possible." Nevertheless, ads with minimally clad males and phone numbers were attention grabbing. In an editorial Boughner lamented, "Well (he said with a sigh), I'm just old enough and cynical enough to believe that principles are great but they don't 'pay the freight,' when it comes to a newspaper." The realities of capitalism held true even in an idealistic movement.[104]

Over the years, *The Wisconsin Light* maintained good relations with *In Step*, its sister publication out of Milwaukee. In 1990, the two publications jointly hosted a media workshop, Getting the Word Out, as part of Gay/Lesbian Press Awareness Month. The workshop effort was recognized with the President's Award from the gay press association. Boughner took editorial note in *The Wisconsin Light* of Geiman as "a great guy" and wished him a belated happy birthday. That same year, *The Wisconsin Light* sent a Valentine with hearts and flowers "to all those in the Lesbian and Gay print and electronic media who strive to keep us informed and raise the consciousness of both straight and Gay people." *The Wisconsin Light* recognized *In Step, Hag Rag, Among Friends, Leaping La Crosse News, Feminist Voices*, and the cable programs *Tri-Cable Tonight* and *Nothing to Hide* with the statement, "Here in Wisconsin it is good to know that we have some of the best examples [of gay media] in the country."[105]

The early success of the paper was reflected in a November 3, 1988, editorial note: "An editor of an eastern Gay paper called praising Wisconsin Lesbians and Gays for our up-front political activity and awareness. 'We didn't ever know you (in Wisconsin) existed,' he said and then added, 'Maybe we can learn from you.'" Boughner mused, "Over and over again in amazement I have asked, 'Doesn't Wisconsin know what it's got?'" To Boughner, the usual answer was, "No, not really." But he certainly did. In a 1988 Thanksgiving meditation, Boughner expressed his gratitude: "I will be thankful too that I am a part of the entire Wisconsin Lesbian/Gay family."[106]

The Wisconsin Light provided a forum for different parts of the LGBT community to engage critically with one another. Subjects that had been taboo in earlier publications were fair game. One letter writer replied to a female letter writer who had asserted that drag typified "sexist stereotypes." Turning the argument around, he argued, "The reason a man—whatever his sexual orientation—can be oppressed for his choice of clothes is because of stereotypes our society holds about what men should be like—who they may sleep with, what they may wear." In his view, drag challenged heterosexist dogma. Identifying himself as a bisexual, he proclaimed, "It is political suicide for the community to sacrifice its internal minorities." The paper also covered the July 14, 1990, meeting in Milwaukee of Midwest Transvestites and Transsexuals, which was a gathering of FTM transsexuals. The report was written by Lou Sullivan, who came back from San Francisco to participate. A letter by Susan Cook of Milwaukee was featured with the prominent heading, "Women Wearing Leather Is Appropriate." She asserted, "There are more Lesbians out here who are differently pleasured than what all the vanilla sexed Lesbians would want the rest of us to think." She closed, "I say, if leather fits. . . ."[107]

Despite this, *The Wisconsin Light* was not on the front lines for sexual freedom. "We believe that Lesbian/Gay Liberation has to do with sex only in a secondary way," Boughner wrote. "The true meaning of what we are fighting for is the freedom to love, and love involves openness, honesty, commitment and fidelity." That its publisher and editor were a loving couple may have colored that view, but it provided the subtext to a newspaper that aspired to journalism rather than the pleasure focus of the bar rag tradition.[108]

This reticence to push sexual boundaries manifested in *The Wisconsin Light*'s response to aggression toward gay men. In response to beatings of "faggots" in Milwaukee's Juneau Park, a gay cruising zone, the paper's advice was to "Stay Out of Juneau Park" because "there is no reason we can see for anyone going there." When male prostitution in Milwaukee's Third Ward was spotlighted in the mainstream news, the paper ran a guest editorial titled "Prostitution Can Not Be Tolerated." The writer argued that "no responsible Gay or Lesbian will or should defend the hustlers."[109]

In early 1989 as the AIDS crisis grew more serious, *The Wisconsin Light* ran an editorial titled "Community Must Go on and Accept Bath Closing as Permanent." The paper thanked the local health department "for safeguarding the health of the entire community." While acknowledging the baths' reputation for "free and untrammeled sex," the paper refused to believe the crackdown was the beginning of an attack on the gay community. Protesting would only further the "idea that we Gays and Lesbians are all about sex and nothing more. This is [as] demeaning as it is wrong." Boughner took up his pen on the issue again in the March 9, 1989, issue, proclaiming the rightness of the decision and calling it "a matter of the most profound insignificance." His sentiment was, "God knows, there's enough homophobia in this world. Let's not invent it where it doesn't exist."[110]

In 1988, Boughner published *Out of All Time: A Gay and Lesbian History*, dedicated "to my beloved spouse, Jerry Johnson, whose love and faith have led me to understand gay love out of all time." The book was a survey scanning the centuries for the commonly understood highlights of gay history with thumbnail sketches (some of which also appeared in *The Wisconsin Light*) of the likes of Alexander the Great, Roman emperor Hadrian, English King Edward II, playwright Christopher Marlowe, Prussian King Frederick the Great, and the English Ladies of Llangollen. He perhaps had less evidence for including several popes, Joe McCarthy, and Jesus of Nazareth. Boughner had a wide cultural reach that picked up the Native American Berdache tradition and Arabian male love poetry.

Beautiful illustrations by Michael Willhoite of the *Washington Blade* accompanied the narrative. Boughner's book, like his editorship of *The Wisconsin Light*, was part of his ongoing work to attack ignorance of gay and lesbian life, which had been culturally suppressed for so many decades before Stonewall.[111]

The Wisconsin Light was one of the bright spots in the early gay liberation effort for its years of in-depth coverage of gay and lesbian news around the state and its literary contributions. For Boughner and Johnson, it was a work of love that provided nourishment for Wisconsin's gay community. After eleven years of faithful publication, in 1998 they sold *The Wisconsin Light* to a new publisher who continued it for another two years before its demise.

High School Journalists Skate on Thin Gay Ice

Journalistic efforts weren't limited to the gay and lesbian communities, and one corollary to the efforts of *OUT!* and similar publications was the effort of high school reporters to expose readers to issues facing the younger generation. In an editorial written for its first anniversary in November 1983, *OUT!*'s editors commented that they hoped gay youth would have role models like those highlighted in their paper. Little did they know they themselves, as gay journalists, would serve as the role models. A month later, Madison East High School principal, Milton McPike, killed an editorial on homophobia from being printed in the high school paper. Jerry Dryer, author of the editorial, vowed to "pursue [the matter] until it's printed." Dryer titled the piece "Homophobia: A Social Disease." He had written it earlier in the fall as co-editor of the *Tower Times*, the East High School newspaper. Dryer wrote that at East he heard "fag" and "faggot" and "queer" commonly used as put downs. He told the *Capital Times*, "I have witnessed a lot of name calling and harassment and have been the victim of it." Dryer indicated there were no openly gay students at East.[112]

Dryer noted in his editorial that "homosexuals have often been thought of as mentally ill" and isolated from society, and even put into mental institutions. "Because of this isolation, most people know very little about gays." To educate his fellow students, Dryer continued, "More recently, though, doctors, lawyers, psychologists and progressive citizens have come to the understanding that homosexuals are not sick, perverted, or ill." Dryer asserted, "Homosexuals are a legitimate part of our society and deserve the same rights and privileges as everyone else. They are vital to us both as individuals and as part of the whole. Yet people continue to discriminate against them, make fun of them, exclude them from activities and even commit violent crimes against them."[113]

The student editorial board had approved the piece but was overruled by faculty supervisor Donna Calvert, who was backed up by McPike, who argued the editorial was accusatory, not educational. Perhaps his real reason surfaced when he stated that he thought it would be disruptive: "I don't want phone calls on the negative side." McPike claimed he only wanted the piece rewritten. He was overruled by his supervisor, Glenn Borland. The Madison district's student bill of rights allowed prior restraint only if materials were obscene, libelous, or disruptive. Borland did not find the topic objectionable.[114]

The story broke with big headlines in the town's two daily papers, which also reprinted Dryer's piece in full. By the time the issue broke in the city's mainstream press, Dryer had transferred to Malcolm Shabazz High School, an alternative program on Madison's east side. Dryer planned to run the editorial in Malcolm Shabazz's paper, *The Alternative*. According to Dryer, the West High School paper also wanted to run it. Jenny Cooke, his former co-editor at East, also voiced support: "The student paper is for the students and they should have a place to voice their opinions." Cooke believed McPike's actions had caused more of a ruckus than the material ever would have. However, she also feared that Dryer might have faced reprisals at East if it had been printed while he was still there.[115]

Several school board members weighed in with comments. Hermine Davidson called McPike's decision "regrettable." Regarding the editorial, she wrote, "Personally I don't see any objection to it." Likewise, Rebecca Young didn't see any problems with the editorial. She noted that calling for gays to be treated in a nondiscriminatory way was not out of the norm in Wisconsin, since "many of our laws ask us to do the same thing." The *Capital Times* wrote its own editorial against the censorship of the piece, commenting that the arguments against it were "so flimsy that they collapse of their own weight."[116]

Yet the wrath of McPike was not done. The school board's attorney threatened *OUT!*, which broke the initial story, with a libel lawsuit for supposedly misrepresenting McPike. In the end, the school system did not file a suit, and the editors noted the attorney never presented evidence regarding how the misrepresentation was made. *OUT!* publisher Peter Klehm issued a press release criticizing the school district's censorship on the matter and its attempt to "chill our investigation."[117]

On the issue of homophobia in the schools, Klehm said the paper had received numerous reports that both students and school personnel freely expressed and even encouraged antigay attitudes, what would later be termed *bullying*. *OUT!*'s editors planned to appear before the Madison Board of Education with their message. "We think lesbian and gay issues need to be addressed openly and without prejudice in the schools, and we urge the Board of Education to take action to this end." Ken Bowling, a former school board member (1980–1983), gave part of the community response and called for the district to conduct extensive in-service training sessions on homophobia for top administrators.[118]

At Stoughton High School, just south of Madison, another student journalist decision caused a flap over the school's paper, *Norse Star*. In November 1987, the paper ran an ad for a lesbian/gay peer support group for high school students. Stoughton school board member Larry Roberts thought the school should cut funding for the paper if the board could not control content. Teacher David Wallner, whose journalism class published the paper, said that under current law, the board could not control what the paper printed. While correct, Wallner was perhaps more than a tad sympathetic. He was a Madison alder and in a previous race had advertised in *OUT!*, identifying himself as a supporter of family rights for gays.[119]

Meanwhile, the owners of the local Stoughton Buggy Scrub carwash were attempting to organize an advertisers boycott. One of the owners, Jane Hill, was quoted as saying, "A lot of people find in-depth discussion of sex and sexual issues offensive." Some advertisers did sign a letter saying they would pull ads. But the owners of Chose A&W and Felland's Mens Wear said they supported the paper. *Norse Star* editor Megan Moriarty believed "there's a lot of support for us." She was correct. The *Wisconsin State Journal* headline on the day following the school board meeting of January 4, 1988, ran: "Gay-ad Critics Silent." With a crowd of sixty on a subzero evening with a wind chill of sixty below, not one of twenty-three speakers urged cutting funding for the paper, and the board took no action against the paper. Wallner had told the board, "Don't seek to cripple and to kill this newspaper. The kids don't deserve that." Student speakers agreed that the issue was homophobia, noting that there were gay and lesbian students at the school. Student Roger Finch said about cutting the funding, "What you are proposing would take us back into the Dark Ages." Moriarty asked, "Where is the censorship going to stop?"[120]

Norse Star supporter the *Capital Times* encouraged the young journalists. In an editorial, the paper noted that for teens, sorting out their sexuality "can be compounded by isolation, fear and loneliness. The peer support groups and counseling services for lesbians and gay teens are designed to help them cope with those feelings." The paper stated such groups are not an effort to round up new recruits. Editor Dave Zweifel, in his column Plain Talk, praised the young journalists for "their editorial integrity." In the paper's Sound Off column, one mother, who knew of a teen suicide, complained about "adults whose shriveled little minds and too-small hearts cannot allow them to see beyond prejudice." In *The Lance*, Madison La Follette High School's paper, staff member Karla Knesting noted that the paper also had run the same ad as the *Norse Star*. Of those opposed to the ad, she thought their "attitude shows pure ignorance."[121]

That high school journalists were addressing LGBT issues by the 1980s is significant. Young people, a generation younger than post-Stonewall activists, presumed gay liberation was a right. The fact that students believed that high school papers should be able to discuss homosexuality and homophobia showed a serious pushback both on the suppression of young journalists and the silence sought by some educators on non-normative sexuality, especially among youth.

SEIZING THE AIRWAVES AND CABLE

Print was not the only medium used by those newly interested in getting out information to and about gay men and lesbians. One of the longest-running broadcast radio programs with strong lesbian content has been *Her Turn*, aired over Madison's alternative radio station, WORT. Begun in 1978, the half-hour show was run by women, including Tara Ayres, who would later become deeply involved in queer theater. According to

Ayres in a 1983 interview, "There [was] never a problem finding ideas." In the 1980s, a different person produced each week's show, often doing the writing, anchoring, and engineering.[122]

Milwaukee pioneered gay radio in 1971 with *Gay Perspective*, broadcast at midnight by WZMF in Menomonee Falls. The show would move to campus station WUWM, where it was given a primetime slot. Alyn Hess, who was involved with the show, recalled, "We realized that once we put the shows together and out over the air, they were gone and eventually those tapes would get lost or erased." Material for the show was often reproduced in articles for *GPU News*. Milwaukee was also home to radio shows focused on women's concerns that likely would have included lesbian topics. In the mid-1970s, *Speaking of Women* aired on 91.1 WNUW FM, and in the late 1970s, *A Woman's Place* aired on 88.9 WYMS FM with moderator Linda Scott, a community broadcast specialist with the Milwaukee Public School System's radio station.[123]

In the 1990s, Madison would have an exclusive gay/lesbian radio show called *Sunday Night Out* on local talk/news station WTSO, Midcontinent Media. The station's general manager, Dave Graupner, commented, "We're hoping to attract a large straight audience as well." Diana Summers was the sparkplug. It began airing June 19, 1994, but ran only briefly.[124]

With the advent of public access cable programming for television, gays and lesbians in both Milwaukee and Madison seized the chance to put their stories on TV, admittedly with a significantly smaller audience than broadcast television. One broadcast show that preceded the cable shows appeared on WHA TV in Madison. Called *Gay Response*, it was organized by the local gay community in 1977 to counter a number of national shows that were considered negative in their portrayal of the gay community. Professor Harvey Goldberg of the UW–Madison campus was one of the featured commentators.[125]

In June 1985, Barbara Williamson led initial efforts in Milwaukee to prepare a cable program called *Rough Cut*, which she optimistically hoped would become a weekly show. Williamson was a Milwaukee native who had returned from New York, where she collaborated in producing a TV show with Vito Russo, the author of *Hollywood Babylon*, a book on gays in the movies. In June 1987, *OUT!* reported that Milwaukee Gay/Lesbian Cable Network producers had produced five programs. In May of the next year, national gay magazine *The Advocate* would include Milwaukee's efforts as evidence that gay cable programming was "a strong force in the Midwest."[126]

In 1988, the Tri-Cable Network replaced Milwaukee Gay/Lesbian Cable Network, with producers planning to produce monthly thirty-minute shows in a magazine format. The Tri-Cable moniker referred to the logo, which featured an inverted triangle, linking it to the pink triangle used by Nazis to identify homosexual prisoners in the camps. Mark Behar and Bryce Clark were early coproducers. They recruited a team of ten volunteers. In 1988, the Milwaukee Access Telecommunications Authority recognized the programming with a Philo Award. Tri-Cable was supported by the fledgling Cream City Foundation with an initial grant of three thousand dollars, because as Don Schwamb, president of the foundation, remarked, "We feel the idea of regular programming is so important."[127]

The focus of *Tri-Cable Tonight* was community activities, especially non-bar activities and news from the thirty gay and lesbian organizations active in Milwaukee. The first show aired October 27, 1987. In addition to the news/issues program, Tri-Cable produced a gay comedy show called *Yellow on Thursday*. Sketches included a gay slumber party, parodies of Pedro Almodovar's movies, and a hilarious look at 1-900 phone calls. W. W. Wells presented a comical news update. Some gay bars ran repeats of the cablecast programs. Tri-Cable ended its monthly programs in December 1989.[128]

In Madison, the United sponsored the weekly half-hour cable show *Glad to Be Gay*. The first show aired in January 1979, and it continued into 1982. Shows included coverage of the 1979 March on Washington, aging in the gay community with Harvey Goldberg, and a drag show produced especially for the program. David Carter was one of the interviewers, and Michael Henry was a coordinator. In 1980, host John Lindert interviewed several transvestites at what was described as "a transvestite party." The episode covered "the differences of being a transvestite and a transsexual." Michael Wisniewski, who crewed for the shows, was active in recruiting support for the program. Wisniewski wrote in 1981 on the occasion of creating a Glad to be Gay Educational Foundation, "We believe that it is important to the continuation of Democracy . . . that minority groups, both ethnic and sexual, have access to the media."[129]

Madison's greatest effort was *Nothing to Hide*, produced by the infamous

David Runyon, an alum of *Glad to Be Gay*. It proved to be one of the nation's longest-running gay cable programs, airing for twenty years with 850 episodes. A former Presbyterian minister who taught in the Art Department at UW–Whitewater, Runyon was director of the school's Crossman Art Gallery. He had come out at age forty-seven, in 1978, through going to the Gay Center in Madison. After splitting with *Glad to be Gay*, he began his own program in December 1981. Runyon estimated he put forty hours a week into his shows. In the beginning, he used Madison public video equipment to create a studio show, but once he got his own port-a-pack camera, he went on the road.

Runyon's idea was "to expose the straight world and the gay world to something respectable, to our joy." He knew a mass media outlet played to both worlds. He hoped that while he was politically sensitive, he could also be politically incorrect. As "the editor, the director, the financer, the producer, and the distributor of the show," he felt entitled to make decisions. When in 1994 he aired Tim Miller's "My Queer Body" performance piece with full frontal nudity, he was suspended for six months from the local cable network. Runyon pushed back at those who criticized

David Runyon, a professor at UW–Whitewater, took to the cable airwaves with regular shows featuring the gay communities of Wisconsin and Chicago.
COURTESY OF SHIH-HSUN LIN

him for showing drag, stating, "I will show drag if and only when it is quality drag."[130]

While Runyon enjoyed the social life of the gay community (he hosted many parties at his Judy Lane home), his sense of gay politics was even stronger. *Nothing to Hide* programs featured social-political events such as filming the Chicago Gay Pride Parade and its Madison attendees. The Madison Gay Men's Chorale, the Windy City Singers, and the Lionheart Theatre of Chicago were also featured. Runyon would cablecast John Boswell of Yale when he spoke on the UW–Madison campus on religion and homosexuality. Programs also featured gay politicians on various issues. Runyon staged and filmed a gentle debate on outing closeted gay political figures with the pro side argued by Dan Savage. Savage worked at Four Star, Madison's local gay video store, and became a writer for *The Onion*, which launched his career as a nationally renowned advice columnist. Perhaps his early experience with videographer Runyon showed him how powerful the handheld camera can be when Savage contemplated his own It Gets Better project to reach gay teens in the 2010s.[131]

Runyon was frustrated that his shows were not more popular with gays and that the gay bars refused to air them. He recalled that one of his regular local watchers was Reverend Richard Pritchard, the local antigay campaigner who would watch his shows "and then call me up and bitch." Runyon expanded the focus from gay issues to other topics in an attempt to gain a broader audience. A few years before the show ended in 2001, Runyon said, "I did the show as an educational process for myself."[132]

IGNORANCE BLOWN AWAY

In early 1975, Madison's *Capital Times* ran a story with the headline "Homosexuality—A Surfacing Reality." Those in the gay community did much of the work of bringing this reality to the surface. For them, coming out was not just a personal act of revelation but a collective endeavor to break down ignorance. The Wisconsin journalists who vigorously presented gay and lesbian lives were on a mission.[133]

Much of this media work came from the larger cities of Madison and Milwaukee. With more resources available, these cities could support the collectives, the volunteers, and the advertising required to sustain these endeavors. Bi-city collectives *OUT!*, *Amazon*, and *Hag Rag* were able to reach a statewide audience, and their directories and stories often covered gay and lesbian life around the state. The reality, however, was excellent Milwaukee and Madison coverage with nods to other parts of the state. Some readers outside these metropolitan areas did feel slighted. In 1992, for instance, James Wallin of Wausau would write to *In Step* complaining of an editorial comment that urged readers to attend Pridefest in Milwaukee: "Explain to me why should we in Northern WI come to Milw. when we are continuously overlooked by you. . . . We are not the country Hillbillies, that you obviously think we are."[134]

Yet the attempt to reach a statewide audience was significant, and it helped grow the perception of a larger Wisconsin identity to the gay and lesbian community. After the 1982 gay rights law was passed, pride in being the first gay rights state became a touchstone for gays and lesbians across the state. It also led to more political content in Wisconsin's gay media. Since the geographic area was also a political entity, features on gays interacting with the state's political culture were frequent. This emphasis on the political was bit more prominent in publications with gay male editors, as they tended to give more space to political-social topics. In contrast, lesbian publications were more socially and culturally focused, as the patriarchy was often seen as the main enemy to combat.

Gay and lesbian media in Wisconsin showcased some outstanding activist writer-journalists, including Eldon Murray, Jamakaya, Ron McCrea, Brooks Egerton, Jeff Kirsch, Sue Burke, Jacob Stockinger, and Terry Boughner, plus the artist Tom Rezza.

There was a joy and humor in the media, as shown by *OUT!*'s spoof with "IN!" and its "Breeders Support Group." *Scarlet Letter* could find the female toilet stall dialogue an "exciting and creative interaction." The *GPU News*'s chaste description of the overlapping lambda symbols as "just marching" surely had a tongue-in-cheek quality. *Hag Rag*'s description of a Lesbian Variety Show act as "mooning the patriarchy" captured some of the raucous energy of these events. Tri-Cable's *Yellow on Thursday* specifically focused on humor.

In his book *Unspeakable*, Rodger Streitmatter shows how some gay media across the nation, while informing, could also titillate, even publishing photos with full frontal nudity. While the Wisconsin gay and lesbian editors certainly pushed some boundaries in discussing the sexual landscape, in general their Midwestern values did not let them go that far. Line drawings of nude figures did appear, but nude photos were very rare. Certainly, the media in open circulation, especially the newspapers that sought to be in public libraries, exercised discretion. On the other hand, a publication such as *Rod's* newsletter, which was sent only to bar patrons, might include full frontal nudity when sent to a presumed closed circulation.[135]

In Wisconsin, the lesbian press had a strong separatist streak. News features favored discussions of womyn's space, including Daughters of the Earth Farm in Norwalk and the SisterMoon Feminist Bookstore in Milwaukee. Gay males were never the audience, nor were male-to-female transsexuals, and at times even straight women were on the outside. Other publications, such as *OUT!* and *The Wisconsin Light*, sought to reach a wider audience, with both gays and lesbians editing and writing features.

This social construction of gay life in Wisconsin was not only significant for residents within the bounds of Wisconsin but was an important part of the developing national story. In April 1983, Virginia Apuzzo, ex-

During a talk at UW–Milwaukee, national leader Ginny Apuzzo praised Wisconsin for its passage of gay-supportive legislation with its first-in-the-nation gay rights law in 1982. *ESCAPE*, MAY 1983

ecutive director of the National Gay Task Force, spoke at UW–Milwaukee's fifth annual Gay/Lesbian Awareness Week. She said, "I should be here listening instead of talking. . . . One of the things we rarely get the opportunity to do—and if anyone is entitled to do it, you certainly are among those folks—is to pause a moment and savor the fact that you are making history." Apuzzo cited an article she had "picked up recently at Harvard University," titled "Only Wisconsin," on the successful passage of the gay rights law. However, she said, much work remained: "Our battle is a war of attrition with ignorance. The most revolutionary thing a gay or lesbian can do is be who they are." The gay and lesbian journalists of Wisconsin agreed and continued the attack on ignorance.[136]

Certainly, after the millions of words and hundreds of thousands of images in the Wisconsin gay and lesbian media, the plea of ignorance would be a hard plea to sustain. Though the publications did reach tens of thousands, most straight Wisconsinites would never see a gay newspaper or hear a gay program. While the attack was vigorous, much of the ignorance remained.

The Wisconsin gay and lesbian media were more influential as an internal community force. In the first decades after Stonewall, despite some coverage of transsexuals and bisexuals, it was very much a gay and/or lesbian media. The repeated cycle of new publications rising from the ashes of failed publications shows there was a great hunger for and a desire to provide such media, and only rarely did a gap remain unfilled. Pride demanded lesbians and gays communicate with each other and that transsexuals and bisexuals claim their voices. The most eager audience for news of coming out was the community itself.

6

THE GOOD ACTS: A LEGISLATIVE DELUGE BEGINS

The changes to eliminate distinctions of race, sex, and sexual prefer-
ences are long overdue. Let us work to effect such changes vigorously
and expeditiously.
— STATE REPRESENTATIVE LLOYD BARBEE, 1973[1]

Ninety-five per cent of the adult population violates these sex laws—
and the other five per cent just don't have any imagination.
— STATE REPRESENTATIVE DAVID CLARENBACH,
ADVOCATING FOR THE CONSENTING ADULTS BILL, 1979[2]

Wisconsin's legislative history on homosexuality, made up of nearly
a century and a half of negative actions, would be substantially
overturned over the course of one decade beginning in 1980. The negative
history began with a bang when the territorial legislature added two years
to the sodomy penalty in 1836, based on laws inherited from Michigan
Territory that were themselves based on Tudor-era laws. As late as 1959,
the legislature was still expanding its antigay legislation, denying a driver's license to anyone convicted of the crime of sexual perversion, which
replaced the sodomy law.

Efforts to unravel this punitive history would be a major task. The
neighboring state of Illinois was the first in the nation to make homosexual
acts between consenting adults legal in 1960 by adopting legal reforms
modeled on the American Law Institute's new penal code, drafted in the

1950s, decriminalizing victimless crimes. Unfortunately for Wisconsin, the state had been ahead of the curve in updating its penal code, but it did not go so far as to repeal penalties for victimless crimes in the McCarthy period. Thus, the 1955 replacement for Wisconsin's sodomy law was a new sexual perversion statute. In the 1972 case of *Jones v. State*, the Wisconsin Supreme court upheld the constitutionality of the statute. But while the law was upheld, winds of change had begun to blow. This chapter details how the Wisconsin gay community and its leaders developed strategic thinking over time and grew in tactical adroitness to achieve two remarkable wins: a statewide nondiscrimination law in 1982 (commonly called the "gay rights law") and consenting adults legislation in 1983. These efforts were not without interactions with national gay groups and leaders, but the effort was locally fueled and benefited from the state's unique progressive past.[3]

LLOYD BARBEE: PROPHET OF WISCONSIN SEX LAW REFORM

Lloyd Barbee, an African American elected to the Wisconsin legislature in 1964, became a pioneer advocate for gay men well before Stonewall. Born in Memphis in 1925, Barbee grew up in the South and joined the NAACP at the age of twelve. During World War II, he served in the Navy, and in 1949 he came to Wisconsin to attend the University of Wisconsin Law School on a scholarship. Barbee was awarded his degree in 1955. He served as chairman of the Madison branch of the NAACP and in 1961 became chair of the statewide NAACP. After moving to Milwaukee in 1962, he led the fight in the lawsuit to desegregate the Milwaukee schools. After a very lengthy judicial process, in 1976 Barbee won the case in federal district court and after further legal maneuvers, there was a settlement to desegregate in 1979.[4]

Barbee's gay advocacy efforts were the first of their kind in the Wisconsin legislature. In the 1967 legislative session, Barbee introduced Assembly Bill (AB) 678. The bill would repeal an extensive list of crimes against sexual morality, among them homosexuality. Analysis of the bill by the Legislative Reference Bureau (LRB) cited the American Law Institute's penal code recommendations, now adopted by Illinois and California. The LRB's unusually favorable analysis also noted: "A recently published

Representative Lloyd Barbee introduced sex reform legislation at the Wisconsin State Capitol even before Stonewall. Following that historic event, he introduced non-discrimination legislation and what may have been the first-in-the-nation same-sex marriage legislation in 1971. WHI IMAGE ID 26539

legal handbook suggests that it might be well to remove criminal sanctions against abnormal sexual connections that . . . are so deeply rooted in the personality of those who practice them as not to be preventable by criminal sanctions. . . . [Such actions] are committed by freely consenting adults and involve no breach of trust or confidence; and are committed privately and therefore do not outrage the public's sense of decency." The analysis further cited a 1963 international conference of criminologists who favored limiting the punishable nature of "homosexuality and other deviant sexual practices." Despite the LRB's tacit support, the bill did not receive a hearing.[5]

The *Milwaukee Journal* quoted Barbee extensively in a May 12, 1967, story, "Barbee Seeks to Liberalize State's Sex Laws." Regarding sexual relations, Barbee argued that people today "do not have the extent of psychological guilt, let alone legal guilt" they once had. He specifically mentioned homosexuals: "They are blackmailed and harassed unnecessarily. The only restrictions that should be placed on them are that they should be 18 years of age or over and should not engage in public and notorious homosexuality." Over the next several legislative sessions (each beginning in the odd-numbered year), Barbee continued his efforts. A few months before Stonewall, the *Journal* reported on February 12, 1969, that Barbee had introduced another bill to liberalize Wisconsin's sex laws. In the post-Stonewall session starting in 1971, he took up sex reform once again, adding a bill to prohibit discrimination based on sexual practices. Another of his proposed bills in that session, AB 1410, included allowing same-sex marriage, perhaps one of the first such legislative efforts in the nation. He also proposed a bill allowing polygamy based on religious belief.[6]

In its coverage of Barbee's proposed bills for the 1971 legislative session, the *Milwaukee Courier*, the state's leading black paper, with forty thousand readers, also reported on Barbee's concern with treatment of homosexuals by law enforcement. "One of the effects of erasing the so-called sexual morality crimes," he said, "would be to reduce police entrapment of prostitutes, male homosexuals, etc., and cut down on the harassment and blackmail of homosexuals. Prostitutes and homosexuals are humans. They should be respected and accorded fair treatment."[7] Later that month, in his Comments column in the *Courier*, Barbee discussed the corrupting effect of enforcing such laws, which required officers "to stick their noses into bedrooms, parks, cars and restrooms, [making] degenerates out of policemen." In June 1971, the *Courier* reported on Barbee's appearance on the radio show *Gay Perspective*, in which he discussed the repeal of sex laws for consenting adults. It quoted him as saying, "The people who suffer under these present laws are the young people, the poor people and the male homosexuals who are subject to harassment and entrapment."[8]

The early bills had not proceeded far through the legislative process, but in the 1973 session, Barbee was chairman of the Assembly Judiciary Committee and could schedule a hearing on his bills. In the 1973 session, he scheduled a hearing on the same-sex marriage bill, timed, as he said, to coincide with Gay Pride Week. Barbee was quoted in the press as saying that it would be "good to permit people who want to marry within their own sex to do so." In a further comment, he said, "I do not like to use the term homosexuality; I call it unisexuality."[9]

While advocates for sex law reform had the chance to test their arguments in a legislative forum at the State Capitol, there was no expectation the committee would vote to take action and report the bill out of committee for further legislative debate. But it was a first step. Barbee remained undaunted. Two days after his 1973 bills failed to move past a hearing, Barbee used his *Milwaukee Courier* column to promote a bill being considered in the Assembly Judiciary Committee to prohibit discrimination on the basis of sex. He opined, "The changes to eliminate distinctions of race, sex and sexual preferences are long overdue. Let us work to effect such changes vigorously and expeditiously."[10]

Barbee's farseeing bills did not elicit groundswells of support in the legislature of the late 1960s and early 1970s. Barbee himself was realistic and philosophical about this, drawing on the experience of how long African Americans had been battling for equality and rights. In his own view, the bills were "imaginative and innovative proposals." The press quoted him as saying, "Measures doomed to failure are capable nevertheless of educating." Further, he said, "I have a different concept of representation; I educate as I legislate." The *Milwaukee Courier* wrote about Barbee in 1974, characterizing him as a reform legislator: "Introducing controversial legislation seems to be Barbee's forte, according to some, but Barbee views such bills as legislation that would not be immediately passed, but might keep politicians abreast of the need for reform in our laws."[11]

THE "GOD ELECTION" ON SAME-SEX MARRIAGE

Barbee's bills were controversial. On July 14, 1973, the *Courier* published a letter to the editor signed "A Senior Citizen, A. Teresa Meuhlenkamp." The letter was headed "Rep. Barbee's Bills Seen as Immoral." Meuhlenkamp wrote, "I am sure [Rep. Barbee] doesn't represent the wishes of the Black Community. Black people are no more immoral than white people. I suggest that you find a man now to replace him at election time—a man who will let it be known that blacks do not condone his immorality and that whites would not flee to the suburbs because of rape, etc. etc." Meuhlenkamp specifically cited the bill to "permit persons of the same sex to marry." A mainstream press article in 1973 on Barbee's bills carried the headline "Un-Christian."[12]

Barbee's forthrightness did not go unchallenged, and the suggestion that he be ousted for his sex reform legislation was taken up in the 1974 Democratic primary. State Senator Monroe Swan's brother, Robert Swan, announced he would challenge Barbee. In putting himself forward, Swan complained that Barbee "had failed to provide true representation of the people in his district by introducing legislation that 'does not reflect the feelings of the 18th district.'" Swan specifically mentioned the measure that would "permit men to marry men"—clearly Barbee's support of gay marriage had hit a nerve. His legislative colleagues came to refer to the battle that followed as the God Election.[13]

In the run-up to the September primary, the *Courier* broke the story of smear tactics being used in the campaign. Swan's campaign had been "distributing a large white poster with red lettering listing some of the bills and accusing Barbee of 'painting a very negative image for our community.'" Among the bills listed were AB 442, eliminating criminal sanctions against sexual acts between consenting adults, and AB 185, allowing persons of the same sex to marry. The *Courier* reported that five hundred posters had been printed, and an effort to get these materials to black churches was underway. In the same edition, an editorial denounced the "moralistic smear campaign" against Barbee and referred to the "red herrings" of the bills. The paper felt "Swan and his backers have resorted to the sad desperate, ancient, and dangerous approach of emotionalism, distortion, and character assassination." Barbee, in contrast, was attributed with courage and brilliance, and the editorial claimed that with his "litany of progressive legislation" he had made blacks "a force to be reckoned with on the Assembly floor." According to the paper, there was "no better Wisconsin legislator."[14]

Despite the smear campaign, Barbee won the support of the black community and the endorsement of the paper, which cited "his distinguished record of struggles against racism, classism, and sexism, through law." He even won support of the church. On August 24, the *Courier* ran a letter with the headline, "Rev. Gregg Asks Support for Lloyd Barbee." B. S. Gregg, the distinguished pastor of the St. Matthew Christian Methodist Episcopal Church, cast Barbee in the light of "a dedicated fighter for our community" who had worked for fair housing laws and with the equal rights division for enforcement of nondiscrimination laws. "We need a person to represent us in the Capitol who is honest, courageous, and uncompromising," he implored. On September 7, the paper ran a guest editorial by Carole Malone titled "Rep. Barbee Still Serves." Malone praised Barbee's "integrity and stamina" and asserted that "he has been involved in every piece of progressive legislation and has fought tirelessly against reactionary and regressive measures." About his bills she was positive: "We understand that his method of introducing bills to educate us as well as legislate is one of the best things going for us."[15]

In reporting on Barbee's 741 to 659 victory in the primary, the *Courier* noted, "A great deal of Swan's support came from precincts with a larger percentage of white voters located on the district's west side boundaries." These white voters would also be highly unlikely to be *Courier* readers. On election night, Barbee noted that he had declined to make the race "a political skunk fight," claiming, "My constituents appreciate me representing them enough not to resort in sewer and garbage politics."[16]

The 1974 primary election showed that the Milwaukee African American community—through both its media and the votes cast by blacks—did not oppose Barbee for his efforts for progressive sex reform decriminalizing homosexuality, nondiscrimination on the basis of sexual orientation, and even marriage equality. From 1967 to early 1977, African Americans as well as gays had their champion in State Representative Lloyd Barbee.

Over the course of his political career, Barbee championed those oppressed by the law and fought to reform oppressive legislation. He spoke out for the Black Panthers and their fights against racism, women and their struggle for equal rights, the Menominee Tribe's efforts for their own self-government, welfare rights, and hippies at smoke-ins. He demanded reform of punitive sex perversion laws and an end to police practices that oppressed the community. He announced in the public realm a vision of equality and fairness that included gays. For that he endured hate mail, public attacks, and an election challenge with smear tactics and dirty tricks. Undaunted, Barbee remained a champion.[17]

David Clarenbach: Champion for a New Generation

In January 1972, at age eighteen, David Clarenbach became the youngest candidate seeking election to the Dane County Board of Supervisors. His early political launch was fueled by the Twenty-Sixth Amendment to the US Constitution, establishing eighteen-year-old voting rights, which had become law on July 1, 1971. David came from a politically active family. His maternal grandfather, Alexander Ernst Frederick of Sparta, Wisconsin, had served in the state assembly from 1913 to 1916. Frederick, a lawyer and an ordained elder of the Methodist Church, was known as "the fighting parson" and was active in Progressive reform. Kathryn (Kay) Clarenbach, David's mother, was appointed by Governor John Reynolds to chair the Governor's Commission on the Status of Women from 1964 to 1969. She helped found the National Organization for Women (NOW) in 1966 and served as chair of NOW's board from 1966 to 1970. Governor Patrick Lucey, elected in 1970 after six years of a Republican governor, appointed her chair of the reconstituted Commission on Women, and she served from 1971 to 1979. David Clarenbach's father, Henry Clarenbach, a teacher and realtor, was a Eugene McCarthy delegate to the 1968 Democratic Convention.[18]

Clarenbach's 1972 race for the Fourth District Dane County Board focused on city–county cooperation, improved environmental policies, and his credentials working with the Wisconsin Civil Liberties Union. He was a freshman at the University of Wisconsin in a district with a large student population, and he easily beat his opponent, a fifty-five-year-old independent contractor. After several months in

David Clarenbach was elected to the Dane County Board of Supervisors as an eighteen year old. He went on to become a member of the Wisconsin assembly where he championed a range of gay issues.
FROM THE AUTHOR'S COLLECTION

office, he would write, "The County Board is clearly in dire need of supervising," perhaps because, as the youngest supervisor, he felt at odds with the mainly older, conservative members. In his 1974 reelection literature (he ran unopposed), he came out strongly: "Any type of discrimination against women, minorities or homosexuals cannot be tolerated. I favor strong safeguards against this sort of discrimination." The issue had surfaced previously in the spring 1974 special election for alder of the Fourth District, for which he served as interim for several months.[19]

In addition to the county board position, Clarenbach was elected to the Wisconsin state assembly in fall 1974 as a Democrat with 43 percent of the vote, winning a three-way race for the Seventy-eighth District against a Republican and a far-left Alliance candidate. He would never again face a serious electoral challenge for the safe Democratic assembly seat. Clarenbach rose quickly in the assembly leadership and became Speaker pro tempore in 1983 at age twenty-nine, frequently presiding over the body's sessions. He gave up the assembly seat in 1994 to run unsuccessfully for Congress and was succeeded by out County Board Supervisor Tammy Baldwin, though she had to win a hotly contested four-way Democratic primary.[20]

While Clarenbach was gay, he did not come out publicly during his electoral career. In a 2001 interview, he explained, "Even in the liberal stronghold of Madison, it would have done more than raise eyebrows. It would've hampered a person's electability. Yet I think it's safe to say that every member of the Legislature and every member of the Capitol press corps knew I was gay. . . . The general consensus was not to intrude into one's personal life." Not unlike many gay men of a slightly earlier generation, David was married to a woman for a period of time. David's ambition to run for Congress in a district that was both urban and rural also played into his personal decision. While weighing the congressional run, he conducted polling that showed being gay would help slightly in Dane County but hurt in nonurban counties. David himself would later note that his political career began the same year longtime Massachusetts Representative Barney Frank ran for his first elected seat, and Frank did not come out until 1987.[21]

There was never any doubt, however, that Clarenbach was a public advocate for the gay and lesbian community. During the 1975 session of the legislature—the only period their service overlapped—Barbee and Clarenbach were joint sponsors of sex reform legislation felicitously named AB 269. When the session ended, Barbee effectively passed the legislative baton to Clarenbach, something Clarenbach would later claim Barbee was comfortable with. The two legislative champions had become good friends, with Barbee taking Clarenbach to his favorite black bars in Milwaukee. Later, Barbee would invite Clarenbach to be his guest at his Jamaican resort. The media seemed to recognize the baton passing, too. During the reelection in 1976, *Renaissance* newsletter proclaimed him "one of the Wisconsin legislature's few vocal advocates for gay rights" and quoted Clarenbach's promise: "The state has a major role to play in breaking down the societal barriers which confront gays on a daily basis." In future sessions, other legislators looked to his leadership on gay issues, and he was integral in the passage of the consenting adults law; the gay rights law; student nondiscrimination protections; hate crimes, including those based on sexual orientation protections; and AIDS confidentiality provisions.[22]

One of Clarenbach's earliest accomplishments was helping to build a core constituency of gays and lesbians. These men and women aided him in hosting and sponsoring fundraisers for his multiple candidacies. In addition to adding to his campaign treasury, these activities built a network of gay fundraisers that aided the broader community. One dimension of network building was among gay staff who worked in the Capitol from both parties, such as Dan Young, a Republican staffer, and Rick Soletski, a Democratic staffer. Later, the two would become a couple. These contacts helped gay staff overcome isolation and provided nurture to gay identities in a world where it was largely suppressed. The network also was useful in obtaining political intelligence, including mailing lists that were culled from gay media and bar contacts. Clarenbach's office was one of the first to invest in repetitive typewriters, a technology that could churn out "personalized" letters, an early example of today's direct mail. This focus on network building was not limited to the legislative district but was statewide and even national. Wisconsin names were identified by their political districts, which enabled them to be used to lobby when bills were pending. Clarenbach nurtured other gay and lesbian political activists around the state, especially Democratic Party members in the Madison area. He reached out to include Dane County supervisors, Madison alders, and

Governor Patrick Lucey signed the Wisconsin ratification of the Equal Rights Amendment in 1975. Onlookers included Representative Lloyd Barbee (left), powerful women members of the assembly Representative Midge Miller (center) and Representative Mary Lou Munts (second from right), and Representative David Clarenbach (far right).
WHI IMAGE ID 97430

even the gay Republican coroner of Iowa County. Clarenbach helped put activists in contact with fledgling national groups such as the gay and lesbian Democratic clubs, helping to grow national networks of like-minded political actors who would shape the national gay agenda.[23]

THE LEGISLATIVE TERRAIN

The legislative fight for gay rights began in earnest in the 1970s but was most powerful when the governor, senate, and assembly were all Democratic. As the table on the next page shows, Democrats dominated the governor's office and the houses of the legislature during the key decades of the 1970s and 1980s.

For two decades, Democrats controlled the assembly, and from 1975 to 1989, they controlled both the senate and assembly. For many of these years, they had control of both houses and the governor's seat. The majority in power would have a great effect on what was brought to the floor for discussion, how extensively it was debated, and what measures made it to

Wisconsin State Government, 1971-1989[24]

Year	Governor	Senate	Assembly
1971	**Dem. Pat Lucey**	Rep. 20/**Dem. 13**	**Dem. 67**/Rep. 33
1973	**Dem. Pat Lucey**	Rep. 18/**Dem.15**	**Dem. 62**/Rep. 37
1975	**Dem. Pat Lucey**	**Dem. 20**/Rep. 13	**Dem. 63**/Rep. 36
1977	**Dem. Martin Schreiber**	**Dem. 23**/Rep. 10	**Dem. 66**/Rep. 33
1979	Rep. Lee Dreyfus	**Dem. 21**/Rep. 12	**Dem. 60**/Rep. 39
1981	Rep. Lee Dreyfus	**Dem. 19**/Rep. 14	**Dem. 58**/Rep. 41
1983	**Dem. Tony Earl**	**Dem. 19**/Rep. 14	**Dem. 60**/Rep. 39
1983	**Dem. Tony Earl**	**Dem. 18**/Rep. 15	**Dem. 52**/Rep. 47
1987	Rep. Tommy Thompson	**Dem. 19**/Rep. 14	**Dem. 55**/Rep. 44
1989	Rep. Tommy Thompson	**Dem. 20**/Rep. 13	**Dem. 56**/Rep. 43

a vote. That said, gay rights legislation was by no means a solely partisan effort. Republican support was crucial in passing both consenting adults legislation and the nondiscrimination gay rights law signed by Republican Governor Lee Sherman Dreyfus. Speaker Tom Loftus recalled how Republican Bill Kraus, communications director at Dreyfus's office, told him and other Democratic legislators when the nondiscrimination law was in the legislature, "If you have the guts to pass it [Dreyfus will] have the guts to sign it." The Democratic Party may have held the rudder, but bipartisan support and pro-gay legislators on both sides of the aisle would determine the outcome.[25]

Democratic assembly speakers were important figures in this legislative battleground. The speaker controlled committee appointments, including the Rules Committee, which decided those issues making it to the floor. Democratic Speakers Ed Jackamonis from Waukesha and Loftus of Sun Prairie, for instance, were supporters of consenting adults bills during Loyd Barbee's tenure, casting votes on the bills' behalf, though the issue was not their highest legislative priority. Jackamonis was respectful of Barbee and, as speaker, was willing to take political risks. His influence helped to gain support for gay concerns in the Milwaukee Democratic delegation. Loftus, who came from Dane County, had no difficulties on the issue.[26]

During the early 1970s, the Wisconsin Democratic Party battled over gay issues and over platforms and adopted party convention resolutions. These debates showed progress was being made in support for key items of the gay agenda, including consenting adults legislation (the old sex plank of the Wisconsin Young Dems) and nondiscrimination legislation based on sexual orientation. While these were important markers, the proposed legislation was by no means controlling of legislative behavior. For one thing, Democratic legislators tended to be more pragmatic and less radical than their activist counterparts. As veteran Capitol journalist John Wyngaard observed, "The democratic party's state conventions, usually composed of the most anxious of the liberal true believers, have devoted most of their time to the discussion and adoption of new and radical legislative proposals that were consistently ignored by the Democratic legislators to whom they were directed." Among the radical issues Wyngaard listed was "the elimination of many of the criminal offenses in the statutory sexual code."[27]

The platform fights had shown there was a vocal gay constituency within the party, one with enough liberal allies to muster convention majorities. Though the party debates were contentious and the majority votes were not overwhelming, a few sentences on sexual issues did not outweigh the entire list of governmental priorities also in the platform. Wyngaard, who noted changes in the atmosphere around sex reform in the 1977 session, expected sex reform to be debated even though he predicted it would not pass. "The mere fact that it has been brought into the open," he said, "is a broad suggestion about the changing temper of the electorate as the state's liberal party sees it."[28]

The Republican Party was also not homogeneous during this period, with some advocates for gay rights within its ranks. Party leadership of the 1970s and 1980s was not rock-ribbed conservative. Ernest Keppler, a Republican leader in the early 1970s, won a gay political endorsement. Republican Senator Tiny Krueger, Senate Minority leader in the late 1970s, had roots in the old Progressive Party Republican tradition. One journalist remembered the professional circus clown turned politician as one of "the strongest supporters" of the gay rights bill. Other Republican legislators were part of that tradition of old progressives who had come back into the Republican Party with Robert M. "Young Bob" La Follette Jr. in 1946. Senator Susan Shannon Engeleiter, a Senate Republican leader in the 1980s, had a strong enough record to be endorsed by the Milwaukee *Courier* over the Democrat in her race. Of course, Governor Dreyfus, the consummate communicator of his day, was an outsider Republican. Many of Dreyfus's circle would be part of the New Republican Conference of Wisconsin trying to prevent the conservative tilt of their party.[29]

During this period, while there were no publicly "out" legislators, there were certainly gay legislators in both parties. Occasionally, they discovered one another at the common venue of gay bars. Clarenbach recalls running into Senator David Berger of Milwaukee and Representative Dick Flintrop of Oshkosh in that manner. Some, like Flintrop and Republican Representative Steve Gunderson, were willing to coauthor favorable gay legislation with Clarenbach. Flintrop, Gunderson, Clarenbach, and Berger lent their names to the letterhead of the Wisconsin Alliance for Sexual Privacy, which was set up to lobby for consenting adults legislation. Berger was the senate sponsor of the sex reform bills. Other legislators, while not as public in their stances, nevertheless had pro-gay voting records. Of course, there were also closeted legislators who covered their identity by antigay votes.[30]

Thus, while not perfectly positioned, by the late 1970s, the generally liberal Democratic leadership of the assembly was ready to bring pro-gay legislation forward. They would be cautious about it, especially at first. On a social issue such as this, there was no party discipline to corral members. Neither did Democrats fear the political power of the gay vote. Yet the momentum from earlier legislation proposed by Representatives Barbee and Clarenbach had opened the floor to much-needed conversation about the rights of gay people. The time was ripe not only for continued conversation but also for legislation to enact much-needed change.[31]

THE CONSENTING ADULTS BILL HELPS FRAME THE ISSUES

The chosen legislative strategy of the gay community in the late 1970s was to push first for the consenting adults bill before moving on to nondiscrimination. Barbee's early bills had combined decriminalizing homosexuality, legalizing prostitution, authorizing polygamy, and lowering the age of consent, measures influenced by the 1960s sexual freedom movement.

While there was some audience for these proposals, it would be a hard push even if the Legislative Reference Bureau tried to cloak some of the changes in penal law reform. On the other hand, to focus on consenting adults legislation worked on the presumption that because this proposed legislation referred to sexual acts practiced by both gays and straights, and even by married couples, it would have broader support.[32]

The proposed consenting adults law would also decriminalize sex outside of marriage for heterosexuals (but not adultery). At the time, there were few prosecutions for heterosexual fornication, but sodomy was still prosecuted. The strategy of grouping gay and straight interests seemed to work. During consideration of the consenting adults bill in the 1981 session, for instance, twenty students from Lawrence University in Appleton turned themselves in to the Outagamie district attorney by sending a statement that they had violated the state's existing fornication law. A student spokesperson called the law "ludicrous." The district attorney declined to prosecute. While keeping the case open, he indicated he needed particulars of when the law was violated, where and with whom, rather than a simple statement of admission. The *Appleton Post-Crescent* noted that the "students who took a put-up-or-shut-up attitude toward the seldom-enforced" law had been effective in pointing out the problem. In another example, an assistant corporation counsel in Waukesha County filed fornication charges against thirteen unwed mothers who were on welfare in 1981. The county hoped to force them to tell the names of the fathers so they could be sued for child support. Instead, the case served to highlight the selective use of the sexual morality laws.[33]

In Wisconsin, naming the bill "consenting adults" and including heterosexual fornication, cohabitation, and oral sex within marriage in its scope was a useful strategy. Minnesota's out gay politicians often talked about their effort on behalf of sodomy repeal. *GPU News* had covered other states' actions similarly, with headlines such as "Sodomy Law Fails." Such discourse perforce was more about homosexuals than Wisconsin's would be. Much of the Wisconsin press bought into the consenting adults strategy, often referring to it as the "cohabitation bill." Other press headlines referred to it as the "Consenting Sex Act bill" or the "Sex bill." Several incidents reported in the press kept the cohabitation issue alive. In 1981, two

Milwaukee police officers, John Buss and Sylvia Johnson, were fired after both the Milwaukee vice squad and the department's internal affairs unit conducted extensive surveillance to prove they were cohabiting, which was against both department policy and state law. The Milwaukee district attorney's office declined to prosecute them. A police commissioner stated the case showed "excessive use of police supervisors for a matter that really didn't have much impact on the community." A year earlier in another high-profile story, an unmarried Wauwatosa couple sought to have their 1978 conviction for sexual intercourse overturned. Circuit Court Judge Laurence Gram denied their effort, opining, "Moses's Ten Commandments provided a basis for the public to regulate morality." Their attorney claimed, "It is the right of the people to engage in conduct intimate and private." The judge's riposte: "Crimes without victims? There's no such thing."[34]

Based on strong gay participation, lobby groups for consenting adults used names such as the Wisconsin Privacy Council and the Wisconsin Alliance for Sexual Privacy to emphasize the private nature of sexual relations for both heterosexuals and homosexuals. Yet while this inclusive claim of privacy for all was publicly advanced, no lobbying efforts were made by organized straights on behalf of their own legal sexual rights. As Judd Marmor and Richard Green, writing in the 1977 *Handbook of Sexology*, observed, "Perhaps the most revolutionary aspect of human homosexuality during recent years has been the role of homosexuals in the forefront of social activism."[35]

Several early gay campaigners helped push the consenting adults fight. In 1976, attorney David Adamany shared with Clarenbach a memorandum of the research on the sodomy law he had prepared for the Paul Safransky case a few years earlier. This research summary was supplemented by a research project done by Dr. Warren Olson, the partner of gay bar owner Rodney Scheel. In 1977, gay member Gridley Hall urged the Madison Equal Opportunities Commission to help put the City of Madison on record in support of consenting adults legislation. His motion would be seconded by out alder James Yeadon. Such self-advocacy would not go unnoticed. Strong opponent Reverend Richard Pritchard noted in 1978 that the gay "community is rising to its own defense." The *Milwaukee Journal* reported on and editorialized about Pritchard's threats to "expose homosexuals in government," warning readers this might result in "an ugly, McCarthy-like atmosphere, with flimsy accusations smearing public reputations indiscriminately."[36]

There were, however, non-gay groups such as the Wisconsin Civil Liberties Union and the League of Women Voters who supported the measure as a good government cause. Madison Police Chief David Couper, who had put his department through training on gay issues and recruiting lesbians and gays, was an early supporter. His police department newsletter of August 1976 included an article titled "The Role of the Police in Regulating Public Morality." Couper wrote, "Our sexual perversion statute includes behavior that is not perverse nor even aberrant, but actually normal sexual behavior." In Couper's view, "the energies and resources of police can be better spent elsewhere." Couper was quite clear in his directive: "Noncommercial sexual conduct between consenting adults in private shall continue *not* to be a concern of the Department."[37]

While the argument that married couples might be swept up into criminal prosecutions for perversion was used to emphasize sexual privacy arguments, the double standard that applied to straight sexual acts was shown in a 1972 Wisconsin Supreme Court ruling in *Jones v. State*. The defendant had been charged with forcibly requiring oral sex from another inmate in the Milwaukee jail. He challenged the newer Wisconsin sexual perversion statute as being unconstitutional because of its vagueness. Part of his argument was that the language could result in prosecution of sexual acts by married couples, an area where some courts were carving out privacy rights. The Wisconsin Supreme Court, in Chief Justice Bruce Beilfuss's opinion, found no vagueness in the legislative language, which stated in section 944.17 that sexual perversion was "an abnormal act of sexual gratification involving the sex organ of one person and the mouth or anus of another." The adjective *abnormal* must have given him the insight that "it is beyond reasonable argument to claim that sec. 944.17(1), Stats., was enacted to control or prohibit the consensual and private sexual intimacies of married persons." In the court's view, he wrote, "We cannot believe this statute can or will be used to threaten or prosecute married couples in violation of their right of privacy."[38]

ENFORCEMENT OF SEX LAWS BY THE NUMBERS

A number of studies in the late 1970s and early 1980s provided data on the prosecution of sexual morality laws and cohabitation. While there was a generally held belief that the antiquated sex laws were seldom enforced, Louie Crew, a gay professor at UW–Stevens Point, undertook to document how the state sex laws were applied to gay men. His research, published in 1981, showed that "each year approximately 86 persons are arrested, 83 (96%) prosecuted, and 71 (83%) convicted of homosexual acts" under Wisconsin law. His data was a projection based on responses from fifty-one of the seventy-one district attorneys in the state who prosecuted criminal violations in 1980. The highest number of reported cases came from Milwaukee and Waukesha counties. Crew found that in the survey, the Milwaukee district attorney made reference only to male homosexuals on sex offenses with no mention of heterosexuals or lesbians being prosecuted. Crew believed that even when the law was not enforced, as a number of district attorneys replied was the case in their jurisdictions, gay men still had "the stigma against them, often to force them into an involuntary kind of self-oppression, making them live in constant fear of exposure and reprisals." In responses to Crew, seven district attorneys supported legislation to decriminalize consenting sex acts.[39]

Professor Martha Fineman, assistant professor at the UW–Madison Law School, found data on heterosexual cohabitation crimes. Though an unnamed source stated that there was "no sense in studying enforcement of a law that wasn't being enforced," Fineman obtained survey responses from fifty-seven of the seventy-one district attorneys on cohabitation cases, though not from the largest, Milwaukee County. The study, released in 1979, showed a range of sixty-five to eighty cases per year in the mid-1970s. The maximum penalty was nine months in prison and a fine of ten thousand dollars. Of the district attorneys who responded, 45 percent had a policy of not prosecuting cohabitation. Yet 51 percent believed "cohabitation is morally wrong and ought to be discouraged with criminal sanctions and prosecutions." Thirty-six percent thought enforcement of the statute meant "that people who cohabit will do so discreetly." In other words, the statute was thought to act as a deterrent to flagrant violators. Fineman observed that the way Wisconsin law was written, "it isn't necessary to prove sexual intercourse, just circumstances which imply sexual intercourse." Dane County District Attorney James Doyle Jr. said of such prosecutions, "Is this something government should be involved in? How much law enforcement resources would you devote to it?" He noted there had not been a cohabitation prosecution in Dane County in "a good many years." During public discussion of the consenting adults bill, the Fineman study and the Sheboygan cohabitation incident were frequently cited. Crew's study received mention only in the gay press.[40]

Another data-driven study came from Stephen Tordella, a demographer at the Applied Population Laboratory connected with the Department of Rural Sociology at UW–Madison. The study, based on census data, was sent March 4, 1980, to the senate committee reviewing consenting adults bill SB 552. Tordella found that "approximately 22,000 Wisconsin households contained unrelated persons of opposite sexes who could be classified as 'living together' in 1976. These households make up between one and two percent of the state's 1.5 million households." The author admitted there was no discernment as to how many were actually "cohabiting" in terms of the sex law or were simply sharing domiciles. The data showed couples "living together" were spread across the educational spectrum, although for those never married under age thirty-five, the number was higher, in the range of 5 percent to 10 percent. The high incidence in the young cohort suggested at least a probability of sexual activity. His conclusion was that " 'living together' is a phenomenon affecting a significant proportion of the population." This study would be cited in the public debate to reinforce the point that cohabitation was not unusual and in fact had become a common social norm.[41]

THE 1977 SESSION: FIRST FLOOR DEBATE

At the beginning of the 1977 Session, Clarenbach and Representative Marcia Coggs (D-Milwaukee), Barbee's successor, introduced one of the Barbee-type bills for comprehensive multiple sex law reforms, perhaps as a tribute to Barbee. Roger Durand, the Milwaukeean heading up the state gay lobbying effort, proclaimed he "hoped the bill would die quickly," citing the need to focus efforts on particular issues. It never emerged from committee. AB 323, introduced later in the session, would better speak to political realities, and Durand and others were working to get Milwaukee sponsors. *GPU News* reported that Durand and Alyn Hess, then head of Milwaukee's Gay People's Union (GPU), "seem optimistic that the new bill will be the first piece of sexual legislation to get out of committee and onto the floor since gays have been fighting for their rights."[42]

AB 323, introduced February 10, 1977, had six sponsors, with Clarenbach as lead sponsor. Other gay men sponsoring were Flintrop (D-Oshkosh) and Gunderson (R-Osseo). Representatives Coggs, Peter Tropman, and Steve Leopold, all Democrats from Milwaukee, also lent support. Leopold was helpful with legislators from Milwaukee's Southside. The senate co-sponsor was Senator David Berger. Prior sessions had seen sex reform bills get a hearing, but none had made it to the floor. This time, there would be floor action. The Assembly Judiciary Committee recommended the bill 8 to 5. When the Assembly Rules Committee put it on the calendar for debate, Reid Beveridge, veteran journalist, noted, "Rep. John Shabaz (R-New Berlin) almost shot out of his chair." Durand told *GPU News* that it was "now or never for this session."[43]

On May 5, 1977, the assembly took up AB 323 and defeated a key motion to kill by laying it on the table with 44 in favor and 55 against. After several amendments were adopted or beaten back, a motion by Republican Minority Leader John Shabaz to indefinitely postpone was defeated by the very close vote of 47 in favor and 50 against. Next, Shabaz moved to refer the bill to the Committee on State Affairs, which lost with 45 in favor and 52 against. The initial vote for passage was 55 in favor and 44 against. The assembly then voted against sending it immediately to the senate, which required a super-majority of two-thirds; the vote was 53 to 44. Clarenbach always believed a secret ballot would have resulted in many more favorable votes.[44]

One of the supporting documents for AB 323 distributed on May 5 was a list of purported endorsers, including 106 clergy, prepared by Reverend Judith Michaels, a Presbyterian minister at UW–Milwaukee. This riled up opponent Richard Pritchard, who contacted some of those listed in the Madison and Milwaukee areas. He claimed they had not seen the assembly bill but had instead had the introductory material read to them over the phone. Donn Edmark, news editor of WRJN in Racine, undertook his own investigation. On air, he claimed there were "startling" misrepresentations: "The circulatory letter . . . in my estimation is false." Upon being contacted by Edmark, respondents generally said they had not been asked about the proposed bill directly. Some organizations admitted they had a general position on the issue of decriminalizing homosexual acts but had not endorsed a Wisconsin-specific bill. An opposition group calling itself the Citizen's League for American Decency (CLAD) in Kenosha distributed printed copies of Edmark's commentary. Needless to say, it did not help public support for the bill.[45]

After the revelations, the *Racine Journal Times* reported that some area legislators were having second thoughts and favored sending the bill back to the finance committee. The paper quoted Edmark as saying that the bill was "just a smokescreen . . . to legalize homosexuality in Wisconsin." The Racine City Council passed a resolution that the assembly "seriously consider all of the implications of Bill 323." On May 11, the assembly referred the bill back to the Assembly Judiciary Committee, which recommended a substitute consenting adults bill by a 7 to 3 vote. The substitute "clean" bill did not include amendments on adultery or prostitution and focused only on consenting adults. On June 13, it was referred to the Joint Committee on Finance, where it died because no action was taken before the legislature adjourned.[46]

1979 SESSION: NEW STRATEGIES

In the next session, Clarenbach, as prime sponsor, with seven cosponsors, reintroduced consenting adults legislation, AB 514, in the assembly. The only action was a hearing that took place on August 2, 1979. In his testimony, Clarenbach explained, "The change this bill presents is one of the most basic principles of our country—the right of protection against unwarranted interference by the government in our private lives." He added, "I find it ironic, on this subject of 'love,' to find those in opposition often so hate filled."

One reason not much was done in the lower chamber was the fallout from the 1978 elections. The election of popular Republican Lee Sherman Dreyfus had increased the Republican seats in the assembly by six. Seven of the Democrats who were no longer there had been supporters of the previous consenting adults bill. On the other side of the issue, none of the Democrats who had voted against the consenting adults bill had trouble with reelection, with several running unopposed. Clarenbach believed the remaining Democrats were not daunted by the losses, as the 1977 majority had been abnormally large and Democratic turnout in the 1978 midterm elections had been lower. However, without those favorable seven votes, the majorities that passed the measure in the lower chamber no longer existed. Prudence suggested not bringing the measure to a quick floor vote. Upon introduction, Representative Gunderson observed its chances were "not very good."[47]

Surprisingly, the Republican members voting for sex reform in 1977 appeared to have suffered no consequences. All five running for reelection had no primary opposition and went on to win their general elections. Susan Shannon Engeleiter (R-Brookfield), Rod Johnston (R-Whitefish Bay), and David Opitz (R-Port Washington) were later elevated to the state senate, and Engeleiter and Patricia Goodrich of Berlin were later part of the leadership team of the Republican legislators. Gunderson, as noted, would go on to win a US House seat from the Third District in western Wisconsin. Engeleiter won a primary battle to become the Republican candidate for the US Senate in 1988 but lost in the general election to Democrat Herb Kohl in a reasonably tight race. She was endorsed in the general election for the US Senate race by The Wisconsin Light, the state's gay newspaper, which noted her votes for consenting adults and the gay rights bills. The editors wrote, "Supporting Engeleiter will send a message to the Republicans. It will tell them that Lesbians and Gays cannot be taken for granted by either party. We are willing to support Republicans who have a record of supporting our issues."[48]

Though Clarenbach's assembly bill did not go far in this session, consenting adults legislation would be tried again in the 1979 legislative session, this time with a new tactic for the senate. Senate Bill (SB) 552 was introduced on February 12, 1980, many months after the assembly bill. Instead of being associated with Clarenbach, who had by this time become personally identified with the assembly bills, the bill was introduced in the senate by the Senate Committee on Human Services upon the request of a number of organizations and individuals. The committee was chaired by Senator Carl Thompson of Dane County, a former Democratic candidate for governor for whom Clarenbach had worked as a young legislative aide. The Thompson and Clarenbach families were close, as Thompson's

wife, Marian, worked at the university in the same area as Kay Clarenbach. The list of requestors printed in the bill included civic groups such
as the League of Women Voters, the Rights and Responsibilities Section of
the State Bar of Wisconsin, the Wisconsin Council on Human Concerns,
and the Dane County Democratic Party. Labor allies were on the list, including American Federation of State, County and Municipal Employees
(AFSCME) Councils 24 and 48, the Wisconsin Federation of Teachers,
Dane County COPE (Committee on Political Education of the Dane County
Federation of Labor), and United Professionals for Quality Health Care.
A number of ministers were listed, mainly from Unitarian Universalist
congregations. Documents existed for specific endorsements to the bill
to avoid the fiasco of the prior session's meltdown.[49]

On February 27, 1980, though it was late in the session scheduled to
end April 2, the senate committee reported recommending the bill by a
vote of 3 to 2, and no one appeared against it. Reverend Tony Larsen, a
Unitarian Universalist minister from Racine, spoke in support, saying, "I
believe the government has no right in the bedroom. . . . Police in some
cities, including Milwaukee, use the sodomy law to entrap homosexuals."
Eunice Edgar of the Civil Liberties Union contended the present cohabitation law "is always applied capriciously." Clarenbach, who testified at the
hearing, told the press, "Undoubtedly most members of the legislature are
violating or have violated the law." He said that did not mean legislators
are "immoral perverts" but simply average people.[50]

The new draft bill replaced references to the value-laden *sexual perversion* with the term *sexual gratification*. The *Janesville Gazette*, citing
Tordella's demographic study on cohabitation, said the present law "is
being increasingly disregarded." Noting that area senators Thompson
and Cullen had voted for the measure, the paper wrote, "The process of
separating secular law from ecclesiastical law requires exceptional insights
and understandings as well as a willingness to persevere." On March 19,
the senate considered the bill but had no debate. They needed and acquired
a two-thirds procedural vote to get to the vote on passage and achieved
that with a 23 to 7 ballot, with a number of Republicans voting favorably
on the procedural matter. The actual vote on passage was eighteen ayes
and twelve nos. Two Republican senators, Johnston and McCallum, voted
aye, and three Democrats voted no. Johnston would later aver his prime

concern was lifting "the ban on the various forms of sexual activity for married persons."[51]

Upon the bill's passage in the senate, Governor Dreyfus indicated he had "no problem with the bill." Martin Schreiber, his predecessor and opponent in the 1978 election, had also publicly said during the campaign that he would sign a consenting adults bill. For Dreyfus, the bill essentially was, in his words, "making the law conform with societal standards," which said he had "seen change . . . in my own lifetime." He added that the law ought to reflect the way police and other law enforcement personnel are enforcing society's standards.[52]

On March 21, the Assembly Committee on Criminal Justice and Public Safety voted to recommend the senate bill by a vote of 7 to 6. Chairperson Representative Edward McClain of Wausau expected the assembly would take it up before adjournment. When the bill hit the floor on March 26, Republican minority leader Shabaz moved non-concurrence, that is, rejection of the senate's passage of the bill, and the motion carried 54 to 41. The bill was dead. The votes lost in the 1978 election might have been the linchpin, but the new tactics practiced in the senate had paid off and would be refined in the future. Dreyfus's comments would help to protect the Republicans who were in support of the bill. Clarenbach called the senate passage "a step toward eventual enactment."[53]

1981 SESSION: THE BIG PUSH

In 1981, organizers for consenting adults legislation again employed the strategy of using legislative committees rather than individuals to sponsor the bill, one in the assembly and one in the senate. The Committee on Criminal Justice and Public Safety sponsored AB 235, and the Committee on Human Services sponsored SB 205. The bills, substantially the same as those attempted in the last session, were introduced in early March 1981. Like the 1979 effort, the committee bills were introduced at the request of organizations and individuals, this time in far greater numbers than in the prior session and again with letters documenting the requests. These included civic and organizational groups such as the League of Women Voters, the Wisconsin Council on Human Concerns, the Wisconsin Chapter of the National Association of Social Workers, and the Madison Police

Department. Labor allies included the Wisconsin Federation of Teachers and AFSCME. Seven district attorneys—six Democrats from Bayfield, Dane, Eau Claire, Green, Marathon, and Polk Counties, and one Republican from Pierce County—were also on the list.[54]

Religious support was also robust. Significantly, the request listed twenty-seven ministers, including Bishop Marjorie Matthews of the Wisconsin Methodist Church, the first woman elected as a bishop for the United Methodists. Matthews was following in the footsteps of her predecessor, Bishop Jesse DeWitt, who in early 1980 wrote a letter of personal support that cited the 1976 statement of Social Principles of the United Methodist Church. That Methodist statement read, "We recognize that sexuality is a good gift of God, and we believe persons may be fully human only when that gift is acknowledged and affirmed." The statement also noted sex "is only to be clearly affirmed in the marriage bond." Matthews said, "It is my understanding that the word of God is available to everyone—to all the children of God. I certainly would not presume to tell God who should receive his grace." In the next session, while consistent in her support, Matthews would note, "I am sure that you realize how much opposition there is to my making such a statement." The supporting ministers ranged from Methodist to Lutheran, Congregational, Unitarian Universalist, Presbyterian, Episcopal, and Disciples of Christ. A portion were associated with campus ministries. Rabbi Lawrence Maher of Mount Sinai in Wausau joined them. Reverend Paul Flucke of Plymouth Church, United Church of Christ, asked other Milwaukee-area clergy to join. Representative Dismas Becker, a Democrat from Milwaukee and a former Jesuit, articulated the importance of the Catholic church endorsing the effort: "The oversight and dominion of this behavior lies within the religious community. It is total ignorance to assume an elected body will be able to do that."[55]

In early 1981, Clarenbach was in contact with Milwaukee Roman Catholic Archbishop Rembert Weakland, who had previously shown support to the gay community through his writings in the Milwaukee *Catholic Herald* and diocesan support for the City of Milwaukee gay rights ordinance. Reluctantly, Weakland declined to add his name to the endorsers. He explained, "I have not had the opportunity to teach and instruct the Catholic population in the way in which I would prefer before such endorsement. So

Milwaukee's Roman Catholic Archbishop Rembert Weakland was a key player in efforts to change Wisconsin's morality laws. On the consenting adults bill decriminalizing homosexual acts, he kept a position of neutrality. On the gay rights bill, he provided crucial support, joining other religious leaders including Lutheran, Episcopalian, and Methodist bishops, as well as Presbyterian, Baptist, Congregationalist, Unitarian, and Jewish faith leaders in Wisconsin. WHI IMAGE ID 119214

often there is great confusion between the moral demands of the Catholic Church and Legislation." While admitting the Church needed to become "more sophisticated" regarding the legislation, he assured Clarenbach, "You can be sure that I will not voice any opposition to it." Charles Phillips, executive director of the Wisconsin Catholic Conference, the Wisconsin bishops' lobbying arm, was also neutral, though he recognized the import of the legislation: "Since laws against fornication and adultery are seldom enforced, the measure would have its most practical effect on statutes pertaining to homosexual acts." Phillips cited the teaching on homosexuals adopted by the National Conference of Catholic Bishops in 1976, *To Live in CHRIST JESUS*. Interviewed in Madison's *Capital Times*, he said, "Yes, we are probably neutral. We have no intention of issuing a position on the bill. . . . The things it wants to legalize are darn near impossible to enforce anyway."[56]

But religious opposition was building. In 1980, Alfred Swan, longtime pastor of Madison's First Congregational Church, wrote a letter to Clarenbach voicing resistance. Swan believed that trends to accept cohabitation and fornication were "so much the worse for our common life." In 1981, an incipient moral majority–type organization formed. Claiming to be a statewide coalition of local morality groups, it called itself PULL, or People Using Legislation Legally. In opposing consenting adults, the group's missive said, "Think of Sodom and Gomorrah—destroyed by fire from heaven because of the wickedness of the people." Also opposing the "open sex" law was Fort Wilderness, tag-lined "A Stronghold of Christian Adventure," in McNaughton. Baptist pastor William Lincoln of Watertown thought the bill would "breed violence, crime and abuse." By April 1981, a formal Wisconsin Moral Majority organization headquartered in Green Bay took the field with a newsletter, the *Moral Majority Eagle*. The group recruited county chairmen and held seminars on civic issues denouncing "humanism." The June issue of the *Eagle* listed assembly votes on consenting adults as a "Report Card," with a minus being a vote for the bill.[57]

For this session, the main action took place in the assembly, as the senate bill made it only to committee. Introduced March 11, 1981, AB 235 was the subject of a hearing on March 26. Longtime sponsor Clarenbach predicted it would pass this session. He commented that most people "didn't even know they were violating the law." He emphasized that the present bill did not decriminalize adultery or prostitution. It was recommended by the Committee on Criminal Justice and Public Safety on April 23, 1981, by a vote of 7 to 5.[58]

A number of amendments saw floor action on April 28. An early motion to table the bill was beaten back with forty-four ayes and fifty-two nos, and consideration of the amendments continued. Clarenbach and a number of Republicans offered an amendment as a statement of intent for the bill. It was a sort of fig leaf for the morally concerned.

944.01 Intent. The state recognizes that it has a duty to encourage high moral standards. Although the state does not regulate the private sexual conduct of consenting adults, the state does not condone or encourage any form of sexual conduct outside of marriage. Marriage is the foundation of family and society. Its stability is basic to morality and civilization, and of vital interest to society and this state.

Though it did not appease naysayers, it did provide some middle ground for those who might be nervous about voting yes.

As was typical of assembly hearings in the spring session, a number of schoolchildren were in the galleries for their annual visits to the Capitol, and legislators became wary about discussing the bills in any detail. As debate proceeded, Shabaz commented, "No amount of amending is going to make it passable." However, a test vote on tabling the bill appeared to point to passage. The crucial vote came on indefinite postponement (which would kill the bill) from a motion at the end of debate by Representative Wayne Wood (D-Janesville). The vote to postpone passed 50 to 49, with eighteen other Democrats joining Wood and thirty-one Republicans to kill it. The press noted that Clarenbach, aware that "there were 49 solid votes for it," had "hoped to pick up the one needed to give it preliminary approval."[59]

Notably, nine Republicans voted with forty Democrats to keep it alive. Republican Mary Panzer of West Bend, who voted in favor, defended her vote as in line with Republican principles. Her father had been a Progressive Party leader in the 1930s. She said, "The Republican Party says government shouldn't be involved in private life. I can't think of anything more private than this." Republican Representative John Merkt, who voted to kill, took the opposite view, though he acknowledged that much of the law was not enforced: "A legitimate purpose of law is to set society standards." A majority of the female legislators supported the bill, with fourteen of the eighteen voting in favor. Strong supporters from the Milwaukee near suburbs included Representatives Betty Jo Nelsen of Shorewood and Lolita Schneiders of Menomonee Falls.[60]

One more attempt was made in the 1981 session. During consideration of the 1981–1983 biennial budget, Clarenbach brought a motion to the Democratic caucus to insert the consenting adults language into the budget document—a strategy based on a long state tradition of loading policy items into the must-pass budget legislation. While he won the caucus vote, at least one conservative Democrat immediately pledged not to vote for passage if it was included. Since no Republican votes could be expected for the caucus version of the budget, the majority party could ill-afford to have members bail. Realizing the divisive character of the move, Clarenbach withdrew the motion. The action showed a political maturity that gained him support in the caucus both for his run as Speaker pro tempore in the next session and for his bills.[61]

1983: OVER THE GOAL LINE

Sixteen years after Barbee first introduced sex reform legislation and eight years after Clarenbach proposed his first consenting adults bill with Barbee, the 1983 session of the legislature would see passage of consenting adults legislation. Although Clarenbach had stepped back from being the main sponsor, he would still be credited with the several-year push that led to the bill's passage.

As in the 1979 session, the Committee on Criminal Justice and Public Safety introduced AB 250, which would decriminalize sexual acts committed by consenting adults in private, to the assembly on March 18, 1983. The committee reported it out with a favorable recommendation for adoption on April 12. The hearing on the bill produced sparks with members of the Moral Majority, whose leaders testified that existing law was needed to "protect the bedrooms" and that the "state law backs up God's law." District Attorney Rod Zemke of Eau Claire told the committee, "I object to someone from the church who says they know everything." Committee member Representative David Prosser said "cohabitation leads to bad things—like children born out of wedlock."[62]

Floor action began April 19. Representative June Jaronitzky (R-Iron River) and nine other Republicans (seven in favor of the bill) introduced the morality statement from the last session as an amendment. The *Green Bay Press Gazette*, while supporting the bill because of the "conviction that government has no business in bedrooms occupied by adults," noted that the morality clause "definitely needed to be said." This was mildly ironic because sponsor Jaronitzky's district included Hurley, a town depicted for prostitution serving miners and lumberjacks in Edna Ferber's novel *Come and Get It*. The vote for moral intent was 96 to 0.[63]

Other amendments were beaten back, including an amendment to have a referendum on the issue before the bill could take effect. Representative John Manske, a closeted gay Republican from Milton, said, "I think we ought to swallow hard and do the voting the people put us here to do." He voted for the bill and later commented, "Nobody was there waiting

In 1983, Governor Tony Earl signed the consenting adults bill, which decriminalized homosexual acts. Standing onlookers included, left to right, Dan Curd, Linda Roovers, Dick Wagner, Representative John Manske, Representative David Clarenbach, Representative Marcia Coggs, Representative Dave Travis, and an unidentified individual. FROM THE AUTHOR'S COLLECTION

with a noose," when he was back in his district. Representative Wood, who killed the bill in the prior session, argued passage would "permit and, in effect legalize homosexual activity that goes on now without the blessing of the law." Representative Cloyd Porter (R-Burlington) claimed the bill would permit "sex in the Brewers' parking lot" during tailgate parties. Following custom, Representative Sheehan Donoghue (R-Merrill) introduced district guests in the gallery. Donoghue told her colleagues, "The ladies are finding it fascinating [to learn] where they can and can't do all these things." She would vote for the bill. The vote on preliminary passage was 55 to 42. Again, Republican votes for passage were key, as seventeen Democrats voted against the bill and thirteen Republicans voted for it, half of them women. The minority leader of the Republicans, Shabaz, and assistant minority leader, Tommy Thompson, were against the bill on all votes. A final vote to send it to the senate on April 21 was 53 to 43.[64]

The senate took AB 250 up on May 3 and, again, all proposed amendments were beaten back except for a technical amendment that reverted sex in public and sex with minors from a misdemeanor to a felony. The senate vote for passage was 20 to 13. Even more so than in the assembly, Republican votes were critical. Thirteen Democrats and seven Republicans made up the majority. The no votes were six Democrats and seven Republicans. Thus, the Republicans were evenly split, and the Democrats were two to one in favor. The assembly quickly concurred on the technical change, and the billed passed. Democratic Governor Earl happily signed the bill into law on May 5, 1983, completing over a decade's struggle.[65]

Clarenbach, in the press spotlight as usual, said passage "reaffirms the willingness of the Legislature to endorse privacy rights." Further, he opined, "It shows a general trend that policy makers in Wisconsin are willing to take some political risks to confront the Moral Majority on their own turf—the religious and moral obligations of government to enforce religious tenets." The *Racine Journal Times* had been skeptical in earlier sessions but accepted the new law with the observation, "The bill apparently will leave moral judgement on activities which may violate conventional moral standards up to a higher authority." The *Capital Times* of Madison proclaimed, "It's about time." Clarenbach got a great deal of recognition for his role in passage. The *Milwaukee Journal* editorialized, "Much credit is due State Rep. David Clarenbach (D-Madison), who waged a long battle for passage." A May 6 story in the *Milwaukee Journal* noted, "In the earlier legislative sessions, Clarenbach was almost alone in his quest for changes in the law." In signing, Governor Earl singled out one legislator for special commendation and said, "I think this moment is a genuine tribute to Dave Clarenbach."[66]

GAY RIGHTS IN WISCONSIN: A NATIONAL FIRST

While the fight for decriminalization was proceeding, an opportunity opened in the 1981 session to advance the other main agenda item: non-discrimination on the basis of sexual orientation or, as it would come to be known popularly, the "gay rights bill." In the press releases for consenting adults legislation, Clarenbach cited support from several Protestant clergy and Jewish leaders; Catholics were generally silent or neutral on the matter. This changed dramatically as focus shifted from consenting adults to nondiscrimination legislation. AB 70, a statewide nondiscrimination bill that included homosexuals as a protected class, was both introduced and passed in the 1981 legislative session. It would be the first such bill passed in the nation.

That discrimination was still an issue was highlighted by the case of Patrick Batt, who in 1977 was fired from the Marion Heights Nursing Home, a Catholic-affiliated home. As with Safransky's case, Batt's case became high profile due to his involvement in the Milwaukee GPU, where he served as chair of the board. *GPU News* reported that in asking for his resignation, the home felt "the common knowledge of his lifestyle had compromised his ability to function as Personnel Director." Batt refused to resign and was fired. While the home tried to claim performance issues as the reason for dismissal, Batt cited a recent evaluation in which he was scored as "very good," the highest classification, in each of the twenty-one areas of

the evaluation. His case was taken up in federal court by the Wisconsin Civil Liberties Union, who argued the case showed the state might not protect the employment rights of individuals who publicly expressed a preference for those of the same sex by joining a gay organization. The federal judge in the matter was former Wisconsin attorney general Robert Warren, who had submitted the brief against Safransky. His unfavorable ruling showed the ongoing lack of employment protections for homosexuals and added fuel to the fire for a state-level nondiscrimination law.[67]

The seeds for the success of the state nondiscrimination bill were planted in 1976 with the American bishops' pastoral letter *To Live*

Patrick Batt's high-profile firing in 1977 from a Milwaukee-area nursing home because of his sexual orientation highlighted the need for a nondiscrimination law in Wisconsin. ARCHIVES DEPARTMENT, UNIVERSITY OF WISCONSIN—MILWAUKEE LIBRARIES

in CHRIST JESUS. This breakthrough document outlined the American Catholic position on homosexuals with this teaching: "Homosexuals, like everyone else, should not suffer from prejudice against their basic human rights. They have a right to respect, friendship and justice." While still against homosexual activity, the bishops' letter saw gay people as a minority with a distinct identity. Many mainline Protestant denominations had already gone on record in the 1970s in favor of nondiscrimination toward homosexuals and, in an era of ecumenical dialogue, many churches were speaking openly about civil rights. Catholic bishops were not immune from recognizing these changes. With the Catholic church's new teaching, homosexuals could be brought into a civil rights discussion. The next step was to translate this teaching into action.[68]

A key to enlisting support of the church was Milwaukee Archbishop Weakland, who had declined to support the consenting adults legislation earlier in the 1981 session. Weakland, who had been heavily influenced by the American bishops' pastoral letter, was already known to be supportive of gay civil rights. On July 19, 1980, the Milwaukee *Catholic Herald* carried his column Herald of Hope, the Archbishop Shares. Under the heading "Who Is Our Neighbor?," he wrote movingly, "We have to see Gay people, then, not as an enemy to be battered down, but as persons worthy of respect and friendship." Tying himself to the pastoral letter, which had been adopted before he was installed as bishop in Milwaukee, Weakland urged readers, "We must be concerned, also, about [gay] rights. Consequently, I cannot believe it is a Christian attitude that would block them from holding responsible positions in the community." In closing he wrote, "I invite all in the Catholic community to join me in showing this kind of respect . . . so that we can assist all members of society in the exercise of their rights, so that no one is treated as a second-class citizen or as somehow 'contaminated.'" Despite this plea, the Archbishop needed to be persuaded, as he had not added his name in support of consenting adults legislation.[69]

A gay activist from Milwaukee would be the linchpin in gaining Weakland's support. In a matter of years, Leon Rouse had become a central figure in the movement. Rouse would recall being impelled to activism by Anita Bryant's victory speech in the 1977 Dade County, Florida, referendum. His first foray into activism was to propose an amendment to

the UW–Milwaukee Student Association's constitution to protect homosexuals; it won by a vote of 33 to 2. In February 1978, as a representative
of the UW–Milwaukee gay community to the statewide Wisconsin Student Caucus, he urged delegates to adopt a resolution against "government regulation of the private sexual behaviors of its adult citizens." The
statement was similar to the 1966 sex plank but went further on record,
stating opposition to "discrimination based on sexual preference" and
calling for legislation to that effect. In the same year, Rouse persuaded the
Academic Staff Committee of UW–Milwaukee to adopt a statement: "We
recommend that the University of Wisconsin–Milwaukee make it publicly
and explicitly known that it adheres to a nondiscrimination policy on the
basis of sexual preference." The faculty senate passed a resolution with
the same wording. Rouse would later be described as both confrontational
and tenacious.[70]

In 1978, Rouse formed the Committee for Fundamental Judeo-
Christian Human Rights and served as its coordinator. His board included
Lutheran, Methodist, Episcopal, and United Church of Christ clergy. The
organization would claim credit for introducing the 1981 nondiscrimination bill through the agency of Representative Steve Leopold of Milwaukee. As legislation for nondiscrimination began to move forward, Rouse
attempted to find an inroad with Archbishop Weakland. Unable to get an
appointment with him, Rouse attended mass at the Cathedral of St. John
the Evangelist for several months before finally approaching the archbishop to ask for his support of AB 70. After reviewing a modified draft of
the bill, Weakland found an indirect way to show support. Reverend John
Murtagh, head of the Archdiocesan Office of Human Concerns, had noted
in correspondence with Clarenbach that his office had not been asked to
take a position in the prior session (on SB 552, the 1979 consenting adults
bill). Now, he wanted be kept abreast of matters for the 1981 session and
asked Weakland's opinion on the nondiscrimination measure. In this environment, the archbishop's letter on AB 70, sent March 2, 1981, played an
important though discreet role. Weakland wrote, "I feel that your commission can in good conscience support this legislation insofar as it bans
discrimination." Citing the 1976 pastoral letter, he continued, "I feel that
support of this Bill would be indeed proper and consistent with previous
positions that the Church has taken."[71]

Weakland, while an authoritative voice, was not unique among Wisconsin Catholics willing to speak out on nondiscrimination as the legislature weighed the matter. Perhaps the most active Catholic around the legislature was Charles Phillips, head of the Wisconsin Catholic Conference, the lobby serving the bishops' interests. He commented favorably in the press that the cities of Madison and Milwaukee had adopted "human rights" bills that protected homosexuals from discrimination, and he quoted the teaching from the bishops' pastoral letter. A particular target of Catholic lobbying was Senator Gerald Kleczka from the Polish Southside of Milwaukee. The Human Concerns Committee of Our Lady of Lourdes Church on South Fifty-Sixth Street wrote him in support of the bill's drive for "God-given human dignity." After the vote, a story circulated that Kleczka's grade school teacher, a nun, was brought to the Capitol and seated in the gallery to encourage a positive vote. Kleczka, later a US congressman, acknowledged the story but denied he needed her presence for a favorable vote.[72]

Other groups voiced support through individuals. Sister Naomi Schoen, of the School Sisters of Saint Francis based in Milwaukee, wrote in support of AB 70 on behalf of the Milwaukee Archdiocesan Sisters Council, as did Father Tony Schumacher on behalf of the Peace and Justice Committee of the Priest Senate of the Diocese of Madison and eighteen signatories of the Catholic Priest District of Racine. Brother Joseph Pfeiffer of the Sacred Heart Fathers and Brothers spoke as a therapist who had worked with gay men, whom he claimed were used as "emotional scapegoat[s]." He wrote, "The real issue is not that of sexual preference but rather, homophobia." Others, including Reverend Steven Scherer of Green Bay, wrote to urge their legislators to vote for the bill. Father Gene Pocernich of the Milwaukee Archdiocesan Office for Human Concerns was present for the assembly vote.[73]

While Weakland was the heavy hitter in a state with an estimated 30 percent Catholic population, a whole chorus line of bishops or bishop-equivalents stood behind AB 70. This overwhelming show included Wisconsin Methodist Bishop Matthews, who had bravely stood alone on the consenting adults issue. Now she was joined in support of nondiscrimination by Episcopal bishops William Wentland of the Eau Claire diocese and Charles T. Gaskell of Milwaukee. Moderate Lutheran traditions were represented by Bishop Robert S. Wilch for the Wisconsin–Upper Michigan

Synod of the Lutheran Church in America, and synod presidents Vernon
Anderson of the American Lutheran Church Northern Wisconsin District
and A. C. Schumacher of the Southern Wisconsin District. Executive Pres-
byters Carl Simon of the Milwaukee Presbytery and Verne Sindlinger of
the Winnebago Presbytery spoke from the Calvinist reformed tradition.
Simon quoted from a recent Presbyterian resolution that stated that "the
Christian community can neither condone nor participate in the widespread contempt for homosexual persons that prevails in our general
culture." Simon placed the action in reference to the Milwaukee nondiscrimination ordinance, which had also included Rabbi Barry Silberg of
Congregation Emanu-El B'ne Jeshurun. Further support came from Ralph
Ley, conference president of the Wisconsin United Church of Christ, and
William Wells, executive minister of the Wisconsin Baptist Convention.[74]

THE GAY RIGHTS BILL TAKES THE FLOOR

On February 3, 1981, AB 70, the nondiscrimination bill, was introduced
in the assembly with sponsors Clarenbach, Leopold, Coggs, Becker, and
Ulichny. Once introduced, the bill was referred to the Judiciary Committee, but as part of legislative management, it was shifted to the Committee on Health and Human Concerns. The committee hearing on May 12
was busy. Clarenbach, as sponsor, led with the question, "Why should
any person be denied a job, a home, or the use of a public place because
he or she is a homosexual?" He closed with what had become his consistent message, "The point is not whether homosexuality is admirable; the
issue is whether discrimination is tolerable." There were fifteen appearances in support for the bill, including Leon Rouse and Barbara Lightner, plus members of civil liberties organizations and religious persons.
Seventeen registered in support, most of them gay advocates. My own
statement quoted from the National Gay Task Force: "It's Time." The only
appearance against came from Reverend Pritchard, and one registration
against came from someone representing a group styled the Un-Gays.[75]

After committee approval by 8 to 6, the bill was scheduled for floor
action on October 27. Clarenbach sought to focus the debate on the issue
of discrimination, noting,

> There's been a good deal of talk . . . that we're going to be debating
> homosexuality today, and I think that that's a serious misinterpreta-
> tion of the issue before us. . . . We live in a land of liberty and justice
> for all. That's what we say every morning in this House—liberty and
> justice for all. And that statement of fact does not read "except gays,"
> any more than it reads "except Jews" or "except Blacks" or "except
> Republicans" or Democrats or any other minority group.

Clarenbach cited the backing of Weakland and others in the chorus of
religious supporters as well as support from Governor Dreyfus's Advisory
Council for Women and Family Initiatives. "It's a matter of bigotry," he
stated in closing.[76]

Minority leader Shabaz responded for the opposition. He compared
the choice of sexual orientation to the choice of whether or not to commit
a felony and stated that discrimination laws should not apply to choices
of behavior. Shabaz urged a vote to kill, "no matter what is going to be
said over you in church." In response, Clarenbach cited the Kinsey report,
which maintained that homosexuality was not a choice but the way people
were born. Even if you reject the biological argument, he stated, "you still
are dealing with a person who did not consciously of their own volition
choose to be a homosexual any more than anyone chooses to be a heterosexual." Then, with passion, Clarenbach continued,

> I find your protestations prejudiced and callous. The very thought
> that homosexuals have not "earned" their right to true minority sta-
> tus in the eyes of the law—the implication that homosexuals have not
> been treated unjustly enough, have not suffered from ignorance and
> hate enough, and have not been the scapegoats of society enough . . .
> is cruel and absurd.

Not to adopt, he concluded, "will give bigots unwritten license to practice
their destructive craft." The motion to kill failed by forty-one ayes to fifty-
five nos. The vote was scheduled for October 23. It passed the assembly by
a close vote of 49 to 45.[77]

One incident during floor consideration was significant. The lobbyist for the School Board Association drafted an amendment to explicitly exempt schools from the legislation, which played on the myth of homosexuals as corrupters of youth. Democrats caught wind of it as the lobbyist shopped around for majority party sponsors. He was directed to go talk to Representative Flintrop, who chaired the Assembly Education Committee. As chair, through scheduling bills for hearings or executive actions, he had control over whether any bills that might be desired by the association would ever see light of day. Flintrop bluntly told the representative to fold it up and put it back in his pocket. The amendment was not introduced.[78]

The night of assembly passage, Clarenbach, who was closely attending to legislative management, wrote Senator Fred Risser requesting the bill's assignment to the Senate Judiciary Committee. It was later reassigned to the Committee on State and Local Affairs and Taxation, which held a hearing on January 28, 1982. The lead speaker in support was Clarenbach. Also speaking for the bill were religious persons and Tom Zander for civil liberties advocates. Longtime gay advocate Alyn Hess spoke, and one of the early GPU organizers, Donna Utke, registered the organization's support. Twelve of the sixteen organizations and people registered in support were gay and lesbian advocates. Rouse's lobbying was credited as "nothing short of amazing and fantastic." Among other efforts, his Committee for Fundamental Judeo-Christian Human Rights had circulated a memo from the Legislative Reference Bureau drafting attorney that made clear the nondiscrimination proposal did not touch the criminal statutes and thus could not be considered a Trojan horse for consenting adults legislation.[79]

The lead speaker against was Max Andrews of the Wisconsin Moral Majority, who spoke for three hundred churches and a mailing list of eight thousand people. His argument was that "those people are not a natural minority and therefore should not be considered for this civil rights legislation." The Committee reported it out by a 4 to 2 vote, with two holdouts, Jerome Van Sistine (D-Green Bay) and Frank Lasee (R-De Pere). During the February 16 floor debate, the senate adopted one amendment by Senator Don Hanaway to specifically state that affirmative action would not be required on the basis of sexual orientation. Attorneys who worked for various state agencies were split over whether the bill might be interpreted this way. To clarify the intent, Clarenbach agreed to accept Hanaway's amendment. The key senate vote, and only roll call, was on a motion by Senator Opitz to kill through nonconcurrence; the motion failed to carry by a vote of 13 to 19. A voice vote accomplished passage, and the bill (with the new amendment) moved to the assembly. On Clarenbach's urging, the assembly concurred with the amendment, and the bill was passed on to Governor Dreyfus.[80]

The Governor's Advisory Council for Women and Family Initiatives had voted in September to support AB 70, but the governor himself had not spoken about the bill. He had a general policy of not commenting on signing until matters reached his desk. In the short time between full legislative passage and the governor's signing, two Christian radio stations mounted a full-scale lobbying effort of phone calls to the executive office. Bill Kraus, a chief aide, commented, "Nine hundred calls to this place is a catastrophe." They received nearly three thousand. Initially, the calls ran against signing, but when Madison's WORT-FM community radio began urging listeners to call in for support, the number balanced out. Whether Dreyfus, a Republican, would veto or sign was not clear, though he did not kowtow to the Moral Majority. When Jerry Falwell visited Madison, his staff made sure the governor was not in town. Still, efforts to persuade Dreyfus not to sign were strong. In Appleton, for instance, the *Post-Crescent*, in a supportive editorial on the bill, mentioned that the Fox Valley Family Forum was among those pressuring Dreyfus not to sign. In the end, Dreyfus signed because, as Kraus explained, he did not think people had the right to inquire into another's sexual orientation. Aide Kraus put it, "He thinks that's an outrageous invasion of privacy." Madison's *Capital Times* praised Dreyfus "for his refusal to bow to a last-minute campaign against the bill." He signed it into law on February 25, 1982.[81]

Dreyfus's embrace of the privacy argument validated part of the gay community's strategy during the long years of lobbying on consenting adults. While acknowledging heavy veto pressure, Dreyfus stated at the signing, "I have decided to sign this bill for one basic reason: to protect one's right to privacy." His reasoning was that "discrimination on sexual preference, if allowed, clearly must allow inquiries into one's private life that go beyond reasonable inquiry and in fact invade one's privacy." For the governor, it was also important that no "gay quotas" be required because of the last-minute affirmative action amendment. Dreyfus noted that the existing nondiscrimination ordinances of Madison, Milwaukee, and Dane County had not led to "problems associated with them, which

Leon Rouse, a community activist, and Representative David Clarenbach looked on as Governor Lee Sherman Dreyfus signed the first-in-the-nation gay rights law in 1982. It would be seven years before another state passed such a law. FROM THE AUTHOR'S COLLECTION

many predicted." Dreyfus's final statement was, "I feel very strongly that one's sexual preferences, either homosexual or heterosexual, have absolutely no place for expression in our classrooms, and should not be tolerated." This set up a future issue regarding schools and sexual orientation that would also play out in the future.[82]

Triumphant with the win, Clarenbach announced to the press, "Wisconsin made history today!" as the first state in the nation with a gay rights bill. The legislator's hope was that "this is only a beginning, and that what happened in Wisconsin will boost gay rights across the country." The *New York Native* and other gay papers had followed the bill's progress with rapt attention. Its story on passage, headlined "Nuns in the Gallery," touted Wisconsin's successful strategy of confronting the Moral Majority with other religious voices on the issue. In a statement from the Madison United, Lightner praised Clarenbach and Rouse and the churches for standing up

New York Native 3/15-28/82

NUNS IN THE GALLERY

The Church, David Clarenbach, and Wisconsin's Gay Rights Bill

by Carol Stroebel

Wisconsin has become the first state in the union to enact a gay civil rights law. The state Senate passed Assembly Bill 70 on a voice vote February 17. (See "Rights Bill Passes Wisconsin Senate; Will Go to Governor for Signature," Native 32.) As expected, Republican Gov. Lee Sherman Dreyfus signed AB 70 February 25.

The driving force behind the bill in the state legislature was its author, state Rep. David Clarenbach (D-Madison). Clarenbach, who was 18 when first elected to public office, is now 28 and has represented downtown Madison in the Assembly for eight years. He has introduced legislation for gay civil rights each year he has been in the statehouse. The Native interviewed him in his legislative offices.

Carol Stroebel: *Wisconsin is the first state to pass such a bill, correct?*

Rep. David Clarenbach: Yes. I don't think it's any fluke or mistake that it occurred in Wisconsin first. One would think that New York or California, with their large and highly politically active gay communities in sensitive environments, would be the place for that first step to be taken. But Wisconsin has a tradition of progressive and innovative legislation.

Is that the only reason?

No, a lot of groundwork was laid here that perhaps other states have not laid. We succeeded in creating an environment of political security by confronting the Moral Majority and their issues. We confronted them and played their game. Naturally, politicians are afraid to offend even a very narrow minority if they are single issue and very vocal. Thus the alleged strength of the Moral Majority. In Wisconsin, our assessment was that if the members of the legislature were allowed to have a secret vote on the gay rights issue—which, of course, they can't—they would vote for it.

Our quest was to create some political security and an environment where we could match the Moral Majority and the ultra-right-wing religious constituency with some equal strength of our own on religious issues. That, more than anything else, was the key to our success.

We generated almost unanimous—literally across-the-board—endorsements of the bill from the leaders and constituencies of the mainstream religions in the state. We got the Archbishop of Milwaukee to endorse the bill. To have the Archbishop writing letters, to have nuns carted in from all over the state to lobby senators and representatives, that counts for a lot. We created a situation so that any legislator who voted for a gay rights bill could run for reelection in the fall or could respond to a reactionary

Wisconsin state representative David Clarenbach.

minister raising trouble in his district by dragging out a dozen letters from the bishops of Catholic, Methodist, Lutheran, and other denominations from around the state.

The issue was not whether homosexuality was admirable or good, because clearly, according to many of the religions, homosexuality is not acceptable conduct. The question was not homosexuality; it was whether discrimination and bigotry were tolerable. The response by mainstream religious leaders was clearly: "We cannot condone discrimination and bigotry against any minority group."

You have been trying to get this bill passed for years. Why did it pass now, when the strength of the regressives appears to be growing?

We confronted the alleged strength of the Moral Majority and found that it was alleged at best. The Moral Majority really represents only a very narrow segment of the population.

Since the state Senate concurred on the bill, the Moral Majority tried to generate an avalanche of phone calls through a Christian radio network that broadcasts "emergency alerts." That network across the state could only generate a little over 1,000 phone calls, which is a pittance. It is a demonstration of their small numbers. Yet they've been able to strike fear in the hearts of politicians all across the country. I think politicians, policy makers, and the public are recognizing that they are no more than fanatics who do not by any means represent the majority sentiment.

No amendments were offered on the bill—not the old exempt-the-school-teachers amendment, not the old exempt-the-National-Guard issue—because you don't want a bunkmate who's a pervert. There are a thousand ways to kill a bill. All sorts of issues could have been raised but weren't.

How difficult was it to get together this coalition?

It was a very long task. In many instances it started at the grassroots level with individuals initiating action in meetings of their denominations.

It led to an interesting contradiction. It was the first session this bill was brought up for a vote and it passed. Yet, the other issue of sex law reform, the consenting adult bill—which would have legalized sex acts that are allowed by law in the majority of states now—has been brought to a vote on numerous occasions and has lost each time. It's illegal to perform homosexual sex acts in Wisconsin yet you are protected by law against discrimination if you are a homosexual.

The Catholic church did not support the consenting adults bill because, in their view, that entered into the moral question of the sex act itself. But the issue is very different when we talk about discrimination, when we talk about denying someone a job or a home. The support we got from the Catholic church was especially instrumental.

Do you see other states following suit?

I think the historic significance is that if Wisconsin—a Midwestern, middle-sized, rural, quasi-conservative state which has nothing particular to offer in terms of a gay rights constituency—if we can do it, any state can do it. Alabama can do it, much less a New York or a California.

While one cannot take the blueprint from the Wisconsin experience and simply transpose it to any state in the union, there are some valuable lessons. If nothing else, the lesson of encouragement and momentum ought to be brought to every state. With the proper groundwork, and the proper understanding that the issue ought not to be articulated as homosexuality good or bad, but as discrimination and bigotry, it can

Continued on page 36

Why the Governor Signed the Bill

Following is a statement issued by Wisconsin Gov. Lee Sherman Dreyfus, a moderate Republican, explaining his decision to sign Assembly Bill 70, the state's gay civil rights bill, into law. Dreyfus signed the measure Thursday, February 25, and it went into effect the following day.

AB 70 prohibits discrimination in employment, housing, and public accommodations based on sexual orientation. This bill has a content that addresses personal rights and privacy. The bill, which I am signing into law, has the support of a wide-ranging group of religious leadership, including leadership of the Roman Catholic Church, several Lutheran synods, and the Jewish community.

I have decided to sign this bill for one basic reason: to protect one's right to privacy. As one who believes in the fundamental Republican principle that government should have a very restricted involvement in people's private and personal lives, I feel strongly about governmentally sanctioned inquiry into an individual's thoughts, beliefs, and feelings.

Discrimination on sexual preference, if allowed, clearly must allow inquiries into one's private life that go beyond reasonable inquiry and in fact invade one's privacy. No one ought to have the right and no one ought to be placed in the position of having to reveal such personal information when it is not directly related to an overriding public purpose.

Be certain to understand that the clear and stated intent expressed by the legislature is that this policy will not require affirmative action or quotas. That was vital to my decision to sign this bill. I was also influenced by the fact that Madison, Dane County, and the City of Milwaukee have ordinances similar to this legislation. The problems associated with them which many predicted just have not arisen.

Let me firmly state that this restriction on discriminatory actions or decisions does not imply approval or encouragement any more than the restriction on discrimination because of a religion or creed implies approval or encouragement of certain religions or creeds.

As to the relationship of this subject to the process of education, I feel very strongly that one's sexual preferences, either homosexual or heterosexual, have absolutely no place for expression in our classrooms generally, and should not be tolerated.

to "the tactics of fear and intimidation." The memory of past antigay witch hunts was not forgotten. As Lightner wrote, those tactics "so frightfully espoused, first by Joseph McCarthy," were echoed in "the state's Moral Majority and other individuals and groups following in that tradition."[83]

REPEAL THE DARN THING

In the months following enactment of gay rights in Chapter 112 (in effect, Act 112, as legislative naming practices changed in 1983), calls for repeal of the nondiscrimination law came from many corners. Some called Governor Dreyfus's privacy issue a phony sellout to gays. At its convention in summer 1982, the Republican Party passed a resolution to repeal the law as a priority for the next legislative session. Much of the opposition came from northeast Wisconsin. A spokesperson for Wisconsin Citizens Against Public Gay Perversion of New Franken, an unincorporated locale in Brown County, trotted out familiar arguments: "Homosexuals promote venereal disease, child molestation and prostitution." On January 10, 1983, pressured by the group, the Brown County Board voted 30 to 14 to pass a resolution supporting repeal. Democrat Representative Lary Swoboda of the nearby Village of Luxemburg agreed to sponsor a repeal bill, arguing that the gay rights bill "forces people who don't ascribe to homosexuality to condone it." This area of the state was dominated by rural Catholics in Door, Kewaunee, and Brown Counties. These Catholics tended to be more conservative than the urban Milwaukee Catholics, many of whom had supported the open housing and welfare rights marches of Reverend James Groppi, a Catholic priest.[84]

The New Franken group, claiming to speak for "the views of the straight 95% majority," rejected charges of homophobia. "Remember, there is nothing wrong with US, but there is something wrong with THEM." A spokesperson said the law gives "preferential treatment for people who don't really deserve it." Following good Catholic theory (but citing no biblical references), their flyer appealed to natural law: the government should not protect "those whose behavior runs contrary to natural law." The Brown County action provoked gay activist Tom Redmond to write an open letter that was published in the *Green Bay Press Gazette*. Redmond had observed that hatred of gays "is a very common attitude around here. . . . I am angry that a small group can evoke homophobia, fear of homosexuality." In his view, gay persons were "workers, blue collar, white collar, truck drivers, business executives, clerics, mother and father, sons and daughters." Redmond argued that the county board vote promoted fear and confessed that he himself was afraid of the simple act of signing his name to the letter. A copy sent to Clarenbach thanked him for his vigilance and included a postscript: "If you are ever in Green Bay you got a hug coming."[85]

As Clarenbach asserted, the repeal effort came "as no surprise," but he believed it could be defeated. He championed the fall 1982 election results as good news for gays, noting that incumbents who voted for the bill "overwhelmingly returned to office." Of the seventeen legislators who were targeted for their pro–gay rights stance, fourteen won reelection. One notable loss was Flintrop, whose district had been greatly changed in a court-drawn redistricting map. Several die-hard foes were also defeated, some replaced by newly elected gay rights supporters. In a November 9 press release, Clarenbach commented, "Things look very good indeed in both houses of the legislature for retention of our new law." The best news, however, was that the election of Governor Earl put a gay-friendly candidate in the state's highest office. Should the legislature not prove an effective firewall, the new governor could veto repeal. Earl's openly gay press secretary, Ron McCrea, commented, "It was a very popular bill and had broad support." Earl himself was on record that he would veto repeal. In the 1983 session, Representative Swoboda did introduce AB 570 to repeal the law, but it died after referral to the Committee on Criminal Justice and Public Safety. Committee chair Representative David Travis (D-Madison) said, "The issue was resolved last session. I really don't see any reason to resurrect it this session."[86]

LEGACY OF THE GAY RIGHTS BILL

In the gay media, the gay rights bill was front page news. *The Advocate*, a national publication, called the nondiscrimination law a "historic move" and even published the state senate roll call. A picture showed Clarenbach with staff and friends celebrating with champagne in the Capitol, and the paper quoted his assertion that that "our state's progressive tradition" carried the day. The *Washington Blade*, the US capital's gay paper, reported

it as an "action without precedent in American political history." Karla
Dobinski of Madison covered it for the Task Force Report of the National
Gay Task Force under the headline, "Getting God on Our Side: How We
Won in Wisconsin," and quoted Senator Jim Moody: "Without this religious support we would not have passed AB 70." Calling it landmark legislation, Dobinski credited Clarenbach's long efforts, writing, "You must
have at least one person in the legislature who will make passage of a gay
civil-rights bill his priority."[87]

Advocates and activists across the country commented on the win.
Justin Osteen, a Madisonian associated with the National Lesbian/Gay
Organization Development Project, proclaimed, "Our success in Wisconsin was not accidental. And strategies used here can be adopted across
the country." From California, Randy Stalling, president of the Alice B.
Toklas Memorial Democratic club, wrote, "You have set an example for
other states to follow and are an inspiration in our fight to pass AB 1 here
in California." Clarenbach himself believed "similar initiatives across the
nation have gotten a big boost from our success." Minnesota Senator Allan
Spear wrote, "Your victory defies the conventional wisdom and gives us all
a tremendous boost." Many other letters and telegrams of congratulations
poured into Clarenbach's office. News stories from multiple states, including Michigan, Indiana, Maine, Connecticut, and Arizona, confirmed the
belief that gay rights were moving forward. Yet it would be seven years
before Massachusetts, the next state to adopt nondiscrimination, passed a
gay rights bill. One letter writer from the University of Sydney wrote that
following Wisconsin, the Australian state of New South Wales had also
passed a nondiscrimination bill on homosexuality in 1982.[88]

In late 1983, now out of office, Dreyfus, at the request of Michigander
James Dressel, wrote to Republicans in the Michigan House of Representatives about Wisconsin's gay rights law as the House's judiciary committee was studying it. The former governor was strongly rebuffed. One
Republican Michigander legislator wrote in response, "I'll not interfere
in Wisconsin's concerns and I hope you'll do the same for us." Another
charged that the Wisconsin bill "led us down the same road as the Roman
Empire." Dreyfus, reverting to his role as a professor of communications,
wryly observed, "He has a very cursory understanding of the period."[89]

Twenty years after the signing, on July 16, 2003, Dreyfus was honored as a special guest at the OutReach Annual Awards banquet with its first Political Courage award. Before the event, Madison's *Capital Times* printed an editorial praising his "foresight" in signing and naming him "among the first to embrace the future." In his introduction, Clarenbach said Dreyfus was "a man that deserves a chapter in the next 'Profiles of Courage.'" Dreyfus, wearing his traditional red vest, demurred. "It didn't have a damn thing to do with courage—it was the right thing to do." This was appropriate modesty for a saint, if the language was a bit salty. Governor James Doyle Jr. added his praise: "The historical record is now even more clear that signing that legislation has made Wisconsin a better state." Congresswoman Tammy Baldwin also praised Dreyfus's "truly historic moment." Later, Dreyfus stayed true to his progressive Republican credentials and issued a 2006 statement with three other former Democratic governors urging a no vote on the proposed Wisconsin constitutional amendment barring marriage equality. When the *Capital Times* ran a cartoon after Dreyfus's passing in 2008, one of the three memories depicted was of the former governor signing the gay rights bill.[90]

Clarenbach also received his due. When he ended his electoral career in Wisconsin, the community recognized the contributions of a major figure. At the 1993 Queer of the Year Dinner, the United of Madison gave him a special award, noting, "During his 18-year career in the Wisconsin State Assembly, David Clarenbach championed the rights of gays and lesbians and bisexuals." *The Wisconsin Light*, a state gay paper, had previously dubbed Clarenbach "the father of the Gay Rights Bill." Now it offered an editorial encomium: "Our community has never had a better friend or ally than David." On Clarenbach going to Washington, DC, as director of the Victory Fund, a national organization promoting the election of lesbian and gay candidates to public office, *The Wisconsin Light* editorialized, "Here is a man of great dynamism, of wide talents, who has used all that and more for the good of our community."[91]

WISCONSIN'S SUCCESS ON GAY AGENDA ITEMS

During the national same-sex marriage battles, Frank Bruni, the first openly gay columnist for the *New York Times*, recalled that in the 1980s you could still be denied a job, and "at that point only Wisconsin and the

District of Columbia provided protection" from discrimination. In 2012, the *Wisconsin Gazette* wrote in another retrospective: "The past as inspiration: Remembering when Wisconsin led the nation with progressive laws."[92]

The landmark victory in Wisconsin became a touchpoint for gays and lesbians across Wisconsin and beyond. In 1985, *The Advocate* published a three-year retrospective on the "milestone," noting that it had been signed by a Republican governor. The story reported, "Since that time gay rights groups, and their supporters in more than a dozen states, have sought passage of similar bills—but despite some near successes, Wisconsin still stands alone." Reporter Peter Freiberg wrote that activists outside the state "feel the state was an odd locale for passage of the nation's first," recalling the "red hunts" and "fag hunts" of Joe McCarthy.[93]

In 2007, Madison's *Capital Times* published a twenty-five-years retrospective with a photograph showing three out Dane County officials carrying a Gay Rights State banner made by Kathleen Nichols for the 1987 march on Washington. The 2007 story noted the memory was bittersweet; a year before, Wisconsin voters had approved a constitutional amendment barring legal recognition of same-sex marriages. Later that year, Madison's OutReach awards banquet used the theme of celebrating twenty-five years of gay rights in Wisconsin with a picture of Dreyfus on the cover. Clarenbach, in retelling the story of passage, capsulized it as "political diplomacy with Republicans and church groups, and decisive leadership among homosexuals."[94]

Wisconsin's passage of gay rights also quickly became a topic of study. In 1987, Pamela Oliver, a UW–Madison sociology professor, led a graduate seminar that included the gay rights legislation as a case study. Students Kirk Kleinschmidt and Nicole Libman focused their research on the speed of the legislation, citing a remark by Barbara Lightner that it was an unexpected "fluke." They also quoted Clarenbach as saying, "We were overwhelmed and shocked that it passed," and quoted opponent Pritchard's statement that it was "a proposal which rushed through the legislative process in a whirlwind of haste." In 2007, William Turner published an article in the *Wisconsin Women's Law Review* on the pioneering legislation, highlighting the analogy from civil rights protections based on race and

At the second national gay rights march in Washington, DC, in 1978, Wisconsin was proudly proclaimed the Gay Rights State. Holding the banner are, left to right, Tammy Baldwin, Dick Wagner, and Kathleen Nichols. FROM THE AUTHOR'S COLLECTION

sex to civil rights protections based on sexual orientation. He stressed the importance of an equality rather than a morality framework and believed "Clarenbach accomplished a feat that many observers at the time doubted he, or anyone else in Wisconsin, could accomplish."[95]

Andrea Rottmann, a German graduate student at the Freie Universitat Berlin, wrote her 2010 master's research paper on "Passing Gay Rights in Wisconsin, 1967–1983," asking, "How is it possible that this Midwestern state took the vanguard in passing state-wide gay rights law?" For her, grassroots work and a place at the table was the answer to passage. Stressing the outsider roles of community activists Rouse and Lightner, Rottmann rejected the claim that Clarenbach "single-handedly got the bill passed"—a claim he himself did not make. Instead, like Clarenbach after the gay rights bill passed, she gave due credit to the state's Progressive Republican tradition and the smart framing of the issues.[96]

DECISIVE VICTORIES LAY THE GROUNDWORK FOR FUTURE CHANGE

Both Barbee and Clarenbach came to politics with civil rights activism in their backgrounds and worked mightily to place the gay struggle in that broad civil rights tradition. In his statements linking the many struggles in America just beginning to emerge, Barbee built bridges for allies. Taking up his mantle, Clarenbach explicitly stated that a vote for gay rights was not simply a vote for blessing or approving homosexuality. He said, "To shy away from a very central involvement in gay rights in the 1980s is like ignoring civil rights and the Vietnam War in the 1960s." Nevertheless, few were unaware that gay people were the major beneficiaries behind his efforts.

Interestingly, the Wisconsin press and others linked these gay struggles to two specific Wisconsin historical traditions. The opposition was not infrequently compared to Joe McCarthy and his witch hunts. And the state's progressive values ran in both political parties, though this was changing as more religious conservatives began to dominate the Republican Party. The gay community showed tactical smarts in finding allies and building support over many years of the legislative battles. The long struggle for consenting adults as the main battleground showed that a vote for homosexuals was not a political death sentences.

The landmark legislation passed with the nondiscrimination gay rights bill of the 1981 session and the hard-fought consenting adults bill of the 1983 session marked a decisive turn in the fight for LGBT rights. After the fall election results of 1984, gays and lesbians began to claim more legislative electoral victories. Kathy Patrick, a lesbian and president of Wisconsin NOW, noted that "at least three candidates with strong gay and feminist support won election to state offices." Patrick said "most of the gay community" supported assembly candidate Barbara Notestein in her first try at public office. Notestein had pledged to give active support to alternative families legislation in an interview with *OUT!* Her primary opponent was Leon Rouse, who had organized in 1982 for the gay rights bill. Rouse lost to Notestein, but another Milwaukee gay man, Tim Carpenter, did gain a seat, though he was not yet out. Representative Ulichny, long "a supporter of lesbian/gay issues in the Assembly," also won a senate seat on Milwaukee's east side.[97]

Though other states were slow to follow on gay rights, passage of consenting adults (Act 17) and the gay rights bill (Chapter 112) were historic wins for Wisconsin's gay community and indeed for the nation. They showed other states what was possible to accomplish through tenacious political action and smart lobbying efforts, and they showcased the significance of building coalitions across the aisle and in the larger community with civic organizations, gay rights groups, and religious stakeholders coming together for common cause. But the work was far from over. Like Stonewall, these victories would serve as a touchstone of memory and become groundwork for more legislative change to come.

7

THE GOOD ACTS:
THE DELUGE CONTINUES

Nabozny introduced sufficient evidence to show that the discrimi-
natory treatment was motivated by the defendants' disapproval of
Nabozny's sexual orientation, including statements by the defendants
that Nabozny should expect to be harassed because he is gay.
—FEDERAL JUDGE JESSE ESCHBACH,
SEVENTH CIRCUIT, *NABOZNY V. PODLESNY* 1996[1]

A test with no right answers.
—*OUT!* MARCH 1985, ON HTLV-III TESTING[2]

Though the passage of sexual orientation nondiscrimination in 1981
and consenting adults in 1983 were triumphant moments in the struggle for gay rights, the fight was by no means over in Wisconsin, particularly
when it came to nondiscrimination. As the previous chapter details, the
gay rights nondiscrimination law came under immediate attack through
repeal efforts and the push for exemptions. After passage, new expansions
of protections were needed for student and school services nondiscrimination and against hate crimes. Additionally, in the 1980s, AIDS came to
Wisconsin, necessitating swift action from the legislature to deal with the
complex public health issues it posed in the state. The hard-won political
skills honed in the 1970s would be greatly tested throughout the 1980s as
the gay community and its legislative allies fought to protect and increase

gay rights and protections, showing that the gay community could advance agenda items in the Wisconsin world of politics.

Rawhide Ranch Seeks Exemption

After outright repeal failed, the next threat to the gay rights bill came
once more from northeast Wisconsin. In April 1985, Rawhide Boys Ranch
of New London in Waupaca County launched a campaign to gut a major
provision in the law. Some legislators, such as Senator Marvin Roshell
(D-Chippewa Falls), saw the proposed exemption bill as a "foot in the
door" to repeal the entire gay rights law.[3] This debate in the mid-1980s
foreshadows an ongoing debate between religious liberty advocates and
supporters regarding nondiscrimination law.

The Rawhide Boys Ranch, a nonprofit residential facility for troubled
male youths, had a capacity of twenty-five. Placements to Rawhide were
made by county social service agencies, so much of its funding was public money. In 1985, it received $354,000 in state and public funds, about 70
percent of its budget. Boys were treated like supposed ranch hands. They
cared for twenty horses and some sheep and learned auto repair. Boys had
to attend church twice a month and go to Wednesday evening "round-
ups" that included scripture lessons. They earned extra grade points when
they recited passages from the Bible. The founder and administrator was
John Gillespie, a fundamentalist Christian. In 1977, the Wisconsin Council
on Criminal Justice had revoked a $110,000 federal grant award because,
though it had no religious affiliation, Rawhide hired only employees "professing a belief in Jesus Christ."[4]

Gillespie believed that "any program working with children (day care
centers, group homes, children's institutions, churches, etc.) that teaches
a specific moral philosophy should be able to use staff who support those
philosophies." Gillespie explained that Rawhide "teaches that marriage
should be a commitment for life if at all possible." Only Christian couples
who had been married five years were hired as house-parents. Further, he
stated, "We feel it is important in our work of rebuilding the lives of children placed with us by the juvenile courts. We believe it should be a bona
fide occupational requirement that our staff support these philosophies."

Rawhide taught that "sexual relations should be within the bonds of marriage." Gillespie averred they were not anti-homosexual, for they were just as against a heterosexual "who believes that open sex among teenagers is OK." He emphasized Wisconsin was the only state to have a gay rights law. [5]

One pastor forwarded the Rawhide letter to the gay community, and in June 1985, *OUT!* alerted its readers to the new attack on the law. Re-

"They've seen their last wayward boy from Dane County until they clean up their act."

Enforcement of Wisconsin's early gay rights measures ran into opposition from those claiming religious liberty to discriminate, such as the Rawhide Boys Ranch. COURTESY OF *THE GREEN BAY PRESS GAZETTE*

porter Sue Burke found a staff member who admitted that "applicants are screened for their religious beliefs." Upon placement, parents signed a release form that permitted Rawhide to offer religious training. This particular staffer's fear was that the law would require Rawhide to hire convicted child molesters. Here again was the appeal to prejudice that gays and lesbians could not be proper role models or be permitted near youth.[6]

The matter was precipitated because, in implementing the 1982 gay rights law, the state was asking contractors to sign nondiscrimination documents to obtain a state license or, as Rawhide put it, "not refuse employment to someone because of their sexual beliefs and practices." Gillespie claimed he just wanted "the legal right to continue to operate as we have for the past 20 years." Citing the football adage "the best defense is a good offense," Gillespie asserted, "This has gone too far. It is time to mount a major offensive—but we will need the help of hundreds of people, churches and other children's organizations." Former governor Dreyfus sent a letter saying he would not have signed the legislation had he known it would affect operations like Rawhide. Holding up a Green Bay Packers helmet, Clarenbach testified against the measure, claiming that removing part of the law was like removing part of the helmet—it would deny the wearer effective protection.[7]

Senator Joe Leean, the chief force behind the Rawhide cause, joined the legislature in 1985 and represented a section of northeast Wisconsin that included New London. A devout Christian, he had previously been president of the Full Gospel Business Men's Fellowship and a director of Youth for Christ. In January 1986, Leean circulated a memo to legislators on the bill he and Representative Wayne Wood were introducing for an exemption for nonprofit organizations that work with youth. It mentioned Rawhide Boys Ranch specifically. In addition, the bill would exempt discrimination over creed and marital status.[8]

During the 1985–1987 session, the Rawhide exemption bills were held in committees controlled by Democrats. Senator Van Sistine of Green Bay said his committee would not act "unless Rawhide backers compromise with gay rights advocates." Leean responded that it was impossible to rewrite the bill without destroying it, so other tactics were tried. Support for the bill showed up prominently in the northeast. The *Appleton Post-Crescent* editorialized "in defense of Rawhide's principles." While recognizing the "importance" of "a law against such discrimination," it wrote, "we support Rawhide in its effort to obtain an exemption." At the senate hearing, Lu Williquette of Green Bay testified for pastors from the Free Methodist, Seventh Day Adventists, and Assembly of God congregations of that city. One former resident who later worked at Rawhide testified favorably at the senate hearing: "The program at Rawhide works. Why mess with it and try and change it?" In contrast, the *Milwaukee Journal* editorialized that while the Rawhide model might claim effectiveness, other programs that did not discriminate also had successes with troubled youths.[9]

The Rawhide case was furthered by a common misunderstanding of the law. Contrary to Rawhide's assertions, churches and church-affiliated associations could, for policymaking and instructional positions, use religious beliefs when making employment decisions. Yet Rawhide was not religiously affiliated. To broaden the political base, Gillespie had tried to sweep churches into his argument, claiming they needed the exemption.[10]

The Wisconsin Civil Liberties Union (WCLU) was "strongly opposed" to Leean's effort, stating in a letter from its legal director, Gretchen Miller, to Senator Adelman, "It severely undermines the fundamental purpose of the Fair Employment Act." The WCLU believed the existing provision on religious associations choosing employees was sufficient to permit them to perform their religious missions. A cook should be judged for culinary qualification, not beliefs. The WCLU separated the discussion of religious groups from tax-exempt child welfare agencies, arguing that "no reason exists for permitting a child welfare agency to assume that homosexuals or bisexuals are unqualified for employment." The fear of employing such persons was asserted as "factually baseless and unfair stereotyping."[11]

Impact, an ecumenical coalition linked to the Wisconsin Conference of Churches, also voiced opposition. Bonnee Voss, the group's director, cited the "firm commitment in the religious community to support the Fair Employment Act." Reflecting on the board's religious support for passage of the state gay rights law, Voss thought board members felt it important "to separate themselves from those in the religious community who do think this is needed."

Leean was stymied both politically and legally. Early in the 1987 session, he tried to find a solution. Representative David Deininger, a moderate Republican from Monroe, took the lead to find a compromise, even researching federal tax code requirements for nonprofits. Meetings were held in fall 1987 and in early 1988 between Clarenbach, Leean, and other legislators, and with staff of the Equal Rights Division, which was part of the state's Department of Industry, Labor and Human Relations. The impetus for a compromise had been given a shove when, in the case of *Corp. of Presiding Bishop v. Amos*, the US Supreme Court had upheld the right of the Mormon Church to favor members of its religion even for some nonreligious jobs. After the Amos case, a Wisconsin legislative attorney wrote an opinion that some of the exemptions in the proposed bill relating to religious organizations might be required on constitutional grounds. The attorney admitted it was "difficult to predict the outcome of a constitutional challenge." The new compromise language would permit "religious organizations to give a preference to an individual who adheres to the religious association's creed for a position that is clearly related to the religious association's teachings and beliefs." The compromise in Assembly Bill (AB) 916 was not to repeal fair employment for sexual orientation, as had been proposed, but to broaden the religious exemption in line with the Supreme Court ruling for positions that could meet a bona fide qualification. Clarenbach would call it a creative alternative. The bill sailed through both houses of the legislature with voice votes.[12]

After passage, some gay advocates claimed that the hard-fought posture of the gay rights state had been abandoned. Clarenbach claimed the expanded, narrowly defined religious exemption, in light of the Supreme Court ruling, was a more realistic stance than defeating everything. The bill avoided a broad exemption on sexual orientation and marital status. Senator John Norquist said passage of AB 916 "was taken on the basis of realities." Eunice Edgar of the WCLU said she was quite sure "the whole matter will be resolved in the courts." Wood, an ardent Rawhide supporter, came back in a later session to try once more for broad exemption and, again, was defeated.[13]

DPI SCHOOL SERVICES FOR GAYS AND LESBIANS IN ACT 29

At the same time gay rights advocates were fending off attacks on the nondiscrimination bill, they sought to expand protections for sexual orientation under the new law. One issue that came up was whether the gay rights bill would have any effect on public schools. While it is common knowledge today that LGBT youth are bullied, it was not so commonly known when, in 1970, a young Mark Hatlen from Cooksville recalled being called a faggot in both late grade and high school in the Evansville school system. Protections did not exist. Kathleen Nichols and I, appointed in 1983 to serve as cochairs of Governor Earl's advisory body on gay issues, sought an early meeting exploring possible enforcement of the law in Wisconsin schools, over which the Wisconsin Department of Public Instruction (DPI) had jurisdiction. The concern was larger than simply nondiscrimination. In July 1983, community concerns were expressed on how we might "determine ways to influence elementary and secondary education regarding lesbian and gay issues." Bert Grover, a former state legislator from Shawano, had been the statewide elected superintendent of public instruction since 1981. Grover averred to Nichols and me that he was no Dane County liberal and could not take an advanced position.[14]

Yet the issues were not invisible to the DPI. In July 1984, the *Milwaukee Journal* reported, "Gay teens say classmates and neighborhood friends . . . have been known to shout ugly remarks, and on occasion even to threaten and physically attack their gay classmates in school." Further, when the DPI spoke publicly on the issue, it indicated that "lesbians and gays are not guaranteed equal access to education in Wisconsin." In fact, as William B. Turner noted in his study of the legal issues around the gay rights bill, the act had failed to cover the area of schools. Earlier state statutes on school discrimination included sex and race but not sexual orientation. DPI official Lond Rodman conceded that at a minimum, the agency would investigate instances of alleged harassment or violence directed at lesbian and gay students.[15]

At the same time these issues were gaining visibility, the Wisconsin Women's Network undertook discussions to add sexual orientation, along with pregnancy status and economic deprivation, to the school nondiscrimination statutes. Kathryn (Kay) Clarenbach, active in the Wisconsin Women's Council, recalled the DPI's fears at the time "that two boys or two girls would want to come to prom together." In December 1984, the DPI admitted it had staff working with the Women's Council on possible legislation but declined to say "whether it will back a new anti-discrimination law that includes protection for gay and lesbians." Superintendent Grover was up for reelection in April 1985. He was so cautious that he did not include nondiscrimination language in the DPI proposals for the up-coming biennial budget submitted in fall 1984. Grover need not have been worried electorally, as he garnered 75 percent of the vote in the nonpartisan spring election.[16]

Despite Grover's reticence to include nondiscrimination in his section of the state budget, it was Governor Earl's budget bill for the 1985–1987 session, Act 29, that became the vehicle to secure nondiscrimination protections for school services. Wisconsin governors for many years had used the state's required biennial budget to embrace all manner of policy proposals in addition to funding state agencies and programs. Earl's advisor on women's issues, Roberta Gassman, understood the DPI would support or at least not object to the matter. The bill created 118.13 of the Wisconsin statues to improve prohibitions on discrimination in schools. Among the proposed classes to be protected were those covered by sexual orientation. The prohibition applied to any discrimination in curricular programs, extracurricular programs, pupil services, and recreational programs sponsored by the school board, on or off school property. Districts had to adopt and disseminate a general policy prohibiting discrimination under the statute. After passage, the DPI proceeded to implement the new statute as required by drafting administrative rules. In 1989, the legislature attached a fine of not more than one thousand dollars, which could be levied against public school officials or teachers who had been found to discriminate.[17]

The DPI statute would prove its worth in the case of Jamie Nabozny, who attended school in Ashland, Wisconsin. As a seventh grader in 1988, he was harassed and bullied because he was gay, having come out at age thirteen. Nabozny told a school counselor he was gay and had been called a "faggot" and that he was subjected to physical abuse. Other records show he was called "queer" and a "fudge packer." In a science classroom, two students performed a mock rape on him while some twenty students watched and laughed. Upon seeking refuge in Principal Mary Podlesny's office, he was told "boys will be boys" and that he should expect such behavior if he was "going to be so openly gay." Distraught, Nabozny ran home. The next day, Nabozny was forced to see the counselor not because he was attacked but because he left school without permission. In the eighth grade, several boys attacked him in a bathroom. Continued attacks led to an attempted suicide.[18]

In high school, the attacks resumed. Nabozny was placed in special education classes, which were the same classes some of the bullies were in. After running away to Minneapolis, he came back with the promise that he would not have to attend the high school, but when his parents tried to homeschool him, they were denied because they did not have high school diplomas. The school district demanded the boy return to classes. After his return, the abuse continued. An assistant principal told Nabozny he deserved the punishment of bullying because of his sexuality. One attack in the school library resulted in internal bleeding from being kicked in the stomach and required surgery. Eventually, Nabozny again ran away to Minneapolis, where he later earned a GED and became a student at the University of Minnesota.[19]

With the help of Lambda Legal, in February 1995 Nabozny sued the school district and a number of its officials. The case claimed violations of federal equal protections under the Fourteenth Amendment and violation of Wisconsin nondiscrimination law, section 118.13(1) Wi. Statute. In compliance with state statute, the Ashland School District had adopted "a policy of prohibiting discrimination against students on the basis of gender or sexual orientation." A federal district court made a summary judgment in favor of the school district, mainly on technical grounds. The matter was then appealed to federal circuit court in Chicago.[20]

In 1996, Judge Jesse Eschbach of the Seventh Circuit Court of Appeals ruled, "We respectfully disagree with the district court's conclusions." Eschbach rejected the federal due process argument, but citing Wisconsin law, he held that the district had infringed Nabozny's equal protection under the grounds of sexual orientation discrimination. The judge found that the record, "combined with the defendants' own admissions, suggests that Nabozny was treated differently from other students." The judge ruled, "The Equal Protection Clause does . . . require the state to treat each person with equal regard, as having equal worth, regardless of his or her status." The judge noted, "Nabozny introduced sufficient evidence to show that the discriminatory treatment was motivated by the defendants' disapproval of Nabozny's sexual orientation, including statements by the defendants that Nabozny should expect to be harassed because he is gay."[21]

Judge Eschbach noted the defense had cited the Supreme Court of case of *Bowers v. Hardwick*, which upheld state sodomy laws in Georgia, finding it a misplaced argument. While not positing that "heightened scrutiny" was necessary regarding discrimination against homosexuals, the judge wrote, "We are unable to garner any rational basis for permitting one student to assault another based on the victim's sexual orientation, and the defendants do not offer us one."[22]

The Nabozny matter was the first case in the nation that found "a public school could be held accountable for not stopping antigay abuse." The case was returned for trial, and a local jury found the school officials liable for failing to stop antigay violence against Nabozny. Before the jury could return to determine the amount of damages, the school district settled with an award of nearly $1 million.[23]

SHUSH! HIV AND CONFIDENTIALITY

While the consenting adults and nondiscrimination acts were on the Wisconsin gay agenda for well over a decade before their enactment, a new crisis raised another issue requiring immediate attention. On March 2, 1985, Margaret Heckler, the Reagan administration secretary of Health and Human Services, announced the licensing of a test for the antibody HTLV-III to help screen the national blood supply for AIDS. The rise of AIDS nationally and the specter of the HTLV-III test to identify its presence raised many issues for the gay community. The fear was that it could be used as a tool for discrimination against gay men by its use as a marker for sexual orientation. Later, the Reagan administration would propose testing the 600,000 immigrants who passed through US borders and deny entry on the basis of the test. A Florida AIDS researcher noted he had been contacted by school districts that thought they might use the test to weed out gay teachers and by country clubs that wanted the test to screen food handlers. The discussion of the possibility of medical quarantine camps stoked some of the worst fears. A study showed one real consequence was that for those who tested positive, 14 percent contemplated suicide.[24]

In August 1984, when the number of confirmed cases of AIDS in the state was at nine, *OUT!* headlined that confidentiality was a prime concern. The story was an interview with Holly Dowling, who had been active with Milwaukee's Brady East STD (BESTD) Clinic and now was the first full-time AIDS worker with the Wisconsin Division of Health. Her concern was that a lack of confidentiality would mean "we would lose a lot of our sources that are critical to conducting epidemiological studies." She noted there had not been many breaches of privacy, "but there have been a couple

BEST NEWS

Published by the BRADY EAST SEXUALLY
TRANSMITTED DISEASE (BEST) CLINIC,
1240 E. Brady Street, Milwaukee, WI 53202, 414/272-2144. EDITORS: Mark
Behar, PA-C, and Doug Johnson, RN, with thanks to Martha Fingleton, RN.
HOURS: Tuesday, 7-10 pm, Saturday, 1-3 pm, walk-in; Monday, 7-9 pm by
appointment for hepatitis program.   September-October, 1984.

BEGINNING OUR ELEVENTH YEAR OF SERVICE TO MILWAUKEE'S GAY COMMUNITY--THE BEST OF HEALTH TO YOU!
          (Founded October, 1974 as Gay Peoples Union VD Screening Program)
   *   *   *   *   *   *   *   *   *   *   *   *   *   *   *   *   *   *   *

WHY BEST NEWS?

Members of the Research & Education Committee and BEST Clinic volunteers felt an urgent need
to provide health information to the Milwaukee gay & lesbian community during the untimely
absence of WisconIn Step magazine. For additional information about health issues and other
important matters, feel free to stop at the BEST Clinic to discuss your concerns or to check
out some of our many gay publications. Let!s hear from you! Please direct your comments,
questions, reactions, and donations to the BEST Clinic or to BEST NEWS, PO Box 239, Milwaukee,
WI 53201. Special thanks to the National Coalition of Gay STD Services (NCGSTDS) for
articles. Although efforts will be made to present accurate, factual information, the BEST
Clinic or its officers, board members, directors, staff, volunteers, friends, or agents cannot
assume liability for articles published or advice rendered.
                    *   *   *   *

BEST CLINIC SEEKS VOLUNTEERS

BEST Clinic needs dedicated, hard-working volunteers to serve in a variety of ways: we need
people to serve on a community advisory council to provide creative input for the development
of an AIDS Resource Guide project (see Cream City Association Foundation Project article below);
we need individuals to work with other Clinic committees (e.g., Program & Development, Research
& Education, Nomination Committees); and we need volunteer staff willing to receive training
and work at the Clinic in providing patient services. Share your talents! Become involved!
Write, phone, or drop in to BEST Clinic. People with AIDS are also needed! Don't be shy!
                    *   *   *   *

BEST WEEK CELEBRATION!

Brady East STD (BEST) Clinic will be celebrating it's 10th anniversary in three separate
activities, September 28-October 5. Wisconsin Governor Tony Earl is expected to issue a
proclamation in honor of the celebration. An open house will initiate festivities, Friday,
September 28, 4:30-6 pm at the Clinic building, 1240 E. Brady St., with wine and cheese
being served. All members of the community are invited to attend! An open discussion
about AIDS and hepatitis B will take place, Wednesday, October 3, 7pm, at the Clinic.
BEST Week culminates with the BEST Clinic 10th Anniversary Harvest Ball & Buffet, Thursday,
October 4, 7 pm at the Crystal Palace, 1925 W. National Av. Advance ticket sales are
available for $7 each at the Clinic or many area bars. All members of the community are
invited to dance to 1950's music, and to dress in your favorite 50s attire (ohh, James Dean!)!
There will be a cash bar, and contests for the BEST dancers, the BEST costumes, the cutest
couples; record spinning provided by "Wild Bill." The Clinic will also be giving away free
condoms during your visit for an STD check-up in October! Come on over for the BEST time!
At the BEST Clinic, we are all volunteers. Our reward is your appreciation. Join us to
celebrate ten years of hard work and let us thank you for your generosity and support!
                    *   *   *

HEPATITIS B TESTING AND VACCINE AVAILABLE AT CLINIC

The BEST Clinic provides a screening and vaccination program for hepatitis B (HBV) on
Monday evenings, from 7-9 pm, by appointment. As HBV is a sexually transmitted disease and
is extremely prevalent in the gay community, the Clinic strongly encourages all gay men
to become vaccinated if they are susceptible. A sexually active gay man has greater than a
60% chance of contracting the disease during his lifetime, which at present, presents a greater
health problem than AIDS. Cost for the program should not be an important consideration, since
the Clinic uses a sliding-scale fee to meet different income levels. The Clinic has also been
successful with insurance reimbursement for those who have health insurance. For further
information, call BEST Clinic, 272-2144, or the HBV Program Coordinator, 342-1630.
                    *   *   *

The newsletter from Milwaukee's Brady East STD Clinic, known as BESTD, was an early
alert mechanism regarding AIDS in the state. *BEST NEWS*, SEPTEMBER–OCTOBER 1984

that have probably affected a few lives." This was the basic conundrum of
the argument between the gay community and traditional public health
workers over use of the test: how to track the progress of the disease and
at the same time respect personal privacy.[25]

In November 1985, *Gay Life,* a paper from Chicago that circulated in
southeast Wisconsin, opined, "We continue to believe that HTLV-III test-

ing is not advisable . . . there is too great a possibility that the results will cause more harm than good." In March 1985, *OUT!* devoted the entire front page to the test with the headline, "A Test with No Right Answers." The paper noted Wisconsin health-care and blood center workers had been briefed in February on the upcoming test release. To avoid people donating blood so they could be tested, the government was trying to establish alternative test sites. Tim Tillotson of Madison's Blue Bus Clinic stated that the issue of informed consent had to be addressed seriously. Wisconsin state epidemiologist Dr. Jeffrey Davis, speaking on behalf of the Division of Health, stated that he and his staff felt the test required "informed, signed consent." But signed consent meant records could be kept on file. *OUT!* reported national gay organizations recommending against taking the test. These included the Gay Rights National Lobby and the National Gay Task Force. Among the cautions from *OUT!* was, "Individuals should be aware of the fact that their blood test results may be requested and obtained by third parties." Gays who wanted to get tested had to weigh many risks. The test "could become part of your medical records, it could be justification for denial of life or health insurance in the future . . . [or it] could become a reason for denying employment." *OUT!* noted the concern that "potential employers may use the test as an indicator of homosexuality." It did not help that national health officials listed homosexuals among the high-risk populations.[26]

Rjurik Golubjatnikov, a gay man, was chief of the immunology section of the state's hygiene testing laboratory. Affectionately called Dr. Rik, he was one of the earliest health-care professionals with data on the local spread of the disease. While maintaining medical confidentiality, he understood the urgency of a community response. In March 1985, the recently formed Madison AIDS Support Network, with Will Handy and Chaz Pope in the lead, distributed an information sheet, stating: "Like most groups which form to meet crisis, we find that the needs exist already, and we are scrambling to meet them." At the same time, a document, not signed but written by Dr. Rik, circulated on the "Prevalence of Antibody to HTLV-III Virus in the Madison Area." The Blue Bus Clinic and the state laboratory had conducted a totally "blind" study on stored blood samples from 113 gay men for whom the clinic had screened for STDs; the samples were from the 1980–1981 and 1984–1985 years. The donor name and the source of the specimens were expunged prior to testing. The 1984–1985 results showed a 28 percent positive result. The test also showed the HTLV-III virus to have been present in the Madison area as early as 1980, with ten persons already showing the antibody. Dr. Rik commented, "Clearly, control and preventive programs must address the concerns and fears of the individuals in the groups at high risk for AIDS to assure success."[27]

On April 19, 1985, Dr. Rik met with leaders in the gay community at my house to discuss how to use the information to best effect. Meanwhile, Brooks Egerton was working on a freelance piece on Rik's report that appeared in the *Capital Times* on April 29. The concern over how to sensitively present the medical information was justified by the headline, written by paper staff, "Tests Show 25% of Gays in Area Exposed to AIDS." The message was misleading: the tests used blood samples from the most sexually active males who went to STD clinics, not a sampling across the gay population. That it was generalized to the entire gay population in Madison showed the hysteria of the day. Egerton's story was more measured, and by the second edition the headline had been changed to "AIDS Exposure Here Lower than Norm, Tests Show." The story cited higher prevalence in New York and San Francisco, the epicenters of the disease, which could hardly be considered the norm. Buried deep in the story was Egerton's observation, "Samples were unavailable from monogamous gays or those with few sexual partners." Inclusion of such samples would mean a significantly lower percentage. Egerton quoted Dr. Rik: "We don't have to be affected by the hopelessness."[28]

By June 1985, free HTLV-III testing was ready at two dozen sites in Wisconsin, including the gay community's favored Blue Bus Clinic of Madison and the BESTD Clinic of Milwaukee. The Wisconsin plan for these alternate sites was that "people with antibody-positive [test results] will be counseled as though they are potentially infectious." In May, reporting low incidences of blood samples with HTLV-III, the spokespersons for Wisconsin's blood banks said that "their centers initially showed far higher positive test rates, and it is believed now many of those early tests were marred by faulty equipment." Dr. Jay Menitove, director of the Milwaukee-based Blood Center for Southeastern Wisconsin, praised the "phenomenal cooperation" from gay men in not donating blood. The Blood Center also said it had not notified any of the persons testing positive because it was not sure "what to tell them." The March issue of *OUT!* reported that the Department of Defense had requested blood banks "to provide the names of all service members who tested positively for the HTLV-III antibody." A spokesperson told a gay newspaper in Washington, DC, that results would "only be used for medical purposes, not disciplinary action." Still, the request confirmed the worst fears of the gay community, that individuals would be publicly exposed.[29]

California was in the forefront of laws related to the HTLV-III test. Assemblyman Art Agnos of San Francisco, whom Harvey Milk had once run against, sponsored carefully considered measures in February 1985 in anticipation of the test. State law required written consent to administer the test, forbade the release of antibody test results, banned employers and insurers from requiring the tests, and required availability for follow-up counseling. This California law became the national model, and its features would be used in Wisconsin. Not all legislators were on such a measured tack. In April 1985, Representative Gus Menos, a Democrat from the Milwaukee area, circulated a draft bill to ensure Wisconsin blood banks would be required to test for HLTV-III and noted in his memo that he sidestepped the issues of concern that had arisen in the gay community. His bill was silent on "the issues of donor notification or sufficiency of the test or tests." He urged legislators to sign up "and be a hero to your constituents."[30]

During deliberations of the proposed 1985–1987 budget, Act 29, the Joint Finance Committee acted on a proposal by Senator John Norquist (D-Milwaukee) to include money for grants for counseling and referral services regarding AIDS. The fiscal bureau memo on the proposal noted, "Local groups have expressed concern about the level of service which can currently be provided in comparison to the general public health problem which AIDS poses." In the Democratic Assembly Caucus's consideration of the Joint Finance Committee's version of the proposal, Clarenbach moved to add further provisions on testing that made it into the adopted bill. The provisions required written consent before an antibody test, imposed confidentiality provisions, and if the results were positive, required information on the disease be provided. The Department of Health and Social Services was to monitor test reliability. Further language was included to "prohibit employers from requiring that such tests be made a condition of employment [and to] prohibit insurers from making such a test a condition of insurance coverage or a factor in determining rates unless H&SS determines such tests to be reliable." The bill provided both criminal penalties and civil liability for violations.[31]

PUBLIC HEALTH AND PRIVATE INFORMATION

Upon passage of the provisions, the issue became public. Dr. Dennis Maki of the UW–Madison Department of Medicine, one of the area's main treatment facilities for AIDS patients, felt the legislative language was dangerous. While acknowledging Clarenbach's courage in proposing such language, Maki's view was that "it was not well advised." In an eight-page letter to Speaker Tom Loftus, he complained there had been no public hearing on the provision and the medical community was unaware of its existence. Maki believed that "the vast majority of legislators who voted for the Budget Bill and implicitly, the amendment, on Mr. Clarenbach's behest, had no input whatsoever from citizens, health care providers, or members of the State Division of Health, many of whom have major reservations regarding the amendment." Like many health professionals, Maki raised the question, "Why should HLTV-III testing be treated differently" from other STDs, and he cited procedures for syphilis.[32]

Mandatory reporting in Wisconsin for AIDS had itself gone into effect in August 1983, with forty-seven cases and twenty-six deaths having been reported by this time. Maki believed that "medical confidentiality is stringently maintained in our health care system with all diseases" and extended to these cases. Since the provisions had been inserted late in the budget process, some echoed the request that the subject be fully discussed by the legislature. Dr. David Kindig, vice chancellor for Health Sciences at UW–Madison, stated, "There is a question of privacy and we haven't thought that through all the way." Wisconsin press accounts acknowledged that "homosexual people feared the test would be used as a sort of a witch hunt." Maki raised the issue that "AIDS testing may be necessary in the future if certain occupations are ever found to present a transmission problem." Clarenbach called Maki's comments "hysterical" and "outrageous."[33]

Governor Earl received pressure from state agencies and health providers for a total veto. Tim Tillotson of the Blue Bus Clinic wrote the governor's office suggesting a middle ground of a partial veto to solve some of the medical community's issues. Earl did a partial veto, but he left many provisions intact. The governor's veto message stated, "I am very sympathetic to the need for confidentiality. But the goal of public health and safety—providing the proper treatment of the disease—has to be considered. My veto strikes a balance between these competing goals." Clarenbach pledged to the governor that he would follow up with a trailer bill; he believed that leaving the provisions in the law would give him leverage with the insurers' lobbyists. Upon signing the budget, Clarenbach was quoted saying, "I'm gratified that we were able to act quickly and provide these much needed protections and assist those who decide to undergo the HTLV-III screening."[34]

John Robinson of Wausau, head of the assembly's Health Committee working with the Division of Health, took the lead for the trailer bill, AB 487, passed in November 1985. A new provision required the reporting of positive HTLV-III test results to the state health agency for use in prevention and control. Among its revised provisions were employer protections that were expanded so no employer could use the test to terminate employment, in addition to the previous requirement of not using it for hiring. The provisions might be lifted if both the state epidemiologist and the federal secretary of health declared HTLV-III infections posed a significant risk of transmitting the disease through employment. Some exceptions were provided for the blanket provision of obtaining prior consent, such as working with donated organs or for research in which "the researcher cannot know the identity of the test subject." Test information could also be provided to emergency care providers, funeral directors, and health-care facilities.[35]

The insurance issue provoked testimony at a September hearing in Milwaukee with insurers asking to use the test in determining underwriting policies. Dr. Robert Gleeson of Northwestern Mutual Insurance argued that not to do so would put a financial burden on the company and its mutual clients. He was joined by testimony from Wausau Insurance, which argued that most of the state's group policies would not be impacted, as no tests were used on individuals in group policies, and others would have recourse to the state's special high-risk pool, which spread risks across insurers operating in the state. Individuals denied regular insurance because of AIDS or other high health risks could apply to the pool. Insurers sought to have the matter determined by the state's insurance commissioner, who regulated their business. Others saw the matter as more complicated because it posed multiple public health concerns that needed to be weighed in the fight against the epidemic. Indeed, Governor Earl, in response to insurers' drive to have access to the test, commented, "Gay and bisexual men have more than their health to think about when they consider being tested for this virus. Despite all our legal protections, those who run the highest risk of the AIDS in Wisconsin are also exposed to a high risk of discrimination if they are identified publicly."[36]

As passed, the final bill did permit the insurance commissioner to authorize the use of other tests as long as they were determined "medically significant and sufficiently reliable." An insurance commission analyst said the use of two enzyme-linked immunosorbent assays (ELISAs) followed by a Western blot test, as were used by blood banks at the time, could be deemed reliable. The question of what was deemed "medically significant" was up to the Division of Health. In March 1986, Linda Reivitz, who as secretary of the Department of Health and Social Services had authority over the Division of Health, outlined a very deliberate process of several months' consideration. Then, a late July report from the state epidemiologist found the ELISA and Western blot tests to be medically significant but suggested caution in their use. On October 1, 1986, the insurance commissioner scheduled a hearing on a proposed rule to allow tests. No resolution resulted. More hearings were scheduled into 1987 under the new Thompson administration. In 1988, testing was permitted for individuals but not for those under group health policies. Robert Hasse, Thompson's appointee as insurance commissioner, supported the request in Thompson's biennial budget that the legislature permit AIDS tests for small group insurance policies.[37]

Since many homosexual men in the state feared the known health consequences of an AIDS diagnosis, and many also feared a concomitant concern of being thus identified as gay, most were very uncertain whether to have a health test. At issue was the need for stringent confidentially about the test and the need for nondiscrimination about the results of the test. The provisions set up in Act 29 with the statutory requirement for written permission to perform screening were an attempt to encourage testing. In the case of positive test results, a referral to a professional counselor was required, another attempt to encourage testing. To ensure that neither test results nor declining to take a test could be used against individuals, the provisions of Act 29 prohibited requiring the test as a condition of employment or insurability. The insurance provisions would later be relaxed. However, most of the gay community's immediate panic over AIDS in the mid-1980s had been addressed at a time of great unease.

HATE CRIMES

The next major legislative act that gays claimed as a victory in the 1980s was the passage of a Wisconsin hate crimes bill that included sexual orientation. As the *Wisconsin Jewish Chronicle* observed in 1988, "Nationwide and in Wisconsin Jewish groups have taken the initiative in advocating hate crimes bills." The Anti-Defamation League (ADL) began publishing an annual audit of "anti-Semitic incidents" beginning in 1979. In December 1986, Nancy Weisenberg, assistant director of the Milwaukee Jewish Council, was in correspondence with state senator Mordecai Lee on his willingness to sponsor what she then termed "ethnic vandalism legislation." On November 12, 1986, the Milwaukee Jewish Council's board passed a draft statement prepared by Robert Friebert, a politically active Jewish community leader, on such legislation, urging penalty enhancement for crimes against persons or property where there was intentional selection based on a minority status. Penalty enhancement did not create a separate crime based on hate intent or hate speech but instead attached a penalty that would result in a greater sentence. In the new hate crimes legislation, such penalty enhancements included status of both creed and sexual orientation. In early development, the proposed bill was called ethnic intimidation legislation. By August 1987, Weisenberg had requested "hate crimes legislation" as the preferred terminology.[38]

In the 1987 session, Brian Rieselman, a gay staffer, requested a draft bill on behalf of Senator Lee's office. The legislative attorney who drafted the bill was in touch with Weisenberg, also an attorney, on the preliminary or working draft. The nuance that the measure was a "penalty enhancer" rather than a separately defined crime was important from a legal standpoint, as penalty enhancers already existed in Wisconsin statutes, such as for masked crimes or crimes with a firearm. Weisenberg indicated that the list of protected groups was taken from existing Wisconsin statutes. This included sexual orientation from the 1982 gay rights bill. In Wisconsin, the equal rights law was a key factor in making sure the proposed new law would also apply to gay hate crimes. The Jewish community, especially Weisenberg and Steve Morrison of the Madison Jewish Community Council, worked hard to build a broad coalition of support. When introduced by Senator Lee on November 25, 1987, the bill, like others we have seen, boasted a long list of requesting groups. Jewish groups included not only the Milwaukee Jewish Council but the Madison Jewish Community Council and the ADL of B'nai B'rith. Other ethnic and racial groups included the NAACP, the Milwaukee Urban League, the Madison Urban League, and the American Indian Peace and Justice League. Because disability was included as a protected class, requestors included United Cerebral Palsy of Southwestern Wisconsin, Access to Independence, and the Association of Retarded Citizens. Gay groups on the list were Milwaukee's Cream City Business Association and Madison's United Political Action Committee.[39]

In Wisconsin, the progress of hate crimes legislation was monitored closely by both the Jewish press and the gay press. As Wisconsin took up the issue in the fall of 1987, the *Wisconsin Jewish Chronicle* noted that the US House of Representatives had passed a measure on reporting hate crimes on October 7 of that year and that Illinois had become the fourth state to enact a bias crimes reporting law. Anti-Semitic incidents and hate crimes were frequently covered in the Jewish paper. The gay press also followed the bill's progress, with *The Wisconsin Light* listing hate crimes on the community's legislative agenda. In 1982, the National Gay and Lesbian Task Force had established its Anti-Violence Project, which began tracking anti-gay violence with its first published report in 1984. Since many gay people were forced to come out over reporting incidents, the task force believed its national report of seven thousand incidents a year in 1989 was very likely underreported. The task force in 1989 also observed that AIDS had become "a focus and justification for anti-gay prejudice and violence."[40]

The Wisconsin Governor's Council on Lesbian and Gay Issues conducted a volunteer state violence survey in 1983–1984 with participation of the state's gay organizations. Following the model of the National Gay and Lesbian Task Force, the Wisconsin survey was part of the council's charge "to make recommendations on improving the public and personal safety of gays and lesbians." A February 1984 status report indicated that 103 surveys were returned. Respondents (57 percent) predominantly lived in Milwaukee or Madison. Three-quarters were male, and most had been out for less than ten years.[41]

Dealing with homophobia was a common refrain in survey comments. "Not being able to live a gay lifestyle openly is harassment," one respondent felt. Another observed, "If my lover and I walked hand-in-hand at the county fair, all kinds of things would happen." Another noted, "The only time we get coverage is when someone dies of AIDS." Results showed that 83 percent had been verbally abused by straight people, most more than once. Of the respondents, 24 percent said they had been punched, kicked, or beaten, and 13 percent had been assaulted with a weapon. Some 10 percent had been harassed or had been victims of violence within their own families. One commented, "Parents disowned me—father threatened life." Perhaps most shocking, 29 percent had been harassed, threatened, or attacked by police. Most did not report the incidents either because they did not believe the justice system would be helpful or they did not want to come out. Milwaukee men accounted for twenty-two of the thirty complaints of police harassment. Of those who went to the police, 47 percent said the police were indifferent or hostile. Only 20 percent found them courteous or helpful. One Milwaukeean said, "Police [make] the 'gay rights state' . . . a joke." A lesbian wrote, "Police Officer called me a dyke and a queer as he beat me."[42]

Lesbians responding were more likely to have been sexually harassed or assaulted. Of those who had experienced this, only three went to the police. According to the press release issued when the survey was made public, Wisconsin lesbians "were much more afraid for their safety, had changed their behavior to avoid trouble, and were more likely to believe that they would have trouble in the future." Indeed, fear was a frequent theme in the survey. One respondent noted, "Being gay involves a constant calculation of risks." Another wrote, "I fear for my safety but try not to let it ruin my life." A respondent said, "Going to and from bars is still very threatening." One felt, "At my size I'm more worried about a gang attack." A non-gay respondent reported, "A friend and myself went to the aid of a gay man in the neighborhood who was being beaten by a gang of youths who were calling him a faggot, sissy, etc." Most wrenching was, "My friend Thomas Buckley was murdered."[43]

When the survey results were released, *OUT!* reporter Sue Burke, who had worked on the survey, argued that sensitivity to homosexual rights should be a criterion in selection of a new police chief for Milwaukee. Disagreement came from Milwaukee's Channel 12 editorial director, Dave Begel, who seemed to discount the survey results. He said, "Now I think gays ought to be able to live in peace. But gee whiz, let's not go overboard." Clearly, however, the survey documented there was a need to deal with gay hate crimes in Wisconsin.[44]

A Tale of Two Versions

In October 1987, the *Wisconsin Jewish Chronicle* editor wrote, "We hope that the Wisconsin legislature will soon enact an anti-hate crimes bill." A later editorial in the paper expressed solidarity with other protected classes: "An attack on someone because of his or her race, religion, ethnic ancestry, disability, or sexual orientation should be considered an attack on all people." To support the effort, the Jewish community had a new tool in the Wisconsin Jewish Conference, a loose group of nine Jewish communities from around the state established the year before with Robert Friebert as president. Michael Blumenfeld, also a Madison alder, served as part-time legislative council. He was to be "the eyes and voice in Madison of Wisconsin's Jewish community."[45]

At a January 7, 1988, hearing of the Senate Judiciary and Consumer Affairs Committee, sponsors Representative Louis Fortis and Senator Lee testified that the bill had symbolic value. Discussion focused on the reasons impelling the bill. Anti-Semitic slogans had been spray painted on a Milwaukee synagogue, and racist epithets on a black woman's home. Fortis called them "inexcusable acts." But the committee chair, Senator Lynn Adelman, was reported to have "doubts about using the criminal law to make symbolic statements." The state's gay press reported that the bill might be bottled up in committee. While calling anti-Semitic crimes outrageous and offensive, Adelman was quoted as saying, "I question whether the criminal law is the appropriate way to express that outrage."[46]

Supporters hoped lobbying would be effective, with three of the six committee members being Jewish (Adelman, Russ Feingold, and Barbara Lorman). Attorney General Don Hanaway also testified in favor of the bill and suggested some amendments, including one for injunctive relief, that is, the use of court orders to stop repeated expressions of prejudice or continued harassment. Lee believed the chances for passage were "good but not great" and pledged to work on Hanaway's issues. At the senate committee hearing, the Midwest ADL spokesperson said of hate crimes, "By making members of minority communities fearful and angry, by making them suspicious of members of other groups and of the power structure that is supposed to protect them, these incidents can damage the fabric of our society and fragment our communities." Weisenberg explained that "the protected groups listed in the Hate Crimes Bill are taken from existing law" and "were chosen because their characteristics put them in the minority and made them vulnerable to harassment." Also speaking in favor at the hearing were two Milwaukee gay groups, the Cream City Business Association and the Lambda Rights Network.[47]

Meanwhile, on October 1, 1987, Clarenbach and others had also introduced AB 599, an assembly hate crimes bill. In promoting the bill, Clarenbach stated, "Violence and harassment toward members of minority groups still rears its ugly head. We see swastikas painted on synagogues, and other signs of race hatred, religious intolerance and gay bashing." The assembly held a hearing on January 14, 1988, and the Committee on Criminal Justice and Public Safety unanimously reported out a substitute bill. The substitute was a weaker version that did not list specifically protected groups and thus included no reference to sexual orientation. The assembly considered the matter on February 24 and, by a vote of 97 to 0, passed the watered-down measure and sent it to the senate. Advocacy groups pushed for the stronger language of the draft senate bill, which named specific groups and included specific protection for cemeteries and synagogues, which were particularly vulnerable to attack. Friebert said, "It's an important statement of public policy that the state of Wisconsin abhors this kind of conduct." Adelman, whose committee had access to both versions, remained dubious: "I predict that if this bill becomes law it will never be applied."[48]

On March 10, after many calls and letters, the Senate Judiciary and Consumer Affairs Committee recommended a substitute version of AB 599 by a vote of 5 to 1 to include the stronger language, with committee chair Adelman in the majority. The committee then voted 4 to 2 to recommend passage. Both Adelman and Feingold voted against recommending the measure over civil liberties concerns, particularly free speech. Rather than advancing the senate's own bill, they believed offering a substitute bill could build off prior passage of the assembly bill and lead to even stronger legislation. This would also eliminate the need for another hearing on the assembly side. Despite his own vote against passage, Adelman got the stronger bill out of his committee. Normally, a standalone bill on a controversial new topic would be debated for several sessions before coming up for passage. This time, there was no such debate. After a minor amendment, the senate adopted AB 599 by a vote of 27 to 3.[49]

In the *Wisconsin Jewish Chronicle*, the early assembly bill had been editorialized as "commendable," but the paper deplored the weakened language, which had taken out the list of protected groups. The weak version also had used the phrase "with intent to intimidate." This raised potential constitutional questions on punishing thoughts and the freedom of opinion. Blumenfeld said, "The bill would have been essentially powerless had the protected classes been removed." The *Chronicle* believed higher fines and longer jail sentences added back in by the senate gave the bill teeth. The paper noted, "The Jewish community fought hard to keep the bill as comprehensive as it is." But the fight was not quite over. When the measure was back in the assembly for a final vote, Wayne Wood, a Democrat from Janesville who had been instrumental in several antigay votes in the past, moved to delete the language that would have protected specific groups, including gays. This amendment was defeated by a vote of 68 to 31. The assembly then concurred with the senate version.

The lesbian publication *Leaping La Crosse News* noted that passage of the senate bill "sends the message that in Wisconsin we consider 'hate crimes' to be especially offensive." Governor Thompson was lobbied with calls and letters to sign, something he indicated privately that he would do. On April 21, 1988, Thompson signed the bill into law as Act 348. Jane Weinberg, assistant regional director of the ADL, praised the governor, saying, "We believe the passage of this bill will be an effective tool against criminal acts of bigotry and prejudice." Wisconsin was among the first states to enact hate crimes legislation that included sexual orientation and was one of the three states to do so before 1989.[50]

RESPONSES TO THE HATE CRIMES LAW

Even after the law passed, there was ongoing concern over hate actions. Hate mail regularly arrived at the offices of the Madison Jewish Council. Madison lesbian police officer Darlene Kemmerer urged gays and lesbians to report hate crimes. "If it stays quiet, then people can say it isn't happening," she told them. Fellow lesbian police officer Alix Olson, police liaison to the gay community, said she was focused on "making the legal process easier for homosexuals who are harassed or bashed." Madison Alder Jim McFarland cautioned that "higher visibility also creates more targets for people to attack."[51]

The first Wisconsin hate crimes case based on sexual orientation occurred near Appleton at the Fox River Mall in Grand Chute in July 1990. The case involved a police cadet in a bar who called a hairstylist a faggot and then beat and bloodied him. While the jury found him guilty of battery, the hate crime label was declined. The victim, Martin Christopher, was glad that at least the jury "refused to accept the defendant's 'bigoted' defense." Christopher stated, "We must stand up for our safety if we expect to have any."[52]

While Adelman doubted the bill would ever be used, it was a Wisconsin case of 1991 that took the matter of hate crimes legislation to the US Supreme Court. Though some had thought a Wisconsin test case might arise from the central Wisconsin vigilante group known as the Posse Comitatus, which was known for espousing antagonism toward minorities, the test case arose in urban Kenosha. A black teenager, Todd Mitchell, was part of a group of older black teenagers in a racially motivated attack of a white fourteen-year-old, leaving him bloodied and unconscious. The young man was comatose for four days, and doctors observed that his injuries might have been fatal had he not received medical treatment. Mitchell was convicted in Kenosha Circuit Court, and the jury added a hate crime penalty enhancer. Mitchell's lawyers appealed to the Wisconsin Court of Appeals. At the appeal level, issues on the constitutionality of the hate crimes law were raised. The appeals court decision upholding the hate crimes law was explicit: "Word, or even beliefs, are not punished here. What is punished is conduct."[53]

Mitchell's attorneys then appealed to the Wisconsin Supreme Court, again challenging the constitutionality of the hate crimes law. While the primary defense of the law was up to Attorney General James Doyle Jr., the Jewish community also weighed in with a friend of the court brief filed by attorney Robert Friebert with help from the ADL. The brief was presented at the request of a coalition of the protected classes. In addition to Jewish groups, the brief was filed on behalf of both the Milwaukee and the Madison Urban League, the NAACP, and the Madison United. The brief identified the purpose of the United as providing "a safe, secure, positive environment for the lesbian and gay communities." Friebert argued that there was a substantial difference in painting the phrase "Kill the Packers" on Lambeau Field and "Kill the Jews" on a synagogue. Friebert argued on behalf of the law "because the legislature had determined that such crimes—motivated by bigotry—are more serious." His brief included ADL reports that showed recent anti-Semitic incidents in Wisconsin, including eight incidents at Madison Hillel.[54]

Gays would be part of the conversation in the decision. Wisconsin Chief Justice Nathan Heffernan noted the facts of the criminal case were not in dispute, only the application of the penalty enhancer under the Wisconsin law of 1988. In reviewing the matter, Heffernan noted, "Statistical sources indicate that incidents of all types of bias-related crime are on the rise." He then proceeded to cite among other sources that "the National Gay and Lesbian Task Force reported 7031 incidents of anti-gay violence in 1989." This has "spawned a growing debate in this country: the constitutionality of legislation that seeks to address hate crimes." Heffernan recognized that adding a word such as *Jew*, *spic*, *nigger*, or *queer* during a crime resulted in possible enhancement. He believed that "opprobrious though the speech may be, an individual must be allowed to utter it without fear of punishment by the state." Writing for the majority, Heffernan ruled that "the statute unconstitutionally infringes upon free speech, and [we] reverse the decision of the court of appeals."[55]

Two dissenting opinions were filed. Justice Shirley Abrahamson held that "the law should be construed narrowly and should be held constitutional." She believed that "our law recognizes the harmful effects of invidious classification and discrimination." Further, she stated, "All members of the group to which the victim belongs may suffer when the individual

Wisconsin Supreme Court Justices Shirley Abrahamson and William Bablitch wrote dissents that supported Wisconsin's hate crimes law, which included penalty enhancements for hate crimes based on sexual orientation. *WISCONSIN BLUE BOOK, 1991–1992*

is victimized." Abrahamson did not think hate crimes law infringed on free speech: "Bigots are free to think and express as they wish, except that they may not engage in criminal conduct in furtherance of their beliefs."[56]

Justice William Bablitch offered an even stronger dissent, opening with a quote from Chicana poet Lorna Dee Cervantes.

> everywhere the crosses are burning,
> sharp-shooting goose-steppers around every corner,
> there are snipers in the schools. . . .
> (I know you don't believe this.
> You think this nothing
> but faddish exaggeration. But they
> are not shooting at you.)

Bablitch contended that the law was not a hate crimes law but a law against discrimination in the selection of a victim. He believed that questioning the hate crimes law questioned all nondiscrimination law. In reviewing precedents, Bablitch cited a Kentucky matter in which "assailants beat a young gay man with a tire iron, locked him into a car trunk with a bunch of turtles and then tried to set the car on fire. He was left with severe brain damage." Bablitch also cited a Madison incident in which counselors at Camp Shalom discovered brake linings had been cut on a bus used to transport children. For Bablitch, "There is ample evidence to support the legislature's conclusion that intentional selection of a victim from a protected class causes a greater harm to its victims as well as to society than do crimes where the victim's status is not a factor."[57]

Attorney General James Doyle Jr. decided to appeal the state supreme court ruling to the US Supreme Court, and oral arguments were heard April 21, 1993. Support for the appeal had come from the attorneys general of forty-nine states. Doyle argued that because the state court had reached "a conclusory constitutional statement" that hate crimes laws impede speech protected under the First Amendment, they had gone beyond merely interpreting a state statute. Thus, the federal court could review the matter. Doyle claimed, "Wisconsin was very careful in drafting this statute. It used language that is found very clearly patterned and found in hundreds of antidiscrimination and civil rights laws, some of them civil, many of them criminal, contrary to the assertion of the Wisconsin Supreme Court."[58]

Again, a friend of the court brief had been filed on the matter at the federal level, with the leading actor the ADL, but also with a broad coalition that included national gay organizations, the Human Rights Campaign Fund, and the National Gay and Lesbian Task Force. The brief also cited the Kentucky incident used by Bablitch and statistics from the National Gay and Lesbian Task Force on incidences of anti-homosexual violence. This was one of the earliest matters in which the US Supreme Court ruled positively that sexual orientation could be included as a protected class, as opposed to rulings on criminal sodomy matters or denial of discrimination protections to gays and lesbians under constitutional or other claims. The next major sexual orientation case, *Roemer v. Evans*, would not arise until 1996. The brief argued for the court to give badly needed guidance, stating, "Penalty enhancement hate crime legislation is no more concerned with motive and no less concerned with conduct than anti-discrimination laws."[59]

The court accepted the Mitchell case "because of the importance of the question presented and the existence of a conflict of authority among state high courts on the constitutionality of statutes similar to Wisconsin's penalty-enhancement provision." Chief Justice William Rehnquist, a native of Milwaukee, writing the decision for the unanimous Supreme Court, mentioned the Doyle and amicus brief argument, stating, "Bias-motivated crimes are more likely to provoke retaliatory crimes, inflict distinct emotional harms on their victims, and incite community unrest." During oral arguments, most justices avoided any mention of gay issues, usually referring to hate on the basis of "race, religion, and so forth." Only one justice, unnamed in court documents, specifically mentioned sexual orientation in listing protected groups. The court's opinion found no merit in the Wisconsin Supreme Court argument regarding the first amendment. Rehnquist wrote in the court's unanimous decision: "The prospect of a citizen suppressing his bigoted beliefs for fear that evidence of those beliefs will be introduced against him at trial if he commits a serious offense against person or property is too speculative a hypothesis to support Mitchell's overbreadth claim." The US Supreme Court reversed the Wisconsin Supreme Court and found "First Amendment rights were not violated by the application of the Wisconsin penalty-enhancement provision." Thus, Wisconsin's passage of a hate crimes law resulted in the US Supreme Court upholding not only the general principle of hate crimes law but specifically that hate crimes based on sexual orientation, one of the protected classes listed, could be legislated.[60]

AIDS BILL OF RIGHTS

The last major legislative action for the gay community in the 1980s was an AIDS Bill of Rights. After the 1988 elections, *The Wisconsin Light* was heartened to find that Democratic majorities in the state legislature had increased slightly, thereby protecting the state's still relatively new gay rights bill. The paper then listed a series of AIDS-related concerns on the community agenda. In November 1988, Clarenbach submitted a drafting request for new AIDS legislation, and in May 1989 he sought sponsors for the bill, called the Wisconsin AIDS Initiative. His plea was that "the AIDS time-bomb has yet to explode here. There are close to 10,000 people in our state who are infected with the HIV virus." Included as sponsors were Milwaukee Democrats Tim Carpenter and Barbara Notestein. The proposal sought to "anticipate the demands on our health care institutions and implement the most cost effective and humane changes." The eleven-point program prohibited health-care providers from refusing service to HIV-positive persons, increased the criminal penalty for intentional disclosure of test results, prohibited local zoning that excluded community-based homes for those with AIDS, and required health policies to cover drugs to treat the disease. There had been an incident where a Milwaukee surgeon had refused to operate because of HIV; this became the vehicle for further non-discrimination provisions over medical services. Several nursing homes in the state had also refused to admit people with AIDS. AB 400 became known as the AIDS Bill of Rights and was introduced on June 6, 1989.[61]

With large bipartisan support, the assembly passed the bill on October 31, 1989. The senate concurred on February 1, 1990, with four dissenting Republican votes. After senate passage, Representative Carpenter called on Governor Thompson to sign AB 400 and other AIDS-related measures, including public school education on the virus and support for clinical trials of new drugs. At the governor's signing, Earl Bricker, who was now executive director of the Madison AIDS Support Network, observed, "This is just one more example of how Wisconsin [has] proven to be a model." Doug Nelson, executive director of the Milwaukee AIDS Project, said, "We are determined to use the new law and see it enforced." Nelson claimed

Four AIDS Related Bills Stalled On Governor's Desk

LOOK TO THE FUTURE

M L G P C

Oscar Wilde　　　Gertrude Stein

THE GAY 90's

Pictured, is the 1990 Milwaukee Pride Logo. See story on page 3.

[Madison]- State Representative Timothy Carpenter (D-Milwaukee) has issued a call for action on AIDS bills passed by the past session of the legislature. Currently, these bills are before Governor Tommy Thompson for his consideration. **Please contact the Governor's office to express your strong support for these initiatives.** Direct your letters to: Office of the Governor, 155 E. State Capitol, Madison, WI 53702; or call (608) 266-1212 (Madison Office) or (414) 227-4344 (Milwaukee Office). Those with facsimile machines can Fax the Governor at (608) 267-8983. The bills are:
　Wisconsin AIDS Initiative-AB 400. (See article, this issue)
　AIDS Education-AB 461. This requires all Wisconsin public school districts to provide AIDS instruction at least once to students in grades 6-8 and once again to

A supportive legislature in the 1980s and early 1990s passed a number of important AIDS-related measures to help the state's residents cope with the epidemic. *THE WISCONSIN LIGHT*, APRIL 5, 1990

only one nursing home out of sixty in the Milwaukee area would accept AIDS patients. He threatened to document cases and refer matters to licensing boards for suspension or revocation. *The Wisconsin Light* asserted, "Credit for the favorable political environment that protects civil liberties and provides a more humane climate in the state rests squarely with the Gay and Lesbian Community. People from across the state have taken an increasingly active role in shaping the public policy that affects them."[62]

REMARKABLE LEGISLATIVE SUCCESSES

The film *MILK* includes a news clip about the Anita Bryant–led effort to repeal nondiscrimination ordinances around the country. In it, news anchor Walter Cronkite and other newscasters talk about the next city where "homosexuality is the issue" facing the voters. By the 1980s, however, most gay activists in Wisconsin had matured politically and no longer wanted homosexuality to be the issue that was addressed head on in the political battles. Instead, they saw value in forming coalitions across issues, in particular those related to protected classes. As the 1980s ended, it was becoming settled policy that sexual orientation was part of the litany of protected minorities in the state. Clarenbach was proud of the legislative gains: "We are making it easier and safer for Gays and Lesbians all across this state to live and to work and to come out."[63]

During this time many, though not most, Wisconsin Republicans were supportive of gay rights. When in 1982 the Republican Party took a position for repealing the gay rights law, Milwaukee Republicans offered some of the strongest dissent. Gay Republican John Rudolph bemoaned the unsuccessful fight against the resolution. John Lyons, chairman of the Twenty-sixth District Republican Club, wrote, "We cannot apologize sufficiently for the utter and unmitigated stupidity of our 1982 State Convention." Efforts to deal with gay issues in schools only began to be addressed with the passage of Act 29 and its provisions on school nondiscrimination. The lesbian publication *Leaping La Crosse News* wrote, "It is particularly important that the state has recognized that there are lesbians and gays under the age of 21!" The Nabozny case showed that school officials could be held accountable. Yet in 2016, the *New York Times* would report that 34 percent of gay teens were likely to be bullied, and 43 percent had considered suicide in the last twelve months.[64]

The AIDS crisis in Wisconsin, as elsewhere, would only deepen, but political leadership over testing showed the state's response could be positive in weighing the gay community's concerns. Notably, this happened at a time when President Ronald Reagan had yet to mention the word. More of the Wisconsin non-legislative AIDS response is covered in chapter 9.

Wisconsin hate crimes law including sexual orientation, another early enactment, showed how building allies during the consenting adults struggle provided long-term dividends. Over time, LGBT individuals would become the most reported target of hate crimes across the nation, even before the 2016 slaughter at the Pulse night club in Orlando.[65]

Combined, the legislative acts of the 1980s showed a remarkable turnaround on legislation regarding homosexuality. Many factors, including the state's unique political tradition of progressivism, played a part. It can certainly be argued that the skills of the gay community and its leaders put Wisconsin at the forefront of national legislation.

8

TONY EARL: PROFILE IN FABULOUS COURAGE

I believe the energy that goes into living a double life and worrying about exposure and possible discrimination on the job is a terrible waste.

—GOVERNOR ANTHONY S. EARL[1]

I don't see civil rights legislation as a panacea, but it's a hell of a good start. Without it, I'd still be back on the massa's plantation. And lord knows that would never do.

—MERRY FRAN TRYON,
EQUAL RIGHTS DIVISION ADMINISTRATOR[2]

When Anthony Earl ran for governor in 1982, he became the first statewide candidate to aggressively seek LGBT support, even including openly gay men and lesbians as part of his campaign. This effort launched the future governor into initiating the first real statewide conversation about the positive contributions of lesbians and gays to the state of Wisconsin. The presence of gays and lesbians working in state government would be one of the key features of his administration.

Anthony Earl grew up in St. Ignace, Wisconsin, at the Straits of Mackinac. He served in the legislature from 1969 to 1973 representing Wausau, including a stint as Democratic majority leader. Once he was out of the legislature, aides to Governor Patrick Lucey let it be known that "they consider[ed] Earl capable of any job in state service." Lucey subsequently appointed Earl secretary of the Department of Administration, where he concentrated on the state budget and used research and analysis to give the governor's office better control over Wisconsin's sprawling state agencies. Later, Earl was appointed secretary of the Department of Natural Resources by that entity's board. Some praised Earl as a true "red shirt," or Wisconsin outdoorsman. He proved to be an effective environmental advocate and would use his natural resources record in the 1982 gubernatorial race.[3]

Perhaps most significant to his efforts during the campaign to broaden an LGBT base of support was that Earl sat down with *Gay Madison* in his headquarters for an in-depth interview with editor Brooks Egerton. This interview appeared in the August edition before the 1982 Democratic primary. The paper had polled other candidates with general questions, but only James Wood, another Democrat, responded. Earl observed that the question of supporting the gay rights bill came up at every debate, and his answer was always an unequivocal yes. He told the paper, "It is not enough to pay lip service [to equal rights] if you don't intend to follow it up." Earl also urged passage for the still-pending consenting adults legislation.[4]

For Earl, it was imperative to follow the passage of the gay rights bill with action. "What kind of enforcement are we going to have?" he asked. Earl and Egerton discussed sexually transmitted diseases and the high incidence of alcoholism in the gay community. "With the appointment of a Secretary of Health and Social Services," Earl said, "I'd make sure it was someone who was sensitive to [that community]." He also promised to appoint a paid staffer as a liaison to the gay community, an issue that would soon become contentious. Regarding education, Earl stated the task was to "not bring children up with the idea that a different sexual orientation is a perversion." He also noted the state's grim financial picture in the next biennial budget—a reality that would define Earl's first two years as governor.[5]

Earl's statements on the inclusion of gays and lesbians in his office were met with strong opposition. During the run-up to the general election, the press reported that Republicans were spreading rumors that Earl would "impose a quota system for hiring gays in state government." To fan antigay sentiment, supporters of Republican candidate Terry Kohler distributed the *Gay Madison* interview in northern counties. With the consenting adults bill still waiting for passage, a spokesperson for Kohler said that Kohler "believes no further gay rights legislation is needed." Crystal Hyslop, writing in *OUT!* before the election, noted, "Anthony Earl has taken a liberal stand and formally addressed the lesbian/gay community issues and concerns." On November 2, 1983, Earl beat Kohler, garnering 57 percent of the vote. His four-year tenure as governor would mark significant advances on gay and lesbian issues, keeping Wisconsin in the forefront of advancing equal treatment of its LGBT citizens.[6]

"Avowed Homosexual" Appointed

In October 1982, San Francisco's Harry Britt, successor to Harvey Milk, speaking in Madison for the Democratic Socialist Alliance, was asked to weigh in on a topic of local importance: the value of a governor's liaison position. In most cases, he responded, these community liaisons have been "coopted," too often "caught between the community's wishes and the office holder's political future." Instead, Britt recommended seeking multiple open gays and lesbians in governmental positions. Earl appeared to see the value of both approaches. Though he still planned to hire a liaison as a paid staffer in the governor's office, Earl appointed several gays and lesbians to state government, even though they were not always formally out. These included Doris Hanson as secretary of the Department of Administration; Katie Morrison, a former state senator, as administrator of the Division of Health; and Dick Flintrop as director of the Council on Criminal Justice. In every case, the appointment was based on merit and a strong public record.[7]

These appointments were not without controversy. In the early staffing of his office, Earl made headlines with the appointment of Ron McCrea as his press secretary. Citizens of Milwaukee woke up on December 2, 1982, with the *Milwaukee Sentinel* declaring, "Avowed Homosexual Named Earl's Press Chief." The governor-elect stated that McCrea's homosexuality "is only one facet of his personality, and hardly the most noteworthy." Hal Bergan of the transition team would recall, "We were astonished at the time that this fact could have been deemed newsworthy, much less headline material." Bergan said the overall reaction had been positive because of McCrea's high standing among journalists. Senator Marvin Roshell, a conservative Democrat from Chippewa Falls, however, was "not pleased," saying, "In my district they don't buy somebody who isn't

Governor Tony Earl (left), who had actively campaigned for gay and lesbian votes in 1982, wanted to have an inclusive administration. His early appointment of openly gay activist Ron McCrea (right) caused a brief press furor. PHOTO BY BRENT NICASTRO

thinking straight." The *Milwaukee Journal* ran a cartoon with a press room labeled "The Daily Sensational." McCrea remarked later, "I had no idea, really, of the kind of storm that would be generated at my appointment."[8]

As the controversy heightened, McCrea offered to withdraw the appointment, but the governor-elect would have none of it. He told McCrea, "Bullshit you will. If I can't deal with a few small-minded people on this, what am I going to do when I have a real problem?" At a meeting of the Milwaukee Cream City Foundation, a gay civic group, McCrea would speak about some of the letters on his appointment from "solid, God-fearing citizens." As he recalled, one student group asked if "the governor shouldn't wear rouge and makeup in the morning to be more attractive to McCrea." Another sarcastically asked, "Isn't your wife jealous?" While his audience responded with laughter at these puerile reactions, McCrea warned, "I want to remind you that the battle out there is still to be won." As an out activist for many years, he reflected, "I used to ask my friends if I really had to put my job on the line as often as I did to make the world safe for disco. But I did."[9]

The controversy over the McCrea appointment and the promised liaison position had a negative impact on the Earl transition team. *OUT!* headlined its editorial of January 1983: "Will Tony Earl Back Down?" In light of the state's fiscal crisis, the transition team balked at putting money toward a gay/lesbian community liaison, saying the governor's office "cannot be expanded to fund this position." (It did, however, find funds for liaisons from the African American, Hispanic, and Native American communities as well as a woman's desk.) The paper voiced concern that if a voluntary board of gay and lesbian advisors was appointed—a much less costly means to include non-straight voices in state government—it would "greatly delay creation of the liaison office." The paper praised Earl for the McCrea appointment, noting he "stood behind that appointment when severely criticized by the homophobic press, something many lesser politicians would not have done." In the end, an official lesbian/gay liaison position would be significantly delayed.[10]

OTHER STATE-LEVEL WORK

Earl's hopes for including gays and lesbians in his administration were not without precedent. In the decade after Stonewall, a small number of elected officials started to pay attention to gay issues. Most were on the municipal level, and one of the frequent actions was to appoint a paid liaison to the lesbian and gay community. Another was to ask volunteers to serve on study or advisory bodies. In April 1976, Democratic Governor Milton Schapp created, by executive order, the Pennsylvania Commission on Sexual Minorities. He also issued an executive order banning discrimination in state employment on the basis of sexual orientation. Two years later, Oregon's Democratic Governor Bob Straub created the Oregon Task Force on Sexual Preference. In a letter of December 12, 1978, Straub praised the task force's resulting report for "systematically identifying and breaking down false fears of our society." Unfortunately, Straub left office in 1979 and was unable to continue the work. On October 9, 1980, Governor Jerry Brown Jr. of California issued an executive order to establish a twenty-five-member Commission on Personal Privacy charged with studying "the problems of discrimination based upon sexual orientation or invasion of the right of personal privacy." The resulting report cited

Wisconsin Governor Dreyfus's signing statement on sexual privacy and recommended that sexual orientation be added to the protected classes under California's nondiscrimination and antiviolence statutes.[11]

COUNCIL FORMED AMID LAVENDER CONTROVERSY

Even though the executive office had determined it could not afford a paid liaison position, Governor Earl still wanted to work with Wisconsin's lesbian and gay communities. The backlash against the decision had been harsh. *OUT!* wrote an editorial called "A Budget Short-Change." They posited that Earl "doesn't want another media splash like the Ron McRae [sic] affair (which, to his credit, he handled admirably)." The *Daily Cardinal* on the UW–Madison campus headlined "Earl Shirks Commitment to Gays and Lesbians." It was at this point that I became involved. By the fall 1982 election, I had already served one full term on the Dane County Board as a gay man; Kathleen Nichols, a lesbian activist, had joined the board in the spring of that year. On December 2, we wrote a joint letter to Governor-elect Earl congratulating him for his forthright support on gay issues and urging a liaison position, reminding him, "All too often lesbians and gay men have suffered discrimination without any redress." This led to a request by the governor for a meeting very shortly after his inauguration. On January 17, we wrote again, outlining a voluntary structure that would retain the "commitment to the liaison function and recognize the need to get on with the work now." We wrote, "Your willingness to add the authority of the executive office to the continuing work for lesbian and gay rights and your personal commitment as Governor are strong indications that Wisconsin's progressive traditions will not falter."[12]

Governor Earl knew the lack of a liaison had been a disappointment, and he wanted to gather information on what other actions might be taken. He asked Kathleen Nichols and me to visit with lesbian and gay communities around the state. We took to the road in mid-January and in four weekends visited Racine, Milwaukee, Stevens Point, La Crosse, Wauwatosa, and Appleton. Some meetings also drew people from Oshkosh, Green Bay, Kenosha, Sturtevant, and Menomonie. In discussing their needs, most gay communities said there was a basic need to convince heterosexual Wisconsinites that there are lesbians and gays in all of Wisconsin. This attitude reflected the gay presumption behind coming out, that if they knew us, they might see us as fellow citizens.[13]

The discussions enabled us to conduct an unofficial survey of the state's gay community as of early 1983, including its local gathering spots, available social services, community support, and public reception. In Appleton, in addition to the local gay bar, a peer counseling organization named Acceptance met biweekly. Lawrence University supported gay-friendly training programs, and the *Appleton Post-Crescent* was thought to be supportive. La Crosse had a small gay bar, a regular women's newsletter, and a UW–La Crosse Gay People's Organization. Though the local paper would not print notices for the community, the available social services run by Catholic Social Services, Lutheran Social Services, and Alcoholics Anonymous (AA) were all thought to be pretty accepting. Racine had one gay bar, but many people preferred the bars in Milwaukee and Chicago. The city's active Gay Lesbian Union was focused around the Racine Unitarian Universalist Church. The Racine local daily paper had stopped listing both gay meetings and the gay hotline, although the Kenosha *News* sometimes printed notices. Gay speakers had visited UW–Parkside several times, and a local AA group catered to gay men. The Racine community was politically sophisticated enough that they had contacted Representative Les Aspin about sponsoring the national gay rights bill. Aspin responded no to sponsorship but committed to voting for it. At UW–Stevens Point, the campus Gay People's Union (GPU) had a small amount of funding from student fees and was able to use campus facilities. It held open forums on homophobia, but posters were regularly torn down. A local visible gay activist reported that he regularly received threatening phone calls. The sheriff of a nearby county reportedly had kicked his gay son out of the house.[14]

We held two meetings in the Milwaukee area and heard many stories of police harassment, including the common practice of police getting a guilty plea by reducing arrest charges to disorderly conduct. Metropolitan Community Church, a Lutherans Concerned group, and a Presbyterian group, along with a Parents and Friends of Gays group, provided support to the community. The local Dignity group was celebrating its eighth anniversary. One of the community's most cherished institutions was Brady East STD Clinic, which had thirty volunteers on a given weekend. Local government agencies could be sympathetic or hostile. There were concerns for gay youth but a wariness regarding how to approach the issue, though a Gay Teens group did exist. Some gay-friendly professional counseling existed. Funding for needed medical services was another concern. The group members discussed their desire for a gay community center building. When we met, Milwaukee had just launched a Gay/Lesbian Film Festival titled Mirroring Our Images, put on by the Lavender Commitment, a group describing itself as "Milwaukee's only gay arts group."[15]

Though we were able to report on some positive relations between the gay and non-gay communities we visited, we also had negative assessments. Our report back to the governor from the travels covered the following points:

1. The new nondiscrimination law was not widely known or acknowledged.

2. Social services frequently funded with public dollars could often be homophobic.

3. Public education on gay issues was badly needed.

4. In law enforcement there was unequal justice and frequent harassment.

5. Overall there was a lack of access to local and state government.

6. There was a real sense that gays and lesbians were disenfranchised in that they paid taxes but had little service or representation.

At this stage, we did not propose solutions to the problems, though we did listen closely to what communities had to say.

Many comments were made during the tour suggesting that if a volunteer council were appointed, the onus would be on volunteers to do the difficult work. At the Milwaukee listening session, longtime gay rights activist Alyn Hess proposed two paid half-time liaison positions, one to be a lesbian and the other a gay male. Then he outlined an agenda of state work, concluding, "As you can see from all of the above, these cannot really be half-time or volunteer positions." Milwaukee activists were upset with the idea of a voluntary council and told Earl's envoys so. Miriam Ben-Shalom of Milwaukee complained, "What chutzpah, unmitigated gall, to come here and ask us to volunteer again." Sharon Devitt, a longtime activist, commented, "They promised us steak and they gave us dog biscuits." Some Milwaukeeans threatened to boycott a volunteer effort. *OUT!* asked in an editorial, "How can volunteer efforts alone manage the huge tasks ahead?" Yet, the editorial also quoted Nichols: "This is an historic moment we can't let pass."[16]

After traveling the state and meeting with more than one hundred people, Nichols and I met with Governor Earl on February 16 to recommend he appoint, by Executive Order, a volunteer Council on Lesbian and Gay Issues. Among the prior examples by states, none had forthrightly chosen the identity-affirming terms *gay* and *lesbian* in their titles. Indeed, when the *Wisconsin Blue Book* listed the council, as it did all the executive bodies, it would be the first time the words *gay* or *lesbian* would appear in this document of historical record for the state.[17]

The governor accepted the recommendation and in turn asked us both to serve as cochairs. Nichols said, "Somebody credible and powerful like a governor saying that you must listen to us gives homosexuals a psychological boost." When the appointments were announced publicly, the *Milwaukee Journal* opined, "It is significant, we think, that both Nichols and Wagner . . . serve in elective public office" and that the appointment "indicates a welcome degree of public enlightenment about homosexuals, at least in their community." The fact that Nichols and I were both from Madison was criticized by Milwaukee activists. The Wisconsin Lesbian and Gay Network (WLGN), based in Stevens Point, also joined the criticism, "concerned that . . . there are rural and metropolitan interests other than Madison's to be considered." Professor Louie Crew, also of Stevens Point, wrote to Nichols and me, "Blessing upon you both for taking on so thorny a chore. I appreciate your efforts to deliver the very attractive booby prize in a responsible way."[18]

Earl's Executive Order No. 9, which I drafted, stated the council "would be of assistance in advising the Governor and executive branch agencies on measures to eliminate discrimination against and victimization of lesbians and gays in Wisconsin" and would "advocate for lesbian and gay interests in general areas of concern throughout the state." There would be fourteen members with gender parity and minority representation. Members were charged, among other items, "to ensure that state funded services are provided in a non-discriminatory manner to lesbians and gay men." In addition, they would "cooperate with educational institutions and public media to present information which shows the contributions lesbians and gays have made and continue to make to our society." The governor signed the order March 29, 1983.[19]

The first appointments ranged from Mark Behar, a male physician's assistant with the Brady East STD (BESTD) Clinic, to Cheryle Williams, a graphic artist with the Wisconsin Women's Building Project; from Crew, an English professor at Stevens Point who had founded the national gay Episcopal group Integrity, to Cynthia Lampman, a Racine activist who edited a national gay newsletter for the Unitarian Universalists; from Lawrence Roeming, an audio specialist at UW–Stout, to Norb Dekeuster, a deputy sheriff in Racine County, to Charlene McLauchlan, a technical writer who also owned a seventeen-acre goat farm in LaValle. Among the group was lawyer Shelly Gaylord, who would go on to be a Dane County Circuit judge, and Sue Burke, a lesbian journalist active in NOW.[20]

Governor Earl spoke at the first meeting on April 23, 1983, offering praise to the members: "By stepping forward to become a part of this council you have already shown the kind of courage and determination necessary to overcome frustration and achieve goals." Earl said of Wisconsin, "Many here are unaware of the size, richness and sophistication of the lesbian and gay community. They are unaware in part because long habits of dislike, disapproval and discrimination—largely the result of ignorance—have made it necessary for gays and lesbians to conceal a part of themselves and lead double lives." In the press, Earl urged a tight focus for the council on implementation of the still-new nondiscrimination law, health issues including AIDS, and domestic concerns such as child custody.[21]

At the first meeting, the council adopted a resolution related to the national AIDS crisis. Though one thousand cases had been reported nationally, none had yet been confirmed in Wisconsin. The resolution requested significant new national funds for research into the transmission and cure of AIDS. Copies were sent to President Ronald Reagan and the Wisconsin congressional delegation. The council was also active in the early AIDS effort in Wisconsin, which is covered in depth in chapter 9.[22]

Formed a year after the nondiscrimination statute was written into law, the council took gay liberation a step further, encouraging and modeling positive recognition of the lesbian and gay communities in the state. The first meeting occurred the same month the legislature finally passed the consenting adults bill, which Earl previously said he would sign, further cementing the import of the moment. Of course, the struggle was ongoing: that same month, the Shawano County Board unanimously adopted a resolution urging a repeal of the state gay rights law. That local debate had offered the assertion that "Wisconsin has attracted more homosexuals since they were granted equal rights." It was a heady time.[23]

COUNCIL ON THE ROAD FOR CHANGE

Representative David Clarenbach urged the council, "Take the struggle for acceptance and gay rights to the village square." Acceptance meant more than nondiscrimination. During its three years, the council met in twenty-two Wisconsin communities, several of them more than once.[24]

Cochair Kathleen Nichols saw the meetings as "a catalyzing occasion for local officials to address the question of what they were doing or could do for the gay/lesbian community." Meetings functioned, as Nichols explained, "to assess the local climate; to see if lesbians and gays are able to function comfortably in their local society; and to determine if there is any discrimination in the workplace, in finding housing, or in dealing with local agencies such as police." Nichols noted that in setting agendas for community meetings, both the gay community and public officials were asked to attend. She stressed the importance of educating officials: "We'd ask them, 'What are you doing for your gay and lesbian constituents?' A lot of times, it was the first time the question had ever been asked."[25]

Among the revelations at the various meetings were indicators of how difficult life in some communities could be. In Eau Claire, a small, covert support group for gays had met at the UW campus, but it disbanded after two members were beaten while returning from a meeting. According to the meeting notes, the perpetrators were "calling [the men] homophobic epithets." In addition, Eau Claire County eliminated funding for a women's center "because it allowed a lesbian support group to meet under its auspices." At the same meeting, we learned that the Chippewa County Mental

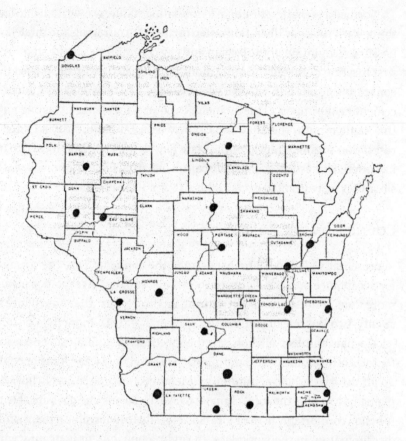

The members of the Governor's Council on Lesbian and Gay Issues, which operated from 1983 to 1986, took seriously their charge to reach all parts of Wisconsin. It held meetings around the state, represented by the dots on this map, in which LGBT community members had a chance to present local officials with concerns that had not been previously addressed. R. RICHARD WAGNER PAPERS, ACC. NO. 2016/014, UNIVERSITY OF WISCONSIN–MADISON ARCHIVES

Health Clinic had no identified programs for gays or lesbians, though in the previous six months inquiries had been made for such services. Of existing programs, meeting attendees said, "None are geared for special problems related to sexual identity." Another frequent theme was the difficulties of lesbians and gay men in obtaining justice in family courts. The Janesville meeting brought up the need for services for gay youth, while in Rhinelander, attendees noted "the disproportionate number of gay and lesbian alcoholics." In Milwaukee, despite the existence of active gay organizations, "services for Hispanic gays, especially young gays" was lacking. A theme expressed in Fond du Lac was the difficulty of "providing services to a dispersed, closeted population." In Monroe, in Green County, no gay residents attended the meeting. And in Menomonie, the home of UW–Stout, no gay students participated.[26]

Yet there were also successes. By fall 1985, as we wrote in our report, Green Bay showed "a remarkable increase in gay and lesbian participation in local services and government in less than two years." Green Bay community members agreed with Captain Wirtz of the police department that harassment of gays leaving the bars had been stopped by police. In Baraboo, home of BAGAL (Baraboo Area Gays and Lesbians), Sauk County deputies impressed the council "with their interest and willingness to receive gay-sensitive training." A two-day stay in Superior hosted by Bob Jansen of the Main Club allowed council members to have many informal discussions with community members. In Sheboygan, gay community members reported "that overall the police in the area were responsive."[27]

Community meetings were generally uneventful but some, such as one in Racine, had a police presence because of threats. The Rice Lake meeting was particularly contentious. Rice Lake had been selected for the meeting as it was the largest population center between Eau Claire and Superior. At the April 1986 meeting, four women, led by Rachel Carson, a pastor's wife, protested. Carson stated, "Creation can't be taught in schools. . . . I'm not going to sit down and let sin override us. I am against Governor Earl's having a Gay-Lesbian Task Force." Carson added, "I can't take my tax dollars and promote things that are wholesome. My rights are infringed upon." According to the *Barron County News-Shield*, the police chief "attempted to calm everyone down to no avail."[28]

RAISING THE RAINBOW FLAG

Even before the new council convened in April 1983, the state press did a quick uptake on it. Many reporters' calls came to the newly visible cochairs on the council's business from both the Wisconsin press and the national gay press. As cochair I made the statement, "The challenge is to reach the minds and hearts of the mainstream population in the state, and use the media to show that gays make up a significant portion of the population and their problems are real."[29]

In April 1983, Bryan Brosamle, a Madison newscaster active with the statewide professional organization, invited the cochairs to address the state's Broadcast News Council annual meeting at Stevens Point. The topic was how to cover this new field of Wisconsin lesbian and gay issues, "matters we will face more and more." We offered some basic dos and don'ts. Use terms such as *gay, lesbian, openly gay, gay-identified*, and *same-sex preference*. Don't use *queers, faggots*, or *avowed homosexual*. We highlighted the issue of personal safety, educating the group about gay bashings and beatings and emphasizing that police ignorance often prevented true stories from being told. We talked about health, noting that STDs and AIDS required sensitive handling. We covered the prevalence of alcoholism and mental health issues in the gay community and talked about the need for social services. Most important, we suggested the need to develop local sources for gay news so that the news didn't simply cover what happened in San Francisco. At least 10 percent of their audience, we told them, was likely interested in lesbian and gay news. Council members offered to serve as contacts for reporters, particularly in areas with few gay activists. Following the meeting, several TV stations did week-long feature series on gay communities. One reporter from Eau Claire published a story on the city's lesbian and gay community that won her an award for best local investigative journalism.[30]

The council also put out forceful reminders to state agencies to make sure the state's new nondiscrimination law was taken seriously. More than a full year after passage of the gay rights bill, a gay man brought the attention of the council to a form issued by UW–Madison that still did not include nondiscrimination on the basis of sexual orientation. About the same time, a survey of Milwaukee-area employers showed that 75 percent "claimed to be unaware that state laws concerning sexual orientation applied to the private sector." Twenty-nine agencies, including the university, were asked to provide actual documents of contracts and forms showing the included sexual orientation language under the equal opportunities requirements. The agency response from the Department of Employment Relations highlighted a problem with state labor agreements.

Fair Employment

For Lesbians

And Gay Men

April, 1983

The Wisconsin Equal Rights Division printed this first-in-the-nation brochure on legal protections for gays and lesbians from discrimination in housing, employment, and public accommodation. R. RICHARD WAGNER PAPERS, ACC. NO. 2016/014, UNIVERSITY OF WISCONSIN—MADISON ARCHIVES

Howard Fuller, the department secretary, reported, "During the recent round of negotiations the State proposed that the recent changes in the State Fair Employment Act be incorporated in all contracts." Fuller reported that certain bargaining units did not agree, though the "absence . . . in the contract language does not limit the state's obligation to comply." He did note, however, that this would limit "an employee's ability to appeal an instance of discrimination based on sexual orientation through the grievance arbitration procedure."[31]

The council supported several efforts related to health, both to educate the public and better determine the health needs of the gay and lesbian population. One effort, discussed in chapter 7, was the survey sent to the gay and lesbian community members as part of the hate crimes legislation effort. In another, the council cooperated with a national women's health project to distribute a lengthy questionnaire on lesbian health concerns. Yet another survey, designed by disabled lesbian Kate Cloudsparks, focused on gays and lesbians with physical or developmental disabilities. Due to requests for accurate information on gays and lesbians, the council prepared a bibliography for academic and public libraries. More than eight hundred libraries in the state received copies.[32]

The council cosponsored the Great Lakes Lesbian/Gay Health Conference in February 1984. This cooperative effort included Milwaukee's BESTD Clinic, Chicago's Howard Brown Memorial Clinic, the Medical College of Wisconsin Infectious Disease Section, the Cream City Association Foundation, and the UW–Milwaukee Gay Community. More than one hundred people attended, and council member Mark Behar was a key organizer. In a keynote, lawyer and activist Karla Dobinski proclaimed, "The steps we take this weekend are breaking the shrouds of silence that surround these problems." Topics included alcoholism, gay/lesbian domestic violence, and AIDS. Dobinski's hope was that "we bring some of our toughest problems out of the closet." At the request of Behar, Governor Earl proclaimed February 1984 as AIDS Awareness Month.[33]

Several members of the council's Health and Social Services Committee took an interest in homosexual prisoners. The head of the Division of Corrections spoke to the council, and committee members followed up with a meeting with the head of Health Services for Corrections. At a visit to the state prison at Waupun, they met with a cross-dressing inmate identified to them as Earnest, though he had legally changed his name to Sandria. The inmate informed them there were many gays in the prison but they remained closeted.[34]

Perhaps the most singular experience during the council's tenure was the sexual assault upon council member Cynthia Lampman and her subsequent treatment by the Racine police. In her report, the assailant was

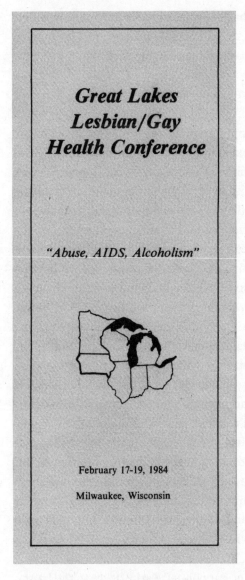

*Great Lakes
Lesbian/Gay
Health Conference*

"Abuse, AIDS, Alcoholism"

February 17-19, 1984

Milwaukee, Wisconsin

As AIDS came to the state, early efforts like this 1984 regional health conference tried to prepare Wisconsin. FROM THE AUTHOR'S COLLECTION

quoted as saying, "You people think you're going to change things. Think again." The assailant referred to her as "the governor's dyke." Lampman complained that the Racine police mishandled the investigation. In her statement, she said the police officer handling the arrest believed the charge "might have been exaggerated" because he referred to her as "an outspoken and readily admitted lesbian." The Racine police chief acknowledged the officer in question was "not what one might call a subtle person replete with an overabundance of tact." Yet the Racine Police and Fire Commission declined to take up Lampman's complaint over the matter.[35]

DON'T SAVE ME FROM MYSELF

As the state's financial health improved in the 1985–1987 biennial budget, Earl proposed to increase the executive office staff by one full-time employee position so he could appoint a full-time gay/lesbian liaison. As with all budget proposals, it was considered by the Joint Finance Committee. At the time, there existed a gentleman's understanding that the governor did not tinker with the legislature's own budget requests and the legislature did not mess with the executive office budget as a courtesy between branches. However, in a stunning 13 to 1 vote, the committee publicly deleted the requested new position from the budget. Only Democrat Joe Strohl of Racine supported Earl. Strohl said the governor "ought to be free to determine what his staff needs are." Ron McCrea was quoted as saying it was "self-evident" that this was an attempt "to prevent Earl devoting any staff time to the lesbian/gay council." Further, he said, "I think it was a way for the legislature to say to the governor, 'You've gone too far' in support of lesbian/gay issues." The apparent ringleader was Senator Roshell. The governor was furious. McCrea recalled, "Earl angrily told the committee members, 'Don't try to protect me from myself.'" The Joint Finance Committee later put the position back in the budget. In reaction to this unexpected pushback from the legislature, McCrea issued a warning to gay and lesbian communities around the state, imploring them to offer the governor "more support and less criticism." They needed to remain aware of Earl's position, otherwise their rights might become "too hot to handle even among Democrats."[36]

In summer 1985, the governor appointed Earl Bricker to the liaison position in the Constituent Relations section of his office. Bricker also provided staff support to the Governor's Council on Lesbian and Gay Issues, but he did not serve as a member. At times, Bricker was assisted by Lynn Haanen, who also worked in constituent relations. Even later in the administration, a young Tammy Baldwin helped as an intern in the Constituent Relations office. Bricker had moved to Madison in 1978 after serving in

Earl liaison urges gays to guard their rights

The governor's liaison to the lesbian and gay communities on Wednesday urged vigilance on homosexual rights, which he said might become a campaign issue.

Earl Bricker said that although Wisconsin was known for its legal protection of homosexuals, they needed to become more politically involved because "what has been given can be taken away."

Bricker spoke at a noon forum at the University of Wisconsin — Milwaukee.

Unlike Gov. Earl, Bricker said, a new governor might not have a staff liaison or a Council on Gay and Lesbian Issues.

A different Legislature might pass a bill such as one recently sought by the New London-based Rawhide Boys Ranch, he said. The organization backed legislation exempting certain non-profit groups from state law prohibiting discrimination based on sexual preference, but the bill died.

Bricker said Earl had chosen Ron McCrea, a homosexual, as his press secretary because the governor considered McCrea the best person for the job. Bricker said he wished such thinking could be a model for all job selections.

Although the governor has not "gone out of his way" to align himself with homosexual rights, he has "done the right thing when it came in front of him," Bricker said. Those choices may provide ammunition for Earl's opponents in the campaign, he said.

Up to now, Wisconsin has not experienced much of the anti-homosexual hysteria that has appeared in other states, he said. But he added that if the number of AIDS cases increased dramatically, such hysteria was a real possibility.

Although there have been no cries for the quarantine of AIDS victims in Wisconsin, for instance, a recent survey by the Council on Gay and Lesbi-

Earl Bricker

an Issues showed that 70% of the respondents thought anti-gay violence was prevalent enough to cause them fear. Fifty-four percent said they had modified their behavior because of violence or the threat of violence, and 88% said they believed they would be the subject of violence, threats or attacks in the future, Bricker said.

During his several years of service as an LGBT liaison for Governor Tony Earl, Earl Bricker worked hard for the appointment of LGBT persons to state government advisory bodies to ensure that the government would reflect the citizens of the state. *MILWAUKEE JOURNAL, APRIL 10, 1986*

the Peace Corps. In 1987, the Cream City Business Association presented Bricker with its Pace Setter Award for "one who by his openness has helped the gay/lesbian community." Subsequently, he was elected to the Dane County Board and, after the Earl administration, served as director of the Madison AIDS Support Network.[37]

In addition to working with the Governor's Council on Lesbian and Gay Issues, Bricker recruited other gays and lesbians for gubernatorial appointments. He wrote to gays and lesbians around the state listing all the various 156 bodies to which the governor made appointments. He tried to reach the "wealth of talent in Wisconsin's gay and lesbian community." Bricker wrote, "I would enjoy being in a position to nominate a lesbian or gay man to serve on the Health Policy Council or the Arbor Month Committee or even the Inland Lakes Protection and Rehabilitation Council." He had some success. Richard Minor of Milwaukee's Black and White Men Together was appointed to the Equal Rights Council of the Department of Industry, Labor, and Human Relations. Katie Morrison indicated that the Department of Health and Social Services had some two hundred advisory committees and appointees and could provide "appropriate linkages to assist and aid the Department on lesbian and gay issues." In 1983, the council had formally moved to accumulate names of persons to submit for appointments. Now, through a cooperative arrangement with the UW–Madison School of Social Work, it also secured two for-credit student interns, Courtney Spitz and Gus May, to provide additional staff support.[38]

Throughout his two-year tenure, Bricker was able to advocate for gays and lesbians from Wisconsin's experience. When New York City was considering a gay rights bill in 1986, he was quoted in the *New York Times* on the effect of Wisconsin's bill: "It has increased the confidence on the part of gay men and lesbians that they are protected." Speaking in 1986 at UW–Milwaukee, Bricker denied there had been an "influx of gays from out-of-state to take advantage of Wisconsin's law." Speaking around the state, Bricker urged vigilance for lesbians and gays, reminding them that "what has been given can be taken away." He speculated that a different governor "might not have a staff liaison or a council on gay and lesbian issues." Bricker warned, "Those choices may provide ammunition for Earl's opponents in the campaign."[39]

DICK FLINTROP'S FOSTER HOME CASE

In November 1982, Representative Richard Flintrop (D–Oshkosh) lost his reelection bid after ten years of service, despite being ranked near the top by newspapers. While in the legislature, he chaired the Education Committee, and in 1977, he authored Wisconsin's reformed Children's Code, a vital piece of legislation that secured rights and fair treatment for youths under the care of the state. In his new administration, Governor Earl appointed him to head the Wisconsin Council on Criminal Justice, which dealt with juvenile justice among other issues.

Flintrop co-owned a house in Oshkosh and also owned a home in Madison. In 1982, his Oshkosh housemates, Byron Malsin and Kathleen Roblee, applied to the Winnebago County Department of Social Services to become foster parents for older troubled teens. Since Flintrop was an owner and resident spending most weekends in Oshkosh, he was listed on the application as well. On December 6, the county foster home coordinator sent a letter denying the foster home license. The first reason listed was "that you presently have living with you a person whose sexual preference is homosexual." Writing for the county, he stated, "We are not in a position to risk exposing a child to this type of behavior as it does not yet fall within minimum acceptable standards of our society." This was just months after the state legislature had passed a gay rights bill. It was not the first time the county had denied a foster application related to homosexuality.[40]

The applicants were not willing to take no for an answer and appealed the matter to the state Department of Health and Social Services. A hearing examiner who adjudicated the matter commented on the county's emphasis on the presence of a homosexual in the home. The examiner stated that "although the homosexual member was interviewed by the county . . . no evaluation of his character or psychological stability was included in the agency's post-hearing report." The examiner went on to note, "The record further shows petitioner and his wife to be highly qualified for foster care of teenage children. He has an M.A. degree in counseling, directs a Center program at the UW–Oshkosh and has worked extensively with troubled teenagers. His wife has a Ph.D. in psychology and teaches in the human services field at the University." The county had stated, "There is likelihood

The Appleton newspaper covered the 1983 story of Dick Flintrop, whom Governor Tony Earl had appointed to head the Wisconsin Council on Criminal Justice, being outed over a foster care case in his hometown of Oshkosh. *APPLETON POST-GAZETTE*, DECEMBER 2, 1983

"There's a certain point where the broader issues merit what is obviously a very substantial personal sacrifice...and a great loss of personal privacy."
— Richard Flintrop

Homosexuality of Flintrop cited in license denial

BY FRANK CHURCH
Post-Crescent staff writer

OSHKOSH — A judge has been asked to decide whether former state Rep. Richard Flintrop's homosexuality should be used as the basis for denial of a foster home license by the Winnebago County Department of Health and Social Services.

Flintrop now serves as the director of the state Council on Criminal Justice. He is part-owner of an Oshkosh residence and lives there when he is not residing in Madison.

The other owners are a married couple who reside at the home and decided to press their efforts to get a foster home license despite the risk of publicity.

The county agency feels it should not be forced to grant a foster home license to the couple because of Flintrop's occasional presence in the home, contending it would be detrimental to the child's well-being.

In a petition filed Nov. 22, the county is asking Circuit Court Branch 3 Judge Tom Williams to reverse a state Department of Health and Social Services order to issue the license.

'It's an issue of broader importance'

MADISON — Richard Flintrop reached about as high as a lawmaker can in his 10 years in the state Assembly.

He became chairman of the Assembly Education Committee. He drew respect from both sides of the political aisle. In every article rating state lawmakers, he was near the top.

A story in a Milwaukee newspaper's Sunday magazine last year called him the "best committee chairman in the Legislature."

He authored the new Children's Code in 1977.

Now, his homosexuality is being cited by the Winnebago County Department of Social Services as a reason to deny an Oshkosh couple a foster home license.

The agency cites sections of that same Children's Code in making its case.

Flintrop was surprised by the county's denial.

"I'm disappointed, particularly because so many of the individuals involved...know me. They know my character. The decision was not based on a judgment of my character."

Six years ago, Flintrop said, he would have never talked to a reporter about his gay lifestyle. Now, he said, he can.

Continued on page 2

The couple — Byron Malsin and Kathleen Roblee — applied for the license more than a year ago. Flintrop's name was added to the application at the insistence of the county agency because he was a frequent resident in the home.

On Dec. 6, Child Foster Home Coordinator Corliss App told them the license was denied.

The couple and Flintrop could have dropped the effort after the county initially turned down the license request, but instead they carried their case to a state Department of Health and Social Services hearing examiner.

A March 16 hearing was held before state Hearing Examiner Shenlah O. Jakobson, an attorney. On Sept. 30, Jakobson reversed the county decision.

On Oct. 25, the state agency denied the county's petition for a rehearing.

Flintrop, who as an Oshkosh assemblyman authored the state Children's Code cited by the county in its court case, said the three decided to be candid about his homosexuality when the application was submitted. He said they felt it important that a youngster knows exactly what home situation he or she will be getting into.

"I see the issue of being able to be judged as a potential foster parent on the merits of my individual character and my personal strengths and weaknesses as a right that I should be entitled to," said Flintrop, who will be 38 on Dec. 15.

Flintrop said staff of Gov. Anthony Earl, who appointed him to the criminal justice post, were told of the decision to appeal the license denial last year.

"No one has ever suggested that it might be judicious to withdraw," said Flintrop when contacted Thursday.

"There's a certain point where the broader issues merit what is obviously a very substantial personal sacrifice...and a great loss of personal privacy," he added.

Flintrop feels there is irony that the state is a co-defendant in the foster license case. In the past, it has been the target of sex discrimination suits.

"In fact, they are the ones that have made a positive, enlightened decision that they know they might have to defend," said Flintrop. "To that extent, it is somewhat unique."

Continued on page 2

observable homosexual behavior could occur within your home." Indeed, Flintrop did invite gay guests to his home, yet the examiner made the crucial distinction between *presence* and the county's assumed *perceived harm*. The examiner ruled, "The county agency presented no evidence that the child would be exposed to any detrimental behavior by members of the household."[41]

The county proved stubborn and appealed the state's ruling to the local court. Then the matter hit the press. In December 1983, the Appleton and Oshkosh papers made the issue of Flintrop's homosexuality front page news, publicly outing him. The Oshkosh paper was already unhappy about the governor's gay appointees. The editors had written, "The trouble with having a governor's council on aberrant behavior is that it gives the practitioners a state soapbox to spout their doctrine." Yet as Flintrop stated, "Most of the key staff in the governor's office were aware of my lifestyle before I was appointed." While his gubernatorial appointment was pending, Flintrop told Earl's staff of the foster home license denial so they would not be blindsided. Staff did not suggest dropping the matter. Indeed, Flintrop felt it should not be an issue. Harkening back as far as the Lucey administration, Flintrop said, "Every governor for the past 12 years has had major important members of their staff and cabinet who were gay and involved in gay activities in the Madison area." Flintrop asserted, "It was not terribly difficult to state [my orientation] publicly at this stage of my life because I've gone through a process of recognizing who I am." Personally, however, Flintrop was disappointed with the county, "particularly because so many of the individuals involved . . . know me. They know my character." Recognizing that it was merely his status as a gay person under consideration, he said, "The decision was not based on a judgment of my character." Flintrop also made sure the press knew that he was raised in a home that had opened its doors to foster children for fifteen years. His conclusion: "I think it was very basic homophobia and a case of very archaic judgment."[42]

As well as the personal dimension, Flintrop spoke to larger issues. He said in the press that it was "a real tragedy that there are so many people . . . in the Fox Valley who don't feel an ability to admit to themselves, much less to their friends and co-workers and acquaintances" that they are gay. He hoped coming out over the matter "might provide some reassurance or encouragement to other gay men and women in our community." The papers noted his characterization of the matter as an "inconvenience." As one who had worked on children's issues, he believed the county should have seen his Oshkosh household "as a real substantial resource for some kids." The press quoted him as saying, "There's a certain point where the broader issues merit what is obviously a very substantial personal sacrifice . . . and a great loss of personal privacy." Flintrop demanded the county apologize and abandon its antigay policy. He noted, after checking with a large number of counties, that they would not have made a gay association a basis for rejection, and some counties had even licensed gay couples as foster parents. For the gay community, Flintrop's outing showed again Earl's willingness to include gays and lesbians among his administration and the notoriety that could entail.[43]

Enforcement of the Law

Merry Fran Tryon, administrator of the Equal Rights Division (ERD) and an African American, was charged with enforcing Wisconsin's new non-discrimination statute. Tryon, described by *OUT!* as the "spunky head of the ERD," was appointed by Governor Dreyfus and continued by Governor Earl. A graduate of Beloit College and a trained psychologist, she characterized herself as "somewhat in the activist mold." Despite the legal charge to work on conciliation for discrimination complaints, in her clear view, ERD was not a social agency but an enforcement and regulation agency. She did not see any inconsistency in being both objective and an advocate. She felt ERD examiners had to level the field when the party being complained about showed up with attorneys. At the same time, Tryon expressed frank concern about dealing with the new sensitive area of sexual orientation, saying, "I think that most of us are homophobic, if we're heterosexual." She planned consciousness raising activities for ERD staff.[44]

Tryon spoke, in addition to Governor Earl, at the first meeting of the Governor's Council on Lesbian and Gay Issues on April 23, 1983. She reported working with the WLGN to educate the gay community about the relatively new gay rights law, saying with candor: "I ask you to be patient if you come into our agency to file a complaint. . . . Recognize that we are ignorant [on the issue of lesbian and gay rights] and help to educate us. Make us more sensitive. Make us do our job." As Tryon observed, in the first year of enforcement there seemed to be a tendency to settle complaints based on sexual orientation rather than go through a formal hearing. In addition, the number of complaints during those early months was low—only twenty in the first ten months of operation. She speculated, "The public just isn't aware

As head of the Equal Rights Division, Merry Fran Tryon was a stalwart in the fight for equal rights for all, including gays and lesbians. *OUT!*, MAY 1983, PHOTO BY BRENT NICASTRO

of the law yet. In time . . . the complaints will rise, as has happened with other equal rights matters." Tryon indicated that her office "received many more calls and inquiries regarding this part of the law" than the complaints that were formally filed. Callers, she said, seemed reluctant to speak about sexual orientation: "Even when asked directly, callers often hesitate to identify themselves as homosexuals." Drawing a comparison, she explained, "We do not have to declare we are black, or we are women [in filing a complaint]. People have to declare they are gay or lesbian."[45]

In an interview with OUT! in May 1983, Tryon expanded on her views of civil rights enforcement: "People say you can't legislate morality, [that] you can't legislate and make people change. All I care about is that their behavior changes." In her view, legislation meant "nothing, until such time that [the public] can see that it is law, that it's being enforced." A particular concern of Tryon's was that the public accommodations section of Wisconsin's nondiscrimination law was weak, with district attorneys bearing the burden of prosecuting cases. In her view, both the law and the enforcement of the law were necessary. Drawing a comparison to civil rights, she said: "I don't see civil rights legislation as a panacea, but it's a hell of a good start. Without it, I'd still be back on the massa's plantation. And lord knows, that would never do." Tryon knew the law well and was able to apply it even when its application seemed unclear. When an antigay ad appeared in the Stevens Point Journal, she said, speaking to the Equal Rights Council, "The ad does not say gays cannot find housing or employment . . . This is a tacky, tacky ad but I don't believe it violates the law." She became an authority on describing Wisconsin's first-in-the-nation law on sexual orientation and was asked to testify at a Michigan legislature committee's hearing.[46]

Another stalwart in the ERD was LeAnna Ware, who had a career of more than thirty years spanning investigation to high-level administration. In the late 1970s, from inside the Department of Industry Labor and Human Relations (now Workforce Development), she supported adding sexual orientation to Wisconsin's law. At the time, she was told it was a "ridiculous idea," and her supervisor said, "Such protections could never be added to the law." In fact, they were, and Ware's professional career included investigating the very first complaint under the new gay rights law. Like Tryon, she had first-hand experiences of gays and lesbians "not eager to say which protected classes" they were part of. Complainants often denied that their employer actually knew they were gay.

In Madison, Ware worked with the United to provide training to ERD staff. The Milwaukee office of ERD, however, was a little slower in coming around. More difficult were the male staff who felt somewhat more threatened than the females. She recalled overhearing comments such as, "I'm not investigating that complaint, you can." As part of its outreach efforts, the ERD conducted labor law clinics to make employers aware of the fair employment law changes. Ware observed it was very rare for any questions to arise about sexual orientation. Like Tryon, Ware became known as an expert in the nondiscrimination law. She was subpoenaed into federal court by the City of Denver when the city challenged the Colorado state ban on local laws regarding nondiscrimination on the basis of sexual orientation. When that state's attorney general asked if it was not tough to enforce the Wisconsin law, her answer was a resounding no. Ware, who was also active with the Madison Equal Opportunities Commission, would end her career as director of the ERD.[47]

RELUCTANCE OVER NEW PROTECTIONS

No one was sure what the dimensions of enforcing the new law on sexual orientation would be. For its 1981 pre-passage fiscal note on AB 70, the ERD looked to the experience of the City of Madison, which had enacted such a law five years earlier. They found the city averaged 1 percent of its 584 employment cases and 2 percent of its housing cases over sexual orientation. The ERD included two assumptions in the fiscal estimate: One, "Madison is somewhat more of a liberal minded community and hence probably not as likely to discriminate against persons on this basis." Two, "While many persons may be discriminated against because of their sexual orientation, these persons may fear attracting public attention to themselves by filing such a charge and thus do not file." The resulting state estimate of twenty employment cases and one housing case could, they expected, "be absorbed within current budget." When the 1983 bill proposing repeal of gay rights surfaced, the state Personnel Commission, which had jurisdiction over state employment, noted it had two hundred complaints in the past year, with approximately 1 percent based on sexual orientation.[48]

In the first year of the new state law, sixteen complaints were filed under sexual orientation, most in the area of employment and a few in the area of public accommodation. For comparison, a Legislative Audit Bureau study on the fiscal year 1987–1988 showed a total of 2,741 complaints for all causes, up from 1,935 in 1980. Complaints based on sexual orientation were 1.4 percent of total complaints. It stayed at this level for quite some time. A review of six years data from 1997–2002 showed sexual orientation at 1.3 percent of all complaints, well within the range predicted when the nondiscrimination law was passed.[49]

Again, the overwhelming number of all discrimination complaints in 1988 (2,484) was in employment. A later survey showed the majority of all equal rights sexual orientation complaints—some 55 percent—came from the urban areas of Madison and Milwaukee, though these counties made up only 25 percent of the state's population. Milwaukee County, with 18 percent of the population, made up 37 percent of the sexual orientation complaints, and Dane County, with 8 percent, made up another 19 percent of complaints. Of all types of complaints about equal rights, the 1988 audit noted probable cause was found in 24 percent of instances, no probable cause in 36 percent, and another 10 percent were settled; the remaining were withdrawn or failed due to a lack of jurisdiction. It is likely sexual orientation complaints fit this pattern.[50]

A number of discrimination cases became high profile. Lake Geneva Country Club fired assistant chef James Taylor, a gay African American man, in 1983, the day after he appeared on a Milwaukee TV news report on gays in Milwaukee. LeAnna Ware of the ERD was the investigator for the complaint. She determined probable cause because the employer, while claiming unsatisfactory performance, had no documentation on his job performance. Taylor, originally from California, said, "Being black and gay in the Midwest, I thought I had a snowball's chance in hell of winning my case." The ERD worked to conciliate the matter and a settlement was reached.[51]

In another high-profile example, Madison United received pushback when it tried to run a classified job ad with the *Milwaukee Journal* for an education/outreach coordinator to "work primarily with gay men." The ERD found probable cause when the *Journal* refused to run the ad, and the matter was referred for conciliation. Eventually, the United accepted a four-hundred-dollar settlement for attorney's fees. The *Green Bay Press Gazette* also received discrimination complaints. The paper turned down an ad from Among Friends, the rural gay referral agency. The paper claimed it was a dating service. When the resubmitted ad specifically said, "Gay/lesbian referrals for medical, legal and professional assistance," it was still refused. The ERD found probable cause of discrimination. Since newspapers fell under the public accommodations section of the law, prosecution was up to the Brown County district attorney, who declined to pursue the issue. The paper subsequently also refused an ad by two women selling gay/lesbian T-shirts. An ad taker said, "We just don't print those kind of ads."

In another instance, a bowling alley in Eau Claire refused to allow two gay men to dance in their associated bar, the Down Under Disco, but had no problem with two lesbians dancing, "because bowlers did not complain when two women went on the dance floor." Again, ERD found probable cause and referred the matter to the district attorney. While this particular district attorney had supported the gay rights law, he declined prosecution of what he termed a "bad case," stating, "Any prosecutor who would take this case would be putting his neck on the line." Merry Fran Tryon had identified the enforcement of public accommodations by district attorneys as a weakness in Wisconsin law for all classes of protected citizens. In 1986, an informal opinion of the attorney general indicated that classified advertising was not a public accommodation, forcing the ERD to reverse itself. Perhaps discretion by outstate district attorneys was warranted, as they likely knew how elected judges might have ruled on the ground-breaking law.[52]

Some discrimination matters did not enter the statistics on complaints. When the real estate agent for a newly hired professor told the dean of a state university that the professor was gay, the dean requested the professor's resignation. "The professor was unwilling to file a formal complaint for fear of its impact on his future job prospects, but after Tryon informed the dean that his request for the professor's resignation violated state law, the dean withdrew the request."[53]

Brooks Egerton, editor of OUT!, commented, "The risks gays take to file a complaint are too high," noting that one must reveal his or her identity, pay for a lawyer, and wait months for resolution. "The penalties are pathetic," he said. "You fight for a shot at getting back where you were two years ago." The law did not provide for any great damages. Yet, a 1983 news story found me expressing optimism. "The law has to be more than mere words on paper," I said. "It has to provide real protection to people in small towns in this state." Eventually, job security for gays and lesbians would become a reality and would outweigh the climate of fear. Other Wisconsin observers felt the law had been helpful, and a number of homosexuals did win settlements through the conciliation process. In Egerton's judgment, "All told, the gay rights bill has strengthened the hand of the lesbian/gay community. It has provided a strong tool for organizing, and many community leaders expect that its use—direct or indirect—will grow in years to come."[54]

CONSERVATIVE OPPOSITION

Conservative opposition based on Governor Earl's pro-gay stance was a constant during his tenure, starting from day one. One of the conservative criticisms of the Earl administration labeled it a "granola" administration composed of "fruits, flakes, and a few nuts." Of course, gays and lesbians were the fruits. In his first months of office, Republican candidate Terry Kohler pointed out, "He promised to appoint queers and he has." When a reporter suggested the public did not seem bothered by the issue, Kohler came back with, "Maybe in your social circle it doesn't." Elaborating, Kohler proclaimed gays were "sick" and "immoral" and "aberrant." Letters to the editor in May 1983, the month the Governor's Council on Lesbian and Gay Issues was created, were often critical. One suggested a recall election. Another denounced the "appeasement of gays and surreptitious condoning of a lifestyle condemned by Scripture." The governor's prepared response letter asserted his belief: "I am confident the Council will provide an important communication link between the Executive Office and the gay and lesbian communities throughout the state. As Governor of all Wisconsin's citizens, I believe this communication is vital."[55]

The drumbeat against Earl for his supportive stance was persistent. A preacher wrote to the *Shawano Evening Leader* complaining, "Our governor boldly appointed to a highly visible position one whose lifestyle is morally malignant in the extreme." In February 1984, the *Dodgeville Chronicle* headlined a viewpoint, "Dump the Gays, Support Families," calling Earl's creation of the council his "ultimate degradation." It continued,

"It is outrageous that Earl has lent his endorsement to a group that carries AIDS." On April 10, 1986, the *South Milwaukee Voice*, faulting the liaison position, gave voice to the anti–"fruits and nuts crowd." It took exception that Earl encouraged "fruits to flaunt it in the face of taxpayers." The *Oshkosh Northwestern* lambasted Earl for creating "a forum for the public proclamation, rather than the private practice, of their particular orientation."[56]

Earl was not unaware of the attacks on his pro-gay policy. In 1985, he accepted a Torchbearer Award from the gay Cream City Business Association for "advancing understanding and acceptance of the gay community." Speaking on harassment, the governor told the group, "People have said they had to change their behavior to avoid being beaten up. The fact that this exists is totally unacceptable." Among his remarks, Earl noted a shift to the right, stating that "it clearly was not a political benefit to be seen as supportive of gay and lesbian issues." But Earl believed it morally right and that "it was intolerable that homosexuals were still subject to harassment and beatings." With an eye forward to reelection, Earl said, "The day will come when gay support will be a political plus. It will be a much healthier society when that day arrives. I hope it arrives soon."[57]

THE CAMPAIGN AGAINST EARL

During the 1986 gubernatorial campaign, Republican candidate Tommy Thompson made the usual partisan attacks on Earl's liberal taxation and spending policies. On this he was backed by the state's major business groups. Due to the state government's fiscal crisis in his first year, Earl had raised the sales tax and put a surcharge on income taxes. "Tony the Taxer" was the moniker used in these attacks. Besides raising taxes, the Republicans charged Earl with making Wisconsin a "social laboratory" by dealing with issues such as marital property reform and comparable pay for female state employees. The social engineering charge was a clear repudiation of their part of the Progressive tradition. Earl responded by saying Wisconsin's Progressivism was at stake. Of course, there was more at stake: the election itself, which would be shaped in large part by the public's reaction to Earl's pro-gay stance.[58]

In early 1986, Ron McCrea warned, "Gay rights will be on the cutting edge of a covert campaign against Tony Earl this year as he runs for reelection." McCrea observed that with the advent of AIDS, "nothing could have been worse for the progress of gay rights." He felt there was "really little respect of what we have made of our lives." If a description of safer sex was considered obscene, he commented, "What would they say about a description of someone dying of AIDS?" Yet Earl did not back down from the issue. He framed the AIDS crisis "the most serious public health problem we face in this nation," stating emphatically, "Unless we recognize that working with the people who are most directly threatened by it and those who are most susceptible to it, we're burying our heads in the sand."[59]

During the Earl administration, the gay community had to deal with two major national events that contributed to the negative climate toward gays. One, signaled by McCrea, was the AIDS crisis, covered more fully in chapter 9. The other was the US Supreme Court *Bowers v. Hardwick* decision upholding the Georgia sodomy law made in summer 1986 during the Wisconsin gubernatorial campaign. Thomas Stoddard of the national Lambda Legal Defense Fund called it "a major disaster." The Governor's Council on Lesbian and Gay Issues requested from the ERD "an analysis of the Court's decision upon Wisconsin law." Though the ERD determined there was no impact upon our state law and disseminated this information to the press, an Associated Press story on the Bowers decision appeared in the Wisconsin press with the headline "Will Concern over AIDS Bring Back Sodomy Ban?" and discussed legislators thinking of proposing changes.[60]

Though the 1982 gay rights law had passed with key bipartisan support, the latter part of the decade saw Wisconsin's political parties becoming polarized over gay and lesbian issues. During Earl's tenure, the Republican Party platform had called for the repeal of the law and failed. Now Thompson and his allies used Earl's forthright support for the LGBT community as an attack on the Democratic incumbent. During the 1986 elections, a group called the Freedom Council put out a Christian Voter Guide in Wisconsin, with three of the eleven questions focused on gays:

1. Do you support treating homosexuals as a minority under state law allowing them benefits now afforded to blacks, Hispanics and other minorities?

2. Would you support repealing the "Gay Rights" measures passed by the 1981–1983 State Legislature which established minority status for homosexuals?

3. Do you support public funds to provide two liaisons from the Governor's office to the "Homosexual Community" at the cost of $104,000 annually?

The tone of the Republican responses was set by their favored gubernatorial candidate, Thompson, who said no to recognizing minority status, no to liaisons, and yes to repealing the gay rights law. Governor Earl's responses in his reelection bid were the exact opposite.[61]

In the end, Earl's bid for a second term fell short. On November 4, 1986, Thompson won the election with 53 percent of the vote, pushing Earl from office and changing the landscape of what was possible for gays and lesbians in state government and in the state of Wisconsin.

THOMPSON THREATENS TO KILL THE COUNCIL

Right before the 1986 election, Tommy Thompson told a gathering of Northwoods realtors, "The gay and lesbian council will not last very long under Tommy Thompson." After his victory, Thompson renewed the issue, stating in a press conference that he would indeed abolish it: "I don't think government should be promoting an alternative lifestyle." (In a later irony, he would lose a 2012 race for the US Senate to out lesbian Tammy Baldwin, who had worked in Earl's office.)[62]

With Earl's defeat, the writing was on the wall. Members of the council considered the matter and resigned en masse, writing individual letters to Governor Earl. In his letter, Will Handy praised Earl for helping "to take Wisconsin's gay rights law out of the statute book and into the reality of daily life." He added, "Our Council, and your support of it, have let the world know that Wisconsin stands behind gays and lesbians as fully legitimate citizens, deserving of dignity and the protection of law." Joy Holthaus of La Crosse wrote that having lesbian and gay issues "listened to with respect was an exhilarating and strengthening experience." Member Jay Jones noted, "What we strived to both attain and maintain was not some special status, but *equal* status." Donald Boychuk commended Earl, saying that his "strong commitment to equal rights for all people has and continues to be outstanding." Mark Behar, who like Kathleen Nichols had served all four years, thanked the governor "for your courage to stand by us and to empower us to speak for ourselves."[63]

The final report of the council stated, "The resignations were tendered with great regret because all members of the Council realize how much more remains to be done. Moreover, we had come to understand what it means to gay men and lesbians to have genuine access to our government and to be included in our state's highest official's vision of a just society." At the last meeting, cochair Nichols voiced a grave concern that "the public's education about the deadly disease AIDS will be set back drastically now that the group has disbanded." She challenged the incoming governor "to uphold the laws of the state, especially regarding sexual orientation." Individual council members pledged to continue being active. Nichols applauded the mobilizing by other groups around the state: "It's important that we not slide backwards in time. Don't mourn, organize."[64]

DEFEAT OF A PROGRESSIVE CHAMPION

The 1986 defeat was more about Earl's policies than his personality. Thomas Still's postelection analysis for the *Wisconsin State Journal* was titled "Earl's Baggage Too Heavy." Veteran statehouse correspondent Matt Pommer of Madison's *Capital Times* wrote of the personal nature of Earl's defeat as Democrats picked up seats in the assembly and the state senate. Pommer attributed the loss to taxes, the unpopular proposal for a Milwaukee prison, and Earl's relationship with Mayor Henry Maier of Milwaukee, a Democrat. Near election eve, Maier, who had a running feud with Earl over state shared revenues with municipalities, said he would not vote for either Earl or Thompson. The Republican challenger believed the mayor's remarks would "work in my favor." Veteran *Milwaukee Sentinel* political reporter Ken Lamke listed among the nine reasons for Earl's defeat, "Many voters are secret bigots, welfare-bashers and gay baiters."[65]

Hal Bergan, a top policy aide in the executive office writing about the loss, stated, "The Earl administration had worried too much about minorities, women, gays and big business and not enough about regular people who work and vote." Bergan said, "Earl had strong views about what he wanted the themes of the campaign to be. He called them the three 'E's': economic development, education, and environmental protection." Yet the election's messages were more than these. As Bergan wrote, "The creation of the Governor's Council on Lesbian and Gay Issues in March 1983 reinforced the 'otherness' of the Earl administration, dealing as it did with a topic that continues to be taboo for most people." Bergan believed the job of the council and other minority desks "was to provide a voice for those who have traditionally been shut out of the political process. But in providing that voice, we seemed to be ignoring mainstream voters." Bergan observed, "The gay issue came up over and over again in our phone calling, particularly in the traditional ethnic neighborhoods of Milwaukee. It was in precisely those neighborhoods that the Earl vote in 1986 fell off most dramatically from our 1982 totals."[66]

In a postelection interview reviewing the administration, Earl talked of the state's many financial issues and his contributions to Wisconsin's environmental traditions. A reporter asked, "But didn't the gay–lesbian issue dominate the equal opportunities issue?" Earl's quick answer was, "Yep. One of the things I discovered was that homophobia runs deep and strong here." A further gubernatorial observation was, "It is very difficult to have a rational discussion of that issue." With only 47 percent of the vote, Earl believed his reelection "just wasn't in the cards." But the governor expressed "nothing but pride and satisfaction for the record of his administration."[67]

Earl Bricker, who had been Earl's liaison, wrote "Tony Earl's Defeat: What It Means for Us." Bricker observed, "Tony Earl was advised to be more cautious in his support of controversial issues (that's us folks)." Seeing the governor as "an outspoken advocate of issues of concern to lesbians and gay men," Bricker admitted that "may have been one of the reasons for his loss, but he's on record as having no regrets." For Bricker, "Tony Earl has been great, and I personally admire him like I've never admired anyone before." Knowledgeable on how state government worked, Bricker lamented that "no one will be as responsive to discrimination against lesbians and gay men as has been Merry Fran Tryon" of the ERD. Despite the loss, Bricker believed the gay community still had viable groups in all parts of the state, fine publications, strong AIDS organizations, and politically active lesbians and gay men.[68]

In their pre-election favorable endorsement, the *Milwaukee Journal* summed up Tony Earl best: "A rare degree of competence, courage, and imagination in leading Wisconsin." Even Thompson spoke well of him, stating after the election, "I consider him a class act." A pre-election poll highlighted Earl's character. Voters gave him the highest rating for integrity of all statewide candidates. Regarding the "moral character befitting a high elected official," 76 percent said yes for Earl and only 14 percent said no. Indeed, he would be remembered for his moral courage and integrity in the face of deep resentment and opposition.[69]

Earl's experiment to open a positive Wisconsin conversation about gays and lesbians was eagerly seized on by the state's gay community, albeit with some caviling. Seeing our visible presence in the halls of power meant we could assert a claim to true citizenship. Knocking on the doors of power meant many, if not all, would be opened. Of course, more visibility meant more pushback. Questions were raised about protections and services available to gay people in their home communities at public forums. This did little to deter the gay and lesbian community, but it did make some possible allies cautious. The conversation once begun, however, could not be stopped. To echo the line made famous at Oscar Wilde's trial, our love *did* dare speak our name.

9

WISCONSIN'S AIDS RESPONSE

[It is] important at this stage of the understanding about AIDS to make these observations: An open, nonjudgmental attitude is basic to all good patient care.
—WISCONSIN MEDICAL SOCIETY STATEMENT, SEPTEMBER 1983[1]

If it's bullshit, we'll shut them down.
—MADISON ACT-UP ACTIVIST DAN SAVAGE ON THE THOMPSON ADMINISTRATION'S TASK FORCE ON AIDS AND PRISONS, 1991[2]

Wisconsin's fight against AIDS was a mere skirmish as compared to the war being fought in the national and global arenas. The major histories of the plague have focused correctly on the most impacted cities and have taken scant notice of non-national and non-coastal responses like Wisconsin's, yet there is a story here. The state's early nondiscrimination law based on sexual orientation provided early protections and aided the LGBT community's call for a fairly inclusive medical approach.

EARLY WARNINGS OF AIDS

Due to the relatively late reporting of AIDS cases in the state, Wisconsin, unlike some other states, had the chance to craft a thoughtful response to the disease. Dr. Roger Gremminger, the medical director of the Milwaukee Brady East STD (BESTD) Clinic, founded in 1974, had already been working in the field of gay health for years when AIDS became known nationally. Based on Wisconsin data, he presented a paper titled "Rural Homosexually Active Men and Hepatitis B Risk" at the American Public Health Association Annual Meeting in November 1982. "Societal prejudice is still a very real factor," he observed, "and the fear generated in a number of homosexually active men is based on real examples of sometimes vicious and unjust treatment." He discussed rural men who came to urban communities. He also found that most men in his study were sexually active by age twenty. As a consequence, he urged high school classes and college organizations to provide sexual health education. By 1982, the Milwaukee clinic Gremminger managed had begun working with Chicago's Howard Brown Clinic on AIDS. Gremminger wrote to Governor-elect Anthony Earl in December 1982 seeking modest support for his clinic. Earl wrote back, "I was favorably disposed . . . toward the grant project for the Brady East Clinic."[3]

On June 24, 1983, Infectious Disease Day, Gremminger presented the paper "AIDS Risk Evaluation for Four Wisconsin Communities" at the Medical College of Wisconsin. He had conducted his study between January and March 1982, before the AIDS crisis loomed over Wisconsin. Since the state was a relatively low-risk area at the time, Gremminger concluded Wisconsin would be "ideal for the study of the natural history of AIDS." From his experience, he knew that "the effect of prejudice, hatred, and irrationality of society, collectively called homophobia," would factor into this history, as well as "the internalized psychic adjustments of gay men to this homophobia." He identified three groups of homosexually active men and deemed only one group out of the three to be accessible for the study—men who accepted their orientation and socialized in gay bars. Gremminger believed this group constituted 50 percent of homosexually active men in the state. Men who rejected their orientation and those who did accept it but did not socialize in bars were deemed inaccessible. His data suggested 66,500 men in Wisconsin would be at risk for AIDS, with some 33,000 of this group accessible for the proposed study. Using information from his earlier hepatitis study, Gremminger made risk estimates based on information he'd collected on the number of each man's sexual contacts, the occurrence of anonymous contacts, and the incidence of non-AIDS sexually transmitted diseases (STDs). In general, he thought the risks would be low in most of Wisconsin's cities, with Milwaukee having the largest number of potential high-risk individuals. His paper emphasized,

"We must avoid the prejudiced assumption that all homosexually active men are at risk for acquiring AIDS and work to create a better environment for homosexually active men and for all men to continue to lead productive lives with satisfying relationships. . . . The fatal disease must not spread to our area."[4]

In the May 1983 issue of *OUT!*, Tim Tillotson, associated with the Blue Bus Clinic of Madison, reported on remarks made by a physician from Northwestern University in Chicago. That area was dealing with twenty-five individuals with AIDS, seventeen of whom had already died. "Now is the time to take action," Tillotson wrote, "before AIDS cases are recognized and reported in this area." A native of Wauwatosa, Tillotson had served as an army medic in Korea. The early dearth of information about AIDS was made apparent in his reported statement, "Current thinking is that a communicable agent such as a virus may be involved." An information card used by Blue Bus presented recommendations for avoiding risks. These included decreasing the number of one's different sex partners (not the frequency of sexual activity) and avoiding intravenous drugs and sex with intravenous drug users. Tillotson advised, "Because of our current incomplete state of knowledge and due to the seriousness of the disease, we believe that it is better to be overly cautious." His research showed that the virus had been present among gay men in Madison as early as 1980. He was an advocate of testing linked with counseling services provided at many alternative health sites. He believed the combination of testing and counseling could create "an empowering situation rather than being slammed with this bad news."[5]

Another key resource for AIDS-related education in Wisconsin was Mark Behar, who was already doing work in the field when AIDS arrived. A physician's assistant, Behar was also a chairperson and founding member of the National Coalition of Gay STD Services in 1979. The organization listed sixty-nine member organizations in 1984, four of which were located in Wisconsin. Behar edited and wrote for the group's newsletter, published for ten years out of Milwaukee. As early as October 1979, in the newsletter's second issue, Tillotson contributed an article titled "Responsible Health Behavior Promoted." He wrote, "My experience has been that people are more receptive to suggestions for improving their health behavior (or for decreasing their risk factors) than they are to suggestions for changing their sexual behavior or lifestyle." By mid-1981, the coalition was attaching copies of the Centers for Disease Control and Prevention (CDC)'s *Morbidity and Mortality Weekly Report* on the new incidences of Kaposi's sarcoma and pneumocyctis pneumonia, early infections found in persons with compromised immune systems. Designated in March 1983 as an "official interim national communication device" for disseminating information on AIDS, the newsletter was an important early source of information about AIDS and the community responses to the disease that were being organized. Since the coalition's member organizations had good working experiences with the gay community regarding STDs, the newsletter highlighted the fact that "local gay community organizations can greatly facilitate the dissemination of factual information regarding AIDS." Behar used *BEST NEWS*, the newsletter of the BESTD Clinic, to further disseminate AIDS information in Milwaukee, including the early advice to use condoms to protect against AIDS, backed up by the distribution of free condoms at the clinic. One newsletter item with the title "What?! Me use a condom?!" assured Milwaukeeans, "They're the rage in New York and San Francisco!!"[6]

Due to Behar's work, UW–Milwaukee hosted ninety-four attendees at the February 1984 Great Lakes Lesbian/Gay Health Conference with the theme Abuse, AIDS, Alcoholism. Participants came mainly from Wisconsin, but Illinois, Indiana, Ohio, and Iowa were also represented. David Ostrow of the Howard Brown Health Center in Chicago gave a speech titled "AIDS: Prevalence, Recognition, Intervention" and discussed support services, hospital/home care, prevention, and risk reduction. This conference was a good example of the gay community marshalling its resources, few as they were, to address the growing crisis. In Wisconsin, as elsewhere, much of the burden of the work fell to those most directly affected by the disease.[7]

On August 1, 1983, the *Appleton Post-Crescent* broke the news of Wisconsin's first reported AIDS death, a man in his fifties who had died the previous week. The paper could not get the local pathologist to comment on the autopsy, and the physician refused to say the cause of death listed on the death certificate. Eventually, the paper was able to confirm that the certificate listed a "'fever of undetermined origin' influenced by an 'immune-compromised host,' without mentioning AIDS." The Outagamie County coroner claimed to be unaware of any AIDS death. The deceased had previously been a patient at the Mayo Clinic in Minnesota. "Gays are scared," the Appleton paper reported.[8]

The *Milwaukee Journal*, on May 31, 1983, reported, "Milwaukee Not Immune to AIDS Outbreak." While there were 1,450 known cases of AIDS nationwide, the paper reported two known cases in Milwaukee, both homosexuals, and six suspected cases. One individual was described as an "active homosexual" and a "promiscuous person" with multiple sexual contacts in Milwaukee. The article also quoted Michael Callen, a diagnosed gay man in New York, as saying, "I am no longer engaging in multiple anonymous sexual contacts." Madison's first AIDS death occurred later in the summer of 1983 when a man traveling through the city was admitted to the Veterans Hospital and died. Dr. Jeffrey Davis, the state epidemiologist, was quoted as saying, "Virtually no cases have been found anywhere outside of the high-risk groups." In this same early period, the *Marinette Eagle Star* ran a syndicated column that discussed the homosexual lifestyle as a "deathstyle" and presented "the premises of gay rights rhetoric" as entirely false. These state newspaper stories help set the tone for the general public of Wisconsin to view AIDS as the gay sexual disease. Journalist Neil Rosenberg, who had written the *Milwaukee Journal*'s pioneering series on the gay community in the 1970s, was now the medical reporter for the paper. In his coverage of the epidemic, he tried to convey "correct messages" about AIDS, as did reporters at many state papers. The *Portage Daily Register*, noting that the *National Enquirer* "is probably not the best source for your information," argued, "Only education will fight the hysteria."[9]

OUT! alerted the gay community to a concomitant worry. "No to the Witchhunt," the paper editorialized. "We worry about another epidemic— an epidemic of homophobia. . . . If every gay man is defined as a *potential* carrier of AIDS, then any and all forms of discrimination against them become possible." "The disease will surely come closer and closer to home," *OUT!*'s reporters warned. "We need assurances that the research dollars and heightened public awareness of AIDS will be used to eradicate the *disease*, not gays." In a letter to the Division of Health in December 1983, Governor Earl expressed similar fears, writing, "I continue to be deeply concerned about the spread of this disease in Wisconsin and the nation. Of equal concern, however, is the anxiety and fear which has accompanied the spread of information about new cases which is often based on misinformation."[10]

At the second meeting of the Governor's Council on Lesbian and Gay Issues, on June 4, 1983, Katie Morrison of the Wisconsin Division of Health and state epidemiologist Davis presented on the state's current situation. The *Milwaukee Journal* story of May 31 had confirmed cases of "the devastating and irreversible disease." Gremminger's hope that Wisconsin could totally avoid the epidemic was not to be. He still believed that Milwaukeeans' conservative lifestyles, unlike "the frenetic lifestyle [of people living in] New York, Los Angeles or San Francisco," could benefit the local gay community. He also acknowledged that, although "the ideal low-risk lifestyle is monogamy," it was not a realistic expectation, since gay men "don't have the societal supports and traditions that help heterosexual couples stay together." Ralph Navarro, president of the Cream City Business Association, said the community was not panicking but that "people are being more cautious about sexual contact." The *Milwaukee Journal*, editorializing on May 7, cautioned, "Don't press the panic button." Gremminger's concern was that gay men would engage in "covert panic and denial which can turn into depression," or what later would be termed "AfrAIDS."[11]

Key figures in Wisconsin's fight against AIDS would be Davis and his staff at the Wisconsin Bureau of Community Health and Prevention. In June 1983, Davis confirmed two cases of individuals who were Wisconsin residents at the time of the illness's onset and two nonresidents who were hospitalized in the state. Some suspected cases were under investigation at the time. Davis urged people to report all suspected cases. The Division of Health, as early as 1981, asked that suspected cases of any "AIDS-like illness" be reported. In 1982, the bureau mailed information to physicians in the state and a network of AIDS information centers began to be established. "People with AIDS or suspect[ed] AIDS obviously have sexual needs," Davis stated. "Dealing with those needs and at the same time preventing additional persons from exposure must be discussed with people who are in positions to provide sensitive and adequate counseling." He recommended that people use condoms and reduce their number of sex partners. In July 1983, Davis told the council, "Increasing numbers of health professionals have come to recognize the importance of sensitive knowledgeable treatment of health problems specific to gay men and lesbians."[12]

To explain the work he was doing within the medical community, Davis shared with the council a draft of a department memo on AIDS that he was planning to send out to physicians and public health officials, providing them with information from the CDC and urging them to cooperate with local public health organizations. The memo's intent was to increase AIDS surveillance and reporting in the state and provide answers to questions and concerns based on known, factual information. The memo also listed gay organizations in the state available for counseling homosexual males in Milwaukee, Madison, Racine, Appleton, Stevens Point, and Menomonie. Behar, a member of the council, praised Davis's draft memo and suggested a few changes, such as replacing "homosexuals/bisexuals" with "homosexually active men."[13]

In 1983, as the state was beginning to grapple with the disease in earnest, Davis sought a federal grant from the National Institutes of Health (NIH) "to step up surveillance." The proposed study would seek to enroll one thousand homosexual men from Dane County and metropolitan Milwaukee through cooperation with the BESTD Clinic and the Blue Bus Clinic. Davis believed, "The state's record in epidemiology research and against discrimination on the basis of sexual preference should help its chances." "Confidentiality will be critical," he explained, and volunteers would enter with informed consent. Governor Earl offered his "full support for your efforts to secure federal support for a longitudinal study." The governor's letter cited the state's nondiscrimination law and the recent repeal of criminal sanctions on homosexuality as positive reasons for federal consideration. Optimistically, he wrote, "The elements of fear and mistrust that might otherwise distort a sensitive study such as this are largely absent in Wisconsin." Ultimately, the grant was not funded because, according to the NIH, Wisconsin "has too few victims."[14]

Much of the real fighting in the battle against AIDS was waged at the local level. In Milwaukee, Gremminger treated patients in 1983 at both the BESTD Clinic and St. Anthony's Hospital. Along with Tim Franson, a physician from the Medical College of Milwaukee, Gremminger spoke to fifty health-care professionals, explaining the need for them "to avoid passing judgment on AIDS victims." Gremminger expressed hope that Wisconsin could avoid the horror stories coming from the coasts, saying, "I don't know how anyone can be so inhumane as to come down hard on a person like that, and moralize and judge them." Though limited space in this book will not allow for full descriptions of the work of the Milwaukee AIDS Project, the AIDS Resource Center of Wisconsin (ARCW), the Madison AIDS Support Network, and the CENTER Project, these organizations were all on the front lines.[15]

THE WISCONSIN MEDICAL SOCIETY LEADS

In the early 1980s, Katie Morrison, administrator of the Division of Health, helped arrange a meeting between the Governor's Council on Lesbian and Gay Issues cochairs and Earl Thayer, the secretary of the Wisconsin Medical Society. As a result, Thayer proposed a statement and a series of initiatives that were adopted by his board of directors on September 17, 1983. The Wisconsin Medical Society, the statement read, "considers it important at this stage of the understanding about AIDS to make these observations: An open, nonjudgmental attitude is basic to all good patient care." The society urged that "individual physicians and their medical societies . . . should seek to keep the AIDS problem in perspective through continuing responsible education of the profession and the public, thus reducing the chance of misinterpretation of facts and ill-founded deprecation of persons or groups." Such a statement was needed, in part, because of an unconfirmed report from Appleton that a physician refused treatment to a Wisconsin AIDS patient. "The statement is meant to prevent that from happening," said the society's communications director. Newspaper accounts noted that the Wisconsin Medical Society praised the efforts of Wisconsin "gay activists for their help in educating both the public and the medical profession about the deadly disease."[16]

After this statement, the Wisconsin Medical Society continued to work hard to coordinate a sensible AIDS response in the state. The President's Page of the October 1983 *Wisconsin Medical Journal* was titled, and focused on, "AIDS and the Physician." The writer, Dr. Chesley Erwin, was Milwaukee County's medical examiner and a professor of pathology at the Medical College of Wisconsin. He noted, "There is some hysteria or near hysteria about AIDS," but, he believed, "the physician must minister to AIDS patients with compassion, with supportive treatment, with general care."[17]

The November issue of the Wisconsin Medical Society's journal was "devoted largely to helping physicians accept their full responsibility for appropriate management of the patient who has or is concerned about Acquired Immune Deficiency Syndrome (AIDS)" and reprinted the society's

Statement concerning AIDS

Adopted by the Board of Directors of the State Medical Society of Wisconsin, September 17, 1983

The first cases of what is now identified as acquired immune deficiency syndrome (AIDS) were reported two years ago. More than 2,000 cases have been reported nationwide, with perhaps as many as 20 confirmed or suspected cases thus far in Wisconsin. The death rate among AIDS cases is very high.

The cause of AIDS is as yet unknown, as is effective treatment. However, the clinical characteristics of the syndrome have been quite well defined, the scientific and clinical studies are growing rapidly, and to some extent the growing body of knowledge is easing some of the disturbing and seldom documented stories of lack of care available to patients who have or suspect they have AIDS.

The Board of Directors of the State Medical Society considers it important at this stage of the understanding about AIDS to make these observations:

• An open nonjudgmental attitude is basic to all good patient care. The sick individual (heterosexual or homosexual) deserves the best care the profession has to offer for all physical or mental conditions.

• There may be clinical situations which for multiple reasons a physician may not choose to treat. When or if such a situation develops, the ethical course is to refer the patient to another physician.

• Both primary and referral physicians should continue to expand their understanding of this syndrome and provide specific advice on how to prevent personal or blood transmission, especially to persons in those groups which show increased incidence of AIDS.

• The individual physicians and their medical societies, including the State Medical Society, should seek to keep the AIDS problem in perspective through continuing responsible education of the profession and the public, thus reducing the chance of misinterpretation of facts and ill-founded deprecation of persons or groups.

The State Medical Society compliments the Section of Acute and Communicable Disease Epidemiology of the Wisconsin Division of Health for its prompt and continuing efforts to update the profession on AIDS. Similarly, the leadership of groups involving homosexually active persons in Wisconsin appear to be acting in a commendably responsible manner to bring about greater understanding of a serious health problem.

Most physicians are aware that the *Journal of the American Medical Association,* the *New England Journal of Medicine,* and Centers for Disease Control publications are highly respected and well read sources for the latest information on AIDS.

Nevertheless, the Society, in support of its expression of policy, will continue to utilize its official publication, the *Wisconsin Medical Journal,* and membership bulletins to provide:

a. widespread dissemination of this statement;
b. updates from the Epidemiology Section of the Division of Health;
c. references to or articles on advice concerning diagnosis, use of lab services, physician referral resources in Wisconsin, information to advise AIDS-susceptible patients, and so on;
d. general information on sexually transmitted diseases and information on how to adequately conduct a sexual activity examination as part of the history and physical;
e. information on medical records and confidentiality;
f. statements by the Wisconsin blood suppliers and processors.

In addition it will encourage professional-sponsored telephone answering services to include in their specialty referral lists physicians or medical centers which have been identified as AIDS referral resources.

At the same time it will encourage all appropriate continuing medical education groups in Wisconsin to give attention not only to the latest scientific and epidemiological updates on AIDS but to the ethical and public educational aspects as well. ■

The Wisconsin Medical Society was an early voice urging compassionate care for AIDS victims. *WISCONSIN MEDICAL JOURNAL,* NOVEMBER 1983

formal statement. The issue was prepared by the journal's medical editor, Dr. Victor Falk, as part of the "Society's broad and vigorous educational and service effort about this grave disease." Falk further noted, "It is a coordinated effort involving the Governor's Council on Lesbian and Gay Issues, many public and volunteer agencies, the Medical Society of Milwaukee County and other medical societies, the two medical schools, and many

other medical individuals and services." Gremminger wrote an article in
the issue called "Taking a Sexual History," in which he argued, "The facts
of a sexual history are important to know as they allow you to intelligently
examine, diagnose, and treat a patient. . . . Judgment and moralistic attitude, however, will always doom the professional encounter with his/her
physician." The final report of the Governor's Council on Lesbian and
Gay Issues described its cooperation with the Wisconsin Medical Society
as "one of the most tangible accomplishments in increasing treatment
resources."[18]

EARL ADMINISTRATION AGAINST AIDS

After the papers reported Wisconsin AIDS cases at the end of May 1983,
Dr. Jeff Davis sent a June 16 memo on AIDS to all Wisconsin physicians,
hospitals, infection control practitioners, and local public health agencies. Of the groups at risk, homosexually active men were listed first. The
memo also included a general fact sheet on AIDS, the CDC's case definition
for epidemiologic surveillance, a questions and answers sheet, and counseling information for at-risk persons including the six Wisconsin cities
offering counseling for homosexually active men. A counseling service
in one of these cities, Stevens Point, would report in August 1983 that it
had received 603 calls for AIDS information; 182 of the 603 callers self-
identified as gay, and another 120 identified as friends or family members
of gay individuals.[19]

At this time, some funeral directors around the country had refused
to deal with the bodies of AIDS victims. To calm their fears, David Rusch,
chairman of the Funeral Directors and Embalmers Examining Board of
Wisconsin, in cooperation with the state Department of Health and Social
Services, provided a memo on appropriate precautions for the transpor-
tation and embalming of AIDS victims, as well as suggestions for safe funeral viewing. The notice, sent in early August, was also sent to Wisconsin
County Coroners and Medical Examiners. These precautions were similar
to those suggested for handling victims of hepatitis B. The viewing suggestions, in particular, were overly cautious: "The family and visitors should
be advised to avoid physical contact with the body during the viewing
and visitation period." However, two years later, some of the intensity

surrounding these practices had lessened. A Racine funeral director in 1985 said, "We've come a long way." Recalling his earlier days working in California, he noted that some funeral directors had used masks and even breathed air from tanks out of fear of contracting the disease.[20]

While the state was trying to educate and encourage the medical community and others to provide compassionate reasoned care, it also established new AIDS policies. Health and Social Services Secretary Linda Reivitz, as of September 1, 1983, promulgated an emergency rule making AIDS a reportable disease. This rule was equivalent to law. The department then offered a permanent rule, which required legislative review. Senator Mike Ellis (R-Neenah) had requested such action following the Appleton-area AIDS death. By late August 1983, the state had acknowledged five AIDS cases, with ten more under investigation. In 1983, the first year of the Earl administration, Morrison, of the Division of Health, reallocated $110,000 in funds to the AIDS fight, focusing on health education and patient follow-up. Confidentiality for the reporting of confirmed and suspected AIDS cases was a key policy. The hope was that early reporting would allow patients to receive counseling with accurate information.[21]

Secretary Reivitz initiated a task force on AIDS in 1985, with the goal of presenting "guidelines for virtually every situation that might involve AIDS and people with AIDS." Dr. David Kindig was named the task force

At a time when President Reagan had yet to utter the word *AIDS*, Governor Tony Earl issued an early AIDS Awareness Proclamation in 1984. FROM THE AUTHOR'S COLLECTION

chair. Will Handy, cochair of the Governor's Council on Lesbian and Gay Issues and founder of the Madison AIDS Support Network, was appointed to the task force despite some opposition from others in the health field. Handy was among several openly gay health-care professionals to serve on the task force. In general, "The task force resulted in primarily progressive policy statements." The council was able to support most recommendations but demurred when it came to the issue of contact tracing, whereby patients were asked to provide the names of all of their sexual contacts so health professionals could conduct follow-up health checks with them. The council explained, "Experience in other states demonstrates that 'contact tracing' dissuades high-risk persons from submitting to antibody testing." Perhaps the council remembered the McCarthy-era witch hunts and the UW–Madison purge of 1962, both of which involved the naming of names in order to accumulate lists of homosexuals. Gay folks argued that alerting people about the risk of AIDS, a worthy goal, was not the same as tracking down individuals and placing their names on lists. Many council members and health professionals involved with the gay community strongly supported "alternate test sites" that were "chiefly administered by gay health professionals because they have the highest usage rate and look upon their mission as equally a testing site and a source of non-homophobic information on risk reduction."[22]

The task force also recommended that hospital workers not be allowed to excuse themselves from treating AIDS patients. Handy said that excusing workers was "a bad idea and ought not be done." Since all health workers are expected to take precautions for blood-borne infectious diseases in general, the task force believed in the "ethical and moral responsibility to treat AIDS patients" and that health workers "should certainly do so in any emergency situation."[23]

AIDS policies within prisons were another complicated issue. On February 17, 1986, Milwaukee's two daily newspapers carried wire stories about a national study with diametrically opposed headlines. The *Milwaukee Sentinel* headline read "AIDS Rate in Prisons Very High," while the *Milwaukee Journal* headline read "AIDS Not Rampant in Prisons, Study Indicates." AIDS was reported to have affected prison populations nationally at a rate sixteen times greater than that of the general population. Yet, 50 percent of prisons were AIDS free because 4 percent of the prisons had 72 percent of the inmate cases. While some state's guidelines called for mass screening and segregation of infected persons, Wisconsin's policy was to make decisions on a case-by-case basis. The state's guidelines stressed education and did not require mandatory segregation of inmates with AIDS nor the blanket testing of prisoners. Inmates were provided with a good amount of information on the disease. In December 1985, Wisconsin Administrator for Corrections Walter Dickey had spoken about Wisconsin's evolving policy, stating, "It is our policy in writing that we will accept AIDS victims . . . and we are going to keep them in the system." Earlier, a Wisconsin inmate with AIDS had been sent to a federal prison that had a medical unit better equipped to handle the patient. But in December 1985, the state prison system accepted an Appleton prisoner who had been exposed to AIDS. Outagamie's sheriff's office had barred the prisoner from the county jail after two "deputies were exposed to blood from slash wounds." Dickey emphasized that the state policy focused on protecting inmates with AIDS and other prisoners from infection with AIDS. He warned that "prisoners who try to 'rile up other inmates' against prisoners with AIDS will be subject to disciplinary proceedings." At least one such instance had already occurred at the Dodge Correctional Institution. State guidelines for the treatment of prisoners with AIDS were focused on information from the National Institute of Justice. Secretary Reivitz of the Department of Health and Social Services, which at the time included the Department of Corrections, said the state followed rules endorsed by the American Correctional Association. Only one Wisconsin inmate was known to be infected as of February 1986.[24]

Wisconsin's policy also focused on prisoners spreading AIDS among themselves. The state task force on AIDS opposed mandatory testing of prison inmates. Dickey, in addressing the council regarding homosexual inmates in early 1985, had noted that the system did not segregate them from the general public. He admitted that prisons try to protect the vulnerable inmates, including homosexuals, from physical violence and sexual assault. In 1984, the Wisconsin prison system received eighteen reported cases of sexual assault and ninety-four reported cases of consensual sexual activity. "Some cases reported as consensual," Dickey added, "may have been assault cases in which the victim was reluctant to testify for fear of reprisal." The next year, 1985, showed a slight uptick in the data with 21 sexual assault reports and 125 consensual sexual activity reports. Again, a corrections official admitted that "the cases of true consent are relatively small." The assaults, in particular, posed a potential for the spread of AIDS.[25]

Some groups responded to the AIDS crisis by encouraging more mandatory testing. In early 1988, a survey reported that the majority of physicians supported the mandatory testing of convicted intravenous drug users, convicted prostitutes, and prison inmates. An analysis of the survey indicated that "nearly half of those surveyed also said that marriage license applicants and homosexual and bisexual males should be tested." State health officials opposed these policies in part because of the cost effectiveness of such expenditures. They favored funding that was directed toward education, which could change behavior: "Widespread public education with voluntary testing and counseling has been accepted by high-risk individuals and is likely to be more successful in reducing high-risk behaviors." When a mandatory testing bill was proposed in 1986, it was killed by the Democrat-controlled Assembly Health Committee.[26]

If the state prison system's approach was generally measured, county jails were another story, as indicated by the 1985 incident in Outagamie. The deputies in that county had been monitoring prisoners for any signs of the disease. None were found. Pre-convicted prisoners and those convicted to serve less than a year were housed in county, not state, facilities. In Milwaukee's House of Corrections in 1986, correctional officers caused a ruckus after they were not told that two workhouse inmates had AIDS. While medical staff had been alerted, not all officers had been informed, partly due to confidentiality concerns. The superintendent responded, "People get crazy about communicable diseases. It sounds like they want a leper colony to ship these poor people off to." In Manitowoc County, after the murder of a gay teacher in rural Two Rivers, the sheriff arrested a suspect also known to be gay who had lived with the murdered man. Since the sheriff knew many AIDS victims were gay, he convinced the inmate to "voluntarily" agree to an AIDS test. The Vernon County sheriff, Geoffrey Banta, borrowed an ambulance mask to be prepared if mouth-to-mouth resuscitation would be required for any inmate with AIDS. He was concerned because two convicted gay prisoners were temporarily being held at his jail while awaiting space in the state system.[27]

The Outagamie incident prompted the Wisconsin Sheriff's and Deputy Sheriff's Association in November 1985 to unanimously call for a "right to know" law. Their request was supported by the Wisconsin Counties Association. Sheriff Banta said, "My jailers are concerned and they want me to take any precautions I can." The La Crosse County sheriff wanted medical screening questions about AIDS to be required as part of jail intake. Outagamie Sheriff Thomas Droostan said, "I have been accused of not being a doctor and not knowing what I am talking about. . . . I am not hysterical; I am concerned." In Milwaukee, the vice squad wanted to test anyone arrested for prostitution or sexual perversion. The captain of the squad expressed concern "about the safety of officers who have to pick up people with high risk of getting AIDS." Sheriffs also complained that they were not told of the state guidelines used in the prison system. Dr. James Vergeront with the State Division of Health weighed in, saying jailers "have a right to know that special precautions need to be taken, but knowing the specific disease is not relevant or important." By December, the state guidelines had been shared with county sheriffs. Winnebago Sheriff Terry Footit said, "Most of the recommendations are basically good common sense in dealing with prisoners. I don't expect any drastic changes in our policies, but we'll review them carefully." When the administrators of the Dane County jail developed their AIDS policies, they worked with the Madison AIDS Support Network and the County Task Force on AIDS chaired by Supervisor Tammy Baldwin. Yet, some individuals were critical of the state's policies. Ron Olm, the Outagamie undersheriff, complained, "First of all, they are worrying about the prisoners. They should be worrying about the employees." He also observed that jails are the feeder system for prisons, and huge numbers of prisoners are first held in jails at the local level. Some years later, a person with AIDS in the advanced stages who was arrested for a traffic violation spent forty-eight hours in the Racine jail lying in his own vomit and feces. He died several days after this non-compassionate imprisonment. As in this tragic instance, confused and worried local jailers failed to receive the information and training that might have led to better management of individuals with AIDS caught up in the law enforcement system.[28]

In the state budget passed in 1989, funding for AIDS/HIV life care services increased to $1.4 million for the two-year fiscal period of 1989–1991, of which $1.2 million was earmarked for expanded case management by AIDS service groups, especially the Milwaukee AIDS Project (MAP), the Madison AIDS Support Network, and the Green Bay CENTER Project. This funding would enable MAP to increase its number of case workers to reach the ideal professional ratio of one to thirty-five. "No other city can make that statement," said Doug Nelson of MAP; he also believed that the organization could "help more PWAs [persons with AIDS] to remain in their homes longer, instead of having to go to hospitals or other institutions." MAP also established a new hospice group for people with AIDS. *The Wisconsin Light* praised Governor Thompson for not exercising a line item veto of the funds.[29]

The planning for the state's next biennial budget revealed continuing concerns over AIDS funding as the number of reported cases in Wisconsin grew. In July 1990, the Assembly Health Committee, now chaired by Representative Tim Carpenter, a gay man, heard Representative David Clarenbach describe AIDS as "a time bomb that has not yet exploded." Through the chairman's efforts, the committee held its next meeting at the Milwaukee AIDS Project's headquarters. At this meeting, Dr. Vergeront, now director of Wisconsin's AIDS/HIV program in the Division of Health, predicted the state would see eight thousand new cases during the 1990s, since it was estimated that ten thousand residents were HIV-positive at that time. "The pace of the epidemic is not letting up," said MAP's Nelson, citing the fact that the number of people MAP was helping in Milwaukee was doubling most years. Witnesses informed the committee that the face of AIDS was changing. Representatives from MAP stated that 34 percent of the people MAP was helping were African American and 12 percent were Hispanic. Vergeront told the committee, "State money to pay for AIDS patients' medications is rapidly running out," due to both increases in the number of patients and the new drugs in patient care. The cost of the drugs had risen to $30,000 a month per patient. Additionally, the committee expected federal cuts in funding related to AIDS, including a cut of $250,000 in prevention education for the state. Both Nelson and Sharon Otto of the ARCW discussed the "ever greater reliance on the private sector to support caregiving" for people living with AIDS. As was the case across the country, Wisconsin's health policy and care systems struggled to keep up with the AIDS epidemic. Overall, the state avoided the hysteria common elsewhere and was guided by humane professional judgments in the provision of services. Yet, the allocation of resources was an ongoing issue.[30]

AIDS AND "WARTIME" VIEWS

For the second gay national march on Washington, on October 8–13, 1987, Wisconsin again sent busloads. In the October 1987 issue of *Feminist Voices*, the magazine's pilot issue as a Madison women's journal, twenty-two-year-old lesbian Dawn Schmitz recorded her reminiscences of the main march, which was held on October 11. (In following years, October 11 would become National Coming Out Day.) As hundreds of thousands gathered, she recalled, "For once, we had ceased to be the invisible minority." She expressed her initial concern that the event could have been focused on white men, but in the end, she was encouraged, saying, "I think we managed to raise the consciousness of people about lesbianism that weekend." Noting that Wisconsin was the only state with a nondiscrimination law on the basis of sexual orientation, she said, "We were cheered as we proclaimed ourselves 'The Gay Rights State.'" She added that the state's delegation sometimes chanted, "Put it on the license plate!" Miriam Ben-Shalom of Milwaukee marched with a group of thirty gay military veterans. Dignity Wisconsin's three chapters were represented. A photo in the article identified Lauren Azar, Karen Booth, and Nancy Geary as Wisconsin marchers.[31]

One of the highlights of the 1987 march was the first national display of the NAMES Project AIDS Memorial Quilt on the National Mall. Noting that much of the media coverage was "predictably homophobic," Schmitz observed that in trying to be compassionate, "much of the media made the action out to be one big AIDS requiem." She believed this "robbed us of our right to be seen as angry as well as sad." But AIDS was a constant theme throughout the weekend of the march. AIDS patients along with friends and lovers were at the head of the march. The seven march demands included an end to discrimination against people with AIDS as well as massive increases in funding for AIDS research and care. That particular demand ended with the phrase "money for AIDS, not for War."[32]

Part of the anger expressed at the 1987 March was targeted at the Reagan administration's slow and insensitive response to the AIDS crisis.

In 1985, Larry Kramer's play *The Normal Heart* appeared off Broadway depicting the escalation of the AIDS crisis in New York. That same year, Michael Callen, one of the founders of the People With AIDS Coalition, published the first issue of *Newsline*, the group's monthly newsletter. In the lyrics of his song "Living in Wartime," which was included on his 1988 album *Purple Heart* and performed in *The Normal Heart*, Callen wrote, "It will not go away / More die every day / This is war!" and "The thunder in the distance / says it's only just begun." Later Callen would tour with the Flirtations, a gay a capella group.[33]

In response to the anger displayed at the march, Kramer and some thirty other activists issued a call for a national "War Conference" to address what they called "a national administration hostile to the cause of lesbian and gay rights and cruelly indifferent to the catastrophe of AIDS." Held at Airlie House in Warrenton, Virginia, just outside Washington, DC, in February 1988, the conference attracted some two hundred gay and lesbian leaders. I was privileged to be able to attend this invitation-only conference. The invitation asserted, "We are fighting for our lives because there are powerful forces making war against us." The final statement crafted during the conference proclaimed,

> Our community is facing unprecedented threats. Not only do we daily face the homophobia that has cost lesbians and gay men their jobs, their housing, the love of their families, their children, their sense of dignity and self-worth and—all too often—their lives, but we have now seen our community decimated by the scourge of AIDS.

The document noted "our twin threats: the disease itself, and the callous and criminal response of our governments to it."[34]

Gay historian John D'Emilio, who also attended the War Conference, penned an opinion piece for *Gay Community News* that appeared in the June 19, 1988, issue. D'Emilio observed a constant conference motif: "Where's our anger?" Observing the tidal waves of grief that have swept the community, he commented, we have learned "all sorts of creative ways to acknowledge and express it." Then, he posed his real question: "Do we want to develop a political strategy for liberation that is based on grief?" He

Facing the increasing death toll from AIDS and drawing on the energy of the 1987 national march on Washington, Larry Kramer and others convened for the War Conference, a meeting of LGBT leaders from across the country, pictured here. R. RICHARD WAGNER PAPERS, ACC. NO. 2016/014, UNIVERSITY OF WISCONSIN–MADISON ARCHIVES

continued, "Terror entered my life the moment I became aware that I was gay. . . . Where would I be if I let gay terror serve as my guide for action? . . . A politics of rage weakens and destroys its proponents and their cause more effectively than it weakens and destroys an oppressive system." Rather than be guided by grief, terror, or rage, D'Emilio concluded, "I would much prefer that we think our way to success." Attendees of the War Conference spent a lot of time focused on crafting four main recommendations. One: a nationwide media campaign for a positive image of gay America. Two: a national network to link organizations across communities, including the AIDS Coalition To Unleash Power (ACT-UP). Three: annual gatherings of gay and lesbian activists. And four: a national Coming Out Day. The movement, attendees felt sure, would bring these things to reality. Back in Wisconsin, along with the other Wisconsin conference-goers, I planned for National Coming Out Day 1988 in a number of ways, including publishing a large display ad in the *Isthmus*. Ultimately, the individuals who attended the War Conference channeled some of the energy from the 1987 march and the general sense of a growing crisis into concrete actions.[35]

DISPARATE STATE AND FEDERAL VIEWS ON DISCRIMINATION

While devising its own responses to AIDS, Wisconsin was also influenced by national actions and responses. As noted previously, Ronald Reagan, who became president in 1981, took an inordinately long time to mention the health crisis, not uttering the word *AIDS* until 1985. His justice department appeared unsympathetic as well. On June 20, 1986, Assistant Attorney General Charles Cooper made a ruling that "federally assisted hospitals or clinics can fire AIDS victims (or non-victims who test positive for AIDS antibodies) without running afoul of federal laws prohibiting discrimination." Some media outlets noted that Cooper interpreted "the legal rights of people with AIDS and related conditions much more narrowly than the department's career civil rights lawyers had recommended." Cooper's new ruling allowed these dismissals because the fear of contagion was so great. In Madison the *Capital Times* denounced the prejudicial policy, publishing an article with the headline, "AIDS Victims Bear a Double Burden."[36]

In Wisconsin in late 1985, Susan Green, the coordinator of the Madison United, wondered if an employer could fire someone because of AIDS under state law. After consulting with attorneys in the Wisconsin Equal Rights Division (ERD), she came to the conclusion that such a firing would be illegal. The issue arose over the matter of a health-care worker in a central Wisconsin town. When he started to show symptoms of an AIDS-related cancer, his employer indicated that he would be fired. Green intervened and, as a result, the employer allowed the man paid disability leave. In January 1986, the ERD ruled that persons with AIDS were protected under the state's Fair Employment Act. The ruling also cited "medical evidence that AIDS cannot be transmitted through casual contact."[37]

Having gone through the struggle to pass the gay rights bill, Wisconsin's equal rights advocates were well-equipped for the AIDS battle. On February 7, 1986, Merry Fran Tryon, the Wisconsin ERD administrator, authored a paper titled "AIDS and the Law." While acknowledging that no rulings had yet been made in Wisconsin's courts, Tryon extrapolated from other Wisconsin court rulings on contagious diseases and came to the definitive conclusion: "Wisconsin under its Fair Employment Law construes AIDS as a legally protected handicap. A job applicant cannot be turned away, or an employee terminated, because he or she has AIDS or tests positive for AIDS, or is merely perceived (or believed) to have AIDS." Tryon also noted the legislature's passage of laws that specifically prohibited termination over an AIDS test or its use as a condition for employment. Showing compassion, she noted, "AIDS sufferers are victimized due to the nature of the disease and to the present climate of misinformation, ignorance and fear in the general population." Dane County Circuit Court Judge George Northrup, a gay man, formed a committee to deal with judicial policy related to AIDS. In 1987, Tim Cullen, the Wisconsin secretary of Health and Social Services, warned nursing homes that they might face lawsuits if they refused AIDS patients. That same year, LeAnna Ware, serving as president of the Madison Equal Opportunities Commission, spoke of a hope "that the citizens of Madison will deal compassionately with the AIDS issue and avoid the abhorrent behavior displayed toward homosexuals in other communities." "Further," she added, "we urge gay men who have been victimized by the public's hysteria regarding AIDS to remember Madison has an ordinance that prohibits discrimination based on sexual orientation." In 1990, with the passage of the Americans with Disabilities Act, federal law finally caught up with Wisconsin state law.[38]

The effects of Wisconsin's progressive policies could be seen when *New Beginnings for Family and Friends*, a magazine published in Westby, near La Crosse, reported extensively on AIDS in the late 1980s. The magazine criticized testing in nearby Minnesota for not being anonymous and listed alternative testing sites that would not hassle someone who made up a name. The March 1990 issue carried a letter from Minnesota ACT-UP activist Dean Amundson, who specifically urged readers to "Take Tests in Wisconsin." Noting that his ACT-UP chapter warned people against taking the Minnesota test, he wrote, "Wisconsin has anonymous testing that is legal; state-wide rights and discrimination protection for gays and lesbians, and no sodomy law. . . . Those who test in Minnesota should be prepared to lie, refuse to answer direct questions and understand they may be incriminating themselves under state drug or sodomy statutes."[39]

Still, during the 1980s, many Wisconsinites did not agree with these progressive policies. The governor's office, in April 1986, received a fundraising letter sent out by the United Families Foundation and signed by Congressman William Dannemeyer (R-CA) protesting laws barring discrimination against AIDS victims. The letter, which was distributed nationally, included this specific complaint: "In Wisconsin, homosexual activists succeeded in passing a law banning employers, insurers, or government agencies from testing for AIDS." Dannemeyer described himself as "angry at public health officials who have caved in to the militant homosexuals and have branded AIDS a civil rights issue rather than a public health issue." As chapter 7 details, despite these detractors, Wisconsin followed its groundbreaking 1982 nondiscrimination law with nondiscriminatory AIDS policies that ensured equal access to professional health services.[40]

Wisconsin Schools and AIDS

When Ryan White—a teenager and hemophiliac who had contracted HIV from a blood treatment—was barred from his school in Kokomo, Indiana, in 1984, he was not the only flash point in the battle over schools' AIDS policies. In late 1985 and early 1986, many Wisconsin schools also grappled with the issue.

In December 1985, the Milwaukee health commissioner Constantine Panagis recommended that "the Milwaukee school system allow children with AIDS to attend classes with healthy children." It was safe, he said. He urged schools to maintain strict hygienic standards for students with AIDS because of their compromised immune systems. The school system's superintendent had sensibly asked the health department for guidelines. Using guidelines issued by the CDC, Panagis said, "When we prepare people with the true facts and say we will review each case, I think we can assure people we'll be very careful and take every precaution." However, such a measured weighing of the health issue was not employed consistently throughout the state.[41]

In March 1986, the Waukesha school board considered the draft of a policy that would allow students or employees diagnosed with or suspected of having AIDS (or any of twenty-two other communicable diseases) to be barred from school by a principal. In one draft, the common cold was on the list. Following a doctor's statement that an individual was suitable to be at school, an appeal could made to the superintendent or school board. One administrator admitted that "concern about acquired immune deficiency was a factor in drafting the policy." The school district said it relied on the county health services for advice. That department had a policy that none of its employees would be forced to work with any clients with AIDS or suspected of having AIDS, though services could continue to be provided by other employees. At the time, this county had no known AIDS patients.[42]

In Sparta, the school superintendent said his administrative policy was to treat students with AIDS as having a communicable disease and to keep them out of school. A doctor could certify that the students were no danger to others, but until such time, they would receive home-bound instruction. The superintendent did acknowledge the hysteria about AIDS in schools, but his fear of legal liability meant he was taking no chances. In Calumet County, the school policy allowed a child with AIDS to attend school with written approval from the family physician and the county director of public health. Marinette Schools barred any students with AIDS from attending.[43]

Sheboygan's schools tried to take a measured approach. The pupil services director decried the "mass-media approach" to the issue that was causing panic. He noted, "At the earliest stage, there is no reason a student who is an active carrier should not be admitted to school." At the next stage, the director believed the goal should be to provide the best care possible for a "student carrier." The district used state and federal guidelines to formulate its policy. Nancy Dorman, policy director for Wisconsin Association of School Boards, said her organization supported state guidelines that recommended allowing students with AIDS to stay in school. Dorman believed public fears were driving the effort to remove students from schools. The Sheboygan Press commented that the state task force on AIDS should be working to "minimize misinformation and the resultant fears." The paper wrote, "The state is on the right track disseminating facts not fear."[44]

Cindy Kontney, a student at Pacelli High in Stevens Point, wrote in a piece for the local newspaper, "Through education we will be able to make rational decisions which concern the victims of AIDS. . . . Education may also lessen the fear we have of AIDS." This was in 1986, before any reported cases had reached this relatively isolated town. The extent to which schools' AIDS policies were being driven by fear and panic rather than the need to respond to real situations can be observed by the fact that the vast majority of schools in Wisconsin had no students with AIDS in the early and mid-1980s.[45]

RACINE SCHOOLS: AN EXTREME CASE

The Racine Unified School District, the third-largest district in the state, proved to be the place where controversy broke out over schools and AIDS policies. In November 1985, the district's board voted 6 to 3 to exclude pupils and district staff with AIDS from the schools. Defending the decision, Superintendent Don Woods said, "Weasel words like 'almost zero possibility of spreading the disease' and 'only minimal chance' would not ensure a safe educational climate for the district's 21,000 pupils and 2,200 employees." Similarly, board member Barbara Scott was among those who thought "state and federal guidelines, which call for keeping AIDS victims in classrooms, are unworkable and unfair." Janice Hand, the director of the Great Lakes Hemophilia Foundation, spoke against the proposed policy. She argued that the district should make its decisions on a case-by-case basis and cited the position of the National Education Association. "My concern," said opposing board member John Graham, "is that the policy as passed by the board is not a policy that's going to elicit cooperation from afflicted individuals or their parents." James Ennis, executive director of the Racine Education Association, claimed that "the policy was developed as part of a purge of homosexual teachers by religious fundamentalists on the board." Board member George Petak (who would later become a Republican state senator) gave credence to Ennis's charge when the press quoted him as saying "he believed homosexuals should not be allowed to teach Unified students." The issue was perhaps fueled by Racine's first reported death from AIDS in November 1985, but board members denied that the death influenced their policy decision. Lampman, a Racine member of Earl's Governor's Council on Lesbian and Gay Issues, described the city as a "homophobic town" that had "very little tolerance for anything that is out of the norm."[46]

The controversy erupted in the letters to the editor of the *Racine Journal Times*. The cartoonist drew a ten-foot pole and labeled it "The Public's Guideline for Dealing with the Victims of AIDS." One reader congratulated the school board for standing "up against the minimization of

AIDS coming out of Hollywood and from the mass media elite." Others praised the idea of quarantine. One reader believed "'AIDS people' should be handled in the same manner as people with leprosy." Protecting the healthy was a common theme among this group. "All known gay teachers or administrators should be given a blood test to check for AIDS," argued one individual. However, those opposed to the policy also wrote in to the paper. One voice on this side of the debate felt the policy was "a return to the discrimination afforded to the lepers of old." Some called it bigoted, nonsensical, and a witch hunt. One writer, who self-identified as a "gay Racine teacher," felt the school board should not make up its own medical guidelines. Others recalled that pupils with disabilities had been barred from school in the past and called for "compassion and understanding to help fellow humans when under attack, especially innocent victims." In like manner, one writer believed this could be a teaching moment: "Encourage students to develop sympathy, empathy and love for the suffering student." Many letter writers believed the guidelines of the Department of Public Instruction and the National Education Association were "sensible and humane," and that the school board had overreacted in giving in to ignorance and hysteria. One pointedly asked, "Don't the AIDS victims have rights?" Another wrote, "As far as I can see, the only thing we, the students, are being 'protected' from is a free society and an educational system where no one is discriminated against."[47]

The editors of the *Racine Journal Times*, on December 13, 1985, joined the discussion with a long editorial titled "AIDS Policy Too Hasty." Noting that the district was the first in the state to bar AIDS victims from classrooms, the paper called attention to the fact that in doing so it went against the proposed policies from the Wisconsin Department of Health and Social Services. The editors also noted that Laura Taff, supervisor of nursing for the Department of Public Instruction, was critical of the Racine board. Pointing out that the guidelines of the federal CDC paralleled the state's information, the editors concluded that the board "had distanced itself from mainstream thinking—both of medical and educational professionals—on how to deal with the potential problem." Most damning was the observation that "the board did not even consult its own medical adviser" before enacting the policy. "Undue haste rather than reasoned judgment appears to have ruled the Unified Board's decision," the editors wrote, as there had been no public hearing and no consultation with teachers or school employees prior to the policy's adoption. In the end, the editors concluded that the board's knee-jerk reaction "smacks of hysteria and does little to allay apprehension."[48]

The Racine Education Association, representing fourteen hundred teachers, filed a complaint with the ERD on February 6, 1986. James Ennis of the association indicated that the complaint alleged the policy violated laws that prohibited discrimination on the basis of sexual preference and disability. The union's attorney stated, "The policy is clearly discriminatory inasmuch as it uniformly and immediately prohibits teachers from their jobs, without making any effort to accommodate the perceived or actual handicap." In mid-April, the ERD made a tentative statement that it believed the policy was illegal. After this "initial Determination" of a violation, the district had the option of either seeking conciliation or seeking a hearing to overturn the decision. The *Milwaukee Sentinel*, in an editorial, urged the board to find a compromise. "Fear must be dealt with before it turns into panic, or a witch hunt of AIDS victims," the editors wrote. As the opinion of the ERD became known, Superintendent Woods continued to defend the policy. "I may wind up in jail for it," he said, "[but] I would rather be safe than sorry. . . . I still see elementary school kids eating out of their paste jar, and sharing their paste jars." This paste jar theory of transmission appears to be unique in the state's discussions about AIDS. The epidemiologist with the state Department of Health and Social Services reaffirmed the "absolute lack of evidence" for arguing that AIDS could be transmitted by casual contact in the classroom. The attorney for the school district said they would seek a hearing to overturn the ruling.[49]

At the April 1986 hearing, an administrative law judge (ALJ) decided in favor of the Racine Education Association. The teacher's union's claim of discrimination on the basis of sexual orientation was accepted. The ALJ relied on the figure that "seventy-three percent of individuals with AIDS/ARC [AIDS-related complex] are homosexual and bisexual" men. Accepted also as evidence was the school board member's statement "that he voted in favor of the policy because he did not believe that homosexuals should be allowed to teach." The ALJ also ruled discrimination on the basis of disability. The union was awarded attorneys' fees and costs, and the school board was ordered to withdraw the policy. The decision focused on the violation

of the employer by "statements which evince an intent to discriminate on a basis forbidden" by Wisconsin's fair employment law. A Racine appeal for further review by the Labor and Industry Review Commission resulted in a decision that also upheld the ruling against the school board. Stubbornly, the school district then sought a Racine Circuit Court review, with the same result. Still not deterred, the district brought the matter to the State Court of Appeals, District II, in 1991. The court observed that while the school district had taken no steps to enforce the AIDS policy, it had refused to rescind or suspend it, so the policy remained on the books and the victory went to the union.[50]

The appeals court set aside the claim of discrimination on the basis of sexual orientation for lack of a complete disparate impact analysis that would have analyzed the number of homosexual employees in the district as compared to heterosexual employees. The court felt the superintendent's claims that the school had no known employees with AIDS was too "soft and potentially self-interested information." Regarding discrimination on the basis on disability, the ALJ had also ruled that an impairment may constitute a handicap even if the condition is communicable. The district did not contest this aspect of previous rulings. The appeals court decision on disability was clear: AIDS represents "real deterioration or loss of bodily function which could make achievement unusually difficult or diminish the capacity to work." The 1991 decision also sadly observed, "AIDS is, as of this writing, ultimately fatal." The court's decision found the district's arguments "disingenuous." The school district's policy "represented a conclusive presumption on the District's part that persons with AIDS or ARC are inherently incapable of performing on the job." The court's final judgment—this was a policy advocating discrimination.[51]

THE QUILT THAT PROVIDED MORE THAN WARMTH

In May 1989, the NAMES Project AIDS Memorial Quilt came to the UW–Madison Fieldhouse, thanks to cosponsors Madison AIDS Support Network and GALVAnize (Gay and Lesbian Visibility Alliance), the group that also organized a march of seven thousand at the Capitol. Tim O'Brien, the volunteer coordinator for MASN, was a strong advocate for bringing the quilt. Two hundred of the more than three thousand individual

The AIDS Quilt visited Madison in 1989. FROM THE AUTHOR'S COLLECTION

panels of the quilt were displayed. As was custom, volunteers in white ceremoniously unfolded the panels and names were read. One Madison visitor seeing the quilt noted that the Fieldhouse was very still and quiet. "I feel so much in this room," he commented. "Joy, sadness, love, caring." He recognized a Madison panel that had been created for the brother of his friend. Julie McGivern, a Madison resident, brought her mother, Genevieve, to see a panel that was made for her two gay brothers, Joseph and Frank, both of whom had lived in Madison but died in New York. Genevieve criticized the Reagan administration as "immoral in their response to the crisis of AIDS." Seeing her brothers' panel in Madison felt, to Julie, like their coming home. Daniel Trzebiatowski, who brought a carload of Milwaukeeans, felt seeing the quilt "was the reality of Gay awareness." As it did elsewhere across the country, the AIDS quilt provided the opportunity for moments of reflection and shared grief in Wisconsin.[52]

GREEN BAY CONTROVERSY

Green Bay proved a flash point for several AIDS-related issues in the mid-1980s. In November 1985, Alder Guy Zima objected to a sexually explicit pamphlet on AIDS transmission. The CENTER (Community Endeavor for Needs in Testing, Education, and Referral) Project, as part of its public education, used a brochure written by the San Francisco Bay Area

Physicians for Human Rights and distributed by the Wisconsin Division of Health. Zima's criticism was joined by complaints from Senators Alan Lasee (R-De Pere) and Joe Andrea (D-Kenosha). They objected to the use of four-letter words for intercourse and "street terms for types of sex in which homosexuals engage." Rallying the support of local physicians and health advocates, the full city council adopted what Mike Belinski called "a pretty intelligent attitude" in regard to the CENTER Project's use of the brochure. Secretary Linda Reivitz responded to the senators by saying, "It is important that we all understand that our objective is not developing materials which are acceptable to the majority of the population, because the vast majority of us are not at risk of this disease." After the controversy, Belinski said, "The shock seems to have worn down." Zima also wanted to enable nurses to refuse to staff the CENTER Project clinic. He said a refusal was "not a matter of insubordination, but a matter of personal moral belief." The city's personnel committee had recommended that the health commissioner should determine staffing assignments at the clinic. Zima wanted to table the personnel recommendation until the pamphlet was rewritten. His motion was defeated on a 17 to 5 vote. Green Bay Health Commissioner Peter Le Mere observed in 1985, "There is really only one program which has become controversial in my 25 years' experience—AIDS. I still feel strongly there is a misunderstanding about the disease and who is at risk."[53]

In early 1986, the issue was reopened. This time, Alder Mike Miller championed the same issue of nurses being able to refuse to staff the clinic. He believed the issue should be negotiated with the union. Commissioner Le Mere reported he was able to staff the clinic with nurses willing to volunteer for the assignment, seemingly making the issue a moot point. But the City Council Personnel Committee directed the health commissioner and personnel director to work on the issue. In council discussion, Alder Sara Thulin said, "We're not going to the union to ask them what (jobs) can be assigned on moral or religious grounds." Zima claimed that "it was an imposition to force nurses to counsel homosexuals when they disapproved of that lifestyle. . . . Management should not force people with Christian beliefs to engage in this type of activity." The council refused by 20 to 2 to reopen its previous decision that staffing was an administrative matter. Mayor Sam Halloin was quoted as saying, "I've heard a lot of bull here tonight and I wouldn't mind if it was the first time. But I've heard it over and over and over again." In March, Zima fought the issue yet again. After abandoning the effort to permit religious and personal beliefs as a basis for objection, he advanced a new proposal: "No employee of the city of Green Bay upon written objection may be required to counsel clients as to how to perform specific sex acts." Le Mere indicated that "all counseling is aimed at disease prevention" at the CENTER Project clinic, as is all other counseling for heterosexuals about venereal diseases. Zima argued, "Normal people should not have to offer counseling on abnormal acts." Yet, seven of the nine community nurses came forward to oppose the proposal. One said, "We deal with a lot of issues with a sexual nature, and this (ordinance) can interfere with our work." Zima again lost his fight.[54]

The next attack on the CENTER Project clinic came later that March from the City of Green Bay Protection and Welfare Committee, which proposed a fee be assessed to out-of-county residents using the clinic. An editorial in the *Green Bay Press Gazette* hoped the city "was motivated by economic concerns and not bias." Though the homosexual lifestyle is "contrary to the values of many in the community," the paper's editors wrote, "there is no room for discrimination against any minority group, especially one most vulnerable to a deadly disease." Belinski was joined in his lobbying efforts against the fee proposal by Le Mere and Brown County nursing director Judy Pinkstaff. Pinkstaff pointed out that "the disease doesn't recognize political boundaries" and that other communicable disease clinics were available regardless of residence. Asking people to state their place of residence would have challenged the reputation the CENTER Project clinic had for maintaining confidentiality. The Brown County Protection Committee unanimously rejected the fee proposal, with the chairman calling it "pretty petty." Belinski praised this responsible attitude.[55]

WISCONSIN ACT-UP

The editors of *The Wisconsin Light*—after observing the national actions of ACT-UP, especially its moving die-ins—encouraged the formation of a Milwaukee chapter in August 1989. "Admittedly, confrontational strategies are not for everyone," the editors wrote, "but we believe that there is a place for those who protest and demonstrate and are not silent." Earlier that year, a candlelight vigil had been held at the Federal Building in Milwaukee "to protest the lack of action by the Federal Government in the fight against AIDS." The Milwaukee chapter was aided in its inception by a visit on August 18 and 19, 1989, from two members of ACT-UP New York's Outreach Committee. Milwaukee organizers and the city's new ACT-UP president, Trzebiatowski, were told the organization "fills the gap between AIDS service organizations and the public." "Forget about good taste," the New York members advised. "Forget about being nice. You don't get anything by saying 'Please.'" *The Wisconsin Light* reported an even more dramatic statement from one New Yorker: "If you're going to die, die with a bullet hole through your open mouth. . . . You cannot wait," they argued. "You can't deal with something only when it becomes a disaster." The New York and local organizers visited gay and lesbian bars to recruit support for Milwaukee's nascent group. At Fannies, women's roles were emphasized. In its heyday, the Milwaukee chapter of ACT-UP had twenty-five active members. They described themselves as "individuals united in anger and compassion, and radically committed to direct action to end the AIDS crisis."[56]

Marquette University, Milwaukee's main Catholic college, was a special target for the Milwaukee chapter. In February 1990, during the distribution of Lenten ashes, at the campus Gesu Church, three hundred condoms and eight hundred pamphlets on AIDS information were distributed. Earlier, ACT-UP had tried to open a dialogue about the university's response to the AIDS crisis, but the vice president of religious affairs had stated that "the university would not compromise the teaching of the Roman Catholic Church." This was understood to mean that there was no possibility of the administration sanctioning safe-sex education on campus, the most effective way after celibacy of avoiding HIV infection. Next, in October 1990, ACT-UP Milwaukee staged a demonstration at a dance held at Marquette University High School to distribute condoms and AIDS information from the State Department of Health. School administrators instructed security guards to physically come between the protestors and the students coming to the dance. Five ACT-UP members were arrested for disorderly conduct. The condoms were a particularly touchy issue for the Catholic school. Subsequent similar high school demonstrations held at Bay View and Whitefish Bay did not result in arrests. A spokesperson for

Milwaukee Public Schools (MPS) said, "While MPS may not like ACT-UP's actions outside the dances, the group was within its constitutional rights of speech and assembly." Students' reactions to the condoms were reported as being either " 'thanks' or 'eeew.' " While some brochures were found discarded afterward, no condoms were found on the ground. ACT-UP member Christopher Fons argued, "If parents and teachers will not teach teen-agers about condoms and will not allow us to teach them, not only are they denying us our rights to free speech and assembly, but they are killing their children." *The Wisconsin Light* proudly saluted Milwaukee ACT-UP for reaching out to high school students. The editors wrote, "Sexual abstinence is a nice ideal, but while we hate to be cynical, for some, especially high school students as well as both younger and older, that's all it is, an ideal. Asking young people to be chaste and expecting all of them to practice it, is kind of like asking the moon not to rise."[57]

ACT-UP Milwaukee conducted an informational protest action at a local dental clinic in 1990. The group had conducted a phone survey of two hundred dentists. The results indicated that one-third were or would be against providing care to people with HIV. Representatives met with the executive director of the Wisconsin Dental Association and with the Marquette Dental School. The action at the clinic was criticized by ultraconservative talk radio host Mark Belling on WISN-AM, who asked the question: "Should dentists be required to treat AIDS patients?" According to *The Wisconsin Light*, Belling "repeatedly stated that the majority of AIDS victims are responsible for their condition; that 95% of people with HIV are personally responsible for their infection and should not complain." ACT-UP alerted the station manager that Belling was spreading "dangerous misinformation about AIDS to the public." The activists also observed that most HIV-infected people are unaware of their status, and they argued that "dentists must use full precautions with every patient, every time and that when such precautions are used, 'the status of both dentist and patients becomes irrelevant.' "[58]

The *Isthmus* ascribed the new "combativeness" of local efforts to the Madison ACT-UP chapter. Gay Wisconsinites were described as "looking to still more confrontational tactics used by gays and lesbians in cities like New York and Washington." In some large cities, ACT-UP protestors chained themselves to doors to block access to offices and staged "die-ins"

One area of concern for many activists in Wisconsin was prisoners with AIDS and their treatment. *MADISON INSURGENT*, APRIL 22–MAY 5, 1991

in streets to block traffic. ACT-UP members from around the country flew in for a major demonstration in Madison in September 1991, protesting Governor Tommy Thompson's failure to respond to a task force report on compassionate and professional health care for persons with AIDS in Wisconsin prisons. Some 150 protestors blew whistles and chanted "shame" at the Capitol. After marching to the Department of Corrections, fifteen individuals were arrested. As a result of the protest, the Department of Corrections appointed a new panel to review the progress being made on the prison recommendations, which included Doug Nelson of MAP and Madison AIDS Support Network coordinator Carole Ahrens. Madison ACT-UP activist Dan Savage said the committee would be closely watched.

ACT-UP activist Dan Savage (center) and others deliver peanut butter and jelly sand-
wiches to Governor Tommy Thompson's office to protest the lack of nutritious meals
being provided to AIDS prisoners. PHOTO BY CAROLYN PFLASTERER, *WISCONSIN STATE JOURNAL*

"If it's bullshit, we'll shut them down," he said. Savage strongly believed
in the need to be "radical" to hold public officials accountable. He told the
press what he preemptively acknowledged was a "horrible thing": "I hope
a lot of straight people get AIDS."[59]

Savage would later become a well-known LGBT activist after creating
the internationally syndicated advice column Savage Love and founding
It Gets Better, a suicide-prevention project for LGBT youth, with his husband. Some of his earliest activism took place in Madison in the early 1990s.
"These are extreme times," he said in 1991, "and gays and lesbians are under
assault. . . . The only way we can get our issues addressed is by acting radical, lying down on sidewalks, screaming and yelling and making radical
demands and saying extreme things, and then when we do that—which is
the only way we can get press—we're dismissed for our extremism." Savage
also became a proponent of outing gay public figures. He and I debated
the outing issue on Madison's local gay cable TV show *Nothing To Hide*.[60]

A new group also briefly making its presence known at the prison
demonstrations in Madison was the Queer Liberation Front of Madison.
Jari Junikka, a graduate student from Finland, got involved with the Front
after he was assaulted by two men who wanted to "do some gay bashing."

Hate crime charges against the men did not stick; Junikka thought this was because the "courts are very homophobic." He stated, "I want to walk hand-in-hand with my lover down State Street." Junikka, who was also active in Madison ACT-UP, claimed, "The government has blood on its hands because of its negligence."[61]

In 1992, some fifteen members of Madison ACT-UP awarded a "Slammie" to Governor Thompson for his "baffling practice of ignoring his own advisers' recommendation for AIDS education and materials distribution in Wisconsin prisons." The mock award was presented during an action in the Capitol protesting the governor's AIDS policies and, in an act of gender balance, denouncing the controversial film *Basic Instinct* for depicting some women "as psycho-killer lesbian/bisexuals." Chants at the protest included, "Suck my dick, lick my clit, Tommy Thompson's full of shit." Among the protesters was Heather Rhoads from Les/bi/femmes, a Madison lesbian bisexual action group. Perhaps because of the strong presence of the prison guards' union, Thompson had taken a harsh line on prison issues and the head of the Department of Corrections was "under fire for inadequate prison guard training." In 1987, Thompson voiced his support

Even in an epidemic, humor was needed to survive, as shown in this cartoon published in the UW–Madison *Daily Cardinal*. DAILY CARDINAL

of "severe penalties" for those who knowingly transmit the disease. And at one point, he supported mandatory HIV testing for inmates in the state's correctional institutions. Later he changed his support to the mandatory testing of only assaultive inmates. The governor's 1992–1993 budget included a $150,000 reduction in funding for the AIDS drug trial program. Dale Tegman, an ACT-UP spokesperson, said, "To be frank, I don't care if Tommy Thompson accepts me as long as he doesn't kill me." In Wisconsin, as elsewhere, the epidemic stirred strong emotions within the gay community as slow government responses resulted in the deaths of friends and lovers. The emergence of ACT-UP in the state provided Wisconsinites with an outlet where frustration and rage could be expressed.[62]

HEART PIECES: WISCONSIN POETS FOR AIDS

The small poetry book *Heart Pieces* was published in January 1987, giving voice to many poets in Wisconsin dealing with lesbian and gay issues, including AIDS. The editor, Norman Richards, conceived of the book as a fundraiser for the Milwaukee AIDS Project. The thirty-two poets featured in the collection hailed from around the state. The diverse group of poets included both men and women, among them a Ho-Chunk and an Iberian-descended poet.[63]

Most of the poetry in this early part of the state's experience of the epidemic was not actually focused on AIDS but on broader issues of gay and lesbian life. Much of it was about love, often lost or unrequited. Bob Tollefson, one of the contributing poets, wrote, "In coming forth / love parallels poetry / the struggle to say what's felt."[64]

Several poets described the challenges of growing up gay in a heteronormative society. In "The Pain of Being Different," Lawrence William O'Connor wrote: "Never exposed to positive aspects of homosexuality. Life as a lie. / Secrecy a way of life." Similarly, Richard Whaley Sims wrote in his poem "Inside" about keeping his true feelings hidden:

I cover my heart with bones and flesh
And believe what the others say,
That i am not who i know i am
And that God would burn me eternally

For loving someone with the whole of my
Heart . . .[65]

Other poems in the collection were written as addresses to lovers. Susan Gregg, in an untitled poem, portrayed the difficulty of coming to terms with homosexuality, writing, "Our sex / the same / Our feelings / confused / Our lives / together." And in "The Rites of Love," Rod Gonsalves wrote:

The way you speak my name so soft
The way you treat me as you do,
I hope someday the time is right,
When I can say I just love you.[66]

The celebration of sexuality was the foremost topic for some. The collection includes a poem called "Boysmell Love" by the well-known Wis-

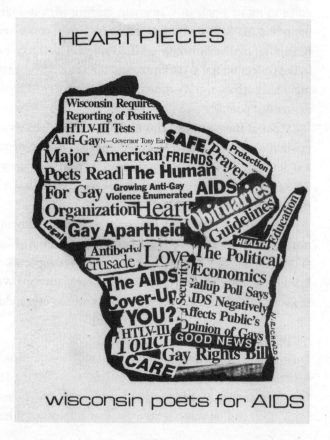

Wisconsin gay and lesbian poets responded to the AIDS crisis with their art in this 1987 collection, a fundraiser for the Milwaukee AIDS Project. MEMORIAL LIBRARY SPECIAL COLLECTIONS

consin gay poet Antler; it includes the lines, "Show me a boy who doesn't love his own smell / Who doesn't get a boner bringing his pubic warmth to his nose when he wakes the first day of vacation."[67]

A few poets addressed the issue of AIDS directly, among them Richards. He wrote, "tonight, / I'm wishing for a miracle / to erase THAT four letter word / from everyone's mind / from everyone's life." Joseph P. Zanoni wrote, "Gay men perish from AIDS, / While the world looks another way. / Constantly teased and insulted / the subject of a dirty joke." David Carroll placed his poem "Never Wearing White" in Milwaukee, the city with bridges, with a river that glitters and factories on the skyline. In a gay bar, he stares at the bartenders' thighs and the other "strange birds / perched on their barstools" and comes to the conclusion: "I'll die of AIDS / or utter frustration." He imagined waking in the morning and wishing "I was a eunuch." Wisconsin was one of the earliest states to enlist artists in the struggle against AIDS. The state had developed enough of a gay literary scene by encouraging and publishing poets in its gay media that by 1987 poets from around the state were ready to mobilize in the fight over AIDS.[68]

Voices from the Wisconsin Battle Lines

While poets addressed the AIDS crisis in their art, other Wisconsinites impacted by AIDS shared their experiences in newspaper and magazine interviews, providing additional perspectives on the epidemic's impact. In 1983, a gay couple, Mark and Jason, returned to the Madison area having caught the virus in San Francisco. Brooks Egerton interviewed them in November 1984. They had been extremely depressed by the stressful panic around AIDS in the Pacific Coast city. Having come out to their families ten years earlier, they had hoped to receive support back in Wisconsin but instead found rejection. "I have not spoken to my mother in 10 months," Jason said. But in Madison, they found health services without prejudice. Chaz Pope with the Gay Center was credited with providing help. Mark said, "I am not afraid of dying, I'm afraid of not living."[69]

In a 1987 story, a man named Tim spoke about his experience nearly two years after his diagnosis. The twenty-five-year-old, who lived with his mother in Milwaukee, asked, "Am I angry? All the time. This is going to sound terrible, but personally I know people who deserve it more than I do." Tim said he was not gay, but "he did not want his real name used because he fears being ostracized or harassed." He believed his sexual contact with women who had been with bisexual men was the likely means of transmission. "I don't trust society to be compassionate enough to understand," he said. Tim, who was African American, was volunteering with the Milwaukee AIDS Project because, as he said, "there is no reason why a 22-year-old black guy should have to go through this again."[70]

One seventy-one-year-old woman from rural Wisconsin told interviewers that she was "plain angry" after her son died of AIDS in Milwaukee. She said Danny "had been so easy to bring up, a good student, the high school class president." He told her he was gay several months before he received his diagnosis. "Much of her anger stems from the fact that her other children, the youngest of whom was 10 years older than Danny, did not offer to help," the interviewer observed. Her grief was compounded by the fact that his siblings "did not attend his memorial service." Danny's oldest sister reputedly said, "He knew what he was getting into when he 'became' a homosexual," and that he had "brought on his condition himself." None of the children helped their mother in what she described as "the worst time of my life." She reached out to Danny's housemate and his friends for support.[71]

Green Bay native Gerald Wagner participated in a lengthy interview with the *Press Gazette* on living with AIDS in his early thirties, eight months after his diagnosis. "He says he knows death is inevitable," wrote his interviewer, "but he prefers not to spend much time thinking about that." After his diagnosis, Wagner lived a lonesome life in a home once owned by his lover, who had died from AIDS. Wagner had suffered bouts of pneumonia and was dealing with forty purple spots from a skin cancer. His work with an AIDS group in Connecticut, where he now lived, was aimed at "breaking down some of the psychological barriers and prejudice [he] believes face the general public when it comes to dealing with homosexuals such as himself." Wagner said, "When I meet someone or meet with a group—and in many cases I'm the first gay person they've ever met—there's quite a difference in their thinking." Wagner felt lucky that his family supported his decision to go public with his disease.[72]

In October 1986, Michael Lisowski wrote a heartfelt Chairman's Notes for the newsletter of the Milwaukee group Black and White Men Together (BWMT). Recalling deaths and diagnoses, Lisowski wrote, "Yes, to me, AIDS is finally hitting home, even here in Beertown." And while some people complained of hearing so much about AIDS, Lisowski said, "My God, I don't think that we have heard enough about AIDS yet." He believed people were still rationalizing their risky sexual behavior as if "AIDS is happening on another planet." He argued, "AIDS is not just a sexual disease: it is also a political and social disease," noting that BWMT had taken the lead nationally to stress the ways in which people of color with AIDS were being neglected. Rather than encouraging gay men to ignore the epidemic and dance the night away, he pleaded, "How long do we crave for Gucci and Calvin before we care for David and Stephen?"[73]

In December 1987, Todd Butler of Milwaukee was featured in the gay magazine *In Step*, providing an "insider's view" of the AIDS experience. It had been three years since his diagnosis. "Everyone I had dealt with in the field of AIDS had told me of the need for confidentiality," he explained, realizing that secrecy was meant to make life easier for him. But then, he said, "Suddenly—something dawned on me. Why am I trying to keep this illness a secret? I had a long fight coming out of the closet, and I wasn't about to climb back into one—especially not a closet with the word AIDS marked on the door." So, two years before the interview, he had gone public. "If they were to see that this illness had hit Milwaukee through someone they knew," he reasoned, "then just maybe people would begin to practice safer sex." Butler eventually participated in a *Milwaukee Journal* series and let the paper print his real name. He reported that 95 percent of the mail and comments he received had been positive and supportive. He closed the personal column in *In Step* by wishing readers a Merry Christmas and thanking them for "the help of a positive and supportive community."[74]

At Milwaukee's 1989 Pride Rally, Trzebiatowski, a Milwaukee ACT-UP founder, gave a speech that was later reprinted in *The Wisconsin Light*. "Nine years into the AIDS epidemic," he said, "we still find ourselves fighting for our civil rights and our lives." He observed that sixty thousand deaths had occurred nationally, with three hundred and counting in Wisconsin. He drew particular attention to "the federal government's lack of awareness, acceptance, response and support to combat the AIDS crisis." Waiting for the majority to act, he believed, had only brought homosexuals "closer to death and extinction." Thus, he made the heart-tugging plea: "Haven't we waited long enough? Haven't we lost enough loved ones and friends to AIDS and AIDS complications? . . . We need to start voicing our rights as citizens of the U.S. We have this right. And this right is the only tool we can use to combat the homo/AIDS-a-phobes." The speech was a prelude to the release of three hundred white balloons, which represented the Wisconsin AIDS deaths. As the balloons floated into the sky, Trzebia-towski quoted a poem that Major Michael Davis had penned over the loss of fallen comrades in Vietnam, including the lines, "Take what they have taught you with their dying and keep it with your own."[75]

THE STATE MOBILIZES FOR FAIR TREATMENT

No community is prepared for an epidemic. Yet Wisconsin possessed resources that were quickly mobilized when the state entered the battle against AIDS in the early 1980s. The professionals who staffed the urban STD clinics in Milwaukee and Madison gave early warnings and provided quick health information to those cities' gay communities. They would go on to promote effective AIDS testing and provide epidemiological data as the disease came to be better understood.

The state's nondiscrimination law on sexual orientation, still the only one in the country in the 1980s, provided many with the hope that discrimination over AIDS might be avoided. The *Milwaukee Journal* edi-torialized, "Now that Wisconsin's first death due to AIDS disease has been confirmed, so has Gov. Earl's wisdom in creating the state's Council on Lesbian and Gay Issues." The gay-friendly Earl administration contributed to efforts by enlisting contacts to mobilize the State Medical Society. Legal confidentiality over testing was another early victory achieved thanks to the gay political advocacy that had previously cohered around consenting adults and gay rights legislation in the state. The efforts of these activ-ists would culminate in the Wisconsin AIDS Bill of Rights in 1990. Both the Wisconsin Equal Rights Division disability ruling, which drew on the state's AIDS confidentiality law, and the Second District Court of Appeals ruling overturning the Racine School Board policy showed that the legal structure of the state would bend to justice. This, of course, did not stop the homophobic panic—especially around schools, prisons, and jails—that accompanied the arrival of AIDS in Wisconsin.[76]

Some people remained optimistic that the state's geographic location would help it evade the epidemic. In 1987, Wisconsin ranked 30th among the states in reported AIDS cases, and Milwaukee ranked 118th among US cities—both well below their comparable population positions. By the time

AIDS Walk Wisconsin, held annually in Milwaukee, was a major fundraiser in the community's efforts to combat the disease and support those impacted by it. ARCHIVES DEPARTMENT, UNIVERSITY OF WISCONSIN– MILWAUKEE LIBRARIES

public health efforts began ramping up, it was known that AIDS came from a virus, and the most likely modes of transmission had been identified. "We know all these things give us an edge that San Francisco didn't have, that New York didn't have," said Sue Dietz of MAP. Most Wisconsin patients who tested for the antibodies reported to the Division of Health that "they have changed sexual practices due to concern about AIDS." In 1990, on a Milwaukee City Cable program, Doug Nelson described the Milwaukee HIV/AIDS situation as less critical than that of the major coastal cities. Paul Nannis, Milwaukee Commissioner of Health for the city, agreed that because of the cooperation of many local organizations, Milwaukee was "ahead of the game" in its AIDS response. Nevertheless, the State Bureau of Community Health was still alarmed by the situation.[77]

Sadly, even well-mobilized resources were no match for the virus. Here, as elsewhere, AIDS service organizations grew out of the gay community's dire need. Increasing needs became a clarion call for a community to mobilize even more resources. Since most of the medical treatment establishments were private companies, advocacy for persons with AIDS was needed. Even with a responsive state government, people with AIDS in Wisconsin needed an organization like ACT-UP. Yet, the Wisconsin response employed more of gay historian John D'Emilio's strategy of "thinking our way" through the crisis than the anger used as motivation by writer Larry Kramer.[78]

Trends in Wisconsin ultimately matched national ones as increasing numbers of women and children acquired the virus. World AIDS Day in 1990 focused on women and AIDS, and Wisconsin groups joined in the effort. Likewise, communities of color would be hard hit. Michael Doylen, head of archives at UW–Milwaukee, which acquired ARCW records, wanted the documents. "The story of how [AIDS] unfolded in the Midwest is really different from the coasts," he said. The number of new infections per year would peak in 1990 with 593 that year. In 2013, Wisconsin, with an HIV diagnosis rate of 4.6 per 100,000, ranked fourteenth from the bottom on the list of states. In 2017, ARCW reported that people with HIV were living longer and Wisconsin had "the lowest HIV mortality rate in America." That was the better news, yet for the period between 2010 and 2014, 422 Wisconsinites with HIV died.[79]

Milwaukee's Dr. Roger Gremminger described AIDS as the Great Moral Debate because it stirred up so much controversy, or as Gremminger said, "because AIDS forced society to deal with some very uncomfortable issues—homosexuality, sexual behaviors, IV drug use, death." Yet, some credit should go to Wisconsin's citizens and its gay community as the state avoided early indifference from its officials and spared many citizens from the worst indignities of the disease. The generally compassionate and medically rational Midwestern approach enabled Wisconsin's gay and lesbian community to leverage scant resources into substantial financial developments, thus cooperating with others to build a caring response.[80]

10

THE FLOWERING OF LGBT WISCONSIN

The only way we can survive is to share each other's ideas and support one another.
—UNITY OF WEST CENTRAL WISCONSIN, EAU CLAIRE[1]

Hiding ourselves from ourselves does no one any good, I know.
—BRIAN SALCHERT, *FOND DU LAC REPORTER*, MAY 21, 1973[2]

The 1983 fact-finding report on the state of the LGBT community in Wisconsin, presented to Governor Anthony Earl by Kathleen Nichols and me, listed only a few flourishing gay communities. However, the passage of the gay rights law and the other good acts (see chapters 6 and 7) unleashed gay community activism across the state. By banding together, gay men and lesbians found mutual support. With legal protections and growing social acceptance, many in the LGBT community felt more comfortable raising their voices. The state's political climate became a unifying force for this minority developing its identity. As the gay community of UW–Stout in Menomonie, Wisconsin, put it in their official slogan, "We've Been Here All Along." This chapter explores the geographic scope of this flowering, while the next focuses on institution building by the Wisconsin LGBT community.[3]

ON THE SUPERIOR SHORE

In 1983, Robert "Bob" John Jansen opened the Main Club, the first gay bar in the Twin Ports area. It remained open for more than thirty-four years, closing in 2017. Jansen has been described as "a trailblazer and pioneer to the LGBT community in the Twin Ports," as well as a "longtime, well-meaning, rabble rouser." Yet, he also faced opposition from local government; when he took over Al's Waterfront Bar in Superior, the city made it difficult for him to secure the original liquor license, and he reached out for the assistance of a gay-friendly attorney from Madison.[4]

The original Jansen bar on Third Street in Superior was destroyed by fire on December 27, 1996. *The Wisconsin Light* reported in its January 2, 1997, edition that the small, close-knit Twin Ports gay community was devastated; one patron said, "I've lost my home." However, the fire department concluded that there was "no reason to suspect arson in this fire." Six months later, Jansen reopened the Main Club on Tower Avenue. The bar hosted drag shows, benefits for people suffering with AIDS, and the Miss Gay Northern Wisconsin pageant. In addition, it served as the outpost for the Northern Wisconsin and Northern Minnesota leather community.

Bob Jansen, standing in the leather tuxedo surrounded by staff at his Main Club, was the leader of Superior's gay community for nearly four decades. KATHRYN A. MARTIN LIBRARY, UNIVERSITY OF MINNESOTA–DULUTH

Jansen was a cofounder of the North Star Gay Rodeo Association, and because the gay rodeo world often overlapped with the leather world, Jansen established a "Leather/Levi Night" at the bar. His signature leather vest with the North Star logo is presented in the online exhibit Wearing Gay History. The Main Club, like some other bars, also screened gay porn films. When some (mainly straight) patrons complained, Jansen responded, "It is our space."[5]

Superior could be a dangerous place for gay people in the 1980s and 1990s. On July 16, 1984, Earl Greely, an Ojibwe man born in Superior, was found beaten to death near the Superior railyards. Greely was a gay poet who had been living in Madison but had recently returned home. Charles Davis, the man charged in Greely's murder, claimed that he was acting in self-defense from Greely's homosexual advances. The OutReach LGBT Library in Madison is dedicated to Greely's memory. Some years later, in 1991, twenty-seven-year-old Kevin E. Dutcher was stabbed to death in the kitchen of his Superior home. The accused killer, Stuart Ellanson, was quoted in the criminal complaint of the Douglas County district attorney's office as saying, "I wanted to kill this fag. My whole life is devoted to killing faggots." In response to this case, Iver Borg, a professor of psychology at the University of Minnesota–Duluth, noted, "There's this tacit support for this violent thinking, for this violence that occurs." In 2017, Jansen reflected, "We still get yelled at today about fag, queer, those kinds of things, but you just kind of let that roll off." He also proclaimed, "The great thing about gay bars is that straight people are always welcome."[6]

In addition to physical violence, the Superior community had to face the AIDS crisis during this era. Jansen recalls, "It was a frightening time for a lot of people." His attempts to make condoms available in the Main Club and other bars were at times rebuffed. The initial AIDS service organization for the northern counties of Douglas, Ashland, Iron, Bayfield, and Sawyer was the Douglas County Health Department. Its efforts for gay men were centered in Superior and Washburn. It held a Safer Sex night with a condom buffet at the Main Club, and it also coordinated events with the Trio Bar, a Superior lesbian bar, especially during the hiatus of the Main Club after its fire. In the early years, the health department conducted some 169 face-to-face encounters with gay people in the region. It also established a buddy program and client advocacy efforts for those with AIDS.[7]

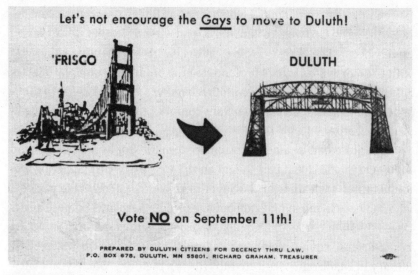

Let's not encourage the <u>Gays</u> to move to Duluth!

'FRISCO   DULUTH

Vote <u>NO</u> on September 11th!

PREPARED BY DULUTH CITIZENS FOR DECENCY THRU LAW.
P.O. BOX 678, DULUTH, MN 55801, RICHARD GRAHAM, TREASURER

Visibility of gays in the Twin Ports of Superior and Duluth sparked a reaction and fear that more gays would move to the area, as demonstrated by this postcard. FROM THE AUTHOR'S COLLECTION

While the Main Club was located in Superior, where liquor laws were more lenient than in Minnesota, Jansen lived in the other Twin Port of Duluth, Minnesota. He refers to himself as "bistatel," presumably a play on *bisexual*. *Land of 10,000 Loves: A History of Queer Minnesota*, a book on the history of gay Minnesota by Stewart Van Cleve, broke its geographic rule to include Jansen's Main Club of Superior in its pages. Even more recognition was given to Jansen when Superior-raised filmmaker Julie Casper Roth created a documentary film about him and the Main Club. Screenings took place in February 2013 in the Twin Ports and later at the OUT Twin Cities Film Festival. Roth believed, "The relevance and the history of trailblazing establishments like Main risk being forgotten as GLBT groups celebrate greater social acceptance, and gay spaces are no longer clearly defined." She credited Jansen with changing "the fabric of our community in far-reaching and meaningful ways."[8]

Up the shore from the Twin Ports in Ashland, Wisconsin, Out Up North (OUN), a gay and lesbian resource and referral organization, was established in the 1990s with a Washburn mailing address. For gay people in this part of the state, a night out on the town meant going to Superior for a drag show or to the bars. The community was so small that OUN regularly printed one hundred copies of its newsletter. The organization focused on how northland gays connected through bars, organizations, friends, and travel to the cities. It ran a helpline and hosted socials, including beach parties and hikes in the woods. OUN also held a Monday Coffee Clutch at the Black Cat Coffee House in Ashland, and newcomers were told to look for the rainbow tablecloth.[9]

A sparkplug and contributor to and editor of the newsletter (also named *Out Up North*) was Dee Tritus, likely a nom de plume. In a newsletter column As Queer As I Wanna Be, Dee, a transplant from the Twin Cities, described a typical burden that lesbians and gay men bear when defined primarily by their sexual orientation. She explained that she was not a hard-core dyke; she stated, "When someone 'outs' me they take away my right of getting to know others in the manner that I see fit." She wanted perhaps to be known as a conversationalist with interesting views on art. Yet, she also acknowledged the "comfort of the unconditional acceptance of other gays and lesbians." In one newsletter, she sent a big thank you and congratulations to Jamie Nabozny "for his persistence and fortitude in the suit brought against three Ashland school district employees" over their non-support of gay and lesbian students.[10]

The *Out Up North* newsletter promoted pride events in Milwaukee, Minneapolis, and Duluth. In May 1997, it took a stand against ads for change ministries and conversion therapy targeting gays in the local paper. The editor denounced these as "fear-based, shame-based and based on self-hatred." Also in 1997, *Out Up North* reported that two lesbian students at Northland College in Ashland took the lead in proposing a new housing choice, Safehaven, for non-heterosexual students. A Drag Dance held to support the effort drew 250 students out of a student body of 900. The Northland Alliance for gays on campus held periodic social events. A gay-friendly book club also existed in Ashland.[11]

FARM FOLKS AND RURAL QUEERS

Though gay men and lesbians in Wisconsin's rural areas often felt more isolated than their urban counterparts, many felt a distinct pride in their ability to live and thrive in the country. One contributor to *Out Up North* in Ashland, who wrote under the name Spike, published an article called

"Pride from a Rural Perspective" in 1997. After opening with a description of attending the Minneapolis pride celebration, Spike affirmed, "Living here in the northland I can say I am proud to be a part of Out Up North." He felt the experience of rural gays "doesn't exactly compare to the goings on found in the cities." Yet, Spike proclaimed, "I possessed an internal pride that people in the cities did not share on the same level." He believed gay people living in rural areas faced more obstacles and hurdles. "Pride for me," he wrote, "is knowing I have gotten over and around many of those hurdles and obstacles, and I am stronger now for it. Pride for me is knowing I have found courage to come out in a rural area where there are only a handful of others who are out." Spike loved living in what he called one of the most beautiful places in the country. He also loved that he possessed "the inner strength and courage to be who I am in an area where there are practically no signs that it is okay."[12]

The true chronicler of gay people in rural Wisconsin is Will Fellows, who wrote *Farm Boys: Lives of Gay Men from the Rural Midwest*, published in 1996 by the University of Wisconsin Press. Fellows grew up on a farm near Evansville in Rock County, Wisconsin. For the book, he conducted autobiographical interviews with seventy-five gay men with rural roots from Midwestern states. His largest sample by far (nineteen men) was from Wisconsin. Fellows believed the lives of gay men "rooted in farm-centered childhoods" had been a "neglected part of U.S. gay culture." One of his hopes for the book was that it would be "helpful to boys and men who are living in rural households and feeling isolated as they deal with issues related to their sexual orientation." *Farm Boys* was edited by Raphael Kadushin, who curated a distinguished and unparalleled line of gay books at the University of Wisconsin Press. Kadushin observed that the stories in *Farm Boys* are "funny and filled with adventure and sex. Growing up gay on a farm . . . wasn't necessarily a celibate youth." The significance of Fellows's pioneering work was underlined when the folks behind the movie *Brokeback Mountain* provided *Farm Boys* to the actors to help them understand rural gay men.[13]

One man who was featured in Fellows's book, Richard Kilmer, was a farm boy from Juneau County who knew he was different. Sexually active at an early age, he remembers confessing to an unsympathetic priest that he had messed around with other rural boys in the barns and woods around his home. As a young man, Kilmer took a cross-continental bike trip to sort out his identity. When he wound up at the Vancouver Gay Center, he took some advice to travel south to the gay mecca of San Francisco, but he was overwhelmed by the urban gay scene there. Kilmer returned to Wisconsin, came out to his parents, bought his aunt and uncle's farm, and converted the chicken coop into a cabin for his dwelling. After becoming a rural landowner, he still maintained ties to Madison, and he had a child with lesbians. Kilmer was a pharmacist by profession, and the AIDS crisis converted him into an activist with Madison AIDS Support Network. As a result of his television interviews about AIDS, Kilmer was nearly fired from his job at a Sauk County health facility for being gay, due to the efforts of a member of the facility's board. The director, who did not want to lose a good pharmacist, had to explain to the board that such a firing would be illegal in Wisconsin. Kilmer's Vernon County farm was the site of gay dances; usually attendees came from farther afield, as local gays hesitated to be identified with such a public activity. Much later in his life, Kilmer became active with the Dairyland Cowboys—a line-dancing gay group with a rural tinge. Presently, his farm has extensive gardens, and he has held very popular plant sales under the business name The Plant Guys.[14]

Todd Larson in rural Green County was another notable gay man from rural Wisconsin, though he embraced his rural and gay identities later than some others who were born on farms. During his high school years, Larson's parents bought what has since become known as Larson Farm, a rural retreat established on the site of a farm that dates back to 1854. He spent summers and weekends in the country and eventually bought and made the farm his own domicile. As a youth, he gained experience haying, handling livestock, working in area cheese factories, and serving as a lifeguard in small-town community swimming pools in New Glarus and Blanchardville. He sensed an aspect of "otherness" in himself but delayed sorting it out. Yet there were some figures in the New Glarus area with whom he sensed a kinship due to their world travels and eccentric natures, such as Edwin Barlow, a founder of the local Wilhelm Tell pageant, and writer Herb Kubly. Having performed as a boy in the Tell pageant, Larson later became an advocate for preserving Swiss culture in the area. He also performed in many other theatrical groups, taking a lead role in several plays. After college, he began his world travels with a stint in the Peace

Corps. Following law school and graduate school, his career working for the United Nations took him to many global hot spots. Larson's partner, who was also involved in international work, was assassinated. During his later career, Larson helped articulate the need for the United Nations to respect the LGBT relationships of its employees. He eventually served three years in the Obama administration, implementing its directive that LGBT rights be part of the United States' global human rights efforts in foreign policy. The farm remains his principal residence.[15]

Of course, in addition to gay men, lesbians also lived and flourished in rural Wisconsin. The Rural Dykes Association in south central Wisconsin was founded in the mid-1990s, hosting gatherings and monthly social events at locations ranging from Hillsboro to Cottage Grove and from Black Earth to Prairie du Sac. They even met in Madison, as urban lesbians were also welcome. Vegetarian potlucks were a popular activity within the association, as were dances, such as the Fall Frolic and Barn Dance, and game nights, including one advertised as "Games, Gossip & Goodies."[16]

Lesbians and gay men living in the rural area along Wisconsin's western border felt the influence of the Twin Cities, according to Stewart Van Cleve, author of *Land of 10,000 Loves*. In Maiden Rock, Wisconsin, a village of two

Todd Larson grew up on a farm near New Glarus and later worked for the United Nations and as an advisor to the White House on international LGBT policies. In this 2015 photo, he poses with President Barack Obama. PHOTO BY PETE SOUZA, COURTESY OF. TODD LARSON

hundred people in Pierce County on the Mississippi, UW–Madison professor Claudia Card pursued feminist topics for her lesbian studies courses at the Minnesota-fueled experimental Women's Learning Institute of the Maiden Rock Collective. Minneapolis was also a major center of American Indian activism; the first two-spirit gathering in the nation, called The Basket and the Bowl, was held there in June 1988 and in Wisconsin the following year. Also in Minneapolis, which is a center of Hmong migration to the United States, an organization called Shades of Yellow formed in 2003, attracting LGBT Hmong people from across the upper Midwest.[17]

For gay men who felt isolated in the era before the Internet, the mail provided a way to connect with others, from war correspondence to the personals published in body magazines to the letters written to *ONE* magazine in the 1950s and 1960s. This method of communicating by mail would continue even after Stonewall. *New Beginnings for Family and Friends*, a magazine published for five years out of rural Westby, Wisconsin, contained hundreds of gay pen pal contacts. The publication listed writing groups from around the globe, such as Gay Mates in Canada, New Pen Friends in Norway, Worldwide Friendship Club in South Africa, Pen Friends in Australia, and the Loving Brotherhood located in Sussex, New Jersey. During the period from late 1987 to 1991, nearly a dozen Wisconsin men sought pen pals through its pages by having their names and addresses published; some of the men lived in cities, but others were from small places such as Neshkoro, Lancaster, and Wisconsin Rapids. One personal ad from Fall Creek, Wisconsin, a village of a thousand in Eau Claire County, was written by a man who self-identified as a "blue collar rural dude 5' 9" not into bars." A different letter to the editor of a gay newsletter complained, "I live in an area of Wisconsin that is so small I'm the only gay person for miles. It's hard to meet people here." While gay folks living in rural areas across the state may have experienced a greater sense of isolation than their urban compatriots did, these stories demonstrate that they nevertheless found ways to affirm their identities and express pride.[18]

GAY GROUPS IN THE NORTHWOODS

Around the woods, fields, and small towns of Wisconsin in the 1980s and 1990s, there were many signs of gay life. A group calling itself the Northwoods Radical Faeries held celebrations for the "Beauty of Mother Earth" at an isolated spot in the woods at the headwaters of the St. Croix River near Gordon, Wisconsin, in 1988 and 1989. At these celebrations, gay men participated in heart circles, nature walks, Taoist erotic massage, poetry, and face painting. According to a group member, the strategy behind using the term *faeries* was "that when we take the very words that others hurl at us in [a] derogatory sense and we make them positive statements about ourselves they lose their sting." For the 1988 gathering, one attraction was the presence of the Radical Faeries' cofounders Harry Hay and John Burnside from California. Attendees from Spooner, Black River Falls, and Mineral Point traveled to the gathering of a hundred in 1988.[19]

South of Gordon in Ladysmith, Wisconsin, two life partners created a unique space for modern dance called Chalice Stream. Barry Lynn, who was originally from North Carolina and had spent his career as a professional dancer in Salt Lake City, moved with his partner, Michael Doran, to Rusk County in 1978. They had met when Lynn performed at a dance workshop for Mount Senario College in Ladysmith and Doran joined Lynn's Utah troupe. The men chose the name Chalice Stream for their home and dance studio in order to "represent man's fashioning of a cup worthy to hold his most precious spiritual values, as we here try to fashion in dance and in life." Doran inherited the eighty-acre wooded site with two

Michael Doran, a Wisconsin native from the area near Ladysmith, established Chalice Stream, a center for expressive dance in northern Wisconsin, with his partner, Barry Lynn, in 1978. The Eau Claire Regional Arts Council recognized them for Outstanding Achievement in Artistic Discipline. PHOTO BY NORMAN REGNIER, COURTESY OF MICHAEL DORAN

Barry Lynn, unlike many modern dance companies of his time, favored abstract gestures and generous use of fabrics as part of his expressive movement. He is pictured here dancing at age ninety-seven in 2011. PHOTO BY MICHAEL HLADILEK, COURTESY OF MICHAEL DORAN

streams running through it from his grandparents. He and Lynn lived in the bell tower of an old school house and used the building's main space as a studio and for performances. According to Doran, Lynn's approach to dance was to bring out its "ritualistic/sacred aspect." This unique style of dance also incorporated the generous use of fabrics. Doran's "body-centric" movements also became part of his theater and teaching work in area schools. The Eau Claire Regional Arts Council recognized their work with an Outstanding Achievement award. Lynn and Doran spent forty years together at Chalice Stream before Lynn died in 2018 at age 103.[20]

In 1983, gay organizing began to occur in another northern Wisconsin town with the establishment of the Rhinelander-Northwoods Gay/ Lesbian Rap group. Founded by the mother of three recent male high school graduates, the initial group consisted of ten members including three from Nicolet College. In an early interview with the *Rhinelander New Times*, members "expressed relief upon abandoning their 'closets' and shedding the mask[s] they once presented to themselves, their families, and society." Though one local tavern was described as having permitted harassing behavior, the article stated that "the management has been notified that a lawsuit under Wisconsin's Gay Rights law will be pursued if the harassment continues." Several members of the group expressed

concerns over being harassed; however, one stated, "I refuse to be intimidated." Another student added, "Being gay in the Northwoods isn't as bad
as one might think." By 1990, area gays had reorganized as the Northern
Wisconsin Lambda Society. With a mailing address in Woodruff, the group
promised all potential members that "any information exchanged will be
strictly confidential, an absolute necessity due to redneck homophobia."
The society hoped to provide a social outlet and informational center to
gay men and lesbians in northern Wisconsin. Knowing the importance of
tourism in Rhinelander, the group also offered to provide information on
recreational resources to any visitors to the area.[21]

ON THE SHORES OF THE BAY

Green Bay had an active gay bar scene for decades, beginning in the 1950s
well before Stonewall (see volume one, *We've Been Here All Along*). One of
the oldest gay bars, operating since 1983, is the Napalese Lounge, originally
located on South Broadway and now on Cedar Street, still functioning after
more than three decades. The Green Bay–based Argonauts Leather Club,
described in more detail in the next chapter, dates back to 1974.

Beyond these social sites, a more organized lesbian and gay community
began to emerge in Green Bay in the 1990s. Founded in the summer of
1992 in a private home on Adams Street, Positive Voice was a membership
organization that would prove to be long lasting. Other area organizations merged into it in the late 1990s, and Positive Voice continued into
the twenty-first century. It was a good place for networking and social interaction, with some meetings drawing up to thirty members. In 1995, the
group reported a total of seventy-one paid members. The organization's
mission statement affirmed, "We must work together as a unified group
to create a positive atmosphere that allows us to share our viewpoints and
feelings to grow, and to gain a greater sense of fulfillment in our lives."
In 1995, Positive Voice sponsored northeast Wisconsin's first-ever gay,
lesbian, and bisexual pride picnic at a pavilion along the Baird Creek Parkway. Folks from nine area bars, the Ten Percent Society of the University
of Wisconsin–Green Bay, Northern Womyn Ink., and the Bay City Chorus
all joined the members of Positive Voice in participating.[22]

For several years, Positive Voice also held Day of Discovery conferences on gay and lesbian political, health, and relationship issues with

Positive Voice
PRESENTS

Brown County Sheriff

MICHAEL DONART

Green Bay Chief of Police

JAMES LEWIS

IN DIALOGUE WITH
THE GAY COMMUNITY

LESBIANS, GAYS & LAW ENFORCEMENT

Monday, October 21
Brown County Central Library
515 Pine Street
Green Bay, Wisconsin
6:30 PM

Refreshment served following the meeting

You are cordially invited to attend!

In fighting homophobia, lesbians and gays sought to encourage positive interactions with law enforcement, here specifically with the Brown County sheriff and the Green Bay chief of police. COURTESY OF RAINBOW OVER WISCONSIN

speakers including State Representative Tammy Baldwin and Scott Evertz, who was affiliated with the Log Cabin Republicans, an organization for gay Republicans. Positive Voice worked with other supportive politicians such as Congressman Steve Kagan, Brown County Executive Nancy Nussbaum, Green Bay Mayor Paul Jadin, and State Senator Dave Hansen. Over the years, Positive Voice membership meetings featured both the Brown County Sheriff and the Green Bay police chief on law enforcement issues. The group also worked to create a gay/lesbian guide to northeast Wisconsin with Lloyd Schaefer and Paul "Cricket" Jacob spearheading the effort. The two men would later take up the Northeast Wisconsin LGBT History Project. Schaefer, a pharmacist and an accompanist at Angels of Hope

Metropolitan Community Church, would later serve in many capacities within Positive Voice, including as president of the organization. In one of his letters from the president, he asserted that the payoff for those volunteering with Positive Voice would be the knowledge that they had served "the GBLT community in a small part in making it a richer environment in which to live, work and play."[23]

The organization published a newsletter called *Positive Voice*, with the redoubtable Mike Fitzpatrick serving as editor for several years. He would write about Green Bay as "the land of cheesehead hats and right-wing wacko writers of letters to the editor." Later Fitzpatrick would be described as "one of Wisconsin's 'shake and bake' activists helping [to] get several LGBT institutions up and running." The newsletter under his editorship downsized to become a smaller, "handy, tavern-friendly size," though subscriptions were also available outside the bars. Fitzpatrick served as the Positive Voice contact in the area and subsequently as the president of Action Wisconsin, the statewide gay lobby, which was later renamed Fair Wisconsin. Along the way, he helped to found Rainbow Over Wisconsin, northeast Wisconsin's LGBT foundation. In 1995, he received a Stonewall Leadership Award from Milwaukee's Pridefest. Fitzpatrick is perhaps best remembered for his AIDS work with the CENTER Project. "I tell people AIDS chose me," he said, as the people he loved were dying. "I did this because no one else would."[24]

Another early and longtime activist in northeast Wisconsin was Paul Jacob. By 1981, Jacob had settled in the Green Bay area, and in 1986, he opened his own gay bar, the Pivot Club, in Menasha as a large dance club. As AIDS made its way into northeast Wisconsin, Jacob joined others in establishing the CENTER Project: The Community Endeavor for Needs in Testing, Education, and Referral. After starting as a volunteer, he eventually

Mike Fitzpatrick, describing himself as a "shake and bake" activist, helped launch numerous LGBT efforts in northeast Wisconsin as the editor of *Positive Voice* and a founder of Rainbow Over Wisconsin, among other roles. COURTESY OF MARK MARIUCCI

While a student at UW–Oshkosh in the late 1970s, Paul Jacob joined the Gay Student Association on campus. He would go on to be involved with Fox Valley bars and then with AIDS work. COURTESY OF MARK MARIUCCI

became part of the staff and served the project for more than twenty-six years. His years in the bar business gave him many valuable contacts for setting up testing facilities and peddling safe-sex goods. He cofounded the group Entertainers Against AIDS, which produced many shows for AIDS awareness and also published the *Urinal Gazette and Tinkle Tribune*, an effective communication device about AIDS that was disseminated in men's rooms in gay bars.[25]

In addition to the *Positive Voice* newsletter, another local gay publication, *Quest*, was founded in 1994 by Mark Mariucci, a freelance professional photographer in Green Bay. The magazine started as a calendar and bar directory with advertising, and it was published with the original subheading "a Wisconsin Gay Entertainment Guide." In 2003, *Quest* expanded to include news and feature articles when other gay media, such as *In Step*, ceased publication. Until it ceased publication in 2019, *Quest* was distributed statewide through bars and businesses focused on the gay community. One of its highlights was coverage of the drag and show scene around the state.[26]

In 1996, Green Bay area activists played a key role in delaying the antigay marriage forces in the state. That February, Dean Kaufert, a moderate Republican representative from Neenah, issued a press release about plans to introduce state legislation against gay marriage. Kaufert had been talked into sponsoring the legislation by two Neenah businessmen, one the head of Promise Keepers, a Christian men's group. Since many members of gay organizations lived in Kaufert's district, gay organizers sprang into action. One such organizer was John Jacob, a gay bar manager with a mailing list of about a thousand, 35 percent of whom, he estimated, lived in Kaufert's district. The Gay/Lesbian Education & Economic Development Association (GLEEDA) based in Appleton; Parents, Families and Friends of Lesbians and Gays (PFLAG); and Appleton's gay bar staff were all enlisted in the campaign. Their targeted calls went to Kaufert's Madison and district offices. Additionally, when Kaufert went on a Wisconsin Public Radio morning call-in show, a staggering number of the calls came in against the possible bill. Finally, Kaufert backed off sponsoring the legislation when the state's Log Cabin Republicans added their voices to the opposition. In the end, the religious right denounced Kaufert's cowardice.[27]

Another tale of Green Bay gays pushing back against and poking fun at antigay efforts was recounted in *Positive Voice*'s March 1996 issue: "'Deep Throat' Reports: I Infiltrated the Christian Coalition." A number of "queers" had infiltrated a meeting of the Brown County Christian Coalition, and *Positive Voice* was delighted to run the "wickedly observant" piece. A staff writer posing as Deep Throat expressed disappointment with the meeting, as he said: "[I'm] expecting hell fire and I'm getting charcoal briquettes." Green Bay Councilman Guy Zima, who made problems for the local AIDS effort, was one politician spotted at the meeting. The local chair was a woman named Barbara Klika. Green Bay Congressman Toby Roth appeared in a national Christian Coalition "slicker than snot recruitment video" that was shown. Deep Throat contrasted the "carefully tooled craftsmanship from the national office and glitter school project quality of the local leadership." Of Klika he wrote, "She could be a den mother; heck she could be MY mother."[28]

On November 20, 1995, thirty Positive Voice members heard five transgender individuals from Green Bay, Fond du Lac, and Milwaukee discuss the many issues they faced. Topics ranged from hormonal therapy to gender reassignment surgery, with participants discussing their individual journeys. Significantly, all four LGBT initials were being used for some gay events in Green Bay and the Fox Valley during this period in the mid- to late 1990s. Later, a Fox Valley transgender group was established.[29]

Campuses in the Green Bay area were active sites for gay programming. At UW–Green Bay in May 1995, five hundred people showed up for a lecture by gay minister and author Mel White with introductory remarks by the campus Ten Percent Society. An area Lutheran evangelical youth group held a prayer service outside the lecture in protest. The college Republicans also circulated flyers condemning the talk. In April 1996, the university celebrated Pride Week on campus with the theme Reclaiming Our History. Later, a Sexuality and Gender Alliance was established at the school. Much later, in 2015, the website College Choice would rank the Green Bay cam-

pus among the top 50 LGBT friendly campuses in the nation. In addition
to UW–Green Bay, St. Norbert College, a Catholic liberal arts college just
south of Green Bay in De Pere, held the CENTER Project's Have a Heart
fundraising dinner for AIDS. For a while, the school also was supportive
of Dignity Northeast Wisconsin, a gay group for Roman Catholics.[30]

A variety of gay and lesbian support and social groups were also
launched in Green Bay in the 1980s and 1990s. The city was home to a chapter of PFLAG as well as to Horizons, a "Lesbigay" teen support group for
the Appleton and Green Bay areas. *Lumber Jane*, described as a "feminist
northern womyn's reader" was published in the mid-1990s out of Green
Bay. The premier issue contained twenty pages of poetry, artwork, and
commentary. An organization called Northern Womyn Ink. was formed
in 1990 by thirty-five area women; it was the brainchild of Barbara Bonini,
who ran the Two Women Café, a popular lesbian space in Green Bay. A
reading group for both men and women called Lavender Salon formed in
1993, with Michael Nitz acting as its primary contact. In 1992, Ted LaPine

Northern Womyn Ink. showed that lesbians in northeast Wisconsin could be organized,
supportive of lesbian parenthood, and literary. COURTESY OF RAINBOW OVER WISCONSIN

and Bob Jarvey founded the Dinettes, a northeast Wisconsin men's gourmet dining group. Menus drawn from food magazines fueled the bimonthly dinner parties. At one event, the host prepared the menu from the last meal served on the *Titanic*. Over the years, the group fluctuated between having thirty and forty members. The Dinettes' last meal was served in 2003.[31]

Green Bay was also home to Angels of Hope Metropolitan Community Church (MCC), which was part of a national denomination founded just before Stonewall specifically for LGBT folks and allies. The church held its first service in 1986 at the Napalese Lounge, a local gay bar, with twenty-eight people attending. Help was provided by the Milwaukee New Hope MCC, and space was borrowed from Green Bay's Union Congregational Church. After some time, meetings moved into a downtown motel space. In 1994, they moved to a storefront site on Forest Street on the east side, a space open to the gay community for meetings of all sorts, where Positive Voice membership meetings were also held. Pastor Ken Hull served Angels of Hope for several years in the 1990s until he was succeeded by Reverend Elaine Thomas. Later, Angels of Hope services were moved to Kaukauna.[32]

Finally, some clubs and social gatherings were established for gay and lesbian citizens in Green Bay during the end of the twentieth century. The Bay City Chorus, which began in 1991 and lasted most of the decade, accepted gay men, lesbians, and all "who are respectful of the gay and lesbian lifestyle" as members. For a period, the group held the NEW (Northeast Wisconsin) Sheepshead Tournament at Appleton and Green Bay, celebrating the card game with central-European origins that is widely played in Wisconsin. Several times, the group performed at St. Norbert College's Hall of Fine Arts. They caroled at nursing homes during the holidays and sang for the gay community's Memorial Day picnic at Baird Creek. The picnic, which has been seen as the first area pride festival, led to the founding of Rainbow Over Wisconsin fundraising group, which has since morphed into a community foundation that continues its work today.[33]

A GREEN BAY MEDIA HEROINE

One of the electronic media heroines of Wisconsin's LGBT community was Eileen Littig, the director of Northeastern Wisconsin In-School Telecommunications (NEWIST), which was part of the Cooperative Educational

Service Agency 7. The educational production group, housed at UW–Green Bay, received awards for its social issues programming. Littig took it as her mission to provide gay and lesbian youth in the schools with media discussing the issues they faced. She was inspired in part by her gay brother, who came out at age twenty-two. "I felt that maybe I didn't understand it as well as I should have," she said, "because no one ever talked about it."[34]

Littig and her staff developed an initial thirty-minute program, *Sexual Orientation: Reading Between the Labels*, with research that included Gilbert Herdt's 1989 book *Gay and Lesbian Youth*. Interviews recorded with leaders at major lesbian and gay youth programs in New York, San Francisco, and Los Angeles were incorporated into the program. Kathryn Jeffers of Iola, Wisconsin, a training consultant for Loyola University who had worked with PFLAG Chicago, was another cited resource. She traveled to Wisconsin and Chicago to provide training for administrators, educators, and counselors with her program about gay youth, *Breaking the Silence about the Invisible Minority*. A brochure promoting the program noted it was designed "to help build respect between individuals of divergent sexual orientation. Ignorance about homosexuality has contributed to a climate of fear, isolation, discrimination and violence toward those perceived as homosexual." Littig believed it was important for the program to provide "a forum for gay and lesbian teens to speak of their concerns," because "the emotional strain of guilt and secrecy robs these youths of energy which could be expended toward development of their full creative and intellectual potential." A teacher's guide supplement was also made available.[35]

Sexual Orientation: Reading Between the Labels aired statewide on instructional television during and after school hours, and it won a gold medal from the Corporation for Public Broadcasting. Warren Gerds, a critic at large for the *Green Bay Press Gazette*, praised the work on this tough topic as "calm, thorough and well made." Gerds said it took courage to make, "but it takes no courage to watch. It's fascinating." Littig, in an interview, said that every time the program aired, she received hundreds of phone calls and letters, most of them negative. "I didn't realize there was so much hate and homophobia," she admitted. Georgia Geise, one of the Wisconsin parents featured in the video who worked in Illinois, was subsequently fired from her job as a home health nurse, which she had held for twelve years. Her son Jed Dietenberger, who also appeared on the show, had horror stories to tell as the only open gay teen in Horicon, Wisconsin. Geise said she was chased around Horicon by a group of teenagers who said they were "going to kill the fag mom so I couldn't make any more fags." Gerds noted, "Littig and others feel homosexual youth are overlooked and suffer too much damage through homophobia." The teen Dietenberger praised Littig, saying she was "doing a fabulous job and I think she's getting the right people on TV."[36]

The NEWIST series *Issues for the '90s* featured a program called *AIDS or Eighty-Something?* The program, produced in 1989, was designed to impress on teens their vulnerability to AIDS, and it was framed as a frank discussion "so teens can decide how they want to live and make those decisions based on facts." This program was also shown on public television around the state. In 1995, Littig created a new program called *Hate, Homophobia and Schools* after being moved by the hateful responses to earlier shows. Teens attending an Upward Bound workshop at UW–Green Bay who were interviewed for the program called gays and lesbians "weird people," with some going as far as saying "they deserve to be shot" and "kill all of them." Littig recounted how one gay teen who had been on the air in one of her earlier programs could not attend the high school in his small home town. He said, "I'm lucky if I make it a few blocks without someone

For teens, their parents and everyone else concerned about young people

Northeastern Wisconsin In-School Telecommunications (NEWIST) produced and distributed early educational materials and classroom TV shows on lesbian and gay issues for teens and concerned adults, as advertised on this promotional brochure. ARCHIVES DEPARTMENT, UNIVERSITY OF WISCONSIN–MILWAUKEE LIBRARIES

screaming something." She wanted *Hate, Homophobia and Schools* to focus on the haters in order to engender tolerance, especially since gay teens were three times more likely to attempt suicide than straight teens at that time.[37]

Early on, Littig introduced a short guide to some gay materials available in northeast Wisconsin for area schools. She noticed that, in 1990, instructional TV in the area had made available *Time to Talk: Homophobia and Sexual Orientation*, a sixty-minute panel program featuring a sociologist from UW–Green Bay, an AIDS educator from Milwaukee, and two high school students. Littig's list of published resources available from NEWIST included Herdt's work as well as Ann Heron's *One Teenager in 10*, Sasha Alyson's *Young, Gay and Proud*, and the memoir written by teenager Aaron Fricke, *Reflections of a Rock Lobster*. By 1993, Littig was providing an eighteen-page list of materials to schools for staff development on gay and lesbian youth. Her efforts were also praised by Green Bay's Northern Womyn Ink. This pioneering, nationally acclaimed work from Green Bay provided resources that enabled classrooms to have thoughtful, informed discussions about homosexuality and homophobia.[38]

DOOR COUNTY, MORE THAN CHERRIES

Before Stonewall, gays and lesbians were living and thriving in Door County. In the 1960s, Maxine Bennett and Martha Peterson built their resort house and ran their antique shop there. The Door County peninsula between Green Bay and Lake Michigan, with its quaint towns, was home to many artists and fine galleries. The area boasted a flourishing summer theater troupe in the Peninsula Players as well as musical performances with the Peninsula Music Festival. In the early twenty-first century, one gay travel writer praised the subtle gay undertones of the Peninsula Players' production *Lumberjacks in Love*. PFLAG Door County, which was founded in 1997, sponsored potluck picnics and raised money for AIDS.[39]

In the late 1980s at Ephraim, Geoff Yeomans and Bruce McKeefry began a landscaping business and added a gardening store that morphed into a shop selling home décor. They initially kept to themselves but eventually became more outgoing as their part of Door County became more gay-friendly with gay condo owners moving in. The two men now live surrounded by forty acres of productive gardens. Since the 1980s, gay residents have settled around the peninsula from Bailey's Harbor to Egg Harbor.[40]

Since 1993, urban gays have found a quieter country life by visiting the Chanticleer gay guest house located on seventy private acres of a working sheep farm near the small city of Sturgeon Bay, the gateway to Door County. The 1915 farmhouse and barn were transformed into bed and breakfast suites by Darrin Day and Bryon Groeschi, known to some as "Door County's gay poster boys." Day and Groeschi met at UW–Madison and both came from farming backgrounds. *The Wisconsin Light* listed other Wisconsin guest houses for gays and lesbians located in Pence in Iron County, Hixton in Jackson County, and Allenton in Washington County. Today, Door County's gay tourism is promoted through an association with the Wisconsin LGBT Chamber of Commerce.[41]

THE FOX VALLEY

LGBT efforts in the Fox Valley began in 1972 with a dinner party in Neenah, which led to the Fox Valley Gay Alliance (FVGA). After a follow-up meeting at the Conway Hotel in Appleton, the organization officially launched with forty to fifty people attending meetings in 1973. Social events were focused around the gay high holidays of Halloween and Mardi Gras. The efforts were spurred by a few prominent activists, including Stan Bracclon, who was a president of the FVGA in the mid-1970s. He also served as editor of *Gay Dialogue*, the alliance's monthly newsletter that appeared in 1977 with a mailing address of Menasha, Wisconsin. During this period, Bracclon acted as the face of the organization doing media appearances on WLUK (broadcast out of Green Bay) and other local radio stations, as well as speaking engagements with organizations including the Unitarian Universalist Fellowship of Appleton. For a while, FVGA ran a helpline also staffed by Bracclon.[42]

In 1973, the *Fond du Lac Reporter* did a two-part series on Fox Valley gays. The writer and the featured gay men remained anonymous. The articles included many quotes from "Simon," the FVGA founder, who had moved to the valley the previous year after being involved with Milwaukee's gay community. Most FVGA members came from Fond du Lac,

Oshkosh, and Appleton. Simon emphasized that they were not a militant group and that most members were under thirty. While no true gay bars existed in the valley at this time, one Appleton bar held one gay night a week. The reporter wrote, "Gays are definitely a minority—but not like minorities as most people tend to identify them. They have no visible differences from the typical person." Simon added, "We are not freaks." Later that year, Brian Salchert of Fond du Lac wrote a letter to the editor stating, "Hiding ourselves from ourselves does no one any good, I know."[43]

The FVGA worked with area libraries to make publicly available "a more expanded and contemporary selection of materials related to the gay theme." The Appleton Public Library agreed to carry *GPU News* among its periodicals. The library director also agreed to purchase more materials "reflecting an honest view of the subjects concerning homosexuality and the gay life-style." Yet, an anonymous "Letter from Fox River Valley" published in the *GPU News* of November 1979 about the cities of Oshkosh, Appleton, and Green Bay stated, "You will have to prove to me that these Wisconsin cities are not inhospitable, intolerant, and outright hostile to gay and bisexual persons. . . . The occasional (perhaps even frequent) anti-gay and Gestapo-like police tactics simply add to the arrogance and bigotry which is already here."[44]

The August 1977 issue of *Gay Dialogue* contained a story on coming out, posing the question, "What is it like to come out in the Fox Valley?" The article described the valley as "an area where the gay community, though certainly not underground, is not nearly as vocal and visible as in the larger metropolitan areas." The piece continued, "Definitely the process is more difficult here, but some have made it through intact." In a further editorial discussion about the FVGA needing more community support, one bar owner said she had tried to be supportive in responding to the call for more funds, but she said, "You must remember that a majority of my customers are not members of the FVGA." This showed the ongoing reality that the subset of LGBT folks who were politically active remained a small minority of the larger community.[45]

A prime focus of the FVGA was to rectify the mainstream public's ignorance about gays and lesbians. Dawn Chase, one of the FVGA's original incorporators on the documents filed with the Register of Deeds in Calumet County, wrote "A Personal Comment" in the March 1977 issue of *Gay*

Dialogue. She pleaded, "We have a job to educate the heterosexual public on homosexuality—to rid them of the myths and their misinformation [and] misguided fears." She also rejected separatism, stating, "We must work together—both men and women in unity." Bracclon echoed her sentiment: "This is exactly what the Fox Valley Gay Alliance is in business for, to change our society so we can all enjoy what life has to offer." With the McCarthy-era red and lavender scares still resonating in Wisconsin, Bracclon wrote, "If we don't want a return to the witch-hunts of the 1950s then we had better get our stuff together."[46]

One month later, *Gay Dialogue* eagerly covered the story when the *Appleton Post-Crescent* came out for the rights of homosexuals, claiming that a "new openness on the matter of homosexuality in American society is probably wholesome." *Gay Dialogue* noted, "While remaining far less than avant-garde in its policy toward gays, the Appleton daily is, at least, willing to openly speak-out on an issue which many public officials and institutions in the Fox Valley are afraid to even think about."[47]

Also in 1977, one of the original incorporators of the FVGA, Gene Kohnke, took over the previous bar that had held one gay night a week

In the 1970s and the 1980s, gay bars were important places for community members to feel safe. As smoking was common at the time, matchbooks were a good way of advertising, even for organizations like the Fox Valley Gay Alliance. COURTESY OF RAINBOW OVER WISCONSIN

since 1973 and made it the first truly gay bar in Appleton. It was given the name Lambda Lounge to "emphasize the idea of gay and proud." Kohnke wanted it to be "part of the gay community." As described by the new institution, the Greek letter *lambda* derives from the pictograph symbol for weighing scales, therefore representing balance and unity. The nature of homosexuals' ongoing struggle for equality also prompted a note that Spartan warriors wore the lambda on their shields. In the 1980s, the bar at 1101 West Wisconsin Avenue became the most popular dance bar in the area. Being the only gay bar in the town, it drew both men and women who shot pool together. In 1983, 1101 West's owner, Andy Leachman, stated, "We're finally starting to get a community that is sticking together for its rights—this is something we've never had before."[48]

By mid-1977, concerned students at Lawrence University, a campus of eleven hundred, formed a Gay Rights Committee "with the hope of increasing gay awareness and addressing specific problems encountered by gay men and women who attend the Lawrence University campus." The group held campus discussions on May 22 and 23 with workshops on emerging scholarship in gay and lesbian studies. Years later, in 1985, a new Gay and Lesbian Alumni group formed. They lobbied for, and the university board of trustees eventually adopted, a policy ensuring "equal opportunity for all." University President Richard Warch said the policy guaranteed "freedom from discrimination based on sexual orientation." A decade later, in May 1995, a Lawrence University Bisexual, Gay, and Lesbian Awareness group was established, holding meetings every Monday. Another group formed a year later: on April 20, 1996, the All Walks of Life Conference at Lawrence featured gay playwright and actor Harvey Fierstein speaking to the campus's Bisexual, Gay, Lesbian and Straight Society.[49]

Other groups popped up around the valley. According to *Positive Voice* in October 1996, there was a Womyn's Potluck & Newsletter. And in 1997, a new Appleton group for teens, the GLBT Partnership, was providing GLBT students between the ages of fourteen and eighteen with "a safe place for support, information sharing, and peer interaction." There was also a PFLAG Appleton/Fox Cities. And the Appleton-based Gay/Lesbian Education & Economic Development Association met monthly. Drag activity continued throughout the area with 1990 seeing the Pivot Club of

Appleton host a pageant for the Miss Gay Great Lakes contest. The winner moved on to the Miss Gay USA Pageant.[50]

The concentration of ongoing efforts in Appleton paid off. In November 2017, one of the regional papers, the *Oshkosh Northwestern*, reported how three cities in northeastern Wisconsin ranked on the Equality Index of the Human Rights Campaign. The headline read, "Appleton Rates High as LGBTQ-Friendly, but Green Bay and Oshkosh Not So Much." Appleton scored 78 out of 100, while the other two scored 40 and 29, respectively. The work during the late 1990s and early 2000s of Appleton's diversity coordinator Kathy Flores was cited. Adding to the city's success in this arena, Vered Meltzer of the Appleton City Council became the state's first openly elected transgender person in 2014. The Fox Valley LGBT community continues to be one of the most active communities in the state, taking up the early work of liberation and forming multiple organizations across the broad spectrum of gay interests.[51]

East Central Wisconsin

Though Oshkosh is situated on the Fox River, the city's gay community developed an identity separate from that of the Fox Valley. Stan Bracclon, a gay rights activist associated with the Fox Valley Gay Alliance, spoke on many occasions, including in an appearance on WOSH-FM's *Zero-In* program on May 2, 1976. Bracclon also cofounded a nascent Gay Student Association at UW–Oshkosh, but due to a large amount of turnover, the group suspended its helpline in May 1977. Still, that same month, the Gay Student Association held its first annual Spring Fling. In 1985, Cher Hanke—the coordinator of the new Lambda Connection in Oshkosh, a group associated with the Women's Resource Center at UW–Oshkosh— felt that "there are a lot of people out there who need the services of a community-minded support and social group."[52]

Before settling in Green Bay, Paul Jacob was another longtime activist in east central Wisconsin. In the late 1970s, while struggling with his sexuality, Jacob transferred from Suomi College in Hancock, Michigan, to UW–Oshkosh because students at Oshkosh could see a psychiatrist free of charge. He remembered barging into the school psychiatrist's office proclaiming, "I'm gay and I don't want to be." Lucky for him, the campus doctor he saw had been involved in the American Psychiatric Association's decision in the early 1970s to discontinue the labeling of homosexuality as a disorder. The doctor advised Jacob, "If you're gay, you're probably not going to change, so you might as well work on accepting it." Jacob went on to join the Gay Student Association on the UW–Oshkosh campus at a time when just two or three people came to meetings. While at college, he tended bar at Appleton's first gay bar and explored gay life.[53]

By 1990, the Ten Percent Society at UW–Oshkosh was publishing the newsletter *ATTENTION*. The newsletter endeavored to provide a creative outlet and an entertaining venue for individuals who are "mad as hell" and "surrounded by meatheads." The editor, Eric J. Reynolds, often wrote about "the oppressive nature of our heterosexist-dominated culture," but he also criticized gays for being spiteful and back-biting. The organization held weekly meetings and sponsored speakers such as Milwaukee's Miriam Ben-Shalom, who visited in 1990. Later in that decade, Sheboygan native Ryan Bemis attended UW–Oshkosh and found the campus to be a good place to come out. While the early gay and lesbian movement gained some traction on the UW–Oshkosh campus, the larger Oshkosh community was less accepting, as evidenced by Dick Flintrop's foster home case (see chapter 8) and later, by national rankings of cities on LGBT issues by the Human Rights Campaign.[54]

Sheboygan on the Lake

The Lakeshore PFLAG group in Sheboygan met monthly in the 1990s at the Wesley Methodist Church. In 1990, the editor of the group's newsletter, which was called the *Lakeshore FLAG*, wrote an article titled "On 'Pretty Good' Parents" about kids who thought their parents were "pretty good" about their homosexuality. The editor, who considered himself a "pretty good" parent, admitted, "PFLAG has made an enormous difference for us." He confessed that it had taken him a long time to come to a meeting, even though his son encouraged him to go. He concluded, "We don't change People, but we can help Parents unload much of the anxiety that lingers even when they are 'Pretty good.'"[55]

A harassment case in Sheboygan mentioned in the November 1990 PFLAG newsletter demonstrated the positive effects of Wisconsin's gay rights law. Jim, a twenty-six-year-old white male, claimed that he was being harassed at his Sheboygan company plant where he had worked for seven years. Rumors had begun circulating that he was gay because his car had been seen parked outside the local gay bar, Sherlock's Home, and now four of his fellow employees would not stop calling out his name in high pitched tones at work. When he reported the incidents to the personnel manager, Jim said his "reports fell on deaf ears." When he contacted the Equal Rights Division in Madison, they told him he could file a complaint because "it was truly illegal to harass people because of their sexual orientation." Probable cause was determined, but the employer declined to seek a solution. When a court hearing was set, the company decided to settle out of court with a monetary payment.[56]

In the article about his case in the Lakeshore PFLAG newsletter, Jim said, "For many years I was told that I could do nothing about this situation, but these people were wrong! STAND UP FOR YOUR RIGHTS IF THIS IS HAPPENING TO YOU!" In the end, he believed he had done something to curb prejudice. The newsletter editor noted that Jim was a "fine young man." Though he himself was not gay, the editor was sometimes mistaken for a gay man and had lost jobs in Iowa where, he said, "the laws do NOT cover similar cases." He noted that harassment, "particularly from bigoted teenage males can be DEVASTATING!"[57]

Other gay community activities in Sheboygan included games of sheepshead, a card game popular in Wisconsin, at the long-lasting Blue Lite Bar, which began running in 1995. And of course, in a town famous for them, brat fries were held to raise money for the northeast Wisconsin gay foundation that later assumed the name Rainbow Over Wisconsin. The force behind the Blue Lite's bar for twenty-two years was Dean Dayton, a native of Shawano, who had studied at UW–Eau Claire. Dayton wore great costumes, including that of a purple wizard and a French maid. He was a major backer of the Rainbow Over Wisconsin Foundation and served as its president for a period, helping it transition to a more traditional foundation. On the whole, the gay and lesbian community in the Sheboygan area did find some support in the 1990s, but it also dealt with a fair amount of antagonism from the larger community.[58]

RACINE AND THE SOUTHEAST

As noted earlier, Racine was among the first Wisconsin cities to have a lesbian and gay group in the early 1970s, well before the gay rights bill had passed. The local Gay/Lesbian Union viewed its purpose as providing "a support group of gay men and lesbians within a city that otherwise offers very little to the gay community." Cochair Cindi Lampman felt that the socializing opportunities in Milwaukee and Chicago filled residents' needs, claiming that "if Racine was not situated between those cities, it would have a stronger sense of community within the gay population." Yet, Jo'Dees bar, serving the gay community from the early 1970s, lasted for more than four decades.[59]

A longtime key figure in the Racine community was Unitarian Universalist minister Reverend Tony Larsen. Originally from California, Larsen

Reverand Tony Larsen, a Unitarian Universalist minister, has been a lifelong advocate for the LGBT community. In this 2011 photo, he is holding a guitar and leading the third annual gay rights march in Racine. PHOTO BY SCOTT ANDERSON, © 2011 *RACINE JOURNAL TIMES*

studied for the Catholic priesthood with the Maryknoll order and earned a master's degree in theology. Catholic liberation theology attracted him, but other church positions did not. Then he discovered the Unitarian Universalists, with their emphasis on "deeds, not creed." In 1975, he was ordained as a minister and became the first full-time pastor of the Unitarian Universalist Church of Racine and Kenosha. After the Kenosha members started their own church, the members of the Racine church changed its name in 1989 to the Olympia Brown Unitarian Universalist Church. Larsen led many Racine Pride marches during his years as a minister. When Reverend Jerry Falwell brought his antigay Moral Majority to Milwaukee in 1985, Larsen was among the fifty picketers at the appearance. When marriage equality arrived in Wisconsin, he and his partner, Craig Matheus, became the first Racine same-sex couple to be married.[60]

When Lampman left the Governor's Council on Lesbian and Gay Issues in 1986, she was replaced by Laura Grisk of Kenosha, who was a member of the Gay and Lesbian Union of Racine. Ironically, she worked at the Southern Wisconsin Center for the Developmentally Disabled in Union Grove, the same institution that had fired Paul Safransky in 1972 for being a homosexual. In 1995, Brent Nance and Christine Pasinski started a Racine book discussion group described as "open to all who wish to grow in their understanding and acceptance of Gay and Lesbian people." By 2009, Racine had become home to the new LGBT Center of Southeast Wisconsin. Larsen, the city's ever-faithful activist, served on its board of directors. There would also be a campus LGBT support group called the UW–Parkside Rainbow Alliance.[61]

Though at times it was overshadowed by Milwaukee, the long-established gay community in southeast Wisconsin found strong leaders, particularly Larsen and Lampman.

West Central Wisconsin:
A Tale of Two Cities—La Crosse

La Crosse and Eau Claire, the two largest cities in west central Wisconsin, developed different gay communities during the latter decades of the century. Linda Zimmerman, who had graduated from high school in Tomah and who had come to La Crosse in 1972, found it very hard to meet other lesbians in the city. Finally, she started to make connections through softball teams, which she says were "a major part of our culture back then." "There was a community here," she observed, but it was "very secretive, very hidden, very closeted." By the mid-1970s, a couple of teams had lesbian members that made up more than half of the players. In 1978, Zimmerman recalled, her "entire team was lesbian—coaches and players, all the way down; managers all the way down. . . . We were a damn good team. I mean, I don't think we lost a game all season." Even as recently as 2001, a big slow-pitch softball state tournament at Sparta was "still very lesbian identified." Zimmerman remembered there used to be a division between the softball lesbians and the lesbians who worked professional jobs until the women's bar Tattoo's opened in La Crosse where they both mixed. After her campus days, Zimmerman worked at printing plants as a bindery worker and then as a press operator. She was not out at work, as she did not consider it safe. In 1996, however, she volunteered at Galaxy, a gay youth group in town, which she saw as a second coming out.[62]

New Beginnings, published in Westby, Wisconsin, near La Crosse, also helped connect gay people in the area. The newsletter's purpose was "providing the support and information that can help through some of the difficulties which occur in a heterosexually dominated civilization." With a print run of one thousand, *New Beginnings* claimed a circulation triangle that stretched from the Twin Cities over to Appleton and down to Davenport, Iowa. The publication mainly focused on gay news from the communities of Eau Claire and La Crosse, with the latter favored over the former. Most of the advertisers (a couple dozen) were from the two west central cities as well, but a few—such as the Frame Corner in Richland Center and Bob Jansen's Main Club in Superior—were from farther afield. In the 1990s, Richland Center was also the locus for the gay group The Pioneers, which billed itself as the Southwest Rural Gay and Lesbian Support Network. The Pioneers benefited from a lesbian-owned bar in Livingston, Wisconsin, that hosted a private party "for fun, fellowship, and frolic" in which they were to be joined by the gay group from Dubuque.[63]

New Beginnings reported on Dubuque's first gay march just across the Mississippi in 1987 when the marchers were pelted with eggs. That year, the Dubuque mayor had refused to declare a gay pride week, claiming the only gay people he had ever known were child molesters. A contributor who published under the name Tony wrote about the second gay march in Dubuque in 1988, sponsored by NOW and PFLAG Dubuque. It attracted folks from western and southern Wisconsin, but it took particular courage for the local Iowa residents to march. Tony observed that "Iowans (unlike Wisconsin residents) can't be shielded from sexual-preference discrimination. Therefore, lesbians legally can be fired from their jobs, and gay males legally can be denied housing—JUST BECAUSE OF THEIR SEXUAL ORIENTATION." One of the organizers, Stacie Nelsdaughter, an open lesbian, was thrown off of her Iowa softball team because the team was harassed in league play due to her sexual orientation.[64]

The drag queen Renn'e was a contributor to *New Beginnings* and wrote the column Coming Out of the Closet with Renn'e. She organized shows to raise money for AIDS research and support through Kira De La Cunte Productions, of which she was one half. The initial shows in 1988 were held at the La Crosse bar Memories. Renn'e was known for saying, "Thanks, you cute little drag queens." She described the life of a drag queen as sometimes overpowering but a lot of fun, adding, "You can be someone different."[65]

The La Crosse County Health Department was an early responder to the AIDS crisis, and Bill Fleming, a health educator, was frequently mentioned in the pages of *New Beginnings*. Born in 1938, he was raised in Viroqua, Wisconsin, where he recalled having a lot of male sex partners in high school. After high school, he briefly studied at the La Crosse Teachers College, which led him to become a Navy corpsman. He was in Washington, DC, in the 1950s and recalled that even though McCarthy had died, "you had to be really careful about things." Remembering the lavender scare, Fleming recalled, "If you were in the military or if you worked in the State Department, whatever, it was just, you know, it was, it was unbelievable." Later, Fleming learned through a friend that he had unknowingly undergone a military investigation but he had escaped suspicion.[66]

Fleming was briefly in Seattle when what was then called the Gay Related Immune Deficiency Syndrome surfaced, and he got involved with the Chicken Soup Brigade, a home meal delivery group for people with the disease. Back in La Crosse, he was hired as the first health educator in the county focusing on AIDS. The phrase "Can We Talk?" was printed on his business card. In 1989, Fleming won the Wisconsin Public Health Association's New Public Health Worker of the Year Award, in part for his work in life care services. Fleming recalled that area lesbians were very useful in providing resources for his AIDS work, while the local gay men were more likely to be diverted by an argument about décor. He found it difficult to patronize gay bars and see men to whom he had provided health information engage in risky behavior. By the late 1980s, La Crosse was home to eight individuals with AIDS, and five AIDS-related deaths had occurred. In 1991, Lutheran Hospital in La Crosse sponsored a Midwest AIDS Conference focusing on how the disease affected small cities and rural areas. The AIDS quilt was displayed as part of the conference. Around this time, *New Beginnings* also reported on the Ho-Chunk Nation's AIDS prevention education aimed at high-risk American Indians, operating out of Tomah, Wisconsin.[67]

Starting as early as 1985, the La Crosse community had a monthly gay/ lesbian support group, which met at the Crossroads Campus Ministry, a student ministry of several mainline Protestant churches. The group held rap sessions for counseling but also offered movie nights and field trips. Another activity in the city that began in the early 1980s was a contest for drag queens, Miss Gay La Crosse. (Drag queens, who had the courage and showmanship to change their public personas, were often the earliest visible members of the community.) The first Mr. Gay La Crosse was crowned in 1987. In 1988, the support group and the La Crosse PFLAG group co-sponsored a workshop on grieving, attended by forty people. It included the mother of a gay man who had died of AIDS. According to contributor Dean Klinkenberg, the session "far exceeded the expectations."[68]

Klinkenberg was a key figure in early La Crosse activities. He came from Albert Lea, Minnesota, and in his senior year of high school, he had a relationship with a guy from his bowling league. He remembered feeling "better off if I was dead than gay" and found solace in heavy drinking. When he came to the La Crosse campus in 1982, student counseling and Alcoholics Anonymous helped him become sober, and he met other gay folks. He was invited to be on a panel about homosexuality that launched him on a path of speaking to four or five classes a semester. He participated in the La Crosse Area Gay Association (LAGA), a gay support group that existed from 1985 to 1994, and he found it therapeutic. The group was not an official campus organization, which is why meetings were held off campus at Crossroads. Keith Kensinger, a sympathetic minister, helped the group, but the posters they put up were often torn down. A typical meeting might draw ten members, with up to twenty-five on a good evening. LAGA also tried to solicit the views of politicians; at first, the group was rebuffed, but then State Representative John Medinger came and spoke to them in 1988.[69]

The student counseling office often passed along Klinkenberg's name as a resource, and at times he felt like the poster boy for the gay community. In the mid-1980s, he spoke to guidance counselors from the local school district after being invited by Rachel Gunderson, a school psychologist with the La Crosse School District. She had come across area high school students struggling with their sexuality. Speaking about one of the high schools, she observed, "Practically every one of the gay young men and a couple of the lesbian women at Logan were suicidal at one point." For Gunderson, a mother to five sons, these struggling youths brought out her maternal instincts. "There are so many heterosexuals who are in the closet," she observed, "who refuse to look out and look around them, and learn."[70]

The year 1987 marked the first gay community picnic in the park at Goose Island, a county park on the Mississippi. The first year was informal, including grills and volleyball and Frisbee. It grew, attracting 250 attendees in its second year, and became an annual tradition. As in many other small communities, gay bars in La Crosse came and went. The downtown bar Players was opened by transplants from southern California around 1990. It served a straight group during lunch but "after dark welcome[d] a festive group to come down and party."[71]

LEAPING LA CROSSE LESBIAN SEPARATISTS

For more than twenty-five years, *Leaping La Crosse News*, also profiled in chapter 5, was an important vehicle of communication and community-building for the very active lesbians in and around the city of La Crosse. Like many such publications, it relied on volunteers and benefits to support itself. One such benefit was "Italian Night at Tattino's," which promised food and dancing to good tunes. An auction in October 1989 raised $680, which exceeded the editors' wildest dreams.[72]

One of the community's events was the Tux Party. Held annually for

LEAPING LA CROSSE NEWS

• NOVEMBER 1983 •

FOURTH ANNUAL TUX PARTY

Attention wild women! Don't get the blues.
Come to the 4th annual tux party instead.

The fourth annual tux party is moving
location and sposorship, but it promises
to be as much fun as ever. The "gayla"
event will start at 8:00 p.m. on November
19, at 133 8th Avenue South in Onalaska
(Joy's new house). There will be plenty
of music, dancing and refreshments --
beer, wine, soft drinks -- and snacks.

You will be asked for a $3.00 donation at
the door. These proceeds will be used to
rescue OUT AND ABOUT WOMEN from dire
financial straights, so there is money to
promote future concerts.

If you don't have a tux, use your imagination. The main object is to have a good
time and come formally attired -- in a
formal or as a punk rocker, for example.
Or, if you are a student, you can rent a
tux at the UW-L Housing Office. Our source
for this piece of information says the
tux rental fees are cheap!

And, there is a third alternative. Come
to the TUX EXCHANGE. There will be a
tux exchange at TATTOO'S on Sunday,
November 13 at 4:00 p.m. This is a chance
for those of us who don't have a tux, to
put an outfit together. It's also a good
oportunity for those who have a tux or
tux accessories that don't fit, to pass
them along to the needy masses.

As you may have noticed, this exchange
takes place just about a week before the
time honored, traditional tux party. So,
it's a good chance to beat the what-to-
wear blues.

One other alternative is that Desmond's
Formalwear has a warehouse where you
can buy a used tux. It's in the Industrial Park on the Northside, and is
open from 8:00 to 12:00 on Saturday
morning.

There will also be a raffle at the tux
exchange, featuring a variety of prizes
for women.

GYM II FIRE

On the night of October 17, the La Crosse
Women's community lost a valuable resource,
and one of the women in our community lost
a dream. GYM II: A Fitness Club For Women
burned that night.

The fire was bad enough that the entire
building was demolished. According to the
owner, Von Piercy, there is no way GYM II
can be rebuilt in the immediate future.

Von appreciates all the support for GYM II
that she has gotten in the past from the
women's community, and is also appreciative
of the support and offers for help that
she has received since the fire.

Watch the LLN for updates on GYM II and
for how you might be able to help Von.

SUBSCRIBE
TO THE LEAPING LACROSSE NEWS!

12 WONDERFUL ISSUES FOR $8.00
(MORE IF YOU CAN, LESS IF YOU CAN'T)

NAME _____
ADDRESS _____

PHONE (OPTIONAL) ____ / ____

PLEASE SEND WITH DONATION TO
LLN · P.O. BOX 932 · LACROSSE, WI·
54601, OR LEAVE AT TATTOOS WITH
BARTENDER. INDICATE IF YOU'D
LIKE IT IN AN ENVELOPE. THANKS!

Leaping La Crosse News, a lesbian feminist publication for western Wisconsin, featured the community's long-running annual women in tuxes party. WISCONSIN HISTORICAL SOCIETY

ten years, the party's locations varied, but for several years it was held at the women-operated Mill Road Café in Galesville in Trempealeau County. "This is the prom we never went to or had a miserable time at," one contributor observed. She continued, "Only a few years before I attended [my all girls] high school, it had been fairly common for the young women of the school to ask each other to the prom. Maybe if that practice hadn't been discontinued, I might have gone." For this writer, the La Crosse Tux Party inspired a frantic "pre-prom flurry" of trying on outfits before the mirror and searching for the flashiest vest. *Leaping La Crosse News* provided information on sources for tuxes, and the women's bar Tattoo's had a Tux Exchange Party, allowing women to assemble outfits from various gently used items. In later years, a group called the Fabulous Cumberbunnies, pimping the Playboy Clubs, performed at the Tux Party and was described as wonderful and funny. One writer observed that the party was not about women in drag but women "dressing in a tux to be the good-looking women they are."[73]

Another annual event that lasted for many years was the Sandbar Party, a July Fourth weekend party held at a "not-often-used sandbar" on the Black River that could be reached only via canoe. Shade tarps and sunscreen were recommended, and some women played naked in the water. In the latter part of the 1980s, *Leaping La Crosse News* reported on efforts to create a designated space for lesbians in La Crosse. Unlike Madison's Lysistrata—a women's space that welcomed lesbians—the La Crosse space was intended to have a specific lesbian focus.[74]

Another social opportunity featured in the publication was DOE (Daughters of Earth) Farm, forty-five miles due east of La Crosse near Norwalk. The Wisconsin Womyn's Land Co-op, the organization that owned the property, had eighty acres and attracted women from around the upper Midwest to camp alone or with women friends without having to worry about being hassled by men. Often described as primitive, the farm included a sauna and a barn with a dance floor. The newsletter debunked the stereotype that the hosts, a few lesbians who lived permanently on the farm, were "a bunch of dogmatic sprout-eating spiritually and politically correct man-hating separatists" and described them as wonderful women. *Leaping La Crosse News* positively identified the co-op as "a growing, evolving example of Lesbian womyn engaging in a cooperative effort." Luna Farm near Soldiers Grove was another rural women's effort—an active farm well known for its French-style goat cheese—that received attention in the pages of the magazine.[75]

In 1985, the group Lesbians United of La Crosse was formed to combat the oppression of lesbians through visibility, education, and by providing

aid to the lesbian community. Brown-bag lunches at the Women's Studies Resource Center of UW–La Crosse were promoted. Lesbian separatist
news, such as the 1988 Wisconsin organizing conference of the National
Lesbian Feminist Organization in Milwaukee, was featured. In May 1984,
a rare item about gay men was printed to announce the formation of the
La Crosse Area Gay Association, which was to have its own newsletter. In
fact, separatism so dominated in this lesbian feminist community that
the man most frequently mentioned in the newsletter in the 1980s was
Governor Earl.[76]

By the mid-1980s, the AIDS crisis required a response from the staff of
Leaping La Crosse News. An editorial in the March 1986 issue asked "Is AIDS
Our Problem?" Despite acknowledging that lesbians had a very low risk of
contracting the disease, the editors wrote, "So, is AIDS our problem? Of
course! . . . We need to be supportive of our gay friends. . . . Discrimination
is insidious and gay oppression reinforces lesbian oppression."[77]

Since many people in the La Crosse area, with its strong Norwegian
roots, were Lutheran, *Leaping La Crosse News* (like *New Beginnings*) reported on the organization Lutherans Concerned, the lesbian and gay supportive effort within that denomination. *LLN* highlighted the Lutheran
documents that stated, "The AIDS crisis calls us to learn that unconditional
love is not a luxury, but a basic need of the human condition." *LLN* was
an important vehicle of communication and community-building for the
very active lesbians in and around the city of La Crosse.[78]

WEST CENTRAL WISCONSIN:
A TALE OF TWO CITIES—EAU CLAIRE

While La Crosse was an early activist center, the Eau Claire community developed more slowly, perhaps in part because the area was so close in prox-
imity to the Twin Cities in Minnesota and that vibrant gay community.
In the late 1980s, the main gay community organization in Eau Claire was
Unity of West Central Wisconsin, a group that met sometimes at the gay
bars and sometimes at the local Unitarian Universalist church. The group
held garage sales to raise money and cooperated with the local bars. An annual Unity Picnic began in 1985 "in the tradition of gay and lesbian pride."
In summer 1988, twenty-five Unity members traveled to the Twin Cities to

see the AIDS quilt. In early 1990, due to various circumstances, all lesbian
and gay bars in the area had closed, so the Unity group tried to host more
social events, including open house parties, card and game parties, and (of
course, in Wisconsin) a bowling party. The group welcomed cheerleading
groups to the bowling party with the line: "All screamers are encouraged
to attend, pom-poms not required but welcome." Women's softball teams
also emerged in the community. By late 1990, a gay bar called Wildwood
Club reopened, welcoming gay men into what had formerly been a wom-
en's space. Like many gay communities in midsized cities, the gay residents
of Eau Claire were starved for "camaraderie and friendship." "It is sad that
we have become separated as a gay community," wrote one community
member in *New Beginnings*, referring to the rift between gay men and
lesbians. "The only way we can survive is to share each other's ideas and
support one another."[79]

A frequent column in *New Beginnings* was Shorts from Soph, written
by a drag performer from Eau Claire who could ruffle some feathers. Performers and audiences from La Crosse and Eau Claire attended shows at
the bars in both cities. For a while, the Eau Claire–based group For Womyn
Only about Western Wisconsin existed. Self-described as a gathering place
where womyn could get "information, help, or guidance," the group's
manifesto proclaimed, "We can be openly friends without announcing our
lesbianism. Friendship is indeed a lesbian act—since it is an act of loving
between women." Activities sponsored by the group included moonlight
bowling, a hayride, sledding, canoeing, a pool tournament, a sweetheart's
dance, and a Leather and Lace dance.[80]

New Beginnings also reported in 1991 on the attempted outing of the area's Republican congressman, Steve Gunderson. He had been tracked down
at an Alexandria, Virginia, gay bar by an activist who urged him to sponsor
the national gay rights bill and publicly come out. As reported, Gunderson
said, "I am out. I'm in this bar, aren't I?" The article also made clear that
Gunderson had an 88 percent pro-gay voting record. At a 1991 Independence Day parade in La Crosse, Minneapolis gay activist Tim Campbell
confronted Gunderson and distributed leaflets outing him. This was not
picked up in the mainline media, and Gunderson was reelected in 1992. In
1994, when a conservative congressman in the House of Representatives
attacked him as gay, Gunderson came out nationally in the *New York Times*

Steve Gunderson, while in the state legislature in the 1970s, lent his name to the Sexual Privacy Coalition seeking to pass consenting adults legislation. Later he came out while serving in the US House of Representatives and won reelection to his western Wisconsin district as an out gay man. WHI IMAGE ID 125409

Magazine. That year, Gunderson, an incumbent Republican congressman, had a primary challenger; he won the primary with 63 percent of the vote and went on to win the general election with 56 percent of the vote. However, in 1996, although he was in line to assume the powerful chairmanship of the Agriculture Committee of the House, Gunderson declined to run for reelection due to the homophobia of his political colleagues and the "character assassination" he had suffered at the hands of conservative forces. Gunderson said, "The reality is that to some people in this country, the possibility of someone who is openly gay assuming the chair of a major committee in Congress . . . they could not accept. . . . We have witnessed some of the most intense and mean-spirited activity I have seen throughout my political career." Remarking on his departure from politics, Gunderson observed, "This marks a victory for bigotry and discrimination." Without the popular Gunderson running in the 1996 election, and perhaps because of the previous primary fight, the Third District seat went to Democrat Ron Kind.[81]

For a period in the 1980s, the Gay & Lesbian Community at Stout (GLCS) also put out a newsletter, which printed, among other things, "Tips on Living with Lesbians and Gays in Residence Halls at Stout." The group held discussion sessions, dances, and a Halloween party and produced a radio program, *We've Been Here All Along*, for the campus radio station. The main organizer of the group, Larry Roeming, who served on the Governor's Council on Lesbian and Gay Issues, provided a brochure to answer many of the "queer queries." The group also put out a GLCS Resource List, which included resources in Minneapolis and Milwaukee. The UW–Stout campus group also provided guidance when a similar campus group was forming at UW–Eau Claire.[82]

UW–EAU CLAIRE: FROM DREARY TO FABULOUS

In the early 1980s, the UW–Eau Claire campus was viewed by gay people as quite conservative. A few gay students set out to change that. Jill Muenich, born and raised in Chippewa Falls, helped spearhead the efforts. In her local high school library, Muenich recalled, the only book on homosexuality had been Anita Bryant's negative tome. (She was likely referring to *The Anita Bryant Story: The Survival of Our Nation's Families and the Threat of Militant Homosexuality*.) In college, she chose to live off campus where she felt more comfortable as a lesbian. The UW–Eau Claire Gay and Lesbian Organization (GLO) was formed by the campus counseling service in the early 1980s; with the students' permission, the counselors shared the names of three gay men and three lesbian students with whom they were working, and those students decided to form the group. Muenich recalled, "I think we surprised a lot of people . . . when we first began to emerge." Early meetings were attended by a dozen or more, and the group used posters to communicate to other students. One woman recalled "even being afraid to stand there and look at [one of the posters]." The organization provided a place for gay students to meet; and one member recalled meeting his life partner there. When Governor Dreyfus signed the gay rights bill in 1982, Muenich felt, "We were in a positive upswing in the early '80s as we were forming." Observing the momentum for gay rights on the state level, she wondered, "Why can this not be happening at the university level?"[83]

Edward Frank (pseudonym), who grew up in Peshtigo, Wisconsin, was another of the GLO's early organizers. He recalled being called a faggot in the UW–Eau Claire cafeteria and that others would not shower at the same time as him in the dorms. His sense was that gay men had a harder time than lesbians on campus. After joining the GLO, Frank found a gay roommate. He participated in one of the main activities of GLO members: speaking when invited to classes in social work, sociology, and psychology. The group tried to send men and women to do the speaking engagements together. This lack of separatism within the organization was functionally required, as there were so few members. As Muenich said, "We needed to be one." At the time, Eau Claire had only one gay bar, which both men and women attended. Gay people had been targeted outside the bar, and some harassers had even entered the bar and poured liquor over the patrons. However, the GLO was a safe place. "It probably was the saving grace for me," Frank said. "I don't know if I could have stayed there" on campus without it.[84]

Robb Jirschelle, who was on campus from 1988 to 1995, recalled that many of the freshman students who came from small towns or rural backgrounds would tell him, "You're the first gay person I've ever known." Jirschelle had come out at age seventeen, but he did not feel comfortable living on campus; he believed most resident assistants were unsympathetic. When publicizing gay events in chalk on the campus foot bridge, he would hear the snickers of passing students. He also attended some of the gay community group meetings at the Unitarian Universalist church in town partly because he believed they sponsored more activities than the campus group. Laura Goetz, a UW–Eau Claire student and Eau Claire native who lived at home, learned of the GLO from a flyer; she thought the group functioned like a support group on campus and could help "de-scare-ify being gay." A few community members occasionally attended the campus meetings. One student in the late 1990s found the group too boring and too political, as he wanted a more social group.[85]

In 1992, a series of four gay bashings occurred during the spring and fall semesters on campus. After these events, the GLO, which had been renamed Gays, Lesbians or Bisexuals for Equality (GLOBE) to include bisexuals, experienced a surge of meeting attendees. One student, Libby, said the issue was "about survival." Because antigay epithets had been used during some of the attacks, the local police treated some bashings as hate crimes. A rally of a hundred students and a roundtable in the campus student center focused on the issue. One lesbian reported being called a "damn dyke," and a gay man declared that his car was almost run off the road. GLOBE advisor Sharon Knopp, who had a black belt in karate, taught self-defense tactics to a group of fifteen or twenty group members. However, the local paper reported, not all UW–Eau Claire students were sympathetic. One said, "I don't think the bashings are all that bad." And another claimed gay students "bring it (violence) onto themselves." Knopp recalled that the bashings "solidified everybody very quickly. When you're under fire then it really does make the organization quite active." The campus police guarded the door during GLOBE meetings. "Those four years were probably the biggest awareness-raising time for the campus on everyone's part," Knopp speculated.[86]

The university responded to the gay bashings in a variety of ways. The Student Senate offered reward money for information leading to an arrest for the crimes. Chancellor Larry Schnack said the violence is "a matter of utmost importance" and "provides us with an additional impetus and motivation to further combat the problem." "Respect Differences" buttons appeared on campus, paid for by university funds. And in response to letters from some Christians who had denounced homosexuality in the campus paper, a coalition of ten campus religious groups issued a statement proclaiming, "The right to live our lives free of violent actions is important to all of us."[87]

In 1997, a whirlwind arrived on the campus in Bob Nowlan, a professor of critical theory and cinema studies in the department of English. The longtime faculty advisor of the campus LGBT group informed Nowlan that he would be the first openly gay professor on campus and suggested that he might feel more comfortable living in the Twin Cities and commuting ninety miles to campus. He rejected the suggestion. In class, he forthrightly announced his sexual orientation to his students. When one student's parents complained to a dean, that administrator said he "saw no reason why anyone should reveal their sexuality to their students." However, with support from students and colleagues, Nowlan persisted in being defiantly out, and the dean shifted his position.[88]

Nowlan taught the English course Studies in Film: Contemporary LesBiGay and Queer Film, which was "the first course ever taught at UWEC to explicitly focus on GLBT issues." *The Spectator*, the campus paper, published an article on the course in the fall of 1999, and a large number of

This illustration by Elizabeth Powell accompanied Bob Nowlan's 2001 article in *Radical Teacher* magazine, "Teaching and Working as an Openly Gay Faculty Member at the University of Wisconsin–Eau Claire." DRAWING BY ELIZABETH POWELL

"hate chalkings" directed at LGBT people appeared on campus in response. For four weeks, *The Spectator* received letters denouncing the chalkings and providing suggestions on how to improve the institution's climate. Nowlan realized, "My role was to press the administration . . . to take responsibility for its own complicity." His course led to the campus's first Human Rights Awareness Conference dealing with sexual orientation in December 1999. The Student Senate followed up with a resolution asking for "courses in GLBT studies as a regular part of the undergraduate general education curriculum." Nowlan, in 1998, circulated a letter to all faculty members that resulted in the forming of the group Equality, UWEC Faculty and Staff in Support of Lesbian, Gay, Bisexual, and Transgender Issues.[89]

Almost two decades later, in 2010, the UWEC campus began the Eau Queer Film Festival, and the campus instituted annual summer seminar trips to San Francisco, where students could study LGBT history. These efforts received exemplary program awards. Chris Jorgenson became the university's LGBT coordinator and enhanced the school's Coming Out Day events with a twenty-by-thirty-foot pride flag. He also boosted the National Day of Silence, an occasion to take a stand against the bullying of LGBT students. The Fireball, a drag performance featuring performers who had appeared on *RuPaul's Drag Race*, became the biggest event his office sponsored. The event, which began in 2012, regularly sold out on campus. One year, the sale of fourteen hundred tickets brought in fifteen thousand dollars to support the LGBT student fund.[90]

Over the years, UW–Eau Claire became mindful of where it might rank on the LGBT-Friendly Campus Climate Index, since its campus vice chancellor had a gay son and was quite aware that there was room for growth. In 2010, the campus put out a press release announcing that it had improved its ranking to four out of five stars. Chancellor Brian Levin-Stankevich emphasized, "Ensuring that everyone feels safe and comfortable on our campus is a university priority." He added, "The Campus Pride Index ranking is an indication we are making progress." By 2017, UW–Eau Claire ranked third in the nation (right after Princeton and MIT) with a score of 95 in the campus rankings of the Fifty Best Colleges for LGBT Students. The school was praised for its "emphatic commitment to equality, diversity, and inclusivity."[91]

An Empowered Community

From farm and hamlet to the state's metropolitan centers, from the Superior shore to the Illinois border, Wisconsin's LBGT residents took up the work of organizing with determination in the 1980s and 1990s. They attempted to change the local cultures where they felt invisible and faced hostility. Among many communities, there existed a strong sense of needing to do this for survival against an all-too-prevalent culture of homophobia. Through the organizations they founded, many gay Wisconsinites explored ways to build mutual support. Even if some groups seemed to have constantly changing names and casts of characters, many persisted thanks to dedicated members who had pride in Wisconsin and a vision of the place it might become.

One article written about the NEWIST TV show on gay teens focused on Georgia Geise, the mother of a gay teen profiled on the show, who had been

fired from her job in Illinois. The story asserted, "Illinois has no prohibition on sexual orientation discrimination, so Geise had no legal resource
to regain the job she'd held for 12 years." Even in Wisconsin, with its unique
legal protections, the sexual orientation of one's child likely would not
provide cause for legal protection. But the quote illustrates the presumed
power of Wisconsin's gay rights law and the pride it could engender. The
NEWIST article is merely one small demonstration that Wisconsin's gay
community felt empowered in the 1980s and 1990s and sought to use its
unique legal standing to build community around the state.[92]

Many LGBT activists throughout Wisconsin were indeed aware of the
legal standing that successful legislation had provided them and sought to
claim their rights as newly empowered citizens. They determined that
their own agency was required to turn the legislation into reality, and
they undertook the work of organizing for liberation. Most efforts were
admittedly modest and based on minimal resources. In the smaller cities,
gay men and lesbian activists often stuck together within organizations,
even if they socialized separately. Even by the end of the twentieth century,
a reputed 98 percent of LGBT Wisconsinites chose not to come out as a
strategy for surviving the oppression of still-rampant homophobia. Nevertheless, there were plenty of Wisconsin heroines and heroes to celebrate.

11

BUILDING LASTING
COMMUNITY INSTITUTIONS

*I believe that sexuality is a gift from God—homosexuality as well as
heterosexuality.*

—REV. PAUL JOHNSON, LUTHERAN
PASTOR FROM VIROQUA IN 1991[1]

*I have dreams of high fantasy, dreams of the perfect mate, dreams of
pleasant days and blissful nights, dreams that far outweigh the consequences of my sexuality. Dreams that I will make a reality.*

—HIGH SCHOOL STUDENT ESSAY FROM 1990
ON SURVIVING HOMOPHOBIA IN SCHOOL[2]

The LGBT community in Wisconsin carried out a series of small, mag-
nificent acts of courage following Stonewall, but it lacked structure
and reach. This chapter outlines the ways in which the constant and repeated efforts of many individuals resulted in a large and diverse community with lasting institutions. Some of these institutions interacted with
national LGBT groups and movements, but most developed a distinctly
local character shaped by Wisconsin's past.

SATURDAY SOFTBALL BEER LEAGUE

As the state's major metropolitan area, Milwaukee, an industrial city that
produces beer and has professional sport teams, has a unique flavor. It

should come as no surprise that one of the state's longest-running gay organizations involved an affinity for both sports and beer. In the summer of
1977, four gay softball teams in the city arranged pick-up games on the field
at the Mitchell Park Domes. The teams were associated with various gay
bars, and it became a tradition that the losing team would buy a half barrel
of beer at their home bar. (For a great review of Milwaukee's gay bars, consult Michail Takach's *LGBT Milwaukee*.) On a cold winter's night in February 1978, several of the ball players, including Tom Theis, Arturo Olazabal,
Norm Schmald, and Tom Salzsieder, hatched an idea for a Memorial Day
weekend softball tournament in Milwaukee. They also talked about for-
malizing gay softball league play in the city. The resulting Saturday Softball
Beer League (SSBL) and its annual tournament have continued up to the
time of this book's publication. Theis, a native of North Prairie, Wisconsin,
was a bartender and waiter. Salzsieder contributed to gay publications and
served the SSBL in many offices over the years, from commissioner to
treasurer. Both men were eventually inducted into the SSBL Hall of Fame.[3]

The SSBL's purpose was "to promote sports in an atmosphere of
friendly competition and to provide social events." The league evolved
over time to include a competitive division, a recreational division, and a
women's division. In a 1995 grant request to the Cream City Foundation,
the league described sports as "the first organized Gay & Lesbian activities.
Sports served as a way for a person, otherwise afraid to venture out, to have
a comfortable acquaintance and welcome into the community."[4]

One of the SSBL's enduring legacies is the Milwaukee Invitational softball tournament. Known variously as the Wreck Room Classic (after a
bar that sponsored a team), Milwaukee Classic, and Dairyland Classic,
the tournament has hosted teams from the Midwest and Toronto. One
of the largest tournaments in 1992 included forty-six teams. In the early
days, teams were supposed to have 80 percent gay members, though this
was later reduced to 50 percent. Reporting on the 1978 tournament mentioned that "many, many friendships were established between the visiting teams." Salzsieder, writing playfully about the 1984 Classic, noted,
"Some of the players will have to get to bed (alone) early as play resumes at
9:00 a.m." In a later comment he noted, "The players bid their goodbyes to
the many friends who they have made (is this the right word?) during the
weekend." League efforts were boosted once the SSBL approached Miller

Milwaukee's gay softball players hosted the Wreck Room Classic, a national gay tournament that attracted teams from around the country. ARCHIVES DEPARTMENT, UNIVERSITY OF WISCONSIN–MILWAUKEE LIBRARIES

Park, home of the Milwaukee Brewers, and established a partnership early in the twenty-first century. League members staffed a concession stand by home plate that raised tens of thousands of dollars for SSBL.[5]

In 1979, the SSBL of Milwaukee became one of the five founding members of the North American Gay Amateur Athletic Alliance (NAGAAA), along with groups from San Francisco, New York City, Los Angeles, and Toronto. On Labor Day weekend of 1979, teams from eight other cities came to Milwaukee for the third Gay World Series in slow-pitch softball, which attracted four hundred spectators. Local gay bars each hosted a team from a different city. The Milwaukee team came in third behind Los Angeles and Minneapolis. In 1985, the ninth Gay World Series was held in Milwaukee, this time featuring nineteen cities and 650 players. It cost twenty thousand dollars to host the games. Former Milwaukeean Ron Burbey became a national commissioner for NAGAAA in 1985 and served a ten-year term. Milwaukee hosted the World Series once again in 2009; the city's tourism agency promoted the bid, as did former SSBL player and gay state legislator Tim Carpenter. Looking back, Bob Melig claimed, "In starting the Classic, we helped others to get organized across the country. We helped everyone see the need for a National Organization, and pioneered the manner in which almost every other tournament is being run."[6]

ROLL THEM BALLS IN THE TEN PIN CAPITAL

Milwaukee's reputation as a bowling capital was confirmed by the popular late 1970s sitcom *Laverne and Shirley*. In the episode "Bowling for Razzberries," the two friends compete for a bowling championship on

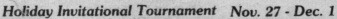

In the Ten Pin Capital of America, lesbian and gay bowling teams partook of local culture, formed bonds, showed pride, and had fun. *IN STEP*, NOVEMBER 14–27, 1985, COURTESY OF TOM REZZA

the fictional Shotz Brewery bowling team. Laverne, characterized as "a tough-talking tomboy," and her roommate, Shirley, both work as bottle cappers at this reputed Milwaukee brewery. The Germanic roots of bowling in Beer City are well documented in *They Came to Bowl: How Milwaukee Became America's Tenpin Capital* by Doug Schmidt. The German word *kegel*, meaning club, was originally used to describe the pins, and bowlers became known as keglers. Milwaukee was such a center for bowling in the late 1800s that the American Bowling Congress, a national organization, operated out of Milwaukee starting in 1907. At the time of World War I, "roughly 17% of Brew City's inhabitants were involved in bowling." During the *Laverne and Shirley* period, "Milwaukee's 100,000 bowling enthusiasts accounted for 9.7% of Milwaukee County's population."[7]

Of course, gay folks were among the many bowlers of Milwaukee; probably most had been raised on the lanes as youths. In 1978, Ken Kurtz and several others decided to invite other gay bowling teams from across the country to come to the Ten Pin Capital for games over the Thanksgiving weekend. Thus, the Holiday Invitational Tournament, or HIT, was born. Kurtz recalled in 1986, "ours was not the first gay tournament, but, it was the first national gay tournament . . . and it's earned us the title of The Grand Daddy of Gay Bowling Tournaments." Gay journalist Bill Meunier reported on the 1981 tourney, observing that 250 keglers "came together to celebrate Gay Bowling, the Thanksgiving Holiday and each other. By the end of the weekend many bowlers found themselves with another reason to give thanks." The event followed the rules of the American Bowling Congress, and a banquet at a major Milwaukee hotel concluded the event. By the mid-1980s, fifty teams were attending. In 1992, a celebration cruise on the lake was added to enhance the social dimension of the tournament. For the twenty-fifth anniversary in 2003, some four hundred bowlers attended, and the prizes included a Harley-Davidson XL 1200 Custom Sportster. One slogan used on a poster with a discreetly placed nude male on the lanes was "Get Your Mind Out of the Gutter."[8]

In 1986, another bowling tournament was established: the MIL-MA-IDS, or the Milwaukee and Madison Bowlers Against AIDS. This tournament alternated between the two cities with proceeds going to the Milwaukee AIDS Project one year and to the Madison AIDS Support Network the next. The Bette Davis Bowling League, which originated the event, hosted in Madison. Bowlers from other cities in the Midwest region also attended. Gay bowling was so popular in Wisconsin that the International Gay Bowling Organization published a newsletter out of Milwaukee.[9]

GAY SPORTS REACH OUT AND TOUCH

Another sports-focused organization in Milwaukee was GAMMA. The initials might have been an acronym for the Gay Athletic Milwaukee Men's Association, but since there was some contention over this, most people simply used the name GAMMA. A touch football game on the lakeshore in 1978 was the origin of this long-lasting group, which still exists at the time of this book's publication. Membership eventually grew to 100–150. The group was created to "provide a social, recreational and cultural outlet for a lonely group of Milwaukeeans who may not have had much of a gay life otherwise. Many were closeted. Some were married and struggling with their identities." Most were generally not the type to join the community's political organizations.[10]

Starting in 1979, volleyball was a mainstay of the early GAMMA group, with competitive and social play occurring at UW–Milwaukee's Engelmann Gym. John Cowles, the early GAMMA president from 1980 to 1986, did a great deal of work to build up the organization. He managed the volleyball activities and even sent teams to tournaments around the country. Cowles came from Michigan to Milwaukee where he obtained a PhD in organic chemistry from Marquette University. He worked for Miller Brewing in the master breweries division and was awarded two patents for brewing research. When he died in 1990 at age thirty-six, GAMMA's volleyball league was renamed the Cowles Volleyball League as a memorial to him.[11]

Another GAMMA sparkplug was Don Schwamb, a native of West Bend, who served on its board for eight years and as a president for the organization. His computer skills helped with organizing mailing lists and the newsletter. Schwamb would go on to play key roles in setting up the Cream City Foundation and the AIDS Resource Center of Wisconsin. His chronicling of the LGBT history of Milwaukee and Wisconsin on a history website around the turn of the twenty-first century created an invaluable community resource.[12]

Don Schwamb (right), shown here with his long-time partner, Gary Williams, was an early Milwaukee community builder active in foundational efforts for GAMMA and the Cream City Foundation. COURTESY OF DON SCHWAMB

Young men in skimpy bathing suits doing water choreography had an appeal for the gay sports fans of Milwaukee's GAMMA. WHI IMAGE ID 142915

Other GAMMA outdoor activities included downhill skiing in Upper Michigan, hiking at Devil's Lake, tennis, golf, biking, camping, and whitewater rafting on the Peshtigo River. The annual boat cruise on Lake Michigan was popular. Water skiing on North Lake included a competition involving skimpy outfits and choreography inspired by the bachelor Tommy Bartlett's famous shows in the Wisconsin Dells. A corn roast with brats in Lake Park occurred every fall. In winter, GAMMA members gathered indoors at the roller rink and outdoors for ice dancing at Wilson Park. For further winter activities, there were nights when members played sheepshead, a popular Wisconsin card game and "one of GAMMA's most popular indoor sports," or traveled to Chicago for theater. As the group's members grew older, activities shifted away from sports and more toward social events.[13]

Brian Pronger, in his book *The Arena of Masculinity* published in 1990, discusses how gay sports groups both built community and explored the gender paradox of homosexuality. He observed that many gays were uncomfortable with regular sports that placed an emphasis on heteronormativity and masculine culture. But in community gay sports, they found camaraderie. Pronger also notes that in the time of AIDS, healthy sports could be an attractive alternative to the seemingly plague-infested bars and baths where many gay men gathered.[14]

LESBIAN ALLIANCE OF METRO MILWAUKEE

Milwaukee was home to lesbian activists going back to Donna Utke in the late 1960s, yet many of the city's homosexual organizations, including the Gay People's Union (GPU), had generally been male dominated. Cheryl Kader, in her article "LGBT Milwaukee" in the *Encyclopedia of Milwaukee*, finds that lesbians "sought to create a culture responsive to their feminist politics and their lesbian identities. Foremost among these endeavors was the publication of *Amazon*." Other early efforts included the Milwaukee NOW chapter and the Women's Coalition of Milwaukee. In 1984, NOW held the Women's Lesbian Rights Conference in Milwaukee. Judy Goldsmith, NOW president at the time, cited the Wisconsin law protecting the rights of lesbians and gay men as the organization's reason for choosing Milwaukee.[15]

In November 1978, more than one hundred women attended the state-wide gathering of the National Lesbian Feminist Organization (NLFO) at UW–Milwaukee. In a move highlighting the perceived vulnerability of lesbians, no Milwaukee lesbians spoke at the associated press conference, and all reporters were barred from the meetings. After the gathering, local NLFO chapters failed to form, and lesbian efforts in the city became less focused. Nevertheless, some prominent community members such as Carol Stevens—a member of the GPU, Grapevine, and many other lesbian groups—can be remembered as founding mothers. Stevens and her partner hosted many "renowned lesbian potlucks" and fundraising events where "all women were welcome, from argumentative political dykes to nervous 'newbie' lesbians taking their first tentative steps to meet other lesbians."[16]

In 1989, lesbians in Milwaukee demonstrated their readiness to claim part of the spotlight with the formation of the Lesbian Alliance of Metro Milwaukee (LAMM). The group's founding mothers are remembered

WISCONSIN LESBIANS MEET

Milwaukee, WI—Over one hundred women met in Milwaukee the week-end of November 10-12 for the first Wisconsin statewide convention of the National Lesbian Feminist Organization (NLFO). The group, organized last spring, described its goals as both personal and political. Barbara Lightner (Madison, WI) added: "The lobbying effort is important, but so is sharing with other lesbians. If you've ever lived in a very isolated way, it's very, very nice to know there are other people in the world you can share with."

The organization's press conference was open to women reporters only. Except for representatives of the gay press, all reporters were barred from the convention meetings; even though the **Milwaukee Journal** had offered to send a woman reporter, and to use neither names nor potographs of the participants. Ms Lightner said that the decision to bar the press was made to protect convention participants.

NATIONAL
LESBIAN
FEMINIST
ORGANIZATION

Some of the topics discussed at the conference workshops included the problems of lesbians whose jobs involve working with young persons, lesbian mothers and co-parents, and lesbian health issues. As an example of how vulnerable lesbians believe themselves to be, Ms Lightner pointed out that no Milwaukee lesbians appeared at the press conference. "This indicates something to you about how lesbians are treated in Milwaukee," she said. A Madison city ordinance protects lesbians from discrimination.

Wisconsin NLFO has resolved that their second convention will take place in the fall of 1979. In the meantime, the members have resolved to establish and exchange of information and support among women of larger communities and smaller communities. In addition, informal exchanges, statewide athletic events, study groups, and support groups to found local NLFO chapters throughout the state are planned. For information, write: NLFO, c/o Women's coalition, Inc., 2211 E. Kenwood Blvd., Milwaukee, WI 53211.

Wisconsin was the first state to try to organize a chapter of the National Lesbian Feminist Organization, holding a statewide meeting in Milwaukee in 1979. *GPU NEWS*, JUNE 1979

as Kitty Barber, Susan Cook, Karen Gotzler, Darla Kashian, and Deb Procknow. Procknow was a lesbian feminist attorney whose address served as the organization's early address. A graduate of Mount Senario College in Ladysmith and president of its alumni association, she was appointed to the college's board of trustees in 1990. The minutes of one of the organizing group's early meetings point out that "nearly 30 organizations exist for Gay and Lesbians that allow people to become involved with issues, but none were solely Lesbian-run and Lesbian-identified."[17]

Early LAMM meetings were held at the Milwaukee Enterprise Center where the group later established offices. Some members still exercised caution regarding their identities as the meeting notes stated, "The appearance of a member's full name in this newsletter is not indication that she is 'out.' We ask that you make no assumptions about how closeted or uncloseted a member is based on either her willingness to hold office in LAMM or the appearance of her name in any newsletter." The *Guide to LAMM Policies* held that "the right to privacy & self-disclosure is a basic Lesbian right." Nevertheless, members Barber and Gotzler often served as spokespersons in the press, and Cook was the group's first chairperson. As part of media relations, Barber spoke to the entire newsroom and editorial staff of the *Milwaukee Journal* in 1993 as part of a symposium entitled "Lesbians and Gays in the News: Beyond Stereotypes." Barber, in attending a Rally for Tolerance at the end of 1993, noted, "We are, all of us, more than just our sexual orientation, more than our religions, more than the color of our skin. We are indivisible not only because we choose to stand together, but because we are, in many ways, the same people."[18]

The LAMM statement on lesbian rights was forthright: "Lesbians in general are family-oriented, civic-minded members of our community; we are among the most productive members of the workforce in all professions & trades." The organization professed to be "working toward more comprehensive & accurate representations of Lesbians in the public arena, with an eye toward a society in which we can safely be out as Lesbians, as our full selves." In 1989, these women were aware of their unique national situation, writing, "while Wisconsin law technically grants us some basic civil rights, in reality we still face numerous forms of discrimination, both blatant and subtle." LAMM called itself a "make-change organization." It ultimately lasted for twenty-four years and gained several hundred members (by 1993 it counted three hundred households as members), making it the largest and longest-lasting lesbian organization in the state.[19]

Part of the impetus to form LAMM arose when a committee of the Milwaukee County Board in 1989 voted to recant a resolution approving Lesbian and Gay Pride Week. After the ensuing fight, some lesbians expressed concern that their voices and issues had not been part of the discussion, so a group referring to itself as "That L Group" came together as the organizing force that resulted in LAMM. The group estimated 50,000 lesbians living in the greater Milwaukee area. Later, in 1992, a LAMM Educational Fund was established. "All across the country," the LAMM newsletter stated, "Lesbians are forming new organizations and establishing agendas for action."[20]

After the group's 1991 pride events, the newsletter noted that "Lesbian visibility increased dramatically." Not only did a large LAMM contingent participate in the parade, but the group held a pancake breakfast for public officials that drew two hundred people. For Pride the following year, LAMM sponsored the "Isle of Lesbos" tent and its members made up the largest contingent in the parade. The circular tent invited all lesbians "to network, schmooze and consort." At an information table staffed "by some of LAMM's most enticing outreach personnel," LAMM was touted as the place to "meet the most exciting Lesbians in Milwaukee." "Our struggle for more visibility is far from over," members stated in the 1990–1991 annual report, "but these activities have been a good start."[21]

In 1991, LAMM members "assumed the leadership in the formation of a network of lesbian and gay groups—the Lavender Network—to respond to police handling of the horrific Jeffrey Dahmer murders." Dahmer's victims were young men, and his criminal behavior began to be conflated with male homosexuality in the press. The Lavender Network, representing some forty different groups, presented a joint statement, and Barber and Gotzler were key figures in pulling together a July 29, 1991, news conference. Lesbian journalist Jamakaya accused the major press of "homosexual overkill" in their reporting. By leading the press campaign against the homosexual sensationalism, the lesbians were able to shift attention away from the male sexual worlds of Milwaukee. A Police Proposal Task Force chaired by Gotzler made recommendations on how the police could improve relations with the gay and lesbian community, calling for a system

Lesbian Alliance ♀ Metro Milwaukee

P.O. Box 93323
Milwaukee, WI 53203
(414) 264-2600

July 1, 1992
Vol. 3, No. 7

"WE'RE OUT FOR OURSELVES"

Isle of Lesbos

Thanks to all who visited the Isle of Lesbos tent at this year's Pride Festival. The benefits of membership continued with free sodas and cake for LAMM card carrying members. Over 200 lesbians stopped at our tent, making this a very successful event. We signed-up many new members and renewed nearly as many old.

The stylish LAMM logo shirts were also extremely popular. These shirts are still available for $15 each. The Isle of Lesbos was definitely a must visit location at this year's Pride Festival. Mark your calendars now for next year's LAMM tent. It promises to be bigger, better, and filled with even more lesbians!

photo by Karen Zimmermann

LAMM WINS PRIDE AWARD

The 1992 Milwaukee Gay and Lesbian Pride Committee awarded LAMM a trophy for the best parade presentation by an organization at this year's Pride Festival held June 14th at Juneau Park. LAMM members and friends were once again the largest contingent in the Pride parade. Hundreds marched behind our new banner and were followed by this year's LAMM truck (complete with balloons, LAMM members, and guests). The three major tv stations all included LAMM coverage. Thanks go to Stephanie Hume and all who organized (and participated in) the contingent.

A rousing round of applause goes to our spokeswoman, Kitty Barber, who inspired thousands with her Pride rally speech following the parade. LAMM then celebrated Kitty's birthday with free cake for all card-carrying members.

Thanks also to Shelli and Anita and the Isle of Lesbos committee for our very popular, shady meeting place and to Margaret Snow and the Police Relations Task Group for hosting the Milwaukee Police Department's Crime Prevention booth.

LAMM's Pride participation continues to grow each year. Stay tuned to this newsletter for 1993 Pride information.

LAMM - LOUD AND PROUD!

The Lesbian Alliance of Metro Milwaukee (LAMM) was represented in the 1992 Pride Parade by this pickup truck full of high energy women. ARCHIVES DEPARTMENT, UNIVERSITY OF WISCONSIN–MILWAUKEE LIBRARIES

of reporting on hate crimes and noting the recent Wisconsin hate crimes law and the survey on harassment of gays and lesbians undertaken by the Governor's Council on Lesbian and Gay Issues.[22]

The task force work included coordinating and organizing testimony for the Mayor's Blue Ribbon Commission, which resulted in the submission of a six-hundred-page document. Having developed a relationship with Milwaukee Police Chief Philip Arreola, LAMM also organized a recruiting session for the police department with the lesbian and gay community—the first-ever such session in Milwaukee. LAMM also helped create a three-hour training curriculum for the city's police recruit classes with Gotzler as one of the trainers.[23]

Many of LAMM's events increased the group's visibility and solidarity, including a presentation by cartoonist Alison Bechdel of her slideshow "Dykes to Watch Out For." In 1991, Kate Clinton attended a reception for twenty-five LAMM supporters, which netted twelve hundred dollars. In 1993, LAMM sponsored buses for the national march on Washington, which one hundred LAMM members attended. Of course, it being Milwaukee, LAMM held a bowling event with a potluck. The group also hosted a huge picnic paired with an all-lesbian softball tournament. Some lesbians formed a volleyball team called SLAMMM, or Some of the Lesbian Alliance of Metro Milwaukee Members. LAMM later arranged a drag show with the Miltown Kings as a fundraising event. "This gang of gender benders consists of kings, queenz, femmes and everything in between," an article later reported. The gender-fluid acts ranged from sexy to humorous.[24]

For several years in the mid-1990s, LAMM sponsored Milwaukee's own Lesbian Variety Show at the Broadway Theatre Center. The press called it "an annual who's who of Lesbian and Gay entertainment." Poet Carmen Murguia recalled reading from her just-published collection *The Voices Inside* and attending the variety show in "full Charro outfit: the hat, the skirt, the tie, the vest, the little jacket, and cowboy boots." Ultimately, the Lesbian Alliance strengthened Milwaukee's female homosexual community over a long period and in a way that showcased powerful women. While still organizing amongst themselves, they avoided remaining distant from the larger LGBT community, as some prior separatists in the NLFO organizing efforts had done.[25]

MILWAUKEE WOMEN GET WILDER: THE CLUB OF TROLLOPS

If the women of LAMM were forceful advocates and organizers, the cohort of Milwaukee women who belonged to the Trollop Club were totally fun loving. Begun in 1987, the club was associated with the lesbian bar Station 2 owned by Shari Wilson and a partner. The bar's décor included a station platform and murals. Just a year earlier, *OUT!* ran an article by Sue Burke titled "Lesbian Bars: Are 5 Too Many for Cream City?" In addition to Station 2, the story also noted the Beer Garden at 3743 West Vliet Street, the oldest existing lesbian bar in the city, which had been operating since the pre-Stonewall days of 1966. At the time of the article's publication, Station 2 (then called the Gay Street Station) had opened recently and offered entertainment by a belly dancer and by lip-sync performers. A year later, the bar moved to new digs and took the name Station 2.[26]

Another lesbian bar of the time, Hot Legs, opened in 1984 and became the only women's disco bar in the city. In addition to hosting a wet T-shirt party, Hot Legs sponsored a women's team in the Saturday Softball Beer League. One of the bar's owners was quoted in Burke's article as saying the owners did not "think five bars will make it" because "women don't drink as much as men." Seemingly proving the point, Burke listed seventeen gay bars for men that existed in town and pointed out that even Chicago, which had six times the population of Milwaukee, had only seven lesbian bars. Following a national declining trend, a 2015 article observed that only one Milwaukee lesbian bar remained, Walker's Pint.[27]

In the *Trollop Club News*, the group's members designated bar owner Wilson as Vice Trollop and Founding Mother. The bar had a mascot, a stuffed parrot called "Snatch." A type of parrot known as a snatch does exist, but these women were certainly playing with the term: Evie Bollinger was designated the President and Keeper of Snatch, the newsletter was nicknamed *Snatch*, and it included a column called Ask Snatch. The goal of the column was "to provide advice to the lovelorn" and about "any of the many things about which Snatch has little or no knowledge." The Trollop Club aimed "to provide social activities to women who enjoy a variety of entertainments." Dues could be paid at the bar.[28]

Groups of up to forty trollops regularly attended Brewers games and held tailgate parties of beer and brats. Busloads of members made annual trips to Chicago for lesbian bar crawls. On one occasion, twenty-four trollops went to a professional hockey game, and a like number attended an outing to a city bowling alley on another. Sometimes the Trollop Club teamed up with its male counterpart, the GAMMA organization, for joint events including dinners out, visits to Great America Park in Chicago, and boat cruises. Trollop members also participated in golf outings and a horse-drawn hayride.[29]

The December 1987 issue of *Trollup Club News* wished all the trollops "a very naughty but nice holiday season." Playing on the dictionary definition of a trollop as a "loose and wanton woman," the newsletter editor redefined a trollop as "a woman who knows what she likes and does it." There was one rule, however: "No trollop shall trollop on another Trollop's trollop." When a reader asked the advice columnist how long one must wait to cruise a trollop's ex, she answered, "I think a good time limit for trolloping on a Trollop's ex-trollop (or ex-non-trollop) is 24 hours." The trollops demonstrated that Milwaukee's lesbian community could embrace newly emerging presentations of female sexuality in a positive, fun, and organized way.[30]

CHEESEHEAD PACKERS, TOO

There is a little-known bit of gay history associated with the Green Bay Packers, the state's iconic National Football League team, and Wisconsin native, Liberace. In his 1986 autobiography, *The Wonderful Private World of Liberace*, the musician titled one chapter "I Lost My Virginity at Sixteen." In this chapter, he claimed that blues singer Miss Bea Haven, who was twice his age, took advantage of him sexually. During this period in Liberace's life, he was playing piano in honky-tonks, developing a "nonchalant attitude toward liquor, cigarettes, and sex," and learning popular music. However, Liberace's longtime companion, Scott Thorson, tells quite a different tale in his tell-all book, *Behind the Candelabra*. While Thorson also placed Liberace's sexual awakening in the period when he played in Wisconsin bars, Thorson wrote, "He was playing in a bar when he met his first adult homosexual—and according to Lee [as Liberace was known to his friends], that man seduced him too." Thorson says Liberace's first lover was "a football hero from the Green Bay Packers. . . . Lee told me, reminiscing about his first lover, 'He was the size of a door, the most intimidating man I'd ever seen. Every time I looked out in the audience there he was smiling at me.'" One night, the footballer drove Liberace home. Thorson remembered Liberace telling him, "That's the night I lost my virginity." According to another published version of the incident, the seduction happened at Wausau's Wunderbar in 1939. After the two men split, Thorson sued Liberace for palimony. Though Liberace never came out, today his flamboyant personality has made him one of the better-known homosexuals from Wisconsin.[31]

David Maraniss, in his 1999 book *When Pride Still Mattered: A Life of Vince Lombardi*, details additional gay connections to the Packers. Maraniss wanted to immerse himself in Vince Lombardi's environment for his research, and he resided in Green Bay for months to get the setting correct. He also conducted extensive interviews as part of his research. Lombardi had a gay brother, Harold, who studied fine arts at Fordham University, where Vince had also gone to school and played football. Vince arrived in Green Bay in 1959, the smallest American city with a big-league team, with a five-year contract as coach and general manager. Harold, the middle brother, shared an artistic nature with his mother, and he would discuss books and opera with his sister-in-law Marie, Vince's wife. After teaching for a while, Harold ended up working as an underwriter for Northwestern Mutual Insurance Company in San Francisco. He later moved to the company's Milwaukee headquarters while Vince was coaching at Green Bay. Harold lived on North Prospect Avenue in Milwaukee. While in San Francisco, Harold had told his parents he was a homosexual. In response to Maraniss's questions, Harold said he was not sure if Vince knew he was gay, but a few of Maraniss's other sources made clear that Vince did know. After leaving the Packers to coach the Washington Redskins in 1969, Vince Lombardi coached a gay player, Ray McDonald, who had been the team's first draft choice in 1967 from the University of Idaho. Lombardi did not tolerate discrimination on his teams and purportedly told his players, "If I hear one of you people make reference to [McDonald's] manhood you'll be out of here before your ass hits the ground."[32]

David Kopay, a Chicago native, was picked up by the Green Bay Packers for the 1972 season, by which time Lombardi had left the team. A Green Bay news story noted he was a different type of player: "A meditative type, he can most often be found exploring a book on philosophy during his free time." The article also called him "free-thinking." After his first year on the team, Kopay said "It was a great experience playing at Green Bay" and that he hoped to make it a ten-year stint in the NFL. Yet, the Packers cut him the next year. Kopay believed he was bisexual for a while, but in the end, he would be the first NFL player to come out as gay. In his 1977 book, *The David Kopay Story*, he wrote, "A lot of coaches and owners already know they have homosexuals playing for them on NFL teams. . . . What they're afraid of—and I think, the only thing they're afraid of—is the publicity about it might affect box-office receipts."[33]

The Milwaukee-based *GPU News* in January 1976 featured a large story, "Star Athlete Comes Out," following Kopay's inclusion in a December 1975 *Washington Star* series on homosexuals in sports. After the series began, Kopay, who was then thirty-three, contacted the reporter to tell his story, resulting in his "becoming the first sports star to come out voluntarily," according to *GPU News*. Kopay appeared on the cover of the May 1977 issue of *GPU News*, and the issue featured an interview by Peter Pherson with Kopay about his book. Kopay said, "I'd like to see the book, and others like it, on the shelves of every school library in the country." Malcolm Snider, a former Green Bay Packer, was the only person who had been one of Kopay's teammates over the years to write him a favorable letter after the news stories.[34]

Esera Tuaolo is another NFL player who has come out and who also played for the Green Bay Packers in the defensive line. Tuaolo, a Samoan raised in Hawaii, was drafted for the Green Bay Packers in 1991 from Oregon State University where he played college football. At the time, he claimed he "didn't even know Green Bay was in Wisconsin." But Tuaolo appreciated the fact that "Packer fans are the number one fans in the league. They show up three hours before the game." Nevertheless, he felt "severe culture shock" in Wisconsin; for a Polynesian, he said, Green Bay was "like going to Siberia." While at Lambeau Field, he once sang the national anthem before a Chicago Bears game in his high tenor voice. By the 1992 season, Tuaolo moved on to play for the Vikings in Minnesota, where he eventually met his partner and made his home.[35]

Tuaolo's autobiography shows he felt he had to hide his gay identity or it would ruin his career as a player. He had an older brother who was also gay and who died young from AIDS. Not knowing any other out football players, Tuaolo tried to convince himself that if he was a football player, he couldn't be gay. In the end, he explored same-sex attraction by going to gay clubs in Honolulu and picking up tourists for one-night stands but never telling them his real name. When he attended the NFL Scouting

Combine, the showcase where college players perform for NFL scouts and coaches, Tuaolo had felt that the league was advanced on racial issues but in the dark ages on sexuality. Reading Kopay's book gave him strength. He recalled going with friends to the Minneapolis gay bar The Saloon. Finally, after leaving the NFL, Tuaolo came out on an episode of *Real Sports with Bryant Gumbel* in 2002, expressing the belief that no active NFL player would come out.[36]

Outsports journalist Cyd Zeigler, in his 2016 book *Fair Play: How LGBT Athletes Are Claiming Their Rightful Place in Sports*, observed, "Men's pro sports are stuck where women's pro sports were in the early eighties, with athletes still afraid of losing endorsement deals and being cut from their teams." Zeigler gives credit to lesbian sports journalists who had been covering lesbian athletes for a decade before him. He heard one suggested statistic that 85 percent of female college basketball coaches were lesbians. Zeigler got a major breakthrough when he approached former Green Bay Packer player Ahman Green in 2012 for an interview about gays in sports. Green acknowledged that his sister was a lesbian and one of his brothers was gay. Later that same day, when Zeigler tried to follow up with Green, a publicist hired by the NFL Players Association tried to block Zeigler from asking any further questions relating to sexual orientation. Green said, "I'm having a conversation with my man Cyd here. So leave us alone and let us finish." In 2017, the *Huffington Post* published an interview with Packers quarterback Aaron Rogers, who identifies as an LGBT ally, saying that "teams are getting closer to fully accepting an openly gay player."[37]

WISCONSIN'S MOTORCYCLE/LEATHER SCENE

One of Milwaukee's iconic industries is Harley-Davidson, and for a long while, the company's factory was located on Juneau Avenue. The Harley tradition in Milwaukee began in 1903, so it is not surprising that Milwaukee's early gay men embraced the concept of motorcycle clubs. To many, Harleys possess a mythical nature that extends beyond that of other transport vehicles. Books on the motorcycles emphasize that they represent rebellion and brotherhood, with a hint of danger—a combination of traits that would certainly appeal to oppressed gay men. In 2003, market data suggested "more homosexuals and lesbians are purchasing

Harley-Davidson motorcycles" than had been previously believed. An auditor for the Zogby International firm observed, "What we are seeing here is a significant change in the percentage of owners of Harley-Davidson motorcycles who happen to be gay." The research suggested these new buyers were motivated by the "masculine image the motor company and its product suggests." The model most favored by gays was the Springer Softtail (owned by 39 percent of gay Harley owners), followed by the Fat Boy model (owned by 33 percent). This trend extended beyond gay men, as lesbian Harley ownership was also thought to be growing. In the 1990s, a loosely affiliated group of gay men called the Great Lakes Harley Riders

Drawing on the ancient Greek myth of a happy crew of men who accompanied Jason on his quest, this Wisconsin gay motorcycle club held an annual cycle run near Hilbert. COURTESY OF RAINBOW OVER WISCONSIN

existed "for the purpose of sharing the Brotherhood of the Machine with our ilk."[38]

One of the longest-running gay motorcycle groups in Wisconsin was the Castaways Motorcycle Club, founded in 1979 after having split from the earlier Silver Star Motorcycle Club. The Silver Stars had formed in 1973 as the region's first gay motorcycle club, and the group was associated with the Wreck Room bar in Milwaukee. Si Smits was involved in both clubs and later founded the Boot Camp Saloon, the city's main leather club. Soon after the Castaways club split off, the Silver Star club folded. In 1981, the Castaways broadened their appeal and became a leather/Levi club. Their first motorcycle run was in 1982. For thirty years, Castaways has been donating to charities, including the AIDS Resource Center of Wisconsin.[39]

The Argonauts of Wisconsin, founded in 1973 and originally located in Milwaukee, claims to be the oldest Wisconsin gay organization. In its constitution, the group aims "to bring together persons with the common purpose and inclination for fellowship and advancement of their interests. The club shall strive at all times to present the leather/Levi image." For many years, the Argonauts and the Castaways held an annual joint run and campout in August, which took place at the Al Kamke farm at Hilbert. Based largely in northeast Wisconsin, the Argonauts held their annual anniversary dinner in Green Bay, and the regular club night was the second Friday of the month at the Napalese Lounge. The club was a founding member of the Mid-America Conference of Motorcycle Clubs, the region's gay leather organization. With a few dozen active members, plus many associate members, the club continues today.[40]

DOLLARS AND SENSE

Wisconsin's early gay institutions and organizations operated mainly on shoestring budgets thanks to the help of just dozens of individuals, especially in the first decade after Stonewall. In many ways, like Blanche DuBois in *A Streetcar Named Desire*, they depended on the kindness of strangers. To fight the legal appeal of Paul Safransky's firing at the Wisconsin Supreme Court, activists took up collections in the gay bars for copying legal briefs and paying filing fees. The 1974 annual report of the GPU of Milwaukee showed revenues of just $12,048 and expenses of just

$10,848. In 1977, *Renaissance* in Madison reported, "Financial Crisis Hits Gay Center and Pledges Drop." The center's regular revenue had been $300 to $400 a month, or about $4,000 annually. The Madison United was a little more flush than some of the other groups by 1981 because it had received city purchase of services money to the tune of $21,250, plus $910 from the Madison Sustaining Fund. But it had raised only $4,251 from contributions and fundraising. Sustaining Fund coordinator Denise Matyka said in the press, "We hope that more lesbian and gay groups will consider applying." The Wisconsin Community Fund was also an early funding source for many gay groups thanks to the involvement of gays and lesbians like Sue Goldwomon and Nancy Dungan. The foundation for Progressive Social Change was another occasional source of funds. Much later, Joseph Pabst, of the Milwaukee brewery family, established a fund in his name and that of his partner, Robert Johnson, that would assist a number of gay organizations.[41]

Milwaukee's BAM

As mentioned earlier, Wisconsin gay bars were some of the early sources of funds for gay efforts in their sponsorships of gay sports teams. In Milwaukee, enough gay bars and bathhouses (the commercial establishments that catered to gay social/sexual life) existed that in 1979 they formed the Business Association of Milwaukee (BAM). In this time of police harassment, early proposed projects included a legal defense fund and legal assistance for patrons of member establishments. Key figures were Bob Schmidt from the M&M Club, Chuck Balistreri (aka Cicerello) from the Factory, Wayne Bernhagen from the Wreck Room, and Paul DeMarco from Club Baths. BAM sponsored bar crawls to Chicago and Madison—it was noted there were fewer passengers on the return bus trip on at least one occasion. BAM also sponsored a Chuck Roast in 1981 of President Balistreri who owned and operated some of Milwaukee's most popular gay bars.[42]

Cream City Business Association

While BAM had a narrow focus, the Cream City Business Association (CCBA) had a broader view, and members described it as "an average cross section of the local professional business community." In 1981, when the association formed, a *Milwaukee Journal* story noted, "They are not likely to be welcomed openly by many other professional groups. That's because the association's members are homosexual." The paper noted that the formation of such associations was a nationwide trend and that CCBA was a member of the National Association of Business Councils. Many members had to remain closeted or discreet in their professions; as one member said, "I must play the role of a heterosexual." The CCBA's members included bankers, corporate executives, and independent business operators. By the first year, fifty members had joined. An early brochure described the association's goal of acting as a body "to further the general welfare of the gay business and professional community as well as the Greater Milwaukee community."[43]

Ralph Navarro was the CCBA's first president. A native of Chicago with Mexican American parents, Navarro was a graduate of Loras College in Dubuque. While he once hoped to be a priest (he had gone to seminary but did not take his final vows, as he found his identity would conflict too much with clerical service—he used the term "almost priest" to describe himself), he worked for a while as a director of youth retreats for the Archdiocese of New Orleans. Navarro became a fundraiser for nonprofit organizations and moved to Milwaukee. He felt that his gay activism flowed from the activism he had been part of his whole life. In Navarro's view, "Working to build a genuine lesbian/gay community is no small task." He saw CCBA as "an opportunity to create an economic block of power to open the mainline society's doors for us a little wider." At national meetings, he would pull out an actual cream-colored city brick to illustrate the source of Milwaukee's nickname as the Cream City for those not familiar with the moniker. By 1985, Navarro had helped CCBA membership grow to two hundred.[44]

Another key figure in the early CCBA was Marc Haupert, who served two years as president following Navarro and edited the association's magazine, *Cream City Special Edition*. Haupert also coordinated the May 1986 meeting in Milwaukee of the National Association of Business Councils. He had moved to Milwaukee in 1972 and worked with arts organizations. In his 1984 president's column in the CCBA newsletter, Haupert stressed that the association spoke "in terms corporate America understands—money and business." Haupert felt it was "on the business front that we can make

One of the Cream City Business Association's early social activities in Milwaukee was gay volleyball. ARCHIVES DEPARTMENT, UNIVERSITY OF WISCONSIN–MILWAUKEE LIBRARIES

significant progress," even though he acknowledged that one Milwaukee lithography company refused to print *Special Edition*. Milwaukee's police chief, Robert Ziarnik, attended his first public meeting hosted by a gay organization when he spoke to CCBA on December 13, 1984. The association was quite pleased when in 1984 the national gay magazine *The Advocate* honored four hundred gay American leaders and, of the seventeen from Wisconsin, eight were CCBA members. Haupert was followed as CCBA president by Jerry Johnson, and then by Karen Gotzler who worked to increase women's participation in the organization. By 1989, the association disbanded but its efforts to organize and engage Milwaukee's gay professional and business communities lived on, most importantly thanks to its establishment of the Cream City Foundation.[45]

A 1984 CCBA membership survey showed that 91 percent of its members were male with a mean annual income of twenty-nine thousand dollars and that 63 percent owned their primary residence. Individual members constituted 52 percent of all CCBA members, and 28 percent were business members. Realizing that many gay folks would embrace the new world of computers, Haupert conducted an interview for the CCBA newsletter with the creator of one of the first online gay bulletin board systems. During his presidency, Haupert noticed he was always being asked for referrals, so in 1984 CCBA put out a directory of businesses and services friendly to the gay community. He urged use of the directory because "financial clout is a major component of our 'gay pride'—is being understood more widely." Their survey had shown that 83 percent of CCBA members attempted to seek out gay-owned or gay-oriented businesses. Annual awards ceremonies were also used to highlight professionals in the Milwaukee community. In a survey of Milwaukee personnel directors, a representative of the local giant Miller Brewing Company said, "Gays are consumers and we need their business just as much as we do everybody else's. We never forget that they, too, buy our products." A spokesperson for Central Ready Mix Concrete said, "We take an evenhanded approach and judge by a person's qualifications and how well they do their job. Heck, for all I know, everyone here could be gay." On the whole, the CCBA made major inroads for gay and lesbian professionals within the larger Milwaukee business community, raising awareness among straight professionals and also encouraging gay folks to be formally out in their workplaces.[46]

CREAM CITY FOUNDATION

An early CCBA project was the Cream City Association Foundation (later renamed Cream City Foundation, or CCF). This was also a dream of Ralph Navarro's, and he became one of the incorporators of the foundation along with James Mauer, Warren Breitlow, and Roger Ravasz. In March 1983, an article in OUT! titled "Fundraising for a Liberated Future" described the formation of the foundation. The story reported that Milwaukee "has something sexual minorities have often lacked—a professional approach to community development and fundraising." The incorporators viewed the foundation as the "Gay United Way" for Milwaukee and southeastern Wisconsin. In the founding documents, they noted a concern regarding "both homophobia and closetism of the gay community" in the area. The foundation's initial goals, after surveying the community, were four: support gay health by combatting sexually transmitted diseases and establish a counseling service, a legal defense fund, and a community center. The first meeting was held October 5, 1982, and the first event was held at the bar This Is It—run by longtime owner and ally Joe Brehm—which had been a gay gathering place since the 1970s. While the event raised only seventy-six dollars, the foundation's incorporators said, "We felt good about it."[47]

Despite its ambitious goals, the foundation's beginnings were modest. In 1983, Don Schwamb, who served as CCF's president during the early years, announced enough fundraising success to enable CCF's first two grants totaling $760 for the creation of two health-related programs in 1984. For the fiscal year ending June 30, 1985, CCF awarded a total of $2,952.47 (up from the grants of $825 the year before). Three of the seven grants awarded that year were AIDS-related, as the community was newly focused on this serious health fight. After ten years in operation, the foundation had awarded a total of $226,000. In 1994, when CCF honored Miller Brewing Company for its support of the community, Miller's director of public affairs, Tom Reed, said, "CCF has continually proven to be an excellent example of how to productively and efficiently take funds and multiply their impact and effectiveness."[48]

In 1995, Milwaukee hosted the National Conference of Gay/Lesbian Foundations (NCGLF) thanks to CCF's efforts. The national group had been founded in 1991 with Milwaukee's Schwamb in attendance. At that time, Milwaukee CCF was listed as one of five foundations that would likely participate in forming a national coalition. In a report to CCF on the founding gathering in San Francisco, Schwamb noted that most participating foundations were male-focused, but special appeals to the lesbian communities were being made. On March 18, 1991, Schwamb wrote to CCF's board urging it to join the new coalition. For the 1995 NCGLF conference held in Milwaukee, the three hosts were the CCF of Milwaukee, the New Harvest Foundation of Madison, and the Philanthrofund of Minneapolis. Through the efforts of Reed, Miller Brewing Company helped underwrite the conference with ten thousand dollars. Still a leader in the field today, CCF achieved success because its incorporators realized the needs of Milwaukee's LGBT community and organized to increase resources for that community.[49]

New Harvest Foundation

In 1983, the efforts underway in Milwaukee inspired a group of Madison's lesbian and gay professionals to meet for six months at my home to discuss community fundraising. The resulting foundation's first brochure noted the need to go beyond bar coat checks and passed donation cans as means of fundraising. The aim would be to found an organization "to fund a broad range of community interests such as arts and culture, social services, spiritual development and communications" for lesbian and gay projects. As a result, the New Harvest Foundation was formally organized on April 29, 1984. All initial members agreed that gender parity would be important on the board, in its officers, and on the grant making committee to ensure that lesbians who had been a key part of the initial discussions would be included. The foundation's first cochairs were Teresa Meuer and me, the first vice cochairs were Marcia Holtz and Ron Sommer, the first treasurer was Thom DeChant, and the first secretary was Deborah Smith.[50]

The discussions in my home revealed that many lesbians and gay men would not feel comfortable writing checks to an outwardly gay foundation. So, following the lead of other gay foundations such as the Horizon Foundation of San Francisco, the group decided on a neutral-sounding name. Since we were focused on a better future for a new, younger crop of gays and lesbians, Karla Dobinski came up with the New Harvest moniker. When the IRS, during the Reagan administration, reviewed New Harvest's tax exemption application, the foundation was admonished not to masquerade as an agricultural group.[51]

The New Harvest Foundation was publicly launched at a January 23, 1985, reception with special guest Mayor Joe Sensenbrenner at the Madison Civic Center. Jerry Dahlke, a native of Ladysmith and professional fundraiser who was helping us get organized, was close to the mayor and secured him for the event. In addition to choosing a neutral-sounding name for the foundation, many early participants felt that "ostensible straights" who were allies in the political world should have a presence on the board. Thus, District Attorney James Doyle Jr. and former Dane County board chairwoman Mary Louise Symon became initial board members, along with several attorneys, a professional firefighter from Madison, and Alder Henry Lufler Jr.[52]

Initially, people thought a three-year goal of raising $10,000 seemed ambitious. When initial quiet inquiries resulted in nearly that amount being collected from board members and a few friends, Dahlke increased the announced goal to $25,000, an unheard-of sum at the time. One key fundraiser was Claire Fulenwider, fondly nicknamed the "Queen Bee" because she was so good at "the sting," or making the actual ask for money. Other strong cochairs included Barb Constans and Paula Bonner. By 1987, New Harvest had given out $21,400 in grants and raised an additional $10,000 to install George Segal's orphaned *Gay Liberation* sculpture in Madison's Orton Park for several years while New York City deliberated about whether to place it near the Stonewall Bar. By 1989, nearly $60,000 had been awarded. In 2009, cochairs Woody Carey and Tret Fure announced that more than $300,000 in grants supporting gay and lesbian efforts had been made since the foundation's inception.[53]

In its second year of public operation, the New Harvest Foundation launched the city's first civic dinner and dance hosted by a gay/lesbian organization on April 19, 1986, reserving the entire Fess Hotel for the event. The evening's featured speaker was former Madison resident Evelyn Beck, author of *Nice Jewish Girls*. Tickets were thirty dollars, and black tie was optional. Using the theme Pride Is Blooming Everywhere, New Harvest for many years sponsored a fundraising garden tour that featured some "gayborhood" gardens such as Scott Thornton's on Jenifer Street. At New Harvest's twenty-fifth anniversary dinner/dance in 2009, Congresswoman Tammy Baldwin spoke. Many of the people who had learned fundraising skills through their work with New Harvest, such as Mary Strickland, were able to use these skills to help in Baldwin's campaigns. Ultimately, these folks raised the dollars that made Baldwin the first member of Congress initially elected as an out person.[54]

PRAYING FOR CHANGE

In earlier chapters, I have described how gay rights advocates in Wisconsin successfully enlisted religious allies in the political fight. A key element was the work of Milwaukee's Council on Religion and the Homosexual in the 1970s. However, the stories of other Wisconsin religious groups are less well known.

When it came to addressing sexuality, the Unitarians of Wisconsin broke ground by adopting a national resolution in 1970 to end discrimination against homosexuals. In 1972, the Milwaukee-area Unitarian Church West in Brookfield sought an injunction against a Waukesha district attorney who had asked to review materials for a Sunday school curriculum titled "About Your Sexuality" for possible violations of Wisconsin's obscenity law. Homosexual behavior was presented via film strips at a time when homosexual activity was illegal in the state. The church board voted not to submit the materials to the district attorney, expressing their belief that there is "no one right norm of sexual behavior for all people." Federal judge John Reynolds granted an injunction against the district attorney. The next year, a follow-up *Milwaukee Journal* story including interviews with many students of the course quoted a fifteen-year-old boy who said, "No one was changed into a sex fiend." The story also reported that the teenage students (who had parental consent to take the course) appreciated "the section on homosexuality—that it was informative and had made them more understanding and tolerant."[55]

After the Unitarian Universalists, the next major denomination to welcome gay folks was the Congregational Church, or the United Church of Christ. The Congregational tradition was strong in Wisconsin, as the church was established in New England before 1800 and many of the state's early settlers came from New England. The faith was reinforced by some of the Swiss Reformed migrants, who appeared in Wisconsin during the nineteenth century. In 1979, the First Congregational Church of Madison hosted a gay dialogue with 113 participants. The first such dialogue in Madison had taken place the year prior during the Reverend Dillabaugh crisis (see chapter 3) and had been attended by sixty-six clergy and twenty-six gay people. In 1980, Reverend Wells Grogan of Madison's First Congregational Church testified in favor of Dane County's ordinance barring discrimination on the basis of sexual orientation. And in 1992, First Congo, as it was sometimes known locally, officially became an open and affirming church. One active member of the Open and Affirming Task Force was Rich Fluechtling, a gay man. In 1997, Reverend Paul Kittlaus of First Congregational coordinated a Madison Affirmation on Homosexuality with more than sixty Christian clergy who were joined by Rabbi Jan Brahms of Temple Beth El. Ripon College, which has historical ties to the Congregational Church, was also the locus of GRANDFLAGS, or the Greater Ripon Area Network Developed for Lesbian and Gay Support, in the mid-1980s. Lois Van Leer, a lesbian and 1978 Ripon graduate, would go on to become a Congregational minister, and in 1999 she returned to give a talk sponsored by Ripon's GLBT student organization. "Even though our denomination was very open and affirming," Van Leer noted in her speech, "the congregations weren't there yet." She also described how she found it hard to accept an "assumption of the superiority of heterosexuality over homosexuality . . . with all the gross arrogance that goes along with it."[56]

In April 1974 *GPU News* ran a story about the group called the Gay United Presbyterians, a caucus within the Presbyterian Church USA (PC-USA) "established to work for change within this denomination of the injustice it perpetuates against people on the basis of sexual orientation." It took a while for their work to bear fruit. Scott Anderson was a gay Presbyterian minister serving a congregation in Sacramento in 1990 when he was threatened with exposure. Deciding to forthrightly tell his congregation he was gay, he gave up his ordination. Later, after her husband died, the wife of the couple that had outed him asked for forgiveness, which he granted. Anderson moved to Madison and in 2003 became executive director of the Wisconsin Council of Churches. In 2006, with the Presbyterian Church's changing rules based on conscience providing a possible opening, Anderson, who had been in a committed relationship for two decades, filed for a new ordination. As a graduate of Princeton Theological Seminary, Anderson in his application wrote that the ministerial prohibition against gays in committed relationships "represents a grievous misapplication of biblical teachings." In 2010, the John Knox Presbytery, comprised of parts of Iowa, Minnesota, and Wisconsin, voted 81 to 25 for his ordination. Reverend Alex Thornburg of Westminster Presbyterian Church in Madison, who voted for Anderson's ordination, said, "I could see it having national implications, for sure." In 1995, Anderson had given his stole, a ministerial garment, to the Shower of Stoles project—a traveling exhibit by the National Gay and Lesbian Task Force. During his reordination on October 8, 2011, at Madison's Covenant Presbyterian Church, the director of the exhibit noted, "Today, for the first time in the life of this collection a stole is being returned, and in so doing, it is transformed from a symbol of loss to a symbol of hope." Anderson became the first openly gay person to be officially ordained in the denomination.[57]

The Lutherans, as one of the largest bodies of Christians in the state derived from German and Scandinavian heritage, are often mentioned in the Wisconsin news. Thus, when Lutherans Concerned for Gay People was formed in 1974, the *Milwaukee Journal* duly reported it. Gay-supportive Lutherans in the upper Midwest organized Lutherans Concerned in Minneapolis "to affirm with joy the goodness of human sexuality which God has given us." *GPU News* in June 1979 also reported on the largest Lutheran body of the time—the Lutheran Church in America (LCA)—having established a Lutheran task force on sexuality. The story noted that one task force appointee—Diane Fraser, a former sociology instructor at Gustavus Adolphus College from the Minneapolis area—was also one of the founders of Lutherans Concerned, which had twenty chapters. In 1978, the first national meeting of Lutherans Concerned was held in Milwaukee. Sixty people gathered at Lake Park Lutheran Church to hear a sermon by Reverend Charles Lewis, a minister for the San Francisco Council of Churches. He urged them to discard the lie that gays are "heretics, lunatics, criminals, sinners, and finally the misfits who are unfit."[58]

A key Milwaukee figure in Lutherans Concerned was Bob Moore, who had cochaired the 1978 national assembly of Lutherans Concerned. He worked at UW–Milwaukee where he served as director of the Executive MBA Program. He was an active member and officer of the Village Church, a congregation of Evangelical Lutheran Church in America (ELCA), a branch of Lutherans resulting from the merger of the LCA with several denominational bodies. In a welcome-to-worship ad in *The Wisconsin Light*, the Village Church proclaimed itself Wisconsin's only registered "Reconciled-in-Christ" congregation due to Lutherans Concerned. In 1988, Moore participated in that church's initial conversations about same-sex weddings. Moore was active in many early gay organizations, and he was a founding member of the Wisconsin Log Cabin Republicans. He was also a president of GAMMA. Mayor John Norquist appointed Moore to serve on the Milwaukee Safety Commission in 1988. His obituary noted that many of the gay organizations he was involved with were still going strong when he died in 1998.[59]

Though Lutherans dominated the religious environment in many Wisconsin cities, this was especially true in western Wisconsin. In 1991, Reverend Paul Johnson of Viroqua resigned under pressure as assistant to the bishop of the La Crosse area Coulee Region synod of the ELCA. Johnson was outed after he confidentially revealed his orientation at a social ministry event in Chicago. Mary Hollister, a Vernon County broadcaster, deplored the church's response to the outing. Johnson, in a statement reputedly reprinted in *The Lutheran*, the denomination's magazine, acknowledged that, according to the church rules, "ordained ministers who are homosexual in their self-understanding are expected to abstain from homosexual relationships" and that he could not "meet these expectations." In the *Westby Times*, Johnson cited parts of the church's "Visions and Expectations" document that affirmed human sexuality as a gift from God. He said he did not believe the church should require ordained gay men to commit to life-long celibacy. Affirming himself as a child of God, Johnson wrote, "I believe that sexuality is a gift from God—homosexuality as well as heterosexuality." He believed gays should experience the fullness of that gift. He asserted that he was not alone, as he believed there could be thousands of gay clergy in the denomination. "I continue to hope things will change in my church," he concluded. "All of us need love and acceptance, not judgement and condemnation." In contrast, an ELCA synod based in Milwaukee encouraged its congregations to accept gay ministers around the same time. Bishop Peter Rognes of Milwaukee said, "The majority felt the church is a welcoming place for all people."[60]

When the Milwaukee press in 1980 first mentioned the Metropolitan Community Church (MCC) of Milwaukee, it described a thirty-five-member congregation "whose membership list is private and whose address is a secret." The congregation began in February 1977 during the first decade of national MCC growth. This gay- and lesbian-affirming denomination began in 1968, right before Stonewall. Milwaukee pastor Valerie Bouchard rejected the label "gay church" because, as she explained, "The emphasis is upon our Christianity, not our sexuality." Bouchard had earned her master's degree in divinity from McCormick Theological Seminary in Chicago, a PC-USA institution. The Milwaukee MCC would perform ceremonies of Holy Union for same-sex couples after three months of counseling. Regarding the church in the city's gay community, the Milwaukee MCC pastor Reverend Steve Stahl said in 1981, "We have the seeds in Milwaukee for dynamic growth and creativity." In 1990, Milwaukee's New Hope MCC welcomed new pastors Chris Pasinski and Nancy Smiegowski, a clergy couple ministry team. Pasinski went on to serve fifteen years in various ministries within in the denomination, and, after a prior experience as a Franciscan sister, Smiegowski served six years in MCC ministry. At the time, they were completing their master's of divinity degrees from Chicago Theological Seminary. Today, the Milwaukee congregation continues as a long-lasting institution with a church at 1239 West Mineral Street. Activities include participation in the Transgender Day of Remembrance and a POZ Spirit Group, a support community for people with AIDS and HIV-positive individuals.[61]

Roman Catholic attitudes regarding homosexuality have too often been perceived only as condemnation. Yet in Wisconsin, many ministers have taken a pastoral approach—one involving patience and gentleness—when interacting with homosexual church members. In 1973, the *Catholic Review* reported that the US province of the Salvatorian priests and brothers based in Milwaukee had developed an eleven-point model for ministry to Catholic homosexuals. Father Ramon Wagner, SDS, head of the Salvatorian Justice and Peace Commission, was quoted as urging "conscientization," or making "people aware of the homosexual as an individual person with human needs and values." Wagner, in the diocesan paper the *Catholic Herald*, said, "Many factors are involved in homosexuality and not all are necessarily abnormal."[62]

An important Roman Catholic approach to homosexuality was undertaken by New Ways Ministry founded in 1977 by Father Robert Nugent, SDS, and Sister Jeannine Gramick, SSND. The fact that Nugent was a Salvatorian showed the continuation of the work begun in 1973. Gramick joined the order of the School Sisters of Notre Dame through its eastern province in Baltimore. The order's western province had its motherhouse in Milwaukee. The tagline that became attached to the work of New Ways came from a bishops' pastoral letter on sexuality describing the need "to find new ways to communicate the truth of Christ because we believe it will make you free." In 1987, Gramick and Nugent spoke at UW–Milwaukee, sponsored by the university's Gay and Lesbian Community. In an interview with *OUT!*, they stressed that the ultimate guide must be one's conscience. Nugent said, "One must follow one's conscience even in the face of the magisterium," or the teachings of the church. In 1986, New Ways Ministry published *Homosexuality and the Magisterium*, which included more than a hundred pages of documents from both the Vatican and US Catholic bishops ranging back to 1975. Some of the documents voiced older traditional viewpoints, but others showed an "emphasis on the Church's responsibility to halt violence and discrimination against gay people." A reviewer in Madison's Integrity/Dignity newsletter observed, "The seeds of change are here in the words of Church leaders themselves."[63]

In 1985, at the Perpetual Help Retreat Center in Oconomowoc, Wisconsin, Gramick and Nugent discussed Vatican officials' attempts to have the two removed from New Ways Ministry. The New Ways ministers saw this crackdown as "different manifestations of homophobia—fear of the topic." Gramick was saddened. "I think it's a grave injustice to the whole church," she said, "because it muzzles part of the church." While in Wisconsin, Gramick and Nugent conducted workshops at the Catholic order School Sisters of Notre Dame in Milwaukee as well as in Madison.[64]

Gramick and Nugent were featured in a 1983 *Milwaukee Sentinel* story with Daniel Maguire, a Marquette University theologian, on homosexual marriage. The article was formulated as a review and interview about Maguire's essay in a book edited by Nugent, *A Challenge to Love: Gay and Lesbian Catholics in the Church*. Maguire wrote that erotic desire is a basic human desire. To say that celibacy "befits homosexuals in any culture, clime or time, is . . . immodest . . . and absurd," he wrote, adding, "If celibacy is so difficult for nuns and priests, how can it be so easy for gay people?" Maguire argued that homosexuals are capable of sustained relationships. Gramick hoped a day would come when acting on homosexuality would no longer be considered a sin, but she observed the church "moves slowly, in terms of centuries."[65]

One welcoming community for a number of gay Catholics in Wisconsin's three metropolitan areas was Dignity, a national ministry for gay and lesbian Catholics. Father Wagner, back in 1973, had observed, "You only have to read a couple of issues of *Dignity* to see how deep the faith commitment is for many of these [people]." Nugent acknowledged that while Dignity had initially been welcomed in some Catholic churches and parish halls, the group was subsequently put out of such spaces by orders from the bishops in the 1980s. Still, he hoped Catholics could find creative new ways "to express their Catholic Christianity."[66]

The largest Dignity chapter in the state was Milwaukee's, formed in February 1975. The group had begun in the apartment of Brother Grant-Michael Fitzgerald, an African American member of the Salvatorians. Fitzgerald did his novitiate at Mount St. Paul College in Waukesha and later attended the Dominican College in Racine. By 1972, he was in Milwaukee teaching black high school–aged youths at the Harambee Education Center and attending meetings of the Gay People's Union. He was not out at Harambee, and his attempts to bring gay speakers to the school were rebuffed. Fitzgerald had worked on position papers for the Salvatorians' ministry to gays. The national gay magazine *The Advocate* featured Fitzgerald in 1973. "How do I show the gay person that God is love," he asked in the article, "not a bookkeeper tabulating sins?" Kevin Mumford, in his book *Not Straight, Not White*, claimed, "Fitzgerald was becoming a national gay rights activist whose unique vantage point as devout, black, and gay increased his political visibility." In 1975, *GPU News* reported on his work in Philadelphia trying to help pass a municipal gay rights bill. Before the bill's passage, he had helped in the formation of Milwaukee's AIDS response.[67]

The northeast Wisconsin Dignity chapter, like the one in Milwaukee, was located in an area of the state with a heavy Catholic population. Reverend Steve Scherer, a St. Jude parish priest, helped to found the chapter in 1983, and he served as one of the spiritual advisors to the group, which met initially in De Pere, Wisconsin, in a rented basement room. The local bishop, while not encouraging, did not block their work. Perhaps this was partly because Scherer upheld the church's position against extra-marital sex. Still, the chapter's first mass was attended by anti-homosexual activists. In a December 1983 article about the local resistance in the *Green Bay Press Gazette*, some area Dignity members were quoted. "On Sunday nights when I'm with Dignity members," said one member, "I feel very much accepted." "Let's put away the Bible-thumping and hatred," said another. A few years later, Scherer, who had since become chaplain at St. Elizabeth Hospital in Appleton, spoke to Catholic high school students at St. Joseph Academy in Appleton. He started with the bishops' 1976 pastoral letter "To Live in Christ Jesus" and focused on the message: "We are all children of God and He understands."[68]

By 1986, Dignity was meeting at St. Norbert's Abbey in De Pere— the same place where Nugent and Gramick had conducted one of their seminars on contemporary studies on homosexuality and the church's response. Scherer passed out leaflets in local gay bars, and he also read to students at St. Joseph Academy from Archbishop Rembert Weakland's open letter of 1980 urging dialogue and respect for homosexuals.

Weakland's personal sexual journey is movingly described in the prologue of his memoir. He clearly outlines the failures of the old, narrow Catholic instruction about sexuality. In a *New York Times* story about the memoir, Weakland stressed the need "to raise questions about the church's teaching that homosexuality is 'objectively disordered.'" Scherer later served as a regional director for Dignity in the early 1990s.[69]

The Madison chapter of Integrity/Dignity (a name referring both to the national Catholic organization Dignity and the national Episcopal group Integrity, also known as I/D) was founded in 1977. It has used the feast of Pentecost—the traditional feast celebrating the beginning of the Church as well as the descent of the Holy Spirit—as its anniversary date, and the celebration continues at the time of this book's publication, making I/D one of the longest-lasting gay groups in the Madison area. It started with worshippers who were mostly Episcopalian, but expanded to include Catholics. The national Dignity director, reflecting on I/D's quarter-century anniversary in 2002, commended the "special warmth and commitment that has long flowed from Madison, Wisconsin, to the rest of Dignity." Louie Crew, a national founder of Integrity for gay Episcopalians, spoke to the Madison chapter of I/D in 1982 in a talk titled "A Heavenly Queer Speaks on Queers in Heaven." Crew attributed many difficulties to "erotophobia—the self-censure that comes from having bodily desires." His view was that God saw all creation, including gay people, and proclaimed "it was good." In a more extended piece on homosexuals and the church, published in the journal *Christianity and Crisis* in 1980, Crew focused not on the issue of whether the church would accept gays but on the issue of whether it would acknowledge their presence. He argued that gay men had been being ordained for centuries. He also emphasized the traditional theological sacramental stance that couples do not get married by the church, but by themselves, and that the church merely solemnizes or blesses the union. Crew believed the church's most basic duty was the "historic mission to minister to all people."[70]

One early I/D convener, Henry Dudek, stressed that the group's most important accomplishment was "promoting the bonds of spiritual friendship among gay people." In its early days, the Madison group was ecumenical in nature. At the national level, I/D maintained connections with both the Catholic organization Dignity and the Episcopal group Integrity. In addition, Lutherans and others joined the group, including Steve Webster, who was associated with Affirmation, a group for gay Methodists. An early brochure stated, "We commit ourselves to welcoming Christians of various traditions and to celebrating our common faith and the richness of our diversity." The liturgy, this brochure explained, was a rite "that can be used by clergy from all faith communities and that will use non-sexist language and imagery." Membership in I/D, while fervent, was never very large. In 1980, the group consisted of just eight people, but by 1992, it had grown to its high point of forty-eight. For the group's tenth anniversary, Right Reverend Roger White, Bishop of Milwaukee (Episcopal), was the celebrant, and he was assisted by Reverend Ellwood Carey of Parkside Presbyterian. In 2010, longtime I/D members Jim Green and Bill Diederich would celebrate their fortieth anniversary with a liturgy at St. Dunstan Episcopal Church, which had since become the home of I/D. The couple was honored by the national Dignity organization for their lifetime contributions of over fifty thousand dollars to Dignity.[71]

Building LGBT-Safe Classrooms

In one story, "A teacher wakes up as a rock is thrown through her window. A note 'Lezzie Bitch' is left in her mailbox. The principal claims it is not a school matter, even though similar notes have been intercepted in her classroom." In another, "A teacher pulls into the parking lot at school to see his name painted on the side of the building, calling him a 'faggot.'" In yet another, "A teacher is denied bereavement leave to be at the side of his hospitalized partner." These tragic LGBT stories appeared in the February 23, 1989, issue of The Wisconsin Light. These and other incidents of harassment were the impetus behind the formation of the Madison-based Gay and Lesbian Educational Employees (GLEE). The initial press account about the group noted that the harassment was occurring in "a city with a stringent nondiscrimination policy," indeed one that had been in effect for the past fourteen years since 1975.[72]

By the time of the The Wisconsin Light story, GLEE had been around for almost a year, since the spring of 1988. The bylaws note it was established "to provide support to gay and lesbian educators." The group's objectives included ensuring educators' rights, lessening homophobia in school systems, and working for changes in curricula and materials. GLEE wanted "to enable all students to gain a realistic and positive concept of the lifestyles and the historic contribution of lesbian and gay people." While the principal mentioned in the first story was not supportive of the teacher, the assistant principal at the same school was a strong source of support. She was Libby Burmaster, who would later become the Wisconsin Superintendent of Public Instruction. The *MTI Reporter*, a newsletter published by the union Madison Teachers Inc. (MTI), was also involved in the early days, letting its members know how to contact GLEE. John Matthews, the director of MTI at the time, was remembered as being "very supportive" of the teachers' efforts.[73]

One of GLEE's initial efforts sparked a minor controversy. On April 7, 1989, a memo with an attached article on homophobia was sent to all Madison Metropolitan School District (MMSD) employees. The memo, which pointed out the homophobic content, was signed by Ruth Guidinas of the MMSD Human Relations Department, Jack Siebert on behalf of GLEE, and Jane LaFlash for PFLAG. Schools Superintendent James Travis had to respond when some parents voiced concern over the memo, and the story got into the hands of reporters in early June. On June 25, 1989, the *Wisconsin State Journal* ran a front-page story on the event under the headline, "Does School's Memo Push Homosexuality?" Some self-identified Christian parents appeared at a school board meeting, and Reverend Richard Pritchard sent a mailing to four hundred people belonging to the group Citizens Concerned for Our Community. Pritchard told the school board that the memo "openly supported and promoted the homosexual lifestyle as normal and acceptable." He then asked the board for permission to distribute his own fact sheet, which called homosexual practices sinful. Terry Cremin, a teacher and GLEE member, defended the distribution of the original memo and, in arguing against Pritchard, pointed out that neither racist nor homophobic comments were appropriate in schools.[74]

Guidinas sent Travis a response memo on June 28, as she was retiring from seventeen years in the district's Human Relations department. She noted that the reason behind sending the original memo was "the harassment of gay and lesbian staff by other staff and by students, as well as the frequent use of homophobic put-downs and name calling by students." Guidinas (whose life partner was Dorothy Davids, a member of the Stockbridge-Munsee Band of Mohican Indians) clarified the distinction between the district's "alleged endorsement of homosexuality" and the district's acknowledgment of homophobia as "unacceptable behavior," stressing that one does not have to endorse homosexuality to decry discrimination against homosexuals. In the press, commenting on Pritchard's fact sheet about homosexuality, Guidinas said, "We don't ask the Nazis to tell us about Jews."[75]

Modest expectations for GLEE were swept aside in the fall of 1989 as the group launched its next major effort. The Wisconsin Education Association Council (WEAC), the largest of the statewide teachers' unions, held an annual conference for educators from around the state in Madison. GLEE had arranged for a subgroup meeting to be held, not on the County Fairgrounds with the other meetings, but at the not-too-distant Madison Franklin School. Organizers recognized that some teachers would not feel comfortable walking into a session with the word *gay* in its title.[76]

The *Milwaukee Sentinel* covered the meeting in an article with the headline, "Homosexual Educators at WEAC Convention Cite Isolation, Fear," but the reporters agreed "not to use names or school districts of the participants unless specific permission was given." Some meeting attendees claimed teaching "is not a safe place to be gay." One lesbian educator noted, "It seems like every morning I cross that line from who I am to who I pretend to be." The *Sentinel* story also noted the group's concerns that extended beyond employee safety. Teachers worried that their students "don't have any role models," and that "as far as they're concerned, homosexuality doesn't exist or if it does, it's something really awful." "God," said one attendee, "if someone had been there when I was 15, it would have made such a difference."[77]

The *Capital Times* of Madison also ran a story on this GLEE meeting titled "Gay Teachers Hold Own Sessions." Despite the state's nondiscrimination law for employment on the basis of sexual orientation, the article stated, "One teacher said he would fear for his job if he acted as a liaison between gay and lesbian students and places where they can get information." After a presentation given by the professional youth services organization PICADA (a group focused on drug and alcohol abuse prevention) about a Madison-based LGBT teen group, one teacher asked, "How do you get more of this in the school district just to prevent suicide of gay teens and offer support?"[78]

The Wisconsin Light reported that the meeting's planners were "elated" with the outcome. It also noted the isolation felt by lesbian and gay teachers from small towns. Dennis Bergren, from Cottage Grove, reported on attending "this affirming group." He wrote, "These are committed teachers who care, who have been the objects of derision and prejudice in their own education and are concerned that their students do not suffer that same pain." GLEE had a banner made with their name on it, and members carried it in Madison gay pride parades. One teacher remembered that "it took a lot of courage for me to march" where students and parents might see them. South Central Wisconsin's LGBT philanthropy organization, the New Harvest Foundation, provided critical early financial support to the group in the form of small grants. A woman librarian helped to create a lesbian and gay bibliography for school use.[79]

By 1994, GLEE had morphed into Gays, Lesbians and Allies for Diversity in Education (GLADE). In another sign of progress, Tom Popp sat on the

Gay and lesbian teachers and educational employees in southern Wisconsin organized for mutual support and to broaden the educational outlooks of their students. Here they are marching in the 1989 Madison Gay Pride Parade. FROM THE AUTHOR'S COLLECTION

Madison Superintendent's Advisory Committee as a representative of the United. Popp, advocating for gays and lesbians and citing the five-point agenda of GLADE, urged Madison schools to create a climate "in which all members of the school community are free from fear, violence and harassment." Pointing out the slowness of even Madison's schools in responding to gay and lesbian issues, Steve Morrison, the advisory council chairman, stated in response, "It's late already."[80]

"We cannot count on intervention by teachers to protect or shield the children," said Sunshine Jones at the United's annual banquet in 1994. Jones was a founding member of the Madison Lesbian Parents Network and worked with GLADE. She and her partner, Jo Ann Kelly, were raising a child who attended Madison's schools. Jones cited cases of children being "subject to homophobic chants and slurs in school with instructors hesitating to halt them." The prior year, gay advocates had presented Madison Superintendent Cheryl Willhoyte with a list of "anti-homophobia strategies." These included mandatory homophobia training for all school principals, a survey of library materials for G/L/B inclusive items, and harassment intervention training for playground and lunchroom supervisors.[81]

GLEE published a newsletter called *New Lessons* in the early 1990s. One lesbian teacher wrote insightfully, "As a lesbian, I live over the edge of political society and the dominant culture. The students I teach are at the edge of the school culture." The newsletter started to carry student tales from that edge.[82]

In April 1993, an article titled "High School Student Speaks Out: Taking a Few Steps Out" appeared. "Throughout my childhood I've been a 'tomboy,'" the student wrote. "In my second grade picture I was wearing a plaid shirt with rainbow colored suspenders and jeans. I hated dresses and nylons." Part of the student's education continued when neighbors moved in on the block: two boys being raised by two moms. "I began to realize that I wanted to live a lifestyle such as theirs rather than the type of life my parents lived," the student reflected. "They have ultimately made me aware of my sexual orientation and I thank them."[83]

In April 1996, LGBT efforts in the Madison schools erupted into a major controversy. A photo essay exhibit called "Love Makes a Family: Living in Gay and Lesbian Families" had been assembled by artist Gigi Kaiser of Amherst, Massachusetts. A heterosexual teacher had learned about the exhibit at a conference and asked to bring it to Madison, specifically to Hawthorne Elementary on the east side. School district administrators expressed concern that it showed only one kind of family, but a teacher at Hawthorne said the excuses from downtown "didn't fly with her." "Schools often pay special attention to certain groups in society," the teacher said, noting Hispanic Heritage Month, Black History Month, and posters of famous women displayed at various schools.[84]

When asked by a reporter for her opinion, school board president Carol Carstensen gave the exhibit a thumbs up based on what she had heard about it. "One of our responsibilities as a school district is to reflect the diversity in the community," she said. A member of the Lesbian Parents Network estimated that at least two hundred district children lived in gay or lesbian households, though this was likely a significant underreporting. At the next school board meeting, one parent called the Kaiser exhibit "a polarizing issue." Tim Valdez, a fourth and fifth grade teacher, saw the exhibit as a form of protection, explaining, "I have witnessed students picked on because of the perception they were gay or lesbian." A GLADE spokesperson said the school district administration had failed to lead. One press report said the exhibit had "become a battleground for those with strong feelings on either side of the debate over the acceptance of homosexual families in society."[85]

Unsurprisingly, the next Madison School Board meeting saw another debate on the issue. Fifteen people spoke in favor of the exhibit and nine against. The record included a letter from Diane Reistroffer, a pastor at University United Methodist Church, who wrote, "I consider the District's contention that the [photo] essay discriminates against heterosexual families phony and ludicrous." In an impassioned statement, community activist Mary Babula (whose partner was a teacher) commended the "heroic teachers and community leaders at Hawthorne." On the other side, outspoken firefighter Ronnie Greer, who had become a well-known LGBT-community opponent, called homosexuality a deceitful and wrong practice. Ultimately, the board took no action against the exhibit going up.[86]

Editorials in the *Capital Times* pointed fingers at the "bumbling school administration." Noting that schools "are literally filled with images of heterosexual parents," one editorial argued that to censor gay and lesbian parents "sends an insulting and despicable message." "The Madison School

Board has a clear policy of promoting tolerance and inclusion toward all groups, including gays and lesbians," the paper stated. The exhibit stayed in school.[87]

Outside of Madison, one of the most moving pieces of writing from this period was republished in a 1990 issue of the GLEE newsletter, *New Lessons*. The piece had originally been written by a Dane County student in a high school paper. It opened, "Dear Editor: I'm sixteen and gay. That's right, queer as a duck. A fairy, Homosexual, homophile, fruitcake, cock-sucker, whatever you want to call it, that's what I am. And I'm not the only one." Referencing the students in his school, the author asks, "Have they ever had a choice but to accept the heterosexual norm? . . . I had none." He continued, "I'll never have children. I won't be allowed to adopt. I'll live in fear of gay bashers, face ridicule of my lifestyle every day. I'll be a reject of society, a monolith of immorality in our perfect America."[88]

This student, like most in the state's educational systems, seemed totally unaware of any effects from the existing legislative protections enacted in 1993 under Statute 118.13 that protected K–12 students from discrimination (including bias, stereotyping, and harassment) on the basis of sexual orientation. Department of Public Instruction administrative rules required school boards to annually provide public notice of any such pupil nondiscrimination policies. The work of educating homosexual and non-binary students about these protections was later taken up by GSAFE (part of the broad movement of gay–straight alliances for safe schools) under its motto: "Creating just schools for LGBTQ+ youth." The organization, which still exists at the time of this book's publication, has supported over two hundred gay–straight student alliances in high schools and middle schools around the state.[89]

Even before these educational networks were established, the student author of the 1990 essay wrote proudly of his sexual orientation: "I wouldn't trade it for the world. I have dreams of high fantasy, dreams of the perfect mate, dreams of pleasant days and blissful nights, dreams that far outweigh the consequences of my sexuality. Dreams that I will make a reality." Building this future, however, would not be his work alone. To the school community, he wrote, "It is your duty as Americans to stand up for the rights of homosexuals, rise out of your homophobia and accept us on the basis of the dreams we share and the hopes we realize."[90]

PRIDE AND COMING OUT CELEBRATIONS

Today some of the most ubiquitous manifestations of the LGBT community are pride parades. They date back to 1970 on the first anniversary of the Stonewall riots. In that year, early gay activists in New York City threw an event called Christopher Street Liberation Day and organized a march from the Stonewall Bar in Greenwich Village (where the bar was proximate to Christopher Street) to the Sheep's Meadow in Central Park. Christopher Street West organized a similar commemorative march in Los Angeles. Thousands attended each march. The parades began as community festivals for the participants. Katherine McFarland Bruce has argued in *Pride Parades: How a Parade Changed the World* that these events were "directed much more at changing culture than politics." In Wisconsin, the pride events have grown from small gatherings to major events.[91]

The earliest gay pride event was MAHE Day sponsored by the Madison Alliance for Homosexual Equality in the spring of 1970, before the big Stonewall anniversary marches. After disappearing for a time, the event later resurfaced in Madison as the Gay Rites of Spring. For many years, the annual summer MAGIC picnic was hosted in Madison's Brittingham Park—an event that attracted hundreds. In Milwaukee, a gay march in 1971 was attended by twenty-five gay men and lesbians who rallied at the War Memorial. In June 1973, Gay Pride Week events were held at UW–Milwaukee with Del Martin of the lesbian group Daughters of Bilitis speaking. In June 1980, Milwaukee's gay community marched from Juneau Park to a rally at MacArthur Square to promote "Gay Pride" and protest police harassment in the city. In the summer of 1980, *Amazon* magazine reported that the Milwaukee Gay and Lesbian Pride Committee had designated June 21–28, 1980, as Lesbian and Gay Pride Week, "the first such celebration in Milwaukee in several years." There was also a picnic at Mitchell Park.[92]

After the October 11, 1987, national gay march at the US Capital, an idea emerged to use the anniversary of the march as a national day for coming out. In 1988, kits of materials were distributed around the country by the National Gay Rights Advocates. Wisconsin's *In Step* magazine ran a story on this effort "to go forward in the campaign for civil rights." Artist Keith Haring designed a national poster.[93]

A follow-up to the War Conference of 1988 was the designation of October 11 as National Coming Out Day. Among other Madison activities, this ad ran in the *Isthmus* encouraging closeted gays and lesbians to come out and get engaged in the community.
ISTHMUS, OCTOBER 7, 1988

Isn't It About Time You Got Engaged?

Maybe so, but how do you tell your family the "special" person in your life is someone of the same sex?

Most of us don't bother. We smile, shrug our shoulders, and answer these well-meaning questions with a polite falsehood or a charming evasion.

What if we told the truth?

What if we were candid with our loved ones—and our friends and co-workers—about our gay or lesbian affections?

Millions of men and women have done just that. Sometimes it's stressful. But more often, "coming out" leads to an honest, close and intimate bond between us and the people we care most about.

Even in difficult circumstances, "coming out" is successful over the long run. It's not just an event—it's a process full of possibilities.

We hope you'll push your possibilities on October 11, which has been designated National Coming Out Day. It is the first anniversary of the national march on Washington.

The theme is "Take Your Next Step."

What is your next step? It may be to admit your homosexual feelings to yourself or one other person. It may be to "come out" to your family, your roommate, or your co-workers.

It may be to do something more public—to show your affection at an airport, or put your lover's picture on your desk, or throw a party for both gay and straight friends.

If you're a public official, maybe this is the time to announce yourself and put the rumors to rest.

But why bother at all? Because the stakes have never been higher.

Bigotry and hate are on the rise—and our invisibility only helps it. As long as most of us don't let society see who we are, responsible people can be led to believe we're marginal or dangerous.

We know different. We know we're numerous—and we're their children, parents, co-workers and neighbors. Our invisibility keeps them in the dark.

"Coming out" is the most powerful act of enlightenment and self-defense we have at our command.

Sure, there are risks. But the payoffs are honest living and greater security—for everyone.

So take the next step October 11. "Come out" in a way that's comfortable for you. And push yourself a little.

It will mean a giant step for all of us.

In Madison, National Coming Out Day is sponsored by the Madison Community United. Call 255-8582 for information.

In Madison, I persuaded the United we needed to do visible things for the first official National Coming Out Day in 1989 and organized for a half-page ad to appear in the weekly *Isthmus*. Since it was fall, the picture showed a family, possibly gathered for the upcoming Thanksgiving dinner, with eyes focused toward an empty place at the table. Since family time was often when lesbians and gay men were asked about possible hetero-normative partners, the large-type caption read, "Isn't It About Time You Got Engaged?" The text explained how gays could get engaged in the next step of coming out rather than hiding with a shrug, because with bigotry and hate on the rise, "the stakes have never been higher." The bold type proclaimed, "'Coming out' is the most powerful act of enlightenment and self-defense we have at our command." Additionally, the *Isthmus* marked the anniversary with a Listening In column by George Vukelich featuring an interview with out county board member Tammy Baldwin. She credited the War Conference—the 1988 crisis gathering of gay and lesbian leaders during the Reagan Administration's homophobic attacks and the devastation of the AIDS epidemic—with coming up with the idea of National

Another Coming Out Day activity was blanketing Bascom Hill on the UW–Madison campus with pink triangles as symbols of gay liberation. In the Nazi concentration camps, homosexuals were designated with pink triangles. The symbol was later proudly adopted to show how oppression could be turned into liberation. JEFF MILLER/UNIVERSITY OF WISCONSIN–MADISON

Coming Out Day. That year's theme was Taking the Next Step. Baldwin said, "Gays simply have to become more visible. We have always been misunderstood. We have always been stereotyped." Quoting Harvey Milk, she asserted, "Like every other group we must be judged by our leaders, by those who are themselves gay and who are visible." Baldwin emphasized that "the 'next step' is not just for the gay community, it's for the straight community as well."[94]

On the campus before dawn on the morning of October 11, 1988, Bascom Hill was decorated with rows of pink triangles put up by the Ten Percent Society in front of the statue of Abraham Lincoln. The pink triangles represented the badges "gays were forced to wear as prisoners in Nazi concentration camps." Stories published in the local papers noted that the former symbol of shame and persecution has "become a symbol not only of gay and lesbian pride, but also as a source of strength." UW–Madison Professor Jim Steakley, an expert on the Nazis' persecution of gay individuals, was quoted about the history in the *Badger Herald* and gave a lecture as part of Coming Out Week. Joe Marx of the Ten Percent Society observed, "Being gay on campus is generally accepted," but others advised, "Don't flaunt it." The *Daily Cardinal* of October 10, 1988, in a lead-up to National Coming Out Day, ran a story titled "The Ins and Outs of America" featuring one UW student's tale. The United newsletter reported, "For a period of a whole week straddling the day, Madison newspapers, television, and radio heralded the event."[95]

MADISON GALVANIZE

Some of the Wisconsin attendees at the 1987 national march in Washington felt impelled to launch a new wave of gay activism on returning to their home communities. In 1988, a group of activists in Madison, including Pam Jacobsen and Richard Kilmer, formed the Gay and Lesbian Visibility Alliance known as GALVAnize. The group, which had begun as the Madison March Committee, quickly grew to seventy-five volunteers who decided to plan a march for spring 1989. The wide-ranging plans included coordinating a week of activities, bringing a section of the AIDS quilt to Madison, and organizing a rally on the State Capitol grounds. The volunteers saw the effort as "a massive visible coming out." Recognizing

the fear many still felt to be out, the group's records show some participants might "choose to march masked." Using the slogan "Come Out for
a Change," the group wanted to "act as a tool for ongoing personal and
political empowerment," emphasizing the agency of the community. By
February 1989, GALVAnize had raised eight thousand dollars. Cosponsors
of the events included the New Harvest Foundation, the CCF, the Wisconsin Community Fund, and the Wisconsin Student Association. The Madison Art Center also helped by sponsoring the AIDS quilt display. Instead of
scheduling the march in June, the group chose Saturday May 6, 1989, so
the event could be held before the university campus shut down at the end
of the spring session. No one would have guessed that light snow would
descend on the marchers in early May.[96]

Many preparations needed to occur throughout 1988 and early 1989,
including fundraising and training peacekeepers. The march was arranged
to go through the campus fraternity area, and some feared there might
be a need "to keep calm between marchers and those watching." In the
end, Fraternity Row on Langdon Street did not pose any challenges, but a
couple dozen counter protesters did show up at the Capitol rally.[97]

GALVAnize events began on Thursday, May 4, with a slideshow by lesbian photographer JEB (Joan E. Biren) on the 1987 lesbian and gay national
march For Love and For Life. She was joined at the Barrymore Theater by
the gay singing duo Romanovsky and Phillips as a fundraiser. On Friday,
Karen Thompson spoke about the process of freeing her lover, Sharon Kow-
alski, and bringing her home as a result of their landmark case about legal
guardianship in Minnesota—a national cause célèbre, but one that received
particular attention in Wisconsin. There was also an opening ceremony
for the AIDS quilt at the UW–Madison Fieldhouse attended by thirty-five
hundred people. The campus *Daily Cardinal* printed a special edition insert
called the "Visibility Alliance" that featured LGBT diversity. Noki Ariki
wrote that Midwest Asian Dykes sponsored a Japanese American lesbian
speaker at Pres House. Cuban-descended Illiminada Amat told the story of
a black woman named "Puddin'" Sterling and her lesbian lover, stressing
that Madison still "needs to work on its own classism and racism."[98]

Initially, organizers of the march were ambitious in setting a goal of seventeen thousand attendees, 10 percent of Madison's population. While this
was wildly optimistic, the actual estimated turnout of seven thousand to

The 1989 GALVAnize march drew at least seven thousand people to the State Capitol, the largest Wisconsin LGBT gathering to date. FROM THE AUTHOR'S COLLECTION

eight thousand was nearly 5 percent of the population and the biggest LGBT celebration in the capital city's history. News coverage described how purple balloons "polka dotted" the crowd of people chanting "Gay Rights State, Put It on the License Plate." Madison police officer Cheri Maples spoke at the march about her loving lesbian relationship. Organizers Meg Gaines and Tony Sheehan led the rally crowd on a march down State Street where one shop displayed multiple pink triangles in its windows. A marcher from Green Bay, who said that in her home city she and her lover were sometimes forced to act like sisters, found the crowd "inspiring." GALVAnize continued to sponsor Madison Pride events for several years and provided renewed vigor to the community with its visible organizing.[99]

PRIDEFEST

Following the 1987 National March, a new Milwaukee Lesbian/Gay Pride Committee was established by folks who had attended the national event. Several hundred people attended the 1988 Rightfully Proud celebration at Mitchell Park. In 1989, the event grew to become a two-mile parade march from the bar district to Cathedral Square, where a rally of five hundred people gathered. This would be the site for an annual rally for four years. In 1994, the event was held at Juneau Park as more of a festival with added food and entertainment and with a new organization called Pridefest as the sponsor. By 1996, Pridefest moved to the lakefront Festival Park.[100]

Confusingly, *The Wisconsin Light* and *In Step* reported the 1989 event both as the first annual parade/rally and as a twentieth anniversary event for Stonewall. Later, people would count the 1988 event as Milwaukee's first pride event. *In Step* observed that thirty-three US cities held pride marches, parades, or events in 1988. Leading up to the 1989 event in Milwaukee, fundraisers were held, including a moonlight cruise aboard the *Edelweiss*. A list of event donors was dubbed the Proud Crowd. Dr. Karen Lamb, a health professional and the wife of Mayor Henry Maier, acted as the parade's grand marshal. She was described (as only a gay journalist with a fashion sense might) as "stunning in a white cartwheel hat, white dress with red highlights, and white shoes with red roses." It was estimated that five hundred people marched and five hundred attended the rally. *The Wisconsin Light* editorialized, "There is no true love without pride; without taking back yourself."[101]

During the 1990s, variations on the pride celebration developed. In 1990, the Milwaukee County Board of Supervisors declined to proclaim Lesbian/Gay Pride Week in Milwaukee. Of course, the event proceeded anyway. Scott Gunkel, the fundraising chair, reported that the event was a success, since revenues totaled $17,148 and expenses were $16,639. Miriam Ben-Shalom acted as grand marshal in 1990. In 1992, Mayor John Norquist vetoed the proposed five thousand dollars in city funds to support Pridefest. In response, Milwaukee's Queer Nation—gay community activists who had gathered under the name to agitate on LGBT issues—"led spirited protests against Norquist." The celebration in 1994 focused on the twenty-fifth anniversary of Stonewall with the theme Our Time To Shine, and it was held north of the War Memorial Art Center. In 1995, fireworks sponsored by Miller Brewing Company were added, and the event, held at Veterans Park, attracted nine thousand attendees. By 1996, Pridefest took place on the Summerfest grounds where all major Milwaukee festivals occur. "Being there is definitely a feather in our cap," said cochair Susan Cook. The move to the new grounds "marked Pridefest's arrival

Milwaukee's 1990 Gay Pride Parade had a joyful feeling, expressed here by some participants. *MILWAUKEE JOURNAL SENTINEL*, JULY 17, 1990, © 2015 JOURNAL SENTINEL INC., REPRODUCED
WITH PERMISSION

into the big leagues of Milwaukee's summer festival season," elevating it to
the status of German Fest and Polish Fest. As the festival grew, attendance
continued to climb with a record-breaking 37,600 in 2017.[102]

WISCONSIN'S ESTABLISHED LGBT COMMUNITY

Shortly after Stonewall, Dale Hillerman, coordinator of the Crossroads
Gay Center in Madison, participated in the Symposium on Homosexuality
at UW–Madison. His words, written in November 1973, provide a snapshot
of the time: "The gay movements are, at best, loose confederations of very
diverse individuals who band together at the local level for various reasons,
and who recognize only the loosest alliances with gay movements elsewhere." While true at the time, the last decades of the twentieth century
witnessed a real transformation from this reality.[103]

Beginning as small, post-Stonewall gatherings, the Wisconsin LGBT
community grew to build lasting institutions. From quiet affirmations
of self to small acts of courage, the movement expanded from engaging

dozens to engaging tens of thousands. In the past fifty years, LGBT institutions formed and flourished, encompassing the worlds of politics, social justice, religion, and education. While the pride events of Madison and Milwaukee remained among the largest in the state, many other Wisconsin communities began to celebrate and show their pride.

Wisconsin leaders and organizations participated in and often helped drive the national agenda. From humble beginnings and often against great odds, the LGBT community came into its own in the Badger State, learning as it grew, overcoming obstacles, and using its voice to promote equality.

"The world is divided into two classes," noted Oscar Wilde, "those who believe the incredible and those who do the improbable." When the noted playwright was tried and convicted in London in 1895, the Wisconsin press and society publicly expressed disgust for the author who wrote about love, but "dare[d] not speak its name."

In the following century, in ways both large and small, Wisconsin's LGBT residents did the improbable. They found their voices, claimed their spaces, and dared to speak the truth. In the process, they built community.

The Miss Guernsey sash went to the winner of a northeast Wisconsin drag contest. The use of the black and white Holstein colors instead of true Guernsey shades was just another aspect of putting on a show. COURTESY OF RAINBOW OVER WISCONSIN

EPILOGUE

S usan Cook, an organizer of the Lesbian Alliance of Metropolitan Milwaukee and Pridefest, said in a 2003 interview, "I think it's important for the younger crowd that they go back to our history. They need to know this stuff." Recalling her own struggle to come out as a lesbian, she commented, "Just because it's this way now doesn't mean it will always be this way." If a century of Wisconsin LGBT history shows us anything, it is that change is indeed possible, but change does not happen without LGBT people exercising their own agency to help bring it about. Moving into the twenty-first century, the earlier work for a more equal society and for an inclusive politics continued to bear fruit. In this epilogue, I want to take a few cultural and political themes into the twenty-first century to better illuminate their development into the present.[1]

A STRONG TRADITION GROWS

In 1992, when David Clarenbach vacated his long-held state legislative seat for a failed bid in US Congress, third-term Dane County Board member Tammy Baldwin announced she would run for his seat. Her stated intent was "to become Wisconsin's first openly gay or lesbian state legislator." With the theme A New Voice, she ran as an out lesbian stressing the need for a seat at the table. Her announcement stated, "Gays and lesbians and other minorities face daily human right struggles that go unchallenged due to inadequate representation. . . . The presence of gays [in political office] is a powerful political statement." Clarenbach had never proclaimed himself as gay and was married at the time of his congressional race; Baldwin, in contrast, was proudly out since her first race for the Dane County Board in 1986. Her 1992 literature was strong on gay issues, including her plan to "introduce legislation to legally recognize and extend full benefits to gays, lesbians and alternative families." But she was also running as a woman. Baldwin proclaimed Belle Case La Follette, an early Progressive feminist, among her role models. She also stressed that only once had her district elected a female representative when in 1949–1953 Ruth Doyle held the seat and that the "good old boys have been running government long enough."[2]

While the *Wisconsin State Journal* sneeringly referred to her as "the most 'politically correct' candidate," the national Gay and Lesbian Victory Fund endorsed her as a progressive who would "give gays and lesbians a presence and a voice that cannot be ignored." Baldwin's argument made sense: "It's time for our legislatures to reflect the diversity of our population." Through her membership in the National Association of Openly Lesbian and Gay and Elected Officials, she had met others aspiring to state-level office. She also drew on the strengths built up in the gay community in prior decades. Tony Sheehan, a gay man, was her treasurer. A major endorsement came from lesbian Margaret McMurray, president of the Wisconsin National Organization for Women. After Baldwin's swearing in, the *Isthmus* ran a story on "How Being 'Out' Helped Tammy Baldwin Get in—the Legislature." The story proclaimed, "Baldwin's swearing into office this week fulfills the promise of Wisconsin's trailblazing 1982 gay-rights bill." Though in appearance she might well have been taken for "a Republican from Fond du Lac," she was "a woman who refuses to conceive of her lesbianism as anything other than an asset."[3]

Baldwin would face three other liberal male candidates in the Democratic Primary. Billy Feitlinger, a former Madison alder and assistant to the county executive, was the early frontrunner. He had a very progressive record of civil rights and antiwar activism and wanted a fairer tax system and universal health care. He too pledged to fight for gay rights and had limited gay and lesbian support. In the end, Baldwin won the Democratic primary with a convincing 43 percent of the vote; Feitlinger, her closest rival, was at 33 percent.[4]

The general election was no cakewalk. A third-party leftist, Mary Kay Baum, was on the ballot, and the central Madison area was the stronghold for her Labor Farm Party. In the primary, the Labor Farm ballot gained only 175 votes, but in the general election, this number swelled to nearly 6,000, higher than Baldwin's primary total but less than the combined 9,000 Democratic primary voters. Baldwin's 59 percent of the general election vote assured her the seat, and when she ran for reelection in 1994 with no Labor Farm opponent, her share zoomed to 76 percent in the district.[5]

In the district next door to Baldwin's, another quiet lesbian would also

Her Story

How being 'out' helped Tammy Baldwin get in — the Legislature.

Early LGBT candidates in Wisconsin and elsewhere feared that being publicly out would harm their electoral chances. By 1992, this analysis in the *Isthmus* suggested Tammy Baldwin's honesty as a lesbian helped her win a seat in the Wisconsin legislature. *ISTHMUS,* JANUARY 8–14, 1993

win office in 1992. Doris Hanson, village president of McFarland, ran in this urban/suburban district for an open assembly seat. Hanson was well known among an older set of lesbians and had served in Governor Anthony Earl's administration as secretary of the DOA from 1983 to 1987. Hanson campaigned as the strong woman's advocate that she was. Several known gay elected officials appeared in her literature, and her campaign materials featured her female softball team, which won the National Softball Tournament in 1954. A sparkplug for both Hanson's and Baldwin's campaigns was the astute political operative and lesbian Linda Willsey. Hanson would win a seven-way Democratic primary and go on to win the general election in the Democratic-leaning district. Unfortunately, Hanson's longtime partner, Ursula Schmitt, was killed shortly after the election in an auto accident. Schmitt's obituary identified her relationship with Hanson, effectively outing the fledgling assemblywoman in the press.[6]

In 1998, Republican Scott Klug retired, leaving an open congressional seat. Again, Baldwin's sharp political instinct told her it was time to run. In this race, she would again face three white men; her strongest challenge came from Rick Phelps, a former executive of Dane County, the largest county in the district. In the end, as the most progressive candidate, Baldwin won the Democratic primary with 37 percent of the vote; Phelps came in second at 34 percent. Baldwin's subsequent win in the general election made her the first out lesbian or gay person to win a congressional office as a nonincumbent. Others, such as Representative Steve Gunderson, had won office, but they came out only after having been in office and/or dragged from the closet.[7]

In 2012, Baldwin decided on her next step and ran for the US Senate in an open-seat contest due to the retirement of Democratic Senator Herb Kohl. Her Republican opponent was former longtime governor and former Health and Human Services secretary Tommy Thompson, whose hard-fought primary consumed a lot of his resources. Baldwin would win the seat with 51 percent of the vote to his 46 percent. President Barack Obama, running for his second term, carried the state by 53 percent, winning thirty-five of the state's seventy-two counties, while Baldwin won thirty-six (though not always the same ones). Baldwin did particularly well in her old congressional district. Again, the Victory Fund supported her, as did Emily's List, which supported her campaign to be the first woman senator from Wisconsin.[8]

With Baldwin's successful Senate run, Wisconsin provided the country with the first out lesbian US Senator. Making it especially sweet, her replacement for the Second Congressional seat was Mark Pocan, a gay man who also had succeeded her in the state assembly seat. Pocan, a Kenosha native like Baldwin, had served on the Dane County Board of Supervisors, a hatching ground for LGBT officials. The tradition for out gay officials that had started with the Judy Greenspan campaign in 1973 now had borne wondrous fruit in Wisconsin.

SCORING HIGH

Americans seem to love using rankings to compare themselves, and true to form, a number of LGBT indexes exist. A 2005 book, *50 Fabulous Gay-Friendly Places to Live*, included Madison as "very gay-friendly." The author called "Madison's GLBT community . . . out and organized." He may have been influenced by a 2004 story "How Gay Is Madison?," which concluded that it was "one of the most open cities in the nation." The article also noted, "Madison has produced more gay and lesbian political leaders than any other city its size, and more than many larger cities." The article mentioned that *Girlfriends* magazine ranked Madison "as the second-best city for lesbians." In 2010, Madison made a list of the fifteen "gayest burgs" put out by the national gay publication *The Advocate*. By 2013, Madison received a score of 100 on the Human Rights Campaign's Municipal Equality Index. In 2015, *The Advocate* placed Madison at number five on the Queerest Cities in America list. Patrick Farabaugh, editor of Madison's *Our Lives* magazine and the founder of gay hockey leagues in Madison, described Madison as a safe space. "You have an LGBT community here that is proud to contribute to keeping us all moving forward. We ask in return that you be proud of us."[9]

Milwaukee has also placed high on gay indices with scores in the 90 percent range. In 2007, *Milwaukee Magazine* tried to gauge how gay-friendly the city was. The story discussed a resident from the east side

THE GAYS NEXT DOOR

The Midwest — with Wisconsin leading the way — has shown the largest increase in people identifying themselves as same-sex couples.

The seeming tranquility of two men holding hands on the lakeshore, here depicted in a Madison story on gays and lesbians, spoke to the achievements of decades of activism. *WISCONSIN STATE JOURNAL*, JULY 8, 2007

who had moved there from Racine because Milwaukee was "relatively gay-friendly, and more livable than places like San Francisco." Walker's Point made the 2006 list of emerging gay ghettos, but as longtime activist Patrick Flaherty noted, "In Milwaukee suburbs being gay is 'still incredibly taboo.'" Milwaukee's Cream City Foundation raised gay awareness in August 2008 with thirty billboards in a Gay Neighbor campaign that also included a website, gayneighbor.org. In 2007, the *Wisconsin State Journal*, reporting on the effects of the city's gay-friendly campaign, reprinted an article from the *Economist* magazine: "The Midwest—with Wisconsin leading the way—had shown the largest increase in people identifying themselves as same-sex couples." Dane County led the way with 2000 census data showing 1.5 percent of population as same-sex couples; some isthmus districts had a 6 percent to 8 percent share. Jason Rae of the Wisconsin LGBT Chamber of Commerce has noted, "It's clear that Wisconsin's major municipalities are leading the way among our nation's cities, but there is still more work to be done."[10]

A Fairer Wisconsin

For most of the twentieth century, Wisconsin, while sharing influences with other parts of the country, fostered its own political traditions. Perhaps the strongest and most particular was its progressive exceptionalism. La Follette Republican progressives envisioned the state as a laboratory of democracy and came together with liberal Democrats, leading to passage of the first-in-the-nation state gay rights law. Yet this unique political climate would erode as the politics of Wisconsin and other states became increasingly polarized. By the 1990s, Republicans in the state had picked up the antigay marriage fever. The initial attempt for marriage equality in 1996, when some eighteen states had anti–gay marriage bills, was beaten back in Wisconsin, as we saw earlier in the discussions of gay organizing in northeast Wisconsin. One of the forces in that fight was Action Wisconsin, a network of gays, lesbians, bisexuals, and allies around the state. Baldwin helped form the group after hearing from Wisconsin gays and lesbians during and after the 1992 election. As Juliet Brodie of Action Wisconsin noted, "Baldwin provided the leadership we have come to rely on." Yet the measure failed, and the legislative fight continued.[11]

In the 2000s, as happened in other states, Wisconsin's Republicans began to use state constitutional amendments as a device to drive conservative voter turnout. In 2006, although state law only permitted marriage between a man and a woman, two successive Republican legislatures passed resolutions to authorize a citizen vote to amend the state constitution. The goal was to make marriage equality impossible through future legislative change. Democratic Governor James Doyle Jr., while opposed, had no power to veto resolutions on constitutional amendments. There was some hope the state's progressive tradition might turn the measure back. Action Wisconsin and the Milwaukee-based Center Advocates joined in a coalition in 2005 to take on the fight. Dubbed Fair Wisconsin, the group raised millions of dollars and organized throughout the state. A high point came when Representative Doris Hanson organized four former governors, three Democrats and one Republican (Lucey, Schreiber, Dreyfus, and Earl) to come out against the prohibitive amendment. A sign of the changing nature of state Republican politics was that former governor Tommy Thompson declined to join the statement. While an impressive group of religious leaders came out against the amendment, it was impossible to organize a Republican group for a no vote. In the end, only two staunchly Democratic counties, Dane and Menominee, voted against it. The amendment passed with 59 percent of the vote statewide. Heavy student turnout organized by Fair Wisconsin over the issue may have helped reelect Doyle and new Democratic legislators.[12]

Actual support for marriage equality, however, remained low even though Fair Wisconsin decided to shoulder on. A 2009 poll showed only 27 percent of Wisconsinites positively supported marriage for same-sex couples; by 2014, however, a Fair Wisconsin poll showed 51 percent in favor. Cultural consensus was changing, and Fair Wisconsin and other advocates saw an opening. During the debate over the amendment, Republican leaders had assured voters that language would not overturn local ordinances such as those in Madison and Dane County that provided domestic partner benefits and protections. Fair Wisconsin continued to fight for these local ordinances as a way to show support for LGBT couples, with the City of Manitowoc passing one by 8 to 1 in 2012.[13]

In the meantime, a new strategy was devised to see what state domestic partner benefits might be conferred without conflicting with the amendment language prohibiting "a legal status identically or substantially similar to that of marriage." Under Executive Director Katie Belanger, Fair Wisconsin, myself included, worked closely with Representative Mark Pocan in 2009 to negotiate with Governor Doyle's office to include a list of domestic partner benefits in the state budget. This passed, and Wisconsin became the first state in the nation with an anti–same-sex marriage amendment to award domestic partner benefits. We had managed to turn the defeat of marriage equality into positive forward momentum.[14]

Another late emerging strategy advanced by the ACLU was to challenge anti-marriage equality provisions both statutorily and constitutionally in a range of federal district courts. Longtime WCLU director Chris Ahmuty, a gay man, helped facilitate a Wisconsin case with eight lesbian/gay couples. On June 6, 2014, US District Court Judge Barbara Crabb ruled the state's ban unconstitutional, saying, "This case is about liberty and equality, the two cornerstones of the rights protected by the United States Constitution." In her decision, she noted, "Plaintiffs are not asking for special rights; they are asking only for the rights that every adult already has." Among many citations, she would cite the Nabozny equal protection case from 1996.[15]

Crabb's decision was issued on a Friday afternoon in June, and she did not immediately issue a stay injunction or a hold on its effects. Dane County Clerk Scott McDonell, defying the attorney general's wish to preserve the status quo, had trained extra persons as deputy registrars to prepare marriage licenses for him to sign. Friday evening and into the weekend, he kept county offices open for a long line of applicant couples to obtain marriage licenses. He also cooperated with Milwaukee County Clerk Joe Czarnezki, who did likewise. In the course of a week, Dane County would issue more than two hundred licenses to same-sex couples, and more than five hundred were issued statewide. Dane County lesbian judges, including Shelly Gaylord, Ellen Berz, and Rhonda Landford, as well as other straight judges, stood ready on the courthouse steps Friday evening to perform the happy ceremonies. Shari Roll and Renee Currie were the first to be married.[16]

A week later, despite having seen "the expression of joy on the faces of so many newly wedded couples," Crabb issued a stay injunction while the state appealed her ruling to the Federal Seventh Circuit Court of Appeals in Chicago. In response, the Wisconsin Civil Liberties Union and Fair

Marriage equality arrived in Wisconsin on June 6, 2014. Fair Wisconsin mobilized in Milwaukee and Madison to help county clerks' offices promptly process the early license requests, like that of Shari Roll and Renee Currie, the first couple to be married, seen here embracing as newlyweds. PHOTO BY MIKE DEVRIES, *CAPITAL TIMES* (MADISON)

Wisconsin launched a new campaign, Wisconsin Unites for Marriage, to help preserve Crabb's ruling. A unanimous decision on the appeal by a three-judge panel of the Seventh Circuit Court upheld Judge Crabb. One of the circuit's leading conservative voices, Judge Richard Posner, attacked the Wisconsin bans because they discriminated "against a minority defined by an immutable characteristic." He scoffed at the attorney general's case: "One would expect the state to have provided *some* evidence, *some* reason to believe, however speculative and tenuous, that allowing same-sex marriage will or may 'transform' marriage." The state attorney general appealed the circuit court decision to the US Supreme Court, which declined to hear the matter, thus putting into effect Crabb's original ruling. Following the process, plaintiffs Judi Trampf, who with her partner, Katy Heyning, worked in Whitewater, proclaimed over the favorable legal outcome: "It made me feel American again."[17]

THE GAY RIGHTS STATE IN THE TWENTY-FIRST CENTURY

In the twenty-first century, the Wisconsin pioneering tradition of out elected LGBT officials continued its robust progress with the election of the first out US senator in Tammy Baldwin. Many municipalities, through their local actions, advanced equality. Despite a loss over a constitutional amendment, Wisconsin advanced legal recognition of lesbian and gay couples with domestic partner benefits. When the federal district court ruled for marriage equality, progressive officeholders and activists sprang into action to make it a reality before other legal moves might prohibit it. This sophisticated maneuver helped to create marriage equality on the ground while further court processes confirmed the Western District of Wisconsin ruling. All in all, the story of Wisconsin's LGBT community gaining and defending their rights is remarkable in the post-Stonewall era.

APPENDIX I:
A SEAT AT THE TABLE

Like every other group, we must be judged by our leaders and by
those who are themselves gay, those who are visible. For invisible,
we remain in limbo—a myth, a person with no parents, no broth-
ers, no sisters, no friends who are straight, no important positions
in employment.

—HARVEY MILK'S "HOPE SPEECH"[1]

The phrase "a seat at the table" was used by early out political candidates to stress the importance of having out gays and lesbians sitting at the official tables where so many decisions about our lives were made. Political power involves large-scale efforts such as nondiscrimination legislation, but it can also be exercised in many ways on a smaller scale. Lesbians and gays at the table could also provide voices to oppose the ever-present homophobes. My own experience shows how having a seat at the table and speaking for the gay community allowed me to become a powerful force for change.

COMING TO THE TABLE

Earlier in this volume, I noted that I ran unsuccessfully for alder in 1974 on a platform of gay rights. Though I had not yet come out in a newspaper of record, I continued to work on the development of Madison's gay institutions. I particularly helped gay rights advocate David Clarenbach with his fundraising. I became part of Clarenbach's support network as we organized a politically active group of liberal Democrat advocates for gay rights. Within this group, we worked to improve our organizing and fundraising skills. The Young Democrats of 1966 had shown us the way to begin. We took up the earlier platform work for gay rights at state Democratic Party conventions in the early 1970s. We were distinctly different

This gathering of Wisconsin LGBT elected officials was a celebration of the fifth anniversary of the Wisconsin gay rights bill. Left to right, Representative David Clarenbach, Dane County Supervisor Dick Wagner, Madison Alderman Henry Lufler Jr., Representative Tim Carpenter, Dane County Supervisor Tammy Baldwin, and Dane County Supervisor Kathleen Nichols. FROM THE AUTHOR'S COLLECTION

from many gay activists in Madison who believed in third-party radical efforts such as the Labor Farm Party, a group that tried to harken back to the old 1930s progressive coalitions of the Midwest.

When I ran for the county board in 1980, my associations with the gay community were definite and known. A factor that might have discouraged one potential opponent in that race was that Clarenbach had promptly circulated my nomination papers in that individual's immediate neighborhood, so if he had circulated his own papers, he would have found that many of his neighbors had already signed mine.

My early political fundraising skills, which primarily involved throwing house parties to raise money, were frequently used in tandem with Dan

A Labor Day gay potluck on Jenifer Street included "the Chucks" (Chuck Beckwith and Chuck Bauer), gay businessmen who operated the very successful Madison store Soap Opera. Beckwith came dressed as the John Waters character Divine in the tiger-print dress, and Bauer is seated at far right. FROM THE AUTHOR'S COLLECTION

Curd, Clarenbach's chief staff member and a tenant of mine in a rental house on the same block where I lived. Curd was and is an excellent cook. His food and clever invitations always drew people to events. Curd's skills were acquired, in part, from working in advertising before joining Clarenbach's staff at the Capitol.

In early 1980, Curd and I threw an Alice B. Toklas Birthday Party at my house as a benefit for the United. We had both joined the Community Advisory Board of the Gay Center a couple of years earlier, and our next two benefits—A Night in Old Key West and San Francisco—were held for the center. At A Night in Old Key West in 1981, both liberal candidates for county executive—chair of the board Rod Matthews and state assemblyperson Jonathan Barry—attended to campaign for gay community votes. This was a first in Dane County's history. Unlike the radical Madison mayoral candidate James Rowen, who had boldly campaigned in gay bars in 1979 seeking gay support, Matthews and Barry were more comfortable at a gay house party hosted by a public official.[2]

FIGHTING THE MORAL MAJORITY

Early out elected officials in some communities around the country noted an interesting phenomenon: that organized gay activity subsided once an electoral victory was won by an out candidate, as many people expected the victorious candidate to carry out the entire community agenda. This was certainly not the case in Madison. In Wisconsin's capital, there always remained an activist gay community to which the out elected officials were important adjuncts.

One of the most harmful ideas to come out of the new Reagan administration in the early 1980s was the Family Protection Act: a grab bag of ideas from the Moral Majority grouped into a piece of legislation whose ostensible aim was refunding the federal Legal Services Corporation, an independent nonprofit providing legal aid to low income Americans. The Gay Rights National Lobby, in an alert, called the grouping of anti-liberal provisions with the bill "a wholesale assault on pluralism and civil liberties" and "a real and dangerous threat to lesbian and gay Americans." A key provision stated that no federal funds could go to any entity that "presents homosexuality, male or female, as an acceptable alternative life style or suggests that it can be an acceptable life style." Additionally, the legislation would exempt teachers from paying union dues, bar legal services clients from receiving assistance for any issues dealing with abortion, and provide protection to private schools at risk of losing tax exempt status for racial discrimination, among many other hobby horses. The National Gay Task Force called it "the centerpiece of the Radical Right's program to restructure American society to conform with the beliefs of a fundamentalist Christian minority." The task force also believed the measure would remove the tax exempt and tax deductible status of all gay organizations. Both national gay organizations began circulating petitions across the country to stop the Family Protection Act. [3]

In Madison, gay activist Gridley Hall took up the cause. Hall had been active as an out gay man on the Madison Equal Opportunities Commission and as part of the early Gay Law Students Association on campus in the 1970s. Sadly, he would later be one the earliest prominent members of the Madison community to die from AIDS.

At Hall's request, and with a draft he provided in early 1982, I prepared a resolution for introduction to the Dane County Board opposing the

Family Protection Act. This would force the board to petition the US Congress. Hall had also approached the Madison City Council. Alder Henry Lufler Jr., a gay man, had introduced a similar resolution petitioning Congress in 1982, which easily passed that body. The draft county resolution noted that the federal proposal would contradict the locally enacted Dane County nondiscrimination protections.[4]

Before the board voted on the resolution, Supervisor Lynn Haanen and I were asked to speak before a membership meeting of the United at the Wil-Mar Community Center in my own neighborhood. The *Daily Cardinal* story of March 15, 1982, covered the meeting and quoted me as saying, "The gay community doesn't need to worry about not being able to lead the type of lifestyle it wants to in Dane County." Haanen added, "Other supervisors' stereotypes about gays were broken down once they started working with gays and lesbians." In addition to the quotes, the paper correctly noted, "Wagner and Haanen are both members of Madison's gay and lesbian community," because we had so identified ourselves in our remarks. My outline notes for the meeting's remarks show I had titled them, "Tales of the County Boring or Life among the Hetro Crowd," with the subtitle "How to Cruise a Committee Meeting."[5]

The Madison *Capital Times* story on my coming out noted that I referred to the Family Protection Act as "a laundry list of the New Right's social agenda." It also mentioned that I had secured twenty sponsors out of the forty-one-member board. One conservative supervisor opposing the resolution commented, "To think these homosexuals are coming out of the woodwork and want to use my tax dollars to advocate their lifestyle. The Bible says this is not a permitted lifestyle. It's perverted." However, his arguments did not prevail, as the board adopted the resolution by a vote of 25 to 11.[6]

Ensuring Serious Enforcement

The attempt by the Rawhide Boys Ranch to gut a major provision of the gay rights bill in 1985 provides another example of the influence that a seat at the table had on Wisconsin's politics. This campaign is covered in detail in chapter 7 but does not include my personal experience with Rawhide's effort to discriminate.

Rawhide was an organization in New London, Wisconsin, where

delinquent youths could be placed by the county social services department. While the ranch was not officially church-affiliated, the owners believed they could claim a religious exemption from the nondiscrimination law in order to continue their practices of giving hiring preference to Christians and of hiring only married couples to be housing unit administrators and only young single males to be child care workers. This placed Rawhide out of compliance with the Dane County Affirmative Action ordinance, and the County Affirmative Action Commission referred the matter to the County Contract Compliance Hearing Board.[7]

The hearing board was made up of five persons representing different county bodies, and each was chosen by the body he or she represented. Mabel Smith represented the Affirmative Action Commission, Supervisor James Amundson represented the Finance Committee, Supervisor William Boyd represented the Personnel Committee, I represented the Public Protection Committee, and the newly elected out lesbian Supervisor Kathleen Nichols was the second representative of the Affirmative Action Commission. The county had clear written rules for contract compliance board hearings. Supervisor Haanen, in her role as chairperson of the Dane County Board of Public Welfare, wrote to the County Contract Compliance Hearing Board that there were other placement alternatives in the state for Dane County to use. The freshly constituted board, at its first meeting on August 3, 1982, elected me its chairperson.[8]

Following the ordinance, we scheduled a quasi-judicial hearing for August 31, 1982, and Rawhide was duly notified. I made sure we proceeded deliberately. The hearing was to determine whether the contractor was in noncompliance with our county ordinance. The board would attempt to determine whether or not Rawhide had (1) failed to file a plan with our contract compliance coordinator, (2) discriminated on the basis of sex, (3) discriminated on the basis of marital status, and (4) discriminated on the basis of religion. We would also consider whether debarment of future contracting to Rawhide should occur.[9]

Rawhide defiantly sent a letter stating that it chose not to appear at the hearing. In the letter, the owners complained about the time it would have taken them to file an affirmative action plan and explained that this was part of their reaction "against government adding cost and employee requirements." What they failed to mention was that county and state dollars were paying for most of the placements. The owners also bemoaned the fact that no other county in the state required contractors to provide such a plan and comply with these equality provisions.[10]

At the hearing on August 31, the county's contract compliance officer presented the evidence. Several other supervisors were present, and one member of the County Affirmative Action Commission indicated that there should not be a "strict" implementation of the county's ordinance. Needless to say, this fell on many deaf ears. The board, in its conclusions, found that Rawhide was not in compliance with the Dane County Affirmative Action ordinance and should be debarred from future contracts. On September 2, I filed a report of the compliance board's actions with the county board. During the whole process, the active roles undertaken by gay and lesbian public officials involved in the matter meant Dane County's fairness policies would be taken seriously.[11]

THE DENTIST WHO NEEDED EXTRACTION

Lynn Haanen and I continued to work as a team for the gay community in the early to mid-1980s. As the Reagan administration did almost nothing in the early fight against AIDS, we sponsored a county resolution "Urging Research into the Cause, Transmission, and Cure of Acquired Immune Deficiency Syndrome (AIDS)." As a supervisor active on health and social services issues, Haanen was the prime sponsor of the measure introduced as a Dane County Board resolution in the first part of 1983. As a gay man, I was most concerned with the health threat to my community and my friends. Noting that there were one thousand AIDS cases nationwide as of March 1983, the resolution urged "that significant new funds be reallocated immediately within the Department of Health and Human Services." An updated version of the resolution noted that while Congress had passed twelve million dollars in supplemental funding, the Reagan administration opposed the funding. The newer version also noted that the Wisconsin Division of Health had initiated an AIDS surveillance program in August 1982 and sought an epidemiological study of one thousand gay men from Wisconsin's metropolitan cities.[12]

As resolution sponsors, Haanen and I attended a June 29, 1983, meeting of the Dane County Board of Health, to which the resolution had been referred. While the board recommended the resolution by a vote of 3 to 2, we were both floored by the remarks made by member Dr. James Pawlisch, a dentist. He stated he would "rather spend $12 million to change human behavior" than cure the disease. Regarding gay sexuality, he said "even animals know better than that." He continued, "With that kind of behavior you have to pay the piper." The county board, ignoring his views, adopted the resolution.[13]

That night after the meeting, Haanen and I wrote to County Executive Jonathan Barry asking for Pawlisch to be removed from the Board of Health, as he was "not concerned about the health and well-being of all citizens of Dane County." Because of his beliefs about the morality and normality of part of the county's population, that is, homosexuals, we questioned his ability to carry out his duties to "protect and improve public health." Section 19.12 of the Dane County Ordinances required that "actions of the committee, commissions, and boards shall complement the Affirmative Action Plan of Dane County." Among the protected groups under the ordinance were those discriminated against because of sexual preference.[14]

On July 13, Pawlisch refused the county executive's request to resign, claiming he had support "from all over the county." One of Pawlisch's friends was pastor Richard Pritchard, who objected to funding studies to cure the disease and approved of funds being used to "help the homosexual recover from his sick life-style."[15]

County Executive Barry booted Pawlisch off the Board of Health in a press release on July 13. In response, a Sunday school teacher at an evangelical church started a petition for Pawlisch's reinstatement. The petition said, "We support the moral criteria that provoked those remarks." "That lifestyle, she said, is 'unclean and unbiblical,'" the Capital Times reported. The parishoner claimed to have collected 1,233 signatures, many of which came from circulating the petitions in churches.[16]

Motivated to respond, Henry Dudek created and circulated a counter petition that stated, "We affirm the moral position that all persons have a right to health care without suffering prejudice based on other's judgments of their behavior. We support Jonathan Barry's decision to remove Dr. James T. Pawlisch from the Dane County Board of Health for publicly expressing discriminatory attitudes that would deprive gay people of that right." In a letter conveying the petition to Rod Matthews, Dane County Board chair, Dudek noted that 1,180 residents had signed it, including 67 identifiable health-care professionals and 17 identifiable church staff. Some of the petitions had been circulated in the city's gay bars, again proving the usefulness of these enduring gay community institutions.[17]

The Pawlisch controversy raged in the press. In an opinion column complaining of Madison's "noisy brand of liberalism," Frank Ryan of United Press International said Barry, Haanen, and I had bordered on "totalitarianism" over the removal of the dentist for his remarks. An anonymous journalist writing as "Capitol Eye" in the *Isthmus* of Madison on July 22 accused us of "Thought Control." He believed politicians should stick to things like filling potholes, burying garbage, and running the jail.[18]

Needless to say, this diatribe provoked a huge response, and parts were printed in subsequent issues of the *Isthmus*. A powerful response signed by then District Attorney James Doyle Jr. and former board chairperson Mary Louise Symon claimed that the individual writing as "Eye" was "shallow and misleading." They noted that the Board of Health was not a debating society where any view might be aired, but an agency of the county government charged by state statute with powers in the area of public health. They wrote, "The county by both law and policy is committed to exercise its powers in a nondiscriminatory fashion." And in closing, they stated, "Barry, Haanen and Wagner acted to ensure that people in this county would be treated fairly."[19]

Brooks Egerton pointed out that "Eye" never took issue with any of the homophobic remarks by Pawlisch and also that "Eye" accepted the implication that "victims of the disease are to be blamed." "What really makes me furious," Egerton fumed in a letter to the *Isthmus* editor, "is realizing that the 'Thought Control' column was virtually the first mention in *Isthmus* of AIDS. For that matter, *Isthmus* has largely ignored the host of other issues that concern lesbians and gay men in Madison." In subsequent years, the paper worked hard to remedy this perception.[20]

Pawlisch filed a lawsuit in early August 1983 seeking reinstatement and claiming his free speech rights and due process rights had been violated. The county moved to dismiss the suit. Lynn Haanen and I filed affidavits on Pawlisch's remarks. The county attorney handling the matter worked closely with me on reviewing legal documents, since I was a member of the Public Protection and Judiciary Committee with oversight of his office. My own document in the case noted that I believed AIDS to be "a disabling condition which your affiant is informed and believes is at epidemic levels among the gay male population and which is often fatal for its victims."[21]

On March 1, 1984, Circuit Court Judge Edward S. Marion ruled in the county's favor against Pawlisch. The court decided that "commonality of political beliefs with the county executive is 'an appropriate requirement for the effective performance of the public office involved.'" The Court of Appeals District IV affirmed the lower court ruling, noting that the remarks "caused Barry to seriously doubt whether Pawlisch could continue to act on health policies without discriminating against the homosexual community." In this case, a seat at the table was able to raise an early alert over how homophobic attitudes could function as roadblocks for public policy on AIDS.[22]

SAVING MAZO BEACH

Noted writer August Derleth attested to the existence of young males using "Bare Skin Beach" on the Wisconsin River as early as the late 1930s. The beach, though little known at that time, continued to be enjoyed for decades. By the 1970s, it was popular with more people in the area and was even known nationally in naturist and counterculture circles. By that point, a specific "gay section" of the beach had developed and was popular with a number of folks in Madison's gay community. Though I never went there myself, I had friends who did. Mazo Beach, as it was known in modern parlance, was tucked just into the northwest corner of Dane County.[23]

Enter Sheriff Jerry Lacke, a moderate appointed to the Dane County Sheriff post by Republican Governor Lee Sherman Dreyfus after Democratic Sheriff Bill Ferris died of cancer. Before his role as sheriff, Ferris had been a bartender at the Pirate Ship, a bar known for its gay crowd in the evening hours. Ferris had been goaded into the sheriff's office by Clarenbach, who dared him to run and potentially get rid of a conservative. Ferris had been concerned, even though he was not gay, that an association with the gay community might rear its head and hurt him electorally. It did not, and he served from 1972 to 1981.

I served with Lacke in county government from his appointment in

1981 to 1990, working closely with him in my role as a member of the Public Protection and Judiciary Committee of the Dane County Board. In his run for election, I endorsed him and campaigned with him at the Willy Street Fair, introducing him to my constituents. When he became sheriff, Lacke became concerned with Mazo Beach as it became more known and used on his watch. Since the beach was located in the town of Mazomanie, the sheriff had primary police responsibilities for this unincorporated area of Dane County. The district attorney's office was the place where charging decisions on arrests were made and cases were selected to be tried in court. Dane District Attorney Jim Doyle Jr., scion of a liberal family, had no interest in spending the county's prosecutorial resources on nudity violations of state statutes if the sheriff's department made an arrest. Lacke came up with a concept for a new county ordinance that, if enacted, would have made nudity at the beach a county ordinance violation and subject to a fine like a parking ticket. The reasoning was that antinudity would be easier for sheriff's deputies to enforce, and most people ticketed would pay the fine and be discouraged from using the beach.

However, all new ordinances to Dane County's code of ordinances had to be adopted by the Dane County Board. To get on the county board's agenda, they had to be recommended either favorably or unfavorably by the appropriate standing committee with jurisdiction, in this case the Public Protection and Judiciary Committee. Since I was chair of the committee when the idea surfaced, I had to agree to place it on the committee's agenda. This was the prerogative of the chair. In this instance, having a seat at the table really worked. I told the sheriff I would not *ever* be placing the ordinance proposal on any agenda of the committee for a vote, so he might as well drop it. Lacke understood this political reality, and the ordinance never saw light of day. The historic Mazo Beach with its connection to the gay community was saved.

GAY LIBERATION COMES TO MADISON

The sculptor George Segal was commissioned in 1979 by a private foundation, the Mildred Andrews Fund based in Louisiana, to create a piece for gay liberation in commemoration of Stonewall. Segal made two castings of his *Gay Liberation* work in his classic style of life-size, white-patina human figures. According to the foundation's wishes, one was initially intended for San Francisco's Harvey Milk Plaza, but it ended up on the Stanford University campus. The other was intended for Sheridan Square in New York City, near the site of the Stonewall Bar. Many people criticized aspects of the commission, complaining that it should have been given to a gay sculptor, as well as the art itself, which was said to portray stereotypical, clone-like men. David Boyce, who served as one of Segal's models for the work, recalled the artist's statement in 1981: "The biggest statement I tried to make was the gentleness and humanity of homosexuals, and it shocks people to express the opinion that a homosexual is a decent, sensitive human being—and I'm shocked at that." Some believed that New York City was not politically ready for the work, so it sat in Segal's chicken coop on his New Jersey farm.[24]

Tom Garver, director of the Madison Art Center, knew Segal and thought the statue could be exhibited in Madison at the Art Center. He made arrangements for it to come to Madison in 1986. Jacob Stockinger, a bisexual and the arts critic for the *Capital Times*, wrote that the display, beginning on January 1, 1986, had been "orphaned by the gay capitals of America." *OUT!*, in its February 1986 issue, proclaimed, "Gay Liberation Statue Finds Madison Home." The piece was generally well received by the city's art scene.[25]

However, even in Madison, Segal's work had its gay critics. In an opinion piece in *OUT!*, L. Aaron Kaufman criticized the Art Center's placement of the three-dimensional work in a third-floor niche. He also suggested that a gay sculptor might have created a work that would present a "more accurate and sensitive representation of gay people's struggle toward enrichment of life and social acceptance as equals." Kaufman cited the critical gay views in New York and San Francisco. He noted that the women in the sculpture were showing affection for each other, while the men barely touched each other, arguing that this played to gender stereotypes.[26]

After the gallery display, the piece was slated to return to Segal's chicken coop, so in the early planning stages of the sculpture's visit, Tom Garver called me as a public figure in both the gay community and in the arts community. (I had served on the Dane County Cultural Affairs Commission and had chaired the Wisconsin Arts Board.) He suggested that the piece might remain in Madison longer than its initial six-month loan period, since New York was still not ready for it. He wondered if we could find a place for it to be publicly displayed outdoors. My good friend and political mentor Sixth District "Boss" Bill Thompson had done many years of service as a member of the Madison Park Commission. He and I strategized that the Marquette neighborhood's Orton Park in the heart of my supervisory district would be an ideal place for the art. We could use our network of political and social contacts to show support. The neighborhood alder, Billy Feitlinger, gladly came on board. Feitlinger and I jointly held a neighborhood meeting on April 29 at the house of Buck Rhyme and Anne Rodgers-Rhyme, who lived on the edge of the park. Feitlinger said he was "optimistic people will accept it." He and I went door to door speaking to all the neighbors around the park to explain the project and urge support.[27]

Meanwhile, Garver and I knew that for such a potentially controversial project we needed to eliminate the question of whether public dollars would be used to cover the sculpture's installation. My involvement with the New Harvest Foundation gave us connections to people who could potentially assume the costs. So Garver arranged for us to have a special fundraising luncheon for donors in the gallery with the Segal piece, and the estimated cost of five thousand dollars was quickly secured.[28]

Next, we needed to obtain permission to place the work in a public park. This meant a vote by the Madison Parks Commission. At a quiet meeting on May 15, by a 6 to 1 vote, the commission approved it. A news story published later in May, noting that the statue was only on loan, said "the Isthmus could be leading the way for the Big Apple." They quoted me as saying, "The fact that Madison is doing this should spur New York to get it together." But then, as the issue of the sculptures being displayed in the park hit the press big time, it became suddenly contentious even in Madison.

The Madison Parks Commission put it back on the agenda for its meeting of June 11. The *Capital Times* described the scene as one in which "opponents quoted the Bible while supporters wore lavender badges." Of the 180 people who registered opinions, 98 were in favor and 81 against. Two-and-a-half hours of testimony occurred. Supporters called Madison the perfect site for the sculpture, as it was the capital city of the only state in the nation with a law protecting gays and lesbians. The placement was supported by the encompassing Marquette Neighborhood Association (of which I had been a past president) and by Judy Olson speaking for the neighborhood's gay-friendly Wil-Mar Center. However, some locals made their opposition known. "As a Christian, a taxpayer and a resident of the east side," said William Goodman, "I'm opposed to seeing homosexuals commemorated." Reverend Richard Conklin warned that the sculpture would make Orton Park a gathering place for homosexuals, which would have been no news for the gay couples who lived on the streets around the park. Feitlinger spoke out against what he termed the "incredible bigotry" of those opposing the project.[29]

On June 11, the commission voted unanimously in favor of the statue being placed in the park. Rumors circulated that the sculpture could be defaced or destroyed by blow torches, grenades, or bombs, according to the press account by Jacob Stockinger of the *Capital Times* on June 12. Linda Bellman, chair of the Parks Commission, noted Segal's stature as an international artist and commented, "I don't think there's anything offensive about it." Bill Thompson, who had quietly lobbied his fellow commissioners, was quoted in the press as saying, "I think the controversy will continue somewhat, but eventually it will die down."[30]

However, press controversy continued. In a letter to the editor of the *Capital Times*, Donna Kirschenmann of Madison wrote, "The sculpture is a sensitive tribute to a significant part of our population—family, friends and acquaintances of us all." But Edmund Zawacki, also of Madison, objected to its presence as "mere propagandistic crap." He suggested it should have a companion piece titled "The Avenging Angel—AIDS." Also in the *Capital Times*, Jack Guzman said if the city denied the placement of Segal's work, it should then erect a monument to "its intolerance and an even more insidious ignorance." Roland DiRienzo of Cross Plains said the sculpture "belongs in Sodom and Gomorrah."[31]

The possibility that a controversial public work of art might be vandalized had always been a consideration in the minds of our planning group. The casting of Segal's *Gay Liberation* piece on the Stanford campus had been attacked with hammers that did little harm to the white coated bronze figures. From the start of the public discourse, Garver had made it known that Segal had volunteered to repair any damage that might occur. Garver had insisted that bollards be placed around the concrete pad of the sculpture

Shown here in the fall of 1988 gathered around George Segal's statue, *Gay Liberation*, in Madison's Orton Park are Dane County Supervisor Dick Wagner, Madison Alderman Jim McFarland, Dane County Supervisor Earl Bricker, Madison Alderman Ricardo Gonzalez, Dane County Supervisor Kathleen Nichols, and Dane County Supervisor Tammy Baldwin. FROM THE AUTHOR'S COLLECTION

to prevent someone from driving a truck into the figures. Within the first couple of months, vandals did indeed attack the art, making black crayon marks on its white surface. However, Segal had provided the Art Center with more of the white coating, and the piece was cleaned and touched up.

Some students from the third and fourth grade classes at the neighborhood's Marquette Elementary School worked with teacher's aide Barb Christopher to create an Orton Park Photo Journal in 1987. Ten-year-old Samira Guyot conducted a survey of forty-five people in the neighborhood, finding that twenty-seven favored the work, nine opposed it, and nine had no opinion. Guyot's peers Anna Gassman, Erin Holm, and Tony Sturm also worked on the photo journal. Christopher believed the project provided the students with a "new awareness and sensitivity to lesbianism and homosexuality."[32]

Madison's adoption of the Segal work was noted across the country. Many gay papers ran photo stories of the work on display in Madison. The *New York Times* of October 31, 1986, noted it was loaned indefinitely to the Madison Art Center. The Parks Commission renewed the annual agreement with the Art Center until New York was finally ready to have it placed in Sheridan Square in time for Pride in 1992.[33]

FOUNDING THE NATIONAL ASSOCIATION OF OUT OFFICIALS

In November 1985, Kathleen Nichols and I joined ten other out American lesbian and gay officials in West Hollywood for the first National Conference of Openly Lesbian and Gay Elected Officials. This identity-based organizing model had been followed earlier by black elected officials. It was amazing to be in the company of this handful of others who were doing the same pioneering work. Harry Britt from San Francisco, who had replaced Harvey Milk as city supervisor, did not join us for the whole conference but spoke at an evening banquet. One of the reported nineteen out officials unable to join us was Gerald Ulrich, the mayor of the small Missouri town of Bunceton. Madison had three out officials, meaning we constituted 16 percent of the nation's total, punching well above our weight. The dean of the group was Minnesota State Senator Allan Spear, who had come out in 1974 following Elaine Noble's first election for two terms as an out lesbian legislator in Massachusetts. The featured keynote speaker at the conference was Chris Smith, an out Labour member of the British parliament. While he was the first member of parliament to publicly acknowledge his homosexuality, he quipped, "I'm gay, just like a hundred other members of parliament. The only difference is, they won't tell you."[34]

The conference, titled "Speaking for Ourselves," had been sponsored through the efforts of Tom Chorlton of the National Association of Gay and Lesbian Democratic Clubs and the Municipal Elections Committee of Los Angeles, one of the first and the largest electorally and locally focused gay groups in the country. Interest also came from the relatively new Human Rights Campaign Fund, and to make it bipartisan, the president of the Log Cabin Republican Club of Los Angeles was a plenary speaker. The conference was held in West Hollywood, a newly incorporated city in Los Angeles County that proclaimed itself as having the first gay government in the nation because two gay men and one lesbian made up the majority of its five-member city council. One of the gay members, Steve Schulte, was a sort of celebrity, as he had been a star of some glossy gay

One of the many political fundraisers held on Jenifer Street included guest of honor
Harry Britt, the successor to Harvey Milk on the San Francisco Board of Supervisors.
Left to right: Kathleen Nichols, Britt, Dick Wagner, and Lynn Haanen. FROM THE AUTHOR'S
COLLECTION

beefcake magazines. John Heilman, mayor of West Hollywood, was the
nation's newest gay mayor.[35]

Within the workshops at this first-ever historic event, attendees discussed ways to identify and articulate a vision of human rights, to develop
a plan of action to boost efforts for the AIDS crisis, and to formulate a
march on Washington to follow up the one held in 1979. Supervisor Britt
argued that we had to overcome the pervasive sense of failure regarding
the movement now that we were in the age of Reagan. Hoping to nurture
and support lesbians and gay men who were potential candidates, the conference offered workshops on political mechanics. Developing a vision for
future out officials in even higher positions was an assumed group agenda.

The conference concluded with a joint statement:

As elected officials, we have a unique opportunity and responsibility
to serve as teachers within the institutions of government . . . and

to demonstrate to our own community that we will always obtain more by reaching for what we need rather than settling for what we can get. . . . We ask not only to be seen and heard, but also to be acknowledged for the work we are doing to provide fair and effective government, and to be supported in our demand that gay and lesbian people be given the respect and justice we deserve. We support and seek to place at the head of our national agenda a vision of human rights which embraces those material and non-material resources which are necessary for each individual to grow into a self-fulfilled, confident, and secure person.[36]

The resulting list of issues developed at the conference showed support for nondiscrimination legislation, repeal of laws on consensual sexual activity between adults, legal recognition of family relationships, equitable treatment in foster care and adoption, support for reproductive freedom, passage of the Equal Rights Amendment, and positive sex education about sexual identity. The major California dailies provided good coverage of the gathering. The *Los Angeles Times* quoted Nichols, saying "she went from being a 'rock-throwing liberal' to an elected official." Nichols followed this up by confirming, "There's nothing like . . . being on the inside." The *San Francisco Chronicle* noted the conference-goers' support for AIDS funding, nondiscrimination laws, and gay marriage. The *Los Angeles Herald Examiner* referred to it as a "first ever 'gay summit'" aimed at more coordination in the electoral arena. The gay *New York Native* reported on the address of Representative Barney Frank, who also keynoted the banquet. Frank, who was not out at the time, urged attendees to push ahead on lesbian and gay issues despite the social backlash. "If you present a bleak landscape," he warned, "there'll be no initiative."[37]

In the conference's concluding statement, the group pledged to "lobby for increased funding for AIDS research and education and to ensure compassionate and informed care for people with AIDS." In March 1986, David Scondras from the Boston City Council and Brian Coyle of the Minneapolis City Council led a delegation of officials who coordinated with the National Gay and Lesbian Task Force on talking with members of Congress. They met with House Speaker Tip O'Neill and Kentucky Representative William Natcher, who headed a key health appropriations subcommittee and strongly opposed the Reagan administration's plans to cut forty-one million dollars of AIDS funding in the 1986 budget.[38]

Following West Hollywood, the next annual conferences were held in the District of Columbia in 1986, Minneapolis in 1987, San Diego in 1988, and Madison in 1989. The conferences let us air our issues as out officials and functioned as a support group for people in our unique positions. Further, they let us see the state of gay and lesbian political and social institutions in other cities. For example, while Nichols worked on the joint statement with a subcommittee of drafters on the Saturday evening of that initial conference, I took advantage of the free passes to Studio One, one of West Hollywood's big discos. The conference would be sustained for several decades, helping to encourage and expand the number of out elected officials across the nation.[39]

MADISON AREA HOMINTERN

In the early 1980s, the Madison-area LGBT officials knew one another well. Kathleen Nichols, Lynn Haanen, and I all worked jointly on county issues. Nichols and I also bonded over being asked to serve as cochairs of Governor Earl's Council on Lesbian and Gay Issues in early 1983 and traveling together all over the state. The three of us had good working relationships with State Representative Clarenbach. Haanen was close to Anne Monks on the Madison City Council; they both represented the Eighth District at a time when city and county districts were coterminous. We would compare line items that were jointly in city and county budgets and examine how they did or did not reconcile. My best friend was Madison Alder Hank Lufler. One year, a fall weekend trip to the Amana Colonies in Iowa saw Haanen, Monks, Lufler, and me (along with other friends) eating sauerbraten and buying handmade brooms. This small group of out elected officials in Madison would change and expand over time.

Haanen left the county board in 1986 but worked to ensure she was succeeded by a lesbian in the Eighth District, the very young supervisor Tammy Baldwin. At the time, Nichols and I were meeting with a group of progressives called together by Alder Billy Feitlinger at Mother Fool's Pub to work on the spring 1985 city elections. After a general session, we broke into working caucuses, and Nichols and I assumed the two of us would be the lesbian/gay caucus. But a young woman came up to join us, introduced herself as Tammy, and stated she had an interest in politics. The rest, as they say, is history.

When Monks left the city council before the end of her term as Eighth District alder, tradition had it that the council (and likewise the county board) would appoint the other body's officeholder to finish the term until the next election, since county districts and aldermanic areas were the same. So, the Eighth District Supervisor Baldwin also became Alder Baldwin. In the subsequent election for a full term, out Republican Jim McFarland was elected as alder. He and his partner, Rick Villasenor, were active in opposing ROTC discrimination on campus. McFarland went on to champion alternative family and domestic partnership recognition in the Madison ordinances. McFarland was not the first out local Republican elected official in the nation, but he was among a very few.

In 1987, Ricardo Gonzalez was elected to Madison's city council as the first out gay Hispanic elected official in the country. Ricardo and his family had fled Cuba after the Castro-led revolution, though his personal sympathies had initially been supportive of Castro. Ricardo himself raised funds for agrarian reform. After landing in Ripon, Wisconsin, he worked for Green Giant in the important Wisconsin canning industry as a personnel manager. He rented his apartment from a gay man who ran a men's clothing store, and Ricardo was brought to Madison to meet the man's friends who were interior decorators. In the small world of Wisconsin's gay circles, he ended up visiting the Jenifer Street house owned by Keith McCutcheon and Joe Korberstein, where many of their gay friends lived, which is now my house.

Then in the spring elections of 1988, Earl Bricker won a seat on the Dane County Board. Bricker had been the liaison for the lesbian and gay community for Governor Anthony Earl. He had also served as a field representative for the Democratic Party. Next, UW–Madison professor John Nees was elected to the Shorewood Hills Village Board, a suburb just west of the university campus. You almost needed a program to keep all of the gay officials straight.

We cooperated in many ways. All of us except McFarland were either Democrats or Socialists (Haanen and Nichols), but we still welcomed McFarland to the work and supported his efforts on gay issues at the city level. To help promote the network, I decided to host an annual Homintern dinner at which officials, along with a partner or guest of their choosing, were welcomed for a social gathering and exchange of ideas. The term *Homintern*, referring to a supposed worldwide conspiracy of homosexuals, was a play on the Communist International, or Comintern, feared by fervid anti-Communists. It harkened back to the witch hunts against commies and queers described in greater detail in my first volume, *We've Been Here All Along*. Ricardo Gonzalez also hosted some Homintern events.

After I became chair of the county board in 1988, I was able to nurture Supervisor Baldwin's career. I gave her influential appointments such as to the County Finance Committee. As the AIDS crisis worsened, we decided to set up a Dane County task force on AIDS to coordinate the many social service programs and public health areas where the county had jurisdiction. I engineered things so that Baldwin would chair the task force. The county worked with many contract providers on AIDS. One Dane AIDS forum included Gridley Hall, then a program officer with the Ford Foundation as well as the chair of the state Medical Society's Task Force on HIV/AIDS. Later, Baldwin was able to use her leadership of the group as a qualification on her literature when she ran for the state assembly for the first time in 1992.

When in 1990 various acts of homophobia occurred in the Madison area, I was able to place a resolution on the county calendar rejecting such violence and expressing appreciation to the United for working against it. Cosponsors of the resolution were Supervisors Baldwin and Bricker. As chair, I could place this issue at the head of the agenda where items were adopted by acclamation without debate, and so it was. Likewise, when Bricker presented a resolution recognizing December 1, 1990, as World AIDS Day, the issue went on the acclamation calendar. When a county agency head told antigay jokes before one meeting, I was able to reprimand him, pointing out the county ordinances for his instruction. At the time of concern in 1989 as to whether nursing homes would accept AIDS patients, I was able to get a ruling from the county's corporation counsel that, in line with our nondiscrimination ordinances, the county nursing home would accept AIDS patients. Big or small, all of these things were accomplished because we had seats at the table and were not going to let our community's concerns go unaddressed.

The Gay Rights State Rolls Out the Pink Carpet

At the 1988 Conference of Openly Lesbian and Gay Elected Officials in San Diego, Madison's out officials made a bid for the next convention in 1989. Our circular noted, "We think it particularly appropriate that our conference should meet in the capital city of the nation's only gay rights state. We wish to show you the future in practice, where nondiscrimination on the basis of sexual orientation is the law of the land." We observed that 1989 would mark seven years of the law working and twenty years of gay and lesbian activism in our city.[40]

To create the conference invitational document, six of the then seven out officials in the Madison area posed amidst the George Segal statue for a cover photo of the brochure designed by Dan Curd. Wisconsin's motto, "Forward," placed in a pink triangle, became the logo. An invitational brochure photo showed Bascom Hill decorated with pink triangles. We noted that out gay/lesbian officials constituted 10 percent of both the Madison City Council and the Dane County Board.

State legislator Clarenbach secured the Wisconsin State Capitol for our sessions, the first time we ever had such a venue, as previous conferences had been held primarily in hotel spaces. Tammy Baldwin and I served as cochairs of the event, and we took seriously the task of showing hospitality to our guests. Friday night we chartered a bus for a Pink Plaque Tour of Madison's lesbian and gay sites, including the Segal statue, serving Wisconsin cheeses and mulled cider on the way. This was followed by a buffet dinner for fifty at my house. The Saturday dinner was hosted at the Wilson Street Grill with entertainment by Lynette and Friends. Ricardo Gonzalez hosted a farewell brunch on Sunday at the Cardinal Bar.[41]

The opening session included a welcome from Clarenbach, which included the admission, "Let's not kid ourselves. Passing laws does not end homophobia." The keynote address was given by Svend Robinson, a recently elected out member of the Canadian Parliament. Robinson, who belonged to the New Democratic Party (a Socialist party), acknowledged that the existence of the group of out officials "gave me a great deal of strength before I [publicly] came out of the closet in February 1988." During his talk, he stressed the fact that "the incidence of gay bashing is still far too high." At the opening, we also had a reading of the historic West

At the Fifth Annual Meeting of Out Elected Officials in 1989, a "Pink Plaque" bus tour of Madison was provided to guests with cheese and cider. Here Dane County Supervisors Kathleen Nichols (left) and Tammy Baldwin (right) offer commentary. FROM THE AUTHOR'S COLLECTION

Hollywood statement by those who had been there. Tribute was paid to drag queen Jose Sarria, who was the first gay person in the nation to run for elected office, in 1961. One particularly special presentation was "The End of Invisibility and the Genesis of the Pink Triangle," given by UW–Madison professor James Steakley on Saturday at noon.[42]

A popular attendee was Keith St. John, who had been elected earlier that month to the Albany, New York, city council. He was the first out gay African American elected official in the nation. Also breaking barriers was our own John Nees, who had been elected as a trustee of the Village of Shorewood Hills. Nees was sixty-five years old, having come out when he was fifty. This put him at the top of the age list of out officials, breaking some ageist stereotypes. He had served as a director of the Wisconsin Environmental Decade, a statewide environmental advocacy organization.[43]

Lou Chibbaro Jr., of the national gay press, attended the conference as a reporter for the *Washington Blade*, and on November 24, he headlined one of his stories, "Madison, Wisconsin, Holds the Record for Openly Gay

Officials." He described this phenomenon as a "series of developments that make even San Francisco pale by comparison." Chibbaro claimed that my welcome remark that the city was "quite friendly" to gays "could have been the understatement of the century."[44]

The *Milwaukee Journal* conference coverage of November 17 noted, "The idea of an openly gay candidate running for office and winning was unthinkable years ago. But times have changed." The story quoted Baldwin as saying that she "expects the task of winning elections to get easier for openly gay candidates as voters observe the performance of those now in office." The story continued, "Once in office, most openly gay officials acknowledge that they represent two constituencies—the general public and the gay community." They ended with a quote from me: "I have more than paid my dues to the community at large. But what a straight politician would not do is address the concerns of the gay and lesbian population. That I can and will do."[45]

THE POWER OF SEATS AT THE TABLE

Lesbian and gay officials in Madison have demonstrated that you can be out, run, and frequently win elections. By doing so many times, and repeatedly, Madison's out elected officials have shown that Judy Greenspan's and Jim Yeadon's experiences in the 1970s were not one-off events. By building and sustaining a strong tradition in the area, they helped create the open climate that has made Wisconsin the only state to elect three out persons to the US Congress: Steve Gunderson (who was reelected after he came out), Tammy Baldwin, and Mark Pocan. Additionally, Baldwin is the first out US Senator.

These officials found ways to be mutually supportive across political lines. On my trips to Washington, DC, as a county official, I also stopped by congressional offices. In a conversation with Gunderson before he was "outed," I was able to tell him I would work against Democrats trying to use his sexual orientation as a campaign issue. As it turned out, conservatives who were his fellow Republicans were the ones who forced him from the closet.

This determined group of officials showed they could assume broad leadership roles and not just be focused on gay agendas. My own work for

Dane County included expanding jail and court space, modernizing the Dane County Airport, solving the tangle of consolidating dispatch and moving to a modern 911 system, sponsoring the county's twelve million dollar participation in Monona Terrace, increasing lake weed cutting for my lakefront district, sponsoring the county's observation of Martin Luther King Jr. Day as a holiday, establishing airport noise abatement policies for my eastside district, and balancing budgetary increases for both human services and public safety.

These experiences show that gay and lesbian local officials can be in contact with national gay rights organizations for information and strategies, and they can find ways to tackle these concerns in their own communities. They made sure equality was part of the public agenda. The national gay press was and would continue to be amazed by the LGBT political successes in Wisconsin. As important as the national accolades, these seats at the table guaranteed that the voices of Wisconsin's LGBT people would be heard in the public debate over issues in their local communities as well as those on the national stage.

Appendix II:
Wisconsin's Elected LGBT Officials

S ince the 1970s, LGBT individuals have held elected office in Wisconsin, one of the state's strong traditions. Some were formally out by self-declaration in the press, while others were generally known within the gay community and provided support on LGBT issues. This list does not include closeted officials. Apologies to any individuals who may have been missed.

United States Senate

Tammy Baldwin (D-Madison), 2013–present

United States House of Representatives

Tammy Baldwin (D-Madison), Second District, 1999–2013
Steve Gunderson (R-Osseo), Third District, 1981–1997
Mark Pocan (D-Town of Vermont), Second District, 2013–present

Wisconsin State Senate

David Berger (D-Milwaukee), 1975–1981
Tim Carpenter (D-Milwaukee), 2003–present
Katie Morrison (D-Platteville), 1975–1979

Wisconsin State Assembly

Tammy Baldwin (D-Madison), 1993–1999
Marisabel Cabrera (D-Milwaukee), 2019–present
Tim Carpenter (D-Milwaukee), 1985–2003
David Clarenbach (D-Madison), 1975–1993
Dick Flintrop (D-Oshkosh), 1973–1983
Steve Gunderson (R-Osseo), 1975–1981

Doris Hanson (D-Monona), 1993–1999
William Murat (D-Stevens Point), 1995–1999
Todd Novak (R-Dodgeville), 2015–present
John Manske (R-Milton), 1981–1987
Mark Pocan (D-Madison), 1999–2013
Mark Spreitzer (D-Beloit), 2015–present
JoCasta Zamarripa (D-Milwaukee), 2011–present

WISCONSIN LOCAL OFFICE

County Officials

Dane County Judge

Ellen Berz, 2012–present
Shelly Gaylord, 2003–present
Rhonda Lanford, 2013–present
George Northrup, 1985–1997
Sarah O'Brien, 1992–2012

Dane County Board Supervisor

Todd Anderson, 1976–1980
Tammy Baldwin, 1986–1994
Kevin Bonds, 1994–1996
Earl Bricker, 1988–1991
Chuck Erickson, 2002–present
Robb Fyrst, 2000–2006
Lynn Haanen, 1979–1986
Kevin Kesterson, 1992–2005 (chair, 1998–2005)
Richard Kilmer, 2016–present
Scott McCormick, 1994–1998
Kathleen Nichols, 1983–1990
Mark Pocan, 1991–1996
Kyle Richmond, 2002–2016
Andrew Schauer, 2014–present
R. Richard Wagner, 1980–1994 (chair, 1988–1992)

Iowa County Coroner

Dr. Tim Correll, 1977–2002

Kenosha County Board

Dayvin Hallmon, 2008–2018

Winnebago County Board

Aaron Wojciechowski, 2016–present

City Officials

Appleton City Council

Teege Mettille, 2011–2013
Vered Meltzer, 2014–present

Ashland City Council

David Mettille 2015–2019

Beloit City Council

Mark Spreitzer, 2011–2015

Dodgeville Mayor

Todd Novak, 2012–to present

Eau Claire School Board

Joe Luginbill, 2015–present

Fond du Lac City Council

Dan Manning, 2013–2015

Madison Mayor

Satya Rhodes-Conway, 2019–present

Madison Municipal Judge

Shelly Gaylord, 1993–2003

Madison School Board

Ken Bowling, 1980–1983

Madison City Council

Tammy Baldwin, 1986 interim appointee
David Clarenbach, 1974 interim appointee
Ricardo Gonzalez, 1989–1995
Lynn Haanen, 1980 interim appointee
Patrick Heck, 2019–present
Eli Judge, 2007–2009
Steve King, 2009–present
Hank Lufler Jr., 1979–1993
Jim McFarland, 1986–1991
Anne Monks, 1980–1986
Judy Olson, 1995–2007
Larry Palm, 2005–2019
Satya Rhodes-Conway, 2007–2013
Matt Sloan, 1999–2005
Napoleon Smith, 1991–1999
John Strasser, 2013–2015
Mike Verveer, 1995–present
Jim Yeadon, 1976–1979

Milton City Council

John Manske, 1973–1977, 1979–1981

Milwaukee Board of School Directors

Jennifer Morales, 2001–2009

Waukesha City Council

Vance Skinner, 2010–2019

Village and Town Officials

Bayfield School Board

Glenn Carlson, 2018–present

La Pointe Town Board

Glenn Carlson, 2019–present
Michael Childers, 2014–2016, 2017–2019

Mazomanie Town Board

Ron Boylan, 2009–2011

McFarland Village President

Doris Hanson, 1991–1995

McFarland Village Trustee

Doris Hanson, 1988–1991
Kevin Kesterson, 1987–1993
Tim Zingraf, 2001–2005

Shorewood Hills Village Trustee

John Nees, 1989–1993

LGBT activism in Wisconsin expanded from a few brave organizers in the fall of 1969 to a mass movement, as shown here in the Wisconsin AIDS Walk occurring in Milwaukee.
ARCHIVES DEPARTMENT, UNIVERSITY OF WISCONSIN—MILWAUKEE LIBRARIES

ACKNOWLEDGMENTS

T he completion of this second volume has only been possible with the assistance and encouragement of many others. I wish to deeply thank them. In mentioning some who have helped with this volume, I fear I will forget others. Try as one might, I am sure there are errors, and I beg the readers' indulgence for my faults.

Thanks go to those who have assisted me with this project. Will Fellows has been invaluable in breaking some of this ground in his books and in providing me with concepts and sources. His early research, hints and tips, and encouragement were stimulating. The late Ron McCrea trod some of this ground himself and pioneered much of our storytelling. Don Schwamb led many community efforts, including the wonderful website on Wisconsin LGBT history. Jamakaya's work of remembering and recording has brought many things to light for our community.

The patience and knowledge of archivists at the UW–Madison Archives, especially David Null, Troy Reeves, and Katie Nash, were most helpful. And thanks to my fellow workers on the community committee for furthering that archive's LGBT special collection: Scott Seyforth, Michele Besant, Pat Calchina, Kalleen Mortensen, and Katherine Charek Briggs. The UW–Milwaukee Archives with its LGBT collection was also invaluable, and its originator and caretaker Michael Doylen encouraged my early efforts by displaying its rich resources. Max Yela of special collections at UW–Milwaukee also was quite helpful. The archivists at the Wisconsin Historical Society assisted with many boxes. The materials at the Legislative Reference Library proved extremely fruitful. The Wisconsin Law Library staff aided me, a non-lawyer, in finding rich documents.

LGBT community members and others made this work possible with their memories and collections. David Clarenbach, whose papers illuminate so much, was particularly helpful, and our many conversations filled in the interstices known only to him. My interviews with Bill Kraus, Steve Morrison, and Michael Blumenfeld helped greatly in my understanding of several matters.

Todd Larson and Richard Kilmer helped articulate rural roots. Paul Soglin, the pioneer in so many progressive things, illuminated the Madison gay rights ordinance passage. Mike Fitzpatrick never let me forget northeast Wisconsin's roles. Doug Nelson, Will Handy, Mary Alice Maury, and others in the AIDS fight provided sustenance when it was desperately needed. Henry Dudek, Jim Green, and all the folks at Integrity/Dignity also lifted spirits.

The late David Adamany several times drew on his memory to share history. Brian Bigler's early research and ongoing clues helped. Patrick Farabaugh and Emily Mills at *Our Lives* magazine encouraged me to write stories of our history and proved to me that an audience exists.

In the days covered in the epilogue, my many friends in Fair Wisconsin—Glenn Carlson and Michael Childers, Robert Starshak and Ross Draegert, Katie Belanger, and Megin McDonell—toiled to prevent past accomplishments from being eroded and to still lead the path forward.

So many colleagues in the Wisconsin Homintern have supported one another, including in many of the efforts here told: my frequent traveling companion Kathleen Nichols, Lynn Haanen, Anne Monks, Tammy Baldwin, Jim McFarland, Earl Bricker, Ricardo Gonzalez, Mark Pocan, and most especially, my dearest friend of forty years, Hank Lufler.

Thanks to all who read a chapter or two. A support has been my faith community that believes the Holy One holds all in mercy. Most of all, my great friend and book coach Mark Webster, who has walked this journey with me, deserves unending appreciation for guidance and insight. Thanks to his husband, Ryan Brown, for sharing Mark's time.

For the production of this book and its companion volume, my heartfelt appreciation goes to the donors who made it possible, and especially the plotters—Kathy Borkowski, Paula Bonner, Ann Schaffer, Mark Webster, and Mary Strickland—who reaped the harvest. The Wisconsin Historical Society staff has opened itself to LGBT history as part of the Wisconsin story, and thanks for that are due to Kathy Borkowski, Brian Thompson, and others. At the Press, Kate Thompson has been there from the beginning. Sara Phillips and Elizabeth Wyckoff, very dedicated editors, have made this volume so much better.

NOTES

Much of the research for this volume comes from the author's extensive personal archives, which have been donated to the LGBTQ Archive at the University of Wisconsin–Madison and are currently being processed as part of the R. Richard Wagner Papers. Many items listed as "in possession of author" are part of this invaluable collection and, in coming years, will be available to researchers and students to continue to learn about and tell these important stories.

Chapter 1

1. Ron McCrea, oral history interview by Brian Bigler, *Gay Madison: A History* project, 1996, Wisconsin Historical Society Archives, Madison, Wisconsin.
2. Eldon Murray, "Gay Liberation: Five Years After Stonewall," *GPU News* (Milwaukee), July 1974, reprinted from *Bugle American* (Milwaukee), June 27, 1974.
3. David Carter, *Stonewall: The Riots that Sparked the Gay Revolution* (New York: St. Martin's Griffin, 2004); see also Martin Duberman, *Stonewall* (New York: Dutton, 1993).
4. Murray, "Gay Liberation."
5. Murray, "Gay Liberation"; Jeremy, "Gay Liberation: An Introduction," *Kaleidoscope* (Milwaukee), February 13, 1970; Edward Alwood, *Straight News: Gays, Lesbians, and the News Media* (New York: Columbia University Press, 1996).
6. Murray, "Gay Liberation."
7. Gay Men's History Panel: Lewis Bosworth, Jess Anderson, Ron McCrea, and Mike Lutz, interview by Scott Seyforth at St. Francis House, Madison, Wisconsin, May 26, 2008, LGBT Civil Rights Collection, UW–Madison; Chuck Bauer and Chuck Beckwith, oral history interview by Brian J. Bigler, *Gay Madison: A History* project, 1996; "March Endorsement," *Gay Madison*, October 1979.
8. Flyers in Kathleen Nichols and Barbara Constans Papers, 1975–1979, Wisconsin Historical Society Archives, Madison, Wisconsin; for other

Wisconsin reflections on Stonewall, see "Gay & Lesbian Rights: Marking
a Quarter Century of Struggle," *Capital Times* (Madison), June 20, 1994;
"Stonewall 25: Pridefest '94," *The Wisconsin Light* (Madison), May 26,
1994; Don Schwamb, "We Have Come So Far Since 1969, but We Still Have
a Long Way to Go," *Queer Life* (Milwaukee), July 2007.

9. "Lesbian Started Stonewall Riots." *Leaping La Crosse News*, July 1989, citing *Lesbian Connection*, July/August 1989.

10. "Stonewall Stories," *In Step* (Milwaukee), July 21, 1994.

11. Theodore Pierce, oral history interview by Brian Bigler, *Gay Madison: A History* project, 1996.

12. Gay Men's History Panel; Jess Anderson, "UW Award Address," Gay, Lesbian, Bisexual and Transgender Alumni Council of the Wisconsin Alumni Association, Pyle Center, University of Wisconsin–Madison, July 17, 2005, transcript at jessanderson.org; "Madison Gays Organize," statement by MAHE, *Kaleidoscope*, February 13, 1970; alternative pronunciation of MAHE raised with author by Ron McCrea, an early member.

13. Gay Men's History Panel.

14. "Organization Instituted for Benefit of Homosexuals," *Daily Cardinal* (UW–Madison), January 7, 1970.

15. Various posters and letter from Sisters of Safo, Judy Greenspan Papers, Faculty Files, UW–Madison Archives, Madison, Wisconsin; Judy Greenspan, "Lesbianism and Feminism," *Daily Cardinal* (UW–Madison), March 6, 1972; Judy Greenspan, "Memoirs of a Tired Lesbian," *Whole Woman* (Madison), October 1972.

16. Greenspan, "Lesbianism and Feminism"; Greenspan, "Memoirs of a Tired Lesbian."

17. Greenspan, "Lesbianism and Feminism"; Gay Men's History Panel; Ron McCrea, oral history.

18. Gay Men's History Panel; Ron McCrea, oral history; "Madison Gays Active in Many Areas," *Capital Times*, June 25, 1973; copy of MAHE statement in George Mosse Papers, LGBT Collection, UW–Madison Archives.

19. "'Windows 27' speak," *Gay Madison*, May 1980; Kathleen Nichols, "A Post Mortem," *Gay Madison*, August 1981.

20. Dale Hillerman, "Gay Counseling Program History," LGBT Collection, UW–Madison Archives, 2015/304, 2–4.

21. Hillerman, "Gay Counseling Program History," 10.

22. Hillerman, "Gay Counseling Program History," 23–27; Jess Anderson, "UW Award Address."

23. Hillerman, "Gay Counseling Program History," 40–43; "Madison Gays Active in Many Areas," *Capital Times*, June 25, 1973.

24. Hillerman, "Gay Counseling Program History," 30–35, 45, 48, 52–53; "Symposium on Homosexuality," *Forum*, November 1973, published by Wisconsin Psychiatric Institute, UW–Madison, copy in Rich Fluechtling Papers, LGBT Collection, UW–Madison Archives.

25. Gay Men's History Panel"; Hillerman, "Gay Counseling Program History," 53–54.

26. "Our History," OutReach (Madison), www.outreachmadisonlgbt.org/our-history.

27. "We're Gay & We're Proud," *Kaleidoscope*, March 20, 1970.

28. "GLF and SAC," *Kaleidoscope*, September 21, 1970; "Freak Parade for Peace," *UWM Post* (UW–Milwaukee), September 10, 1971; "Bombing the Ave.," *Kaleidoscope*, September 9, 1971.

29. "Gay History," *Bugle American*, September 10, 1975; "Gay March," *Kaleidoscope*, January 8, 1971; "Milwaukee YIP . . . ," *Kaleidoscope*, September 21, 1970; "GLF and Sac"; "Gay Liberation Front Male Workshop Statement," *Kaleidoscope*, September 21, 1970; "Raid, Riot Marked Turning Point for Movement," *Milwaukee Journal*, February 29, 1972.

30. Eldon Murray, "GPU: 5 Years of Teaching," *Bugle American*, September 10, 1975; "Boys in the Band," *Kaleidoscope*, November 6, 1970.

31. "'Cruising,' 'Windows' Protested," *Amazon* (Milwaukee), April/May, 1980; copy of flyer "Stop the Movie 'Cruising,' Join the Protest" in possession of author.

32. Murray, "GPU: 5 Years of Teaching."

33. Murray, "GPU: 5 Years of Teaching."

34. Alyn Hess letter to Channel 6, Milwaukee, n.d., in possession of author; "Deaths: Alyn Hess," *Milwaukee Journal*, April 3, 1989; "In Loving Memory: Alyn W. Hess," BWMT (Black and White Men Together) Milwaukee newsletter, April 1989; "In Memoriam: Alyn W. Hess, 1939–1989," *In Step*, April 13, 1989; "Milwaukee Activist Alyn Hess Dies of AIDS Complications, *The Wisconsin Light*, April 6, 1989.

35. "Gay Peoples Union to Hold Conference," *Milwaukee Journal*, March 21, 1972; "Homosexuals Urge Fight for Acceptance," *Milwaukee Journal*,

April 9, 1972; "Homosexual Bill of Rights," *Kaleidoscope*, September 27, 1968; Midwest Homophile Conference Notes, in GPU [Gay People's Union] Papers, UW–Milwaukee LGBT Collection, Milwaukee, Wisconsin.

36. "Homosexuals Urge Fight for Acceptance"; program from Midwest Homophile Conference, GPU Papers.

37. Notes from Midwest Homophile Conference, GPU Papers.

38. Notes from Midwest Homophile Conference, GPU Papers.

39. "Gay Union Plans Party," *Milwaukee Journal*, February 7, 1974; MASQUE-RAID flyer in GPU Papers; "Gay People Slate Event," *Milwaukee Sentinel*, January 21, 1974; "Gay Crowd Holds Masquerade Ball," *Milwaukee Journal*, February 10, 1974; GPU Annual Report 1974, in GPU Papers.

40. GPU Annual Report 1974; "Homosexual Clinic to Deal With VD," *Milwaukee Journal*, October 6, 1974.

41. "The Gay Revolution," six-day series in the *Milwaukee Journal*, February 27–March 3, 1972, including: "Homosexuals Seek End to Persecution," February 27, "Causes of Homosexuality Still A Mystery," February 28, "Raid Riot Marked Turning Point for Movement," February 29, "Does the Law Prosecute or Persecute?," March 1, "Churches Easing Stand on Gays," March 2, and "Sex Identity Ills Cause Problems," March 3; "Praise for Gay Series," *Milwaukee Journal*, March 13, 1972; "Life Not So Gay," *Milwaukee Journal*, March 22, 1972; "'Closet Queens' at Work," *Milwaukee Journal*, March 23, 1972.

42. "Sex Identity Ills Cause Problems"; "Homosexual Stigma Lifted," *Milwaukee Journal*, April 8, 1974.

43. "Homosexuals Seek End to Persecution"; "Homosexuality Lifted from List of Mental Disorders," *Sheboygan Press*, December 15, 1973.

44. "Does the Law Prosecute or Persecute?"

45. "Homosexuals Seek End to Persecution."

46. "Churches Easing Stand on Gays."

47. "Churches Easing Stand on Gays."

48. "Out of the Closet: Milwaukee's Gay Scene," special issue, *Bugle American*, September 10, 1975; "Gay Perspective," *Bugle American*, September 4, 1974.

49. "Out of the Closet."

50. "Out of the Closet."

51. Murray, "GPU: 5 Years of Teaching"; "Out of the Closet"; "Gay Objections," *Milwaukee Sentinel*, June 21, 1973.

52. "Out of the Closet."

53. "The Gay Revolution," in "Out of the Closet: Milwaukee's Gay Scene."

54. "Homosexuals Seek End to Persecution"; "Toward Human Liberation"; "Gay History."

55. GPU Annual Report 1974; "The Gay Revolution"; *Bugle American*, September 10, 1975.

56. "The Gay Revolution."

57. Editorial, *GPU News*, October 1971.

58. "Letter from Fox River Valley," *GPU News*, November 1979.

59. "L.A. Activist Visits GPU," *GPU News*, March 1974; "Jack Baker at Oshkosh," *GPU News*, December 1973.

60. "Activist Dr. Kameny to Speak," *GPU News*, March 1974; "Voeller Speaks at GPU," *GPU News*, July 1976; "Symposium: Gays and the Law," *GPU News*, June 1976.

61. "Elaine Noble to Speak in Madison," *GPU News*, March 1977; "Bell to Speak," *GPU News*, June 1979; "Bell Speaks at U.W.M.," *GPU News*, June 1979.

62. "Ben Shalom Speaks at Appleton," *GPU News*, December 1977.

63. "Fox Valley 'Gay Libs'—Their Lives, Their Aims," *Fond du Lac (WI) Reporter*, January 26, 1973; "Fond du Lac Homosexual 'Tells All About It,'" *Fond du Lac Reporter*, January 27, 1973; "Hiding Ourselves from Ourselves," *Fond du Lac Reporter*, May 21, 1973.

64. "Appleton Library to Carry GPU News," *GPU News*, December 1976.

65. "Merle Miller Visits Whitewater," *GPU News*, October 1973; Edward Alwood, *Straight News: Gays, Lesbians, and the News Media* (New York: Columbia University Press, 1996), 109; "A Homosexual's Story," *Milwaukee Journal*, February 21, 1971.

66. "'Gay' G.I. 'Undesirables,'" *The Royal Purple* (UW–Whitewater), October 31, 1972, in Eldon Murray Papers, UW–Milwaukee LGBT Archives.

67. "UWSP Confab," *GPU News*, June 1980; "Gay Pride Week Planned," *Amazon*, June/July, 1980; "Lesbian/Gay Conference," *Amazon*, August/September 1981.

68. "Flaunting Our Virtues" and "We Shall Go Forth" conference materials in possession of author; "Going Forth at the Annual Conference," *OUT!* (Madison), May 1983; "WLGN Sets Conference for State's Activists," *OUT!*, September 1984.

69. "Sparks Fly over Anti-Gay Letter," *OUT!*, April 1984.

70. "Fear and Loathing in Rural Wisconsin: A Conversation With Sandra Lipke," *OUT!*, February 1983; "Dear Friend: Letter from WLGN State Council," November 4, 1982, copy in possession of author.

71. "Fear and Loathing in Rural Wisconsin"; Kay Springstroh, "We Must Refuse to be Silent: Commentary from WLGN," *OUT!*, March 1984; "Homophobes Hit the Streets," *OUT!*, February 1984; Eleanor Roosevelt PAC, early 1983, minutes in possession of author; "State-wide Organization Needed to Build Unity and Support," *The Wisconsin Light*, July 27, 1989.

72. Callen Harty, *My Queer Life* (Madison, WI: self-pub., 2013), 29–32.

73. "Gay Lib Attracts Few," *Newscope* (UW–Parkside), March 13, 1972, in Murray Papers.

74. "Student Describes Life of Homosexual," *UW–Milwaukee Post*, November 19, 1971; "Being Gay: One Experience," *crossroads* (UW–Milwaukee), February 15, 1973, March 15, 1973, April 12, 1973, and May 3, 1973, in Murray Papers.

75. Peter Ehrmann, "Minority: Exercise Discretion," *crossroads*, October 3, 1974, in Murray Papers.

76. Alyn Hess, "Counter Point," *crossroads*, October 10, 1974; Gay Students Association, "To the Editor," *crossroads*, October 10, 1974; Louis Stimac, "Dear Peter Ehrmann, alias Archie Bunker," *crossroads*, October 10, 1974; all in Murray Papers.

77. "Here and There," *GPU News*, July 1980; *Gay Comix*, No. 2, 1981, also carried the heading, "Lesbian and Gay Men Put It On Paper"; "Denis Kitchen," Wikipedia entry, wikipedia.org; "Kitchen Sink Press," Wikipedia entry, wikipedia.org; Denis Kitchen, speech at UW–Parkside Big Read in 2014, rebroadcast on University Place, March 30, 2016; "Comics Code Authority," Wikipedia entry, wikipedia.org.

78. Reverend Wilbur C. Cain, "In My Opinion," *Milwaukee Journal*, March 14, 1973; Council on Religion documents in Murray Papers.

79. "Sex Law Repeal Urged at Hearing," *Milwaukee Sentinel*, February 29, 1972; "Bill to Liberalize Sex Laws Discussed," *Milwaukee Journal*, February 29, 1972; "Times Change; Sex Behavior Bill Unopposed," *Wisconsin State Journal* (Madison), February 29, 1972.

80. Minutes of Milwaukee Council on Religion and the Homosexual (CRH), June 24, 1972, in the Murray Papers.

81. "Bridge to Homosexuals," *Advance* (Milwaukee), May 1972, in CRH, Murray Papers.
82. "The Church as Advocate for the Gay," undated paper, CRH documents in Murray Papers.
83. "ALPAC to Develop Guidelines for Ministry to Homosexuals," *Badger Lutheran* (Milwaukee), February 17, 1972, in Murray Papers; letter from Cain to Mrs. Taege, February 23, 1973, CRH documents in Murray Papers; "Homosexuality Is Sin, Synod Rules," *Milwaukee Sentinel*, July 10, 1973; "Synod Condemns Homosexuality," *Milwaukee Journal*, July 10, 1973.
84. CRH Minutes, September 4, 1973, CRH documents in Murray Papers; letter from Charles Schinlaub to Eldon Murray, July 8, 1974, CRH documents in Murray Papers; letter from Schinlaub to Murray, June 10, 1976, CRH documents in Murray Papers; "Churches, Homosexuals Uneasy," *Milwaukee Journal*, June 22, 1974; letter from Charles Schinlaub to Friends and Members [of the Council on Religion and the Homosexual, Inc.], October 23, 1974, CRH documents in Murray Papers.
85. Ron McCrea oral history.

Chapter 2

1. "Amicus Brief," filed on behalf Paul R. Safransky, August Term 1973, in Supreme Court Reports for August Term 1973, No. 349, on appeal *Safransky v. State Personnel Board*, held in Wisconsin Law Library, Madison, Wisconsin.
2. Judy Greenspan, "Memoirs of a Tired Lesbian," *Whole Woman* (Madison), October 1972.
3. "State Can Can Gays," *GPU News* (Milwaukee), March 1973.
4. "Abridgement of Testimony at State Personnel Board," October 27, 1972, and "Respondent's Supplemental Appendix," in the matter before the State Personnel Board of Paul R. Safransky, Appellant v. Wilbur J. Schmidt, Secretary, Department of Health and Social Services, respondent, in Supreme Court Reports for August Term 1973, No. 349, on appeal *Safransky v. State Personnel Board*; both held in Wisconsin Law Library, Madison, Wisconsin.
5. "Abridgment of Testimony" and "Respondent's Supplemental Appendix."
6. "Abridgment of Testimony" and "Respondent's Supplemental Appendix."
7. "Abridgment of Testimony" and "Respondent's Supplemental Appendix."
8. "Abridgment of Testimony" and "Respondent's Supplemental Appendix."

9. "Abridgment of Testimony" and "Respondent's Supplemental Appendix."

10. "Editorial," *GPU News*, November/December 1973; "Gay Worker Challenges Firing," *Milwaukee Journal*, October 31, 1974.

11. "Abridgment of Testimony" and "Respondent's Supplemental Appendix."

12. "Abridgment of Testimony" and "Respondent's Supplemental Appendix."

13. "Abridgment of Testimony" and "Respondent's Supplemental Appendix."

14. "Abridgment of Testimony" and "Respondent's Supplemental Appendix."

15. "Abridgment of Testimony" and "Respondent's Supplemental Appendix."

16. "Abridgment of Testimony" and "Respondent's Supplemental Appendix."

17. "Abridgment of Testimony" and "Respondent's Supplemental Appendix."

18. "Abridgment of Testimony" and "Respondent's Supplemental Appendix"; "State Panel Sustains Homosexual's Firing," *Milwaukee Journal*, February 7, 1973.

19. "Madison G.L.F. Files Brief," *GPU News*, May/June 1973; "WCLU Lets Down Gays," *GPU News*, November/December 1973; "Gay Lib Enter Court Fight Here," *Capital Times* (Madison), April 7, 1973; "Homosexual Appeals Firing," *Milwaukee Journal*, February 22, 1973.

20. *Badger Pride*, newsletter of UW–Madison GLBT Alumni Council, Fall 1988.

21. W. L. Jackman, *Paul R. Safransky v. State Personnel Board*, Dane County Circuit Court 138-412, May 17, 1973; "Gay Lib Enters Court Fight Here."

22. Jackman, *Paul R. Safransky*; "Firing of Homosexual Upheld," *Milwaukee Journal*, June 6, 1973; "Homosexual Asks Help of High Court," *Milwaukee Journal*, February 12, 1974; "Justices Uphold Dismissal of Gay," *Milwaukee Journal*, March 6, 1974.

23. "WCLU Lets Down Gays," *GPU News*, November/December 1973; "Gay Worker Challenges Firing," *Milwaukee Journal*, October 31, 1972.

24. "WCLU Lets Down Gays"; "Gay Worker Challenges Firing."

25. "WCLU Lets Down Gays"; "Gay Worker Challenges Firing."

26. "WCLU Lets Down Gays"; "Gay Worker Challenges Firing"; "Feedback," *GPU News*, November/December 1973.

27. "Editorial," *GPU News*, November/December 1973.

28. Author's conversations with David Adamany, n.d., Madison, Wisconsin.

29. Author's conversations with David Adamany; "State Supreme Court Hears Job Loss Case," *GPU News*, February/March 1974.

30. "Appellants Brief and Appendix," *Paul R. Safransky v. State Personnel Board*, Wisconsin Supreme Court, August Term 1973, No. 349, submitted by

Todd J. Mitchell and David Adamany, Attorneys for Appellant, Wisconsin Law Library; "Homosexual Asks Help of High Court," *Milwaukee Journal*, February 12, 1974.

31. "Appellants Brief and Appendix."
32. "Appellants Brief and Appendix."
33. "Appellants Brief and Appendix."
34. "Appellants Brief and Appendix."
35. "Appellants Brief and Appendix."
36. "Respondent's Brief," *Paul R. Safransky v. State Personnel Board*, Wisconsin Supreme Court, August Term 1973, No. 349, submitted by Robert Warren, Attorney General, Robert J. Vergeront, Assistant Attorney General, Wisconsin Law Library.
37. "Respondent's Brief."
38. "Respondent's Brief."
39. "Respondent's Brief."
40. "Editorial," *GPU News*, December 1973.
41. Justice Hanley decision, *Paul R. Safransky v. State Personnel Board*, filed March 5, 1974; Justices Uphold Dismissal of Gay," *Milwaukee Journal*, March 6, 1974.
42. Hanley decision.
43. Hanley decision; author's conversations with David Adamany.
44. Louis Stimac, "Open Letter from Frustrated Liberationist," 1974, letter in Louis Stimac Papers, UW–Milwaukee LGBT collection.
45. Sheila (Lou) Sullivan and Alyn Hess, "Supreme Court Upholds Gay Firing," *GPU News*, April 1974.
46. Sullivan and Hess, "Supreme Court Upholds Gay Firing"; "300 Hear Report on School Sexism, *Milwaukee Sentinel*, May 22, 1974.
47. "Gay Men's History"; Ron McCrea oral history interview by Brian Bigler, *Gay Madison: A History* project, 1996, Wisconsin Historical Society Archives, Madison, Wisconsin; "Madison Gays Active in Many Areas," *Capital Times*, June 25, 1973.
48. "Judy Greenspan to be Candidate for School Board," *Wisconsin State Journal* (Madison), February 7, 1973; "Vote Greenspan for School Board," *Whole Woman*, February 1973; Greenspan campaign flyer, n.d., in Judy Greenspan Papers, LGBTQ Archive, UW–Madison, "Greenspan Stresses Re-structuring," *Daily Cardinal* (UW–Madison), March 2, 1973; "A

Crowded School Board List Starts Sorting Out," *Capital Times*, February 15, 1973.

49. "School Board Candidate Runs on Gay Platform," *Capital Times*, February 5, 1973; "Vote Greenspan for School Board."

50. "Vote Greenspan for School Board"; "Local Lesbian-Feminist School Board Candidate," *Daily Cardinal*, February 7, 1973; "Greenspan Stresses Re-structuring."

51. Jackman, *Paul R. Safransky*; Hanley decision.

Chapter 3

1. "Liberty and Homosexuality," *Milwaukee Journal*, July 8, 1977.

2. Organizing Statement of Madison Community United, 1978, in possession of author.

3. "Homosexual Agenda," Wikipedia entry, wikipedia, org; "Homosexual agenda," RationalWiki entry, rationalwiki.org; "The Homosexual Agenda!," Liberty University, www.bettybowers.com/homoagenda.html; "Homosexual Agenda," Conservapedia entry, www.conservapedia .com; "What Is the 'Gay Agenda' in America?," MassResistance, www .massresistance.org/docs/gen/08a/barber_gayagenda.html; "Gay Agenda," Uncyclopedia entry, uncyclopedia.wikia.com.

4. "Liberty and Homosexuality."

5. "Liberty and Homosexuality."

6. "Liberty and Homosexuality."

7. "Liberty and Homosexuality."

8. Madison Equal Opportunities Commission (EOC) Minutes, November 8, 1973, at City of Madison EOC Offices, Madison, Wisconsin; "Gay Rights Protections United States and Canada," May 1982, pamphlet published by National Gay Task Force, copy in possession of author. The EOC records have been digitized and can be accessed through the EOC office in the Department of Civil Rights, Madison, Wisconsin.

9. "Milestone for Equal Opportunities Ordinance," *Wisconsin State Journal* (Madison), December 11, 2013.

10. EOC Minutes, November 8, 1973.

11. Notes on remarks by Ricardo Gonzalez on January 14, 2016, at Outreach Senior Alliance, in possession of author; Cardinal Bar History, cardinalbar .com/history.

12. EOC Minutes, November 8, 1973.

13. EOC Minutes, November 8, 1973.

14. EOC Minutes, January 13 and February 10, 1972; Bed-In postcard, in possession of author.

15. EOC Minutes, February 14, 1974.

16. Richard Wagner, fourth district alderperson campaign literature, in possession of author.

17. EOC Minutes, November 14, 1974.

18. EOC Minutes, December 12, 1974; author's conversations with Jim Yeadon. Informal conversations with Jim took place in Madison, Wisconsin, over several years.

19. Jonathan Thompson, "Progressive Innovation in the 1970s: Madison, WI, and the Conference on Alternative State and Local Public Policies," *Progressive Planning Magazine*, www.plannersnetwork.org/2007/01/; author's notes on discussion with Mayor Paul Soglin, Madison, Wisconsin, December 23, 2011.

20. Madison Common Council Proceedings, March 11, 1975, Madison City Clerk's Office, Madison, Wisconsin. The ordinance was published March 25, 1975.

21. "New Massage Parlor Curb Pushed," *Wisconsin State Journal*, December 13, 1974; discussion with Mayor Soglin.

22. "Ordinance by Petition," presented January 28, 1975, on file at the Madison City Clerk's Office; "Council to Confront Massage Problems," *Capital Times* (Madison), February 15, 1975; "God or Satan? Voters Will Choose," *Capital Times*, February 18, 1975.

23. "Soglin Reelected Mayor," *Wisconsin State Journal*, April 2, 1975; detailed election returns, Madison City Clerk's Office.

24. "Volunteers Needed in Gay Civil Rights Projects: Madison's Gay Community Answers Challenge of Anita and Company," *Renaissance* (Madison), June 1977; "Yeadon to Speak at GPU Meeting," *GPU News* (Milwaukee), May 1977; Anti–Anita Bryant Bash flyer in Kathleen Nichols and Barbara Constans Papers, Wisconsin Historical Society Archives, Madison, Wisconsin; Soglin letter copy in Nichols and Constans Papers; "Gay Arts Festival Set for May Day in Madison," *GPU News*, April 1977.

25. Andrea Rottman, "Passing Gay Rights in Wisconsin, 1967–1983" (master's thesis, Freie Universitat Berlin, 2010), Section 3.4, 1978: A Year of Crisis,

the Effort to Repeal Madison's Gay Rights Ordinance; "Defeat in Eugene?,"
GPU News, July 1978; "Madison Drive Will Support Gays," *Milwaukee Journal*, May 11, 1978.

26. "United Petition Aims at Protecting Gay Rights," *Daily Cardinal*
(UW–Madison), May 11, 1978; Frank Custer, "Dillabaugh Wants Gun,"
Madison Press Connection, May 3, 1978.

27. "Know Your Madisonian: Kathleen Nichols," *Wisconsin State Journal*,
April 6, 2006; Kathleen Nichols, "Now We Are Five," in Madison Commu-
nity United newsletter, October 1983; Madison Community United Bylaws,
in possession of author; "Defeat in Eugene?"; " United Petition,"; Virginia
Mayo, "Groups Join to Save Equal Rights Ordinance," *Capital Times*,
May 11, 1978; EOC, "Report of the Equal Opportunities Commission on
Dane County Association of Evangelicals Petition to Permit Discrimination
on the Basis of Sexual Orientation," in possession of author.

28. "Gay Rights Activists Says Bryant Helps Cause," *Daily Cardinal*, May 2,
1978; Bill Christofferson, "Gay Issues May Split City," *Madison Press
Connection*, May 3, 1978; "Local Coalition Is Backing Homosexuals' Civil
Rights," *Wisconsin State Journal*, May 12, 1978; Rosemary Kendrick, "Pro-
rights Coalition to Launch Drive," *Madison Press Connection*, May 11, 1978.

29. Songsheet from the United, in possession of author.

30. Rottman, "Passing Gay Rights," Section 3.4.

31. Rottman, "Passing Gay Rights," Section 3.4; "M.A.G.I.C Picnic: Hot Fun in
the Summertime," *Gay Madison*, July 1982.

32. Reverend James Wright remarks from a transcript of "Meditation on Civil
Liberties," his speech at MAGIC picnic, in Nichols and Constans Papers,
Box 1, Folder 13, quoted in Rottman, "Passing Gay Rights," Section 3.4.

33. EOC, "Report of the Equal Opportunities Commission."

34. Kathleen Nichols, "Interview With Hizzoner Paul Soglin," *The Gay Endeavor* (Madison), March 1978; "Madison Stands Pat," *GPU News*, May
1979; "History of the United," n.d., in possession of author.

35. Various Madison Community United newsletters, brochures, and annual
reports of the early 1980s, in possession of author.

36. "Sex Law Reform Update: A Report by Lobbyist Barbara Lightner," *Gay
Madison*, October 1979; "Barbara Lightner Resigns from the United!," *Gay
Madison*, September 1982; Duane Kolterman, "Barbara Lightner Lauded:
'Incomparable Efforts' for the Community," *Gay Madison*, September 1982.

37. Various Madison Community United newsletters, brochures, and annual reports from the early 1980s, in possession of author.

38. "Madison Organizes against Gay Assault," *Free for All* (Madison), September 10, 1981; "Gay Women-Gay Men—If You Have Been Assaulted You Are Not Alone," brochure funded by City-County Committee on Sexual Assault, in possession of author; "Lesbian and Gay-Directed Assault," poster for forum at Pres House, December 28, 1981, in possession of author; "Crisis Phone Line Going Strong," *Madison Insurgent*, April 10, 1989; "History of the United."

39. United Political Action Committee (UPAC) program, brochure in possession of author; "History of the United."

40. The United Annual Report, 1981, in possession of author.

41. "UPAC, Madison's Lesbian/Gay Political Action Committee," flyer, n.d.; "Dane County Issues for the United Program," handwritten document for 1982 election; Memo to Candidates for the Dane County Board of Supervisors from the United Political Action Committee, undated document for the 1982 election; "Proposed Bylaws of the United Political Action Committee (UPAC)," February 27, 1983, all in possession of author; Madison Common Council Proceedings, March 2, 1976, Madison City Clerk's Office.

42. "UPAC Steering Committee Agenda," December 21, 1982; "UPAC Steering Committee Agenda," February 21, 1983; "United Political Action Committee Endorsement Guidelines," January, 1983; Memo to Candidates for City of Madison Common Council, from the United Political Action Committee, undated document, ca. early 1983; flyer for Mayoral Forum, March 15, 1983, sponsored by UPAC; "The Origins of Brunch" invitation, March 13, 1983; "Dear Friend" letter, March 13, 1983; "United Political Action Committee, Financial Report for the Period from January 1, 1983 to July 15, 1983"; memo to members, supporters and volunteers of UPAC, prior to meeting of July 27, 1983; all in possession of author.

43. Artwork and slogan on early United materials, in possession of author.

44. "Susan Green: A Spirit Vibrantly Alive," notes in Queer of the Year 1993 Awards program, in possession of author; "New Coordinator Hired," Madison Community United newsletter, November/December 1985; "Kathy Patrick Named Pres. of Wis. NOW," *OUT!* (Madison), July 1984; "Big Brothers/Sisters Challenged for Bias," *OUT!*, May 1985; "Big Brothers

Votes out Anti-gay Policy," *OUT!*, June 1986; "Susan Green 1954–1986," statement issued on the United letterhead, in possession of author; letter from Susan Green to Dick Wagner, June 3, 1986, in possession of author; "State Law Forbids Firing People with AIDS," *OUT!*, December 1985; "The United Wins Major Advocacy Case: Big Brothers/Big Sisters Drops Ban on Gay & Lesbian Volunteers," Madison Community United newsletter, May/June 1986.

45. "Broadway Health Club Raided," *GPU News*, June 1978; "Bath Raid Followup," *GPU News*, July 1978.

46. "Bath Raid Followup"; "More Police Harassment in MKE," *GPU News*, August 1978; "Editorial," *GPU News*, November 1979; Alyn Hess, "Scenario for: 'The Great Bath Raid,'" *GPU News*, July 1978; "Bookstore Arrests," *GPU News*, September 1979; "Legal Defense Fund," *GPU News*, February 1979; "Club Raided," *GPU News*, October 1979.

47. "Second Raid on Club MKE," *GPU News*, March 1979; "Editorial," *GPU News*, May 1979; "Bookstore Arrests," *GPU News*, September 1979; "Club Raided," *GPU News*, October 1979; "Update Milwaukee," *GPU News*, December 1979; "Update Milwaukee," *GPU News*, January 1980; "Bath Raid," *GPU News*, July 1980.

48. "Response to D. A. McCann," *OUR HORIZONS* (Milwaukee), January 7, 1982; "Guest Editorial: McCann Must Enforce Law, Fairly, Evenly," *The Wisconsin Light* (Milwaukee), October 6, 1988.

49. Hess, "Scenario for: 'The Great Bath Raid.'"

50. "Editorial," *GPU News*, May 1979; "Update Milwaukee," *GPU News*, December 1979; "Gays Rally to Protest Police Harassment," *Milwaukee Journal*, June 29, 1980.

51. "Editorial," *GPU News*, November 1979; "Update Milwaukee," *GPU News*, July 1980; "Oust Breier Petitions Filed," *GPU News*, September 1980.

52. "Feminists Fight City Hall—Task Force Formed," *Amazon* (Milwaukee), December 1979/January 1980; "Oust Breier Petitions Filed"; "Gay Groups Meet Ziarnik," *OUT!*, November 1984.

53. "View: Sexual Silence," *Isthmus* (Madison), January 31, 1986.

54. "Syphilis Rate Increasing Among Homosexuals," *Milwaukee Journal*, August 14, 1974.

55. "Homosexual Clinic to Deal with VD," *Milwaukee Journal*, October 6, 1974; "BESTD Clinic," Milwaukee LBTG History, www.mkelgbthist.org; "Roger

Gremminger," Milwaukee LGBT History, www.mkelgbthist.org; "Taking Care of Ourselves: BEST Clinic Celebrates 10th Anniversary," *OUT!*, October 1984. Many individuals, organizations, businesses, media outlets, and events are profiled on the Milwaukee LGBT History website.

56. "Services Slated for Hospital Head," *Milwaukee Journal*, July 8, 1974; "'Shook Up' Community to Get Inquest," *Waukesha Freeman*, July 11, 1974; "Eggum Stymied by McConnell," *Waukesha Freeman*, July 12, 1974; "Waukesha Judge Reaffirms Secrecy," *Milwaukee Journal*, August 8, 1974; "Sex Case Information Sought," *Milwaukee Journal*, August 14, 1974; "Waukesha Judge to Reopen Probe," *Milwaukee Journal*, August 16, 1974; "Probe Testimony Disclosure Sought," *Milwaukee Sentinel*, August 24, 1974.

57. "Looming AIDS Specter Puts Porn Dens in Dangerous Light," *Capital Times*, December 8, 1986; "AIDS Forcing Porn Shop Regulation," and "Mayor [Sensenbrenner] Calls for Parlor, Porn Probe," *Capital Times*, December 9, 1986.

58. "Looming AIDS Specter Puts Porn Dens in Dangerous Light"; "Mayor [Sensenbrenner] Calls for Parlor, Porn Probe."

59. "Jason's Story: Street Hustler Selling Sex," *Capital Times*, December 10, 1986.

60. "'Gay Life' Was No Life at All," *Milwaukee Star Times*, January 24, 1974; "Judge Rules Man Can't Be Prostitute," *Milwaukee Journal*, May 24, 1974; "Man Convicted as Prostitute," *Milwaukee Journal*, May 30, 1974.

61. "Gays Thrive Here, but Male Prostitution Scarcely Exists," *Milwaukee Journal*, August, 1, 1976; "Big Increase Seen in Gay Prostitution," *Milwaukee Journal*, February 27, 1981.

62. "Male Prostitutes, Clients Frequent Third Ward Area," *Milwaukee Sentinel*, July 24, 1989; "Milwaukee Sentinel Apologies to Community for Misleading Article," *The Wisconsin Light*, July 27, 1989.

63. "RODS Tenth Anniversary Booklet, 1979-1989," in possession of author.

64. "Madison's Historic Hotel Washington, Nationally Known Gay Mecca, Burns," *The Wisconsin Light*, February 29, 1996; "Rising From the Ashes: The Hotel Washington," *The Wisconsin Light*, July 4, 1996; "Good-By Hotel Washington," *The Wisconsin Light*, September 26, 1996; "A Service in Remembrance of a Long Standing Friend: Hotel Washington and the Life It Represented," in possession of author.

65. An example can be found in the *Isthmus*, August 22, 1986; Alternative Connections, Inc. invitation, in possession of author.

66. Postcard invitation to Bivouac '96, in possession of author.

67. Sunny Schubert, "Life Gets Too Wild in Olin Park," *Wisconsin State Journal*, November 1, 1991; Sean T. Wherley, "Society's Hangups Cause Gay Sex in Park," *Wisconsin State Journal*, July 8, 1995; "Alderman Verveer Defends the Right of All People to Use Madison's Parks," *The Wisconsin Light*, July 4, 1996; Police Try to Crack Down on Public Sex," *Wisconsin State Journal*, November 24, 2009.

68. "Arrests Continue on Wauwatosa Park," *OUT!*, October 1986;

69. "Tosa Resumes Arrests of Homosexuals," *Milwaukee Journal*, May, 22, 1987; "Park Surveillance Stepped Up," *OUT!*, July 1987; "Sexual Activity in Park Continues; 23 Arrested," *Milwaukee Journal*, August 5, 1987; "Psychiatrist Says Secrecy Lures Some Gays to Park," *Milwaukee Journal*, September 28, 1987.

70. "Sweep of Gays Protested," *Milwaukee Journal*, August 6, 1986.

71. Richard Jacobson, "TCT Reporting on Club 3054 Has Been One-Sided, Unfair," *Capital Times*, June 1, 1994; "City, Club 3054 Reach Compromise," *Capital Times*, June 9, 1994.

72. "Special Offer to Lovers," *Take Over*, October 4, 1976; Laurie Burnstein, Dawn Howes, and Marcia Weisman, "Shirt-free Victory," *The Edge* (Madison), June/July 1991.

73. Lisa M. Diamond, *Sexual Fluidity: Understanding Women's Love and Desire* (Cambridge: Harvard University Press, 2008); Ritch C. Savin-Williams, *Mostly Straight: Sexual Fluidity Among Men* (Cambridge: Harvard University Press, 2017); Jacob Stockinger oral history interview by Brian Bigler, *Gay Madison: A History* project, 1996, Wisconsin Historical Society Archives; Ron McCrea, remarks at OutReach History Group, December 2015, attended by author.

74. Bisexual Women's Support Group, "Alternative to the Alternative," *Feminist Voices* (Madison), April 1991; Kate Loftus, "Bisexuality: A Two-Part Series," *Capital Times*, October 28–29, 1991.

75. Bisexual Women's Support Group, "Alternative to the Alternative"; Kate Loftus, "Bisexuality."

76. Loftus, "Bisexuality."

77. Loftus, "Bisexuality."

78. "We Have Money to Start a Newsletter," *Bi-Lines* (Madison), November/December 1992; "MAGIC Picnic," *Bi-Lines*, November/December 1992; *Bi-Lines*, February/March 1993; "On a Personal Note," *Bi-Lines*, April/May 1993. Bi-Lines newsletters, clippings, flyers, and posters can be found in the LGBT Collection, UW–Madison Archives, Madison, Wisconsin.
79. "A Bisexual Community in Madison," *Bi-Lines*, November/December 1992; "It's Our Anniversary," *Bi-Lines*, February/March 1993; "Not Just Cows and Corn: Bi Activism in the Midwest," *BiNet News* (Seattle), Winter 1994.
80. "A Variety of Biphobia," *Bi-Lines* February/March 1993; "Lesbian and Bisexual Woman's Dialogue," *Bi-Lines* April/May 1993; David O'Donnell, "Coming Out: From Where and Why?," *Bi-Lines*, November 1993/January 1994; "Blatancy, Balance, and Being Bi," *Bi-Lines*, February/March 1993.
81. "Milwaukee Bi Groups," *Bi-Lines*, Summer/Fall 1995; letter, BiNet Midwest newsletter (Minneapolis), March 1994.

Chapter 4
1. "Women Discuss Gay Marriage," *UWM Post* (UW–Milwaukee), December 3, 1971.
2. Quoted in "Yeadon Campaign Fag-Baited by *Badger Herald* Editors," *Renaissance* (Madison), March 1977.
3. "Assembly Candidates Speak Out," "Maps of 25th & 26th Assembly Districts," "Registration Information," "18th District Candidate Also Speaks Out on Issue," all in *GPU News* (Milwaukee), September 1976; "Candidates Polled on Gay Rights," *GPU News*, October 1976; "Gay Votes Equal Gay Power," *GPU News*, October 1976.
4. *GPU News*, September 1976.
5. *GPU News*, September 1976.
6. *GPU News*, September 1976.
7. *GPU News*, September 1976.
8. "Candidates Polled on Gay Rights," *GPU News*, October 1976, "Gay Votes Equal Gay Power," *GPU News*, November 1976.
9. "Candidates Polled on Gay Rights"; "Gay Votes Equal Gay Power."
10. "Candidates Polled on Gay Rights"; "Gay Votes Equal Gay Power."
11. "Election Results: The Winners," *GPU News*, December 1976.
12. "Sex Laws Introduced in Wisconsin," *GPU News*, February 1977.
13. UPAC brochure, in possession of author; "P.A.C. Formed," *OUR HORIZONS*

(Milwaukee), February 5, 1982; "Feminist, Gay Votes Were Felt," *OUT!* (Madison), December 1984; "New Political Action Group Forms," *OUT!*, May 1987.

14. "Confab Sparks State Lobby," *GPU News*, July 1976; "Gay-Lesbian Coalition," *Amazon* (Milwaukee), April/May 1978; "WASP to Work for New Sex Law," *GPU News*, March 1977; "Committee Says 'Change Law,'" *GPU News*, January 1977.

15. "Legislature Conducts Sex Hearings," *Daily Cardinal* (UW–Madison), March 30, 1977; "Assembly Bill 323 Hearings Held," *GPU News*, April 1977.

16. "Wisconsin Bill Clears Committee," *GPU News*, May 1977; recorded vote on AB 323 from Assembly Journals, Legislative Reference Bureau, Madison, Wisconsin.

17. "Sex Law Delayed But Still Alive," *GPU News*, June 1977; "Update on AB 323," *GPU News*, September 1977.

18. "Yeadon New Alderman," *Wisconsin State Journal* (Madison), October 13, 1976; "Council Vacancy Won by Yeadon," *Capital Times* (Madison), October 13, 1976; "Gay Activist on City Council," *Renaissance*, March 1977; "Madison Blazed a Gay Trail," *Wisconsin State Journal*, December 12, 2008; Manitowoc PFLAG, https://sites.google.com/site/pflagmanitowocwi/yes-manitowoc.

19. "Gay Activist on City Council."

20. "Yeadon Campaign Fag-Baited by *Badger Herald* Editors," *Renaissance*, March 1977; "Open Gay Runs for Alderperson in Madison," *GPU News*, March 1977.

21. "Yeadon Campaign Fag-Baited."

22. "Yeadon Campaign Fag-Baited."

23. "Yeadon Campaign Fag-Baited."

24. "Yeadon Campaign Fag-Baited"; election results in Madison City Clerk's Office.

25. "Yeadon to Speak at GPU Meeting," *GPU News*, May 1977; "Gay Person of the Year—Elaine Noble," *GPU News*, January 1977; "Elaine Noble to Speak in Madison," *GPU News*, March 1977.

26. "Yeadon to Retire," *GPU News*, March 1979.

27. "Jack Baker at Oshkosh," *GPU News*, Nov/December 1973; "Men Married,

Leave on Honeymoon" *Milwaukee Journal* September 7, 1971: "'Gay' No Bar on Baker's Career," *Minneapolis Star*, May 5, 1971; "Gay Liberationist Speaks," *Oshkosh Advance-Titan*, October 4, 1973.

28. "Legality of Gay Marriage," *GPU News*, April 1973.

29. "Milwaukee Woman Broke Ground on Gay Marriage—in 1971," *Milwaukee Journal Sentinel*, October 7, 2014; Donna Burkett oral history, Milwaukee LGBT History Project, UW–Milwaukee Libraries; "Today in History: 1 October 1971," Skepticism, www.skepticism.org/timeline.

30. "Gay Women Wed on Christmas Day," *GPU News*, January 1972; "Women Lose Bid to Marry," *Milwaukee Journal*, January 11, 1972; "Women Discuss Gay Marriage," *UWM Post*, December 1971.

31. "Gay Wedding," *GPU News*, June 1973; Roy Badger, "Opinion & Commentary: If You Think Marriage Doesn't Matter, Think Again," *Capital Times*, February 19–25, 2014.

32. Circular letter from Madison Institute for Social Legislation (MISL) to "Dear Friend," January 24, 1984, in possession of author; Alternative Family Rights Task Force Report, October 21, 1987, Madison Equal Opportunities Commission (EOC) records; Alternative Family Rights Task Force minutes, November 3, 1987, EOC Records; MISL newsletter, November 1987, in possession of author.

33. "New Family Legislation Boosted at Forum," *OUT!*, October 1984; Families May Gain an Alternative," *Milwaukee Journal*, July, 8, 1985.

34. EOC Alternative Family Rights Task Force minutes.

35. "YMCA Won't Budge; Case Goes to Hearing," *OUT!*, October 1984; "Lesbian Family's Struggle with YMCA Nears Climax," *OUT!*, December 1984; "The Red Rose of Courage," MISL newsletter, n.d., in possession of author; Program for First Annual Alternative Families Recognition Day Picnic, August 31, 1985, in possession of author.

36. "Crazy-Making in the School?," MISL newsletter, November 1987.

37. EOC Alternative Family Rights Task Force minutes.

38. "Local Alderman's Revelations May Have Political Impact," *Capital Times*, November 21, 1987.

39. "Incumbents Retain City Council Seats," *Capital Times*, April 8, 1987; McFarland memo of July 6, 1987, copy in possession of author; letter circulated by Rick Villasenor and Jim McFarland July 12, 1988, in possession

of author; Rick Villasenor letter, "Support Alternative Families," in *OUT!*,
August 1987; Report of the Equal Opportunities Commission, November 3,
1987, copy in possession of author.

40. Robert Sharp, letter to Alder Wayne Bigelow, August 1, 1988, copy
in possession of author; *Issues in Review* (Greater Madison Chamber
of Commerce bulletin), December 19, 1987, in possession of author;
"'Family' Plan Dead?," *Capital Times*, January 2, 1988; "'Family' Plan
Strategy Sought," *Capital Times*, January 23, 1988.

41. "Council Goes Halfway on 'Kate & Allie' Law," *Wisconsin State Journal*,
August 3, 1988; "Aldermen on Record on Alternative Families," *Wisconsin
State Journal*, August 3, 1988; "Alternative Families Gain a Little Ground,"
Capital Times, August 3, 1988.

42. "Council Goes Halfway on 'Kate & Allie' Law"; "Aldermen on Record on Alternative Families"; "Alternative Families Gain a Little Ground."

43. "'Domestic Partner' Pool Pass Fee OK'd," *Capital Times*, August 21, 1990;
"Madison Approves Domestic Partners Legislation," *The Wisconsin Light*
(Madison), June 28, 1990; "Gay Couple Shares Parenthood Duties,"
Capital Times, April 27, 1991; Alternative Family Ordinance introduced
March 20, 1990, Madison, Wisconsin, copies provided to author.

44. "Miriam Ben-Shalom," Wikipedia entry, wikipedia.org; "Miriam Ben-
Shalom," Milwaukee LGBT History, www.mkelgbthist.org. Many individuals, organizations, businesses, media outlets, and events are profiled on
this site.

45. "Ousted Lesbian Files Suit," *Milwaukee Journal*, July 12, 1978; "Milwaukee's
Miriam Ben-Shalom Receives Prestigious National Stonewall Award,"
The Wisconsin Light, April 28, 1994; Miriam Ben-Shalom, "Lesbian and
Gay Soldiers Get the Cold Shoulder," *OUT!*, October 1984.

46. "Army Ban Unconstitutional," *GPU News*, June 1980; "Terence T. Evan,"
Wikipedia entry, wikipedia.org.

47. "Army Ban"; "Appeal Sought in Ruling on Gays," *Milwaukee Sentinel*,
May 21, 1980; "Lesbian Wins Army Back Pay," *Milwaukee Journal*, June 8,
1984; "Miriam Ben-Shalom's Example Is a Glorious Light for Millions," *The
Wisconsin Light*, March 21, 1990.

48. Baldwin press release, March 31, 1993; Baldwin letter to Wisconsin Congressional Members, March 24, 1993, copies in possession of author.

49. Brice D. Smith, *Lou Sullivan: Daring to Be a Man among Men* (Lexington,

KY: Transgress Press, 2017), 6–7; "Becoming Men: Activist Brice Smith Pens the Story of Female-to-Gay Male Trans Pioneer," *Wisconsin Gazette* (Milwaukee), August, 25, 2011; "Milwaukee Gender Pioneer Put Gay Trans Men on the Radar," *Wisconsin Gazette*, June 1, 2017; Susan Stryker, "Portrait of a Transfag Drag Hag as a Young Man: The Activist Career of Louis G. Sullivan," in *Reclaiming Genders: Transsexual Grammars at the Fin de Siecle*, edited by Kate More and Stephen Whittle (New York: Cassell, 1999), 62; Julian Carter, "Embracing Transition, or Dancing in the Folds of Time," in *The Transgender Studies Reader 2*, edited by by Susan Stryker and Aren Z. Aizura (New York: Routledge, Taylor & Francis Group, 2013).

50. Sheila (Lou) Sullivan, "A Transvestite Answers a Feminist," *GPU News*, August 1973; Smith, *Lou Sullivan*, 9, 10, 16, 28.

51. Smith, *Lou Sullivan*, 12–14.

52. Smith, *Lou Sullivan*, 17, 22, 27, 43.

53. Smith, *Lou Sullivan*, 47–49; Stryker, "Portrait of a Transfag," 64; Susan Stryker, *Transgender History* (Berkeley, CA: SEAL Studies, 2008), 116.

54. Smith, *Lou Sullivan*, 98, 141; Louis Sullivan, *From Female to Male: The Life of Jack Bee Garland* (Boston: Alyson Publications, 1990), 3, 131, 165–174.

55. Joanne Meyerowitz, *A History of Transsexuality in the United States* (Cambridge, MA: Harvard University Press, 2002), 276; Stryker, *Transgender History*, 120; Stryker, "Transfag," 63.

56. Meyerowitz, *A History of Transexuality*, 276; Smith, *Lou Sullivan*, 166; Sullivan quoted in Stryker, *Transgender History*, 120.

57. "B.W.M.T-Milwaukee Formally Structures," BWMT (Black and White Men Together) Milwaukee newsletter, Spring 1991; Black and White Men Together—Milwaukee Records, 1981–1989, Milwaukee Manuscript Collection 208, Wisconsin Historical Society, Milwaukee Area Research Center, University of Wisconsin–Milwaukee Libraries, Milwaukee, Wisconsin. Hereafter BWMT Records.

58. "Black and White Men Together—Purpose," BWMT Milwaukee newsletter, Spring 1981.

59. "B.W.M.T. Milwaukee Membership Application," BWMT Records.

60. "1st Anniversary Celebration to Feature 1st Public Meeting; Prof. Louie Crue [Crew] Keynote Speaker," BWMT Milwaukee newsletter, October/November 1981; "Guest Speaker Lloyd Barbee," BWMT Milwaukee news-

letter, March 1985; "Milwaukee Police Department Speakers at August BWMT Meeting," BWMT Milwaukee newsletter, September 1985.

61. "Mondale Endorses Gay Rights Bill," BWMT Milwaukee newsletter, April 1984; Michael S. Lisowski, "Martin Luther King Jr.: Through the Looking Glass," BWMT Milwaukee newsletter, February 1987; Tony Brown, "Black/ White Men Together," *OUR HORIZONS*, November 5, 1981; Michael Lisowski, "Blacks, Gay, Whites: Common Fiction?," *OUR HORIZONS*, December 9, 1981.

62. Michael Adams, "Mom, Dad; I'm Gay!," BWMT Milwaukee newsletter, April 1984.

63. "BWMT Conference Draws a Crowd," *OUT!*, November 1984.

64. "Welcome to Milwaukee and We're Celebrating," BWMT Milwaukee newsletter, June 1987; "Milwaukee Hosts National BMWT Convention," *OUT!*, June 1987; News release from Milwaukee NABWMT Convention, 1987, BWMT Records.

65. Alyn Hess, "What We Propose to Do for Love," letter to Louis Stimac, ca. February/March 1978, in Louis Stimac Papers, LGBT Archives, UW–Milwaukee.

66. Louis Sitmac letter to Alyn Hess, March 8, 1978, Stimac Papers.

67. "Gay Rights Measure Still Alive, Officials Say," *Milwaukee Journal*, June 21, 1980; "Milwaukee Rights Law?," *GPU News*, June 1980.

68. "Gay Rights Measure Still Alive, Officials Say"; "Milwaukee Rights Law?"; "Rights Law," *GPU News*, July 1980; "Proposed Gay Rights Law Backed," *Milwaukee Sentinel*, July 8, 1980.

69. "Panel Changes Vote on Plan for Gay Rights," *Milwaukee Sentinel*, June 24, 1980; "Gays, Feminists Build Family Life," *Milwaukee Journal*, July 3, 1980.

70. "City Council Passes Gay Rights Ordinance," *Milwaukee Journal*, July 8, 1980.

71. "Milwaukee Rights Ordinance Passed," *GPU News*, August 1980; "City Council Passes Gay Rights Ordinance."

72. "Drive Starts to Repeal Homosexual Provision," *Milwaukee Sentinel*, July 8, 1980; "Waukesha Says No," *GPU News*, September 1980.

73. Author's correspondence with the Archdiocese of Milwaukee, August 1980, in possession of author; Archbishop Weakland, "Who Is Our Neighbor," *Catholic Herald* (Milwaukee), July 8, 1980.

74. "County Adds Job Protection for Homosexuals," *Wisconsin State Journal*,

August 22, 1980; "Dane Board Oks Gay Hire-Fire Rule," *Capital Times*, August 22, 1980.

75. Proceedings of the Dane County Board of Supervisors for August 21, 1980.

Chapter 5

1. Barb C., "Between Closets," *Amazon* (Milwaukee), November 1972. *Amazon* is available online at Independent Voices: An Open Access Collection of an Alternative Press, http://revealdigital.com/independent-voices/.

2. Mark McNary, "Ginny Vida Speaks," *Renaissance* (Madison), July/August/September 1976. *Renaissance* is available on microfilm at the Wisconsin Historical Society, Madison, Wisconsin.

3. The interviews were transcribed into a book of the same title. Nancy Adair and Casey Adair, *Word Is Out: Stories of Some of Our Lives* (New York: New Glide Publications, 1978); "Word Is Out: Stories of Some of Our Lives," Wikipedia entry, wikipedia.org; "Prologue," *Word Is Out*.

4. Graham Robb, *The Discovery of France: A Historical Geography from the Revolution to the First World War* (New York: W. W. Norton, 2007); Rodger Streitmatter, *Unspeakable: The Rise of the Gay and Lesbian Press in America* (Boston: Faber and Faber, 1985), xiii.

5. "Prologue," *Word Is Out*, ix.

6. "Say It Loud, Gay Is Proud," *Red Star Express: Revolutionary Youth Movement Beer City, Amerika* (Milwaukee), December 1970–January 1971.

7. "Quest Turns 15 with This Issue: A Message from Quest Publisher, Mark Mariucci aka ZA," *Quest* (Green Bay), February 14, 2008.

8. "Rethinking Scarlet Letter," *Scarlet Letter* (Madison), September 1971.

9. Judy Greenspan, "Come Out, Come Out, Wherever You Are," *Scarlet Letter*, September 1971.

10. Untitled article, *Scarlet Letter*, March/April 1972.

11. "GPU News," Milwaukee LGBT History, www.mkelgbthist.org. Many individuals, organizations, businesses, media outlets, and events are profiled on the Milwaukee LGBT History website; "Editorial," *GPU News* (Milwaukee), October 1971.

12. "Editorial by Alyn Hess," *GPU News*, April 1974; "You and Lambdas" cartoon, *GPU News*, June 1974.

13. "Researchers Find Children of Lesbians No Different," *GPU News*, December 1976; "Election Results," *GPU News*, December 1976.

14. "Erotic S&M Among Gays," *GPU News*, August, 1976.

15. "Eldon Murray," Dictionary of Wisconsin History online, www .wisconsinhistory.org/Records/Article/CS10893.

16. "Editorial," *GPU News*, October 1971, "Editorial," *GPU News*, July 1976; "Appleton Library to Carry GPU News," *GPU News*, December 1976; "Editorial," *GPU News*, July 1980.

17. "Editorial," *GPU News*, October 1976; "Editorial," *GPU News*, March 1977.

18. "Dear Subscriber," letter from Alyn Hess to GPU readers, Spring 1981, Milwaukee LGBT History, www.mkelgbthist.org.

19. Susan Stryker, *Transgender History* (Berkeley, CA: SEAL Studies, 2008), 114; Sheila (Lou) Sullivan, "A Transvestite Answers a Feminist," *GPU News*, August 1973; Introduction to Sullivan reprinted August 1973 GPU article in *The Transgender Studies Reader*, edited by Susan Stryker and Stephen Whittle (New York: Routledge, 2006), 159.

20. Sheila (Lou) Sullivan, "Looking toward Transvestite Liberation," *GPU News*, February/March 1974. He quoted from Dennis Altman, *Homosexual Oppression and Liberation* (1971), Esther Newton, *Mother Camp: Female Impersonators in America* (1972), Harry Benjamin, *The Transsexual Phenomenon* (1966), Arno Karlen, *Sexuality and Homosexuality* (1971), and V. Grant, "The Cross Dressing: A Case Study," *Journal of Nervous & Mental Diseases* 130, no. 8 (1960).

21. "Looking toward Transvestite Liberation,"

22. Sheila (Lou) Sullivan, Review of *Emergence: A Transsexual Autobiography* by Mario Martino, *GPU News*, February 1978; Brice Smith, *Lou Sullivan: Daring to be a Man among Men* (Lexington, KY: Transgress Press, 2017), 86; Louis Sullivan, *From Female to Male: The Life of Jack Bee Garland* (Boston: Alyson Publications, 1990).

23. "Amazon 10th Anniversary," *Amazon*, April/May, 1982; letter from Angela Peckenpaugh in "Feedback," *Amazon*, June/July/August 1978.

24. *Amazon*, July 1972; "Why Amazon?" *Amazon*, April/May 1980.

25. Barb C., "Between Closets"; "SISTERS?," *Amazon*, March 1973; "How to Identify a Real Lesbian," *Amazon*, October 1973.

26. "Dyketatics!," *Amazon*, February 1976; "N.O.W. Embraces 'Dykes,'" *Amazon*, October 1974; "Milwaukee Lesbian Poetry," *Amazon*, November 1975; "Random Thoughts of a Lesbian/Feminst Masturbator," *Amazon*, March 1973.

27. Kitty, "Letter under Madness," *Amazon*, February/March 1978; Vicki, "On Coming Out," *Amazon*, March 1976.

28. "Building a Lesbian Nation: National Lesbian Feminist Conference," *Amazon*, May 1976; Karen Voltz, "Womonspace Sisternews," *Amazon*, June/July/August 1978; "NLFO: Update," *Amazon*, Summer 1979; "NLFO State Conference: Focus on the Resolutions," *Amazon*, Fall 1978/Winter 1979.

29. "Grapevine, A Lesbian-Feminist Action Core," *Amazon*, May 1974; "Grapevine to N.O.W.," *Amazon*, March 1975; "Through the Grapevine," *Amazon*, June, October, and November 1975, and January and September 1976; "Grapevine Yard Party" poster, *Amazon*, June/July 1976; "Women's Grapevine Group Begins Meeting at New Location," *The Wisconsin Light* (Madison), March 1990.

30. "From the Northwoods: A Journal," *Amazon*, December 1983/January 1984; "Women Make History," *Amazon*, February/March 1984; "Sister-Moon," *Amazon*, April 1981; "Sistermoon Closes," *Amazon*, April/May 1983;"Goodbye Sistermoon," *Amazon*, October/November 1983.

31. "Fantasy Realized: or,—a Home for Our Cow," *Amazon*, April/May 1977; "Wisconsin Womyn's Land," *Amazon*, February/March 1978; "W.W.L.C.," April/May 1978; "Womyn's Land," *Amazon*, Summer 1979; "Arkansas Wimmin on Land News," *Amazon*, June/July/August 1978; "More on D.O.E. Farm," *Amazon*, June/July 1988.

32. "More on D.O.E. Farm"; "D.O.E. Farm, One Womyn's View," *Amazon*, June/July 1988.

33. "Collective Statement," *Amazon*, February/March 1978; "Transexuality: Rap Response," *Amazon*, April/May 1978.

34. "Collective Statement," *Amazon*, February/March 1978; "Transexuality: Rap Response," *Amazon*, April/May 1978.

35. "Through the Grapevine," *Amazon*, April 1975.

36. "Dear Amazon Readers," *Amazon*, November 1974; "Old Amazons: Lance in Her Truck," *Amazon*, October/November 1976; "Salute to Old Amazons," *Amazon*, April/May, 1982.

37. "The New Amazon," *Amazon*, October/November 1976.

38. "Sisternews and Views: Perserving Our History," *The Wisconsin Light*, March 9, 1989; "From the Editor's Desk," *The Wisconsin Light*, January 25, 1990.

39. "Men Face a 'Moment of Reckoning,'" *Wisconsin Gazette* (Milwaukee), November 30, 2017; "We Were Wild Once," *Wisconsin Gazette*, January 24,

2103; "LGBT History from the Trenches," *Wisconsin Gazette*, July 29, 2010; "Adventures in Queer Journalism," *Wisconsin Gazette*, August 12, 2010; "History of the Women's Coalition 1972–1987," *Hag Rag* (Milwaukee), January/February 1988; "Sisternews and Views: Preserving Our History," *The Wisconsin Light*, March 9, 1989; "Jamakaya Wins UWM Award," *The Wisconsin Light*, December 15, 1988; Jamakaya website, www.jamakaya.com.

40. "The Right to Be Gay," *Free for All* (Madison), March 28, 1973; "Bisexual Chic," *Free for All*, July 18, 1973; "Gay Rap," *Free for All*, January 24, 1974; "Gay Confab," *Free for All*, September 6, 1974.

41. "Wanted: Women & Men in Print," *Renaissance*, February 1978.

42. "Editorial Note," *Renaissance*, June 1977; Mark McNary, "Ginny Vida Speaks," *Renaissance*, July/August/September 1976.

43. "The Dynamics of Drag," *Renaissance*, November 1977; "The Gay Poor: A Challenge for the Gay Liberation Movement," *Renaissance*, December 1977; Lenny Tropp, "Some Friends of Mine and Yours," *Renaissance*, January 1978; David Smith, "Gay Library News," *Renaissance*, November 1977; David Smith, "The Library Is Growing," *Renaissance*, December 1977; David Smith, "Mad City Bookstores," *Renaissance*, February 1978; "A.R.T.: Gay Community Theater," *Renaissance*, July/August/September 1976; "Gay Arts Festival Set for May Day in Great Hall," *Renaissance*, March 1977.

44. Chuck Rhodes, "Get Your Priorities Gay," *Renaissance*, January 1978.

45. Letter, *Renaissance*, March 1977; Clark Williams, "The Other Side/ 'Beautiful Is Ugly,'" *Renaissance*, November 1977.

46. Ron McCrea, "Disco Debate: First Response, *Renaissance*, January 1978.

47. Lenny Tropp, "Disco: Second Response," *Renaissance*, January 1978; "McCrea Replies," *Renaissance*, February 1978.

48. *The Gay Endeavor: A Publication for Gay Women and Gay Men* (Madison), March 1978.

49. "Last Issue?," *Gay Madison*, October 1979.

50. "Gay Madison Editors Form New Paper—Growing Up and OUT!," *Gay Madison*, September 1982; "Unfit to Print," *Gay Madison*, August 1982.

51. "Pinning Him Down: An Interview with Tony Earl," *Gay Madison*, August 1982; "James Wood," *Gay Madison*, August 1982.

52. "A-MUSE-ING AMAZON: Interview with Cheryl G.," *Leaping La Crosse News*, March 1984.

53. "A-MUSE-ING AMAZON," *Leaping La Crosse News*, December 1983; Mary O'Sullivan, oral history interview by John Magerus, July 24, 2001, La Crosse, Wisconsin, UW–La Crosse Oral History Program; Margaret Larson, *For the Common Good: A History of Women's Roles in La Crosse County, 1920–1980* (La Crosse, WI: League of Women Voters Education Fund, 1996), 96–97.

54. "LLN Bankrupt," *Leaping La Crosse News*, October 1983; "LLN Benefit: Italian Night at 'Tattinos,'" *Leaping La Crosse News*, May 1983; "Vote to Keep Your Newsletter Coming: Donate to the LLN," *Leaping La Crosse News*, July 1992.

55. "Report on the National March on Washington," *Leaping La Crosse News*, November 1987; "Wisconsin Gay Republican Group," *Leaping La Crosse News*, September 1988.

56. "Guess Who Got Left Out Again," *Leaping La Crosse News*, October 1983.

57. "Publisher Klehm Departs," *OUT!* (Madison), September 1984.

58. Albert Hertzfelt (pseudonym), "Yes, Dear, There Is Life after Madison . . ." *OUT!*, November 1982; Brooks Egerton, "Inside OUT!," *OUT!*, November 1983.

59. On Rice Lake, "Ignorance Isn't Bliss," *OUT!*, August 1984.

60. "Outward Bound," *OUT!*, November 1982.

61. "IN!," *OUT!*, November 1983; "Breeders Support Group Forming," *OUT!*, November 1983; "Wisconsin Records Its First HETS Death," *OUT!*, November 1983; "Straight Revolt at Stone Hearth," *OUT!*, November 1983; "IN!," *OUT!*, April 1984.

62. "Keep It Up," *OUT!* December 1982.

63. Brooks Egerton, "What Do Gays and Transsexuals Have in Common," *OUT!*, February 1983.

64. Dragonfly, "What Does a Sex-Change Operation Change?," *OUT!*, February 1983; "Transsexual Prisoner Thwarted by Officials," *OUT!*, July 1984.

65. "Paying the Price," *OUT!*, March 1983; "Media Myopia," *OUT!*, April 1984.

66. Steve Starkey letter to "Dear Supporter of *OUT!*," n.d., *OUT!* letterhead; "Helping OUT! Helps the Community," *OUT!*, July 1987.

67. "Amazon, Thanks," *OUR HORIZONS* (Milwaukee), January 7, 1982.

68. Ralph Navarro obituary, *Milwaukee Journal*, June, 12, 2001; "A Very Gay Vision," *OUR HORIZONS*, December 9, 1981.

69. Michael Lisowski, "Chicago Dynamic," *OUR HORIZONS*, November 5, 1981; Michael Lisowski, "Anything but Moral," *OUR HORIZONS*,

November 5, 1981; Roger Gremminger, "Gay Elected President of Public Health Association," *OUR HORIZONS*, December 9, 1981.

70. "Why Two?," *OUR HORIZONS*, December 9, 1981.

71. "For the Moment UNTIL LATER," *OUR HORIZONS*, February 5, 1982.

72. "For the Moment UNTIL LATER."

73. "A Letter from 'GayLife/Escape' to Our Readers," *ESCAPE* (Milwaukee), July 14, 1983.

74. "A Letter from 'Gay Life/Escape' to Our Readers"; Paul Cotton, "Issues of Racism, Sexism Grappled at NABC [National Association of Business Councils] Meeting," *ESCAPE*, May 19, 1983; "Roll Out the Carpet for HIT [Holiday Invitational Tournament]," *ESCAPE*, November 18, 1982; "Milwaukee Has First Gay-Lesbian Film Fest," *ESCAPE*, January 13, 1983; "Crisis at Dunes," *In Step* (Milwaukee), April 18, 1984.

75. "Crisis at Dunes."

76. "Obituaries: David Paul Iraci," *The Wisconsin Light*, November 1, 1990; "Geiman Was Publisher for Gay Community," *Milwaukee Journal Sentinel*, May 19, 2004.

77. "In Step Back on Feet," *OUT!*, November 1984; "History of In Step News," www.instepnews.com/history.

78. "In the Mailbox," *In Step*, April 5, 1984; "Publication Statement," *In Step*, April 5, 1984.

79. See, for example, Kim Zweibohmer, "Madonna Fever," *In Step*, April 5, 1984; Tom Salzsieder, "Wreck Room Classic Softball Tournament," *In Step*, May 17, 1984; "Graffiti," *In Step*, April 5, 1984.

80. Antler, "Bringing Zeus to His Knees," *In Step*, April 5, 1984.

81. W. W. Wells, III, "Juicy Bits: 1069EZ Gay Income Tax Return," *In Step*, May 30, 1989.

82. Editor's Note on "Governor's Council Urges Full-Time Liaison," *In Step*, May 3, 1984; "Comment: In Step's Program for Our Concerns," *In Step*, May 31, 1984; "AIDS Find Reported," *In Step*, April 5, 1984; "AIDS Is Here," *In Step*, May 17, 1984; "Geiman Was Publisher for Gay Community."

83. "Comment: Barflies," *In Step*, June 28, 1984.

84. "Comment: Barflies," Miriam Ben-Shalom, "No Small Potatoes: Even in Our Own House," *In Step*, June 28, 1984.

85. "Letters," *In Step*, November 21, 1990.

86. "New Lesbian-Feminist Paper Launched," *OUT!*, January 1987; "Crone" cover, *Hag Rag*, January/February 1988.

87. "Call for Articles on Creating Lesbian Community," *Hag Rag*, January/February 1988.

88. Mary Frank, "Myths about Separatism," *Hag Rag*, January/February 1988.

89. "Kissing Girls Popular in Madison," *Hag Rag*, January/February 1988; "Kissing Girls?! Who Dunnit?!," *Hag Rag*, January/February 1989; "Lesbian Variety Show: 'I Got This Way from Kissing Girls,'" *Hag Rag*, January/February 1989.

90. Lance, "The Discussion of Sex in the Lesbian Press," *Hag Rag*, September/October 1988; Sue Burke, "*Lesbian Sex* and *Lesbian Passion*: Laugh a Little and Improve Your Sex Life," *Hag Rag*, September/October 1988.

91. Mary Klobucar, "Frozen in Fear or Filled with Power," *Hag Rag*, November/December 1988.

92. Justice Fire, "Pudbusters," *Hag Rag*, November/December1988.

93. "Among Friends References Referrals Networks for the Gay and Lesbian Communities of Rural Wisconsin," brochure, n.d., in possession of author; "Rural Gays: Loneliness Marks Their Dual Lifestyle," *Capital Times* (Madison), February 8, 1986.

94. "Among Friends References Referrals Networks"; "Will New Tourism Slogan Make Us the 'Gay State,'" *Capital Times*, January 15, 1988,

95. "Among Friends References Referrals Networks"; "Editor's Corner," *Among Friends* (Madison), March 1986.

96. Beck Schwitz, "Small Town Advantages," *Among Friends*, March 1986; "Editor's Corner," *Among Friends*, March 1986; "Bodoh Quartz: Ron Bodoh and Larry Henke's Relationship Was Founded on Stone," *Among Friends*, April 1988; "Complaints Filed against 2 Newspapers," *Capital Times*, February 8, 1986.

97. "And in This Corner . . . We're Back," *Among Friends*, October 1987.

98. "Thanks," *The Wisconsin Light*, November 20, 1987.

99. "*The Wisconsin Light* Succeeds *OUT!*," *The Wisconsin Light*, November 20, 1987.

100. "Editorial," *The Wisconsin Light*, November 20, 1987; "Thanks."

101. Bill Meunier, "Wisconsin Marches on Washington, D.C.," *The Wisconsin Light*, November 20, 1987.

102. "Humorous 'Dykes to Watch Out For' Cartoon Debuts in *Light*," *The Wisconsin Light*, September 20, 1990.

103. "Bigotry Snaps Its Head," *The Wisconsin Light*, December 18, 1987.

104. "The Editor's Desk," *The Wisconsin Light*, May 13, 1988.

105. "Light and In Step to Hold Media Workshop on February 24," *The Wisconsin Light*, January 11, 1990; "Wisconsin Light and In Step Receive National Award," *The Wisconsin Light*, May, 17, 1990; "From the Editor's Desk," *The Wisconsin Light*, September 1990; "Valentines to Wisconsin's Gay Media for Press Month," *The Wisconsin Light*, February 9, 1990.

106. "From the Editor's Desk," *The Wisconsin Light*, November 3, 1988; "From the Editor's Desk," *The Wisconsin Light*, November 17, 1988.

107. "Drag Need Not Slow Progress," letter to *The Wisconsin Light*, December 14, 1989; "Midwest Transvestites and Transsexuals Meet in Milwaukee," *The Wisconsin Light*, August 23, 1990; Susan Cook, "Women Wearing Leather Is Appropriate," *The Wisconsin Light*, December 14, 1989.

108. "Fidelity Reigns Supreme," *The Wisconsin Light*, July 27, 1987.

109. "As Violence Increases, Stay out of Juneau Park," *The Wisconsin Light*, July 26, 1990; "Guest Editorial: Prostitution Can Not Be Tolerated," *The Wisconsin Light*, July 27, 1989.

110. "Community Must Go On and Accept Bath Closing as Permanent," *The Wisconsin Light*, January 12, 1989; "City Used Sound Judgement Permanently Closing Bath," *The Wisconsin Light*, March 9, 1989.

111. Terry Boughner, *Out of All Time: A Gay and Lesbian History* (Boston: Alyson Publications, 1988).

112. "Inside 'OUT!,'" *OUT!*, November 1983; "East High Axes Gay-Issues Editorial," *OUT!*, January 1984; "Ban of Editorial on Homosexuality Stirs Protest," *Wisconsin State Journal* (Madison), January 27, 1984; "This Is the Controversial Article on 'Homophobia,'" *Wisconsin State Journal*, January 27, 1984; "Editorial Ban 'Disrupts' East High," *Capital Times*, January 27, 1984; "Text of Banned Editorial," *Capital Times*, January 27, 1984.

113. "Text of Banned Editorial."

114. "Ban of Editorial on Homosexuality Stirs Protest"; "East High Censorship Decision Is Appealed," *OUT!*, February 1984; "Debate on Schools' Homophobia Rages," *OUT!*, March 1984.

115. "Editorial Ban 'Disrupts' East High"; "Ban of Editorial on Homosexuality Stirs Protests."

116. "Editorial Ban 'Disrupts' East High"; "Censored: A Plea for Tolerance," *Capital Times*, January 30, 1984.

117. "East High Censorship Decision Is Appealed"; Peter Klehm, "*OUT!* Criticizes School District on Censorship Case," press release reprinted in *OUT!*, February 1984.

118. "*OUT!* Criticizes School District on Censorship Case"; "Debate on Schools' Homophobia Rages."

119. "Funding Cut to School Paper Urged," *Wisconsin State Journal*, January 4, 1988; "School Paper Stands to Lose over Gay Ads," *Milwaukee Journal*, January 4, 1988.

120. "Funding Cut to School Paper Urged"; "School Paper Stands to Lose over Gay Ads"; "Gay-Ad Critics Silent at Board Meeting," *Wisconsin State Journal*, January 5, 1988; "Speakers Back Stoughton Paper," *Capital Times*, January 5, 1988.

121. "Ignoring the Realities of Sex Is Risky," *Capital Times*, January 2, 1988; Dave Zweifel, "Plain Talk: A Tip of Our Hats to Stoughton High Journalists," *Capital Times*, January 6, 1988; "Sound Off: Gay Ad," *Capital Times*, January 5, 1988; Karla Knesting, "Gay Life and Controversy Go Hand in Hand," *The Lance* (La Follette High School, Madison), January 19, 1988.

122. "Now It's Her Turn," *OUT!*, March 1983.

123. "Milwaukee Has 1st Gay Radio Program, Newspaper, in Early 1970's," *The Wisconsin Light*, February 23, 1989; "Every Time She. . . ." *Amazon*, March 1975; "A Woman's Place . . . 88.9 FM," *Amazon*, October/November 1979.

124. "Gay Talk Show to Air on WTSO," *Wisconsin State Journal*, June 5, 1994; press release from WTSO, October 20, 1995 and letter from Diana Summers to author, May 22, 1994, in possession of author.

125. "Gay Show on Channel 21," *Renaissance*, February 1977, "Greeting Herstorian," letter dated August 1991, Judy Greenspan files, University of Wisconsin–Madison Archives, Madison, Wisconsin.

126. "Gay/Lesbian Cable Network Underway," *OUT!*, June 1987; "Advocate Praises Tri-Cable Tonight," *The Wisconsin Light*, May 13, 1988.

127. "Milwaukee Gay/Lesbian Cable Wins Awards," *OUT!*, October 1988;

"Milwaukee Gay/Lesbian Calbe Network a.k.a. Tri-Cable Tonight," Milwaukee LGBT History, www.mkelgbthist.org.

128. "Milwaukee Tri-Cable Films 'Gay & Lesbian Voice '88'" *OUT!*, September 1988; "Tri-Cable to Cease Monthly Cable Programs," *The Wisconsin Light*, November 16, 1989.

129. "Glad to Be Gay," *Gay Madison*, October 1979; "Glad to Be Gay" list of shows in George Mosse Papers, Box 2, LGBT Collection, UW–Madison Archives; letter from Wisniewski to Dick Wagner, mid-September 1981, in possession of author.

130. "Working from One End to the Other, and All Points in Between," *OUT!*, December 1982; "Dave Runyon Has Nothing to Hide," *The Wisconsin Light*, January 15, 1988; letter to Runyon, August 24, 1994, in possession of author; "Advocate Praises Tri-Cable Tonight."

131. "Dave Runyon Has Nothing to Hide."

132. "Dave Runyon Has Nothing to Hide."

133. "Homosexuality—A Surfacing Reality," unidentified clipping, ca. 1975, in possession of author.

134. James Wallin letter, *In Step*, June 1993.

135. Streitmatter, "Introduction," *Unspeakable*, x; *Rod's* newsletter, Fall 1991, in possession of author.

136. "You Are Making History," *ESCAPE*, May 5, 1983.

Chapter 6

1. Lloyd Barbee, "From the Legislature," *Milwaukee Courier*, January 27, 1973.

2. "Who Hasn't Broken Laws on Private Sex?," *Madison Press Connection*, January 29, 1979.

3. George Painter, "The Sensibilities of Our Forefathers: The History of Sodomy Laws in the United States—Wisconsin," Gay and Lesbian Archives of the Pacific Northwest, www.glapn.org/sodomylaws/sensibilities/wisconsin.htm.

4. Barbee's legislative biographies, *Wisconsin Blue Book*, 1966–1975; "Biography/History," Lloyd Barbee Papers, UW–Milwaukee Archives, Milwaukee, Wisconsin. The *Wisconsin Blue Books* are compiled biennially by the Wisconsin Legislative Reference Bureau and published by the Wisconsin Department of Administration.

5. Analysis by the Legislative Reference Bureau, Wisconsin Assembly Bill 678, 1967, Legislative Reference Bureau, Madison, Wisconsin. All bills introduced during a legislative session, along with drafting files and draft amendments, are in the Legislative Reference Bureau (LRB) Library, Madison, Wisconsin, held in bound volumes and organized by the opening year of the biennial session. Hereafter they will be listed by bill number and session year.

6. "Barbee Seeks to Liberalize State's Sex Laws," *Milwaukee Journal*, May 12, 1967; "Sex Crimes," *Milwaukee Journal*, February 12, 1969.

7. "Bill Takes Government out of Bedroom," *Milwaukee Courier*, April 3, 1971.

8. Lloyd Barbee, "Comments," *Milwaukee Courier*, April 17, 1971.

9. "Legislature Will Study Bills on Trade, Homosexuals," *Capital Times* (Madison), June 25, 1973; "Barbee's Bills Labelled 'Un-Christian,'" *Capital Times*, June 26, 1973.

10. Lloyd Barbee, "From the Legislature," *Milwaukee Courier*, January 27, 1973.

11. "Barbee's Bills Labelled 'Un-Christian'"; "A Choice for 18?," *Milwaukee Courier*, November 2, 1974.

12. "Rep. Barbee's Bills Seen as Immoral," *Milwaukee Courier*, July 14, 1973.

13. "Robert Swan to Vie against Barbee," *Milwaukee Courier*, July 13, 1974.

14. "For Assembly Seat, Smear Tactics Being Used in Campaign," *Milwaukee Courier*, August 17, 1974; "Dirty Tricks," *Milwaukee Courier*, August 17, 1974.

15. "Endorsement," *Milwaukee Courier*, September 7, 1974; "Rev. Gregg Asks Support for Lloyd Barbee," *Milwaukee Courier*, August 24, 1974; Carol Malone, "Rep. Barbee Still Serves," *Milwaukee Courier*, September 7, 1974.

16. "Barbee Turns Back Swan Challenge," *Milwaukee Courier*, September 14, 1974.

17. "Bill to Repeal Sex Laws," *Milwaukee Courier*, June 12, 1971; Lloyd Barbee, "From the Legislature," *Milwaukee Courier*, May 19, 1972.

18. "A. E. Frederick Legislative Biography," *Wisconsin Blue Book*, 1915, 526–27; "Clarenbach, Kathryn," American National Biography, www.anb.org.

19. David Clarenbach, District 4 Supervisor, "County Board Report," Spring 1974, copy in possession of author; "Clarenbach Reports," Fourth Ward Organization newsletter, August 1972, copy in possession of author; "Young Candidates Facing 1st Test," *Milwaukee Journal*, March 5, 1972; campaign

flyer for March 7, 1972, county board supervisor election, copy in possession of author; "District 4 Candidates Have Major Differences in Ideas," *Capital Times*, March 24, 1972.

20. "Vote for Representative to the Assembly by District, November 5, 1974," *Wisconsin Blue Book* (1975), 831; "Vote for Representative to the Assembly by District, General Election," *Wisconsin Blue Book* (1993–1994), 923.

21. Paul D. Cain, "David Clarenbach," *Leading the Parade, Conversations with America's Most Influential Lesbians and Gay Men* (Lapham, MD: Scarecrow Press, 2007), 297; Kurt Chandler, "Out Politician Tim Carpenter Goes on the Record about His Sexuality," *Milwaukee Magazine*, August 1, 2001.

22. Cain, "David Clarenbach," 297; "Clarenbach Seeking Reelection," *Renaissance* (Madison), July/August/September 1976; letter from Warden R. L. Gray to Clarenbach, March 2, 1976, David Clarenbach Papers, Box 5, Folders 9–10, Wisconsin Historical Society, Madison, Wisconsin. The author's political experience with Clarenbach goes back to the 1972 county supervisor race. They were also briefly roommates in the Mansion Hill District.

23. Author's conversation with Clarenbach, July 1, 2016, Madison, Wisconsin; author's recollections as a member of the growing gay political circle.

24. Data on partisan identification compiled by author from *Wisconsin Blue Books* for the decades of the 1970s and 1980s.

25. "Strategist Had Respect of Allies, Foes: Obituary Bill Kraus, 92," *Wisconsin State Journal* (Madison), December 15, 2018.

26. Author's conversation with Clarenbach, July 1, 2016.

27. John Wyngaard, "Legislative Atmosphere Changes," undated clipping about 1977 session, Clarenbach Papers, Box 3, Folder 2.

28. For Party Platforms, see the *Wisconsin Blue Books*. For example, the Wisconsin Democratic Party Platform, adopted June 12, 1976, and printed in the 1977 *Wisconsin Blue Book*, 838: "We support the extension of full civil rights to people of variant sexual inclinations, and the abolition of criminal sanctions on the private sexual activity of consenting adults." The 1975 *Wisconsin Blue Book*, 765–72, printed the party's platform from 1974 which had no such language. Author's knowledge from attending state party conventions as a delegate; "Candidate Opposes Taxes, Sex Laws," *Milwaukee Journal*, April 19, 1974; Wyngaard, "Legislative Atmosphere Changes."

29. Senator Clifford Kreuger is listed as Republican Minority Leader in the

Wisconsin Blue Books of 1975, 1977, and 1979–1980; "Candidates Polled on Gay Rights," *GPU News* (Milwaukee), October 1976; John Nichols, "Lawton Reasserts Progressive Vision," *Capital Times*, August 5, 2003.

30. "WASP to Work for New Sex Law," *GPU News*, March 1977; letterhead of Wisconsin Alliance for Sexual Privacy, Clarenbach Papers, Box 3, Folder 8; Steve Gunderson and Rob Morris with Bruce Bawer, *House and Home* (New York: Dutton, Penguin Group, 1996), 291, 306–8.

31. Tim Cullen describes tensions serving as Senate Democratic Majority Leader in *Ringside Seat: Wisconsin Politics, the 1970s to Scott Walker* (Mineral Point, WI: Little Creek Press, 2016), 45–47.

32. Dan Curd, recollections to author, Madison, Wisconsin.

33. "20 Students Admit Violating Fornication Law," unidentified clipping dated June 23, 1981, Clarenbach Papers, Box 3, Folder 2; "The Pros and Cons of Cohabitation," *Appleton Post-Crescent*, July 11, 1981.

34. "Sex & Sin in Sheboygan," *Playboy*, August 1972; "Cohabitation Bill Could Finally Pass," *Capital Times*, March 24,1981; "Police Criticized for Cohabitation Probe," *Milwaukee Journal*, June 19, 1981; "Couple Lose Appeal in Tosa Sex Case," *Milwaukee Journal*, February 19, 1980.

35. Judd Marmor and Richard Green, "Homosexual Behavior," *Handbook of Sexology* (Amsterdam: Elsevier/North-Holland Biomedical Press, 1977), 1065.

36. David Adamany, Memorandum on SB 14, to David Clarenbach, January 15, 1976; Gridley Hall, Memorandum on Equal Opportunities Commission (EOC), February 22, 1977; EOC Legislative Committee Minutes; "Bulletin" from Citizens Concerned for Our Community, n.d., all in Clarenbach Papers, Boxes 3 and 4; *Milwaukee Journal*, n.d., "For Madison: A Matter of Human Rights," reprinted in *Capital Times*, May 15, 1978.

37. Madison Police Department newsletter, August 17, 1976, in Clarenbach Papers, Box 3, Folder 4.

38. *Jones v. State*, 55 Wis 2d 742–748, Supreme Court of Wisconsin.

39. Louie Crew, "Homosexuals and Wisconsin Law," *OUR HORIZONS* (Milwaukee), December 9, 1981.

40. Memo from Lynn Sarko of UW–Madison Law School to Criminal Justice and Public Safety Committee members, August 15, 1979, in Clarenbach Papers, Box 2, Folder 3; "Is Cohabitation Really a Crime?," *Wisconsin State Journal*, October 15, 1979.

41. Memo from Stephen Tordella, March 4, 1980, Clarenbach Papers, Box 2,

Folder 3; "System Finds Population Facts," *Milwaukee Sentinel*, July 11, 1983.

42. "Sex Laws Introduced in Wisconsin," *GPU News*, February 1977.

43. "Wisconsin Bill Clears Committee," *GPU News*, May 1977; Reid Beveridge, "Was the Veterans Board Intimidated?," *Wisconsin State Journal*, April 25, 1977.

44. Assembly *Journal*, 1977 Session, 889–93, 920–22. The Legislative Reference Bureau holds the journals of the state assembly and senate, organized by year based on the first year of the biennial session. Actions of each house are recorded by date. During the session these are distributed daily to each legislative office for inclusion in a legislator's office binder, and after the biennial session they are put together in bound volumes for each house. Indexes to the journals provide topical information and a listing of bills by the main legislative sponsor under the legislator's name. Hereafter, the journals will be cited by session year and page number.

45. Citizen's League for American Democracy (CLAD) document with Edmark attachment and Pritchard memo to members of the Wisconsin State Assembly, June 14, 1977, both in Clarenbach Papers, Box 3, Folder 5; "Sex Privacy Bill Stirs up a Dispute," *Milwaukee Journal*, June 5, 1977.

46. "Controversial Sex Bill Deserves Closer Scrutiny," *Racine Journal Times*, May 10, 1977.

47. "Vote for Representatives to the Assembly by District, Primary Election September 12, 1978," *Wisconsin Blue Book* (1979–1980), 905–8; "Vote for Representatives to the Assembly by District, Primary Election November 7, 1978," *Wisconsin Blue Book* (1979–1980), 923–26; Clarenbach Remarks, August 2, 1979, Clarenbach Papers, Box 3, Folder 7; author's conversation with Clarenbach, July 1, 2016; "Who Hasn't Broken Laws on Private Sex?"

48. "Vote for United States Senator by County, September 13, 1988," *Wisconsin Blue Book* (1989–1990), 904; "Vote for United States Senator by County, November 8, 1988, *Wisconsin Blue Book* (1989–1990), 918; Eagle Forum PAC letter, May 12, 1988, in possession of author; "Dukakis and Engeleiter Are Deserving of Our Support," *The Wisconsin Light*, October 20, 1988.

49. Author's conversation with Clarenbach, July 1, 2016; the legislative drafter's file for SB 552, housed at the LRB, shows requestors for SB 552 with several handwritten annotations as names were added. The basic bill was

drawn from the prior session at the request of Senator Carl Thompson to the LRB drafter.

50. "Reform Sought in Sex Laws," *Milwaukee Sentinel*, February 28, 1980; "State Urged to Revise Laws on Sexual Conduct," *Milwaukee Journal*, February 28, 1980.

51. "Sex-Consenting Bill Gets State Senate's Approval," *Wisconsin State Journal*, March 20, 1980; "Local Legislators Oppose Sex Bill 3-1," *West Bend News*, March 30, 1981; "Deregulating Sex," *Janesville Gazette*, March 12, 1980.

52. "Dreyfus Says Sexual Law Overhaul is OK by Him," *Capital Times*, March 20, 1980; "Dreyfus Likely to Approve Cohabitation Bill," *Milwaukee Sentinel*, March 21, 1980; Author's discussion on campaign with Governor Martin Schreiber, Executive Residence, Madison, Wisconsin, 1978; "WCS Passes Resolution," *GPU News*, March 1978.

53. Assembly *Journal*, 1979 session, 2970, 3119–3120; "Senate OKs Decriminalizing of Sex by Consenting Adults," *Capital Times*, March 19, 1980.

54. Drafting files for 1981 bills AB 325 and SB 205, LRB; Roger Durand letter to Clarenbach, February 26, 1979, Clarenbach Papers, Box 3, Folder 6; Dane Prosecutors letter to Clarenbach, May 11, 1977, Clarenbach Papers, Box 3, Folder 8.

55. Drafting files for 1981 bill, LRB; Jesse DeWitt letter to Clarenbach, January 25, 1980, Clarenbach Papers, Box 3, Folder 8; Majorie Mathews letter to Clarenbach, February 17, 1983, Clarenbach Papers, Box 2, Folder 25; "Lesbian/Gay Rights Advocate, Bishop Dies," *OUT!*, August 1986; circular letter by Paul Flucke, February 17, 1981, Clarenbach Papers, Box 3, Folder 8; "It's Not State's Job to Regulate Sexual Morality," *Wisconsin Rapids Daily Tribune*, April 7, 1981.

56. Rembert Weakland letter to Clarenbach, March 2, 1981, Clarenbach Papers, Box 3, Folder 8; Charles Phillips, "Legislators to Reconsider State Laws Regarding Sex," *Times Review* (La Crosse), February 5, 1981; "Cohabitation Bill Could Finally Pass," *Capital Times*, March 24, 1981; Howell Williams, *Homosexuality and the American Catholic Church: Reconfiguring the Silence, 1971–1999* (PhD Diss., Florida State University), 20.

57. Alfred Swan letter to David Clarenbach, March 27, 1980; R. Charles Weier, Associate Chairman of People Using Legislation Legally (PULL), letter draft to state legislators, October 3, 1981; R. Charles Weier letter to Dear

Representative, March 21, 1982; Truman H. Robertson, Fort Wilderness, letter to Sanator [*sic*] David Clarenbach, May 21, 1981; *Moral Majority Eagle* (Wisconsin), April 1981 and June 1981; copies of all in Clarenbach Papers, Box 3, Folder 5.

58. "Cohabitation Bill Could Finally Pass."

59. "Assembly Rejects Bill Changing Sex Laws," *Milwaukee Sentinel*, April 29, 1981; "Local Legislators Oppose Sex Bill 3-1," *West Bend News*, March 30, 1981.

60. "Assembly Rejects Bill Changing Sex Laws"; "Local Legislators Oppose Sex Bill 3-1."

61. Author's conversation with David Clarenbach, July 1, 2016.

62. Reverend Max Andrews and Reverend Harley Keck quoted in "Adult Sex Measure Draws Crossfire," *Capital Times*, April 1, 1983; "Clarenbach, Prosser at Odds over Cohabitation Measure," *Wisconsin State Journal*, April 2, 1983; "Note of Purpose a Good Addition," *Green Bay Press Gazette*, n.d., clipping in Clarenbach Papers, Box 3, Folder 3; Edna Ferber, *Come and Get It* (Madison, WI: Prairie Oak Press, 1991).

63. "Note of Purpose a Good Addition"; Ferber, *Come and Get It*.

64. "Bill to Legalize More Adult Sex Acts Advances," *Wisconsin State Journal*, April 20, 1983; "Consenting-Adults Bill Approved by Assembly," *Milwaukee Sentinel*, April 22, 1983; "Assembly Endorses Bill Permitting Cohabitation," *Milwaukee Sentinel*, April 20, 1983; "Clarenbach Feels Vindicated," *Milwaukee Journal*, April 24, 1983; Assembly *Journal*, 1983 session, 144–47, 153–55, 161.

65. Senate *Journal*, 1983 session, 185–86.

66. "Your Bedroom Now a Safer Place," *Milwaukee Journal*, May 9, 1983; "Sex Acts Law Focus: Legality, Not Morality," *Racine Journal Times*, May 12, 1983; "Repeal an Intrusive Law," *Capital Times*, April 27, 1983; "Earl Signs Bill on Sex Acts," *Milwaukee Journal*, May 6, 1983; "Earl Signs Consenting Sex Law," *Capital Times*, May 6, 1983.

67. Ernest P. Cuneo, "Homosexuals, Their Jobs and the Law," *Milwaukee Journal*, October 26, 1973; "Gay Fired for 'Lifestyle,'" *GPU News*, June, 1977; "WCLU Intervenes in Suit by Gay," *Milwaukee Sentinel*, November 4, 1977; WCLU Foundation press release, November 4, 1977; memo from Eunice Edgar, "ACLU Activities on Behalf of Gay and Lesbian Rights," November 9,

1987, copy in possession of author; "Fired Gay Fights Back," *Renaissance*, December 1977.

68. *To Live in CHRIST JESUS*, pamphlet, Publications Office, United States Catholic Conference, Washington, DC, 1976; "Pope Francis Says Church Should Apologize to Gays," *New York Times*, June 27, 2016.

69. Reverend Weakland, "Who Is Our Neighbor?," *Catholic Herald* (Milwaukee), July 19, 1980; "Rights of Homosexuals Become Issue Again," *Catholic Herald*, June 13, 1981.

70. Andrea Rottmann, "God Loves Them as They Are," *Wisconsin Magazine of History* 99, no. 2 (Winter 2015–2016): 5; "WSC Passes Resolution," *GPU News*, March 1978; "Leon Rouse," Milwaukee LGBT History, www.mkelgbthist.org. Many individuals, organizations, businesses, media outlets, and events are profiled on the Milwaukee LGBT History website.

71. Rottmann, "God Loves Them as They Are," 8–9; Commission on Human Concerns Committee Memo, May 11, 1981, Clarenbach Papers, Box 2, Folder 24; Drafting file for AB 70, LRB; "The Case of Leon Rouse," *In Step* (Milwaukee), October 29, 2002; Reverend Weakland letter to John Murtaugh, March 2, 1981, Clarenbach Papers, Box 5, Folder 11.

72. "Legislators to Reconsider State Laws Regarding Sex," *Times Review*, February 5, 1981; Reverend James L. Dameir letter to Senator Kleczka on behalf of Our Lady of Lourdes Congregation Human Concerns Committee, December 4, 1981, Clarenbach Papers, Box 5, Folders 9–12; Sister Naomi Schoen letter to Senator Garald Kleczka on behalf of the Milwaukee Archdiocesan Sisters Council, January 4, 1982, Clarenbach Papers, Box 2, Folder 25; Rottmann, "God Loves Them as They Are," 11.

73. Sister Schoen letter; Father Tony Schumancher letter to David Clarenbach on behalf of Justice and Peace Committee, Priest Senate, Dioceses of Madison, February 17, 1981; "11 Religious" letter to Representatives Rooney, Neubauer, and Ladwig on behalf of the Second Priest District of the Archdiocese of Milwaukee, n.d.; Brother Joseph Peiffer, Dehon House Milwaukee of the Sacred Heart Fathers and Brothers, letter to Governor Dreyfus, n.d.; Reverend Steven J. Scherer, St. Jude Catholic Church, Green Bay, letter to Jerome Van Sistine, February 2, 1982; all in Clarenbach Papers, Box 5, Folder 11.

74. Verne E. Sindlinger, Executive Presbyter, Winnebago Presbytery, letter to

Members of the Wisconsin Legislature, August 20, 1981, copy in possession of author; information packet on Chapter 112, Laws of 1981, prepared
by Clarenbach's office in 1982, copy in possession of author.

75. Statement given before the Assembly Health & Human Services Committee, May 12, 1981, by Representative David Clarenbach, copy in author's
possession; "Committee Record of Assembly Committee on Health &
Human Services," Clarenbach Papers, Box 5, Folder 7; author's own statement of May 12, author's possession.

76. "Document on Debate on AB 70, Friday, October 23, 1981," Clarenbach
Papers, Box 5, Folder 11. Assembly debates were not printed in the Assembly *Journals*, only actions, but the Assembly Democratic Caucus would tape
debates for soundbites that members could send home to radio stations.
This unusual debate transcript would have been made from that taping.

77. "Document on Debate on AB 70"; Assembly *Journal* for Votes, 1356–58,
1441–43.

78. Author's conversation with Clarenbach, July 12, 2016.

79. David Clarenbach letter to Senator Risser, October 27, 1981, Clarenbach
Papers, Box 5, Folder 15; "Moral Majority Attacks AB 70," *OUR HORI-
ZONS*, February 5, 1982; memo from Richard Sweet, Senior Staff Attor-
ney, Wisconsin Legislative Council, on Analysis of a Proposed Amendment
to 1981 Assembly Bill 70, February 4, 1982, in Clarenbach Papers, Box
5, Folder 6; "Record of Committee Proceedings," Senate Committee on
Taxation, State and Local Affiars, January 28, 1982, in Clarenbach Papers,
Box 5, Folder 19.

80. "Record of Committee Proceedings"; "Moral Majority Attacks AB 70." On
affirmative action see letters to Clarenbach from Claudean Roehmann,
Department of Employment Relations, October 26, 1981, from Ed Main,
Department of Administration, October 26, 1981, and from Roberta
Gassman, October 26, 1981, all in Clarenbach Papers, Box 5, Folder 6.

81. "Radio Stations Spur Calls to Governor," *Milwaukee Sentinel*, February 23,
1982; "Governor Signs Wisconsin Rights Bill," *Washington (DC) Blade*,
March 5, 1982; "Law Protects Sexual Preference," *Appleton Post-Crescent*,
March 2, 1982; "A Human Rights Victory," *Capital Times*, February 26, 1982;
author's discussion with Bill Kraus, July 6, 2016, Madison, Wisconsin.

82. "New 'Gay Rights' Law Sadly Necessary," *Milwaukee Journal*, February 26,

1982; Dreyfus signing statement issued by Clarenbach, Clarenbach Papers, Box 5, Folder 11.

83. Clarenbach press release, February 25, 1982, Clarenbach Papers, Box 5, Folder 15; "Nuns in the Gallery," *New York Native*, March 15–28, 1982, copy in Clarenbach Papers, Box 5, Folder 22; Madison United statement, February 25, 1982, Clarenbach Papers, Box 5, Folder 17.

84. "'Privacy' Phony Issue, Sellout to Gays," *Wisconsin Property Owner's News*, March 10, 1982; "Gay Rights Bill Is Under Fire," *Gay Life* (Chicago), February 1983; www.luxemburgusa.com; "Gay Rights Is the Theory, Discrimination Still the Practice," *OUT!* (Madison), March 1983; drafting file for AB 570, LRB; "Repeal of Gay-Rights Law Faces Tough Opposition," *Milwaukee Journal*, July 22, 1983; The Wisconsin Cartographers' Guild, *Wisconsin's Past and Present: A Historical Atlas* (Madison: University of Wisconsin Press, 1998), 22–23; Swoboda legislative biography, *Wisconsin Blue Book*, 1981–1983, 23.

85. "Gay Rights Bill Is under Fire"; flyer of Wisconsin Citizens Against Public Gay Perversion, Clarenbach Papers, Box 5, Folder 18; "Wisconsin Citizens against Special Rights for Homosexuals," *Denmark (WI) Press*, July 14, 1983; "Homophobes Still on the Loose," *OUT!*, July 1983; Tom Redmond, open letter originally published in *Green Bay Press Gazette*, January 28, 1983, Clarenbach Papers, Box 5, Folders 9–10.

86. Clarenbach press release, November 9, 1982, Clarenbach Papers, Box 5, Folder 17; "Gay Rights Bill Is under Fire"; "Presbyterians Back Rights Law," *OUT!*, April 1983; "Gay Rights Is the Theory"; Assembly *Journal*, 1983 session, 297; "Repeal of Gay-Rights Law Faces Tough Opposition."

87. "Wisconsin First State to Pass Gay Rights Law," *The Advocate* (Los Angeles), April 1, 1982; "Wisconsin Senate Backs Gay rights," *Washington Blade*, February 19, 1982; National Gay and Lesbian Task Force Report, March/April 1982.

88. Allan Spear to Clarenbach, February 25, 1982, Randy Stalling to Clarenbach, October 10, 1983, Craig Johnston to Clarenbach, December 3, 1982, Clarenbach Papers, Box 5, Folders 9–10.

89. "Dreyfus Tells of Rebuff by Michigan Legislature," *Wisconsin State Journal*, December 13, 1983.

90. "Honoring Lee Dreyfus," *Capital Times*, July 16, 2003; "Dreyfus Accepts

OutReach Award," *Wisconsin State Journal*, July 17, 2003; "Ex Gov. Dreyfus Honored by Gays," *Capital Times*, July 17, 2003.

91. Program for 1993 Queer of the Year, in possession of author; "Clarenbach Plans 1992 Run for Congress in Second District, *The Wisconsin Light* (Madison), November 29, 1990; *The Wisconsin Light* editorial quoted in Cain, "Clarenbach."

92. Frank Bruni, "To Know Us Is to Let Us Love," *New York Times*, June 26, 2011; "The Past as Inspiration: Remembering When Wisconsin Led the Nation with Progressive Laws," *Wisconsin Gazette* (Milwaukee), May 31, 2012.

93. "Wisconsin: Gay Rights," *The Advocate*, September 3, 1985; "Wis. Becoming First Gay Rights State in '82 Highlights 1980s," *The Wisconsin Light*, January 11, 1990.

94. Clarenbach press release, January 22, 1987, Clarenbach Papers, Box 5, Folder 5; "Ex-Gov. Dreyfus Accepts OutReach Award"; "Behind the Curve, 25 Years after Becoming the First 'Gay Rights' State, Wisconsin Regresses," *Capital Times*, April 11, 2007.

95. Kirk Kleinschmidt and Nicole Libman, "A Case Study in the Gay Movement: Wisconsin's Gay Rights Law," May 16, 1987, copy in possession of author; William B. Turner, "The Gay Rights State: Wisconsin's Pioneering Legislation to Prohibit Discrimination Based on Sexual Orientation," *Wisconsin Women's Law Journal* 22, no. 1 (Spring 2007): 93–94.

96. Andrea Rottmann, "Introduction," *Passing Gay Rights in Wisconsin, 1967–1983* (master's thesis, Freie Universitat Berlin, 2010).

97. "Feminist, Gay Votes Were Felt," *OUT!*, December 1984.

Chapter 7

1. *Nabozny v. Podlesny*, US Court of Appeals, Seventh Circuit, 92 F.3d466 (1996).

2. "A Test with No Right Answers," *OUT!* (Madison), March 1985.

3. Memo from John Gillespie to Wisconsin Churches, April 1985, copy in possession of author; "Rawhide Bill Almost Passes, Will Return," *OUT!*, April 1986.

4. "Starr Endorses Exemption Bill," *Milwaukee Sentinel*, March 6, 1986; "Riding Herd at Rawhide," *Milwaukee Journal Magazine*, January 18, 1987.

5. Memo from Gillespie.

6. "Change in Law Urged by Christian Group," *OUT!*, June 1985.

7. "Starr Endorses Exemption Bill"; "Rawhide Bill Almost Passes."

8. Senator Joe Leean memo to All Lesgislators, January 30, 1986, copy in possession of author; list of sponsors on AB 825, Assembly *Journal*, 1985–1987 session, 661, Legislative Reference Bureau (LRB) Library, Madison, Wisconsin. See chapter 6, note 44, for an explanation of the state assembly and senate journals.

9. "Compromise on Rawhide Bill Sought," *Green Bay Press Gazette*, March 6, 1986; "Rawhide Bill Almost Passes"; "In Defense of Rawhide Principles," *Appleton Post-Crescent*, March 4, 1986; "Rawhide Battles for Its Values," *Oshkosh Northwestern*, March 7, 1986; "Fairness for Everyone," *New Holstein (WI) Reporter*, January 8, 1987; "Former Rawhide Resident Says He Needed 'Structure,'" *Fond du Lac (WI) Reporter*, March 6, 1986; "Rawhide's Record in Rehabilitating Kids Can't Justify Bias in Hiring," *Milwaukee Journal*, March 14, 1986.

10. Howard Bellman letter to Senator Leean, October 30, 1986, copy in possession of author.

11. Gretchen Miller, legal director of WCLU, letter to Senator Lynn Adelman, September 24, 1987, copy in possession of author.

12. "Fair-Hiring Law Exception Eyed for Rawhide," *Wisconsin State Journal* (Madison), December 28, 1987; memo from Dave Deininger to Tim Carpenter et al., October 26, 1987; memo from Dave Deininger to Tim Carpenter et al., December 22, 1987; Legislative memo, LRB-4140/1dn (drafter's note), July 29, 1987, prepared by Jeffrey J. Shampo, Legislative Attorney; memo from Carol Lobes and LeAnna Ware to David Clarenbach, December 16, 1987; memo from LeAnna Ware to Clarenbach et al., January 6, 1988; all memos in possession of author; AB 916 actions in *Journals* of Senate and Assembly; "Rawhide Amendment Dies in Madison," *The Wisconsin Light*, March 11, 1988.

13. "Rawhide Amendment Dies in Madison"; "State Assembly Defeats 'Rawhide Exemption' Bill," *The Wisconsin Light*, March 22, 1990.

14. Author's remembrances of Hatlen and Grover conversations, minutes of the Governor's Council on Lesbian and Gay Issues, July 23–24, 1983.

15. "Teenage Gays Share a Dreadful Isolation," *Milwaukee Journal*, July 1984; minutes of the Governor's Council on Lesbian and Gay Issues, July 23–24, 1983; William B. Turner, "The Gay Rights State: Wisconsin's Pioneering

Legislation to Prohibit Discrimination Based on Sexual Orientation," *Wisconsin Women's Law Journal* 22, no. 1 (Spring 2007): 97–98; "No Equal Access in Schools," *OUT!*, April 1984.

16. "No Equal Access in Schools"; "Is DPI Dragging Its Feet on Discrimination?," *OUT!*, December 1984; "Vote for Superintendent of Public Education," *Wisconsin Blue Book* 1985–1986, 883. The *Wisconsin Blue Books* are compiled biennially by the Wisconsin Legislative Reference Bureau and published by the Wisconsin Department of Administration.

17. On the Wisconsin governor's use of the state budget, see Dick Wagner et al., *DOA, the Story: Four Decades of Wisconsin's Department of Administration* (Madison: DOA, 2002); "New Discrimination Statute for DPI," *OUT!*, October 1986; Legislative Fiscal Bureau, 1987–1989 session, Biennial Budget document analyzing Act 29, 994. Legislative Fiscal Bureau and Biennial Budget documents are filed by session at the Legislative Reference Bureau Library.

18. *Nabozny v. Podlesny*, US Court of Appeals, Seventh Circuit, 92 F.3d466 (1996).

19. *Nabozny v. Podlesny*, US Court of Appeals; "Nabozny v. Podlesny," Wikipedia entry, wikipedia.org.

20. Eschbach decision, *Nabozny v. Podlesny*.

21. Eschbach decision, *Nabozny v. Podlesny*.

22. Eschbach decision, *Nabozny v. Podlesny*.

23. Lambda Legal, "Nabozny v. Podlesny," Lambda Legal, www.lambdalegal.org/in-court/cases/nabozny-v-podlesny.

24. Randy Shilts, *And the Band Played On: Politics People and the AIDS Epidemic* (New York: St. Martin's Press, 1987); "Reagan Favors Tests for AIDS, Aide Says," *Milwaukee Journal*, May 12, 1987.

25. "AIDS Worker: Confidentiality Prime Concern," *OUT!*, August 1984.

26. "HTLV-III Is Here," *Gay Life* (Chicago), November 28, 1985; *OUT!*, March 1985.

27. Rjurik Golubjatnikov, "Prevalence of Antibody to HTLV-III Virus in the Madison Area," unpublished research paper, copy in possession of author.

28. "Test Show 25% of Gays in Area Exposed to AIDS," *Capital Times* (Madison), April 29, 1985; "AIDS Exposure Here Lower than Norm," *Capital Times*, April 29, 1985.

29. "State Opens Free Sites for HTLV-III Test," *OUT!*, June 1985; "Officials

Question Usefulness, Cost of AIDS Antibody Test," *Capital Times*, May 9, 1985; "AIDS No Great Threat to Blood Centers Here," *Wisconsin State Journal*, July 30, 1985.

30. Shilts, *And the Band Played On*, 542; Representative Menos memo and attachment, April 9, 1985, in possession of author.

31. Memo from Ken Johnson of Legislative Fiscal Bureau to Senator Norquist, April 16, 1985, copy in possession of author; author's conversation with David Clarenbach, July 29, 2016, Madison, Wisconsin; 1985–1987 Biennial Budget, Fiscal Bureau Documents, LRB.

32. Dennis Maki letter to Representative Loftus, June 25, 1985, copy in possession of author.

33. "Doctors Weigh Pros, Cons of AIDS Test," *Wisconsin State Journal*, July 1, 1985; "AIDS Test Reporting Ban Sparks Debate," *Capital Times*, July 23, 1985.

34. Tim Tillotson to Ron McCrea, July 2, 1985, copy in possession of author; 1985–1987 Biennial Budget, Fiscal Bureau Documents; "Privacy Provision Signed into Law," *OUT!*, August 1985; "Wisconsin: Gay Rights," *The Advocate* (Los Angeles), September 3, 1985; author's conversation with Clarenbach, July 29, 2016.

35. AB 487, 1985–1987 session; "Bills Will Change HTLV-III Blood Test Laws," *OUT!*, October 1985; "Insurance Tests Possible with HTLV-III," *OUT!*, November 1985.

36. "Bills Will Change HTLV-III Blood Test Laws."

37. "Insurance Tests Possible with HTLV-III Law"; Linda Eivitz letter to Thomas Fox, Commissioner of Insurance, March 20, 1986, copy in possession of author; "AIDS Testing for State Insurance Companies?," *OUT!*, September 1986; Clarenbach press release on October hearing, n.d., copy in possession of author; "Hearings Held on Insurance HIV Tests," *OUT!*, February 1986; "Expanded AIDS Tests Proposed," *Capital Times*, January 7, 1988; "Insurance AIDS Test Supported," *Capital Times*, February 25, 1988.

38. "A Bill for All Wisconsinites," *Wisconsin Jewish Chronicle*, January 15, 1988; Nancy Weisenberg letter to Senator Mordecai Lee, December 2, 1986; Weisenberg letter to Attorney Bruce Feustel, March 4, 1987; Weisenberg to Feustel, August 7, 1987; all in SB 442 drafting file, 1985–1987 session, LRB; Robert Friebert, first draft of hate crimes bill per statement of January 7, 1988, to Senate Committee Hearing, copy furnished by Michael Blumenfeld.

39. Copy of SB 442 showing list of requestors as introduced in drafters file for AB 599, LRB; the same LRB attorney, Bruce Feustel, worked on both bills.

40. "Illinois Becomes Fourth State to Enact a Bias Crimes Reporting Law," *Wisconsin Jewish Chronicle*, November 27, 1987; "Anti-Semitic Vandalism in US Last Year up for the First Time Since 1980," *Wisconsin Jewish Chronicle*, January 29, 1988; "3,000 Hate Crimes in US Between 1980 and 1986," *Wisconsin Jewish Chronicle*, January 22, 1988; "Election Brings Added Security to Gay Rights Law," *The Wisconsin Light*, December 1988; National Gay & Lesbian Task Force, "Anti-Gay Violence, Victimization & Defamation in 1989," 1990.

41. Draft press release on volunteer state violence survey, February 25, 1984, in possession of author. The survey was conducted from 1983–1984 by the Governor's Council on Lesbian and Gay Issues.

42. Draft press release on volunteer state violence survey.

43. Draft press release on volunteer state violence survey.

44. Draft press release on volunteer state violence survey; "Dave Begel Commentary," June 14, 1984, copy in possession of author.

45. "A Stroke against Hate Crimes," *Wisconsin Jewish Chronicle*, October 9, 1987; "A Bill for All Wisconsinites"; "State Jewish Group Hires Legislative Consultant," *Wisconsin Jewish Chronicle*, October 16, 1987.

46. "Extra Fines Urged for Hate Crimes," *Milwaukee Journal*, January 8, 1988; "Attorney General Supports State Hate Crimes Bill," *Wisconsin Jewish Chronicle*, January 15, 1988.

47. "Attorney General Supports State Hate Crimes Bill"; "Lee, Fortis to Introduce State Hate Crimes Bill," *Wisconsin Jewish Chronicle*, November 6, 1987; statement by Michael Lieberman, Midwest Civil Rights Director, Anti-Defamation League of B'nai B'rith, Greater Chicago Regional Office, copy provided by Michael Blumenfeld; "Wisconsin Hate Crimes Bill in Serious Trouble," *The Wisconsin Light*, February 12, 1988.

48. David Clarenbach press release, October 23, 1988, copy in possession of author; Assembly *Journal*, 1987–1989 session, 591, 721–22; "Two Bias Crimes Bills Now Await Action by State Senate," *Wisconsin Jewish Chronicle*, March 4, 1988.

49. Senate *Journal*, 1987–1989 session, 679, 706; "Two Bias Crimes Bills Now Await Action"; Clarenbach press release, October 23, 1988.

50. "1988 Lesbian/Gay Issues," *Leaping La Crosse News*, April 1988; author's

conversation with Steve Morrison, April 1988, Madison, Wisconsin; letter from Jane Weinberg to Governor Tommy G. Thompson, April 21, 1988; "A Stronger Hate Crimes Bill," *Wisconsin Jewish Chronicle*, March 4, 1988; author's conversation with Steve Morrison, July 21, 2016, Madison, Wisconsin; author's conversation with Clarenbach, July 12, 2016; National Gay and Lesbian Task Force, "Anti-Gay Violence"; "Hate Crime Laws in the United States," Wikipedia entry, wikipedia.org; Jane Weinberg, Anti-Defamation League Greater Chicago Regional Office, letter to Governor Tommy G. Thompson, April 21, 1988, copy furnished by Michael Blumenfeld.

51. Author's conversation with Steve Morrison, July 21, 2016; "Gays, Lesbians Fear Hate-Crime Upsurge Here," *Capital Times*, September 20, 1990.

52. "State Hate Crimes Law Tested in Appleton Trial," *The Wisconsin Light*, March 7 1991; "Cop Faces Felony Count in Attack," *Wisconsin State Journal*, July 31, 1990; "First Hate Crimes Prosecution Ends with Mixed Results," *The Wisconsin Light*, March 21, 1991.

53. Interview with Steve Morrison, July 21, 2016; Court of Appeals Opinion, filed June 5, 1991 in *State v. Mitchell*, 163 Wis.2d 652 (1991).

54. Amici Curiae brief, November, 25, 1991, *State v. Mitchell*, 169 Wis. 2d 153, Wisconsin Law Library, Madison, Wisconsin.

55. Heffernan decision, *State v. Mitchell*, 169 Wis.2d 153 (1992).

56. Abrahamson dissent, *State v. Mitchell*, 169 Wis.2d 153 (1992).

57. Lorna Dee Cervantes, "Races," in M. Sanchez, ed., *Contemporary Chicana Poetry* 90 (1986), quoted in Bablitch dissent, *State v. Mitchell*, 169 Wis.2d 153 (1992).

58. James Doyle press release, January 29, 1993, copy furnished by Michael Blumenfeld; oral arguments in *Wisconsin v. Mitchell*, 1993 WL 751845 (1993).

59. Amici Curiae brief, *Wisconsin v. Mitchell*, 1992 WL 12012031 (US) (Appellate Petition, Motion and Filing), Supreme Court of the United States, November 4, 1992.

60. Rehnquist opinion, *Wisconsin v. Mitchell*, 508 U.S. 476 (1993).

61. "Election Brings Added Security to Gay Rights Law," *The Wisconsin Light*, December 1, 1988; Clarenbach's drafting request, November 11, 1988, copy in possession of author; Clarenbach, "Dear Colleague" letter, May 16, 1989, copy in possession of author; "AIDS Initiative Introduced in Assembly," *In Step* (Milwaukee), June 8, 1989; "State AIDS Bill of

Rights Passes Senate; Goes to Governor," *The Wisconsin Light*, February 8, 1990.

62. "Four AIDS Related Bills Stalled on Governor's Desk," *The Wisconsin Light*, April 5, 1990; "Thompson Signs AIDS Bill of Rights into Law," *The Wisconsin Light*, April 19, 1990; "MAP to Take Tough Stand on Enforcing New AIDS Bias Law," *The Wisconsin Light*, April 19, 1990; "Rep. David Clarenbach," *The Wisconsin Light*, June 13, 1990.

63. "Wisconsin Assembly Passes Gay Rights Bill," *Chicago Gay Life* 7, no. 20 (February 1982); "Activists Honored at 'Queer of the Year' Banquet," *In Step*, June 17, 1993.

64. "New State Statutes Protect Young Lesbians and Gays," *Leaping La Crosse News*, May 1986; "High Risk," *New York Times Magazine*, September 11, 2016.

65. "Hate Crimes Now Directed at L.G.B.T. People the Most," *New York Times*, June 18, 2016.

Chapter 8

1. Governor's quote in draft Annual Report of Governor's Council on Lesbian and Gay Issues, 1984, copy in possession of author.

2. "Fighting for Justice from within the System, ERD Head Speaks," *OUT!* (Madison), May, 1983.

3. Dick Wagner et al., *DOA, The Story: Four Decades of Wisconsin's Department of Administration* (Madison: Department of Administration, 2002), 44–46.

4. "Pinning Him Down: An Interview with Tony Earl," *Gay Madison*, August 1982.

5. "Pinning Him Down."

6. "Mud-Slinging and Queer-Baiting," *OUT!*, November 1982; "Making Campaign Promises a Reality," *OUT!*, November 1982.

7. "One Foot in the White House, One Foot in a Concentration Camp," *OUT!*, November 1982.

8. "Wisconsin Governor-Elect Appoints Gay Journalist to Top Press Post," *The Advocate* (Los Angeles), January 20, 1983; Hal Bergan, "The Morning After," *Milwaukee Magazine*, January 1987; Ron McCrea oral interview, #903, January 14, 23, and 28, 2008, Madison, Wisconsin, UW–Madison Archives Oral History Program.

9. Ron McCrea oral interview; "Gay Rights Law Contradicts State Statutes," *Capital Times* (Madison), undated clipping in David Clarenbach Papers,

Box 3, Folder 2, Wisconsin Historical Society Archives, Madison, Wisconsin; "Social Progress Lagging for Gays, Earl Aide Says," *Milwaukee Journal*, May 15, 1983; Ron McCrea remarks to Outreach Senior Alliance, 2016, Madison, Wisconsin; "McCrea Warns of Anti-Gay Smear Campaign," *OUT!*, January 1986.

10. "Will Tony Earl Back Down?" *OUT!*, January 1983.

11. Mark Segal, *And Then I Danced: Traveling the Road to LGBT Equality* (New York, Akashic Books, 2015), 110; "40th Anniversary of PA Council for Sexual Minorities to Be Commemorated April 12," LGBT Center of Central Pennsylvania, www.centralpalgbtcenter.org/news; "New PA Panel," *GPU News* (Milwaukee), October 1978; "The Oregon Report," *OUT!*, March 1979; "Robert W. Straub," Wikipedia entry, wikipedia.org; "Report of the Commission on Personal Privacy," December 1982, copy in possession of author; "Brown Supports Gays," *GPU News*, April 1980.

12. "A Budget Short-Change," *OUT!*, February 1983; "Earl Shirks Commitment," *Daily Cardinal* (UW–Madison), February 18, 1983; Kathleen Nichols and Dick Wagner letter to Tony Earl, December 2, 1982; Tony Earl letter to Dick Wagner, December 6, 1982; Kathleen Nichols and Dick Wagner letter to Tony Earl, January 17, 1983, all in possession of author.

13. Notes from meetings with Kathleen Nichols and Governor Tony Earl, January–February 1983, in possession of author; "Mirroring Our Images: The First Annual Milwaukee Gay/Lesbian Film Festival," pamphlet; Alyn Hess memo, January 29, 1982, in possession of author; poster benefiting WLGN (Wisconsin Lesbian and Gay Network) for Music for a New Age concerts, February 1983; "The Gay Center's Guide to Madison, Wisconsin," pamphlet, all in possession of author.

14. Author's notes and documents from travels.

15. Author's notes and documents from travels.

16. Author's notes; Alyn Hess memo; Council on Lesbian and Gay Issues, First Annual Report, 1984, in possession of author; "Anger over Call for Volunteer Gay Liaison," *Gay Life* (Madison), February 3, 1983; "Milwaukee Angry over Volunteer Appointments," *OUT!*, February 1983; "A Budget Short-Change."

17. "Earl Is Urged to Form Group on Gay Issues," *Wisconsin State Journal* (Madison), February 16, 1983; "Governor's Council on Lesbian and Gay Issues," *Wisconsin Blue Book*, 1983–1984, 368.

18. "Gay Council Leaders Feel Sense of Mission," *Capital Times*, February 24, 1983; letter from Wisconsin Lesbian/Gay network to Governor Earl, February 22, 1983, copy in possession of author; "Appointments Coming Soon, But Earl Refuses to Meet With WLGN," *OUT!*, March 1983; "2 on Panel Say Madison Open about Homosexuals," *Milwaukee Sentinel*, February 21, 1983; Louie Crew to Dick Wagner and Kathleen Nichols, February 11, 1983, copy in possession of author.

19. Author's file on drafting the Executive Order.

20. "12 Appointed to Governor's Lesbian, Gay Issues Council," *Wisconsin State Journal*, April 2, 1983.

21. "It's Official, Folks—A Volunteer Council, And Milwaukee Wants to Name Its Own Reps," *OUT!*, March 1983; "Governor's Council Holds First Meeting," *OUT!*, May 1983.

22. Minutes of Council on Lesbian and Gay Issues, April 23, 1983, Wisconsin State Capitol, in possession of author.

23. "Governor's Council Holds First Meeting."

24. "Final Report of the Wisconsin Governor's Council on Lesbian and Gay Issues," January 2, 1987, in possession of author.

25. "Governor's Council Resigns, Issues Challenge to Thompson," *OUT!*, January 1987; "Lesbian, Gay Issue Debated," *Barron County (WI) News-Shield*, April 30, 1986; "Gay Issues Group's Breakup Seen as Setback," *Capital Times*, December 8, 1986.

26. Draft Annual Report for Council on Lesbian and Gay Issues, 1984, in possession of author; "Final Report of the Wisconsin Governor's Council"; Minutes of Council on Lesbian and Gay Issues, June 25, 1983, and October 22, 1983, in possession of author.

27. "Final Report of the Wisconsin Governor's Council."

28. "Lesbian, Gay Issue Debated," *Barron County News-Shield*, April 30, 1986; "Final Report of the Wisconsin Governor's Council."

29. "Governor's Council on Lesbian & Gay Issues," *Cream City Special Edition* (Milwaukee), May 1982.

30. Author's notes on broadcast speech; "Final Report of the Wisconsin Governor's Council."

31. "2 on Panel Say Madison Open about Homosexuals"; minutes of the Governor's Council, September 24, 1983, in possession of author; "Final Report of the Wisconsin Governor's Council"; Howard Fuller, Secretary Dept.

of Employment Relations, to Dick Wagner and Kathleen Nichols, November 2, 1983, in possession of author; Draft Annual Report of Governor's Council on Lesbian and Gay Issues, 1984, copy in possession of author.

32. "Final Report of the Wisconsin Governor's Council."

33. "Historic Health Conference Held," *OUT!*, March 1984; "Final Report of the Great Lakes Lesbian/Gay Health Conference, February 17–19, 1984," copy in possession of author.

34. Minutes and Committee Reports of the Council, March 24, 1984, and July 28, 1984; Greg Quindel, report on Waupun visit, April 28, 1984; both in possession of author.

35. Draft Annual Report of Governor's Council, 1984; Lampman and Racine Police Chief James Corvino quoted in "Racine Panel Won't Discipline Investigator," *Capital Times*, July 14, 1984.

36. "Liaison Position on Critical List," *OUT!*, May 1985; "Sharon Metz for Lieutenant Governor," *OUT!*, September 1986; "McCrea Warns of Anti-Gay Smear Campaign," *OUT!*, January 1986.

37. "Earl Bricker," Milwaukee LGBT History, www.mkelgbthist.org. Many individuals, organizations, businesses, media outlets, and events are profiled on this site.

38. Minutes of Governor's Council, June 4, 1983 and July 23 and 24, 1983, in possession of author; "Final Report of the Wisconsin Governor's Council."

39. "Earl Liaison Urges Gays to Guard Their Rights," *Milwaukee Journal*, April 11, 1986; "Legality, Psychology and the Homosexual Rights Bill," *New York Times*, March 16, 1986.

40. "It's an Issue of Broader Importance," *Appleton Post-Crescent*, December 2, 1983; "Gay in Foster Home Leads to License Appeal," *Capital Times*, December 6, 1983; Crolliss App, Winnebago County Dept. of Social Services, letter to Byron Malsin and Kathleen Roblee, December 6, 1982, copy in possession of author; "County Proceeds in Flintrop Case," *Appleton Post-Crescent*, December 6, 1983.

41. "It's an Issue of Broader Importance"; "Gay in Foster Home Leads to License Appeal"; App letter to Malsin and Roblee; hearing examiner ruling of September 29, 1983, copy in possession of author; "County Proceeds in Flintrop Case."

42. "Shout About It," *Oshkosh Northwestern*, April 22, 1983; "Homosexuality of Flintrop Cited in License Denial," *Appleton Post-Crescent*, December 2,

1983; "Flintrop's Homosexuality Becomes Public Issue," *Oshkosh Northwestern*, December 4, 1983; "It's an Issue of Broader Importance"; "Homosexuality at Issue in Foster Home License," *Marinette (WI) Eagle-Star*, December 8, 1983.

43. "It's an Issue of Broader Importance"; "Homosexuality of Flintrop Cited."

44. "Fighting for Justice"; Report, Dane County Affirmative Action Communication Training Program, July 1981, in possession of author.

45. "Governor's Council Holds First Meeting"; "Few File Complaints under State's New Gay Rights Law," *Capital Times*, May 7, 1983; "Few Gays in State Filing Bias Complaints," *Milwaukee Journal*, June 20, 1983.

46. "Fighting for Justice"; "Ad on Lesbians, Gays Discussed by Council," *Stevens Point Journal*, July 21, 1984.

47. "2007 Ally of the Year," OutReach Program, 2007, in possession of author; author's notes on 2003 discussions with LeAnna Ware and Merry Fran Tryon, in possession of author.

48. Department of Industry, Labor, and Human Relations, fiscal estimate for AB 70, AB 70 Drafting File, Legislative Reference Bureau (LRB), Madison, Wisconsin; Personnel Commission, Fiscal Estimate for LRB-1944/1, LRB-1944/1 drafting file, LRB.

49. Kirk Kleinschmidt and Nicole Libman, Appendix C and D, "A Case Study in the Gay Movement," *Sociology* 626 (May 16, 1987); Wagner review of DILHR data on discrimination cases, 1997–2002.

50. Wagner review of data.

51. "Firing Was Discriminatory: Gay," *Janesville Gazette*, November 28, 1983.

52. "Homosexual Rights: Wisconsin Only State with Law on Books," *San Jose Mercury News*, February 29, 1984; "Lawsuit May Test State Gay Rights Law," *OUT!*, July 1986; "*Green Bay Press Gazette*: No Gay Ads," *OUT!*, September 1986.

53. "Gay Rights Is the Theory, Discrimination Still the Practice," *OUT!*, March 1983; "Prejudice Locks Many Homosexuals into Closet," *Eau Claire Leader-Telegram*, February 2, 1983; William B. Turner, "The Gay Rights State: Wisconsin's Pioneering Legislation to Prohibit Discrimination Based on Sexual Orientation," *Wisconsin Women's Law Journal* 22, no. 1 (Spring 2007): 93–94.

54. "Homosexual Rights: Wisconsin Only State with Law on Books"; "Few Gays in State Filing Bias Complaints"; "Gay Rights Is the Theory."

55. "Kohler Rips Earl on Tax, Homosexual Appointees," *Milwaukee Sentinel*, March 12, 1983; "Gov. Earl's Efforts on Behalf of Gay Community Draw Criticism," *Milwaukee Journal*, May 19, 1983; Executive Office, response letter, February 22, 1983, copy furnished by Kathy Fullin.

56. "Comments on Editorial Concerning Appointment," *Shawano (WI) Evening Leader*, April 20, 1983; "Dump the Gays, Support Families," *Dodgeville (WI) Chronicle*, February 9, 1984; Editorial, *South Milwaukee Voice*, April 10, 1986; "Enlightened Kids and Homophobic Adults," *OUT!*, May 1980; "Shout About It"; "Fundamentalist Protestors in Rice Lake," *OUT!*, June 1986.

57. "Earl Gets Award, Vows Support for Gays," *Milwaukee Journal*, April 16, 1985; "Shift to Right Hurts Gays, Earl Says," *Wisconsin State Journal*, April 16, 1985; "Earl Says Political Climate Shifting away from Support of Gay Rights," *Milwaukee Sentinel*, April 16, 1985.

58. "Gov. Earl Philosophic in Defeat," *Wisconsin State Journal*, November 6, 1986; "Earl Scores Higher in Paper's Integrity Poll," *Wisconsin State Journal*, November 1, 1986; "Progressivism at Stake, Earl Says," *Milwaukee Sentinel*, November 1, 1986; "Thompson Strategy Works: Hammering at Record of Old Friend Earl Leads to Victory," *Milwaukee Journal*, November 5, 1986.

59. "McCrea Warns of Anti-Gay Smear Campaign," *OUT!*, January 1986.

60. "Final Report of the Wisconsin Governor's Council"; "Friend and Foe See Homosexual Defeat," *New York Times*, July 1, 1986; "Gay Community Still Subjected to Double Standard on Rights" *Milwaukee Journal*, April 20, 1986; Arthur Srb, "Will Concern over AIDS Bring Back Sodomy Ban?," *Capital Times*, July 7, 1986.

61. Wisconsin Christian Voter Guide, pamphlet, 1986, copy in possession of author.

62. "Thompson Vows End to Gay-Lesbian Council," *Wisconsin State Journal*, November 1, 1986; "Thompson Would Create Jobs for Welfare Recipients," *Milwaukee Sentinel*, November 8, 1986.

63. "Governor's Council Ponders Options," *OUT!*, December 1986; "Governor's Council Resigns, Issues Challenge to Thompson," *OUT!*, January 1987.

64. Copies of some resignation letters in Mark Behar Papers, LGBT Collection, UW–Milwaukee Archives.

65. Thomas Still, "Earl's Baggage Too Heavy," *Wisconsin State Journal*,

November 6, 1986; Matt Pommer, "Why Earl Lost," *Capital Times*, November 5, 1986; "Maier Snubs Thompson and Earl," *Milwaukee Sentinel*, November 1, 1986; Kenneth Lamke, "Explanations for Earl's Defeat Are Many," *Milwaukee Sentinel*, November 7, 1986.

66. Hal Bergan, "The Morning After," *Milwaukee Magazine*, January 1987; "Wisconsin Voters Full of Surprises," *Capital Times*, November 5, 1986.

67. "Earl Reflects on His Four Years," *Capital Times*, December 8, 1986; "Earl: 'It Wasn't in the Cards,'" *Capital Times*, November 8, 1986.

68. "Tony Earl's Defeat: What It Means for Us," *OUT!*, December 1986; "Goodbye to Wisconsin Governor Anthony Earl," *Windy City Times* (Chicago), January 8, 1987, reprinted in *Historic Speeches and Rhetoric for Gay and Lesbian Rights (1892–2000)*, Robert B. Ridinger, ed. (New York: Harrington Park Press, 2003), 535–37.

69. "UW Faculty Bitter over Pay Freeze Idea," *Capital Times*, July 1, 1983; "Editorial," *Milwaukee Journal*, reprinted in "Views from Wisconsin," *Capital Times*, November 1, 1986.

Chapter 9

1. State Medical Society of Wisconsin Statement, September 17, 1983, published in *Wisconsin Medical Journal*, November 1983.

2. "ACT UP Forces State Response on Prisons," *Madison Insurgent*, September 9, 1991.

3. Roger Gremminger, "Rural Homosexually Active Men and Hepatitis B Risk," paper given at American Public Health Association Annual Meeting, November 1982; Roger Gremminger, "Prospectus for Grant Consideration [to Control New Sexually Transmitted Diseases]," December 1, 1982, all in possession of author.

4. Gremminger, "Rural Homosexually Active Men"; "Milwaukee Not Immune to AIDS Outbreak," *Milwaukee Journal*, May 31, 1983.

5. "AIDS: 'It's Time to Take Action,'" *OUT!* (Madison), May, 1983; "No Trend Yet in Tests for HTLV-III Antibody," *OUT!*, December 1985.

6. Newsletter of the National Coalition of Gay STD Services, and early pamphlet of 1983, in possession of author; other copies in National Coalition of Gay Sexually Transmitted Disease Service Records, 1979–1993, Wisconsin Historical Society, held as part of LGBT collections, Golda Meier Library, UW–Milwaukee, Milwaukee, Wisconsin; "What?! Me use a condom?!,"

BEST NEWS (Milwaukee), September/October 1984, copy in possession of possession of author; "Mark Behar," Milwaukee LGBT History, www .mkelgbthist.org. Many individuals, organizations, businesses, media outlets, and events are profiled on the Milwaukee LGBT History website.

7. Minutes of the Great Lakes Lesbian/Gay Health Conference (GLLGHC) Steering Committee, July 25, 1983, August 22, 1983, September 6, 1983; GLLGHC conference brochure, GLLGHC conference packet; all in possession of author.

8. "Valley Man's Death Was First in State Attributed to AIDS," *Appleton Post-Crescent*, August 1, 1983; "GAYA: AIDS Investigation Should Not be Kept Quiet," *Green Bay Press Gazette*, August 11, 1983; "AIDS Valley Gay Community Scared, Angry," *Appleton Post-Crescent*, August 7, 1983.

9. "Milwaukee Not Immune to AIDS Outbreak," *Milwaukee Journal*, May 31, 1983; "State Finds 2nd AIDS Case; More Likely, Doctor Says," *Capital Times* (Madison), July 2, 1983; "The Significance of Aids as It Relates to Gay Liberation," *Marinette (WI) Eagle Star*, June 2, 1983; "Word's Getting out about AIDS Risk," *Milwaukee Journal*, December 16, 1985; "Only Education Will Fight the Hysteria," *Portage (WI) Daily Register*, December 4, 1985.

10. "No to Witchhunt," *OUT!*, June 1983; Governor Earl letter to Kathryn Morrison, December 22, 1983, copy in possession of author; "Democratic Candidates for U.S. Senate on the Issues," *Capital Times*, September 10, 1988.

11. "Milwaukee Not Immune to AIDS Outbreak"; "The Deadly Menace of AIDS," *Milwaukee Journal*, May 7, 1983; "Interview with Roger Gremminger, M.D. and Mark Behar, P.A.," *Cream City Special Edition* (Milwaukee), May, 1983.

12. "State Epidemiologist Expects Many New AIDS Cases," *OUT!*, July 1983; "AIDS Identification Outlined by Official," *Oshkosh Northwestern*, August 26, 1983; "Council Focuses on Health Issues," *OUT!*, July 1983.

13. Jeffrey P. Davis, draft memo on Acquired Immune Deficiency Syndrome, presented at Governor's Council meeting of June 4, 1983, final memo issued June 16, 1983, to Wisconsin health providers and agencies, copy in possession of author; Governor's Council files for meeting of June 4, 1983.

14. "The Natural History of Acquired Immune Deficiency Syndrome (AIDS) in Homosexual Men, Wisconsin: A Cooperative Proposal (Wisconsin Division of Health, Brady East STD Clinic, Blue Bus Clinic, State Laboratory of

Hygiene, and the Milwaukee County Medical Complex), July 1983, in possession of author; "State Seeks Federal AIDS Study Grant," *Wisconsin State Journal* (Madison), July 2, 1983; "AIDS Study Would Need 450 Gay Men Here," *Capital Times*, July 2, 1983; Governor Earl letter to Jeffrey Davis, July 6, 1983, copy in possession of author; "State Won't Get Federal AIDS Grant; Lack Victims," *Capital Times*, September 16, 1983.

15. "Doctor Warns of AIDS Stigma," *Milwaukee Journal*, December 4, 1983.

16. Minutes of Governor's Council of September 24, 1983, and attachment of Medical Society statement, in possession of author; "Medical Society Urges Awareness to Combat AIDS," *Capital Times*, September 21, 1983; "Medical Group Asks Awareness Concerning AIDS," *Wisconsin State Journal*, September 22, 1983.

17. "President's Page: AIDS and the Physician," *Wisconsin Medical Journal*, October 1983.

18. Victor Falk, "Editorial Statement: AIDS, Acquired Immune Deficiency Syndrome"; "Statement Concerning AIDS," adopted by the Board of Directors of the State Medical Society of Wisconsin, September 17, 1983; Roger A. Gremminger, "Taking a Sexual History"; all in *Wisconsin Medical Journal*, November 1983.

19. Jeffrey Davis, memo on AIDS, June 16, 1983, copy in possession of author; Don Fink and Richard Noonan, Wisconsin Lesbian/Gay Network, letter to Governor's Council on Gay and Lesbian Issues, September 27, 1983, copy in possession of author.

20. Funeral directors memo of August 3, 1983, in possession of author; "State Issues Precautions on AIDS," *Appleton Post-Crescent*, August 4, 1983; "Precautions Limited, Mortician Reports," *Racine Journal Times*, November 27, 1985.

21. Linda Reivitz letter to Mike Ellis, August 17, 1983, copy in possession of author; "Five AIDS Cases Diagnosed, State Investigating 10 More," *Shawano (WI) Evening Leader*, August 25, 1983; "State Gears up for Fight against AIDS," *Milwaukee Journal*, August 21, 1983.

22. Governor's Council minutes, April 20, 1983, in possession of author; "Equal Rights Effectiveness, AIDS Concern Addressed by Gubernatorial Representative," *UWM Post* (Milwaukee), April 15, 1986; "AIDS Task Force Calls for Tracing of Sexual Partners," *Stevens Point Journal*, June 20, 1986; "Gay Group Hits Plan to Trace AIDS Contact," *Capital*

Times, April 5, 1986; "Final Report: Wisconsin Governor's Council on Lesbian and Gay Issues."

23. "Excuses Opposed in Treating AIDS," *Milwaukee Sentinel*, April 11, 1986.

24. "AIDS Rate in Prisons Very High," *Milwaukee Sentinel*, February 17, 1986; "AIDS Not Rampant in Prisons, Study Indicates," *Milwaukee Journal*, February 17, 1986; "Prison to Accept Ailing Burglar," *Milwaukee Journal*, December 6, 1985; "State Will Not Change AIDS Policy," *Oshkosh Northwestern*, February 19, 1986; "AIDS Not a Threat to Prisoners." *Kenosha News*, December 16, 1985; "Prison Guidelines for AIDS Adopted," *Milwaukee Journal*, February 20, 1986.

25. "Homosexual Assault in Prisons a Problem," *Wisconsin State Journal*, January 29, 1985; "State Prisons: Rape Issue Less Serious," *Capital Times*, May 19, 1986.

26. "Doctors, State Differ on Testing for AIDS," *Milwaukee Journal*, January 15, 1988.

27. "Deputies 'Clear' in AIDS Exposure," *Appleton Post-Crescent*, April 29, 1986; "Not All Were Told about Inmate with AIDS," *Milwaukee Journal*, August 8, 1986; "Murder Suspect to Get AIDS-Exposure Test," *Capital Times*, November 3, 1986.

28. "AIDS Threat in Jails Worries Sheriff," *La Crosse Tribune*, November 21, 1985; "AIDS-Inmate Data Sought by Sheriff," *Wisconsin State Journal*, November 17, 1985; "AIDS Policy Studied for Winnebago Jail," *Oshkosh Northwestern*, December 3, 1985; "County Jail Developing AIDS Guidelines," *Capital Times*, January 13, 1988; "State Group Backs Bill on AIDS Testing," *Appleton Post-Crescent*, December 13, 1985; "ACT-UP," Milwaukee LGBT History, www.mkelgbthist.org.

29. "Clarenbach Scores Stunning Victory for Wisconsin AIDS Fight," *The Wisconsin Light*, August 10, 1989; "Thompson Signs $1.4 Million AIDS Funding," *The Wisconsin Light*, August 10, 1989; "Rep. Clarenbach's Hard Work Brings Jubilation to AIDS Groups," *The Wisconsin Light*, August 10, 1989.

30. "State Lack Funds to Support AIDS Caseload Increase," *The Wisconsin Light*, July 26, 1990.

31. "Love, Pride, Anger in D.C.," *Feminist Voices* (Madison), October 1987.

32. "Love, Pride, Anger in D.C."; pamphlet on Gay March on Washington, in possession of author; response from Senator Robert Kasten, November 16, 1987, in possession of author.

33. Album lyrics, *The Flirtations: Live Out on the Road* (1992, Flirt Records); Martin Duberman, *Hold Tight Gently: Michael Callen, Essex Hemphill, and the Battlefield of AIDS* (New York: The New Press, 2014), 93.

34. "War Conference Set for February 26–27," *The Wisconsin Light*, February 12, 1988; author's notes from the War Conference, February 26–27, 1988, Warrenton, Virginia, in possession of author.

35. John D'Emilio, "You Can't Build a Movement on Anger: Feeling Our Way toward Failure, Thinking Our Way toward Success," reprinted in *Speaking for Our Lives: Historic Speeches and Rhetoric for Gay and Lesbian Rights (1892–2000)*, ed. Robert B. Ridinger (New York: Harrington Park Press, 2004), 582–84.

36. "Anti-AIDS Policy OK on the Job," *Appleton Post-Crescent*, June 23, 1986; Michael Moore, "An Invitation to Senseless AIDS Bias," unidentified clipping, June 29, 1986, in possession of author; "AIDS Victims Bear a Double Burden," *Capital Times*, June 25, 1986.

37. "State Law Forbids Firing People with AIDS," *OUT!*, December 1985; "Hiring Law Protects AIDS Victims," *Capital Times*, January 12, 1986.

38. Merry Fran Tryon, "AIDS and the Law," typesheet, February 7, 1986, copy in possession of author; "EOC Head Takes Note of Anti-bias Safeguards," *Capital Times*, August 18, 1983; "Nursing Homes Warned to Take AIDS Patients," *Capital Times*, December 8, 1987.

39. "Minnesota AIDS Testing," *New Beginnings for Family and Friends* (Westby, Wisconsin), October 1989; "Take Test in Wisconsin," *New Beginnings*, March, 1990.

40. Letter from United Families Foundation signed by William E. Dannemeyer, sent to Wisconsin Governor's Executive Office, received April 1, 1986; "AIDS: America's New Plague," pamphlet, copies furnished by Executive Office.

41. "City Official: Allow AIDS Pupils in Class," *Milwaukee Sentinel*, December 4, 1985.

42. "AIDS Policy for Schools Studied," *Waukesha Freeman*, March 25, 1986; "Committee Approves AIDS Policy to Allow Exclusion from Schools," *Waukesha Freeman*, May 1, 1986; "Waukesha Schools OK Ban on Kids with AIDS, Other Ills," *Capital Times*, June 5, 1986; "Volunteers Will Treat AIDS Cases," *Waukesha Freeman*, March 24, 1986.

43. "AIDS Policy Pondered in Sparta," *La Crosse Tribune*, January 28, 1986;

"Children's Board Backs AIDS Policy," *Appleton Post-Crescent*, January
1986; "School Board Sets AIDS Policy," *Marinette Eagle Star*, February 2,
1986.

44. "Schools Ponder Guidelines for Dealing with AIDS," *Sheboygan Press*, June
11, 1986; "Time for an AIDS Policy," *Sheboygan Press*, May 7, 1986; "AIDS
Policy Urged," *Racine Journal Times*, December 4, 1985.

45. "Time to Educate Selves on AIDS," *Stevens Point Journal*, March 26, 1986.

46. "Racine OKs Excluding Pupils, Teachers with AIDS or Herpes," *Milwaukee
Sentinel*, November 19, 1985; "Unified AIDS Ban," *Racine Journal Times*,
November 27, 1985; "Kids, Teachers with AIDS Voted Out of Racine
Schools," *Windy City Times* (Chicago), November 28, 1985.

47. "Questions Posed on AIDS Policy," *Racine Journal Times*, December 12,
1985; "Man, 30, Dies of AIDS Here," *Racine Journal Times*, November
27, 1985. "Opinion: About Unified's AIDS Policy," *Racine Journal Times*,
December 12, 1985.

48. "AIDS Policy Too Hasty," *Racine Journal Times*, December 13, 1985.

49. "AIDS Rule Spurs REA Complaint," *Racine Journal Times*, February 7, 1986;
"Bias Panel Studies AIDS Plan," *Milwaukee Journal*, February 13, 1986;
"AIDS Policy Defended," *Racine Journal Times*, April 20, 1986; "AIDS Policy
Mistaken; Rule Must be Re-done," *Milwaukee Sentinel*, May 9, 1986; "AIDS
Policy Too Hasty."

50. *Racine Unified School District v. Labor and Industry Review Commission*,
case no. 90-1969, Court of Appeals Decision, September 11, 1991, copy in
possession of author

51. *Racine Unified School District v. Labor and Industry Review Commission*
decision.

52. "Personal Reflection on the Quilt," MASN *(Madison AIDS Support Network)
News*, May, 1989, in possession of author; "AIDS Quilt Honors 2 Brothers
Who Died," *Capital Times*, May 6, 1989; "Seeing the Names Project Quilt Is
Overwhelming Experience," *The Wisconsin Light*, May 18, 1989.

53. "Flap over Pamphlet Won't Stop CENTER Project," *OUT!*, December
1985; "Council Say City Nurses Should Staff AIDS Clinic," *Green Bay Press
Gazette*, November 20, 1985; "AIDS Brochure Called Too Explicit," *Milwaukee Journal*, December 10, 1985; "Assisting AIDS Clinic Is Just One of
Many Jobs for Le Mere," *Green Bay Press Gazette*, November 30, 1985.

54. "Committee Votes to Assign Nurses for AIDS Screening," *Green Bay Press*

Gazette, January 30, 1986; "Nurses-AIDS Issue Bypassed," *Green Bay Press Gazette*, February 5, 1986; "Council Stands Pat on AIDS Screening," *Green Bay Press Gazette*, February 18, 1986; "Panel OKs Zima's Sex-Counseling Proposal," *Green Bay Press Gazette*, March 13, 1986; "Back Again: City Council Should Reject Proposal on Sex Counseling," *Green Bay Press Gazette*, March 18, 1986; "Council Retains AIDS-Clinic Policy," *Green Bay Press Gazette*, March 19, 1986.

55. CENTER Project ad, *In Step* (Milwaukee), October 8, 1992; "Green Bay Announces AIDS Conference," *The Wisconsin Light*, December 15, 1988.

56. "Milwaukee ACT-UP Deserves Strong Citizen Involvement," *The Wisconsin Light*, August 10, 1989; "AIDS Protest Vigil at Federal Building," *The Wisconsin Light*, May 18, 1989; "ACT-UP Milwaukee Receives Help from New York City Group," *The Wisconsin Light*, August 24, 1989; "ACT-UP," Milwaukee LGBT History, www.mkelgbthist.org.

57. "ACT-UP Distributes Condoms and AIDS Pamphlets at Marquette," *The Wisconsin Light*, March 8, 1990; "ACT-UP Members Plead Not Guilty for Distributing AIDS Information," *The Wisconsin Light*, November 1, 1990; "ACT-UP Commended in Helping Our Youth Learn Safe Sex," *The Wisconsin Light*, October 18, 1990.

58. "ACT-UP Survey Finds Dentists Discriminate Against HIV+ People," *The Wisconsin Light*, September 6, 1990; "Milwaukee ACT-UP Demonstrates Against Wisconsin Dental Community's Discriminatory Response to AIDS," *The Wisconsin Light*, September 20, 1990; "WISN Radio Accused of Spreaing AIDS Misinformation to the Public," *The Wisconsin Light*, October 4, 1990; "Does the World Still Recognize a Holocaust?," flyer, Jerry Johnson Papers, Box 1, Folder 1, UW–Milwaukee LGBT Archives.

59. "In Your Face," *Isthmus*, September 13, 1991; "ACT-UP Forces State Response on Prisons," *Madison Insurgent*, September 9, 1991; "ACT-UP Shakes up AIDS Awareness," *Wisconsin State Journal*, July 29, 1991; letter from Daniel Fons (ACT-UP) to Terry Boughner, July 27, 1990, Johnson Papers, Box 1, Folder 1.

60. "AIDS Activists Vow to End Local Silence," *Madison Insurgent*, February 25, 1991; "ACT-UP Shakes Up AIDS Awareness," *The Wisconsin Light*, July 29, 1991.

61. "In Your Face"; "AIDS Activists Vow to End Local Silence."

62. "ACT-UP Awards 'Slammies' to Gov.," *Daily Cardinal* (UW–Madison), March 31, 1992; "AIDS Criminalization for Wisconsin?," *OUT!*, April 1987; "ACT-UP Protests Prison Practices," *Daily Cardinal*, September 10, 1992.

63. "Wisconsin 'Poets for AIDS' Releases New Anthology," *In Step*, February 5, 1987; Norman Richards, ed., *Heart Pieces: Wisconsin poets for AIDS* (Milwaukee: Namron Press, 1987).

64. Richards, *Heart Pieces*, 48–49.

65. Richards, *Heart Pieces*, 6, 46.

66. Richards, *Heart Pieces*, 11, 45.

67. Richards, *Heart Pieces*, 14–15.

68. Richards, *Heart Pieces*, 20, 65, 70–72.

69. "Fighting for Their Lives," *OUT!*, November 1984.

70. "He's Bitter about Disease, but is Adjusted to His Fate," *Milwaukee Sentinel*, October 21, 1987.

71. "'Plain Angry' about Disease That Killed Son," *Milwaukee Sentinel*, October 21, 1987.

72. "AIDS Sufferer Keeps on Crusading," *Green Bay Press Gazette*, February 20, 1986.

73. Michael Lisowski, "Chairman's Notes," BWMT (Black and White Men Together) Milwaukee newsletter, October 1986, LGBT Collections, UW–Milwaukee Archives.

74. "An Insider's View by Todd Butler," *In Step*, December 17, 1987.

75. "We Must Bond Together to Live and Overcome Ignorance and Hatred," *The Wisconsin Light*, June 29, 1989.

76. D'Emilio, "You Can't Build a Movement on Anger"; "Gay-Issues Council Helps Fight AIDS," *Milwaukee Journal*, September 2, 1983.

77. "State Given Edge on AIDS Epidemic," *Milwaukee Sentinel*, October 21, 1987; "AIDS Awareness in Milwaukee," City of Milwaukee Cable TV News, 1990, Digital Collection, UW–Milwaukee Archives.

78. D'Emilio, "You Can't Build a Movement on Anger."

79. "World AIDS Day December 1 Focuses on Women," *In Step*, December 12, 1990; "ARCW Donates Its Archives to UWM Libraries," *Wisconsin Gazette* (Milwaukee), May 8, 2015; Wisconsin Department of Health, "Wisconsin HIV: Integrated Epidemiology Profile 2010–2014," July 2016, copy in possession of author; form letter from Michael Gifford (ARWC) to Dick Wagner, March 31, 2017, copy in possession of author.

80. Roger Gremminger, "Medically Speaking: AIDS Provokes the Great Moral Debate of the Century," *The Wisconsin Light*, May 13, 1988.

Chapter 10

1. "Unity," *New Beginnings for Family and Friends* (Westby, Wisconsin), August 1990; hereafter, *New Beginnings*.

2. "Hiding Ourselves from Ourselves," *Fond du Lac (WI) Reporter*, May 21, 1973; copy in the Eldon Murray papers, LGBT Collection, UW–Milwaukee Archives, Milwaukee, Wisconsin.

3. GLCS Resource List, flyer from the Gay & Lesbian Community at UW–Stout, ca. early 1980s; GLCS newsletter, ca. early 1980s; both in possession of author.

4. "Bob Jansen's Gay Activism Predated Northland Pride," *Lavender Magazine* (Edina, MN), August 13, 2010, www.lavendermagazine.com/archives/uncategorized/bob-jansen%E2%80%99s-gay-activism-predated-northland -pride; Historical Note (Biographical), Jansen, Robert J., Archives and Special Collections, Kathryn A. Martin Library, University of Minnesota– Duluth; author's personal correspondence with Robert J. Jansen, 1983.

5. "Superior's Main Club Burns," *The Wisconsin Light* (Madison), January 2, 1997; Joey Norton, "Twin Ports' First Openly Gay Bar, The Main Club, Closing After 34 Years," August 22, 2017, Fox21 (Duluth–Superior), www .fox21online.com; Steve Lenius, "Minnesota's Leather History," May 30, 2003, Leather Life blog, www.leathercolumn.blogspot.com/2003/05; Mockups for Main Club ads for *The Wisconsin Light* and flyer for mayoral candidate Dan O'Neill to speak at club, both in Main Club file, Jerry Johnson Papers, LGBT Archives, UW–Milwaukee, Box 2, Folder 7; Jansen Rodeo Vest, Wearing Gay History online exhibit, www.wearinggayhistory. com/items/show/1765.

6. "Twin Ports Gay Bar Owners Reflect on Civil Rights Movement," WDIO-DT (Duluth, MN), February 27, 2017, www.WDIO.com/news/flame-main -club-lgbt-duluth-superior/4411754; "Earl Greely Memorial Library," OutReach flyer, ca. 1990s, in possession of author; email to author from Steve Starkey, OutReach Director, September 22, 2015; "Superior Man Brutally Killed by Openly Homophobic Attacker," *The Wisconsin Light*, June 13, 1991.

7. Douglas County Health Department Grant file, Cream City Foundation Papers, LGBT Archives, UW–Milwaukee, Box 4, Folder 14.

8. "Bob Jansen's Gay Activism"; "Documentary Explores Gay History in Twin Ports," *Duluth (MN) News Tribune*, February 28, 2013; Stewart Van Cleve, *Land of 10,000 Loves: A History of Queer Minnesota* (Minneapolis: University of Minnesota Press, 2012), 152–54.

9. *Out Up North* (Washburn) newsletter, various issues from 1997, Out Up North file, Johnson Papers, Box 4, Folder 18.

10. *Out Up North*, February 1997.

11. *Out Up North*, February 1997; *Out Up North*, May 1997.

12. Spike, "Blue Valentine," *Out Up North*, February 1997; Spike, "Pride From a Rural Perspective," *Out Up North*, May 1997.

13. Will Fellows, *Farm Boys: Lives of Gay Men from the Rural Midwest* (Madison: University of Wisconsin Press, 1996), 3–7; *Farm Boys* grant application, Cream City Foundation Papers, Box 4, Folder 23; "The Buzz: The Local Literary Scene," *Isthmus* (Madison), June 7, 1996; "Growing up Gay: Author Collects Stories from the Heartland of America," *Janesville Gazette*, May 13, 1996; "UW–Madison News Release—A 'Brokeback' Connection," January 10, 2006, in possession of author.

14. Author interview with Richard Kilmer, Madison, Wisconsin, February 23, 2018.

15. Author interview with Todd Larson, Madison, Wisconsin, February 19, 2018; Todd Larson, *Larson Farm* (self-published, 2017), 25, 30.

16. Rural Dykes Association materials, Johnson Papers, Box 4, Folder 35.

17. Van Cleve, *Land of 10,000 Loves*, 10, 258–59, 192–94, 273–74; Claudia Card, *Lesbian Choices* (New York: Columbia University Press, 1995), 12.

18. Author's survey of all issues of *New Beginnings for Family and Friends*, 1987–1991, held at the Wisconsin Historical Society Serials Collection, Madison, Wisconsin.

19. "The First Northwoods Faerie Gathering!," *New Beginnings*, June 1988; "The First Northwoods Midsummer Faerie Gathering: The Circle Comes Home," *New Beginnings*, September 1988; "Northwoods Radical Faeries Will Gather," *New Beginnings*, July 1989.

20. "About Chalice Stream," Rusk Area Arts Alliance, https://sites.google .com/site/ruskareaartsalliance2/aboutchalicestream; Barry Lynn

obituary, *Ladysmith (WI) News*, January 28, 2018; "Dance Icon Lynn Remembered," *Eau Claire Leader Telegram*, January 28, 2018.

21. "Area Gays Reject 'Closets,'" *Rhinelander New Times*, December 1983; "New Organization to Fill Voids in Northern Wisconsin," *The Wisconsin Light*, November 29, 1990.

22. Author's review of *Positive Voice* (Green Bay) issues from May, 1995–February 1998, Johnson Papers, Box 4, Folder 26.

23. "Winter Conference Date Set," *Positive Voice*, October 1995; "Angel of Hope Moves," *Positive Voice*, January 1996; "Positive Voice," Milwaukee LGBT History, www.mkelgbthist.org. Many individuals, organizations, businesses, media outlets, and events are profiled on this site.

24. "From the Editor's Desktop," *Positive Voice*, May 1995; "Gay Guide Moves toward Publication," *Positive Voice*, October 1995; "Shaking It Up with Mike Fitzpatrick," *Quest* (Green Bay), December 2012.

25. "LGBT Activist Paul (Cricket) Jacob," *Quest*, December 2012.

26. "Quest," Milwaukee LGBT History, www.mkelgbthist.org; list of topics comes from various issues of *Quest*, 1990s and 2000s.

27. "Insider's Report: How Northeast Wisconsin's Gay Community Helped Scuttle the Anti–Same Sex Marriage Bill in Just Five Days . . . Part One," *Positive Voice*, March 1996; "Insider's Report: Part Two of How Northeast Wisconsin's Gay Community Helped to Overturn the Anti–Same Sex Marriage Bandwagon," *Positive Voice*, April 1996.

28. "'Deep Throat' Reports: I Infiltrated the Christian Coalition," *Positive Voice*, March 1996.

29. *Positive Voice*, January 1996; *Positive Voice*, April 1996; "Fox Valley Transgender Group," Milwaukee LGBT History, www.mkelgbthist.org.

30. "Mel White Calls for Dialogue: 500 Attend Speech at UW GB," *Positive Voice*, May 1995; "PVN News Notes—Tammy Baldwin, Miriam Ben-Shalom, Harvey Fierstein and Denise Brown to Speak in Area This Month," *Positive Voice*, April, 1996; "'Have a Heart' Dinner Set for February 10," *Positive Voice*, January, 1996; "Sexuality and Gender Alliance at UW–Green Bay," Milwaukee LGBT History, www.mkelgbthist.org; "50 Best Colleges for LGBTA Students," College Choice, www.collegechoice.net/rankings/best-lgbt-friendly-colleges-and-universities.

31. PFLAG Green Bay, Horizons, and Northern Womyn Ink. appear in regularly scheduled events listings in *Positive Voice* throughout 1995 and 1996;

"Lavender Salon," Milwaukee LGBT History, www.mkelgbthist.org; "New Green Bay Women's Group Plans December 2 Fundraiser," *The Wisconsin Light*, November 29, 1990; "Dinettes," Milwaukee LGBT History, www .mkelgbthist.org.

32. "Angels of Hope: MCC Church Site on Green Bay's East Side," *Positive Voice*, January 1996; "MCC Rummage Sale Wraps Up," *Positive Voice*, June/ July 1997; "Angels of Hope Xmas Bazaar," *Positive Voice*, October 1997; "Angels of Hope—MCC News," *Positive Voice*, February 1998; "Angels of Hope," Milwaukee LGBT History, www.mkelgbthist.org.

33. "Bay City Chorus," Milwaukee LGBT History; " 'Alive with Pride' Picnic May 28," *Positive Voice*, May 1995.

34. NEWIST flyer, Cream City Foundation NEWIST Grant File, UW–Milwaukee LGBT Collection, Box 6, Folder 2; hereafter NEWIST Grant File.

35. NEWIST flyer.

36. Warren Gerds, "Show on Gay Teens Took Courage," *Green Bay Press Gazette*, January 26–February 1, 1992; Clipping beginning "Eileen Littig Was Geared Up," undated clipping, NEWIST Grant File; "Wisconsin TV Producer Airs a Message of Tolerance," undated clipping, Cream City Grant File.

37. "High Schools, Homophobia and Hate: A Proposed Video Presentation," copy in NEWIST Grant File; "Wisconsin TV Producer Airs a Message of Tolerance."

38. "Issues Facing Gay and Lesbian Youth," NEWIST Grant File.

39. "The Boys behind the Door: Gays Have Helped Make Door County a Top Destination," *Wisconsin Gazette* (Milwaukee), September 22, 2011; "PFLAG-Door County," Milwaukee LGBT History, www.mkelgbthist.org.

40. "The Boys behind the Door."

41. "25 Years and Counting: The Unique History of the Chanticleer Guest House," October 17, 2017, Chanticleer Guest House, www.chanticleer guesthouse.com/25-years-counting-unique-history-chanticleer-guest -house/; Annie Tobey, "Cool Travels to Door County," July 25, 2011, Gay Richmond News, www.gayrva.com/guides/travel/cool-travels-to-door -county-wi/; "LGBTQ+ Travel in Door County," Door County Wisconsin, www.doorcounty.com/experience/lgbt-travel/; Guest House ad, Johnson Papers, LGBT Collection, UW–Milwaukee, Box 2, Folder 5.

42. "Fox Valley Gay Alliance," Milwaukee LGBT History, www.mkelgbthist.org;

Gay Dialogue (Menasha, WI), issues of January, March, April, May/June, August 1977, part of the Eldon Murray Collection, UW–Milwaukee Golda Meier Library Special Collections, Milwaukee, Wisconsin.

43. "Fox Valley 'Gay Libs'—Their Lives, Their Aims," *Fond du Lac (WI) Reporter*, January 26, 1973; "Fond du Lac Homosexual 'Tells All About It,'" *Fond du Lac Reporter*, January 27, 1973; "Hiding Ourselves from Ourselves," *Fond du Lac Reporter*, May 21, 1973.

44. "Appleton Library to Carry GPU News," *GPU News* (Milwaukee), December 1976.

45. "Coming Out," *Gay Dialogue*, August 1977; letter from Doris Colavecchi of Doris's Super Bar, *Gay Dialogue*, May/June 1977.

46. "A Personal Comment," *Gay Dialogue*, March 1977; "The Mourning After," *Gay Dialogue*, May/June 1977.

47. "Rights of Homosexuals," *Appleton Post-Crescent*, April 5, 1977; "PC [*Appleton Post-Crescent*] Comes Out for Gay Rights," *Gay Dialogue*, April, 1977.

48. "The New Lambda Lounge," *Gay Dialogue*, August, 1977; "1101 West: From Community, to the Community," *OUT!* (Madison), July 1983.

49. "Lawrence University Gay Rights Committee," *Gay Dialogue*, May/June, 1977; Regularly Scheduled Events, *Positive Voice*, April, 1966; "Lawrence University Promises Full Equality," *OUT!*, December 1985; "Gay and Lesbian Alumni Groups Increasing," *New Beginnings*, July 1988.

50. "Positive Voice," Milwaukee LGBT History, www.mkelgbthist.org; author's review of community calendar of events and regularly scheduled events in *Positive Voices*, May 1995–February 1998; "Miss Gay Great Lakes Pageant," *New Beginnings*, February 1990; "GLBT Partnership Celebrating 15 Years of Changing Our Community," *Quest*, September 2012.

51. "Appleton Rates High as LGBTQ-friendly, but Green Bay and Oshkosh Not So Much," *Oshkosh Northwestern*, November 2, 2017; "Transgender Candidate Elected to Wis. City Council," *USA Today*, April 2, 2014; "50 Best Colleges for LGBTQ Students."

52. "President Stan Bracclon Speaks at Unitarian Universalist Fellowship," *Gay Dialogue*, January 1977; "Gay Student Association UW–Oshkosh Sponsored First Annual Spring Fling," *Gay Dialogue*, May/June 1977; "Oshkosh Offers Lambda Connection," *OUT!*, May 1987.

53. "LGBT Activist Paul (Cricket) Jacob," *Quest*, December 2012.

54. *ATTENTION*, December 1990, Johnson Papers, Box 4, Folder 17; "Wisconsin's Newest Spanish Teacher, Ryan," *Quest*, June 12, 2003.

55. "On 'Pretty Good' Parents," Lakeshore (Sheboygan) PFLAG newsletter, September 1990, Johnson Papers, Box 4, Folder 23.

56. "Justice Is Served," Lakeshore PFLAG newsletter, November 1990.

57. "Editor's Comment," Lakeshore PFLAG newsletter.

58. "Memorial Day Brat Fry Sizzles up $1300 for ROW," *Quest*, June, 2005; "Remembering Dean Dayton," *Quest*, November 2014.

59. "GLU: Still Going After All these Years," *OUT!*, October 1983; "Jo'Dee's International," Milwaukee LGBT History, www.mkelgbthist.org.

60. "Pastoring to Generations," *Kenosha News*, November 11, 2017; "Minister's Retirement Brings Sweet Sorrow," *Racine Journal Times*, March 26, 2017; "Celebrating Pride and Successes," *Racine Journal Times*, June 29, 2015; "Larsen Joins Picketers," *OUT!*, June 1985; "Gay Marriage in Racine," *Racine Journal Times*, October 7, 2014.

61. "Governor's Council Gets New Member," *OUT!*, May 1986; "LesBiGay Book Discussion Group in Racine County," *In Step* (Milwaukee), October 12, 1995; "Racine LGBT Center Sets Gala Opening April 4," *Quest*, March 26, 2009.

62. Linda Zimmerman, oral history interview conducted by John Magerus, July 26, 2001, La Crosse, Wisconsin, UW–La Crosse Oral History Program.

63. "Editorial," *New Beginnings*, December 1987; Pioneers organization flyer, in author's possession.

64. "Dubuque March," *New Beginnings*, April 1988; "Dubuque to Hold Third Pride March/Rally," *New Beginnings*, September 1989.

65. "Coming Out of the Closet with Renn'e," *New Beginnings*, May 1988; "Coming Out of the Closet with Renn'e," July 1988.

66. Bill Fleming, oral history interview conducted by John Magerus, September 18, 2000, La Crosse, Wisconsin, UW–La Crosse Oral History Program.

67. "Coming Out of the Closet With Renn'e," *New Beginnings*, September 1988; "Bill Fleming Wins WPHA Award," *New Beginnings*, November 1989; Fleming, oral history interview; "Winnebagos Awarded Grant," *New Beginnings*, January 1990; AIDS: Issues in Rural America, conference notice, *New Beginnings*, April/May 1991; AIDS: Issues in Rural America, conference notice, *New Beginnings*, June/July 1991.

68. "Workshop a First for La Crosse," *New Beginnings*, March, 1988.

69. Dean Klinkenberg, oral history interview conducted by John Magerus, November 6, 2000, La Crosse, Wisconsin, UW–La Crosse Oral History Program.

70. Rachel Gunderson, oral history interview conducted by John Magerus, October 16, 2000, La Crosse, Wisconsin, UW–La Crosse Oral History Program.

71. Notice, *New Beginnings*, June 1988; "Thanks," *New Beginnings*, July 1988; letter from K.P., February 1990.

72. "LLN Bankrupt," *Leaping La Crosse News*, October 1983; "LLN Benefit: Italian Night at 'Tattinos,'" *Leaping La Crosse News*, May 1983; "Vote to Keep Your Newsletter Coming: Donate to the LLN," *Leaping La Crosse News*, July 1992.

73. "A-MUSE-ING AMAZON: Prom and Tuxedos," *Leaping La Crosse News*, November 1985; "Eighth Annual Tux Party," *Leaping La Crosse News*, September 1987; "Ninth Annual Tux Party," *Leaping La Crosse News*, November 1988, "Tenth Annual Tux Party," October/November 1989.

74. "The 9th Annual Sandbar Party," *Leaping La Crosse News*, July 1984; "Lesbian Space," *Leaping La Crosse News* issues of July, August, September, and October 1989; Mary O'Sullivan, oral history interview conducted by John Magerus, July 24, 2001, La Crosse, Wisconsin, UW–La Crosse Oral History Program.

75. "Katherine Hepburn at DOE Farm??????????," *Leaping La Crosse News*, March 1983; "DOE Farm Today," *Leaping La Crosse News*, August 1989.

76. "Lesbians United: A New Political/Social Organization," *Leaping La Crosse News*, May, 1985; "News from the Men's Community," *Leaping La Crosse News*, May, 1984.

77. "Is AIDS Our Problem?," *Leaping La Crosse News*, March 1986.

78. "Lutherans Concerned," *Leaping La Crosse News*, June 1986.

79. "To Cities," *New Beginnings*, August 1988; "Wildwood and Share," *New Beginnings*, August 1990.

80. "For Womyn Only" flyer, in *New Beginnings*, January 1990.

81. "Congressman Steve Gunderson Outed," *New Beginnings*, August/September 1991; "Gunderson Bows Out Again; Blames Anti-Gay Bigotry," *In Step*, July 25, 1996.

82. GLCS Resource List; GLCS newsletter.

83. Jill Muenich, oral history interview, November 30, 2013, Fitchburg, Wisconsin; Edward Frank (pseudonym), telephone interview, November 20, 2013; Carla Johnson, oral history interview, November 22, 2013, Hudson, Wisconsin; Steve (pseudonym), oral history interview, December 1, 2013, Madison, Wisconsin; all conducted by Melissa Schultz, UW–Eau Claire Gay and Lesbian Oral History Project (GLOHP), 2013–2014, UHC 351, Special Collections and Archives, McIntyre Library, UW–Eau Claire, Eau Claire, Wisconsin.

84. Frank, oral history interview; Muenich, oral history interview.

85. Robb Jirschelle, oral history interview, January 13, 2013, Eau Claire, Wisconsin; Crystal Martin, oral history interview, November 30, 2013, Madison, Wisconsin; Laura Goetz, telephone interview, January 21, 2014; Dan Hillis, oral history interview, January 28, 2014, Eau Claire, Wisconsin; all conducted by Melissa Schultz, UW–Eau Claire GLOHP.

86. Sharon Knopp, oral history interview, December 13, 2013, Eau Claire, Wisconsin, conducted by Melissa Schultz, UW–Eau Claire GLOHP; "Gay Bashing Reported at University," *Eau Claire Leader-Telegram*, March 25, 1992; "Four Bashings Reported," *Eau Claire Leader Telegram*, October 4, 1992; "Some Students Bash Sexual Orientation," *Eau Claire Leader Telegram*, October 4, 1992.

87. "Administration Ponders Gay-Bashings," *Eau Claire Leader-Telegram*, October 8, 1992; "Reward Offered in Hate Crimes Incidents," *Eau Claire Leader-Telegram*, March 26, 1992; "Groups Decry Hate Crimes," *Eau Claire Leader-Telegram*, May 8, 1992.

88. Bob Nowlan, "Teaching and Working as an Openly Gay Faculty Member at the University of Wisconsin–Eau Claire," *Radical Teacher* (Pittsburgh, PA), May 2001, 27.

89. Nowlan, "Teaching and Working," 28, 30.

90. Christopher Jorgenson, oral history interview, December 17, 2013, Eau Claire, Wisconsin, conducted by Melissa Schultz, UW–Eau Claire GLOHP; series of press releases from UW–Eau Claire, including "English Faculty Co-edit Essay on New Queer Cinema," January 6, 2011; "Film Presentation and Discussions to Highlight World AIDS Day," November 22, 2006; "New Women's Studies Travel Seminar Accepting Applications," March 29, 2010; "'Children of God' to Headline Eau Queer Film Festival," September 29, 2010; "Travel Seminar, Film Festival Receive Examplary

Program Awards," January 19, 2011; "Eau Queer Film Festival Set for Octo. 13-16," September 29, 2011, all in Box 2, Folders 6 and 14.

91. Beth Hellwig, oral history interview, December 17, 2013, Eau Claire, Wisconsin, conducted by Melissa Schultz, UW–Eau Claire GLOHP; "UW–Eau Claire Improves Ranking on LGBT-Friendly Campus Climate Index," UW–Eau Claire press release, October 11, 2010, UW–Eau Claire LGBT Oral History Collection, Box 2, Folder 14; "50 Best Colleges for LGBTQ Students."

92. "Wisconsin TV Producer Airs a Message of Tolerance," undated, unidentified clipping, in Cream City Foundation NEWIST Grant File.

Chapter 11

1. "Gay Minister Resigns Post," *New Beginnings for Family and Friends* (Westby, Wisconsin), June/July 1991. Hereafter, *New Beginnings*.

2. "High School Student Speaks Out," *New Lessons* (Madison), December 1990, provided by Dennis Bergren, in possession of author.

3. "History of SSBL," Saturday Softball Beer League, www.ssblmilwaukee.com/pages/ssblhistory; "History of NAGAAA Fest," NAGAAA Fest, www.nagafest.com/about/history.phplw; "Hall of Fame," NAGAAA Softball, www.nagaaasoftball.org/hall-of-fame/; "Milwaukee's Saturday Softball Beer League [SSBL] Started It All," *The Wisconsin Light* (Madison), May 13–June 9, 1988; "Tom Theis," Milwaukee LGBT History, www.mkelgbthist.org. Many individuals, organizations, businesses, media outlets, and events are profiled on the Milwaukee LGBT History website.

4. "Opening Day 1998," SSBL newsletter, Saturday Softball Beer League file, Jerry Johnson Papers, LGBT Collection, Golda Meier Library, UW–Milwaukee, Milwaukee, Wisconsin, Box 5, Folder 1; Grant application from SSBL, Cream City Foundation Papers, LGBT Collection, Box 6, Folder 13, UW–Milwaukee.

5. "History of NAGAAA Fest"; "Team Cops MKE Title," *GPU News* (Milwaukee), July 1978.

6. "Softball Gay World Series III," *GPU News*, October 1979; "World Series Softball Comes to Milwaukee," *OUT!* (Madison), August 1985; "SSBL Milwaukee Wins 2009 World Series Bid," *Quest* (Green Bay), February 14–27, 2008; Tom Salzsieder, "Milwaukee Wreck Room Classic Softball Tourna-

ment," *In Step* (Milwaukee), May 3, 1984; "Milwaukee's Saturday Softball Beer League [SSBL] Started It All."

7. "Laverne and Shirley," Wikipedia entry, wikipedia.org; Doug Schmidt, *They Came to Bowl: How Milwaukee Became America's Tenpin Capital* (Madison: Wisconsin Historical Society Press, 2007), 2–3, 10, 32.
8. "Holiday Invitational Tournament," Milwaukee LGBT History, www.mkelgbthist.org; Ken Kurtz, "Jock Shorts, Welcome H.I.T. Bowlers!!," *In Step*, November 20, 1986; Ken Kurtz, "Jock Shorts H.I.T. '87," *In Step*, December 17, 1987; Jerry Warzyn, "Holiday Invitational Tournament X a Great Success," *The Wisconsin Light*, December 1, 1988; Bill Meunier, "H.I.T. a Major Win," *OUR HORIZONS* (Milwaukee), December 9, 1981.
9. Ken Kurtz, "Jock Shorts," *In Step*, November 20, 1986; Ken Kurtz, "MIL-MA-IDS '87," *In Step*, February 5, 1987; International Gay Bowling Organization newsletter, 1988, Johnson Papers, Box 3, Folder 18.
10. "GAMMA," Milwaukee LGBT History, www.mkelgbthist.org; Paul Masterson, "Milwaukee GAMMA 37 Years and Counting," *Shepherd Express* (Milwaukee), November 17, 2015.
11. Pat Callen letter to Cream City Foundation, October 20, 1992, Cream City Foundation Papers, Box 4, Folder 10; "John M. Cowles, Served on Cream City Foundation Board and as GAMMA President," *The Wisconsin Light*, January 25–February 7, 1990.
12. "Don Schwamb," Milwaukee LGBT History, www.mkelgbthist.org.
13. Survey of activities from GAMMA newsletters, June 1992, December 2000, and June 2001, GAMMA file, Johnson Papers, Box 3, Folder 2.
14. Brian Pronger, "Gay Culture in Gay Sports," *The Arena of Masculinity: Sports, Homosexuality, and the Meaning of Sex* (New York: St. Martin's Press, 1990), 233–50.
15. Cheryl Kader, "LGBT Milwaukee," Encyclopedia of Milwaukee, https://emke.uwm.edu/entry/lgbt-milwaukee/; NOW Lesbian Rights Conference program brochure, in possession of author.
16. "Wisconsin Lesbians Meet," *GPU News*, June 1979; "Carol Stevens Remembered as Lesbian Pioneer"; Jamakaya, "Carol Stevens: A Wonderful Life," *Wisconsin Gazette* (Milwaukee), July 15, 2010.
17. Minutes variously titled of the Network, of That Lesbian Group, of Lesbian Alliance of Metro Milwaukee, and of LAMM Planning Committee,

August 22, 1989, September 24, 1989, October 19, 1989, November 20, 1989, December 18, 1989, and January 26, 1990, LAMM (Lesbian Alliance of Metropolitan Milwaukee) Papers, LGBT Collection, UW–Milwaukee Archives, Box 2, Folder 12; Carol von Ott, "A Brief Incomplete History of the Lesbian Alliance," in LAMM 20th Anniversary Program, LAMM Papers, Box 2, Folder 8.

18. "Guide to LAMM Policies," LAMM Papers, Box 5, Folder 2; "LAMM Speaks against Hate," LAMM newsletter, May 1994. This and other LAMM newsletters are housed in the LAMM Papers, Box 3, Folder 1.

19. "Guide to LAMM Policies"; "LAMM Speaks Against Hate."

20. "Lesbian Organizing in Milwaukee," in LAMM 20th Anniversary Program; grant application to Cream City Foundation, ca. 1990, LAMM Papers, Box 1, Folder 23.

21. "Pride '91 a Success!!," LAMM newsletter, July 1991; "Isle of Lesbos," LAMM newsletter, July 1992; "LAMM to Have an 'Isle of Lesbos' Tent at Pride Fest," *The Wisconsin Light*, June 11–24, 1992; LAMM annual report 1990–1991, LAMM Papers, Box 1, Folder 3.

22. "Lesbian Organizing in Milwaukee"; "Four Arrested at Queer Nation Demonstration," *The Wisconsin Light*, October 17–30, 1991.

23. "Lavender Network's Proposals Adopted by Commission Report," *The Wisconsin Light*, October 17–30, 1991; Gotzler file in Johnson Papers, Box 3, Folder 12; "Karen Gotzler: Our Woman of the Year," *The Wisconsin Light*, January 16–29, 1997.

24. "Bechdel," LAMM newsletter, May 1990; "Kate Clinton Fundraiser Nets $1,200," LAMM newsletter, January 1992; "Ronnie Gilbert Fundraiser a Success," LAMM newsletter, June 1992; "Celebrating with Us," in LAMM 20th Anniversary Program; LAMM annual reports, 1990–1994, LAMM Papers, Box 1, Folder 3.

25. "Lesbian Variety Show Set for August 24," *In Step*, August 7–20, 1996; Theresa Delgadillo, *Latina Lives in Milwaukee* (Champaign: University of Illinois Press, 2015), 200.

26. "Lesbian Bars: Are 5 Too Many for Cream City?," *OUT!*, September 1986.

27. "Lesbian Bars: Are 5 Too Many for Cream City?"; Molly Snyder, "Where Have All the Lesbian Bars Gone?," On Milwaukee, August 14, 2015, www.onmilwaukee.com/bars/articles/lesbianbarsdisappers.html.

28. *Trollop Club News*, November 1987, December 1987; all issues in Wisconsin Historical Society Pamphlet Collection.

29. *Trollop Club News*, November 1987, April/May 1988, December/January 1988–1989.

30. *Trollop Club News*, December 1987, April/May 1988, October/November 1988.

31. Liberace, *The Wonderful Private World of Liberace* (New York: Harper and Row, 1986), 40; Scott Thorson with Alex Thorleifson, *Behind the Candelabra: My Life with Liberace* (New York: E. P. Dutton, New York, 1988), 17–18; Duane Dudek, "Liberace Lover was Green Bay Packer, HBO Movie Asserts," *Milwaukee Journal Sentinel*, May, 21, 2013; "Behind the Candelabra and the Queerness of Liberace," *Los Angeles Review of Books*, May 27, 2013.

32. David Maraniss, *When Pride Still Mattered: A Life of Vince Lombardi* (New York: Simon and Schuster, 1999), 73, 234, 343–44, 471; Robert W. Wells, *Vince Lombardi: His Life and Times* (Madison: Wisconsin House, Ltd., 1971); David Kopay and Perry Deane Young, *The David Kopay Story: An Extraordinary Self-revelation* (New York: Bantam Books, 1977), 129–130.

33. Kopay and Young, *The David Kopay Story*, 178–179, 215.

34. "Star Athlete Comes Out," *GPU News*, January 1976; Peter Pheron, "Interview with Dave Kopay Regarding a Particular Attitude," *GPU News*, May 1977; Kopay and Young, *David Kopay Story*, 131, 193.

35. Esera Tuaolo with John Rosengren, *Alone in the Trenches: My Life as a Gay Man in the NFL* (Naperville, IL: Sourcebooks, 2006), 73, 85, 89, 106–7.

36. Tuaolo and Rosengren, *Alone in the Trenches*, 168, 172, 257–63, 276.

37. Cyd Zeigler, *Fair Play: How LGBT Athletes are Claiming Their Rightful Place in Sports* (New York: Edge of Sports, 2016), 10, 80, 83, see especially chapter 10, "Ahman Green Unlocks the Media Fear of 'The Question,'" 158–71, 203; "Coming Out: A New Book Explores the World of LGBT Athletes," *Isthmus* (Madison), June 2–8, 2016; "Aaron Rodgers: I Think The NFL Is 'Getting Closer' To Welcoming A Gay Player," *Huffington Post*, August 31, 2017.

38. Mac McDiarmid, *The Ultimate Harley-Davidson: The Complete Book of Harley-Davidson Motorcycles: Their History, Development and Riders* (London: Lorenz Books, 2000); Peter Henshaw, *Harley-Davidson: The Making of a Cult* (Stamford, CT: Longmeadow Press, 1994), 10; Oluf F. Zierl,

Ride Free Forever: The Legend of Harley-Davidson (Cologne, Germany: Konemann, 1998); "Great Lakes Harley Riders," Milwaukee LGBT History, www.mkelgbthist.org; Reuters News Service, "Harley Demographic Seeing Increase in Gay Riders," July 12, 2003; Chicagoland Sports Bikes, www.chicagolandsportbikes.com/forums/8-open-forum/22316-harleys-gone-gay.html.

39. "Castaways M.C.'s History," Castaways M.C. of Milwaukee, www.castwaysmc.org/castways_mcs_history; "Castaways M.C.," Milwaukee LGBT History, www.mkelgbthist.org; "An Interview with Community Activist Si Smits," *Quest*, October 2012.

40. "Funds Raised from Annual Holiday Candy Sale Benefit the CENTER Project." *Positive Voice* (Green Bay), October 1995; "Argonauts Leather Club," Milwaukee LGBT History, http://www.mkelgbthist.org; Paul Masterson, "Argonauts of Wisconsin, One of the Oldest LGBT Organizations in Wisconsin," *Quest*, May 2103.

41. Wisconsin Community Fund letter of April 1989, in possession of author; Denise Matyka, "MSF supports gays," *OUT!*, August 1986; "Interview with Joseph Pabst," Joseph Pabst Papers, Box 4, Folder 1, LGBT Collection, UW–Milwaukee Archives; "Johnson and Pabst LGBT Humanity Fund-Grant History," Pabst Papers, Box 4, Folder 3.

42. "Business Association," *GPU News*, February 1979; "Business Association of Milwaukee," Milwaukee LGBT History, www.mkelgbthist.org.

43. "Homosexuals Form Business Unit," *Milwaukee Journal*, July 21, 1981; "The Business of Being Gay," *Milwaukee Magazine*, January 1982.

44. "Homosexuals Form Business Unit"; "The Business of Being Gay"; "Gay Activist Ralph Navarro Dies at 51," *In Step*, June 14, 2001; "Brewing a Gay Community," *Cream City Special Edition* (Milwaukee), May 1983, copy of this and other issues of *Cream City Special Edition* in possession of author; memo from Ralph Navarro to Members of Cream City Business Association (CCBA), August 7, 1986, Ralph Navarro Papers, LGBT Collection, UW–Milwaukee; Ralph Navarro, "Why a Cream City Business Association?," in Cream City Business Association Papers; 1985/86 Cream City Business Association directory, copy in possession of author.

45. "Marc Haupert," Milwaukee LGBT History, www.mkelgbthist.org; "President's Column," *Cream City Special Edition*, December 1984; "President's Column: We're Listening," *Cream City Special Edition*, September 1984;

Marc Haupert, "Is There Anybody Out There?," *Cream City Special Edition*, September 1984; "Invitation to CCBA Dinner with Robert Ziarnik," *Cream City Special Edition*, December 1984; CCBA newsletter, September 1984; "Cream City Business Association," Milwaukee LGBT History, www.mkelgbthist.org; "CCBA Forms Women's Group," *OUT!*, July 1987.

46. Lee C. Rice, "CCBA 1984 Membership Survey: Summary and Overview," *Cream City Special Edition*, December 1984; CCBA 1984 Membership Survey, copy in author's possession; "Gay Milwaukee Works," *Cream City Special Edition*, May 1983.

47. "Fundraising for a Liberated Future," *OUT!*, March 1983; "Cream City Foundation Celebrates: 14 Years of Helping the Community," *The Wisconsin Light*, June 6, 1996; Cream City Foundation minutes, 1982–1998, Cream City Foundation Papers, Box 1, Folder 3; Cream City Foundation incorporation papers, Cream City Foundation Papers, Box 1, Folder 20; "Beloved LGBT Ally Joe Brehm Left behind Milwaukee's Oldest Operating Gay Bar, as Well as a Legacy of Support," *Wisconsin Gazette*, June 2, 2016.

48. Don Schwamb letter to Dear Friends of the Gay Community, December 20, 1983, Cream City Foundation Papers, Box 1, Folder 21; "Major Grants Made in the Fiscal Year Ending June 30, 1985" and "Cream City Foundation Grants Given (as of August 8, 1984)," both in Cream City Foundation Papers, Box 2, Folder 5; "Schwamb to Retire as CCF Plans for New Decade," *The Wisconsin Light*, August 24, 1989; "Cream City Foundation Celebrates 14 Years"; author's notes on Holbrook remarks to OPEN, May 19, 2016, in possession of author.

49. "National Conference of Foundations," Cream City Foundation Papers, Box 2, Folder 8.

50. New Harvest Foundation brochure, ca. 1984; bylaws for New Harvest, adopted April 29, 1984, both in possession of author.

51. New Harvest Foundation brochure.

52. Jerry L. Dahlke obituary, Oregonlive, https://obits.oregonlive.com/obituaries/oregon/obituary.aspx?pid=174617344; invitation to New Harvest Foundation reception, January 23, 1985, in possession of author.

53. New Harvest Foundation founding documents, in possession of author; "Grant Recipients Announced," *OUT!*, March 1987; "Gay Foundation to Mark 5 Years," *In Step*, March 30, 1989; Woody Carey and Tret Fure letter to Dear Friends, December 2009, copy in author's possession.

54. Invitation to New Harvest gala of April 19, 1986, in possession of author; "Pride was Blooming Everywhere," *New Harvest Gleaner*, Fall 2003, www .newharvestfoundation.org/newsletter.php.

55. "Sex Course Stirs Protests," *Milwaukee Journal*, January 2, 1972; "Unitarians Get Support on Sex Class," *Milwaukee Journal*, January 25, 1972; "Former Students Reflect on That Unitarian Sex Class," *Milwaukee Journal*, November 22, 1973; "UULGC [Unitarian Universalist for Lesbian/Gay Concerns]—Where We Came From," *Unitarian Universalist Lesbian/Gay World* (Boston), June 1, 1985, copy in possession of author.

56. "Clergy/Gay Dialogue II Planned," *Gay Madison*, October 1979; "Clergy/Gay Dialogue II Reviewed," *Gay Madison*, December 1979; First Congregational United Church of Christ (Madison), "A Madison Affirmation on Homosexuality and Christian Faith," May 12, 1997, in possession of author; sermon by Reverend Paul Kittlaus, First Congregational Church, January 31, 1993, copy in possession of author; "You Are Welcome Here," *Isthmus*, April 18, 2014; "Rural Lesbians/Gays Form Support Groups—GRANDFLAGS," *OUT!*, August 1985.

57. "Gay United Presbyterians," *GPU News*, April 1974; "Re-ordination Caps Long Journey," *Wisconsin State Journal* (Madison), October 9, 2011; "Gay Ordination Would Open Doors," *Wisconsin State Journal*, February 23, 2010.

58. "Lutheran Gays Organize Group," *Milwaukee Journal*, June 29, 1974; Stewart Van Cleve, *Land of 10,000 Loves: A History of Queer Minnesota* (Minneapolis: University of Minnesota Press, 2012), 95–97; "Fraser Named to Church Unit," *GPU News*, June 1979; "Lutherans Meet in MKE," *GPU News*, June 1978; "Gay Lutherans Meet in Milwaukee," *GPU News*, September 1978.

59. "J. Robert Moore," Milwaukee LGBT History, www.mkelgbthist.org; Village Church ad in *The Wisconsin Light*, September 22, 1988; "Same Sex Weddings?," *The Wisconsin Light*, September 8, 1988; "Mayor Norquist Appoints Moore to Safety Commission," *The Wisconsin Light*, September 8, 1988.

60. "San Francisco Gay Ordination Set," *New Beginnings*, January 1990; "Gay Minister Resigns Post," *New Beginnings*, June/July 1991.

61. "Church Quietly Serves Homosexuals," *Milwaukee Sentinel*, July, 19, 1980; "Pastor's Job Demanding; Gays and the Spirit," *OUR HORIZONS*, December 21, 1981; "New Hope Church Appoints Two Women as Pastoral Leaders," *The Wisconsin Light*, October 18, 1990.

62. "Order Develops Model Ministry to Homosexuals," *Catholic Review* (Bal-

timore), March 9, 1973, and "Salvatorians to Study Ministry to Homo-
sexuals," *Catholic Herald* (Milwaukee), February 24, 1973; "Salvatorians
Develop Model for Ministry to Homosexuals," *Catholic Week* (Mobile, AL),
February 23, 1973.

63. "UW–M Speakers See Church Slow to Change," *OUT!*, May 1987;
Integrity/Dignity (I/D) newsletter (Madison), February 1986, in possession of author.

64. "Priest, Nun Tell of Trials over Work with Gays," *Milwaukee Sentinel*,
April 20, 1985.

65. "Theologian Addresses Homosexual Marriage," *Milwaukee Sentinel*,
March 12, 1983; *Catholic Herald* (Madison) quoted in "The Other Task
Force Report—The Milwaukee Report on Women," I/D newsletter, Spring
1983; "Review: The Church and the Homosexual, by John J. McNeil, S.J.,"
GPU News, October 1978.

66. "Salvatorians Develop Model for Ministry to Homosexuals."

67. "Local Dignity Group Formed," *GPU News*, March 1975; "Brother
Grant-Michael Fitzgerald SDS," LGBTQ Religious Archives Network,
www.lgbtqreligiousarchives.org/profiles/grant-michael-fitzgerald-sds;
Kevin J. Mumford, *Not Straight, Not White: Black Gay Men from the March
on Washington to the AIDS Crisis* (Chapel Hill: University of North Carolina
Press, 2016), see esp. chapter 5, "The Disavowal of Brother Grant-Michael
Fitzgerald," 99–124; "Fitzgerald, Grant Michael," Gay History Wikispace,
https://gayhistory.wikispaces.com/Fitzgerald%2C+Grant+Michael; Dig-
nity Milwaukee newsletter, May 1978 and September/October 1979, in
Jerry Johnson Papers, Box 2, Folder 21.

68. "Dignity Milwaukee 20 Years Old," *In Step*, March 16, 1995; Kevin-Richard
Quader, "Milwaukee Dignity to Celebrate Fifteenth Anniversary February
17," *The Wisconsin Light*, January 11, 1990; "CCBA Gives 'Hall of Fame'
Awards," *OUT!*, May 1987; "Catholic Gays' Group Meets Local Resistance,"
Green Bay Press Gazette, December 18, 1983; "Priest Talks about Gays,
Church," *Green Bay Press Gazette*, March 22, 1986.

69. "Priest Talks about Gays, Church"; Rembert Weakland, O.S.B., *A Pilgrim
in a Pilgrim Church: Memoirs of a Catholic Archbishop* (Grand Rapids, MI:
William B. Eerdmans Publishing, 2009), 3–20; "Years After Resigning in
Disgrace, an Archbishop Is Speaking Out," *New York Times*, May 15, 2009;
"AIDS: Remembering & Hoping," I/D newsletter, Summer 1990.

70. "I/D—A History to Live By," I/D newsletter, Spring/Summer 2002, "Crew," I/D newsletter, Mid-fall, 1982.

71. "I/D Celebrates Tenth Anniversary in Madison," *OUT!*, July 1987; I/D Fall Programs Brochure, 1982, copy in possession of author; "Integrity/Dignity Moves Onward," I/D newsletter, Fall 1981; I/D Tenth Anniversary program, copy in possession of author; "Madison Couple Sustains National Movement," I/D newsletter, Spring 200; "25th Anniversary Liturgy," I/D newsletter, Spring/Summer 2002; "Jim & Bill Celebrate 40 Years," Integrity/Dignity liturgy, March 13, 2010, copy in possession of author.

72. "Educational Employees in Madison Organize," *The Wisconsin Light*, February 23, 1989, based on draft submitted by group of Madison Area Gay and Lesbian Educational Employees (GLEE), draft among papers from Dennis Bergren in possession of author.

73. Transcript of oral history tape by GLEE founders Dennis Bergren, Mary Mastaglio, and Mary Babula, April 10, 2000; copy of GLEE bylaws, ca. 1988; "An Historical Perspective of GLEE," *New Lessons* (Madison), December 1991; all among papers from Dennis Bergren in possession of author. These include numerous issues of the GLEE newsletter, *New Lessons*.

74. GLEE oral history; "Does Schools' Memo Push Homosexuality?," *Wisconsin State Journal*, June 25, 1989.

75. Memo from Ruth Gudinas to James L. Fullin Jr. (president of Madison School Board), June 28, 1989, among papers from Dennis Bergren in possession of author; obituary for Ruth Anna Gudinas, Madison.com, host.madison.com/news/local/obituaries/gudinas-ruth-anna.

76. GLEE oral history; "Sectional for Gay and Lesbian Education Employees," from Educating for the Next Century," WEAC Convention Program, October 25–27, 1989, among papers from Dennis Bergren in possession of author; "Madison Educators Share Concerns, Plan Spring Meeting," *The Wisconsin Light*, November 16, 1989; Dennis Bergren, "Teachers Attend Gay Session at Convention," *The Wisconsin Light*, November 16, 1989.

77. "Homosexual Educators at WEAC Convention Cite Isolation, Fear," *Milwaukee Sentinel*, October 25, 1990.

78. "Gay Teachers Hold Own Sessions," *Capital Times* (Madison), October 24, 1991.

79. GLEE oral history.

80. "Respect Gays, Group Urges Schools," *Capital Times*, January 7, 1994; Gays, Lesbians and Allies for Diversity in Education (GLADE) letter to Dear Friends, January 1994; GLADE brochure, n.d.; GLADE flyer, n.d, GLADE Goals flyer, n.d., all among papers from Dennis Bergren in possession of author.

81. "Gay Honorees Rip City Schools," *Capital Times*, undated clipping, among papers from Dennis Bergren in possession of author.

82. "One Person's Story," *New Lessons*, April 1993.

83. "High School Student Speaks Out," *New Lessons*, April 1993.

84. Jim Maraniss, "Photog: Gay Show Worth the Pain," *Capital Times*, June 6, 1996; "Critics: Gay Photo Show Excludes Heterosexuals," *Capital Times*, April 30, 1996; "No Decision as Gay Photos Spark Uproar at School," *Capital Times*, May 2, 1996.

85. "Critics: Gay Photo Show"; "Gay Photo Controversy Settled at Hawthorne Elementary," *Wisconsin State Journal*, May 5, 1996; "Gay Photo Exhibit OK'd," *Capital Times*, May 3, 1996.

86. "Gay Photos, Other Woes Dog School Board," *Capital Times*, May 7, 1996; Dianne Reistroffer statement, May 1, 1996, copy among papers from Dennis Bergren in possession of author.

87. "Gay Families and Schools," *Capital Times*, May 1, 1996; "Peace at Hawthorne," *Capital Times*, May 4, 1996.

88. "High School Student Speaks Out," *New Lessons*, December 1990.

89. GSAFE, 2017 Celebration of Leadership brochure, in possession of author.

90. "High School Student Speaks."

91. Katherine McFarland Bruce, *Pride Parades: How a Parade Changed the World* (New York: New York University Press, 2016), 8, 49.

92. "Gay March," *Kaleidoscope* (Madison), January 8, 1971; "Gay Pride Week to Begin Friday," *Milwaukee Journal*, June 29, 1973; "Del Martin to Speak," *Milwaukee Sentinel*, July 6, 1973; "Gays Rally to Protest Police Harassment," *Milwaukee Journal*, June 29, 1980; "Gay Pride Week Planned," *Amazon* (Milwaukee), June/July 1980; "Update Milwaukee," *GPU News*, June 1980.

93. "National Coming Out Day October 11," *In Step*, September 1, 1989; National Coming Out Day Kit, ca. 1987, in possession of author.

94. Coming Out Day ad, *Isthmus*, October 7, 1988; George Vukelich with Tammy Baldwin, "Taking the Next Step," *Isthmus*, October 7, 1988.

95. "Gays 'Come Out'" *Badger Herald* (UW–Madison), October 12, 1988; "Pretty in Pink," *Capital Times*, October 11, 1989; "Bascom Badges," *Wisconsin State Journal*, October 12, 1989; "Signs Mark Homosexuals' March," *Milwaukee Sentinel*, October 12, 1988; "Bascom Hill: Pink Triangles Represent Gay/Lesbian Pride," *Daily Cardinal* (UW–Madison), October 11, 1988.

96. "Thousands Expected for Madison's May 6 Lesbian and Gay Pride March," *Feminist Voices* (Madison), April 1989; GALVAnize Program booklet, 1989, copy in possession of author.

97. "Get Ready to March!," *Insurgent* (Madison), April 24, 1989; "Gay, Lesbian Marchers are Welcome," *Capital Times*, April 29, 1989.

98. GALVAnize Program booklet; "Visibility Alliance," *Daily Cardinal*, May 6, 1989.

99. "Thousands Come Out for Gay, Lesbian Rights," *Wisconsin State Journal*, May 7. 1989; "7,000 Marchers Fill Madison Streets with Pride and Enthusiasm," *The Wisconsin Light*, May 18, 1989; "Action=Life," *Feminist Voices*, May 1989.

100. "Pride Celebrations," Milwaukee LGBT History, www.mkelgbthist.org.

101. "Everyone Should Show Their Pride in Milwaukee June 17," *The Wisconsin Light*, June 1, 1989; "Special Edition: Milwaukee Pride Celebration '89," *The Wisconsin Light*, June 1, 1989; "Milwaukee Pride Week '89 Special Section," *In Step*, June 8, 1989; "Pride Week Notes," *In Step*, June 8, 1989; "First Milwaukee Pride Parade and Rally a Great Success," *The Wisconsin Light*, July 13, 1989; Michail Takach, *LGBT Milwaukee* (Charleston, SC: Arcadia Publishing, 2016), 88–94.

102. Pride Celebration program booklet: "Look to the Future: The Gay 90s, 1990, June 16–24, 1990"; program for MLGPC (Milwaukee Lesbian Gay Pride Committee) Annual Meeting, September 10, 1990; "Parade and Rally Suggested Chants" flyer; and MLGPC financial statement, 1990, all in Johnson Papers, Box 3, Folder 36; Jamakaya, "The Rough Road to Pridefest," *Wisconsin Gazette*, June 13, 2013; "Pridefest Books Romanovsky & Phillips, Unveils '96 Logo: Excitement Builds about New Summerfest Site," *In Step*, April 4, 1996; "Summerfest Ground Here We Come!!," *The Wisconsin Light*, November 23, 1995; Takach, *LGBT Milwaukee*, 88–94; "30 Years Later . . . An Interview with Pridefest Founder Bill Meunier," *Quest*, July 2017.

103. Dale Hillerman, "A Personal Perspective of the Gay Movement," from "Symposium on Homosexuality," *Forum* (Wisconsin Psychiatric Institute, UW–Madison), November 1973.

Epilogue

1. "Susan Cook," Milwaukee LGBT History, www.mkelgbthist.org. Many individuals, organizations, businesses, media outlets, and events are profiled on this site.

2. Tammy Baldwin 1992 campaign materials including two undated letters to Dear Friends, sent to voters; pamphlet, Gay and Lesbian Victory Fund, Recommended Candidates: Tammy Baldwin for Wisconsin State Assembly; campaign brochure, "Take a Stand for Change!"; campaign brochure, "With a Vision for Our Community"; campaign flyer, "Tammy Baldwin, State Assembly On the Issues," all in the Linda Willsey Papers, LGBT Collection, UW–Madison Archives, Madison, Wisconsin; "Lesbian Banking on Voter Approval in Assembly Race," *Milwaukee Sentinel*, May 4, 1992.

3. "Primary Perspectives," *Wisconsin State Journal* (Madison), September 3, 1992; Baldwin campaign materials; Kent Williams, "Her Story," *Isthmus* (Madison), January 8, 1993.

4. Billy Feitlinger campaign materials, Willsey Papers; *Wisconsin Blue Book*, 1993–1994, 905. The *Wisconsin Blue Books* are compiled biennially by the Wisconsin Legislative Reference Bureau and published by the Wisconsin Department of Administration.

5. *Wisconsin Blue Book* 1993–1994, 923.

6. Doris Hanson campaign materials, Willsey Papers; "Enrolled Joint Resolution Relating to the Life and Public Service of Doris J. Hanson," 2007, Wisconsin Assembly, http://docs.legis.wisconsin.gov; *Wisconsin Blue Book*, 1993–1994, 904, 923.

7. *Wisconsin Blue Book*, 1999–2002, 859, 862.

8. *Wisconsin Blue Book*, 2013–2014, 880, 920.

9. Gregory A. Kompes, *50 Fabulous Gay-friendly Places to Live* (Franklin Lakes, NJ: Career Press, 2005); Frank Burres, "How Gay Is Madison?," *Madison Magazine*, February 2004; "Gayest Cities in America," *The Advocate* (Los Angeles), February 2010; "Madison Gets Perfect Score on Equality Index," *Wisconsin Gazette* (Milwaukee), November 28, 2013; Patrick Farabaugh, "Madison a Safe Space," *Spectrum* (Madison), 2009.

10. "Gay in the City," *Milwaukee Magazine*, August 2007; "Milwaukee, a Gay and Lesbian Travel Guide," brochure, n.d., in possession of author; "The Gays Next Door," *Wisconsin State Journal*, July 8, 2007; "Isthmus a Haven for Gay Couples," *Wisconsin State Journal*, August 15, 2001; "Milwaukee, Madison Score High for LGBT-Friendly Policies and Programs," *Wisconsin Gazette*, December 13, 2012.

11. Juliet Brodie, Action Wisconsin letter, February 19, 1996, copy in author's possession.

12. Author's recollections of Doris Hanson and Fair Wisconsin.

13. Greenberg Quinlan Rosner Research, "Survey of Wisconsin Voters," January 29, 2009, copy in possession of author; "Wisconsin Support for Marriage Equality Rising," *Wisconsin Gazette*, April 12, 2014; "Benefit Brawl: Were Marriage Ban Supporters Gunning for Domestic Partner Protections after All?," *Capital Times* (Madison), February 25–March 3, 2009; "Fair Wisconsin Applauds Manitowoc City Council Passage of Domestic Partner Benefits," Fair Wisconsin press release, March 20, 2012, copy in possession of author.

14. Draft for 2009–2011 Budget provision on Domestic Partnership, Legislative Reference Bureau-1308/3, 2009–2011 session, copy in possession of author; "Doyle's Budget Aids Gay Couples," *Wisconsin State Journal*, February 20, 2009; Conway Strategic, "Message Compass—Domestic Partners," 2009, copy in possession of author.

15. Judge Barbara Crabb, *Virginia Wolf et al. v. Scott Walker, et al.*, 14-C-00064-SLC, Western District of Wisconsin.

16. Author's recollections of work as deputy registrar; "Clerk Key Player for Gay Marriages," *Wisconsin State Journal*, June 22, 2014; "City of Love: Dane County Clerk's Prep for Gay Marriage Ruling Paid Off," *Capital Times*, June 11, 2014; "First Same-Sex Marriage Certificate Fit for History Books," *Wisconsin State Journal*, September 28, 2014.

17. "Equality Campaign Starts as Gay Marriage Ban Heads to Court," *Capital Times*, August 13, 2014; "A Formidable Argument for Same-Sex Marriage: Leading Conservative Judge Richard Posner Dares the Supreme Court to Take Wisconsin's Case," *Isthmus*, September 11, 2014; "It Made Me Feel American Again," *Isthmus*, August 28, 2014.

Appendix I

1. Harvey Milk, "The Hope Speech," quoted in Randy Shilts, *The Mayor of Castro Street: The Life & Times of Harvey Milk* (New York: St. Martin's Press, 1982), 362.

2. Copies of invitations in possession of author.

3. "Fact Sheet on the 'So-Called' FAMILY PROTECTION ACT," prepared by Gay Rights National Lobby, ca. 1981; "Family Protection Act, IPO0149, Info Pack, Background Material," Congressional Research Service, Library of Congress, 1981; "Summary of Selected Sections of the Family Protection Act," prepared by National Gay Task Force, 1981, all in author's possession; *Congressional Record–Senate*, June 17, 1981, S 6329-6335; "The Family Protection Act: Handle with Care," *Christian Science Monitor*, July 23, 1981; "Campaign against the Radical Right Kicks Off with 'Stop the FPA' Press Conference," National Gay and Lesbian Task Force Report, September/October 1981.

4. Copies of city resolution drafted by Gridley Hall, December 16, 1981, and introduced by Alderman Lufler February 1, 1982, in possession of author.

5. "Speakers Rip Family Protection Act," *Daily Cardinal* (UW–Madison), March 15, 1982; copies of my speaking notes for Madison Community United panel, in possession of author.

6. "Wagner Leads Fight against 'Family' Act," *Capital Times* (Madison), March 17, 1982; "Dane Board Turned Off by Family Protection Act," *Capital Times*, April 2, 1982.

7. Masthead, *Rawhide Reporter* (New London, WI), Fall 1982; "Dane Advised to End Boys' Ranch Ties," *Capital Times*, July 14, 1982; "Rawhide Defends Self against Charges," *Press-Star* (New London), August 12, 1982; "County Severs Rawhide Ties," *Wisconsin State Journal* (Madison), September 1, 1982; John Gillespie letter to Leslie Hamilton, August 25, 1982, copy in possession of author.

8. Lynn Haanen letter to R. Richard Wagner, August 16, 1982, in possession of author.

9. Debarment Report of the Dane County Contract Compliance Board, September 2, 1982, copy in possession of in author.

10. Gillespie letter to Hamilton, August 25, 1982; "Rawhide Officials Won't

Be at Hearing," *Capital Times*, August 16, 1982; "Rawhide Won't Fight Charges of Bias," *Wisconsin State Journal*, August 15, 1982.

11. Minutes of the Dane County Contract Compliance Board, August 31, 1982, copy in possession of author.

12. Dane County Board of Supervisors minutes, Res. 5, 1983–84 and Sub. 1 to Res. 5, Proceedings of the Dane County Board, Office of the Dane County Clerk, Madison, Wisconsin; Governor Anthony S. Earl letter to Dr. Jeffrey Davis, State Epidemiologist, July 6, 1983, copies in possession of author.

13. "County Health Board Member to Be Asked to Resign," *Wisconsin State Journal*, July 1, 1983; "Health Board Member Asked to Quit," *Capital Times*, July 1, 1983.

14. Letter from Supervisors Lynn Haanen and R. Richard Wagner to County Executive Jonathan Barry, June 29, 1983, copy in possession of author.

15. Dane County Executive Jonathan Barry letter to James Pawlisch, June 30, 1983, copy in possession of author; "County Official Won't Quit over Homosexual Remarks," *Wisconsin State Journal*, July 7, 1983; "Anti-gay Dane Official Won't Quit," *Capital Times*, July 12, 1983.

16. "Barry Ousts Appointee over Homosexual Remarks," *Wisconsin State Journal*, July 14, 1983; "Barry Boots Pawlisch for Anti-gay Remarks," *Capital Times*, July 14, 1983; Jonathan Barry press release of July 13, 1983, copy in possession of author; "Petition Seeks Pawlisch Reinstatement," *Wisconsin State Journal*, September 15, 1983; "Petitions Ask Return of Anti-gay Dane Official," *Capital Times*, September 21, 1983.

17. Letter and petitions Henry X. Dudek to Rod Matthews, County Board Chair, November 15, 1983, copies in possession of author.

18. Frank Ryan, "Fired for His Opinions," *Waukesha Freeman*, July 26, 1983; "Capitol Eye: Thought Control," *Isthmus* (Madison), July 22, 1983.

19. "Capitol Eye," letter from James E. Doyle Jr. and Mary Louise Symon, *Isthmus*, July 25, 1983, copy in possession of author.

20. "Eye Revisited," letter from Brooks Egerton, *Isthmus*, August 5, 1983.

21. "Man Fired by Barry over Anti-gay Remarks Sues," *Wisconsin State Journal*, August 9, 1983; "Ex-Health Board Member Claims Free Speech Violated," *Capital Times*, August 9, 1983; Cal Kornstedt, Senior Assistant Corporation Counsel, letter to Supervisor Richard Wagner, October 17, 1983, copy

in possession of author; copy of notes and Court Affidavit by Supervisor Wagner in possession of author.

22. Circuit Court Branch 8 Decision, March 1, 1984, copy in possession of author.

23. August Derleth, *The Wisconsin: River of a Thousand Isles* (New York: Rinehart, 1942), 325.

24. "Statue Planned for NYC," *GPU News* (Milwaukee), November 1979; "George Segal's *Gay Liberation*," GLBTQ Arts, www.glbtqarchive.com/arts/segal_g_A.pdf; David B. Boyce, from "The Making of *Gay Liberation* (the Statue)," in Richard Schneider Jr., *In Search of Stonewall: The Riots at 50, The Gay & Lesbian Review at 25, Best Essays, 1994–2018* (Boston: G&LR Books, 2019).

25. Tom Garver, memo to Richard Wagner and others, December 19, 1985, copy in possession of author; Jacob Stockinger, "Gay Liberation Work Finds a Home Here," *Capital Times*, January 11, 1986; "Gay Liberation Statue Finds Madison Home," *OUT!* (Madison), February 1986.

26. L. Aaron Kaufman, "'Gay Liberation': Hardly Either," *OUT!*, June 1986.

27. Memo of December 19, 1985, to Richard Wagner; "Art in Orton Park" meeting notice for April 29, 1986, copies in possession of author; "Sculpture Finds Home in City," *Wisconsin State Journal*, May 28, 1986.

28. "Orton Park to Get Pro-gay Statue," *Capital Times*, May 27, 1986.

29. "Park Site for Gay Statue Re-affirmed," *Wisconsin State Journal*, June 12, 1986; "Pro-gay Statue OK'd Despite Opposition," *Capital Times*, June 12, 1986.

30. "Pro-gay Statue OK'd"; "Gay Statue Move is Criticized," *Capital Times*, June 3, 1986.

31. Letter from Donna Kirshenmann, "Orton Park Sculpture is a Sensitive Tribute," *Capital Times*, June 10, 1986; letter from Edmund Zawacki, "'Gay Lib' Statue is Propagandistic Junk," *Capital Times*, June 13, 1986; letter from Jack Guzman, "'Gay Lib' Sculpture Reaction Intolerant," *Capital Times*, June 11, 1986; letter from Roland Di Renzo, "Pro-gay Statue Sets Poor Example," *Capital Times*, June 5, 1986.

32. "Orton Park Project Expands Pupils' Educational Horizons," *Capital Times*, June 4, 1987.

33. Agreement between Madison Art Center and Madison Parks Commission, June 25, 1986, copy in possession of author; "Madison Parks

Commission OKs 'Gay Liberation' Statue," *The News* (Los Angeles), June 27, 1986; "Collage" in Douglas C. McGill, "Art People," *New York Times*, October 31, 1986.

34. Materials on West Hollywood Conference in possession of author; "Just Doing His Job: Mayor Gerald Ulrich Is a Reluctant Celebrity," *The Advocate*, April 25, 1989; "Gay Member of British Parliament to Speak at Historic West Hollywood Conference," *Gay Writes* (Los Angeles), November/ December 1985.

35. "Schulte Speaks: A Conversation with the Mayor of West Hollywood," *The Advocate*, May 26, 1987, 42–50.

36. "Elected Officials Press Statement," November 24, 1985, copy in possession of author.

37. "Conference Urges More Gay Elected Officials," *Los Angeles Times*, November 24, 1985; "Gay Officials Group Backs 'Marriage' Law," *San Francisco Chronicle*, November 25, 1985; "Homosexual British Official Sees 'Signs of Progress' Abroad," *Los Angeles Herald Examiner*, November 25, 1985; " 'Gay Summit' Draws Elected Officials from across Nation," *New York Native*, December 16–22, 1985.

38. "Update on Elected Officials Lobbying," memo from Tom Chorlton to Lesbian & Gay Elected Officials, February 25, 1986; National Gay Task Force, "AIDS Advisory: President's Budget Calls for 20% Cut in AIDS Funding," ca. early 1986; Brian Coyle letter to Richard Wagner, February 13, 1986, all in possession of author.

39. Materials on the first dozen annual Openly Lesbian and Gay Elected Officials conferences, which became a formal support organization known as the Victory Fund, are part of the author's materials donated to UW–Madison LGBTQ Archive, Madison, Wisconsin.

40. Letter of invitation to the Fifth Annual International Conference of Gay and Lesbian Officials, November 17, 1988, signed by Richard Wagner, Kathleen Nichols, Tammy Baldwin, Earl Bricker, and Alder James MacFarland, copy in possession of author.

41. Invitation brochure for the Fifth Annual International Conference of Gay and Lesbian Officials, copy in possession of author.

42. "Unity, New Laws Urged to End 'Gay Bashing,' " *Capital Times*, November 20, 1989; "Gay Officials Urged to Combat Violence," *Milwaukee Journal*,

November 20, 1989; conference brochure with schedule, copy in possession of author.

43. "Lesbian, Gay Officials Edge towards Diversity," *Madison Insurgent*, November 20, 1989; "Nees' Entry to Politics: Breaking Age Barrier," *Madison Insurgent*, November 20, 1989.

44. "Elected Gays Nervously Eye Redistricting," *Washington (DC) Blade*, November 24, 1989; "Madison, Wisconsin, Holds the Record for Openly Gay Officials," *Washington Blade*, November 24, 1989.

45. "Gay Officeholders Tell of Progress as They Meet in Madison," *Milwaukee Journal*, November 17, 1989.

INDEX

Note: Page numbers in *italic type* refer to illustrations.

From Female to Male (Sullivan), 129
FTM (female-to-male) transsexuals,
    131–132, 148–151, *149*, 190
Fuller, Howard, 297

Gagalaino, Nick, 122
GALVAnize (Gay and Lesbian Visibility
    Alliance), 167, 344, 451–453, *453*
GAMMA (Milwaukee sports
    organization), 411–413, 419
Garland, Jack, 150
Garstecki, John, 48, 49, 50, 51–53, 55
Garver, Tom, 478–479, 480–481
gay (term), 147
Gay & Lesbian Community at Stout
    (GLCS), 399–400
Gay and Lesbian Alliance (GALA)
    (UW–Platteville), 39
Gay and Lesbian Center (Madison),
    18, 78, 158
Gay and Lesbian Educational
    Employees (GLEE), 441–442. *See
    also* Gays, Lesbians and Allies for
    Diversity in Education (GLADE)
gay and lesbian film festival
    (Milwaukee), 175, 176, 290
Gay and Lesbian Organization (GLO)
    (UW–Eau Claire), 400–401
Gay and Lesbian Youth (Herdt), 379,
    381
Gay Arts Festival (Madison, 1977), *160*
gay bars
    and AIDS crisis, 95, 375
    Fox Valley area, 35–36, 384–385
    Green Bay area, 372
    Milwaukee, 33, 93, 406–408
    in the press, 30–31, 161–162, 168,
        179–180
gay bashings, 86–87, 296, 298–300,
    351–352, 401–402
Gay Center (Madison). *See* Madison
    Gay Center
Gay Comix, *41*, *42*
gay community centers, 15, 290
Gay Community News, 335
Gay Dialogue (FVGA newsletter),
    382–384

Gay Endeavor (Madison publication),
    162, *163*
gay institutions and organizations,
    budgets and funding, 425–426,
    429–432
gay kissing booth, *30*, 31
Gay Law Students Association
    (UW–Madison), 35, 78, 116, 118,
    470
"Gay Liberation: Five Years after
    Stonewall" (Murray), 5
Gay Liberation Front (GLF), 10, 13, 53.
    See also Madison Gay Liberation
    Front (GLF)
Gay Liberation (Segal sculpture), 432,
    477–482, *481*
Gay Life (Chicago newspaper),
    262–263
Gay Madison (publication), 162–165,
    164
gay media. *See* LGBT media
gay men, 10–11, 155–156
Gay People's Union (GPU), 18, 32
    1976 survey on gay issues, 112–113
    and Coalition to Oust Chief Breier,
        92
    flyer for Safransky fundraising, *57*
    legal defense fund, 90–91
    Milwaukee, 50, 70, 93–94, 131,
        425–426
    and police harassment, 92
    publications. *See GPU News*
        (publication)
    Sullivan and, 130
Gay Perspective (radio show), 20–21,
    196, 206
gay political efforts, 109
    alternative families legislation,
        120–127
    Dane County legislation, 137–138
    and McFarland, 124–126
    and military service, 127–129
    Milwaukee legislation, 135–137
    racism and homophobia, 132–135
    role of Yeadon, 116–120
    sexual reform legislation, 114–116
    and statewide leverage, 110–114